ΠΡΟΚΛΟΤ ΔΙΑΔΟΧΟΤ
ΣΤΟΙΧΕΙΩΣΙΣ ΘΕΟΛΟΓΙΚΗ

PROCLUS
THE ELEMENTS OF
THEOLOGY

ΠΡΟΚΛΟΥ ΔΙΑΔΟΧΟΥ
ΣΤΟΙΧΕΙΩΣΙΣ ΘΕΟΛΟΓΙΚΗ

PROCLUS
THE ELEMENTS OF
THEOLOGY

A REVISED TEXT
with Translation, Introduction
and Commentary

by

E. R. DODDS

Formerly Regius Professor of Greek in the
University of Oxford

SECOND EDITION

CLARENDON PRESS · OXFORD

This book has been printed digitally and produced in a standard specification
in order to ensure its continuing availability

OXFORD
UNIVERSITY PRESS

Great Clarendon Street, Oxford OX2 6DP

Oxford University Press is a department of the University of Oxford.
It furthers the University's objective of excellence in research, scholarship,
and education by publishing worldwide in

Oxford New York

Auckland Bangkok Buenos Aires Cape Town Chennai
Dar es Salaam Delhi Hong Kong Istanbul Karachi Kolkata
Kuala Lumpur Madrid Melbourne Mexico City Mumbai Nairobi
São Paulo Shanghai Taipei Tokyo Toronto

Oxford is a registered trade mark of Oxford University Press
in the UK and in certain other countries

Published in the United States
by Oxford University Press Inc., New York

© Oxford University Press 1963

The moral rights of the author have been asserted

Database right Oxford University Press (maker)

Reprinted 2004

ISBN 0-19-814097-5

PREFACE TO SECOND EDITION

BESIDES correcting a number of misprints and other minor errors in the text, I have taken advantage of this reprint to bring the work more nearly up to date by providing an appendix of 'Addenda et corrigenda'. Asterisks in the body of the book refer the reader to this appendix. My thanks are due to Father H. D. Saffrey, O.P., and to Mr. Lionel Strachan for helpful corrections; to Professor S. Pinès and Dr. Richard Walzer for information about a fragmentary Arabic version; and above all to Dr. D. M. Lang and the Georgian Academy of Sciences, whose generous assistance has enabled me to give a fuller account of Petritsi's Georgian translation.

E. R. D.

OXFORD,.
12 *April* 1962.

PREFACE TO FIRST EDITION

THIS edition owes its inception to Professor A. E. Taylor, who indicated to me the need for something of the kind more years ago than I care to remember. Its publication has been rendered possible by the generosity of the Delegates of the Clarendon Press. I wish to take this opportunity of thanking all those who have helped me in the work of preparation, including the many librarians who have assisted me with information or by arranging, often at considerable personal trouble, for the loan of MSS. or their photographic reproduction. I owe an especial gratitude to Monsignor Mercati, for his courteous help in connexion with Vatican MSS.; to Mr. J. L. Zimmerman, for the loan of rotographs; to Mr. Stephen Gaselee, who arranged for me the transport of MSS. from abroad; to the Birmingham University Research Committee, who contributed to the cost of having MSS. photographed; to Mr. R. P. Blake, Director of the Harvard University Library, Professor R. P. Casey of the University of Cincinnati, and my colleague Professor S. Konovalov, who aided me to trace the history of the little-known Georgian and Armenian versions; and to Dr. S. Kauchtschischwili of the University of Tiflis, who has allowed me to use a portion of his unpublished collation of the Georgian. In the later stages of the work my prime helpers have been Professor A. D. Nock of Harvard, who read the whole book in manuscript and made a number of valuable suggestions; Mr. B. S. Page of this university, whose vigilant proof-reading has saved me from many inaccuracies; and the admirably patient Readers of the Press. For the imperfections which remain I alone am responsible.

E. R. D.

BIRMINGHAM,
12 *November* 1932.

CITATIONS

In citing ancient texts for which custom has not yet established a universally recognized system of reference, I have usually specified the edition referred to. The following are the chief exceptions:

PROCLUS' commentaries on the *Alcibiades I* and the *Parmenides*, also the *de decem dubitationibus, de providentia et fato* and *de malorum subsistentia*, are cited by pages and lines of Cousin's 2nd edition (*Procli Opera Inedita*, Paris 1864); the other commentaries by pages and lines of the Teubner texts—*in Cratylum* sometimes also by paragraphs (small roman numerals); the *Elements of Physics* (*El. Phys.*) by paragraphs. For the *Platonic Theology* (*Th. Pl.*) I have where possible cited the book and chapter in addition to the page of the *editio princeps*; but the chapter numeration in the text of the edition is often faulty. Chapter numbers in brackets, e.g. *Th. Pl.* III. (vi.) 126, refer to the more correct numbering given in the table of contents.

PLOTINUS is cited by the traditional subdivisions or by Volkmann's pages and lines. For the convenience of readers I have usually given both references, the latter in brackets.

PORPHYRY's ἀφορμαί (*sententiae*) by Mommert's pages and lines, or by paragraphs (sm. rom. nums., Mommert's numeration); fragments of the *de regressu* from Bidez's *Vie de Porphyre*; other works by paragraphs.

IAMBLICHUS *de mysteriis* by Parthey's pages and lines, or by book and chapter; other works by pages and lines of the Teubner editions.

SALLUSTIUS by Nock's pages and lines, or by chapters (sm. rom. nums.).

DAMASCIUS by Ruelle's pages and lines (the fragments of the *Life of Isidorus* by those of Asmus).

STOBAEUS by Wachsmuth and Hense's subdivisions, or by the pages and lines of their edition: Heeren's pages are added in brackets.

ALBINUS (Alcinous) *didascalicus* (εἰσαγωγή) by C. F. Hermann's pages and lines (*Appendix Platonica*, Teubner).

NICOLAUS METHONENSIS ἀνάπτυξις τῆς θεολογικῆς στοιχειώσεως
Πρόκλου by pages and lines of Voemel's text (in Creuzer's *Initia
Philosophiae*, pars iv, Frankfurt, 1825).
Patristic texts by pages of the *Patrologia*, unless otherwise stated.

Modern works are cited by pages.   The only abbreviations which
need explanation are:

Arnou = R. Arnou, *Le Désir de Dieu dans la Philosophie de Plotin*
(Paris, Alcan, n.d.).

Bidez, *C.M.A.G.* = *Catalogue des MSS. Alchimiques Grecs*, vol. vi.
(containing Bidez's Introductions to various works of Psellus
and to Proclus' fragment περὶ τῆς καθ᾽ Ἕλληνας ἱερατικῆς τέχνης).

Geffcken, *Ausgang* = J. Geffcken, *Der Ausgang des griechisch-
römischen Heidentums*, 1920.

Inge [3] = W. R. Inge, *The Philosophy of Plotinus*, 3rd ed., 1929.

L.S. [8] = Liddell and Scott's *Lexicon*, 8th ed.

Praechter, *Richtungen* = K. Praechter, *Richtungen u. Schulen im
Neuplatonismus* (in *Genethliakon Robert*, pp. 105–56).

Reitzenstein, *H.M.-R.* [3] = R. Reitzenstein, *Die Hellenistischen
Mysterien-Religionen*, 3rd ed., 1927.

Taylor, *Phil. of Pr.* = A. E. Taylor, *The Philosophy of Proclus*,
in Proc. Aristotelian Society XVIII (1918).

Ueberweg-Geyer [11] = Ueberweg's *Grundriss der Geschichte der
Philosophie*, Band II, 11th ed.

Whittaker [2] = T. Whittaker, *The Neoplatonists*, 2nd ed., 1918
(reprinted 1928).

Zeller III [4] = E. Zeller, *Die Philosophie der Griechen*, Teil III,
4th (and 5th) ed.

CONTENTS

INTRODUCTION

CHAPTER I

§ 1. *Character and purpose of the ' Elements of Theology '.*

He who presents the world with an elaborate edition of a book dating from the last age of Graeco-Roman decadence labours *prima facie* under the suspicion of contributing to that most extensive of all sciences, the *Wissenschaft des Nichtwissenswerthen.* My justification lies partly in the historical significance of Proclus as one of the chief links between ancient and medieval thought ; partly in the unique position of the *Elements of Theology* as the one genuinely systematic exposition of Neoplatonic metaphysic which has come down to us.

For the student, and especially for one who is grappling for the first time with this complicated body of thought, its systematic character lends it an importance second only to that of the *Enneads* of Plotinus. The *Enneads*, though they stand on an incomparably higher philosophical level than any subsequent product of the school, are in form a collection of occasional essays or lectures. Originating as they did in school discussions,[1] they are not, and were not meant to be, either individually or collectively, the ordered exposition of a system : each essay presupposes a large body of doctrine common to the writer and his audience, and proceeds at once to illuminate some particular aspect of it which has been discussed at the seminar (τὰς ἐμπιπτούσας ὑποθέσεις, Porph. *vit. Plot.* 4) or to examine some ἀπορία which has been raised in connexion with it. The general logical principles which form the structural skeleton of the system are for the most part referred to only incidentally, and their structural significance remains implicit, becoming clear only upon a comparison of a number of different passages. Among later works, neither Porphyry's ἀφορμαὶ πρὸς τὰ νοητά nor the little treatise of Sallustius περὶ θεῶν καὶ κόσμου presents the system as a structurally coherent unity. Both seem designed rather for the general public of their time than for professional students of philosophy ; and in both the selection of material is governed less by considerations of logic than by an ethical or religious purpose. The ἀφορμαί, as we have it now,[2]

---

[1] Cf. Bréhier, *La Philosophie de Plotin*, 15 ff.

[2] The conjecture that our text is incomplete has been confirmed by the discovery of a σχόλιον in the Mediceus B of the *Enneads* which cites a passage of the ἀφορμαί as from the *first book* of τὰ περὶ νοητῶν ἀφορμῶν (Bidez, *Vie de Porphyre*, 106, n. 1).

is a disjointed and lop-sided collection of edifying thoughts, mainly quotations from or paraphrases of Plotinus, some in the form of brief apophthegms, others expanded into little essays. The περὶ θεῶν καὶ κόσμου is 'an official catechism of the pagan Empire',[1] the work of a man interested in philosophy less for its own sake than as a means of fortifying the minds of the next generation against the corrupting influence of Christianity.

In strong contrast with these earlier manuals, the *Elements of Theology* is a purely academic and theoretical work, containing little or nothing that appears to be directed either to spiritual edification or to religous controversy. It is, as Bréhier observes,[2] an 'œuvre de professeur assagi par une longue tradition scolaire'. And it is nothing if not systematic. We may regard it, in fact, as an attempt to supply the comprehensive scheme of reality desiderated by Plato in the seventh book of the *Republic*—to exhibit, that is to say, all forms of true Being as necessary consequences derived in conformity with certain general laws from a single ἀρχή. It is not, indeed, a complete epitome of Neoplatonism ; for the constitution of the changing world beneath the moon belongs not to θεολογία but to φυσιολογία, and ethics too are touched on only incidentally, since the main concern of θεολογία is with 'procession' and not with 'reversion'. But it is a complete system of 'theology' in the Aristotelian sense of 'first philosophy' or metaphysic.[3] The book falls into two main sections. The first of these (props. 1 to 112) introduces successively the general metaphysical antitheses with which Neoplatonism operated —unity and plurality, cause and consequent, the unmoved, the self-moved and the passively mobile, transcendence and immanence, declension and continuity, procession and reversion, *causa sui* and *causatum*, eternity and time, substance and reflection, whole and part, active and passive potency, limit and infinitude, being, life, and cognition. The remaining part (props. 113 to 211) expounds in the light of these antitheses the relations obtaining within each of the three great orders of spiritual substance, gods or henads, intelligences, and souls ; and the relations connecting each of these orders with the lower grades of reality. The emphasis throughout is on structure ; and for this reason, abstract and dessicated as the treatise appears on a first acquaintance, it has for the student of Neoplatonism the same sort of value relatively to the *Enneads* which the study of anatomy has for the zoologist relatively to the examination of the living and breathing animal.

---

[1] Cumont in *Rev. de Phil.* 16 (1892) 55.   Cf. also Nock, *Sallustius*, pp. ci ff.
[2] *Philos. de Plotin*, 10.   [3] See Commentary, p. 187.

The style[1] and method of the book are in strict conformity with its systematic purpose, and therefore differ considerably from those employed by Proclus in his longer works. The vast prolixities of exposition which uncoil their opulence in the bulky and shapeless sentences that fill most of the 1100 pages of the *Timaeus* commentary, and riot unchecked in the jungle of the *Platonic Theology*, are here pruned to a brevity which leaves no room for parenthetic digression or rhetorical ornament. And in place of the constant appeals to authority—now to Plato, now to 'Orpheus' or the *Chaldaean Oracles*—which irritate the reader of the major works and confuse him by their ingenuity of misinterpretation, in the *Elements of Theology* Proclus has adopted, at least in appearance, the method of pure *a priori* deduction known to the ancient mathematicians as synthesis and familiar to us from Euclid and Spinoza. It is substantially, as Professor Taylor points out,[2] the Platonic method of hypothesis; and Proclus found a model for it in the hypothetical argumentations put into the mouth of Parmenides in Plato's dialogue of that name.[3] As a means of exhibiting succinctly the logical presuppositions on which a system of belief implicitly rests it has great and obvious advantages. To carry the method through a philosophical work with the degree of formal precision attempted in the *Elements of Theology* is, however, no easy task, whatever the system expounded. Ingenious as Proclus is, too often his 'demonstration', though formally correct, in fact merely repeats the 'enunciation' at greater length; and lapses even from formal correctness of reasoning may be detected here and there,[4] though less frequently than one might have expected. These weaknesses are inherent in the method: the coherence of a body of philosophical thought cannot be fully expressed in a chain of logically flawless syllogisms.

A more serious fault is Proclus' trick of confusing the accidental with the essential by introducing in the guise of *a priori* deductions doctrines which owe their form, and even sometimes their being, to

[1] Under 'style' I do not include Pr.'s technical vocabulary, which is a heritage from his predecessors, and remains, so far as I have observed, fairly constant throughout his philosophical writings.
[2] *Phil. of Pr.* 606 ff. It may be doubted, however, whether Pr. fully realized the hypothetical character of his postulates, to which centuries of unquestioned tradition had given the appearance of self-evidence.
[3] Cf. *Th. Pl.* I. x χρῆται γὰρ ἀεὶ (sc. ὁ Παρμενίδης) τοῖς πρώτοις συμπεράσμασιν εἰς τὰς τῶν ἐχόντων (lege ἐχομένων) ἀποδείξεις, καὶ τῆς ἐν γεωμετρίᾳ τάξεως ἢ τοῖς ἄλλοις μαθήμασι παράδειγμα προτείνει νοερόν, τὴν τῶν συμπερασμάτων τούτων πρὸς ἄλληλα συνάρτησιν.
[4] For examples of circular arguments cf. props. 3 and 77 nn.; prop. 169 n.

a chance phrase in the *Timaeus* or the *Chaldaean Oracles*. Although no authorities are directly quoted in the *Elements of Theology*, its pages are haunted by the ghosts of authorities. Genuinely 'free' thought was no more possible to a pagan writer in the fifth century after Christ than it was to his Christian contemporaries. There is, it is true, a substantial difference of method between Proclus and, for example, his Christian imitator 'Dionysius': the latter makes no pretence of reaching any of his conclusions by argument, but is content, when he cannot find a suitable scriptural text, to quote 'Hierotheus' as sole and sufficient authority. But when Mr. Whittaker in his zeal for Proclus' reputation goes so far as to deny that he is a scholastic 'in the sense that he in principle takes any doctrine whatever simply as given from without',[1] he forgets for the moment that Proclus too had his scriptures. Plato is to Proclus something more than the supreme master and teacher which he is for Plotinus: he is definitely an inspired writer. His philosophy is an 'illumination' ($\ddot{\epsilon}\kappa\lambda\alpha\mu\psi\iota\varsigma$), 'according to the beneficent purpose of the higher powers, which to the souls that haunt generation, in so far as it is lawful for them to enjoy blessings só high and great, revealed therein their secret intelligence and the truth which is as old as the universe'.[2] Nor is this the only revelation which the gods have vouchsafed. Have they not spoken to us more directly in the *Chaldaean Oracles*, uttered by them through the entranced lips of their servant Julianus, the theurgist 'whom it is unlawful to disbelieve'[3]? All that they tell us, and all that Plato tells us, we must 'take as given': our task is only to interpret. Where the two revelations appear to conflict, as unfortunately happens in some passages,[4] the appearance is due to the crudity of our interpretation. The rest of Greek philosophy is in a different class: its chief usefulness is to enable us 'to explain the obscure passages in Plato by the help of the nearest analogies in the doctrine of others'.[5] All this is strictly parallel to Christian proceedings; and it accounts for the odd saying attributed to Proclus by his biographer Marinus,[6] 'If I had it in my power, out of all ancient books I would suffer to be current ($\phi\acute{\epsilon}\rho\epsilon\sigma\theta\alpha\iota$) only the *Oracles* and the *Timaeus*; the rest I would cause to vanish from the world of to-day ($\ddot{\alpha}\nu \ldots \dot{\eta}\phi\acute{\alpha}\nu\iota\zeta o\nu \dot{\epsilon}\kappa \tau\hat{\omega}\nu \nu\hat{\upsilon}\nu \dot{\alpha}\nu\theta\rho\acute{\omega}\pi\omega\nu$), because certain persons suffer actual injury from their

---

[1] *Neoplatonists*[2] 161. [2] *Th. Pl.* I. i.
[3] $\mathring{\psi} \mu\grave{\eta} \theta\acute{\epsilon}\mu\iota\varsigma \mathring{\alpha}\pi\iota\sigma\tau\epsilon\hat{\iota}\nu$, *in Tim.* III. 63. 24 *
[4] Despite the fact that, according to Psellus ($\pi\epsilon\rho\grave{\iota} \tau\hat{\eta}\varsigma \chi\rho\upsilon\sigma\hat{\eta}\varsigma \dot{\alpha}\lambda\acute{\upsilon}\sigma\epsilon\omega\varsigma$, *Rev. des Ét. Gr.* 1875, p. 216), Julianus had the advantage of personal consultation with the ghost of Plato.
[5] *Th. Pl.* I. ii.   [6] *vit. Proc.* xxxviii.

undirected and uncritical reading'. This remarkable pronouncement has often been misunderstood. It does not mean that the most learned Hellenist of his day wished to make a holocaust of Greek literature; he only wished to restrict its circulation for the time being to the initiates of Neoplatonism. Nor does it, I fear, mean, as Mr. Whittaker suggests it may,[1] that Proclus had 'seen the necessity of a break in culture if a new line of intellectual development was ever to be struck out'. New lines of intellectual development were as inconceivable to Proclus as to his Christian adversaries. Their business was to preserve the uninstructed from the poison of pagan philosophy; his, to preserve them from the deadly errors of such as put Aristotle on a level with Plato or set up Moses as a rival to the Chaldaeans. To either end a drastic censorship of literature was in an uneducated world the only practical expedient. When the gods have told us what to think, the study of man-made opinions becomes for the commonalty both unnecessary and dangerous, though scholars may profit by it.[2] 'In fact', as Bidez has recently said, 'this anti-Christian philosophy was more like the new faith which it attacked than like the ancient religion which it defended'.

§ 2. *The place of the ' Elements of Theology' in the work of Proclus* *.

If we group the philosophical writings of Proclus according to their method and content they fall naturally into the following classes :—

1. The extant commentaries on the *Republic, Parmenides, Timaeus*, and *Alcibiades I*; and the commentary on the *Cratylus*, of which we possess only excerpts. All these show clear traces of their origin in lecture-courses; and the *Cratylus* excerpts may well be taken not from any published work of Proclus but from a pupil's notebook. Among the lost writings are commentaries on the *Phaedo, Gorgias, Phaedrus, Theaetetus*, and *Philebus* and on the *Chaldaean Oracles*, and possibly others.[3] The ἐπίσκεψις τῶν πρὸς τὸν Τίμαιον Ἀριστοτέ-

---

[1] *Neoplatonists*[2] 159.
[2] It has been asked why Pr. extends his proposed censorship to all but one of Plato's dialogues. The answer is, I think, that in his judgement, as in that of Iamblichus, all the essentials of Plato's philosophy are contained in the *Parmenides* and the *Timaeus (in Tim.* I. 13. 14); and the former of these dialogues has been the subject of so much misunderstanding (*in Parm.* 630 ff., *Th. Pl.* I. viii) that it must be presumed unsuitable for popular study. Zeller rightly compared the mediaeval exclusion of the laity from the study of the Bible.
[3] The line between 'published' commentaries and 'unpublished' lecture-courses is difficult to draw; notes of the latter taken by pupils were doubtless current within the school. All the lost commentaries mentioned above are referred to by

λους ἀντιρρήσεων and the συναγωγὴ τῶν πρὸς τὸν Τίμαιον μαθηματικῶν θεωρημάτων appear to have been respectively prolegomena and appendix to the *Timaeus* commentary.

2. The *Platonic Theology*, which shares to a great extent the exegetic character of the commentaries. Of the *Orphic Theology* and the *Harmony of Orpheus, Pythagoras and Plato* (both now lost) Proclus seems to have been editor rather than author.[1]

3. A group of lost works on religious symbolism[2] (περὶ τῶν μυθικῶν συμβόλων), on theurgy (περὶ ἀγωγῆς), against the Christians, on Hecate and on the myth of Cybele. These are represented for us only by the fragment περὶ τῆς καθ᾽ Ἕλληνας ἱερατικῆς τέχνης (*de sacrificio et magia*), which, previously known only in Ficino's Latin version, has now been published in the original Greek by Bidez (*Cat. des MSS. Alchimiques Grecs*, VI. 148 ff.).

4. A number of occasional essays, three of which, the *de decem dubitationibus circa providentiam*, the *de providentia et fato*, and the *de malorum subsistentia*, survive in the mediaeval Latin version of William of Morbecca. To this class belonged the περὶ τόπου and (if this was an independent work) the περὶ τῶν τριῶν μονάδων: also perhaps the controversial πραγματεία καθαρτικὴ τῶν δογμάτων τοῦ Πλάτωνος, which was directed against Domninus.

5. The two systematic manuals, the *Elements of Theology* and the *Elements of Physics* (formerly known as περὶ κινήσεως). These are distinguished from the other extant works by the use of the deductive method and the absence of reference to authorities.[3]

The attempt to determine the order of composition of these multifarious works is beset with difficulty. None of them contains any reference to external events by which it can be dated; and Proclus' biographer supplies no such full chronological materials as

Proclus himself. A commentary or lecture-course on Plotinus is cited by Damascius II. 253. 19 (ἐν τοῖς εἰς Πλωτῖνον) and by scholiasts on the *in Remp.* and the *de mysteriis*.

[1] Suidas attributes works under these two titles both to Proclus and to Syrianus. According to Marinus (*vit. Pr.* 27) Proclus merely added scholia to the commentary of his master on the *Orphica*; and the double attribution of the *Harmony* probably has a similar explanation. Cf. *Th. Pl.* pp. 203, 215; Olympiod. *in Phaed.* 52. 18 Norvin.

[2] For the meaning of σύμβολον in Proclus see prop. 39 n.

[3] The view suggested by Bardenhewer in his edition of the *de causis*, and apparently accepted in one place by Ueberweg-Geyer[11] (p. 303: contrast pp. 149, 285, 409 etc.), that the *El. Th.* is probably not the work of Pr. himself but originated in his school, is not supported by any argument and hardly needs refutation. I can find nothing in the style or content of the treatise which lends colour to it; and the unanimous testimony of our MSS. is confirmed by Psellus and by the Arabic and Armenian tradition (see below).

Porphyry gives in the *Life of Plotinus*. He tells us (c. xiii) that Proclus had composed the commentary on the *Timaeus*, 'and much else', by his twenty-eighth year (A.D. 437–8); this is the only 'absolute' date which we possess,[1] and, as will presently appear, it is not really absolute. At first sight it would seem that the numerous references to other works of the author which occur in the commentaries furnish an easy means of fixing the relative dates of his writings ; and a chronological arrangement based mainly on this evidence was proposed by Freudenthal.[2] In this arrangement the *Elements of Theology* appears as the earliest of Proclus' extant works (with the possible exception of the *Elements of Physics*) ; seven further works intervene between it and the *Timaeus* commentary, so that it is presumably a product of its author's early twenties. Considerable doubt, however, is cast on these conclusions by a circumstance to which Praechter has called attention,[3] viz. the existence of cross-references from the *in Tim.* to the *in Remp.* and *vice versa*—showing that Proclus was in the habit of making additions to his commentaries after they had already been made public either in book-form or (more probably) as lectures. This fact seems to render futile any attempt to 'date' the commentaries as we have them ;[4] and it invalidates many of the arguments by which Freudenthal supported his dating of the other extant works. As regards these latter almost the only *certain* conclusion to be drawn from the data collected by Freudenthal is that the *Platonic Theology* presupposes the publication in some form of the commentaries on the *Timaeus* and the *Parmenides*, both of which it cites. In the three Latin treatises no earlier works are mentioned by name ; the *de mal. subsist.* contains, however, what is probably, though not certainly, a reference to the *Elements of Theology*.[5] There are also possible

---

[1] We are not justified in assigning the commentary on the *Phaedo* to 432–4 on the evidence of Marinus c. xii, though it may have been begun at that date. Marinus' language in c. xiii rather implies that the *in Tim.* was the first of the commentaries to be made public.

[2] *Hermes* 16 (1881) 214 ff.

[3] *Göttingische gelehrte Anzeigen* 167 (1905) 505 ff.

[4] The most that can be said with any confidence is that the commentaries on the *Parmenides, Alcibiades I* and *Cratylus* probably received their present form later than the *in Tim.* and *in Remp.*, as (*a*) they are never cited in the two latter (except for a very doubtful reference to *in Crat.*, *in Tim.* I. 451. 8) ; (*b*) *in Tim.* III. 12. 29 seems to refer to a *prospective* commentary on the *Parmenides* ; (*c*) these three (esp. the *in Crat.*) stand closer in style and phraseology to the rather senile *Th. Pl.* than do the other two.

[5] *de mal. subsist.* 203. 39, cf. *El. Th.* prop. 63. The alleged reference at 255. 17 to prop. 8 is too vague to carry any conviction, and the same thing is true of the supposed allusions in the *de mal. subsist.* to the other two Latin treatises ; in all these cases the reference may well be to one of the lost works.

allusions to the *Elements of Theology* in the *in Tim.* and the *in Parm.* ;[1] but we have no assurance that these references, even if they have been rightly identified, were not first introduced in a later revision of the commentaries. And the fact that the *Elements of Theology* itself contains no references to earlier works is (*pace* Freudenthal) of no evidential value whatever, since the method of the book precluded such references.

Freudenthal's contention as to the early date of the *Elements* does not, however, rest entirely on evidence of this type. He asserts that Proclus is here still completely dependent on Plotinus and Porphyry, and that a wide gulf separates the doctrine of the manual from that of the *Platonic Theology* (which he places, probably rightly, at or near the end of Proclus' literary career). The statement about the complete dependence of the *Elements of Theology* on Plotinus and Porphyry is repeated with little qualification by Zeller and others after him, but is rightly challenged by Mr Whittaker. How far it is from being true will be shown in the next section: it is sufficient to say here that the treatise is not only coloured throughout by the language and thought of Iamblichus but gives a prominent place to doctrines, such as that of the divine henads, which are peculiar (so far as we know) to the Athenian school. It is, however, true that there are considerable differences, though little in the way of direct contradiction, between the doctrine of the *Elements of Theology* on the one hand and that of the *Platonic Theology* and the commentaries on the other. In the first place, a number of secondary elaborations which appear in the latter are entirely missing from the former: among these may be mentioned the interposition between the 'intelligible' and the 'intellectual' gods of an intermediate class who are both intelligible and intellectual ; the subdivision of the 'supra-mundane' order of gods into ἀρχικοί (ἀφομοιωματικοί) and ἀπόλυτοι θεοί; and the subdivision into subordinate triads of the fundamental triad Being–Life–Intelligence.[2] Secondly, certain of the late Neoplatonic doctrines which do appear in the *Elements* seem to have an insecure place there or to be rather carelessly combined with the Plotinian tradition: the most striking example of this is the twofold usage of the term νοῦς, sometimes for the Plotinian hypostasis (as in props. 20, 57, 109, 112, 129, 171), sometimes for the lowest member of the

---

[1] *in Tim.* I. 385. 9, cf. prop. 92 ; II. 195. 27, cf. props. 67 ff. ; *in Parm.* 1147. 36, cf. prop. 17. Pr. nowhere cites the *Elements of Theology* by name.

[2] For the first two of these refinements see note on props. 162–5 ; for the third cf. esp. *Th. Pl.* III. xiv. ff.

triad ὄν-ζωή-νοῦς (prop. 101 &c.), without any warning to the reader
or the addition of any distinguishing adjective; so too the Iamblichean doctrine of ἀμέθεκτα, accepted elsewhere in the *Elements*,
seems to be ignored in prop. 109; and echoes of Plotinus' teaching
about the status of the human soul survive in imperfect harmony
with theorems derived from Iamblichus.[1] Such loose joints are
discoverable elsewhere in Proclus' work, but they are as a rule
more skilfully concealed.   Finally, all direct reference either to
personal mysticism or to theurgy is absent from the *Elements*.

The importance of these facts for the dating of the *Elements* will
be variously estimated. Those in the second category seem to me
the most significant.   The absence of certain subordinate distinctions may well be due merely to a desire for brevity and lucidity,
though it is less easy to account in this way for the omission of the
θεοὶ νοητοὶ καὶ νοεροί.[2]   In a voluminous writer who has an elaborate
system to expound some minor variations and even inconsistencies
are in any case to be expected; and in fact such variations may be
observed, not only on comparing the commentaries with one another
and the *Platonic Theology*, but sometimes even within the limits of
a single work.[3]   Direct reference to mystical experiences or to
occult practice may have been felt to be out of keeping with the
rationalist character of the *Elements* or to infringe upon its *a priori*
method of argument : that Proclus in fact believed in theurgy when
he wrote it can hardly be doubted (cf. notes on props. 39 and 145).
Nevertheless, the evidence as a whole seems to me to point definitely, if not quite decisively, to the conclusion that the *Elements* is
a relatively early work.   This is not to say, however, that it should
be assigned with Christ-Schmid to the year 432 (when Proclus was
twenty-two !) : to regard it as the prentice essay of an undergraduate
who has not yet developed ' his own system ' is a complete miscon-
ception.   The system expounded in the *Platonic Theology* and the
metaphysical commentaries is *substantially* the same as that of the
Elements ; and, as we shall see in a moment, scarcely anything in it
is of Proclus' own invention.

A minor question concerns the relationship of the *Elements of
Theology* to the *Elements of Physics*.   From the fact that the latter
is based almost exclusively on Aristotle's *Physics* its latest editor,

---

[1] See notes on props. 193 and 195.

[2] That this particular doctrine is not an invention of Proclus' latest period may,
however, be inferred from *in Parm.* 949. 38 ff. δεδείχαμεν γοῦν πάλαι διὰ τῶν εἰς
τὴν παλινῳδίαν γραφέντων (i.e. in the *Phaedrus* commentary) ὅτι πᾶσαι αἱ τάξεις
ἐκεῖναι μέσαι τῶν νοερῶν εἰσι θεῶν καὶ τῶν πρώτων νοητῶν.

[3] Examples will be found in the notes on prop. 20, l. 18, and props. 75, 116, 167.

Ritzenfeld, argues that it was composed at a very early stage in
Proclus' philosophical education, when he was reading Aristotle
with Syrianus (Marin. *vit. Proc.* c. xiii): he would therefore separate
it from the relatively mature *Elements of Theology.* But the argument is not cogent ; for in physics Aristotle is accepted by all the
later Neoplatonists, no less than by their medieval successors, as
the supreme authority. And the discrepancy alleged by Ritzenfeld
between *El. Phys.* II. prop. 19 and *El. Th.* prop. 14 disappears on
examination.[1] The two manuals resemble each other so closely in
style and phraseology that I am inclined to accept the usual and
natural view that they were composed about the same period of
Proclus' life and were intended to be complementary.

§ 3. *Proclus and his Predecessors.*

The body of thought whose structure is anatomized for us in the
Elements of Theology is not the creation of one individual or of one
age ; it represents the last result of a speculative movement extending over some five centuries. If we look at this movement as a
whole we can see that its direction is throughout determined mainly
by two impulses, one theoretical and the other practical or religious.
On the theoretical side it reflects the desire to create a single Hellenic
philosophy which should supersede the jarring warfare of the sects
by incorporating with the Platonic tradition all that was best in
Aristotle, in Pythagoreanism and in the teaching of the Porch. On
the practical side we can best understand it as a series of attempts
to meet the supreme religious need of the later Hellenistic period
by somehow bridging the gulf between God and the soul ; to con-
struct, that is to say, within the framework of traditional Greek
rationalism a scheme of salvation capable of comparison and rivalry
with those offered by the mystery religions.

In recent years we have learned to recognize with increasing
clearness the directive influence of both these motives upon the
teaching of Poseidonius, the first of the three dominant personalities
who have left their individual impress upon Neoplatonism. But the
Poseidonian synthesis was neither wide enough nor sufficiently
coherent to win permanent acceptance ; and the Poseidonian
solution of the religious problem was too deeply infused with Stoic
materialism for an age which was coming more and more to demand

[1] See note on prop. 14; and for another discrepancy, which again is more
apparent than real, prop. 96 n.

a purely spiritual conception both of God and of the soul. It was reserved for the dialectical genius of Plotinus to translate into achievement the ideal of philosophic unity, and for his mystical genius to transfer the 'return of the soul' from the domain of astral myth to that of inner experience. Though Plotinus is commonly treated as the founder of Neoplatonism, in the wider movement we are considering he stands not at the point of origin but at the culminating crest of the wave. Formally, the later Neoplatonic school owes more to him than to any other individual thinker save Plato; yet spiritually he stands alone. He left to his successors a dialectical instrument of matchless power and delicacy and a vivid tradition of personal mysticism in the proper sense of that term, as the actual experience of the merging of the self at certain moments into some larger life. But within two generations the dialectical tension of opposites which is the nerve of the Plotinian system was threatening to sink into à meaningless affirmation of incompatibles; and 'unification' (ἕνωσις) had ceased to be a living experience or even a living ideal and had become a pious formula on the lips of professors. At this point the history of Greek philosophy would have come to an end but for the introduction of new methods, both theoretical and practical, by the Syrian Iamblichus (d. *circa* 330).

The historical importance of Iamblichus has hardly been sufficiently recognized, no doubt because his metaphysical works have perished and the outlines of his doctrine have to be reconstructed mainly from Proclus' report of his teachings together with the fragments preserved by Stobaeus and the semi-philosophical treatise *On the Mysteries of the Egyptians*.[1] Mystagogue and thaumaturgist though he was, and in intellectual quality immeasurably inferior to a Poseidonius or a Plotinus, his contribution to the final shaping of Neoplatonism is scarcely less than theirs. With him, as Praechter has said,[2] begins not merely a new school but a fresh direction of thought. Not only can we trace to him many individual doctrines which have an important place in the later system, but the dialectical principles which throughout control its architecture, the law of mean terms,[3] the triadic scheme of μονή, πρόοδος and ἐπιστροφή,[4] and the

---

[1] The traditional ascription of this treatise to Iamblichus is rejected by Zeller and others; but the arguments adduced by Rasche (*de Iamblicho libri qui inscribitur de mysteriis auctore*, Münster 1911) and Geffcken (*Ausgang*, 283 ff.) have convinced me that it is justified.

[2] *Richtungen*, 114. Cf. also Bidez, *Vie de Julien*, chaps. XI and XII.

[3] *apud* Pr. *in Tim.* II. 313. 15 ff. The formal use of this principle is also implied in the *Theologumena Arithmeticae* (10. 9 ff. de Falco), a work which if not by Iamb.'s hand certainly reflects his teaching; and cf. Sall. 28. 31.

[4] *apud* Pr. *in Tim.* II. 215. 5 (cf. III. 173. 16).

mirroring at successive levels of identical structures,[1] though in part derived from earlier origins, appear to have received at his hands their first systematic application. To him rather than to Proclus belongs the honour or the reproach of being the first scholastic. Not less important is the new religious outlook, which discovered the key to salvation not in the Plotinian θεωρία, but in θεουργία, a form of ritualistic magic whose theoretical text-book was the *Chaldaean Oracles*, and whose procedure has its nearest parallels in the Graeco-Egyptian magical papyri. This change is a natural corollary to the humbler cosmic status assigned by Iamblichus and most of his successors to the human soul.[2] As the ancient world staggered to its death, the sense of man's unworthiness grew more oppressive, and the mystical optimism of Plotinus came to seem fantastic and almost impious: not by the effort of his own brain and will can so mean a creature as man attain the distant goal of 'unification'. 'It is not thought', says Iamblichus,[3] 'that links the theurgist to the gods: else what should hinder the theoretical philosopher from enjoying theurgic union with them? The case is not so. Theurgic union is attained only by the perfective operation of the unspeakable *acts* correctly performed, acts which are beyond all understanding; and by the power of the unutterable symbols which are intelligible only to the gods.' With that the whole basis of the Plotinian intellectual mysticism is rejected, and the door stands open to all those superstitions of the lower culture which Plotinus had condemned in that noble apology for Hellenism, the treatise *Against the Gnostics*.[4]

In the light of this necessarily brief and incomplete outline of the development of Neoplatonism, and especially of the part played in it by Iamblichus, we may turn to consider what personal contribution was made by Proclus and in what relation he stands to his predecessors. On both questions widely different opinions have been expressed. Geffcken[5] describes Proclus and his school as 'philosophasters sleep-walking in a Utopian world', and Christ-Schmid[6] calls him 'an apologist who nowhere seeks to promote the

---

[1] *apud* Pr. *in Tim.* I. 426. 20 ff.; cf. Praechter, *op. cit.* 121 ff.

[2] Cf. notes on props. 184 and 211; also *in Tim.* III. 165. 7, 231. 5 ff., 244. 22 ff.; *in Parm.* 948. 12 ff.

[3] *de myst.* II. 11. The interest in occultism appears already in Porphyry's early work *On the Philosophy of the Oracles* (written before he knew Plotinus); but the distinctive features of Iamblicho-Procline theurgy do not.

[4] To speak, as even Hopfner does in his recent *Gr.-Aegyptischer Offenbarungszauber* (II. §§ 44, 79), of 'theurgic excursions of the soul' in Plotinus is to commit a capital error in religious psychology by confusing mysticism with magic. Still commoner is the opposite error which lumps together as 'mystics' the whole of the Neoplatonic school.

[5] *Ausgang*, 197.   [6] *Gesch. d. Griech. Lit.* II. ii. 1061.

knowledge of truth, a compiler without spiritual independence'. To Whittaker,[1] on the other hand, he is 'not only a great systematizer but a deep-going original thinker'; and Prof. Taylor[2] considers that 'for the historian of thought his significance is hardly second to that of Plotinus himself'. Again, while Zeller[3] represents the Athenian school (of which Proclus is for us the leading representative) as returning from the more extreme aberrations of Iamblichus to 'a stricter dialectical procedure', Praechter[4] denies that there is any foundation for such a view: 'the Athenian school goes full sail in the wake of the Syrian'.

As regards the second point, an analysis of the sources of the *Elements*, such as I have attempted in my commentary, tends generally to confirm Praechter's opinion. It is true that the greater part of the treatise agrees with Plotinus in substance if not in form, and that occasional verbal echoes both of the *Enneads*[5] and of Porphyry's ἀφορμαί[6] are not wanting. But (a) even the 'Plotinian' theorems not infrequently betray intermediate influences both in their language and in the hardening to a 'law' of what in Plotinus is the tentative expression of an individual intuition. (b) There are a number of particular doctrines which we can trace with more or less confidence to Iamblichus either as their originator or as the first to give them systematic importance: among them are the doctrine of 'unparticipated' terms (prop. 23, &c.); that of αὐθυπόστατα or 'self-constituted' principles (props. 40–51); much of Proclus' teaching about time and eternity (props. 52–5); the classification of gods (props. 162–5) and of souls (props. 184–5); the definite denial that the soul ever attains release from the circle of birth (prop. 206) and that any part of it remains 'above' (prop. 211). (c) Even more important than these are the general structural

---

[1] *Neoplatonists*[2] 233. [2] *Phil. of Pr.* 600.
[3] *Phil. der Griechen* III. ii[4]. 805.
[4] *Richtungen* 119. The close dependence of Pr. on Iamb. had already been emphasized by Simon (*Hist. de l'école d'Alexandrie* II. 428 ff.), although he failed to recognize its full extent.
[5] The following is perhaps the most striking verbal parallel:

El. Th. prop. 168 οὐκ ἄλλου μὲν (νοῦ) ἴδιον τὸ νοεῖν, ἄλλου δὲ τὸ νοεῖν ὅτι νοεῖ. εἰ γάρ ἐστι κατ' ἐνέργειαν νοῦς καὶ νοεῖ ἑαυτὸν οὐκ ἄλλον ὄντα παρὰ τὸ νοούμενον, οἶδεν ἑαυτὸν καὶ ὁρᾷ ἑαυτόν. ὁρῶν δὲ νοούντα καὶ ὁρῶντα γινώσκων, οἶδεν ὅτι νοῦς ἐστι κατ' ἐνέργειαν.

Enn. II. ix. 1 πάντως γε ὁ αὐτὸς ἔσται τῷ ὅσπερ ἐνόει ὁ νοῶν ὅτι νοεῖ... ὅταν δὲ δὴ ὁ νοῦς ὁ ἀληθινὸς ἐν ταῖς νοήσεσιν αὐτὸν νοῇ καὶ μὴ ἔξωθεν ᾖ τὸ νοητὸν αὐτοῦ... ἐξ ἀνάγκης ἐν τῷ νοεῖν ἔχει ἑαυτὸν καὶ ὁρᾷ ἑαυτόν· ὁρῶν δὲ ἑαυτὸν οὐκ ἀνοηταίνοντα ἀλλὰ νοοῦντα ὁρᾷ.

[6] e.g. *El. Th.* prop. 30 πᾶσα πρόοδος μενόντων... γίνεται τῶν πρώτων.
prop. 142 ὡς πάρεστιν, οὕτως ἐκείνων ἀπολαύει.

ἀφ. xxiv. αἱ πρόοδοι μενόντων τῶν προτέρων... γίνονται.
xxxiii. § 2. οὕτως αὐτοῦ ἀπολαύει, ὡς αὐτὸ πέφυκεν.

principles mentioned above as having been developed by Iamblichus. Again and again in the *Elements* Proclus justifies his multiplication of entities, like Iamblichus in the same circumstances,[1] by reference to the ' law of mean terms ', viz. that two doubly disjunct terms AB and not-A not-B cannot be continuous, but must be linked by an intermediate term, either A not-B or B not-A, which forms a ' triad ' with them.[2] Not less frequently does he save the unity of his system or reconcile conflicting traditions with the help of the principle—perhaps Neopythagorean, but first systematically applied, so far as we know, by Iamblichus—that 'all things are in all things, but in each according to its proper nature '.[3] And the exploitation at successive levels of the triad μονή–πρόοδος–ἐπιστροφή, which Zeller regarded as especially characteristic of Proclus, seems to be again a legacy from his too ingenious predecessor.[4] Finally, (*d*) a comparison of the *Elements* with the *de mysteriis* shows that a considerable proportion of Proclus' technical terminology was inherited from Iamblichus.[5]

The impression thus gained from the *Elements* is strengthened when we turn to Proclus' other works. Iamblichus is for him ὁ πάντας ἐν πᾶσιν ὀλίγου δέω φάναι κρατῶν;[6] he shares with Plotinus the honorific epithet θεῖος or θειότατος (whereas Aristotle is merely δαιμόνιος). Proclus ventures to criticize him but rarely, and then with a hint of apology in his tone.[7] In the matter of superstitious respect for theurgy there seems little to choose between the two writers. According to Proclus it is ' a power higher than all human wisdom, embracing the blessings of divination, the purifying powers of initiation, and in a word all the operations of divine possession '.[8] Like Iamblichus, he thinks that ' it is not by an act of discovery, nor by the activity proper to their being, that individual things are united to the One ',[9] but by the mysterious operation of the occult

---

[1] *apud* Pr. *in Tim.* II. 313. 19 ff.
[2] The principle is laid down in prop. 28. For examples of its application cf. props. 40, 55, 63, 64, 132, 166, 181. On its historical importance see Taylor, *Phil. of Pr.* 608 f.
[3] Prop. 103, where see note. This principle underlies props. 121, 124; 125, 128, 129, 134, 140, 141, 170, 176, 177, 195, 197.
[4] Prop. 35 note. How much of the detailed working out of these ideas was done by Iamb. himself, and how much by Syrianus or Pr., it is hard to say, as the remains of the two former are relatively so scanty.
[5] Technical terms characteristic of the *de mysteriis* which appear in the *El. Th.* include ἀλληλουχία, ἀρχηγικός, αὐτοτελής, ἄχραντος, γενεσιουργός, διακόσμησις, διάταξις, ἰδιάζω, περιοχή, πλήρωμα, προόν(τως), πρωτουργός, συναφή, τελεσιουργός (-γεῖν *El. Th.*), ὑπερηπλωμένος: to which we can add from other works of Iamb. ἀοριστταίνω and ὁμοταγής.
[6] *in Tim.* III. 34. 5.
[7] e.g. *in Tim.* I. 307. 14 ff. esp. 308. 17; III. 251. 21.
[8] *Th. Pl.* I. (xxvi.) 63.
[9] *ibid.* II. vi. 96.

'symbols' which reside in certain stones, herbs and animals.[1] It is true that he is fond of introducing into his descriptions of 'theurgic union' Plotinian tags such as μόνος μόνῳ συνεῖναι; but what for Plotinus was the living utterance of experience seems to be for him literary tradition. It is significant that Marinus never claims for his hero that he enjoyed direct union with God, as Plotinus and on one occasion Porphyry had done: instead he tells us that he was an expert in weather-magic and in the technique of evocation, and that while practising 'the Chaldaean purifications' he was vouchsafed personal visions of luminous phantoms sent by Hecate.[2] The fundamental change of outlook after Porphyry is clearly recognized and stated by Olympiodorus, who remarks that 'some put philosophy first, as Porphyry, Plotinus &c.; others the priestly art (ἱερατικήν), as Iamblichus, Syrianus, Proclus and all the priestly school'.[3]

After making deduction of all theorems directly derived from Plato,[4] Aristotle[5] and Plotinus, and also of such as we have positive grounds for attributing to Iamblichus or other fourth-century writers,[6] there is still in the *Elements* a substantial residue of ἀδέσποτα. But it must not be assumed that this residue represents the personal contribution of Proclus. Behind Proclus stands the figure of his master Syrianus, that teacher 'filled with divine truth' who 'came to earth as the benefactor of banished souls . . . and fount of salvation both to his own and to future generations'.[7] Proclus is said to have been chosen by Syrianus as 'the heir capable of inheriting his vast learning and divine doctrine';[8] and to this rôle he remained faithful throughout his life. Seldom in the commentaries does he

---

[1] See the passages quoted in my notes on props. 39 and 145.

[2] *vit. Proc.* xxviii.

[3] *in Phaed.* 123. 3 Norvin. Compare the remark of Psellus that when Iamb. and Pr. read the *Chaldaean Oracles* they abandoned Greek for Chaldaic doctrine: ὁμοῦ τε γὰρ τούτοις συνεγένοντο καὶ καταιγίδας τὰς Ἑλληνικὰς μεθόδους περὶ τὸν συλλογισμὸν ὠνομάκασι (C. M. A. G. VI. 163. 19 ff.). Psellus' source for this exaggerated statement is Procopius of Gaza (the Christian adversary of Proclus), as appears from the passage quoted by Bidez on p. 85.

[4] The direct influence of Platonic texts and especially of the *Timaeus* and the *Parmenides* is, as we should naturally expect, very strong.

[5] The influence of Aristotle, especially in the domain of logic, increased steadily from the time of Plotinus down to that of the last Alexandrine philosophers, who are almost as much Aristotelians as Neoplatonists. In the *Elements* it is seen especially in props. 20 (ll. 16 ff.), 76, 77–9, 94, 96, and 198.

[6] To Iamblichus' pupil and rival, Theodore of Asine, may be due the formal discrimination of the three types of wholeness (props. 67–9); but apart from this I find nothing in the *Elements* to justify the *obiter dictum* of F. Heinemann, '(Proclus fühlt) dass der Weg von Plotin zu ihm mehr über Amelius und Theodor von Asine, als über Porphyr und Jamblich führt' (*Plotin* 107). Amelius and Theodore are frequently and sharply criticized in the *in Tim.*, e.g. II. 274. 10, 277. 26 ff.; 300. 23, III. 33. 33, 104. 8, 246. 27, 32 ff. and 333. 28.

[7] *in Parm.* 618. 3 ff.   [8] Marinus, *vit. Proc.* xii *fin.*

venture to innovate substantially upon earlier tradition without appealing to the authority of his teacher, guide and spiritual father (ὁ ἡμέτερος διδάσκαλος, καθηγεμών, πατήρ), whose doctrine is his 'trusty anchor'.[1] Zeller and others have suspected him, it is true, of using Syrianus as a stalking-horse, or at any rate of unconsciously introducing his own ideas into reports of Syrianus' teaching; but Olympiodorus makes the opposite accusation, that he put forward as his own certain of his master's ideas, even perhaps of his master's writings (in Phaed. 5². 18 Norvin). As no systematic treatise from the hand of Syrianus is preserved to us it is impossible fully to confirm or dispose of these conflicting suggestions. But sufficient evidence can be gleaned from Syrianus' extant commentary on Aristotle's *Metaphysics* to show that most of the theories commonly regarded as characteristic of Proclus were in fact anticipated, at least in part, by his master (who in turn *may*, of course, have taken them from some predecessor now lost *). This appears to be the case with the most striking of all the later innovations, the doctrine of 'divine henads', which fills about a quarter of the *Elements* : [2] I have tried to show in the commentary (note on sect. L) that these henads come from Plato's *Philebus* by way of Neopythagoreanism, and that they were identified with the gods by Syrianus, though much secondary elaboration was no doubt contributed by Proclus. In the same category are the important principles that the causal efficacy of the higher hypostasis extends further down the scale of existence than that of the lower,[3] and that generic characters in the effect proceed from a higher source than the specific ; [4] the exaltation of πέρας and ἀπειρία into cosmogonic ἀρχαί (again a borrowing from Neopythagoreanism) ; [5] the curious doctrine of relative infinitude ; [6] and the modification of earlier views on the relation of the Intelligence to the Forms.[7] Were Syrianus' other works preserved, this list could probably be extended; but even as it stands it suffices to prove that, in so far as a new direction was given to Neoplatonism after it took up its headquarters at Athens, that direction had already been deter-

---

[1] *in Tim.* III. 174. 14. In its earliest form the *Timaeus* commentary seems to have been a 'critical summary' of Syrianus' lectures on the subject (Marinus xiii). Original additions are commonly prefaced by apologetic phrases like εἴ με δεῖ τοὐμὸν εἰπεῖν.

[2] Props. 113-165.

[3] Prop. 57. This is not actually stated by Syr. as a general law, but he affirms it formally of the relation between τὸ ἕν and τὸ ὄν (in *Metaph.* 59. 17).

[4] Props. 71, 72; Syr. *l. c.* 29. 4 ff.   [5] Props. 89-92; Syr. 112. 14 ff.

[6] Prop. 93; Syr. 147. 14.

[7] Prop. 167. Pr.'s profession that he is following Syr. here (in *Tim.* I. 310. 4, 322. 18) is partly confirmed by Syr. himself, 110. 5.

mined before Proclus succeeded to the chair of Plato. And the view that Proclus was not an innovator but a systematizer of other men's ideas is strongly confirmed by the evidence of Marinus. Anxious as the latter naturally is to make the most of his hero's originality, the best example of it which he can find is a minor change in the classification of ψυχαί ;[1] the main claim which he makes for him as a philosopher is that he expounded and harmonized all earlier theologies 'both Greek and barbarian', and critically sifted the theories of all previous commentators, keeping what was fruitful and rejecting the rest.[2]

Proclus, then, is not a creative thinker even in the degree of Iamblichus, but a systematizer who carried to its utmost limits the ideal of the one comprehensive philosophy that should embrace all the garnered wisdom of the ancient world. To attempt an absolute valuation of the system which he expounded lies outside the scope of this edition. I will only say that its fundamental weakness seems to me to lie in the assumption that the structure of the cosmos exactly reproduces the structure of Greek logic. All rationalist systems are to some extent exposed to criticism on these lines; but in Proclus ontology becomes so manifestly the projected shadow of logic as to present what is almost a *reductio ad absurdum* of rationalism. In form a metaphysic of Being, the *Elements* embodies what is in substance a doctrine of categories: the cause is but a reflection of the ' because ', and the Aristotelian apparatus of genus, species and differentia is transformed into an objectively conceived hierarchy of entities or forces.[3]

Yet as the extreme statement of that rationalism which dominated European thought longer and to deeper effect than any other method, the *Elements* remains a work of very considerable philosophical interest. And its author was certainly something more than the superstitious pedant pictured for us by certain writers. Superstitious he unquestionably was, and pedantic also : in the fifth century after Christ it could hardly be otherwise. He believes in mermaids and dragons,[4] in goat-footed Pans,[5] in statues that move without contact like the tables of the spiritualists ;[6] from the fact that the Man in the Moon has eyes and ears but no nose or mouth he can argue seriously that astral gods possess only the two higher senses ;[7] and his interpretative zeal is such that a personage in a Platonic dialogue

[1] *vit. Proc.* xxiii.   [2] *ibid.* xxii, cf. xxvi.
[3] Cf. notes on props. 6, 8, 67–9 and 70.
[4] *in Tim.* II. 202. 24.   [5] *in Crat.* lxxiv.
[6] *in Tim.* III. 6. 12.   [7] *in Crat.* lxxviii.

has but to smile for him to scent a profound symbolic meaning.[1]
Yet the man who was capable of these puerilities reveals not only in
the *Elements* but in many passages of the commentaries a critical
acumen and a systematic grasp not easily to be matched within the
post-classical period in any philosophical writer save Plotinus. The
paradox of Proclus has been well expressed by Freudenthal,[2] ' in
Proklus' Lehren ist Tiefsinn mit grenzenlosem Aberglauben,
haarscharfe Dialektik mit unlogischer Verschwommenheit der
Begriffe, gesunde Kritik mit naiver Glaubensseligkeit, mathematische
Gedankenstrenge mit der Unvernunft eines wundersüchtigen Mysti-
zismus [3] zu einem unauflöslichen Knäuel in einander gewirrt '. But
critics are inclined to forget that Proclus' qualities were all but
unique in an age when his defects were all but universal. Standing
as he does on the desert frontier between two worlds, with his face
turned towards the vanishing world of Hellenism, he makes in the
perspective of history a figure rather pathetic than heroic; to see his
achievement in its true proportion we must set it against the im-
poverished and tormented background of his own century and those
that followed. In this sense historians of Greek philosophy have in
general done him considerably less than justice. Historians of the
Middle Ages, on the other hand, are beginning to realize his importance in another aspect, as one of the fountain-heads of that
Neoplatonic tradition which, mingling unrecognized with the slow-
moving waters of medieval thought, issued beyond them at last to
refertilize the world at the Renaissance. Wholly preoccupied as he
was with the past, the philosophy of Proclus is not merely a summa-
tion of bygone achievement : the accident of history has given it
also the significance of a new beginning.

§ 4. *The Influence of Proclus.*[4]

The influence which Proclus exercised upon early medieval
thought may be called accidental, in the sense that it would scarcely
have been felt but for the activity of the unknown eccentric who within
a generation of Proclus' death conceived the idea of dressing his
philosophy in Christian draperies and passing it off as the work of a

---

[1] *in Parm.* 1022. 10 ff.
[2] *Hermes* 16 (1881) 218 ff.
[3] i.e. occultism. The genuine mystic is seldom ' wundersüchtig '.
[4] All that is attempted here is to indicate a few salient points, with special
reference to the *El. Th.* A detailed study of the subject would require a book to
itself, and would demand a far more intimate knowledge of medieval and
renaissance literature than I possess [*].

convert of St. Paul. Though challenged by Hypatius of Ephesus and others, in official quarters the fraud[1] met with complete and astonishing success. Not only did the works of 'Dionysius the Areopagite' escape the ban of heresy which they certainly merited, but by 649 they had become an 'Urkunde' sufficiently important for a Pope to bring before the Lateran Council a question concerning a disputed reading in one of them. About the same date they were made the subject of an elaborate commentary by Maximus the Confessor, the first of a long succession of commentaries from the hands of Erigena, Hugh of St. Victor, Robert Grosseteste, Albertus Magnus, Thomas Aquinas and others. 'Dionysius' rapidly acquired an authority second only to that of Augustine. In the East his negative theology and his hierarchical schematism exercised a powerful influence on John of Damascus (d. *circa* 750), who in turn influenced the later scholastics through the Latin version of his ἔκδοσις τῆς ὀρθοδόξου πίστεως made in 1151. But 'Dionysius' also affected western thought more directly, first through the clumsy translation made by Erigena in 858, and later through the versions of Johannes Saracenus and Robert Grosseteste. In Erigena's own treatise *de divisione naturae* the Neoplatonism of 'Dionysius'[2] became the basis of a comprehensive world-system; it reappears in later writers like Simon of Tournai and Alfredus Anglicus, and influenced Bonaventura, Aquinas and Descartes.[3] The authenticity of Dionysius' works was denied by the renaissance humanist Laurentius Valla, but was not finally disproved until the nineteenth century (there are still Catholic theologians who profess belief in it).

The extent of ps.-Dion.'s dependence on Proclus was first fully revealed by the work of the Jesuit Stiglmayr and especially by the elaborate study of H. Koch, *Pseudo-Dionysius Areopagita in seinen Beziehungen zum Neuplatonismus u. Mysterienwesen.* They show that not only did he reproduce with a minimum of Christian disguise the whole structure of Athenian Neoplatonism and take over practically

[1] It is for some reason customary to use a kinder term; but it is quite clear that the deception was deliberate (cf. H. Koch, *Pseudo-Dionysius* 3).

[2] Ps.-Dion. appears to be his main source in this work, though he used also Augustine and Gregory of Nyssa: see J. Dräseke, *Joh. Scotus Erigena u. dessen Gewährsmänner* (Stud. z. Gesch. d. Theol. u. Kirche Bd. ix, H. 2). The extent of his debt to Neoplatonism has recently been investigated by H. Dörries, *E. u. d. Neuplatonismus*, who, however, treats as original certain doctrines of E. which are in fact Neoplatonic, such as the simultaneous affirmation of divine transcendence and divine immanence (pp. 25, 29: cf. *El. Th.* props. 98 n., 145 l. 20 n.) and the emphasis laid on the '*vita*-Begriff' (p. 43 n. 1: cf. props. 101–2 n.).

[3] Descartes owed much to his contemporary and intimate friend, the theologian Gibieuf, who was steeped in ps.-Dion. (E. Gilson, *La Liberté chez Descartes* 193, 201).

the whole of its technical terminology,[1] but he followed Proclus slavishly in many of the details of his doctrine. A single example from Koch must here suffice :

Pr. *in Alc.* II. 153 Cousin[1]: καὶ θεοὶ τοίνυν θεῶν ἐρῶσιν· οἱ πρεσβύτεροι τῶν καταδεεστέρων, ἀλλὰ προνοητικῶς· καὶ οἱ καταδεέστεροι τῶν ὑπερτέρων, ἀλλ᾽ ἐπιστρεπτικῶς.

ps.-Dion. *Div. Nom.* 4. 10 : καὶ τὰ ἥττω τῶν κρειττόνων ἐπιστρεπτικῶς ἐρῶσι . . . καὶ τὰ κρείττω τῶν ἡττόνων προνοητικῶς.

Many other borrowings are noted in the commentary. The effect of his imitations is not infrequently grotesque, as when he transfers to Christ and the Holy Ghost the epithets with which Proclus had adorned his henads.[2]

While Proclus was thus conquering Europe in the guise of an early Christian, in his own person he seems to have been studied at first only for the purpose of refuting his system and then not at all. At Alexandria the heritage of the Neoplatonic school passed without any breach of continuity into the hands of such Christian successors as Johannes Philoponus;[3] but the resolute paganism of Proclus and the other Athenian Neoplatonists[4] precluded any such evolution in their case. In the sixth century Proclus' teaching was still sufficiently influential to call for detailed refutation—witness the extant work of Philoponus *de aeternitate mundi contra Proclum*, and the treatise composed by Procopius of Gaza in answer to Proclus' commentary on the τελεστικά of Julianus.[5] But thereafter, as Aristotle became the one officially licensed philosopher of the Byzantine world, Proclus and his brother Platonists sank into an obscurity from which they were retrieved only by the humanist revival under the Comneni.

During this period of eclipse, however, the knowledge of Proclus' work was diffused in the East. His commentaries on *Rep.* Book X,

[1] To the long list of borrowed terms given by Koch may be added ἀγελαρχία, ἄζως, ἀνεκφοιτήτως, ἄσχετος, αὐτοτελής, οὐσιοποιός, περιοχή, πηγαῖος, προαιωνίως, προόν, ὑπέρζωος, ὑφειμένος, &c.

[2] Pr. *de mal. subsist.* 209. 27, the henads are ' velut flores et supersubstantialia lumina ': hence for ps.-Dion. Jesus and the Πνεῦμα are οἷον ἄνθη καὶ ὑπερούσια φῶτα (*Div. Nom.* 2. 7).

[3] See Praechter, *Richtungen*; and P. Tannery, *Sur la Période Finale de la Philosophie Grecque*, in *Rev. Philosophique* XXI (1896) 266 ff.

[4] Pr.'s attitude cost him a year's banishment from Athens (Marinus xv). Direct criticism of the established religion was exceedingly dangerous in the fifth century, but he comes very near to it in such passages as *in Remp.* I. 74. 4 ff., *in Alc.* 531. 39, *in Crat.* cxxv. The same tone is perceptible in Damascius (*vit. Isidor.* 48. 11 ff., 92. 26 ff., 103. 12 ff.) and Simplicius (*in Arist. de caelo* 370. 29).

[5] This is referred to by a scholiast on Lucian, *Philopseudes* 12 (IV. 224 Jacoby): cf. Bidez in *C.M.A.G.* VI. 85 n. 1.

the *Gorgias*, the *Phaedo* and (unless this is a misattribution) the *Golden Verses*, are known to have been translated into Syriac.[1] Fragmentary Arabic versions of the two last-named are also recorded;[2] and various others of his works were known at least by name to Mohammedan scholars.[3]   We hear also of an Arabic work by the physician Razi, entitled 'Concerning Doubt, in connexion with [or, against] Proclus'; and of an Arabic version of the *de aeternitate mundi contra Proclum*.[4]   The *de causis*, of which we shall have occasion to speak in a moment, is thought by O. Bardenhewer, the editor of the Arabic text, to have been compiled from an Arabic translation of the *Elements of Theology*;[5] but no record of such a translation has as yet been discovered, unless, with August Müller, we interpret in this sense an obscure entry in Haji Khalfa's *Lexicon Bibliographicum et Encyclopaedicum*.[6]   The *Elements of Theology* was, however, translated into Georgian, with a commentary,[7] by John Petritsi early in the twelfth century; thence[8] into Armenian by the monk Simeon of Garni in 1248; furnished with a new Armenian commentary by bishop Simeon of Djulfa in the seventeenth century; and finally retranslated from the Armenian into Georgian in 1757.[9] On these versions, which are still extant, see below, pp. xli–ii. They are of interest as showing a fairly continuous study of Proclus in the Near East from the later Middle Ages down to the eighteenth century.

Of much greater historical importance than these is the *Liber de*

---

[1] Baumstark, *Geschichte der Syrischen Literatur* p. 231.

[2] M. Steinschneider, *Die Arabischen Uebersetzungen aus dem Griechischen* (= Beihefte z. Centralblatt f. Bibliothekswesen 12) 92 f.

[3] See especially the list given in the *Fihrist* of Muhammed ibn Ishâq (pp. 22–3 of the German translation by August Müller published under the title *Die Griechischen Philosophen in der Arabischen Ueberlieferung*, Halle 1873). It includes a θεολογία and a 'Lesser στοιχείωσις', which Müller identifies respectively with the *El. Th.* and the *El. Phys.* As, however, the latter appears to figure elsewhere in Muhammed's list as 'A work on the definitions of the natural elements', it is perhaps more probable that the 'Lesser στοιχείωσις' is the *El. Th.* and the θεολογία the *Th. Pl.*

[4] Steinschneider *op. cit.* pp. 93, 105.   [5] P. 47 of his edition.

[6] Tom. V, p. 66 Fluegel, no. 10005 : Kitâb-el-thálújiyá, liber theologiae, i.e. doctrinae religionis divinae, auctoribus Proclo Platonico · et Alexandro Aphrodisiensi. Hunc librum Abu Othmán Dimeshcki anno . . . mortuus, transtulit. The date is lacking. Steinschneider, *op. cit.* p. 92, thinks that the title is corrupt and the ascription to Proclus due to a confusion *.

[7] Attributed in the Georgian MSS. to 'John' (Petritsi); in the Armenian to Amelachos or Iomelachos or Homelachos (? Iamblichus), 'the Athenian bishop and philosopher and rhetor ' *.

[8] Dashien's view, that the Armenian version was made direct from the Greek, is controverted by N. J. Marr, *John Petritski*, in Proc. Russ. Archaeol. Acad. (Zapiski Vostochnago) 19 (1909).

[9] See Marr, *op. cit.*, and P. Peeters, *Traduction et Traducteurs dans l'hagiographie orientale*, in Analecta Bollandiana 40 (1922) 292.

causis, which passed in medieval times for the work of Aristotle, but is in fact (as Aquinas recognized [1]) a translation of an Arabic work based on the *Elements of Theology*. The original Arabic book, which has been published with a German version by O. Bardenhewer, would seem to have been composed by a Mohammedan writer in the ninth century. It was rendered into Latin between 1167 and 1187 by Gerhard of Cremona, and is constantly cited as an authority from Alanus ab Insulis (end of the twelfth century) onwards. It exists also in an Armenian [2] and in no fewer than four Hebrew [3] versions. The additions made to it by Albertus Magnus contain further material derived ultimately from the *Elements*, doubtless again, as Degen [4] thinks, through an Arabic intermediary. In this extended form it was used by Dante, and is probably the main source of the Neoplatonic ideas which appear in the *Convito* and the *Divine Comedy*.[5]

Proclus' ideas were thus for the second time introduced to Europe under a false name of singular inappropriateness. His direct influence upon the Byzantine world begins only with the renaissance of Platonism in the eleventh century, upon the Latin West with Aquinas and William of Morbecca in the thirteenth. The Byzantine Neoplatonist Michael Psellus (1018–78 or 1096) was steeped in Proclus, and has preserved for us much curious matter taken from his lost commentary on the *Chaldaean Oracles* (as does also Nicephorus Gregoras in his scholia on the *de insomniis* of Synesius).[6] In his *de omnifaria doctrina* Psellus makes abundant use of the *Elements of Theology*, which he quotes as τὰ κεφάλαια.[7] But despite the authority of ' Dionysius ', whose pagan imitator he was thought to be,[8] the vogue of Proclus was looked upon with suspicion by the orthodox. Hence the next century saw the elaborate Ἀνάπτυξις τῆς θεολογικῆς στοιχειώσεως Πρόκλου by the theologian Nicolaus, Bishop

---

[1] Aquinas' words are : ' Videtur ab aliquo philosophorum Arabum ex praedicto libro Proculi (sc. the *El. Th.*) excerptus, praesertim quia omnia quae in hoc libro continentur, multo plenius et diffusius continentur in illo '. His commentary on the *de causis* is variously dated between 1268 and 1271 *.

[2] In the Mechitaristen-Bibliothek at Vienna, no. 483[6].

[3] Steinschneider, *Die Hebraischen Uebersetzungen des Mittelalters* §§ 140 ff.

[4] E. Degen, *Welches sind die Beziehungen Alberts des Grossen* ' Liber de causis et processu universitatis ' *zur στοιχείωσις θεολογική* . . . ? (München, 1902 *.

[5] M. Baumgartner, *Dantes Stellung zur Philosophie*, in Zweite Vereinschrift d. Görresgesellschaft (1921) 57 ff.

[6] See Bidez in *C. M. A. G.* VI. 83 n.11, 104 ff. ; and on Psellus' Neoplatonism in general, C. Zervos, *Un Philosophe néoplatonicien du XI⁰ siècle, Michel Psellos.*

[7] Cap. 74 (cf. *El. Th.* props. 38, 39). Other borrowings from *El. Th.* appear in cap. 16 (= prop. 124) and caps. 19-26 (= props. 62, 166, 167, 169, 171, 173, 176, 177).

[8] Suidas s.v. Διονύσιος ὁ Ἀρεωπαγίτης : Psellus *de omnif. doct.* cap. 74.

of Methone,[1] which is directed against τινὲς τῆς ἔνδον ταύτης καὶ ἡμετέρας γεγονότες αὐλῆς who 'think the propositions of Proclus worthy of admiration' (p. 2 Voemel). This 'refutation' was accompanied by a text of the original work, and is the source of a number of our MSS. of it (see below, pp. xxxiii–v).

The first work of Proclus to be made directly accessible in Latin was the *Elements of Physics*, which was translated from the Greek in Sicily somewhere about the middle of the twelfth century. The *El. Th.* was introduced to the West in 1268, when the Flemish Dominican William of Morbecca or Moerbeke, friend of Aquinas, papal chaplain, and afterwards Archbishop of Corinth, produced a Latin version of it (see below, p. xlii), followed later by a part of the *in Tim.*, the *de dec. dub.*, the *de prov. et fat.* and the *de mal. subsist.* The recently discovered version of the *in Parm.* may or may not be from the same hand; it belongs in any case to the latter part of the thirteenth century.[2] These translations appeared at a time when Plotinus, and Plato himself (save for the *Phaedo*, the *Meno*, and part of the *Timaeus*), were still unknown in the West; and they played a decisive part in shaping the later medieval notion of 'Platonism'.[3] From them springs the prestige of Proclus as (in Tauler's words) 'the great pagan Master'—a reputation which he continued to enjoy down to the time of Leibniz. The translation of the *Elements of Theology* was used by Aquinas in his last years,[4] and its influence

[1] A fragment contained in a Vatican MS. of the fourteenth and fifteenth centuries and there ascribed to Procopius of Gaza was published by A. Mai in 1831 and discovered sixty years later to be word for word identical with a passage in the Ἀνάπτυξις. On this basis J. Dräseke (*Byz. Zeitschr.* VI [1897] 55 ff.) erected the theory that Procopius is the real author of the Ἀνάπτυξις, which must therefore have been composed within a generation of Proclus' death or even (as D. prefers to think) during his lifetime. This conclusion, if sound, would obviously have a very important bearing on the history of the text of the *El. Th.*; but the objections urged by Stiglmayr (*Byz. Zeitschr.* VIII [1899] 263 ff.), which need not be recapitulated here, seem to me decisive. Additional arguments against D.'s view are the following: (a) the confusion of dates by which Origen is said to have derived his heretical doctrine of ἀποκατάστασις from the *El. Th.* (Ἀνάπτ. p. 57) is surely impossible for a writer almost Proclus' contemporary; (b) Ἀνάπτ. p. 187 ὡς ἐν τοῖς περὶ ὅρου πλατύτερον ἡμῖν διευκρίνηται would have to be treated as an interpolation, since it unmistakably refers to the treatise of Nicolaus πρὸς τὸν ἐρωτήσαντα εἰ ἔστιν ὅρος ζωῆς καὶ θανάτου p. 224 Demetrakopoulos (Ἐκκλησιαστικὴ Βιβλιοθήκη, Lpz. 1866); (c) at *El. Th.* page 70 l. 35 f. and several other passages the reading *implied in the text of the* Ἀνάπτ., as well as given by our N MSS. of the *El. Th.*, involves a complex corruption such as could hardly have arisen by the date which D. assumes.
[2] R. Klibansky, *Ein Proklos-Fund u. seine Bedeutung* (Abh. Heidelberger Akad. 1929, no. 5), 30 ff. The *Platonic Theology* seems to have been first translated in the fifteenth century (*ibid.* 26 n.2).
[3] Klibansky, *op. cit.* 18 ff.
[4] He quotes the book by name more than once in the *de substantiis separatis*. For parallels between the *Elements* and the teaching of Aquinas see on props. 28, 30, 50–4, 57, 124, 190.

was soon reflected in the German Dominican school : Dietrich of Freiberg (*c.* 1250–1310) repeatedly quotes it by name[1]; another Dominican, Berthold of Mosburg, composed a lengthy commentary upon it which still exists in manuscript[2]; and we ought probably to recognize in it one of the main sources of Eckhart's peculiar type of negative theology.[3] In the fifteenth century it formed with the *Platonic Theology* and the *in Parm.* the favourite reading of Nicholas of Cusa,[4] who derived from Proclus important elements of his own doctrine and often cites him as an authority.

In the renewed popularity of the Neoplatonists at the Renaissance Proclus had a full share. For the *Elements of Theology* this is sufficiently attested by the great number of fifteenth- or sixteenth-century copies which have survived: over forty are known to me, and there are probably others still. In the importation of Proclus manuscripts from the East, Cardinal Bessarion was especially active,[5] and no fewer than three of our MSS. of the *Elements* come from his library; another was written by Marsilio Ficino, the translator of Plato and Plotinus; another was owned by Pico della Mirandola, whose celebrated Fifty-five Propositions seem to be based exclusively upon Proclus.[6] A new Latin translation of the *Elements of Theology* by Patrizzi was printed in 1583; but the first printed edition of the Greek text (with the *Platonic Theology* and the *Life* by Marinus) did not appear until 1618. Beyond this point I cannot attempt to carry the present survey. It shall end with two quotations which may be of interest to students of English literature.

The first is taken from Nature's answer to Mutability at the end of the *Faerie Queen* (VII. vii. 58):

> I well consider all that ye have said,
> And find that all things stedfastnesse do hate
> And changed be; yet, being rightly wayd,
> They are not changed from their first estate;
> But by their change their being do dilate,
> And turning to themselves at length againe,
> Do work their owne perfection so by fate.

---

[1] See the passages cited in Ueberweg-Geyer[11] 556 f. De Wulf says that he put Proclus on a level with Augustine and Aristotle.

[2] In the library of Balliol College, Oxford, no. 224[b]; also Vat. Lat. 2192.

[3] E. Krebs, *Meister Dietrich*, 126 ff.; Klibansky 12 n. 2.

[4] His friend Giovanni Andrea de Bussi says of him 'his ille libris veluti thesauris suis et propriis maxime recreabatur, ut nulli alii rei tantopere vigilaret' (quoted by Klibansky, 26 n. 3; cf. 29 n. 1). His copy, with autograph comments, of William of Morbecca's version of *El. Th.* is preserved at Cues (no. 195 Marx, ff. 34ʳ–66ʳ).

[5] Klibansky, 24.   [6] See chap. II § 1, nos. 2, 14, 37; 45; 24.

This strange-sounding doctrine becomes intelligible when we realize that it is a distant echo of Proclus' theory that 'every effect remains in its cause, proceeds from it, and reverts upon it' (*El. Th.* prop. 35). Spenser may possibly have read Patrizzi's translation of the *Elements*, but more likely he came by the idea indirectly, through some Italian Neoplatonist (cf. Renwick, *Edmund Spenser*, 164).

The second is from Coleridge: 'The most beautiful and orderly development of the philosophy which endeavours to explain all things by an analysis of consciousness, and builds up a world in the mind out of materials furnished by the mind itself, is to be found in the *Platonic Theology* of Proclus'.[1]

CHAPTER II.

§ 1. *Manuscripts* *.

The MSS. which I have examined with a view to the present edition fall for the most part into three well-marked families, though some of the later copies show signs of conflation. The complete list (including a few known to me only from earlier collations) is as follows :—

FIRST FAMILY, representing the text used by Nicolaus of Methone in the twelfth century (see above, p. xxx f.). These MSS. contain props. 1–198 only.[2]

B   1. *Vaticanus graec. 237* (formerly 171), ff. 76–181ᵛ, saec. xiv, chart. (see Mercati and Cavalieri, *Codices Vaticani Graeci Descripti*, T. I.). Very few corrections or marginalia. I have made a full collation (from photographs).

2. *Marcianus graec. 403* (formerly 193), ff. 60–100ᵛ, saec. xv init., perg. (see Zanetti and Bongiovanni, *Graeca D. Marci Bibliotheca Codicum Manu Scriptorum*). Formerly in the possession of Bessarion. No corrections or marginalia. A full collation (which I had made before I had seen B) shows that this MS. has a number of errors and *lacunae* peculiar to itself, but otherwise (save for occasional correction of obvious miswritings) agrees very closely with B, on which it is mainly if not wholly dependent.

To this family belong also the MSS. (nos. 3–13) of Nicolaus of Methone's Ἀνάπτυξις τῆς θεολογικῆς στοιχειώσεως, which includes a complete text of props. 1–198 of Proclus' work, but neither text of nor commentary on the remaining propositions.

[1] *Memorials of Coleorton II*, Jan. 1810.
[2] Except D, where props. 199–209 mid. were added by a later hand, and the copies of D (nos. 6–10).

C 3. *Vaticanus graec. 626*, ff. 121–213ᵛ, saec. xiv (vel xiii fin.), chart. The earlier portion has been corrected by another hand (a contemporary διορθωτής?); in the later portions the διόρθωσις seems to have been carried out by the scribe himself. This MS. gives a text of Proclus closely similar to B; but it is clearly independent of B, as B of it.[1] I have made a full collation (from photographs).[2]

(B Voemeli) 4. *Lugdunensis B. P. graec. 23*, saec. xvi (?), chart. (see Voemel in *Initia Philosophiae ac Theologiae, Pars IV*, Frankfurt am Main 1825, pp. viii–ix). Contains only the opening and closing words of each proposition; Voemel gives a collation of these (*op. cit.* pp. 252–4). Claims to be copied from a Vatican MS., which can with certainty be identified with C.

D 5. *Ambrosianus graec. 648, ff. 1–26+727, ff. 193–237*, saec. xiv fin. et xv, chart. (see Martini and Bassi, *Catalogus codicum graecorum Bibliothecae Ambrosianae*). This MS. is a patchwork product. (*a*) Props. 1–77 and 98–115 were written by one hand, props. 78 and 116–20 by another, props. 79–97 by a third. These three hands are contemporary, and seem to belong to the end of the fourteenth century. (*b*) Props. 121–98 are in a fourth and perhaps somewhat later hand. (*c*) A fifteenth-century hand (*d*) added props. 199–209 mid. (without commentary).[3] (*d*) Finally, the book was rebound in two parts, with several leaves misplaced; and the leaf containing props. 6 and 7, which had been lost at some earlier stage, was replaced first by a faulty Latin version (not William of Morbecca's) and then by the Greek in a sixteenth-century hand. Correctors: (i) in the earlier propositions occur sporadic corrections in at least two different hands, D² (perhaps the scribe of props. 78 and 116–20) and D³; (ii) a further hand (D⁴) has corrected the work of all scribes down to prop. 198. This MS. is on the whole inferior to C, but is probably independent of it, being free from some of its characteristic errors.[4] I have collated it for props. 1–198.

6, 7, 8, 9, 10. *Ambrosiani graec. 203, 204, 207, 1016, 212*, are sixteenth-century copies of D, made after stage (*c*) and before stage (*d*). The first four were written by Camillus Venetus.

E 11. *Parisinus 1256*, chart., saec. xv (see Omont, *Inventaire*

---

[1] Cf. e.g. p. 6 ll. 18–19; p. 20 l. 17.
[2] A collation by Holsten is preserved in his copy of Portus' edition, Biblioteca Barberina J.iv. 31.
[3] The text of these props. is clearly borrowed from one of the copies of M classed below as group m. i, and has therefore no independent value.
[4] Cf. e.g. pp. 64 l. 5; 158, l. 15. At p. 54 l. 19 DE alone have the true reading.

INTRODUCTION xxxv

Sommaire des MSS. grecs de la Bibliothèque Nationale). I have
made a full collation of this MS.; but it is distinctly inferior to
BCD, and its value as a source for the text is questionable. It has
most but not all of the readings characteristic of D (stage (*b*) after
correction), while in a few passages it reproduces the erroneous
reading of D *before* correction. Where it differs from D, it either
agrees with the older representatives of the family, or, more often,
introduces errors of its own. It may be either a cousin of D or
a descendant derived through a copy embodying occasional corrections from B or C.

(A 12. *Lugdunensis B. P. graec. 4*, chart., saec. xvi (see Voemel,
eli) *l. c.*). This is the only MS. of the first family, if we except the
fragmentary no. 4, of which a collation has hitherto been published
(by Voemel, *op. cit.* pp. 233 ff.). It appears to be derived from D;
but if Voemel's collation is a complete one (I have not examined
the MS.), it has been contaminated with readings from the second
family.

13. *Laurentianus plut. IX cod. 12*, ff. 1–127, chart., saec. xv vel
xvi (see Bandini, *Catalogus Codicum Graecorum Bibliothecae Lauren-
tianae*, T. i, p. 406, where it is wrongly ascribed to saec. xiv).
A partial collation indicates that this MS. is very closely related to E,
though neither appears to be dependent on the other.

M SECOND FAMILY. 14. *Marcianus graec. 678* (formerly 512),
ff. 128–76ᵛ, chart., saec. xiii fin. vel xiv init. (see Zanetti and Bongiovanni, *op. cit.*). From Bessarion's library. Two leaves, containing
respectively props. 10 init.–12 εἴτε γὰρ ἐφίεται κἀκείνου and 20 ἐπέκεινά
ἐστιν ἡ ψυχῆς οὐσία–21 καὶ τῇ νοερᾷ οὐσίᾳ, have been lost at some
date since the beginning of the fifteenth century. Props. 203 αἱ δὲ
ἔσχαται κατὰ τὴν τάξιν–211 fin. are in another hand contemporary
with the first. There are a number of glosses, marginal and interlinear, in the first hand, mostly of little interest. The MS. has been
much tampered with, and many of the original readings have been
wholly or partially erased; but most of these can be recovered with
greater or less certainty by the help of nos. 15–23, which descend
from a copy of M made before correction. In the corrections
themselves two stages can be distinguished. (*a*) Before 1358 (the
date of O) two hands had been at work. One of these (M²) introduced a large number of readings, which agree sometimes with the
first family, sometimes with the third, occasionally with neither (in
the last case they are with the rarest exceptions worthless). To the
other hand (M³) are due a few marginal variants, mostly from the

first family. (*b*) Between 1358 and about 1400 additional corrections were made (from the third family?) by another hand or hands (M⁴), the most important being the filling of the extensive lacuna in prop. 209.—I have made a full collation (partly from photographs).

The remaining MSS. of the second family are all dependent primarily on M, though many of them embody also a certain number of readings from other sources. They may be classified according to their derivation (*a*) from M before correction (group m i), (*b*) from M as corrected by M¹ and M³ (group m. ii–iii), (*c*) from M as further corrected by M⁴ (group m. iv).

Group m. i. Arg (= A Creuzeri) 15. [*Argentoratensis*]: see Creuzer¹ (= *Initia Phil. ac Theol. Pars* III), p. xvii, and Haenel, *Catalogus librorum MSS. qui in bibliothecis Galliae etc. asservantur.* This MS. perished in 1870, and no adequate description of it exists; but we have a collation by Schweighäuser, which with Portus's readings constitutes the whole *apparatus criticus* of Creuzer's earlier text. Creuzer calls it 'quantivis pretii codicem', and it in fact preserved many sound readings of M¹ which were unknown to Portus, as well as a few incorporated from other sources (if the collation can be trusted); but it also exhibited many corruptions peculiar either to itself or to group m. i. It broke off at the lacuna in prop. 209, as do the other members of the group (except nos. 19 and 21–23).

16. *Parisinus 2045*, ff. 51ᵛ–106ᵛ, chart., saec. xv (see Omont, *op. cit.*). Props. 153–end are in another hand. Appears, so far as I have collated it, to be a representative of M¹ slightly less corrupt than Arg.

(L a Creuzeri) 17. *Lugdunensis Voss. graec. 14*, chart., saec. xv vel xvi. Resembles, but is inferior to, no. 16 (of which, however, it is apparently independent). A few readings from this MS. are given in an appendix to Creuzer's first edition.

18. *Parisinus graec. 1885*, chart., saec. xvi, is a copy of no. 17.

19. *Vaticanus graec. 1036*, ff. 101–204, chart., saec. xvi fin. Breaks off at prop. 208 fin., and is otherwise faulty.

(H Creuzeri) 20. *Hamburgensis phil. graec. 25*, saec. xvi, written by A. Darmarius and formerly in the possession of Lucas Holsten, who states that he 'emended Portus's whole edition' from it: see H. Omont, *Catal. des MSS. grecs. . . . des Villes Hanséatiques.* I have not seen this MS., but there is a partial collation by J. Gurlitt in Cr.¹ pp. 319 ff. Creuzer's assumption that it is a copy of a Vatican MS. seems to be mistaken.

21. *Parisinus 2028* contains the Στοιχείωσις Θεολογική (ff. 74–106), perg., saec. xiv, bound with paper MSS. of later origin (see Omont, *Invent.*, where it is wrongly described as *Theologicae Institutionis libri sex*). Props. 1–4 have been lost and supplied in a later hand on paper (apparently from O); prop. 211 is missing. This MS. is not the parent of nos. 15–20, but appears to be derived like them (through a common ancestor, as is shown by common omissions) from M¹. It is not, however, a satisfactory representative of the text of M¹, as it exhibits a large number of readings introduced from other sources.

22. *Vaticanus 1444*, ff. 45–90, chart., a. 1542. Prop. 211 is missing, as in no. 21, of which this MS. appears to be a corrupt descendant.

23. *Parisinus 1842*, ff. 156ᵛ–318ᵛ, chart., saec. xvii. Lacks prop. 211, and abounds in the grossest errors.

oup
–iii.   All these MSS., while based on M²⁻³, agree in certain passages with BCD against all the hands in M. We may suppose them derived from M²⁻³ through a common ancestor which was occasionally corrected from the first family.[1]

O   24. *Bodleianus Laud. graec. 18*, ff. 242–88ᵛ, chart., a. 1358: written by Stelianos Choumnos, and formerly in the possession of Pico della Mirandola : see Coxe's *Catalogue* (where it is wrongly described as containing 209 props. instead of 211). This MS., of which I had made a complete collation before I was acquainted with M, has some corruptions shared by the rest of the group, and a large number of others peculiar to itself and no. 25. Many of these errors figure in Portus's text, and not a few are retained by Creuzer. Corrections have been introduced by several later hands. These are sometimes hard to distinguish ; but O² seems to have used a MS. of the first family, while O³ often emends conjecturally and wildly.

25. *Parisinus 1830*, ff. 279–330, chart., a. 1539 : written by Valeriano Albino. Derived from O after that MS. had been corrected.

26. *Riccardianus graec. 70*, ff. 217–56, chart., saec. xv (see Vitelli's catalogue). This and the following MSS. are independent of O. They have one or two sound readings peculiar to them which seem to be due to conjecture.

---

[1] E.g. the missing words in prop. 78, l. 15 were supplied, and a characteristic reading of BCD introduced in prop. 198, l. 25.

27. *Monacensis graec. 502*, ff. 1–38, chart., saec. xv : formerly at Augsburg. Derived from no. 26.

28. *Parisinus 2018*, ff. 260–305, chart., saec. xv. Closely resembles no. 26.

29. *Ambrosianus 38*, chart., a. 1581 : written by F. Patrizzi, who records that it was copied from a MS. written 112 years earlier. Closely resembles. nos. 26–8, but appears to be independently derived from the common source of this sub-group.

30. *Ambrosianus 1010*, ff. 361ᵛ–429, chart., saec. xvi : written for Pinelli by Georgius Aetolus. An inferior copy.

31. *Ambrosianus 812*, ff. 31–84, chart., saec. xvi : written by Camillus Venetus, and formerly in the possession of F. Patrizzi. Copy of 30 ?

32. *Bodleianus Misc. 84* (formerly 3036), chart., contains props. 1–32 πᾶσα ἄρα ἐπιστροφή (not 1–29 as stated by Coxe), bound with various late MSS. This fragment, in a fifteenth-century hand, resembles nos. 30–1.

33. *Monacensis graec. 547*, ff. 304–51, chart., saec. xv (init.?): formerly at Augsburg. Written in 3 hands: (i) props. 1–122 ; (ii) props. 123–4 ; (iii) props. 125-end. This MS. and the three following embody some further corrections of the text of M²⁻³, in addition to those found in nos. 24–32. Moreover, no. 33 has itself been extensively corrected from the first family.

34. *Parisinus 1828*, ff. 239–80ᵛ, chart., claims to be a copy 'transcriptus et recognitus ex antiquo exemplari Bibliothecae D. Marci Venetiarum' by Nicholas de la Torre in 1562. It proved on examination to be a copy, not of any MS. now at Venice, but almost certainly of no. 33 (made after that MS. had been corrected).[1]

35. *Laurentianus plut. LXXXVI cod. 8*, ff. 271ᵛ–92, chart., saec. xv. Resembles the original text of no. 33 ; but the two appear to be mutually independent.

(L b Creuzeri) 36. *Lugdunensis B. P. graec. 59*, ff. 15–70, chart., saec. xvi. Faulty copy of no. 35. Here again a corrector has introduced variants from the first family. A few readings from this MS. are given by Creuzer[1], pp. 319 ff.

Group m. iv. 37. *Marcianus graec. 613* (formerly 192), ff. 265–310ᵛ, perg., saec. xv (init. ?). Formerly in the possession of Bessarion.

---

[1] E.g. a scholion on prop. 5 from the margin of M was inserted in the text after ἄμα (p. 6, l. 16) in the archetype of nos. 33 and 35 : in no. 33 it was struck out by the corrector, with the note τοῦτο σχόλιον ἦν : in no. 34 the gloss appears in the margin and the words τοῦτο σχόλιον ἦν in the text (subsequently deleted).

38. *Vindobonensis graec. 38* (formerly 14), ff. 268–318, chart., c. 1548. Bought at Venice in 1672, and formerly in the possession of Sebastianus Ericius. Derived from no. 37.

Here should probably be classified also the two following:

39. *Vaticanus 1737* (formerly 45), ff. 15–89, chart., saec. xv vel xvi? Formerly in the possession of Aloysius Lollinus.

40. *Palatinus 347*, ff. 1–4, pap. Contains props. 1–15 οὐδὲν ἄρα σῶμα in a sixteenth-century hand.

THE THIRD FAMILY is represented, so far as I know, by three MSS. only, nos. 41–3. These offer a text which often differs very substantially (especially in order of words) from that of all other MSS. Many of their peculiarities appear to be due to deliberate and reckless 'correction' of the tradition[1]—a vice which imposes great caution in the use of these MSS. At the same time they show some signs of contamination from the first family: cf. especially p. 126, ll. 5–6. In a number of passages, however, they and they alone offer what is unmistakably the true reading (cf. e.g. pp. 18, ll. 24–5; 94, l. 4; 160, l. 22; 164, ll. 6, 9; and esp. 70 l. 35); and it is at least doubtful whether conjecture is in every case responsible for this.

P   41. *Parisinus 2423*, ff. 51ᵛ–8ᵛ, chart., saec. xiii (see Omont, *Invent.*). Contains only props. 1–78 ἀτελής. δεῖται γάρ—. Injured here and there by worms. No marginalia, but one or two traces of correction by another hand.

Q   42. *Marcianus graec. 316* (formerly 521), ff. 52–73ᵛ, chart., saec. xiv init. (?) (see Zanetti and Bongiovanni, *op. cit.*). Has a few marginalia and interlinear corrections in the original hand; and a number of wild readings, apparently due to conjecture, in a later hand (Q²). This MS. and the preceding appear to be mutually independent, though closely related: Q is on the whole the better. I have made a full collation of both.

43. *Parisinus 1734*, ff. 343–81ᵛ, chart., saec. xv. Badly faded in places. I had collated this MS. before seeing Q; but it has probably no independent value. It bears convincing marks[2] of derivation from Q as corrected by Q²; and where it departs from

---

[1] Such 'corrections' are sometimes stylistic: these MSS. fairly systematically try to avoid hiatus by elisions, transpositions, and writing γοῦν for οὖν. They also introduce Atticisms like γιγνώσκω for γινώσκω of the other MSS. Variants of this class are not as a rule recorded in my *apparatus*. Sometimes the motive is grammatical, e.g. p. 90, ll. 8 and 12, p. 102, l. 1; often a corruption is complicated by an attempted remedy, as p. 34 ll. 8–11, p. 68 ll. 13–15. Sometimes, again, the intention is to improve the sense, as p. 22 l. 3.

[2] Many of its corruptions are directly traceable to peculiarities in the handwriting of Q or to misreading of contractions in Q.

this text its readings are to all appearance either borrowed from the second family [1] or the result of conjecture.[2]

There remain to be mentioned two incomplete MSS. apparently of mixed origin, viz. :

44. *Laurentianus plut. LXXI cod. 32*, ff. 81ᵛ–3ᵛ, chart., saec. xiv. Contains props. 1–13 ἔστιν ἄρα καὶ ἡ ἀγαθότης—. Agrees sometimes with M²⁻³, sometimes with BCD ; has also one reading found only in PQ, a number of errors and *lacunae* peculiar to itself, and several insertions in the text which evidently originated in glosses.

45. *Ambrosianus 329*, chart., saec. xv, is a book of extracts inscribed ' Marsilii Ficini florentini', and written in his hand. Ff. 214ᵛ–26 contain a number of passages from the Στοιχείωσις Θεολογική. Ficino perhaps used no. 26 in conjunction with a MS. of the first family ; but if so the result reflects little credit on his scholarship.

I append a list of other renaissance copies for the benefit of any one who thinks it worth while to examine them, and also in order to indicate the wide diffusion of the work during the sixteenth century.

Bibl. Bongarsiana, Berne, no. 150, containing props. 11–14 only, attributed by Hagen to saec. xvi–xvii init.; no. 362, containing props. 1–138 mid., attributed by Hagen to saec. xv and by Omont to saec. xvi.

Monastery of the Holy Sepulchre, Constantinople, no. 326 (Papadopoulos Kerameus, Ἱεροσολυμιτικὴ Βιβλιοθήκη, vol. IV), written in 1580 by A. Darmarius.

Offentl. Bibl., Dresden, no. Da 56, containing props. 1–29, attributed by v. Carolsfeld to saec. xvii.

Bibl. Escorialensis, Σ III 8 (104), ff. 1–47, claims to have been copied from a recent exemplar in the possession of Pinelli [perhaps no. 30] by Sophianus Melessenus (*sic*) in 1569.[3]

Hamburgensis phil. graec. 26 : a copy of C made for Lucas Holsten in 1636 (see Omont, *Catalogue des MSS. grecs . . . des Villes Hanséatiques*).

---

[1] E.g. p. 126, l. 4 παρόντων ὡσαύτως, as M ; p. 164, l. 8 τὸ τῆς ψυχῆς μετέχον, as M²BCD (suprascript. as Q).

[2] E.g. p. 20, l. 11 τὸ μὲν γὰρ πρώτως for πρώτως γάρ (ω) ; p. 24 l. 18 ἄλλου . . . ἄλλο for ἄλλου . . . ἄλλο PQ (ἄλλο . . . ἄλλου BCD[M]W).

[3] Another Escurial MS., catalogued by N. de la Torre in the sixteenth century, perished in the fire of 1671.

Royal Library, Madrid, no. O 37 : claims to have been copied in Rome by Camillus Venetus in 1552.

Monacensis graec. 91, ff. 383–432ᵛ, containing props. 1–198 (and hence presumably of the first family), ascribed by Mommert to saec. xvi ; 59, a copy of the Ἀνάπτυξις which claims to have been made by Michael Maleensis at Florence in 1550 [from no. 13?].

Bibl. Borbonica, Naples, graec. 343 (III E 21), written at Naples in 1582.

Bibl. Vallicellana, Rome, no. 51 (D 6), ascribed by Martini to saec. xvi.

Bibl. du Pilar, Saragossa, no. 3109, written in 1583 by A. Darmarius.

Bibl. Nazionale, Turin, no. 247 (Pas. graec. 345), attributed by Pasini to saec. xvi and described by Stampini as a fragment in bad condition.[1]

Parisinus supp. grec 450 contains only the beginning of a table of contents of the Στ. Θ.

I have failed to trace Bernard 4184 (misprinted 4183) *Procli Elementa Theologiae*, which is no. 4 in his *Catalogus librorum manuscriptorum Edward Browne M. D. Londinensis* ; nor have I found the *Gottorpiensis antiquissimus* which Portus claims to have used.[2]

The above list could doubtless be still further enlarged if search were made in the smaller European libraries; but it seems improbable that anything of fresh value would be added.

§ 2. *Translations.*

eo 1. The old Georgian version of John Petritsi (*supra*, p. xxix) represents a Greek text at least a century older than our earliest Greek MSS. I understand that Dr. S. Kauchtschischwili of Tiflis has in preparation a full study of this version. His work is unfortunately not yet available, but he has very kindly sent me a preliminary collation of propositions 1–5 from a MS. in the University Library at Tiflis. It would seem from this that Petritsi took a certain amount of liberty with the original, sometimes supplying words which are not expressed in the Greek, varying the order of words or the construction, or using two Georgian words to represent one

---

[1] Another copy, no. 316, was destroyed in the fire of 1904.
[2] No. 207 in the Royal Library, Copenhagen, is merely Portus's autograph draft of his edition of 1618. Harleianus 5685, which is stated by Christ-Schmid, *Griech. Literaturgeschichte*⁶ II. 2, p. 1061, to be the oldest and best MS. of the Στ. Θ., does not contain the Στ. Θ. at all, but only the Στοιχείωσις Φυσική.

Greek one. This increases the difficulty of reconstituting the Greek text used by him, and I have included in my *apparatus* such readings only as seemed to me fairly certain. They are sufficient to show that Petritsi's text belonged to the MPQW group, not to the BCD group, and they suggest that its nearest congeners may be PQ; but the material at present available is too scanty to justify me in assigning it a more definite place in the *stemma codicum*. The collation of props. 1–5, while it exhibits a number of corruptions peculiar to the Georgian tradition, offers us no acceptable readings not otherwise evidenced; but here again a generalized inference would be rash *.

2. The Armenian version of the monk Simeon of Garni exists in MSS. in the Mechitaristen-Bibliothek of Vienna (no. 372), in the Biblioteca San Lazaro at Venice, and at Eschmiadzin in the Caucasus. It appears to be derived from Petritsi's Georgian (*supra*, p. xxix, n. 8), and not directly from the Greek.

3. The second Georgian version is a retranslation from the Armenian (*supra*, p. xxix, n. 9).

W   4. The Latin version of William de Morbecca [1] exists, like the three just mentioned, only in manuscript *. It was completed, as the colophon tells us, at Viterbo on June 15, 1268. It thus represents a text at least as old as the earliest extant MSS. of the original; and it can be shown not to be based on any of the latter. Being, like most medieval translations, perfectly literal, it constitutes a valuable *subsidium* (a fact first recognized by Holsten). But before it can be so used it is of course necessary to distinguish and discount errors which have arisen in the transmission of the Latin itself. Such errors are surprisingly numerous, considering that two of our MSS. appear to have been written within a generation of de Morbecca's autograph, viz. Peterhouse 121, saec. xiii fin. (α) and Vaticanus 2419, c. 1300? (β). In addition to these I have used Vaticanus 4426, saec. xiv (γ), which is sometimes more correct than either.[2] Even after comparing these three, there remain a number of passages where it is not easy to determine what de Morbecca

---

[1] See above, p. xxxi. The name in its Latinized form is variously spelt : α and β give 'Morbecca'.

[2] Of the later MSS., I have examined two in the Library of Balliol College, Oxford (one of which includes Berthold of Mosburg's commentary, and is the 'Berealdus' erroneously regarded by Fabricius as an independent version) ; and one in the Bibliothèque Publique at Poitiers (no. 137). All these are exceedingly corrupt ; but all of them here and there seem to imply a Greek original different from that implied by αβγ : see for example page 22 l. 31, page 56 l. 19, page 94 l. 1. Has the tradition been corrected from another version, or from a Greek MS.?

wrote, still less what he read.[1] There can be no doubt, however, that his text implies (a) a large number of readings, sound and unsound, shared by M¹ only; (b) a much smaller number, sound and unsound, shared by the third family only; (c) a few sound readings found only in MSS. of the first family. In addition, we can infer with more or less confidence at least a few readings not found in any extant MS.; and one or two of these merit serious con sideration.   De Morbecca's own scholarship was not of a high order : e.g. at page 64, l. 27, he takes τὸ ὅλον as nominative and τὰ μέρη (l. 26) as accusative; at page 128, l. 2, he takes γένεσιν as accus. of γένεσις; at page 134, l. 13, he is content to make nonsense of a sentence by reading ἀλλ' for ἄλλ'.   It seems unlikely that he ever had recourse to conjecture, though some of the copyists have done so.

5. A Latin version of the Ἀνάπτυξις and Στ. Θ. by Bonaventura Vulcanius, autograph,[2] saec. xvi, is preserved at Leyden (B.P. lat. 47). I have not seen this, but it is described by Voemel (*Praef.*, p. ix) as a paraphrase of no critical value.

6. The Latin version of F. Patrizzi, printed at Ferrara in 1583, is based, so far as I have examined it, on renaissance copies of the second family.

7. Subsequent translations are numerous but unsatisfactory. Most of them suffer from an inadequate understanding of the subject-matter, and all are based on corrupt texts.   Those known to me are :

Latin, Aem. Portus 1618; Creuzer 1822 (based on Portus), reprinted with a few changes 1855.

German, Engelhardt 1823 (in *Die Angeblichen Schriften des Areopagiten Dionysius*, vol. ii, pp. 139 ff.).

English, T. Taylor 1816 (based on Patrizzi); Thos. M. Johnson 1909; A. C. Ionides 1917.

Italian, M. Losacco 1917.

The *Liber de Causis* (see above, p. xxix f.) is not a translation, a paraphrase, or even a systematic abridgement of Proclus' work, and much even of the substance has been modified to suit the requirements of a different theology; hence it has little or no value as a *subsidium* to the Greek text.   The same may be said of the additions made to it by Albertus Magnus.

---

[1] I have not cited in my critical notes readings of these MSS. which are obviously due to corrupt transmission of de Morbecca's Latin : e.g. page 2, l. 11, where for ἐστί τι τῶν ὄντων αβ give 'est aliquid totum' ('est aliquid entium' γ recte); page 104, l. 29, where for ὥσπερ all MSS. give 'sed' (read 'sicut').

[2] See the new catalogue, *Codd. MSS. Bibl. Universitatis Leidensis.*

§ 3. *Editions, &c.*

Port. 1. The *editio princeps*, Aemilius Portus, 1618. I have failed, as Creuzer did, to trace the *codex Gottorpiensis* which Portus claims to have used; but it is evident that his text is based on an inferior MS. or MSS. of the second family. It is closely akin to O, many of whose characteristic errors it shares or corrupts further; it also contains a good many errors which I have not noted in any MS.[1] There are no signs that Portus was acquainted with BCD or PQ, or W; and his emendations are seldom of any value.

Cr.[1] 2. F. Creuzer, 1822 [= *Initia Philosophiae ac Theologiae ex Platonicis Fontibus Ducta, Pars Tertia*].[2] The text of this edition is based solely on Portus and Arg. In more judicious hands Arg would have been of considerable value (*vide supra*); but Creuzer had neither critical instruments nor critical acumen to sift the wheat from the chaff, and his text is often actually worse than Portus's. His notes consist mainly of irrelevant references.

Cr.[2] 3. F. Creuzer, 1855 [printed in the Didot *Plotinus*, pp. xlix-cxvii]. The chief change is the absence of any *apparatus criticus*, though Creuzer asserts in the preface to this edition that it is 'much more accurate' than its predecessor, as he has used codd. Leidensis A (my 17), Hamburgensis (my 20), and Leid. B (my 36),[3] as well as Taylor's translation. None of these would have helped him much had he indeed used them; but that he should have ignored Voemel's published collation of no. 12,[4] a MS. of the first family though a corrupt one, is astonishing.

4. There has been no edition since Cr.[2], and of other critical contributions I know only a few emendations by Schweighäuser (quoted in the notes to Cr.[1]) and T. Taylor (in notes to his translation). Holsten's unpublished collations have already been mentioned.

5. The text of the present edition is based mainly on six MSS., viz. BCD of the first family, M of the second,[5] and PQ of the third, together with de Morbecca's version (W). The later MSS. seem to contribute only one or two plausible conjectures; and the Georgian

---

[1] In my *apparatus* I have as a rule recorded only those errors of Portus to which Creuzer has given currency by repeating them.

[2] Erroneously described by Christ-Schmid, *l. c.*, as the *editio princeps.*

[3] A partial collation of these three MSS. is given in an Appendix to Cr.[1]

[4] Styled codex A by Voemel: not to be confused with Creuzer's A (= my 'Arg') and Leidensis A (= my 17).

[5] I have cited Arg and O to supply the gaps in M, and occasionally to account for the readings of the printed editions. Where the reading of M[1] cannot be made out with certainty, but the present state of the MS. supports the hypothesis that M[1] read as Arg, I have used the symbol [M] for M as represented by Arg.

version (Geo) is available only for props. 1–5. If we symbolize the archetype of BCD by [N] and that of PQ by [Π], then our sources are [N], M, [Π] and W. It will, I think, be fairly clear from my collation (a) that in the main these four sources are mutually independent, though [Π] *may* be contaminated here and there from [N]; (b) that if allowance is made for the influence of conjectural emendation upon the text of [Π], M[Π]W are more closely related to each other than any of them is to [N]; (c) that MW are more closely related to each other than either of them is to [Π]. From (b) follows the important corollary that readings common to [N]M or to [N]W [1] will usually be those of the common archetype [X] of all our MSS.

I cannot determine the date of [X] with any precision. If I am right in my view that the text used by Petritsi, the Georgian translator, belonged to the group M[Π]W, then 1100 or thereabouts is the *terminus ad quem* for the archetype of this group, and *a fortiori* for [X]. Again, if it could be assumed that B (which does not contain the Ἀνάπτυξις) is not derived from a MS. of the Ἀνάπτυξις, then [N], the common ancestor of B and the Ἀνάπτυξις MSS., could not be later than the twelfth century. But this assumption is hardly warranted: a copyist more interested in pagan than in Christian philosophy might well extract the Proclus text from Nicolaus and leave the rest. And the abrupt manner in which Nicolaus' commentary ends, together with the mention in the superscription to the Proclus text in C of 211 propositions (200 in B, no numeral in D), points rather to a mutilation of our text of Nicolaus than to Nicolaus' having used a mutilated text of Proclus: if so, [N], which had this mutilation, must have been written *later* than the time of Nicolaus. [X] must in any case be a good deal earlier than [N], to allow for the development of the fairly complicated corruptions which the first family exhibits. On Dräseke's view, that the Ἀνάπτυξις is the work of Procopius of Gaza, republished practically without alteration by the Bishop of Methone seven centuries later, we should expect the N text of Proclus to go back also to Procopius; so that [X] would be pushed back to a date in Proclus' own life-time or shortly after. But see above, p. xxxi, n. 1.

Only a very small fraction (probably not five per cent) of the errors which disfigure the editions of Portus and Creuzer go back to [X], so that the passages which call for conjectural emendation are

[1] Whether in any particular passage [N][Π] has more authority than [N] is of course doubtful, if I am right in my suspicion that [Π] has in places been contaminated from [N].

relatively few. The chief part of my work has been in removing corruptions of late origin, attempting the reconstruction of [X], and endeavouring to introduce a system of punctuation which shall not needlessly obscure the author's thought.—The *stemma codicum* facing this page makes no claim to complete accuracy : to obtain certainty as to the mutual relationship of the various renaissance copies would have involved a vast and unremunerative labour. But it may be useful as indicating what I conceive to be the main lines of affiliation. —In orthographical matters I have not deemed it prudent to impose a rigid consistency where the MSS. did not authorize it. But I have adopted γενητός,[1] ἀγένητος, γίνομαι, γινώσκω, and -ττ- not -σσ- throughout, also ἑαυτό (ἑαυτοῦ &c.) not αὐτό except in the phrase καθ' αὑτό, these being the spellings of BCDM in a large majority of passages. To avoid making the *apparatus criticus* too unwieldy, I have refrained from recording (*a*) variations of punctuation, (*b*) unimportant variations of orthography (such as those just mentioned) and accentuation, (*c*) presence or absence of -ν ἐφελκυστικόν, (*d*) a few obvious errors which are peculiar to *one* of the closely related MSS. BCD and are therefore unlikely to have stood in [N], their archetype, e.g. prop. 1, l. 6, καθ' ὅλου B. With these exceptions the collation of BCDM[2] is, I hope, complete. As regards PQ, considerations of space prohibited printing a complete list of the errors peculiar to these MSS. ; but I trust that I have ignored no reading of this group which has any possible bearing on the constitution of the text.

[1] In origin, γενητός and γεννητός are of course distinct words ; but I can trace no distinction of usage in Proclus.

[2] Miswritings by the first hand in M which were corrected *by the same hand* are occasionally ignored : e.g. p. 164, l. 22, where the scribe first wrote ἡ ψυχὴ ἄρα αὐθυπόστατον—evidently out of carelessness—and then encircled this with a dotted line to indicate deletion and continued with the true text καὶ ἡ ψυχὴ ἄρα αὐθυπόστατος.

STEMMA CODICUM

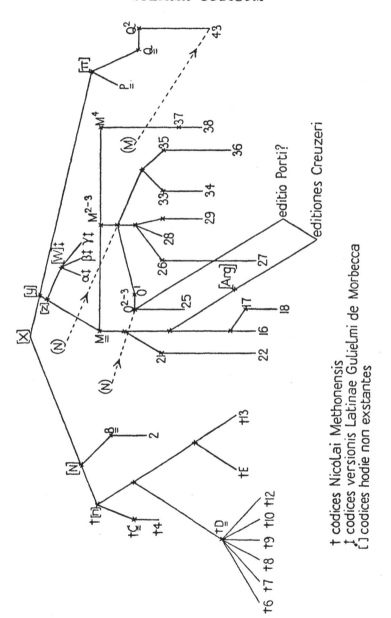

† codices Nicolai Methonensis
‡ codices versionis Latinae Gulielmi de Morbecca
[ ] codices hodie non exstantes

SIGLA

CODICES

B   Vaticanus 237, saec. xiv.   ⎫
C   Vaticanus 626, saec. xiii–xiv.   ⎬ familiae primae.
D   Ambrosianus 648 + 727, saec. xiv exeuntis. ⎭
    d   continuator codicis D (capp. 199–209), saec. xv.
M   Marcianus 678, saec. xiii–xiv, familiae secundae.
M¹   primae manus lectiones a correctoribus oblitteratae vel commutatae, ita tamen ut etiamnunc legi possint (sim. C¹ etc.).
[M]   primae manus lectiones a correctoribus oblitteratae vel commutatae, ita tamen ut apographorum ope satis certe restitui possint.
   M² M³ similibus designantur manus correctrices.

P   Parisinus 2423, saec. xiii. ⎫
                                ⎬ familiae tertiae.
Q   Marcianus 316, saec. xiv. ⎭
ω   consensus codicum BCDMPQ (post cap. 77 BCDMQ).

Nonnunquam citantur:
E   Parisinus 1256, primae familiae, saec. xv.
O   Bodleianus Laud. 18, secundae familiae, a. 1358.
Arg   lectiones codicis Argentoratensis secundae familiae, hodie non exstantis, a Schweighaeusero descriptae.
dett.   consensus omnium vel plurium apographorum secundae familiae.

W   versio Latina Gulielmi de Morbecca, a. 1268, in his libris tradita:
   a   Cantabrigiensis, bibl. Dom. S. Petri 121, saec. xiii.
   β   Vaticanus 2419, saec. xiii–xiv.
   γ   Vaticanus 4426, saec. xiv.
Geo   versio vetus Georgica, cuius specimen per amicam S. Kauchtschischwilii benevolentiam ad capp. 1–5 adhibere licuit.

EDITORES

Port.   Aemilius Portus, a. 1618.
Cr.¹   Fridericus Creuzer, a. 1822.
Cr.²   Fridericus Creuzer, a. 1855.
edd.   consensus editorum.

ΠΡΟΚΛΟΥ ΔΙΑΔΟΧΟΥ

ΠΡΟΚΛΟΥ ΔΙΑΔΟΧΟΥ

ΣΤΟΙΧΕΙΩΣΙΣ ΘΕΟΛΟΓΙΚΗ.

1. Πᾶν πλῆθος μετέχει πῃ τοῦ ἑνός.

εἰ γὰρ μηδαμῇ μετέχοι, οὔτε τὸ ὅλον ἓν ἔσται οὔθ᾽ ἕκαστον τῶν πολλῶν ἐξ ὧν τὸ πλῆθος, ἀλλ᾽ ἔσται καὶ ἐκείνων ἕκαστον πλῆθος, καὶ τοῦτο εἰς ἄπειρον, καὶ τῶν ἀπείρων τούτων ἕκαστον ἔσται πάλιν πλῆθος ἄπειρον. μηδενὸς γὰρ ἑνὸς μηδαμῇ μετέχον 5 μήτε καθ᾽ ὅλον ἑαυτὸ μήτε καθ᾽ ἕκαστον τῶν ἐν αὐτῷ, πάντῃ ἄπειρον ἔσται καὶ κατὰ πᾶν. τῶν γὰρ πολλῶν ἕκαστον, ὅπερ ἂν λάβῃς, ἤτοι ἓν ἔσται ἢ οὐχ ἕν· καὶ εἰ οὐχ ἕν, ἤτοι πολλὰ ἢ οὐδέν. ἀλλ᾽ εἰ μὲν ἕκαστον οὐδέν, καὶ τὸ ἐκ τούτων οὐδέν· εἰ δὲ πολλά, ἐξ ἀπειράκις ἀπείρων ἕκαστον. ταῦτα δὲ ἀδύνατα. 10 οὔτε γὰρ ἐξ ἀπειράκις ἀπείρων ἐστί τι τῶν ὄντων (τοῦ γὰρ ἀπείρου πλέον οὐκ ἔστι, τὸ δὲ ἐκ πάντων ἑκάστου πλέον) οὔτε ἐκ τοῦ μηδενὸς συντίθεσθαί τι δυνατόν. πᾶν ἄρα πλῆθος μετέχει πῃ τοῦ ἑνός.

2. Πᾶν τὸ μετέχον τοῦ ἑνὸς καὶ ἕν ἐστι καὶ οὐχ ἕν. 15

εἰ γὰρ μὴ ἔστιν αὐτοέν (μετέχει γὰρ τοῦ ἑνὸς ἄλλο τι ὂν παρὰ τὸ ἕν), πέπονθε τὸ ἓν κατὰ τὴν μέθεξιν καὶ ὑπέμεινεν ἐν γενέσθαι. εἰ μὲν οὖν μηδέν ἐστι παρὰ τὸ ἕν, μόνον ἐστὶν ἕν· καὶ οὐ μεθέξει τοῦ ἑνός, ἀλλ᾽ αὐτοὲν ἔσται. εἰ δ᾽ ἐστί τι παρ᾽ ἐκεῖνο, ὃ μὴ ἔστιν ἕν, [τὸ μετέχον τοῦ ἑνὸς καὶ οὐχ ἕν ἐστι καὶ 20 ἕν, οὐχ ὅπερ ἓν ἀλλ᾽ ἓν ὄν, ὡς μετέχον τοῦ ἑνός] τούτῳ ἄρα οὐχ ἕν ἐστιν, οὐδ᾽ ὅπερ ἕν· ἓν δὲ ὂν ἅμα καὶ μετέχον τοῦ ἑνός, καὶ διὰ τοῦτο οὐχ ἓν καθ᾽ αὐτὸ ὑπάρχον, ἕν ἐστι καὶ οὐχ ἕν, παρὰ τὸ ἓν ἄλλο τι ὄν· ᾧ μὲν ἐπλεόνασεν, οὐχ ἕν· ᾧ δὲ πέπονθεν, ἕν. πᾶν ἄρα τὸ μετέχον τοῦ ἑνὸς καὶ ἕν ἐστι καὶ οὐχ ἕν. 25

TITULUS. Πρόκλου διαδόχου πλατωνικοῦ φιλοσόφου στοιχείωσις θεολογική (στοιχειώσεις θεολογικαί M¹) κεφάλαια σια´ (κεφάλαια σ´ B : om. D) ω
1. 2 μετέχει BCP (ex μετέχοι BP) τό om. PQ 3 ἐκείνων BCDPQ Geo : ἐκ τινων MW ἕκαστον del. M² 4 καὶ τῶν ... 5 ἄπειρον om. M¹ 4 ἑκάστων Geo 5 τὸ πλῆθος PQ γὰρ non agnoscit Geo ἑνός om. PQ 7 τῶν πολλῶν non agnoscit Geo 8 λάβῃς M : λάβοις cett. καὶ εἰ οὐχ ἕν om. M¹ 10 et 11 ἐξ ἀπειράκις ἀπείρων) infinite infinitum Geo 11 οὔτε γάρ ... 14 ἑνός in DE hic omissa in D post refutationem Nicolai ad hoc caput appositam inveniuntur 11 τι om. PQ 13 συντίθεταί τι PQ 14 πῃ in rasura M², om. Arg
2. 15 τό PQ: om. BCDM 19 τι] τό P dett. 19-20 παρ᾽ ἐκείνῳ dett., edd. 20 ὅ] ᾧ Geo 20-24 locus nimis plenus: quae uncinis inclusi e margine illata

PROCLUS THE PLATONIC SUCCESSOR

THE ELEMENTS OF THEOLOGY.

A. OF THE ONE AND THE MANY.

PROP. 1. *Every manifold in some way participates[1] unity.*

For suppose a manifold in no way participating unity. Neither this manifold as a whole nor any of its several parts will be one; each part will itself be a manifold of parts, and so to infinity; and of this infinity of parts each, once more, will be infinitely manifold; for a manifold which in no way participates any unity, neither as a whole nor in respect of its parts severally, will be infinite in every way and in respect of every part. For each part of the manifold— take which you will—must be either one or not-one; and if not-one, then either many or nothing. But if each part be nothing, the whole is nothing; if many, it is made up of an infinity of infinites. This is impossible: for, on the one hand, nothing which is is made up of an infinity of infinites (since the infinite cannot be exceeded, yet the single part is exceeded by the sum); on the other hand, nothing can be made up of parts which are nothing. Every manifold, therefore, in some way participates unity.

PROP. 2. *All that participates unity is both one and not-one.*

For inasmuch as it cannot be pure unity (since participation in unity implies a distinct participant), its 'participation' means that it has unity as an affect, and has undergone a process of becoming one. Now if it be nothing else but its own unity, it is a bare 'one' and so cannot participate unity but must *be* pure unity. But if it has some character other than oneness, in virtue of that character it is not-one, and so not unity unqualified. Thus being one, and yet (as participating unity) in itself not-one, it is both one and not-one. It is in fact unity with something added, and is in virtue of the addition not-one, although one as affected by unity. Everything, therefore, which participates unity is both one and not-one.

---

[1] The transitive use of *participate* throughout the translation is dictated by the convenience of the passive form: the authority of Milton and Hooker may serve to excuse it.

---

esse suspicor   20–1 καὶ ἕν ἐστι καὶ οὐχ ἕν PQArg   21 ἀλλ' ἕν ω (tacite
om. Cr.)   τούτῳ scripsi: τοῦτο ω

3. Πᾶν τὸ γινόμενον ἓν μεθέξει τοῦ ἑνὸς γίνεται ἕν.

αὐτὸ μὲν γὰρ οὐχ ἕν ἐστι, καθὸ δὲ πέπονθε τὴν μετοχὴν τοῦ ἑνός, ἕν ἐστιν. εἰ γὰρ γίνοιτο ἓν ἃ μή ἐστιν ἓν καθ᾽ αὐτά, συνιόντα δήπου καὶ κοινωνοῦντα ἀλλήλοις γίνεται ἕν, καὶ ὑπομένει τὴν τοῦ ἑνὸς παρουσίαν οὐκ ὄντα ὅπερ ἕν. μετέχει ἄρα τοῦ ἑνὸς 5 ταύτῃ, ᾗ πάσχει τὸ ἓν γενέσθαι. εἰ μὲν γὰρ ἤδη ἐστὶν ἕν, οὐ γίνεται ἕν· τὸ γὰρ ὂν οὐ γίνεται ὃ ἤδη ἐστίν. εἰ δὲ γίνεται ἐκ τοῦ μὴ ἑνὸς πρότερον, ἕξει τὸ ἓν ἐγγενομένου τινὸς ἐν αὐτοῖς ἑνός.

4. Πᾶν τὸ ἡνωμένον ἕτερόν ἐστι τοῦ αὐτοενός.

εἰ γάρ ἐστιν ἡνωμένον, μετέχοι ἄν πῃ τοῦ ἑνὸς ταύτῃ, ᾗ καὶ 10 ἡνωμένον λέγεται· τὸ δὲ μετέχον τοῦ ἑνὸς καὶ ἕν ἐστι καὶ οὐχ ἕν. τὸ δ᾽ αὐτοὲν οὐχὶ καὶ ἕν ἐστι καὶ οὐχ ἕν. εἰ γὰρ καὶ τοῦτο ἕν τε καὶ οὐχ ἕν, καὶ τὸ ἐν αὐτῷ πάλιν ἓν τὸ συναμφότερον ἕξει, καὶ τοῦτο εἰς ἄπειρον, μηδενὸς ὄντος αὐτοενὸς εἰς ὃ στῆναι δυνατόν, ἀλλὰ παντὸς ἑνὸς καὶ οὐχ ἑνὸς ὄντος. ἔστιν ἄρα τι τὸ 15 ἡνωμένον τοῦ ἑνὸς ἕτερον. ταὐτὸν γὰρ ὂν τῷ ἡνωμένῳ, τὸ ἓν πλῆθος ἄπειρον ἔσται, καὶ ἕκαστον ὡσαύτως ἐκείνων ἐξ ὧν ἐστι τὸ ἡνωμένον.

5. Πᾶν πλῆθος δεύτερόν ἐστι τοῦ ἑνός.

εἰ γὰρ ἔστι πλῆθος πρὸ τοῦ ἑνός, τὸ μὲν ἓν μεθέξει τοῦ 20 πλήθους, τὸ δὲ πλῆθος τὸ πρὸ τοῦ ἑνὸς οὐ μεθέξει τοῦ ἑνός, εἴπερ, πρὶν γένηται ἕν, ἐστὶν ἐκεῖνο πλῆθος· τοῦ γὰρ μὴ ὄντος οὐ μετέχει· καὶ διότι τὸ μετέχον τοῦ ἑνὸς καὶ ἕν ἐστιν ἅμα καὶ οὐχ ἕν, οὔπω δ᾽ ὑπέστη ἕν, τοῦ πρώτου πλήθους ὄντος. ἀλλ᾽ ἀδύνατον εἶναί τι πλῆθος μηδαμῇ ἑνὸς μετέχον. οὐκ ἄρα πρὸ 25 τοῦ ἑνὸς τὸ πλῆθος.

εἰ δὲ δὴ ἅμα τῷ ἑνί, καὶ σύστοιχα ἀλλήλοις τῇ φύσει (χρόνῳ γὰρ οὐδὲν κωλύει), οὔτε τὸ ἓν καθ᾽ αὐτὸ πολλά ἐστιν οὔτε τὸ πλῆθος ἕν, ὡς ἀντιδιῃρημένα ἅμα ὄντα τῇ φύσει εἴπερ μηδέτερον θατέρου πρότερον ἢ ὕστερον. τὸ οὖν πλῆθος καθ᾽ 30 αὐτὸ οὐχ ἓν ἔσται, καὶ ἕκαστον τῶν ἐν αὐτῷ οὐχ ἕν, καὶ τοῦτο εἰς ἄπειρον· ὅπερ ἀδύνατον. μετέχει ἄρα τοῦ ἑνὸς κατὰ τὴν

3. 2 αὐτὸ μὲν γὰρ οὐχ ἕν ἐστι BCD: καθ᾽ αὐτὸ μὲν κτλ. Par. 2028 in additamento saec. xv, O² : om. MPQWGeo   3–4 καθ᾽ αὐτά, συνιόντα δήπου καί om. Geo   7 ἤδη] εἴδει Geo   8 prius ἑνός MPQWGeo, suprascr. ἐκ τῆς στερήσεως M⁸ (unde orta est Porti lectio) : ἓν εἶναι BCD   ἐγγινομένου PQ αὐτῷ BCD
4. 10 μετέχει ἄν CPQ   12 τὸ δ᾽ αὐτοὲν . . . ἐστι καὶ οὐχ ἕν om. C¹ 15 τι om. PQ   18 ad finem capitis lacunam perperam statuerunt Port., Cr.¹
5. 20 εἰ γάρ . . . ἑνός om. C¹   20 τὸ μὲν . . . 21 πρὸ τοῦ ἑνός om. PQWGeo 22 ἐκεῖνο τὸ πλῆθος PQ : ἐκεῖνο non agnosc. Geo   23 καὶ διότι BCD : διότι cett.   ἅμα om. C¹   24 ἀλλὰ καί D¹   28 πολλά ἐστιν BCD[M] : πολλὰ εἶναι M²PQWGeo   29 οὔτε τὸ πλῆθος ἕν om. Geo   30 τὸ γοῦν PQ

PROP. 3. *All that becomes one does so by participation of unity.*

For what becomes one is itself not-one, but is one inasmuch as it is affected by participation of unity : since, if things which are not in themselves one should become one, they surely do so by coming together and by communication in each other, and so are subjected to the presence of unity without being unity unqualified. In so far, then, as they undergo a process of becoming one, they participate unity. For if they already *are* one, they cannot *become* one : nothing can become what it already is. But if from a former not-one they become one, their unity must be due to a ' one ' which has entered into them.

PROP. 4. *All that is unified is other than the One itself.*

For if it is unified, it must in some way participate unity, namely, in that respect in which it is said to be unified (prop. 3) ; and what participates unity is both one and not-one (prop. 2). But the One itself is not both one and not-one : for if it also be one and not-one, then the unity which it contains will in its turn contain this pair of elements, and there will be infinite regress, since we shall find no simple unity at which our analysis can stop, but everything will be one and not-one. The unified, therefore, is something other than the One. For the One, if identical with the unified, will be infinitely manifold, as will also each of the parts which compose the unified.

PROP. 5. *Every manifold is posterior to the One.*

For suppose a manifold prior to the One. The One will then participate the manifold, but the prior manifold will not participate the One, seeing that, in the first place, it exists as manifold before the One comes to be, and it cannot participate what does not exist ; and secondly, because what participates the One is both one and not-one (prop. 2), but if the First Principle be plurality, no ' one ' as yet exists. But it is impossible there should be a manifold in no way participating the One (prop. 1). Therefore the manifold is not prior to the One.

Suppose now a manifold coexistent with the One ; and that the two principles are co-ordinate in nature (to their temporal co-ordination there is no such objection): then the One is not in itself many, nor the manifold one, but they exist side by side as contra-distinguished principles, inasmuch as neither is prior or posterior to the other. The manifold, then, will be in itself not-one, and each of its parts not-one, and so to infinity : which is impossible (prop. 1).

ἑαυτοῦ φύσιν, καὶ οὐδὲν ἔσται αὐτοῦ λαβεῖν ὃ μὴ ἔστιν ἕν· μὴ
ἐν γὰρ ὄν, ἐξ ἀπείρων ἄπειρον ἔσται, ὡς δέδεικται. πάντῃ ἄρα
μετέχει τοῦ ἑνός.

εἰ μὲν οὖν τὸ ἕν, τὸ καθ' αὑτὸ ἓν ὄν, μηδαμῇ μετέχει πλήθους,
ἔσται τὸ πλῆθος πάντῃ τοῦ ἑνὸς ὕστερον, μετέχον μὲν τοῦ ἑνός, 5
οὐ μετεχόμενον δὲ ὑπὸ τοῦ ἑνός.

εἰ δὲ καὶ τὸ ἓν μετέχει πλήθους, κατὰ μὲν τὴν ὕπαρξιν ὡς
ἓν ὑφεστός, κατὰ δὲ τὴν μέθεξιν οὐχ ἕν, πεπληθυσμένον ἔσται
τὸ ἕν, ὥσπερ τὸ πλῆθος ἡνωμένον διὰ τὸ ἕν.   κεκοινώνηκεν
ἄρα τό τε ἓν τῷ πλήθει καὶ τὸ πλῆθος τῷ ἑνί· τὰ δὲ συνιόντα 10
καὶ κοινωνοῦντά πῃ ἀλλήλοις εἰ μὲν ὑπ' ἄλλου συνάγεται,
ἐκεῖνο πρὸ αὐτῶν ἐστιν, εἰ δὲ αὐτὰ συνάγει ἑαυτά, οὐκ ἀντί-
κειται ἀλλήλοις· ἀντικείμενα γὰρ οὐ σπεύδει εἰς ἄλληλα. εἰ οὖν
τὸ ἓν καὶ τὸ πλῆθος ἀντιδιῄρηται, καὶ τὸ πλῆθος ᾗ πλῆθος οὐχ
ἕν, καὶ τὸ ἓν ᾗ ἓν οὐ·πλῆθος, οὐδέτερον ἐν θατέρῳ γενόμενον, 15
ἓν ἅμα καὶ δύο ἔσται. ἀλλὰ μὴν εἰ ἔσται τι πρὸ αὐτῶν τὸ συν-
άγον, ἢ ἕν ἐστιν ἢ οὐχ ἕν. ἀλλ' εἰ οὐχ ἕν, ἢ πολλὰ ἢ οὐδέν.
οὔτε δὲ πολλά, ἵνα μὴ πλῆθος ᾖ πρὸ ἑνός· οὔτε οὐδέν· πῶς
γὰρ συνάξει τὸ οὐδέν; ἐν ἄρα μόνον· οὐ γὰρ δὴ καὶ τοῦτο τὸ
ἓν πολλά, ἵνα μὴ εἰς ἄπειρον. ἔστιν ἄρα τὸ αὐτοέν· καὶ πᾶν 20
πλῆθος ἀπὸ τοῦ αὐτοενός.

6. Πᾶν πλῆθος ἢ ἐξ ἡνωμένων ἐστὶν ἢ ἐξ ἑνάδων.

ἕκαστον γὰρ τῶν πολλῶν ὅτι μὲν οὐκ ἔσται καὶ αὐτὸ πλῆθος
μόνον καὶ τούτου πάλιν ἕκαστον πλῆθος, δῆλον. εἰ δὲ μὴ ἔστι
πλῆθος μόνον, ἤτοι ἡνωμένον ἐστὶν ἢ ἑνάς. καὶ εἰ μὲν μετέχον 25
τοῦ ἑνός, ἡνωμένον· εἰ δὲ ἐξ ὧν τὸ πρώτως ἡνωμένον, ἑνάς. εἰ
γὰρ ἔστι τὸ αὐτοέν, ἔστι τὸ πρώτως αὐτοῦ μετέχον καὶ πρώτως
ἡνωμένον. τοῦτο δὲ ἐξ ἑνάδων· εἰ γὰρ ἐξ ἡνωμένων, πάλιν τὰ
ἡνωμένα ἔκ τινων, καὶ εἰς ἄπειρον. δεῖ δὴ εἶναι τὸ πρώτως ἡνωμένον ἐξ ἑνάδων· καὶ εὕρομεν τὸ ἐξ ἀρχῆς.   30

5. 1 ἑαυτοῦ scripsi : αὐτοῦ ω (ex corr. D²)   2 ἄπειρον ω (om. Cr.)   4 τὸ
ἕν om. BCD¹   μετέχοι M, participabit W   7 τό] αὐτό D¹
8 ὑφεστός.M : ὑφεστώς cett.   9 ὥσπερ ... τὸ ἕν om. PQ   14 ἀντιδιῄρηνται
Q, ἀντιδιῄρωνται P   15 οὐδ' ἕτερον M   16 ἕν ... δύο ἔσται om. Geo
18-19 πῶς γὰρ συνάξει τὸ οὐδέν ; om. B (in mg. M¹)

6 et 7. In D deperdito folio cc. 6 et 7 suppl. manus recentior (saec. xvi)

6. Titulum περὶ ἑνάδων praebent BCD : περὶ ἑνάδος M : capitum titulos
omnes om. PQW   23 μὲν οὖν οὐκ M   καὶ om. PQ   24 τούτου]
τοῦτο M¹ : τούτων Arg fort. recte   25 ἑνάς scripsi : ἑνάδες ω   25 καὶ
εἰ ... 26 ἑνάς om. C¹   26 ἑνάς scripsi : ἑνάδες ω   28 τοῦτο ex ἔσται δέ (?)
factum P   29 δὴ scripsi : δέ ω   30 εὕρωμεν PQ   lacunam post ἀρχῆς
perperam statuerunt edd.

By its own nature, therefore, it participates the One, and it will be impossible to find any part of it which is not one; since if it be not one, it will be an infinite sum of infinites, as has been shown. Thus it participates the One in every way.

If then that One whose unity is not derivative in no way participates plurality, the manifold will be in every way posterior to the One, participating the One but not participated by it.

If on the other hand the One in like manner participates plurality, being indeed one in substance, but by participation not-one, then the One will be pluralized because of the manifold as the manifold is unified because of the One. Thus the One communicates in the manifold and the manifold in the One. But things which come together and communicate in each other, if they are brought together by a third principle, have that principle as their prior; if on the contrary they bring themselves together, they are not opposites (for opposites do not tend towards opposites). Now on the supposition that the One and the manifold are contradistinguished, and the manifold *qua* manifold is not one, and the One *qua* one is not manifold, neither arising within the other, they will be at once one (by participation) and two (in substance). But if something prior to both is required to bring them together, this prior is either one or not-one; and if not-one, either many or nothing. But it cannot be many (else we have a manifold prior to the One); nor can it be nothing (how should a nothing draw them together?). It is one, therefore—and nothing but one; for plainly *this* One cannot be many, or we have infinite regress. It is, then, the One itself; and from the One itself every manifold proceeds.

PROP. 6. *Every manifold is composed either of unified groups or of henads (units).*

For it is evidently impossible that each constituent of a manifold should be in its turn a pure plurality, and each constituent of this plurality again a plurality (prop. 1). And if the constituent part is not a pure plurality, it is either a unified group or a henad: a unified group if it have unity by participation, a henad if it be a constituent of the first unified group. For if there is a ' One itself' (prop. 4), it must have a first participant, which is the first unified group. And this first group is composed of henads: for if it be composed of unified groups, these in turn will be composite, and so to infinity. The first unified group, then, is composed of henads; and we have found true what we enunciated.

7. Πᾶν τὸ παρακτικὸν ἄλλου κρεῖττόν ἐστι τῆς τοῦ παραγομένου φύσεως.

ἤτοι γὰρ κρεῖττόν ἐστιν ἢ χεῖρον ἢ ἴσον. ἔστω πρότερον ἴσον. τὸ τοίνυν ἀπὸ τούτου παραγόμενον ἢ δύναμιν ἔχει καὶ αὐτὸ παρακτικὴν ἄλλου τινὸς ἢ ἄγονον ὑπάρχει 5 παντελῶς. ἀλλ᾽ εἰ μὲν ἄγονον εἴη, κατ᾽ αὐτὸ τοῦτο τοῦ παρ-άγοντος ἡλάττωται, καὶ ἔστιν ἄνισον ἐκείνῳ, γονίμῳ ὄντι καὶ δύναμιν ἔχοντι τοῦ ποιεῖν, ἀδρανὲς ὄν. εἰ δὲ καὶ αὐτὸ παρακτι-κόν ἐστιν ἄλλων, ἢ καὶ αὐτὸ ἴσον ἑαυτῷ παράγει, καὶ τοῦτο ὡσαύτως ἐπὶ πάντων, καὶ ἔσται τὰ ὄντα πάντα ἴσα ἀλλήλοις 10 καὶ οὐδὲν ἄλλο ἄλλου κρεῖττον, ἀεὶ τοῦ παράγοντος ἴσον ἑαυτῷ τὸ ἐφεξῆς ὑφιστάντος· ἢ ἄνισον, καὶ οὐκέτ᾽ ἂν ἴσον εἴη τῷ αὐτὸ παράγοντι· δυνάμεων γὰρ ἴσων ἐστὶ τὸ τὰ ἴσα ποιεῖν· τὰ δ᾽ ἐκ τούτων ἄνισα ἀλλήλοις, εἴπερ τὸ μὲν παράγον τῷ πρὸ αὐτοῦ ἴσον, αὐτῷ δὲ τὸ μετ᾽ αὐτὸ ἄνισον. οὐκ ἄρα ἴσον εἶναι δεῖ τῷ 15 παράγοντι τὸ παραγόμενον.

ἀλλὰ μὴν οὐδ᾽ ἔλαττον ἔσται ποτὲ τὸ παράγον. εἰ γὰρ αὐτὸ τὴν οὐσίαν τῷ παραγομένῳ δίδωσιν, αὐτὸ καὶ τὴν δύναμιν αὐτῷ χορηγεῖ κατὰ τὴν οὐσίαν. εἰ δὲ αὐτὸ παρακτικόν ἐστι τῆς δυνάμεως τῷ μετ᾽ αὐτὸ πάσης, κἂν ἑαυτὸ δύναιτο ποιεῖν 20 τοιοῦτον, οἷον ἐκεῖνο. εἰ δὲ τοῦτο, καὶ ποιήσειεν ἂν ἑαυτὸ δυνατώτερον. οὔτε γὰρ τὸ μὴ δύνασθαι κωλύει, παρούσης τῆς ποιητικῆς δυνάμεως· οὔτε τὸ μὴ βούλεσθαι, πάντα γὰρ τοῦ ἀγαθοῦ ὀρέγεται κατὰ φύσιν· ὥστε εἰ ἄλλο δύναται τελειότερον ἀπεργάσασθαι, κἂν ἑαυτὸ πρὸ τοῦ μετ᾽ αὐτὸ τελειώσειεν. 25

οὔτε ἴσον ἄρα τῷ παράγοντι τὸ παραγόμενόν ἐστιν οὔτε κρεῖττον. πάντῃ ἄρα τὸ παράγον κρεῖττον τῆς τοῦ παραγο-μένου φύσεως.

8. Πάντων τῶν ὁπωσοῦν τοῦ ἀγαθοῦ μετεχόντων ἡγεῖται τὸ πρώτως ἀγαθὸν καὶ ὃ μηδέν ἐστιν ἄλλο ἢ ἀγαθόν. 30

εἰ γὰρ πάντα τὰ ὄντα τοῦ ἀγαθοῦ ἐφίεται, δῆλον ὅτι τὸ πρώτως ἀγαθὸν ἐπέκεινά ἐστι τῶν ὄντων. εἰ γὰρ ταὐτόν τινι τῶν ὄντων, ἢ ταὐτόν ἐστιν ὂν καὶ τἀγαθόν, καὶ τοῦτο τὸ ὂν οὐκέτι ἂν ἐφιέμενον εἴη τοῦ ἀγαθοῦ, αὐτὸ τἀγαθὸν ὑπάρχον· τὸ

7. Tit. περὶ παραγόντων καὶ παραγομένων BCDM   4 ἔστω πρότερον ἴσον MPQW : om. BCD dett.   6 εἴη ex corr. M², om. Arg   7 καὶ ante ἐκείνῳ add. P 8 δύναμιν ἔχοντι MPQ, potentiam habenti W : ἔχοντι δύναμιν BCD   9 ἄλλου Arg, alterius W   11 ἄλλου ἄλλο E dett.   12 αὐτοῦ primitus M : αὐτῷ P   13 παραγαγόντι PQ   τό om. PQ   14 εἴπερ] εἰ tum lacunam 3 fere litt. PQ   παράγον PQArg : παραγαγόν BCDM   τῷ] τό BCD   15 αὐτὸ δὲ τῷ PQW   17 παράγον PQ : παραγαγόν BCDM   19 αὐτό] eius W 25 ἑαυτό scripsi : αὐτό ω : sibi W : αὐτὸ (ἑαυτὸ) coni. Cr.   26 τὸ παραγόμενον

9

B. Of Causes.

PROP. 7. *Every productive cause is superior to that which it produces.*

For if not superior, it must be either inferior or equal. Let us first suppose it equal. Now, either the product has itself power to produce a further principle, or it is altogether sterile. But if it be supposed sterile, it is thereby proved inferior to its producer: the impotent is not equal to the fecund in which is the power of creation. And if it be productive, the further product will again be either equal to its cause or unequal. But if it be equal, and if this be true universally, that the producer generates a consequent equal to itself, then all beings will be equal one to another, and no one better than another. And if it be not equal, neither was the former product equal to the former producer. For equal powers create equals ; but if a cause, not being equal to its consequent, were yet equal to its own prior, we should have here equal powers creating unequals. Therefore it is impossible the product should be equal to the producer.

Again, it is impossible the producer should ever be inferior. For as it gives the product existence, it must furnish also the power proper for that existence. But if it is itself productive of all the power which is in its consequent, it is able to create a like character in itself, that is, to increase its own power. The means to this cannot be lacking, since it has force sufficient to create ; nor can the will be lacking, since by nature all things have appetition of their good. Therefore, were it able to fashion another thing more perfect than itself, it would make itself perfect before its consequent.

Since, then, the product is neither equal to the producer nor superior to it, the producer is necessarily superior to the product.

PROP. 8. *All that in any way participates the Good is subordinate to the primal Good which is nothing else but good.*

For if all things which exist desire their good, it is evident that the primal Good is beyond the things which exist. For if it be identified with any existent thing, either an existent thing is identical with the Good, and by this identity excluded from desiring the

---

9

τῷ παράγοντι dett., Cr. (τῷ τὸ παράγοντι παραγόμενον exhibet Port.)   27 πάντῃ
MPQW : πᾶν BCD, sed cf. p. 14, l. 17
  8. Tit. περὶ τοῦ πρώτου ἀγαθοῦ, ὃ καὶ τἀγαθὸν καλεῖται BCDM   30 prius
ἀγαθόν om. C¹   alt. ἀγαθόν PQ (cf. p. 10, ll. 9 et 28): τἀγαθόν BCM, τὸ
ἀγαθόν D   33 τό om. PQ   34 αὐτοαγαθόν PQ

γὰρ ὀρεγόμενόν του ἐνδεές ἐστιν οὗ ὀρέγεται, καὶ τοῦ ὀρεκτοῦ
[ἕτερον καὶ] ἀπεξενωμένον· ἢ τὸ μὲν ἄλλο, τὸ δὲ ἄλλο· καὶ τὸ
μὲν μεθέξει, τὸ ὄν, τὸ δὲ ἔσται μετεχόμενον ἐν τούτῳ, τὸ ἀγαθόν.
τὶ ἄρα ἀγαθόν ἐστιν, ἐν τινὶ τῶν μετεχόντων ὄν, καὶ οὗ τὸ
μετασχὸν ἐφίεται μόνον, ἀλλ᾽ οὐ τὸ ἁπλῶς ἀγαθὸν καὶ οὗ πάντα 5
τὰ ὄντα ἐφίεται. τοῦτο μὲν γὰρ κοινὸν πάντων ἐστὶ τῶν ὄντων
ἐφετόν· τὸ δὲ ἐν τινὶ γενόμενον ἐκείνου μόνον ἐστὶ τοῦ μετα-
σχόντος.
    τὸ ἄρα πρώτως ἀγαθὸν οὐδὲν ἄλλο ἐστὶν ἢ ἀγαθόν. ἂν γάρ
τι ἄλλο προσθῇς, ἠλάττωσας τῇ προσθέσει τὸ ἀγαθόν, τὶ 10
ἀγαθὸν ποιήσας ἀντὶ τοῦ ἀγαθοῦ τοῦ ἁπλῶς· τὸ γὰρ προστεθέν,
οὐκ ὂν τὸ ἀγαθὸν ἀλλ᾽ ἔλαττον ἢ ἐκεῖνο, τῇ ἑαυτοῦ συνουσίᾳ τὸ
ἀγαθὸν ἠλάττωσεν.

    9. Πᾶν τὸ αὔταρκες ἢ κατ᾽ οὐσίαν ἢ κατ᾽ ἐνέργειαν κρεῖττόν
ἐστι τοῦ μὴ αὐτάρκους ἀλλ᾽ εἰς ἄλλην οὐσίαν ἀνηρτημένου τὴν 15
τῆς τελειότητος αἰτίαν.
    εἰ γὰρ ἅπαντα τὰ ὄντα τοῦ ἀγαθοῦ κατὰ φύσιν ὀρέγεται, καὶ
τὸ μὲν ἑαυτῷ παρεκτικόν ἐστι τοῦ εὖ, τὸ δὲ ἐπιδεὲς ἄλλου, καὶ
τὸ μὲν παροῦσαν ἔχει τὴν τοῦ ἀγαθοῦ αἰτίαν, τὸ δὲ χωρὶς
οὖσαν, ὅσῳ δὴ οὖν ἐγγυτέρω τοῦτο τῆς τὸ ὀρεκτὸν χορηγούσης, 20
τοσούτῳ κρεῖττον ἂν εἴη τοῦ τῆς κεχωρισμένης αἰτίας ἐνδεοῦς
ὄντος καὶ ἀλλαχόθεν ὑποδεχομένου τὴν τελειότητα τῆς ὑπάρξεως
ἢ τῆς ἐνεργείας. ἐπεὶ οὖν [ὅτι καὶ ὅμοιον καὶ ἠλαττωμένον] καὶ
ὁμοιότερόν ἐστιν αὐτῷ τῷ ἀγαθῷ τὸ αὔταρκες καὶ ἠλαττωμένον
τῷ μετέχειν τοῦ ἀγαθοῦ καὶ μὴ αὐτὸ εἶναι τὸ ἀγαθὸν πρώτως, 25
συγγενές πώς ἐστιν ἐκείνῳ, καθόσον παρ᾽ ἑαυτοῦ δύναται τὸ
ἀγαθὸν ἔχειν· τὸ δὲ μετέχον καὶ δι᾽ ἄλλου μετέχον μειζόνως
ἀφέστηκε τοῦ πρώτως ἀγαθοῦ καὶ ὃ μηδέν ἐστιν ἄλλο ἢ ἀγαθόν.

    10. Πᾶν τὸ αὔταρκες τοῦ ἁπλῶς ἀγαθοῦ καταδεέστερόν
ἐστι. 30
    τί γάρ ἐστιν ἄλλο τὸ αὔταρκες ἢ τὸ παρ᾽ ἑαυτοῦ καὶ ἐν
ἑαυτῷ τὸ ἀγαθὸν κεκτημένον; τοῦτο δὲ ἤδη πλῆρές ἐστι τοῦ
ἀγαθοῦ καὶ μετέχον, ἀλλ᾽ οὐχὶ αὐτὸ τὸ ἁπλῶς ἀγαθόν. ἐκεῖνο

---

8. 2 ἕτερον καὶ ἀπεξενωμένον BCD Par. 2028 : καὶ ἀπεξενωμένον om. MPQW
(ἀπεξενωμένον in mg. M³): ἕτερον καί omissa voluit Port.   4 ἔστιν ἄρα τὶ
ἀγαθόν PQ   6 κοινόν ἐστι πάντων dett., Cr.   7 μόνου BCD   12 αὐτοῦ
BCD (αὐτῇ primitus D?)   συνουσίᾳ MPQ, coexistencia W : οὐσίᾳ BCDM³
9. Tit. περὶ αὐτάρκους BCDM   15 οὐσίαν scripsi : αἰτίου M¹ ut videtur :
αἰτίαν cett.   ἀνηρτημένου M¹ ut videtur, PQ : ἠρτημένου BCM², ἠρτυμένην D
16 αἰτίαν BCDPQ, M² in rasura : αἰτίον (sic) Arg : οὐσίαν Lugd. Voss. 14 etc.
18 καί PQ : om. cett.   20 οὖν om. M (add. M³)   23 οὖν [M], quidem W :
ὅτι cett.   καὶ ὅμοιον καὶ ἠλαττωμένον om. BCD   ὅτι καὶ ὅμ. κ. ἠλ. ex
margine illata   23 alt. καί . . . 24 ἠλαττωμένον om. M¹   24 καί om.

Good (since all appetite implies a lack of, and a severance from, the object craved); or (since this is impossible) its existence is to be distinguished from its goodness, and the latter will be immanent in the former and participated by it. If so, it is not *the* Good, but *a* good, being immanent in a particular participant: it is merely the good which this participant desires, not the unqualified Good desired of all existing things. For that is the common object of all yearning, whereas an immanent good belongs to the participant.

The primal Good, then, is nothing else but good. Add to it some other character, and by the addition you have diminished its goodness, changing it from the Good unqualified to a particular good. For that added character, which is not the Good but some lesser thing, by its coexistence has diminished the Good.

PROP. 9. *All that is self-sufficient either in its existence or in its activity is superior to what is not self-sufficient but dependent upon another existence which is the cause of its completeness.*

For if all things which exist have a natural appetition of their good; and if further there are things which derive their well-being from themselves and things which demand another's help, things which have the cause of their good within them and things to which it is external: then in proportion as the former are nearer to the giver of their desire, so must they be superior to that which needs an extraneous cause of good and has its existence or its activity completed only by reception from without. Since, then, the self-sufficient has more likeness to the Good itself (yet falls short, in that it participates good and is not itself the primal Good), it is in some way akin to the Good, inasmuch as it can furnish its good out of its own being, whereas that which not only participates, but does so through an external medium, is at a further remove from the primal Good which is nothing else but good.

PROP. 10. *All that is self-sufficient is inferior to the unqualified Good.*

For what else is the self-sufficient than that which has its good from and in itself? And this means that it is indeed fulfilled with goodness, and participates good, but is not the unqualified Good itself: for the latter, as has been shown (prop. 8), transcends

---

dett., edd. : autem W   24 ἠλαττωμένον μὲν ... 26 συγγενὲς δέ Laur. 71. 32
25 τὸ μετέχειν dett., edd.   26 παρ' αὐτοῦ PQ   26–7 ἔχειν τὸ ἀγαθόν PQ
27 μετέχειν (bis) edd.
    cc. 10 init.–12 l. 19 κἀκείνου hodie in M requiruntur
10. 29 τό om. BCDO   31 alt. τό om. PQ   32 ἐστι om. dett., edd.

γὰρ καὶ τοῦ μετέχειν καὶ τοῦ πλῆρες εἶναι κρεῖττον, ὡς δέδεικται. εἰ οὖν τὸ αὔταρκες πεπλήρωκεν ἑαυτὸ τοῦ ἀγαθοῦ, τὸ ἀφ' οὗ πεπλήρωκεν ἑαυτὸ κρεῖττον ἂν εἴη τοῦ αὐτάρκους καὶ ὑπὲρ αὐτάρκειαν. καὶ οὔτε ἐνδεές τινος τὸ ἁπλῶς ἀγαθόν. οὐ γὰρ ἐφίεται ἄλλου (εἴη γὰρ ἂν ἐλλιπὲς ἀγαθοῦ κατὰ τὴν ἔφεσιν)· 5 οὔτε αὔταρκες· εἴη γὰρ ἂν πλῆρες ἀγαθοῦ, καὶ οὐ τἀγαθὸν πρώτως.

11. Πάντα τὰ ὄντα πρόεισιν ἀπὸ μιᾶς αἰτίας, τῆς πρώτης.

ἢ γὰρ οὐδενός ἐστιν αἰτία τῶν ὄντων, ἢ κύκλῳ τὰ αἴτια πεπερασμένων τῶν πάντων, ἢ ἐπ' ἄπειρον ἡ ἄνοδος καὶ ἄλλο 10 ἄλλου αἴτιον καὶ οὐδαμοῦ στήσεται ἡ τῆς αἰτίας προϋπόστασις.

ἀλλ' εἰ μὲν μηδενὸς εἴη τῶν ὄντων αἰτία, οὔτε τάξις ἔσται δευτέρων καὶ πρώτων, τελειούντων καὶ τελειουμένων, κοσμούντων καὶ κοσμουμένων, γεννώντων καὶ γεννωμένων, ποιούντων καὶ πασχόντων· οὔτε ἐπιστήμη τῶν ὄντων οὐδενός. ἡ γὰρ τῶν 15 αἰτίων γνῶσις ἐπιστήμης ἐστὶν ἔργον, καὶ τότε λέγομεν ἐπίστασθαι ὅταν τὰ αἴτια γνωρίσωμεν τῶν ὄντων.

εἰ δὲ κύκλῳ περίεισι τὰ αἴτια, τὰ αὐτὰ πρότερα ἔσται καὶ ὕστερα, δυνατώτερά τε καὶ ἀσθενέστερα· πᾶν γὰρ τὸ παράγον κρεῖττόν ἐστι τῆς τοῦ παραγομένου φύσεως. διαφέρει δὲ οὐδὲν 20 τὸ διὰ πλειόνων ἢ δι' ἐλαττόνων μέσων συνάπτειν τῷ αἰτιατῷ τὸ αἴτιον καὶ ποιεῖν ἀπ' ἐκείνου· καὶ γὰρ τῶν μεταξὺ πάντων ἔσται κρεῖττον ὧν ἐστιν αἴτιον, καὶ ὅσῳ ἂν πλείω τὰ μέσα, τοσούτῳ μειζόνως αἴτιον.

εἰ δ' ἐπ' ἄπειρον ἡ τῶν αἰτίων πρόσθεσις, καὶ ἄλλο πρὸ 25 ἄλλου ἀεί, πάλιν οὐδενὸς ἐπιστήμη ἔσται. τῶν γὰρ ἀπείρων οὐδενός ἐστι γνῶσις· τῶν δὲ αἰτίων ἀγνοουμένων οὐδὲ τῶν ἑξῆς ἐπιστήμη ἔσται.

εἰ οὖν καὶ αἰτίαν εἶναι δεῖ τῶν ὄντων, καὶ διώρισται τὰ αἴτια τῶν αἰτιατῶν, καὶ οὐκ εἰς ἄπειρον ἡ ἄνοδος, ἔστιν αἰτία πρώτη 30 τῶν ὄντων ἀφ' ἧς οἷον ἐκ ῥίζης πρόεισιν ἔκαστα, τὰ μὲν ἐγγὺς ὄντα ἐκείνης, τὰ δὲ πορρώτερον· ὅτι γὰρ μίαν εἶναι δεῖ τὴν ἀρχήν, δέδεικται, διότι πᾶν πλῆθος δεύτερον ὑφέστηκε τοῦ ἑνός.

10. 1 ὡς om. PQ   2 γοῦν DPQ   2 τοῦ ἀγαθοῦ . . . 3 ἑαυτό om. PQO¹
5 ἐλλειπές edd.
11. Tit. περὶ αἰτίου BCDO   10 πεπερασμένα PQ   10–11 ἄλλου ἄλλο edd.
11 οὐδαμῶς P   αἰτίας] οὐσίας O   12 αἰτία BDE : αἴτιον CPQOArg, sed
cf. ll. 9 et 29   13–14 κοσμούντων καὶ κοσμουμένων om. PQ   21 μέσων
(μέσον B) συνάπτειν BCD dett. W : transp. PQ (μέσον P)   23 τὰ πλείω τά O
primitus   25 πρόσθεσις BC²O, appositio W : πρόθεσις C¹DEArg : πρόσοδος
PQ   25–6 πρὸς ἄλλον Q, ab alio W   26 τῶν γὰρ . . . 28 ἔσται om. O
30 πρώτη] προτέρα PQ   31 ἕκαστον PQ   32 δεῖ μίαν εἶναι PQ

participation and fulfilment. If, then, the self-sufficient has fulfilled itself with goodness, that from which it has fulfilled itself must be superior to the self-sufficient and beyond self-sufficiency. The unqualified Good lacks nothing, since it has no desire towards another (for desire in it would be a failure of goodness); but it is not self-sufficient (for so it would be a principle fulfilled with goodness, not the primal Good).

Prop. 11. *All that exists proceeds from a single first cause.*

For otherwise all things are uncaused; or else the sum of existence is limited, and there is a circuit of causation within the sum; or else there will be regress to infinity, cause lying behind cause, so that the positing of prior causes will never cease.

But if all things were uncaused, there would be no sequence of primary and secondary, perfecting and perfected, regulative and regulated, generative and generated, active and passive; and all things would be unknowable. For the task of science is the recognition of causes, and only when we recognize the causes of things do we say that we know them.

And if causes transmit themselves in a circuit, the same things will be at once prior and consequent; that is, since every productive cause is superior to its product (prop. 7), each will be at once more efficient than the rest and less efficient. (It is indifferent whether we make the connexion of cause and effect and derive the one from the other through a greater or a less number of intermediate causes; for the cause of all these intermediaries will be superior to all of them, and the greater their number, the greater the efficiency of that cause.)

And if the accumulation of causes may be continued to infinity, cause behind cause for ever, thus again all things will be unknowable. For nothing infinite can be apprehended; and the causes being unknown, there can be no knowledge of their consequents.

Since, then, things cannot be uncaused, and cause is not convertible with effect, and infinite regress is excluded, it remains that there is a first cause of all existing things, whence they severally proceed as branches from a root, some near to it and others more remote. For that there is not more than one such first principle has already been established, inasmuch as the subsistence of any manifold is posterior to the One (prop. 5).

12. Πάντων τῶν ὄντων ἀρχὴ καὶ αἰτία πρωτίστη τὸ ἀγαθόν ἐστιν.·

εἰ γὰρ ἀπὸ μιᾶς αἰτίας πάντα πρόεισιν, ἐκείνην τὴν αἰτίαν ἢ τἀγαθὸν χρὴ λέγειν ἢ τἀγαθοῦ κρεῖττον. ἀλλ' εἰ μὲν κρείττων ἐκείνη τοῦ ἀγαθοῦ, πότερον ἥκει τι καὶ ἀπ' ἐκείνης εἰς τὰ 5 ὄντα καὶ τὴν φύσιν τῶν ὄντων, ἢ οὐδέν; καὶ εἰ μὲν μηδέν, ἄτοπον· οὐ γὰρ ἂν ἔτι φυλάττοιμεν αὐτὴν ἐν αἰτίας τάξει, δέον πανταχοῦ παρεῖναί τι τοῖς αἰτιατοῖς ἐκ τῆς αἰτίας, καὶ διαφερόντως ἐκ τῆς πρωτίστης, ἧς πάντα ἐξήρτηται καὶ δι' ἣν ἔστιν ἕκαστα τῶν ὄντων. εἰ δέ ἐστι μετουσία κἀκείνης τοῖς οὖσιν, 10 ὥσπερ καὶ τἀγαθοῦ, ἔσται τι τῆς ἀγαθότητος κρεῖττον ἐν τοῖς οὖσιν, ἐφῆκον ἀπὸ τῆς πρωτίστης αἰτίας· οὐ γάρ που, κρεῖττων οὖσα καὶ ὑπὲρ τἀγαθόν, καταδεέστερόν τι δίδωσι τοῖς δευτέροις ὧν τὸ μετ' αὐτὴν δίδωσι. καὶ τί ἂν γένοιτο τῆς ἀγαθότητος ·κρεῖττον; ἐπεὶ καὶ αὐτὸ τὸ κρεῖττον τὸ μειζόνως ἀγαθοῦ μετ- 15 ειληφὸς εἶναι λέγομεν. εἰ οὖν οὐδὲ κρεῖττον ἂν λέγοιτο τὸ μὴ ἀγαθόν, τοῦ ἀγαθοῦ πάντως δεύτερον.

εἰ δὲ καὶ τὰ ὄντα πάντα τοῦ ἀγαθοῦ ἐφίεται, πῶς ἔτι πρὸ τῆς αἰτίας ταύτης εἶναί τι δυνατόν; εἴτε γὰρ ἐφίεται κἀκείνου, πῶς τοῦ ἀγαθοῦ μάλιστα; εἴτε μὴ ἐφίεται, πῶς τῆς πάντων 20 αἰτίας οὐκ ἐφίεται, προελθόντα ἀπ' αὐτῆς;

εἰ δὲ τἀγαθόν ἐστιν ἀφ' οὗ πάντα ἐξήρτηται τὰ ὄντα, ἀρχὴ καὶ αἰτία πρωτίστη τῶν πάντων ἐστὶ τἀγαθόν.

13. Πᾶν ἀγαθὸν ἑνωτικόν ἐστι τῶν μετεχόντων αὐτοῦ, καὶ πᾶσα ἕνωσις ἀγαθόν, καὶ τἀγαθὸν τῷ ἑνὶ ταὐτόν. 25

εἰ γὰρ τὸ ἀγαθόν ἐστι σωστικὸν τῶν ὄντων ἁπάντων (διὸ καὶ ἐφετὸν ὑπάρχει πᾶσι), τὸ δὲ σωστικὸν καὶ συνεκτικὸν τῆς ἑκάστων οὐσίας ἐστὶ τὸ ἕν (τῷ γὰρ ἑνὶ σώζεται πάντα, καὶ ὁ σκεδασμὸς ἕκαστον ἐξίστησι τῆς οὐσίας), τὸ ἀγαθόν, οἷς ἂν παρῇ, ταῦτα ἓν ἀπεργάζεται καὶ συνέχει κατὰ τὴν 30 ἕνωσιν.

καὶ εἰ τὸ ἓν συναγωγόν ἐστι καὶ συνεκτικὸν τῶν ὄντων, ἕκαστον τελειοῖ κατὰ τὴν ἑαυτοῦ παρουσίαν. καὶ ἀγαθὸν ἄρα ταύτῃ ἐστὶ τὸ ἡνῶσθαι πᾶσιν.

12. 3 πάντα om. PQ   5–6 τὰ ὄντα καί fort. secludenda   6 τὴν φύσιν] τὰ φύσει Q   μέν] καί O   8 αἰτιατοῖς BCDPQ (coni. T. Taylor): αἰτίοις Arg O¹   9 ἧς ω (ἐξ ἧς edd.)   10 κἀκείνης BC²DO : καὶ ἐκείνης PQ : κἀκείνοις C¹Arg   11 τι om. PQ   12 ἀφῆκον DE, deveniens W, sed cf. c. 136, l. 29   που PQ, utique W : πω cett.   κρεῖσσον O primitus   13 ἀγαθόν PQ   15 μείζονος BCD   16 οὖν om. D : γοῦν PQ   ἂν ω (om. edd.) 18 πῶς . . . 19 ἐφίεται om. PQ   22 τἀγαθόν ω (ἀγαθόν dett., edd.)
13. 26 σωστικόν ἐστι PQ   28 ἑκάστου PQ   τὰ πάντα BCD   32 καὶ συνεκτικόν om. M¹   33 παρουσίαν ex ἐνέργειαν factum P

Prop. 12. *All that exists has the Good as its principium and first cause.*

For if all things proceed from a single cause (prop. 11), we must hold that this cause is either the Good or superior to the Good. But if it be superior to the Good, does it or does it not exercise some force upon things and upon the nature of things? That it does not would be a strange view: for thus it would forfeit its title to the name of cause. For something must in every case pass over from the cause to the effect; and especially must this be true of the first cause, from which all things depend and to which all things owe their several existence. But if things have participation in this supposed superior cause, as they have in the Good (prop. 8), they will possess some character higher than goodness, some character derived from this first cause: for surely the superior principle, transcending the Good, does not bestow upon secondary beings a meaner gift than does the Good which it transcends. And what should this character be which is higher than goodness? For by the very term 'higher' we mean that which in greater measure participates good. If, then, the not-good cannot be called 'higher', it is necessarily posterior to the Good.

Again, if all things which exist have desire towards the Good, how can there be a further cause beyond it? For if they desire that other also, how can their desire be pre-eminently towards the Good? And if they desire it not, how .comes it that they have no desire towards the universal cause whence they proceeded?

Again, if the Good is that from which all things depend, the Good must be the principium and first cause of all things.

Prop. 13. *Every good tends to unify what participates it; and all unification is a good; and the Good is identical with the One.*

For if it belongs to the Good to conserve all that exists (and it is for no other reason that all things desire it); and if likewise that which conserves and holds together the being of each several thing is unity (since by unity each is maintained in being, but by dispersion displaced from existence): then the Good, wherever it is present, makes the participant one, and holds its being together in virtue of this unification.

And secondly, if it belongs to unity to bring and keep each thing together, by its presence it makes each thing complete. In this way, then, the state of unification is good for all things.

εἰ δὲ καὶ ἡ ἔνωσις ἀγαθὸν καθ' αὑτὸ καὶ τὸ ἀγαθὸν ἑνοποιόν,
τὸ ἁπλῶς ἀγαθὸν καὶ τὸ ἁπλῶς ἐν ταὐτόν, ἑνίζον τε ἅμα καὶ
ἀγαθῦνον τὰ ὄντα. ὅθεν δὴ καὶ τὰ τοῦ ἀγαθοῦ τρόπον τινὰ
ἀποπεσόντα καὶ τῆς τοῦ ἑνὸς ἅμα στέρεται μεθέξεως· καὶ τὰ
τοῦ ἑνὸς ἄμοιρα γενόμενα, διαστάσεως ἀναπιμπλάμενα, καὶ τοῦ 5
ἀγαθοῦ στέρεται κατὰ τὸν αὐτὸν τρόπον.

ἔστιν ἄρα καὶ ἡ ἀγαθότης ἔνωσις, καὶ ἡ ἔνωσις ἀγαθότης,
καὶ τὸ ἀγαθὸν ἕν, καὶ τὸ ἐν πρώτως ἀγαθόν.

14. Πᾶν τὸ ὂν ἢ ἀκίνητόν ἐστιν ἢ κινούμενον· καὶ εἰ κινούμενον, ἢ ὑφ' ἑαυτοῦ ἢ ὑπ' ἄλλου· καὶ εἰ μὲν ὑφ' ἑαυτοῦ, αὐτο- 10
κίνητόν ἐστιν· εἰ δὲ ὑπ' ἄλλου, ἑτεροκίνητον. πᾶν ἄρα ἢ
ἀκίνητόν ἐστιν ἢ αὐτοκίνητον ἢ ἑτεροκίνητον.

ἀνάγκη γὰρ τῶν ἑτεροκινήτων ὄντων εἶναι καὶ τὸ ἀκίνητον,
καὶ μεταξὺ τούτων τὸ αὐτοκίνητον.

εἰ γὰρ πᾶν τὸ ἑτεροκίνητον ὑπ' ἄλλου κινουμένου κινεῖται, ἢ 15
κύκλῳ αἱ κινήσεις ἢ ἐπ' ἄπειρον· ἀλλ' οὔτε κύκλῳ οὔτε ἐπ'
ἄπειρον, εἴπερ ὥρισται τῇ ἀρχῇ τὰ ὄντα πάντα καὶ τὸ κινοῦν
τοῦ κινουμένου κρεῖττον. ἔσται τι ἄρα ἀκίνητον πρῶτον
κινοῦν.

ἀλλ' εἰ ταῦτα, ἀνάγκη καὶ τὸ αὐτοκίνητον εἶναι. εἰ γὰρ 20
σταίη τὰ πάντα, τί ποτε ἔσται τὸ πρώτως κινούμενον; οὔτε
γὰρ τὸ ἀκίνητον (οὐ γὰρ πέφυκεν) οὔτε τὸ ἑτεροκίνητον (ὑπ'
ἄλλου γὰρ κινεῖται)· λείπεται ἄρα τὸ αὐτοκίνητον εἶναι τὸ
πρώτως κινούμενον· ἐπεὶ καὶ τοῦτό ἐστι τὸ τῷ ἀκινήτῳ τὰ ἑτεροκίνητα συνάπτον, μέσον πως ὄν, κινοῦν τε ἅμα καὶ κινούμενον· 25
ἐκείνων γὰρ τὸ μὲν κινεῖ μόνον, τὸ δὲ κινεῖται μόνον.

πᾶν ἄρα τὸ ὂν ἢ ἀκίνητόν ἐστιν ἢ αὐτοκίνητον ἢ ἑτεροκίνητον.
ἐκ δὴ τούτων κἀκεῖνο φανερόν, ὅτι τῶν μὲν κινουμένων τὸ
αὐτοκίνητον πρῶτον, τῶν δὲ κινούντων τὸ ἀκίνητον.

15. Πᾶν τὸ πρὸς ἑαυτὸ ἐπιστρεπτικὸν ἀσώματόν ἐστιν. 30

οὐδὲν γὰρ τῶν σωμάτων πρὸς ἑαυτὸ πέφυκεν ἐπιστρέφειν.
εἰ γὰρ τὸ ἐπιστρέφον πρός τι συνάπτεται ἐκείνῳ πρὸς ὃ ἐπιστρέφει, δῆλον δὴ ὅτι καὶ τὰ μέρη τοῦ σώματος πάντα πρὸς
πάντα συνάψει τοῦ πρὸς ἑαυτὸ ἐπιστραφέντος· τοῦτο γὰρ ἦν τὸ
πρὸς ἑαυτὸ ἐπιστρέψαι, ὅταν ἐν γένηται ἄμφω, τό τε ἐπιστραφὲν 35

---

13. 1 ἀγαθόν, καὶ καθ' αὑτό dett., Cr.   2 τε ω (om. edd.)   3 τἀγαθοῦ BCD
5 γιγνόμενα M   5-6 τἀγαθοῦ M
14. Tit. περὶ ἀκινήτου καὶ (ἢ D) αὐτοκινήτου ἀρχῆς ἢ αἰτίας (αἰτίου D, οὗ C)
BCDM   9 aut motum aut immobile est W   14 καὶ τὸ μεταξὺ PQ
15 κινουμένου BCEQW : κινούμενον DMP   16 ἀλλ'... 17 ἄπειρον om. BCD
21 ἐστι PQ   25 μέσον· πῶς οὖν; [M]PQ   28 μὲν om. M¹
15. Tit. περὶ ἀσωμάτου οὐσίας, καὶ τί ἴδιον αὐτῆς BCDM   33 δή om. M¹

But again, if unification is in itself good, and all good tends to create unity, then the Good unqualified and the One unqualified merge in a single principle, a principle which makes things one and in doing so makes them good. Hence it is that things which in some fashion have fallen away from their good are at the same stroke deprived of participation of unity ; and in like manner things which have lost their portion in unity, being infected with division, are deprived of their good.

Goodness, then, is unification, and unification goodness ; the Good is one, and the One is primal good.

C. OF THE GRADES OF REALITY.

PROP. 14. *All that exists is either moved or unmoved ; and if the former, either by itself or by another, that is, either intrinsically or extrinsically : so that everything is unmoved, intrinsically moved, or extrinsically moved.*

For since there are things extrinsically moved it follows that there is also something unmoved, and an intermediate existence which is self-moved.

For suppose all extrinsic movement derived from an agent which is itself in motion ; then we have either a circuit of communicated movement or an infinite regress. But neither of these is possible, inasmuch as the sum of existence is limited by a first principle (prop. 11) and the mover is superior to the moved (prop. 7). There must, then, be something unmoved which is the first mover.

But if so, there must also be something self-moved. For imagine all things to be at rest : what will be the first thing set in motion ? Not the unmoved, by the law of its nature. And not the extrinsically moved, since its motion is communicated from without. It remains, then, that the first thing set in motion is the self-moved, which is in fact the link between the unmoved and the things which are moved extrinsically. At once mover and moved, the self-moved is a kind of mean term between the unmoved mover and that which is merely moved. Everything which exists, therefore, is unmoved, intrinsically moved, or extrinsically moved.

Cor. From this it is apparent also that of things moved, the self-moved has primacy ; and of movers, the unmoved.

PROP. 15. *All that is capable of reverting upon itself is incorporeal.*

For it is not in the nature of any body to revert upon itself. That which reverts upon anything is conjoined with that upon which it reverts : hence it is evident that every part of a body reverted upon itself must be conjoined with every other part—since self-reversion is precisely the case in which the reverted subject and that upon

καὶ πρὸς ὃ ἐπεστράφη. ἀδύνατον δὲ ἐπὶ σώματος τοῦτο, καὶ
ὅλως τῶν μεριστῶν πάντων· οὐ γὰρ ὅλον ὅλῳ συνάπτεται
ἑαυτῷ τὸ μεριστὸν διὰ τὸν τῶν μερῶν χωρισμόν, ἄλλων ἀλλαχοῦ
κειμένων. οὐδὲν ἄρα σῶμα πρὸς ἑαυτὸ πέφυκεν ἐπιστρέφειν,
ὡς ὅλον ἐπεστράφθαι πρὸς ὅλον. εἴ τι ἄρα πρὸς ἑαυτὸ ἐπι- 5
στρεπτικόν ἐστιν, ἀσώματόν ἐστι καὶ ἀμερές.
16. Πᾶν τὸ πρὸς ἑαυτὸ ἐπιστρεπτικὸν χωριστὴν οὐσίαν ἔχει
παντὸς σώματος.
εἰ γὰρ ἀχώριστον εἴη σώματος οὐτινοσοῦν, οὐχ ἕξει τινὰ
ἐνέργειαν σώματος χωριστήν. ἀδύνατον γάρ, ἀχωρίστου τῆς 10
οὐσίας σωμάτων οὔσης, τὴν ἀπὸ τῆς οὐσίας ἐνέργειαν εἶναι χω-
ριστήν· ἔσται γὰρ οὕτως ἡ ἐνέργεια τῆς οὐσίας κρείττων, εἴπερ
ἡ μὲν ἐπιδεής ἐστι σωμάτων, ἡ δὲ αὐτάρκης, ἑαυτῆς οὖσα καὶ
οὐ σωμάτων. εἰ οὖν τι κατ᾽ οὐσίαν ἐστὶν ἀχώριστον, καὶ κατ᾽
ἐνέργειαν ὁμοίως ἢ καὶ ἔτι μᾶλλον ἀχώριστον. εἰ δὲ τοῦτο, οὐκ 15
ἐπιστρέφει πρὸς ἑαυτό. τὸ γὰρ πρὸς ἑαυτὸ ἐπιστρέφον, ἄλλο ὂν
σώματος, ἐνέργειαν ἔχει χωριζομένην σώματος καὶ οὐ διὰ
σώματος οὐδὲ μετὰ σώματος, εἴπερ ἥ τε ἐνέργεια καὶ τὸ πρὸς ὃ
ἡ ἐνέργεια οὐδὲν δεῖται τοῦ σώματος. χωριστὸν ἄρα πάντῃ
σωμάτων ἐστὶ τὸ πρὸς ἑαυτὸ ἐπιστρέφον. 20
17. Πᾶν τὸ ἑαυτὸ κινοῦν πρώτως πρὸς ἑαυτό ἐστιν ἐπιστρεπτικόν.
εἰ γὰρ κινεῖ ἑαυτό, καὶ ἡ κινητικὴ ἐνέργεια αὐτοῦ πρὸς
ἑαυτό ἐστι, καὶ ἐν ἅμα τὸ κινοῦν καὶ τὸ κινούμενον. ἢ γὰρ
μέρει μὲν κινεῖ, μέρει δὲ κινεῖται, ἢ ὅλον κινεῖ καὶ κινεῖται, ἢ
ὅλον μὲν κινεῖ, μέρει δὲ κινεῖται, ἢ ἔμπαλιν. ἀλλ᾽ εἰ μέρος 25
μὲν ἄλλο ἐστὶ τὸ κινοῦν, μέρος δὲ ἄλλο τὸ κινούμενον, οὐκ
ἔσται καθ᾽ ἑαυτὸ αὐτοκίνητον, ἐκ μὴ αὐτοκινήτων ὑφεστός,
ἀλλὰ δοκοῦν μὲν αὐτοκίνητον, οὐκ ὂν δὲ κατ᾽ οὐσίαν τοιοῦτον.
εἰ δὲ ὅλον κινεῖ, μέρος δὲ κινεῖται, ἢ ἔμπαλιν, ἔσται τι μέρος ἐν
ἀμφοτέροις καθ᾽ ἓν ἅμα κινοῦν καὶ κινούμενον, καὶ τοῦτό ἐστι 30
τὸ πρώτως αὐτοκίνητον. εἰ δὲ ἓν καὶ ταὐτὸν κινεῖ καὶ κινεῖται,
τὴν τοῦ κινεῖν ἐνέργειαν πρὸς ἑαυτὸ ἕξει, κινητικὸν ἑαυτοῦ ὄν.

15. 1 τὸ πρὸς ὅ Q fort. recte (cf. l. 18)   ἐπεστράφη ω (ἐπιστράφη Cr. errore
preli)   3 ἑαυτῷ BCPQ, sibi W : ἑαυτό D : αὑτῷ M   ἄλλον P, ἀλλ᾽ vel
ἀλλ᾽ M¹, om. Arg
16. 9 τινοσοῦν PQ, qui ante hoc verbum scholion textui inserunt τὸ τινοσοῦν
προσέθηκε τῷ ἀχωρίστῳ (sic)· τὸ εἴτε συνθέτου ἐστὶν ἀχώριστος εἴτε ἁπλοῦ ἢ
ὀστριωδοῦς ἢ τοῦ αἰθερωδοῦς· τοσαῦτα γὰρ τὰ φυσικά.   10 χωριστόν preli errore
Cr.   15 ἢ om. P Q   16 τὸ γὰρ πρὸς ἑαυτό ω (om. dett., edd.)
17. 23 ἢ] εἰ M   24-5 ἢ ὅλον κινεῖ καὶ κινεῖται om. BCDM¹ : ἢ ὅλον μὲν κινεῖ,
μέρει δὲ κινεῖται om. M¹ : integrum textum tradunt PQM²W (fere similia coni.
T. Taylor)   27 ὑφεστός M : ὑφεστώς cett.   30 fort. τοῦτο ἔσται
31 ταὐτόν BCD (ἐν κατ᾽ αὐτόν D¹) : τὸ αὐτό PQ : αὐτό M : per se W (cod. Ball.
'idem')   32 ἑαυτό] αὑτό PQ

which it has reverted become identical. But this is impossible for a body, and universally for any divisible substance : for the whole of a divisible substance cannot be conjoined with the whole of itself, because of the separation of its parts, which occupy different positions in space. It is not in the nature, then, of any body to revert upon itself so that the whole is reverted upon the whole. Thus if there is anything which is capable of reverting upon itself, it is incorporeal and without parts.

PROP. **16.** *All that is capable of reverting upon itself has an existence separable from all body.*

For if there were any body whatsoever from which it was inseparable, it could have no activity separable from the body, since it is impossible that if the existence be inseparable from bodies the activity, which proceeds from the existence, should be separable : if so, the activity would be superior to the existence, in that the latter needed a body while the former was self-sufficient, being dependent not on bodies but on itself. Anything, therefore, which is inseparable in its existence is to the same or an even greater degree inseparable in its activity. But if so, it cannot revert upon itself : for that which reverts upon itself, being other than body (prop. 15), has an activity independent of the body and not conducted through it or with its co-operation, since neither the activity itself nor the end to which it is directed requires the body. Accordingly, that which reverts upon itself must be entirely separable from bodies.

PROP. **17.** *Everything originally self-moving is capable of reversion upon itself.*

For if it moves itself, its motive activity is directed upon itself, and mover and moved exist simultaneously as one thing. For either it moves with one part of itself and is moved in another ; or the whole moves and is moved ; or the whole originates motion which occurs in a part, or *vice versa*. But if the mover be one part and the moved another, in itself the whole will not be self-moved, since it will be composed of parts which are not self-moved : it will have the appearance of a self-mover, but will not be such in essence. And if the whole originates a motion which occurs in a part, or *vice versa*, there will be a part common to both which is simultaneously and in the same respect mover and moved, and it is this part which is originally self-moved. And if one and the same thing moves and is moved, it will (as a self-mover) have its activity of motion directed

πρὸς ὃ δὲ ἐνεργεῖ, πρὸς τοῦτο ἐπέστραπται. πᾶν ἄρα τὸ ἑαυτὸ
κινοῦν πρώτως πρὸς ἑαυτό ἐστιν ἐπιστρεπτικόν.

18. Πᾶν τὸ τῷ εἶναι χορηγοῦν ἄλλοις αὐτὸ πρώτως ἐστὶ
τοῦτο, οὗ μεταδίδωσι τοῖς χορηγουμένοις.

εἰ γὰρ αὐτῷ τῷ εἶναι δίδωσι καὶ ἀπὸ τῆς ἑαυτοῦ οὐσίας 5
ποιεῖται τὴν μετάδοσιν, ὃ μὲν δίδωσιν ὑφειμένον ἐστὶ τῆς
ἑαυτοῦ οὐσίας, ὃ δέ ἐστι, μειζόνως ἐστὶ καὶ τελειότερον, εἴπερ
πᾶν τὸ ὑποστατικόν τινος κρεῖττόν ἐστι τῆς τοῦ ὑφισταμένου
φύσεως. τοῦ δοθέντος ἄρα τὸ ἐν αὐτῷ τῷ δεδωκότι προυπάρχον κρειττόνως ἔστι· καὶ ὅπερ ἐκεῖνο μέν ἐστιν, ἀλλ' οὐ 10
ταὐτὸν ἐκείνῳ· πρώτως γὰρ ἔστι, τὸ δὲ δευτέρως. ἀνάγκη γὰρ
ἢ τὸ αὐτὸ εἶναι ἑκάτερον καὶ ἕνα λόγον ἀμφοτέρων, ἢ μηδὲν
εἶναι κοινὸν μηδὲ ταὐτὸν ἐν ἀμφοῖν, ἢ τὸ μὲν πρώτως εἶναι, τὸ
δὲ δευτέρως. ἀλλ' εἰ μὲν ὁ αὐτὸς λόγος, οὐκ ἂν ἔτι τὸ μὲν
αἴτιον εἴη, τὸ δὲ ἀποτέλεσμα· οὐδ' ἂν τὸ μὲν καθ' αὐτό, τὸ δ' 15
ἐν τῷ μετασχόντι· οὐδὲ τὸ μὲν ποιοῦν, τὸ δὲ γινόμενον. εἰ δὲ
μηδὲν ἔχοι ταὐτόν, οὐκ ἂν τῷ εἶναι θάτερον ὑφίστατο τὸ λοιπόν,
μηδὲν πρὸς τὸ εἶναι τὸ ἐκείνου κοινωνοῦν. λείπεται ἄρα τὸ μὲν
εἶναι πρώτως ὃ δίδωσι, τὸ δὲ δευτέρως ὃ τὸ διδόν ἐστιν, ἐν οἷς
αὐτῷ τῷ εἶναι θάτερον ἐκ θατέρου χορηγεῖται. 20

19. Πᾶν τὸ πρώτως ἐνυπάρχον τινὶ φύσει τῶν ὄντων πᾶσι
πάρεστι τοῖς κατ' ἐκείνην τὴν φύσιν τεταγμένοις καθ' ἕνα
λόγον καὶ ὡσαύτως.

εἰ γὰρ μὴ πᾶσιν ὡσαύτως, ἀλλὰ τοῖς μέν, τοῖς δ' οὔ, δῆλον ὡς
οὐκ ἦν ἐν ἐκείνῃ τῇ φύσει πρώτως, ἀλλ' ἐν ἄλλοις μὲν πρώτως, 25
ἐν ἄλλοις δὲ δευτέρως, τοῖς ποτε μετέχουσι. τὸ γὰρ ποτὲ μὲν
ὑπάρχον, ποτὲ δὲ μή, οὐ πρώτως οὐδὲ καθ' αὐτὸ ὑπάρχει, ἀλλ'
ἐπεισοδιῶδές ἐστι καὶ ἀλλαχόθεν ἐφῆκον, οἷς ἂν οὕτως ὑπάρχῃ.

17. 1-2 ἑαυτοῦ κινοῦν M, αὐτὸ κινοῦν PQ
18. Tit. περὶ ὄντος BD   3 τὸ τῷ εἶναι scripsi : τὸ τὸ εἶναι M : τὸ εἶναι cett.
(ex corr. D)   5 αὐτῷ τῷ εἶναι [M] : αὐτὸ τὸ εἶναι cett. (τό om. P) : ipsi
dat esse W   6 μετάθεσιν PQ   7 αὐτοῦ dett., Cr.   ὃ δέ ἐστιν αὐτῶ,
'Ανάπτ. 34. 24   τελειότερον M, τελεώτερον BCD : τελειοτέρως PQ   9 τό
om. C¹ : τῷ dett., Port. Cr.¹   9-10 προυπάρχον ω (om. dett., edd.)   14 δευ-
τέρος (sic) D, δεύτερον P   15 ἂν ω (αὖ dett., Cr.)   τῷ δέ M   16 ἐν τῷ
BCDM : ἐν τινι PQ, in aliquo W   πάσχοντι BCD   17 ἔχοι BDEP
(ex ἔχει)Q : ἔχει CM   ὑφίσταιτο B, ὑφίστατο C, statuit W :
ὑφίσταιτο DEM : ὑφίσταται PQ   post λοιπόν usque ad finem capitis deficit C
18 πρὸς τῷ εἶναι edd.   19 alt. ὃ om. PQ   τὸ διδὸν (δίδον M) ἐστιν ω :
τὸ διδόμενόν ἐστιν Par. 2028, Arg ex ci. (in mg. εἶχε τὸ διδόν), quod datum est
W ; sed cf. ll. 10-11 supr.   20 αὐτῷ τῷ M : αὐτὸ τό BPQ, ipsum esse W :
ὃ   ὃ
αὐτῷ τῷ D, αὐτὸ τῷ E   θάτερον ω (θατέρῳ Port. Cr.¹, om. Cr.²)
28 ὑφῆκον Q   ὑπάρχει BC dett.

upon itself. But to direct activity upon anything is to turn towards that thing. Everything, therefore, which is originally self-moving is capable of reversion upon itself.

PROP. 18. *Everything which by its existence bestows a character on others itself primitively possesses that character which it communicates to the recipients.*

For if it bestows by mere existence, and so makes the bestowal from its own essence, then what it bestows is inferior to its essence, and what it is, it is more greatly and more perfectly, by the principle that whatever is productive of anything is superior to its product (prop. 7). Thus the character as it pre-exists in the original giver has a higher reality than the character bestowed : it is what the bestowed character is, but is not identical with it, since it exists primitively and the other only by derivation. For it must be that either the two are identical and have a common definition ; or there is nothing common or identical in both ; or the one exists primitively and the other by derivation. But if they had a common definition, the one could not be, as we have assumed, cause and the other resultant ; the one could not be in itself and the other in the participant ; the one could not be the author and the other the subject of a process. And if they had nothing identical, the second, having nothing in common with the existence of the first, could not arise from its existence. It remains, then, that where one thing receives bestowal from another in virtue of that other's mere existence, the giver possesses primitively the character which it gives, while the recipient is by derivation what the giver is.

PROP. 19. *Everything which primitively inheres in any natural class of beings is present in all the members of that class alike, and in virtue of their common definition.*

For if it be not present in all alike, but be found in some and not in others, it is evident that it did not primitively reside in that class, but resides primitively in some, and by derivation in others whose participation of it is transient. For a character which at one time belongs to a subject, and at another does not, does not belong to it primitively nor in virtue of the subject's nature, but is adventitious and reaches its possessor from an alien source.

20. Πάντων σωμάτων ἐπέκεινά ἐστιν ἡ ψυχῆς οὐσία, καὶ πασῶν ψυχῶν ἐπέκεινα ἡ νοερὰ φύσις, καὶ πασῶν τῶν νοερῶν ὑποστάσεων ἐπέκεινα τὸ ἕν.

πᾶν γὰρ σῶμα κινητόν ἐστιν ὑφ' ἑτέρου, κινεῖν δὲ ἑαυτὸ οὐ πέφυκεν, ἀλλὰ ψυχῆς μετουσίᾳ κινεῖται ἐξ ἑαυτοῦ, καὶ ζῇ διὰ 5 ψυχήν· καὶ παρούσης μὲν ψυχῆς αὐτοκίνητόν πώς ἐστιν, ἀπούσης δὲ ἑτεροκίνητον, ὡς ταύτην ἔχον καθ' αὑτὸ τὴν φύσιν, καὶ ὡς ψυχῆς τὴν αὐτοκίνητον οὐσίαν λαχούσης. ᾧ γὰρ ἂν παραγένηται, τούτῳ μεταδίδωσιν αὐτοκινησίας· οὗ δὲ μεταδίδωσιν αὐτῷ τῷ εἶναι, τοῦτο πολλῷ πρότερον αὐτή ἐστιν. ἐπ- 10 έκεινα ἄρα σωμάτων ἐστίν, ὡς αὐτοκίνητος κατ' οὐσίαν, τῶν κατὰ μέθεξιν αὐτοκινήτων γινομένων.

πάλιν δὲ ἡ ψυχὴ κινουμένη ὑφ' ἑαυτῆς δευτέραν ἔχει τάξιν τῆς ἀκινήτου φύσεως καὶ κατ' ἐνέργειαν ἀκινήτου ὑφεστώσης· διότι πάντων μὲν τῶν κινουμένων ἡγεῖται τὸ αὐτοκίνητον, πάν- 15 των δὲ τῶν κινούντων τὸ ἀκίνητον. εἰ οὖν ἡ ψυχὴ κινουμένη ὑφ' ἑαυτῆς τὰ ἄλλα κινεῖ, δεῖ πρὸ αὐτῆς εἶναι τὸ ἀκινήτως κινοῦν. νοῦς δὲ κινεῖ ἀκίνητος ὢν καὶ ἀεὶ κατὰ τὰ αὐτὰ ἐνεργῶν. καὶ γὰρ ἡ ψυχὴ διὰ νοῦν μετέχει τοῦ ἀεὶ νοεῖν, ὥσπερ σῶμα διὰ ψυχὴν τοῦ ἑαυτὸ κινεῖν. εἰ γὰρ ἦν ἐν ψυχῇ τὸ ἀεὶ νοεῖν 20 πρώτως, πάσαις ἂν ὑπῆρχε ψυχαῖς, ὥσπερ καὶ τὸ ἑαυτὴν κινεῖν. οὐκ ἄρα ψυχῇ τοῦτο ὑπάρχει πρώτως· δεῖ ἄρα πρὸ αὐτῆς εἶναι τὸ πρώτως νοητικόν· πρὸ τῶν ψυχῶν ἄρα ὁ νοῦς.

ἀλλὰ μὴν καὶ πρὸ τοῦ νοῦ τὸ ἕν. νοῦς γὰρ εἰ καὶ ἀκίνητος, ἀλλ' οὐχ ἕν· νοεῖ γὰρ ἑαυτὸν καὶ ἐνεργεῖ περὶ ἑαυτόν. καὶ τοῦ 25 μὲν ἑνὸς πάντα μετέχει τὰ ὁπωσοῦν ὄντα, νοῦ δὲ οὐ πάντα· οἷς γὰρ ἂν παρῇ νοῦ μετουσία, ταῦτα γνώσεως ἀνάγκη μετέχειν, διότι ἡ νοερὰ γνῶσίς ἐστιν ἀρχὴ καὶ αἰτία πρώτη τοῦ γινώσκειν. ἐπέκεινα ἄρα τὸ ἓν τοῦ νοῦ.

καὶ οὐκέτι τοῦ ἑνὸς ἄλλο ἐπέκεινα. ταὐτὸν γὰρ ἓν καὶ 30 τἀγαθόν· ἀρχὴ ἄρα πάντων, ὡς δέδεικται.

20. a l. 1 ἐπέκεινα usque ad cap. 21, l. 27 οὐσίᾳ deficit M ut nunc est
1 ψυχῆς BCDOW : ψυχή PQArg: an ψυχική? 2 τῶν ante ψυχῶν add. PQ
3 ἐπέκεινα τὸ ἕν] ἐπέκεινα ὁ νοῦς· καὶ πάντων τῶν ὄντων ἐπέκεινα ἐστι τὸ ἕν PQ
5 ἑαυτοῦ BDE : αὑτοῦ CPQ dett. 6 καὶ παρούσης) ἢ παρουσίᾳ PQ 7 καθ'
αὑτήν dett. 8 τήν om. BCD dett. 10 αὐτή Q, ipsa W : αὕτη cett.
11 σωμάτων. αὕτη ἐστίν Arg 12 γενομένων O 13 ἀφ' ἑαυτῆς dett.
15 διό Arg 17 ἀφ' ἑαυτῆς O ἀκίνητον Arg 18 τά om. D¹PQ
19 διὰ νοῦ PQ τὸ σῶμα O 20 τοῦ] τό dett. 21 post πρώτως ins.
ἤτοι καὶ ταῖς (τοῖς P) ἀλόγοις PQ 22 ψυχή QArg. 26 νοῦ δὲ οὐ πάντα
om. dett. (τοῦ δὲ νοῦ οὐ πάντα Cr.² sine libris) 27 ἄν Ricc. 70 Amb. 38 :
om. ω νοῦς μετουσίᾳ edd. 29 τοῦ νοῦ τὸ ἕν PQ 31 ἀρχὴ ἄρα
PQ, principium ergo Waβγ : τἀγαθὸν δὲ ἀρχή BCD dett. (et sic W secundum
codd. Poit. Ball.)

PROP. 20. *Beyond all bodies is the soul's essence; beyond all souls, the intellective principle; and beyond all intellective substances, the One.*

For every body is moved by something not itself: self-movement is contrary to its nature, but by communication in soul it is moved from within, and because of soul it has life. When soul is present, the body is in some sense self-moved, but not when soul is absent: showing that body is naturally moved from without, while self-movement is of soul's essence. For that in which soul is present receives communication in self-movement; and a character which soul by its mere existence communicates must belong in a far more primitive sense to soul itself (prop. 18). Soul is therefore beyond bodies, as being self-moved in essence, while they by participation come to be self-moved.

Soul again, being moved by itself, has a rank inferior to the unmoved principle which is unmoved even in its activity. For of all things that are moved the self-moved has primacy; and of all movers, the unmoved (prop. 14 *cor.*). If, therefore, soul is a self-moved cause of motion, there must exist a prior cause of motion which is unmoved. Now Intelligence is such an unmoved cause of motion, eternally active without change. It is through Intelligence that soul participates in perpetuity of thought, as body in self-movement through soul: for if perpetuity of thought belonged primitively to soul it would inhere, like self-movement, in all souls (prop. 19); hence it does not belong primitively to soul. Prior to soul, then, must be the first thinker: that is, the Intelligence is prior to souls.

Yet again, the One is prior to the Intelligence. For the Intelligence, though unmoved, is yet not unity: in knowing itself, it is object to its own activity. Moreover, while all things, whatsoever their grade of reality, participate unity (prop. 1), not all participate intelligence: for to participate intelligence is to participate knowledge, since intuitive knowledge is the beginning and first cause of all knowing. Thus the One is beyond the Intelligence.

Beyond the One there is no further principle; for unity is identical with the Good (prop. 13), and is therefore the principium of all things, as has been shown (prop. 12).

21. Πᾶσα τάξις ἀπὸ μονάδος ἀρχομένη πρόεισιν εἰς πλῆθος τῇ μονάδι σύστοιχον, καὶ πάσης τάξεως τὸ πλῆθος εἰς μίαν ἀνάγεται μονάδα.

ἡ μὲν γὰρ μονάς, ἀρχῆς ἔχουσα λόγον, ἀπογεννᾷ τὸ οἰκεῖον ἑαυτῇ πλῆθος· διὸ καὶ μία σειρὰ καὶ μία τάξις, ἢ ὅλη παρὰ 5 τῆς μονάδος ἔχει τὴν εἰς τὸ πλῆθος ὑπόβασιν· οὐ γὰρ ἔτι τάξις οὐδὲ σειρά, τῆς μονάδος ἀγόνου μενούσης καθ' αὑτήν.

τὸ δὲ πλῆθος ἀνάγεται πάλιν εἰς μίαν τὴν κοινὴν τῶν ὁμο- ταγῶν πάντων αἰτίαν. τὸ γὰρ ἐν παντὶ τῷ πλήθει ταὐτὸν οὐκ ἀφ' ἑνὸς τῶν ἐν τῷ πλήθει τὴν πρόοδον ἔσχε· τὸ γὰρ ἀφ' ἑνὸς 10 μόνου τῶν πολλῶν οὐ κοινὸν πάντων, ἀλλὰ τῆς ἐκείνου μόνης ἰδιότητος ἐξαίρετον. ἐπεὶ οὖν καθ' ἑκάστην τάξιν ἐστί τις καὶ κοινωνία καὶ συνέχεια καὶ ταυτότης, δι' ἣν καὶ τάδε μὲν ὁμοταγῆ λέγεται, τάδε δὲ ἑτεροταγῆ, δῆλον ὡς ἀπὸ μιᾶς ἀρχῆς ἥκει πάσῃ τῇ τάξει τὸ ταὐτόν. ἔστιν ἄρα μονὰς μία πρὸ τοῦ 15 πλήθους καθ' ἑκάστην τάξιν καὶ εἱρμὸν τὸν ἕνα λόγον τοῖς ἐν αὐτῇ τεταγμένοις παρεχομένη πρός τε ἄλληλα καὶ πρὸς τὸ ὅλον. ἄλλο μὲν γὰρ ἄλλου αἴτιον ἔστω τῶν ὑπὸ τὴν αὐτὴν σειράν· τὸ δὲ ὡς μιᾶς τῆς σειρᾶς αἴτιον ἀνάγκη πρὸ τῶν πάντων εἶναι, καὶ ἀπ' αὐτοῦ πάντα ὡς ὁμοταγῆ γεννᾶσθαι, μὴ 20 ὡς τόδε τι ἕκαστον ἀλλ' ὡς τῆσδε τῆς τάξεως ὑπάρχον.

ἐκ δὴ τούτων φανερὸν ὅτι καὶ τῇ φύσει τοῦ σώματος ὑπάρχει τό τε ἓν καὶ τὸ πλῆθος, καὶ ἥ τε μία φύσις τὰς πολλὰς ἔχει συνηρτημένας καὶ αἱ πολλαὶ φύσεις ἐκ μιᾶς εἰσι τῆς τοῦ ὅλου φύσεως, καὶ τῇ τάξει τῶν ψυχῶν πάρεστιν ἐκ μιᾶς τε ἄρχεσθαι 25 ψυχῆς τῆς πρώτης καὶ εἰς πλῆθος ψυχῶν ὑποβαίνειν καὶ τὸ πλῆθος εἰς τὴν μίαν ἀνάγειν, καὶ τῇ νοερᾷ οὐσίᾳ μονάδα τε εἶναι νοερὰν καὶ νόων πλῆθος ἐξ ἑνὸς νοῦ προελθὸν καὶ εἰς ἐκείνην ἐπιστρέφον, καὶ τῷ ἑνὶ τῷ πρὸ τῶν πάντων τὸ πλῆθος τῶν ἑνάδων καὶ ταῖς ἑνάσι τὴν εἰς τὸ ἓν ἀνάτασιν. μετὰ τὸ ἓν 30 ἄρα τὸ πρῶτον ἑνάδες, καὶ μετὰ νοῦν τὸν πρῶτον νόες, καὶ μετὰ τὴν ψυχὴν τὴν πρώτην ψυχαί, καὶ μετὰ τὴν ὅλην φύσιν αἱ πολλαὶ φύσεις.

21. Tit. περὶ τοῦ (om. BCD) : τοῦ om. O) ὅτι οὐ πρῶτον αἴτιον ὁ νοῦς BCDArgO tum ἐντεῦθεν ἄρχεται τὴν περὶ τῶν ἰδεῶν δόξαν τῶν πλατωνικῶν συνιστᾶν (συστᾶν C) BCD   4 μέν om. O   5 αὐτῇ Arg, ἑαυτῆς PQ[2]   alt. μία om. O   ἢ scripsi : ἡ ω   9 αἰτίων Arg   τῷ om. O   14 ἀρχῆς om. O   ἥκει om. dett.   16 καὶ εἱρμὸν τὸν ἕνα λόγον PQ : τὸν ἕ. λόγ. κ. εἱρμόν BCD dett. W (τὸν ἕ. λόγ. om. C[1])   17 αὐτῷ O   παρεχομένη τεταγμένοις PQArg   18 ἄλλο ... ἄλλου BCDArgW : ἄλλω ... ἄλλου PQ : ἄλλο ... ἄλλῳ O   τῶν] τό Arg   19 τῆς μιᾶς edd.   20 πάντων] πραγμάτων O   πάντα] πάντως PQ : πάντων Arg   γίνεσθαι PQ   24 εἰσι om. BCD dett.   27 post οὐσίᾳ add. οὖν O   30 ἥ ... ἀνάτασις O[2] vel O[3]   32 primum τήν om. BCDO   32-3 αἱ om. PQ : αἱ πολλαί om. O

PROP. **21**. *Every order has its beginning in a monad and proceeds to a manifold co-ordinate therewith; and the manifold in any order may be carried back to a single monad.*

For the monad has the relative status of an originative principle, and so generates the appropriate manifold. Hence a series or order is a unity, in that the entire sequence derives from the monad its declension into plurality: if the monad abode sterile within itself, there could be no order and no series.

And in the reverse direction the manifold may be carried back to a single common cause of all the co-ordinate terms. For that which is identical in every member of the manifold did not proceed from one of those members: that which proceeds from one out of many is not common to all, but is peculiar to the single individuality of that one. Since, then, in every order there is some common element, a continuity and identity in virtue of which some things are said to be co-ordinate and others not, it is apparent that the identical element is derived by the whole order from a single originative principle. Thus in each order or causal chain there exists a single monad prior to the manifold, which determines for the members of the order their unique relation to one another and to the whole. It is true that among members of the same series one is cause of another; but that which is cause of the series as a unity must be prior to them all, and *qua* co-ordinate they must all be generated from it, not in their several peculiarities, but as members of a particular series.

Cor. From this it is apparent that in the nature of body unity and plurality coexist in such a manner that the one Nature has the many natures dependent from it, and, conversely, these are derived from one Nature, that of the whole; that the soul-order, originating from one primal Soul, descends to a manifold of souls and again carries back the manifold to the one; that to intellective essence belongs an intellective monad and a manifold of intelligences proceeding from a single Intelligence and reverting thither; that for the One which is prior to all things there is the manifold of the henads (divine units), and for the henads the upward tension linking them with the One. Thus there are henads consequent upon the primal One, intelligences consequent on the primal Intelligence, souls consequent on the primal Soul, and a plurality of natures consequent on the universal Nature.

26 THE ELEMENTS OF THEOLOGY

22. Πᾶν τὸ πρώτως καὶ ἀρχικῶς ὂν καθ' ἑκάστην τάξιν ἕν ἐστι, καὶ οὔτε δύο οὔτε πλείω δυεῖν, ἀλλὰ μονογενὲς πᾶν.

ἔστω γάρ, εἰ δυνατόν, δύο· τὸ γὰρ αὐτὸ ἀδύνατον καὶ πλειόνων ὄντων. ἢ οὖν ἑκάτερον τούτων ἐστὶν ὃ λέγεται πρώτως ἢ τὸ ἐξ ἀμφοῖν. ἀλλ' εἰ μὲν τὸ ἐξ ἀμφοῖν, ἓν ἂν εἴη πάλιν καὶ 5 οὐ δύο τὰ πρῶτα. εἰ δὲ ἑκάτερον, ἢ ἐκ θατέρου θάτερον, καὶ οὐ πρῶτον ἑκάτερον· ἢ ἐπίσης ἄμφω. ἀλλ' εἰ ἐπίσης, οὐδέτερον ἔτι ἔσται πρώτως. εἰ γὰρ τὸ ἕτερον πρώτως, τοῦτο δὲ οὐ ταὐτὸν τῷ ἑτέρῳ, τί ἔσται τῆς τάξεως ἐκείνης ; ὃ γὰρ μηδὲν ἄλλο ἐστὶν ἢ ὃ λέγεται, τοῦτο ἔστι πρώτως· τούτων δὲ ἑκάτερον 10 ἕτερον ὄν ἐστί τε ἅμα καὶ οὐκ ἔστιν ὃ λέγεται. εἰ οὖν ταῦτα διαφέρει μὲν ἀλλήλων, οὐ καθόσον δέ ἐστιν ὃ λέγεται πρώτως διαφέρει (τοῦτο γὰρ πρώτως ταὐτὸν πέπονθεν), οὐκ ἄμφω ἔσται πρώτως, ἀλλ' ἐκεῖνο, οὗ ἄμφω μετασχόντα πρώτως εἶναι λέγεται. 15

ἐκ δὴ τούτων φανερὸν ὅτι καὶ τὸ πρώτως ὂν ἕν ἐστι μόνον, ἀλλ' οὐ δύο τὰ πρώτως ὄντα ἢ πλείω· καὶ ὁ πρώτιστος νοῦς εἷς μόνος, ἀλλ' οὐ δύο οἱ πρῶτοι νόες· καὶ ἡ πρωτίστη ψυχὴ μία· καὶ ἐφ' ἑκάστου τῶν εἰδῶν, οἷον τὸ πρώτως καλόν, τὸ πρώτως ἴσον, καὶ ἐπὶ πάντων ὁμοίως· οὕτω δὲ καὶ τὸ τοῦ ζῴου εἶδος ἓν 20 τὸ πρῶτον, καὶ τὸ τοῦ ἀνθρώπου· ἡ γὰρ αὐτὴ ἀπόδειξις.

23. Πᾶν τὸ ἀμέθεκτον ὑφίστησιν ἀφ' ἑαυτοῦ τὰ μετεχόμενα, καὶ πᾶσαι αἱ μετεχόμεναι ὑποστάσεις εἰς ἀμεθέκτους ὑπάρξεις ἀνατείνονται.

τὸ μὲν γὰρ ἀμέθεκτον, μονάδος ἔχον λόγον ὡς ἑαυτοῦ ὂν καὶ 25 οὐκ ἄλλου καὶ ὡς ἐξῃρημένον τῶν μετεχόντων, ἀπογεννᾷ τὰ μετέχεσθαι δυνάμενα. ἢ γὰρ ἄγονον ἑστήξεται καθ' αὑτό, καὶ οὐδὲν ἂν ἔχοι τίμιον· ἢ δώσει τι ἀφ' ἑαυτοῦ, καὶ τὸ μὲν λαβὸν μετέσχε, τὸ δὲ δοθὲν ὑπέστη μετεχομένως.

τὸ δὲ μετεχόμενον πᾶν, τινὸς γενόμενον ὑφ' οὗ μετέχεται, 30 δεύτερόν ἐστι τοῦ πᾶσιν ὁμοίως παρόντος καὶ πάντα ἀφ' ἑαυτοῦ πληρώσαντος. τὸ μὲν γὰρ ἐν ἑνὶ ὂν ἐν τοῖς ἄλλοις οὐκ ἔστιν· τὸ δὲ πᾶσιν ὡσαύτως παρόν, ἵνα πᾶσιν ἐλλάμπῃ, οὐκ ἐν ἑνί ἐστιν, ἀλλὰ πρὸ τῶν πάντων. ἢ γὰρ ἐν πᾶσίν ἐστιν ἢ ἐν ἑνὶ

22. 2 δυεῖν BMPQ : δεῖν CD   4 prius ἥ] εἰ dett.   ἕν ante ἑκάτερον add. CDE   ἐστίν om. dett.   6 ἐκ θατέρου ωW (ἑκατέρου dett., edd.)   7 ἑκάτερον ὄν· ἤ M²   8 τούτω M   13 καὶ οὐκ ἄμφω PQ   13–14 ἔσται πρῶτα BDO   16 καὶ ω (om. edd.)   τὸ πρῶτον ὄν PQ   20 ἐπὶ πᾶσιν PQ
23. Tit περὶ τοῦ ἀμεθέκτου BCDM   23 ἀμεθέκτου PQ   25 λόγον ἔχον PQ   26 ὡς ω (om. edd.)   ἐξῃρημένον M²   27 ἥ BCDW (coni. T. Taylor) : εἰ M (in rasura) PQ   30 post μετέχεται rep. τινὸς γενόμενον Cr. sine libris   33 ἵν' ἅπασιν PQ   καὶ οὐκ PQ

PROP. 22. *All that exists primitively and originally in each order is one and not two or more than two, but unique.*

For, if possible, let it be two (there will be the same impossibility if it be more than two). Either, then, each of these two is primitively what it is called, or the combination of both is so. But if the combination is so, what is primitive will be one again and not two. And if each severally, either one is derived from the other, and so only one is primitive; or else the two are on a level. But if they be on a level, neither will now be primitive. For if either be primitive yet distinct from the other, why should it belong to the same order as the other? For the primitive is that which is nothing else than what it is called; but each of these two, being distinct from its fellow, both is, and at the same time is not, what it is called. If, then, they differ, but not in respect of their primitive quality (for both have this common quality as a primary affect), the primitive existent will be not the pair, but that by participation of which both are described as existing primitively.

Cor. From this it is apparent that primal Being is one only, and there are not two or more primal types of Being; that primal Intelligence is one only, and there are not two primal Intelligences; that the primal Soul is one, and so with each of the Forms, as the primal Beautiful, the primal Equal, and all the rest in like manner; that so again the primal Form of animal is one, and that of man. For the same proof applies to all.

PROP. 23. *All that is unparticipated produces out of itself the participated; and all participated substances are linked by upward tension to existences not participated.*

For on the one hand the unparticipated, having the relative status of a monad (as being its own and not another's, and as transcending the participants), generates terms capable of being participated. For either it must remain fixed in sterility and isolation, and so must lack a place of honour; or else it will give something of itself, whereof the receiver becomes a participant, whilst the given attains substantial existence as a participated term.

Every participated term, on the other hand, becoming a property of that particular by which it is participated, is secondary to that which in all is equally present and has filled them all out of its own being. That which is in one is not in the others; while that which is present to all alike, that it may illuminate all, is not in any one, but is prior to them all. For either it is in all, or in one out of all,

28 THE ELEMENTS OF THEOLOGY

τῶν πάντων ἢ πρὸ τῶν πάντων. ἀλλὰ τὸ μὲν ἐν πᾶσιν ὄν,
μερισθὲν εἰς πάντα, πάλιν ἄλλου ἂν δέοιτο τοῦ τὸ μερισθὲν
ἐνίζοντος· καὶ οὐκέτ' ἂν τοῦ αὐτοῦ μετέχοι πάντα, ἀλλὰ τὸ μὲν
ἄλλου, τὸ δὲ ἄλλου, τοῦ ἑνὸς μερισθέντος. εἰ δὲ ἐν ἑνὶ τῶν
πάντων, οὐκέτι τῶν πάντων ἔσται, ἀλλ' ἑνός. εἰ οὖν καὶ κοινὸν 5
τῶν μετέχειν δυναμένων καὶ τὸ αὐτὸ πάντων, πρὸ τῶν πάντων
ἔσται· τοῦτο δὲ ἀμέθεκτον.

24. Πᾶν τὸ μετέχον τοῦ μετεχομένου καταδεέστερον, καὶ τὸ
μετεχόμενον τοῦ ἀμεθέκτου.

τὸ μὲν γὰρ μετέχον, πρὸ τῆς μεθέξεως ἀτελὲς ὄν, τέλειον δὲ 10
τῇ μεθέξει γενόμενον, δεύτερόν ἐστι πάντως τοῦ μετεχομένου,
καθὸ τέλειόν ἐστι μετασχόν. ᾗ γὰρ ἀτελὲς ἦν, ταύτῃ τοῦ
μετασχεθέντος, ὃ ποιεῖ τέλειον αὐτό, καταδεέστερον.

τὸ δὲ μετεχόμενον, τινὸς ὂν καὶ οὐ πάντων, τοῦ πάντων ὄντος
καὶ οὐ τινὸς πάλιν ὑφειμένην ἔλαχεν ὕπαρξιν· τὸ μὲν γὰρ τῷ 15
πάντων αἰτίῳ συγγενέστερον, τὸ δὲ ἧττον συγγενές.

ἡγεῖται ἄρα τὸ μὲν ἀμέθεκτον τῶν μετεχομένων, ταῦτα δὲ
τῶν μετεχόντων. ὡς γὰρ συνελόντι φάναι, τὸ μέν ἐστιν ἓν
πρὸ τῶν πολλῶν· τὸ δὲ μετεχόμενον ἐν τοῖς πολλοῖς, ἓν ἅμα καὶ
οὐχ ἕν· τὸ δὲ μετέχον πᾶν οὐχ ἓν ἅμα καὶ ἕν. 20

25. Πᾶν τὸ τέλειον εἰς ἀπογεννήσεις πρόεισιν ὧν δύναται
παράγειν, αὐτὸ μιμούμενον τὴν μίαν τῶν ὅλων ἀρχήν.

ὡς γὰρ ἐκείνη διὰ τὴν ἀγαθότητα τὴν ἑαυτῆς πάντων ἐστὶν
ἑνιαίως ὑποστατικὴ τῶν ὄντων (ταὐτὸν γὰρ τἀγαθὸν καὶ τὸ ἕν,
ὥστε καὶ τὸ ἀγαθοειδῶς τῷ ἑνιαίως ταὐτόν), οὕτω καὶ τὰ μετ' 25
ἐκείνην διὰ τὴν τελειότητα τὴν ἑαυτῶν ἄλλα γεννᾶν ἐπείγεται
καταδεέστερα τῆς ἑαυτῶν οὐσίας. ἥ τε γὰρ τελειότης τἀγαθοῦ
μοῖρά τίς ἐστι καὶ τὸ τέλειον, ᾗ τέλειον, μιμεῖται τἀγαθόν.
ἐκεῖνο δὲ πάντων ἦν ὑποστατικόν· ὥστε καὶ τὸ τέλειον ὂν
δύναται παρακτικόν ἐστι κατὰ φύσιν. καὶ τὸ μὲν τελειότερον, 30
ὅσῳ περ ἂν ᾖ τελειότερον, τοσούτῳ πλειόνων αἴτιον. τὸ γὰρ
τελειότερον μᾶλλον τἀγαθοῦ μετέχει· τοῦτο δέ, ἐγγυτέρω τἀγα-
θοῦ· τοῦτο δέ, συγγενέστερον τῷ πάντων αἰτίῳ· τοῦτο δέ,
πλειόνων αἴτιον. τὸ δὲ ἀτελέστερον, ὅσῳ περ ἂν ἀτελέστερον ᾖ,
τοσῷδε μᾶλλον ἐλαττόνων αἴτιον. πορρώτερον γὰρ ὂν τοῦ 35

23. 2 τοῦ τό CM² : τοῦτο BDM¹ : om. PQ
24. 10 μέν om. O, neque agnosc. W   11 γινόμενον D, γενόμενον ex γινόμενον P   12 καθ' ὅ BD   post γάρ ins. ἓν PQ   ταύτῃ ω, hac W :
suprascr. κατὰ τοῦτο M, unde κατὰ τοῦτο ταύτῃ O¹, καὶ τοῦτο edd.   14 prius
πάντων] πάντως M¹
25. Tit. περὶ τελείου BCDM   25 τὸ ἀγαθοειδές PQ   τῷ] τό BPQ
32-3 τἀγαθοῦ MQ : τοῦ ἀγαθοῦ BCDP

or prior to all. But a principle which was in all would be divided amongst all, and would itself require a further principle to unify the divided ; and further, all the particulars would no longer participate the same principle, but this one and that another, through the diremption of its unity. And if it be in one out of all, it will be a property no longer of all but of one. Inasmuch, then, as it is both common to all that can participate and identical for all, it must be prior to all : that is, it must be unparticipated.

PROP. **24.** *All that participates is inferior to the participated, and this latter to the unparticipated.*

For the participant was incomplete before the participation, and by the participation has been made complete : it is therefore necessarily subordinate to the participated, inasmuch as it owes its completeness to the act of participation. As having formerly been incomplete it is inferior to the principle which completes it.

Again, the participated, being the property of one particular and not of all, has a lower mode of substance assigned to it than that which belongs to all and not to one : for the latter is more nearly akin to the cause of all things, the former less nearly.

The unparticipated, then, precedes the participated, and these the participants. For, to express it shortly, the first is a unity prior to the many ; the participated is within the many, and is one yet not-one ; while all that participates is not-one yet one.

D. OF PROCESSION AND REVERSION.

PROP. **25.** *Whatever is complete proceeds to generate those things which it is capable of producing, imitating in its turn the one originative principle of the universe.*

For that principle because of its own goodness is by a unitary act constitutive of all that is : for the Good being identical with the One (prop. 13), action which has the form of Goodness is identical with unitary action. In like manner the principles consequent upon it are impelled because of their proper completeness to generate further principles inferior to their own being (prop. 7). For completeness is a part of the Good, and the complete, *qua* complete, imitates the Good. Now we saw that the Good was constitutive of all things (prop. 12). Accordingly the complete is by nature productive within the limits of its power. The more complete is the cause of more, in proportion to the degree of its completeness : for the more complete participates the Good more fully ; that is, it is nearer to the Good ; that is, it is more nearly akin to the cause of all ; that is, it is the cause of more. And the less complete is the cause of less, in proportion to its incompleteness : for being more remote from that which produces

πάντα παράγοντος, ἐλαττόνων ἐστὶν ὑποστατικόν. τῷ γὰρ
πάντα ὑφιστάνειν ἢ κοσμεῖν ἢ τελειοῦν ἢ συνέχειν ἢ ζωοποιεῖν
ἢ δημιουργεῖν τὸ μὲν ἐπὶ πλειόνων ἕκαστα τούτων δρᾶν συγγενές, τὸ δὲ ἐπὶ ἐλαττόνων ἀλλοτριώτερον.

ἐκ δὴ τούτων φανερὸν ὅτι τὸ πορρώτατον τῆς ἀρχῆς τῶν 5
πάντων ἄγονόν ἐστι καὶ οὐδενὸς αἴτιον· εἰ γάρ τι γεννᾷ καὶ ἔχει
τι μεθ' ἑαυτό, δῆλον ὡς οὐκέτ' ἂν εἴη πορρώτατον, ἀλλ' ὃ παρ-
ήγαγε πορρωτέρω ἐκείνης, αὐτὸ δὲ ἐγγύτερον τῷ παράγειν καὶ
ὅτι ἄλλο, μιμούμενον τὴν πάντων παρακτικὴν τῶν ὄντων αἰτίαν.

26. Πᾶν τὸ παρακτικὸν αἴτιον ἄλλων μένον αὐτὸ ἐφ' ἑαυτοῦ 10
παράγει τὰ μετ' αὐτὸ καὶ τὰ ἐφεξῆς.

εἰ γὰρ μιμεῖται τὸ ἕν, ἐκεῖνο δὲ ἀκινήτως ὑφίστησι τὰ μετ'
αὐτό, καὶ πᾶν τὸ παράγον ὡσαύτως ἔχει τὴν τοῦ παράγειν
αἰτίαν. ἀλλὰ μὴν καὶ τὸ ἓν ἀκινήτως ὑφίστησιν. εἰ γὰρ διὰ
κινήσεως, ἢ ἐν αὐτῷ ἡ κίνησις, καὶ κινούμενον οὐδὲ ἓν ἔτι ἔσται, 15
μεταβάλλον ἐκ τοῦ ἕν· ἢ εἰ μετ' αὐτὸ ἡ κίνησις, καὶ αὐτὴ ἐκ
τοῦ ἑνὸς ἔσται, καὶ ἡ ἐπ' ἄπειρον, ἢ ἀκινήτως παράξει τὸ ἕν.
καὶ πᾶν τὸ παράγον μιμήσεται τὸ ἓν καὶ τὴν παρακτικὴν τῶν
ὅλων αἰτίαν. ἐκ γὰρ τοῦ πρώτως πανταχοῦ τὸ μὴ πρώτως·
ὥστε καὶ ἐκ τοῦ πάντων παρακτικοῦ τὸ τινῶν παρακτικόν. καὶ 20
ἅπαν ἄρα τὸ παράγον μένον ἐφ' ἑαυτοῦ παράγει τὰ ἐφεξῆς.

ἀνελαττώτων ἄρα τῶν παραγόντων μενόντων, τὰ δεύτερα
παράγεται ὑπ' αὐτῶν· τὸ γὰρ ὁπωσοῦν ἐλαττούμενον μένειν
ἀδύνατον οἷόν ἐστιν.

27. Πᾶν τὸ παράγον διὰ τελειότητα καὶ δυνάμεως περιουσίαν 25
παρακτικόν ἐστι τῶν δευτέρων.

εἰ γὰρ μὴ διὰ τὸ τέλειον, ἀλλ' ἐλλεῖπον κατὰ τὴν δύναμιν
παρήγαγεν, οὐδ' ἂν τὴν ἑαυτοῦ τάξιν ἀκίνητον ἠδύνατο
φυλάττειν. τὸ γὰρ δι' ἔλλειψιν καὶ ἀσθένειαν ἄλλῳ τὸ εἶναι
παρεχόμενον τῇ ἑαυτοῦ τροπῇ καὶ ἀλλοιώσει τὴν ὑπόστασιν 30
ἐκείνῳ παρέχεται. μένει δὲ οἷόν ἐστι πᾶν τὸ παράγον· καὶ
μένοντος, τὸ μετ' αὐτὸ πρόεισι. πλῆρες ἄρα καὶ τέλειον

---

25. 1 παντός M   3 τοῦτο M   ἐρᾶν BCD   8 ἐκείνου BCD   τῷ
παράγειν PQArg et fort. M¹, eo quod producat W : τῷ παραγαγεῖν BCDM²
9 ὅτι BCM, quodcumque W : ὁ ὅτι DE, ὃ ἔτι Laur. 9. 12 : τι Mon. 547 : om.
PQ   πάντων om. PQ   τὴν post παρακτικήν ins. M¹ sup. lin.   ὄντων]
πάντων PQ
26. 15 ἢ ἐν αὐτῷ BCDM : ᾖ ἐν ἑαυτῷ PQ   ᾖ κίνησις M   16 τοῦ
ἕν MPQ, ex eo quod unum W : τοῦ ἑνὸς BCD   ᾖ εἰ μετ' αὐτό [M] PQW : εἰ ᾖ
μετ' αὐτό M² : ᾖ οὐκ ἐν αὐτῷ BCD   ᾖ κίνησις BCDPQ : ᾖ κίνησις M : sit motus W
αὐτή PQ : om. BCDMW   21 τὸ παράγον μένον BCD : τὸ παραγόμενον
MPQW   ὑφ' ἑαυτοῦ PQ, a seipso W
27. 25 τελειότητα BCDOW : τελειότητος MPQ   29 ἄλλα [M]   31 πᾶν
om. PQ   32 μετ' αὐτοῦ M

all, it is constitutive of fewer things ; since to constitute or regulate or complete or maintain or vitalize or create a large class of things approaches nearest to the universal performance of these functions, while a like service to a smaller class stands at a further remove.

Cor. From this it is apparent that the principle most remote from the beginning of all things is sterile and a cause of nothing. For if it generate and have a consequent, it is plain that it can no longer be the most remote : its product is more remote than itself, and itself is brought nearer by the fact of producing another, whatever that other be, and thus imitating that cause which is productive of all that is.

PROP. 26. *Every productive cause produces the next and all subsequent principles while itself remaining steadfast.*

For if it imitates the One, and if the One brings its consequents into existence without movement, then every productive cause has a like law of production. Now the One does create without movement. For if it create through movement, either the movement is within it, and being moved it will change from being one and so lose its unity ; or if the movement be subsequent to it, this movement will itself be derived from the One, and either we shall have infinite regress or the One will produce without movement. And secondly, every productive principle will imitate the One, the productive cause of the sum of things : for the non-primal is everywhere derived from the primal, so that a principle productive of certain things must derive from the principle which produces all things. Therefore every productive principle produces its consequents while itself remaining steadfast.

Cor. It follows that the productive principles remain undiminished by the production from them of secondary existences : for what is in any way diminished cannot remain as it is.

PROP. 27. *Every producing cause is productive of secondary existences because of its completeness and superfluity of potency.*

For if it had produced not because of its completeness, but by reason of a defect of potency, it could not have maintained unmoved its own station : since that which through defect or weakness bestows existence upon another furnishes the substance of that other by a conversion and alteration of its own nature. But every producer remains as it is, and its consequent proceeds from it without change in its steadfastness (prop. 26). Full and complete, then, it

ὑπάρχον, τὰ δεύτερα ὑφίστησιν ἀκινήτως καὶ ἀνελαττώτως, αὐτὸ
ὂν ὅπερ ἐστὶ καὶ οὔτε μεταβάλλον εἰς ἐκεῖνα οὔτε ἐλαττούμενον.
οὐ γὰρ ἀπομερισμός ἐστι τοῦ παράγοντος τὸ παραγόμενον·
οὐδὲ γὰρ γενέσει τοῦτο προσῆκεν, οὐδὲ τοῖς γεννητικοῖς αἰτίοις.
οὐδὲ μετάβασις· οὐ γὰρ ὕλη γίνεται τοῦ προϊόντος· μένει γὰρ 5
οἷόν ἐστι, καὶ τὸ παραγόμενον ἄλλο παρ' αὐτό ἐστιν. ἀναλ-
λοίωτον ἄρα τὸ γεννῶν ἵδρυται καὶ ἀνελάττωτον, διὰ γόνιμον
δύναμιν ἑαυτὸ πολλαπλασιάζον καὶ ἀφ' ἑαυτοῦ δευτέρας ὑποστάσεις παρεχόμενον.

28. Πᾶν τὸ παράγον τὰ ὅμοια πρὸς ἑαυτὸ πρὸ τῶν ἀνομοίων 10
ὑφίστησιν.

ἐπεὶ γὰρ κρεῖττον ἐξ ἀνάγκης ἐστὶ τοῦ παραγομένου τὸ
παράγον, τὰ αὐτὰ μὲν ἁπλῶς καὶ ἴσα κατὰ δύναμιν οὐκ ἄν
ποτε εἴη ἀλλήλοις. εἰ δὲ μὴ ἔστι ταὐτὰ καὶ ἴσα, ἀλλ' ἕτερά τε
καὶ ἄνισα, ἢ πάντη διακέκριται ἀλλήλων ἢ καὶ ἥνωται καὶ 15
διακέκριται.

ἀλλ' εἰ μὲν πάντη διακέκριται, ἀσύμβατα ἔσται, καὶ οὐδαμῇ
τῷ αἰτίῳ τὸ ἀπ' αὐτοῦ συμπαθές. οὐδὲ μεθέξει τοίνυν θατέρου
θάτερον, πάντη ἕτερα ὄντα· τὸ γὰρ μετεχόμενον κοινωνίαν
δίδωσι τῷ μετασχόντι πρὸς τὸ οὗ μετέσχεν. ἀλλὰ μὴν ἀνάγκη 20
τὸ αἰτιατὸν τοῦ αἰτίου μετέχειν, ὡς ἐκεῖθεν ἔχον τὴν οὐσίαν.

εἰ δὲ πῇ μὲν διακέκριται, πῇ δὲ ἥνωται τῷ παράγοντι τὸ
παραγόμενον, εἰ μὲν ἐπίσης ἑκάτερον πέπονθεν, ἐπίσης ἂν
αὐτοῦ μετέχοι τε καὶ οὐ μετέχοι· ὥστε καὶ ἔχοι ἂν τὴν οὐσίαν
παρ' αὐτοῦ καὶ οὐκ ἔχοι τὸν αὐτὸν τρόπον. εἰ δὲ μᾶλλον εἴη 25
διακεκριμένον, ἀλλότριον ἂν εἴη τοῦ γεννήσαντος μᾶλλον ἢ
οἰκεῖον τὸ γεννηθέν, καὶ ἀνάρμοστον πρὸς αὐτὸ μᾶλλον ἤπερ
ἡρμοσμένον, καὶ ἀσυμπαθὲς μᾶλλον ἢ συμπαθές. εἰ οὖν καὶ
συγγενῆ τοῖς αἰτίοις κατ' αὐτὸ τὸ εἶναι καὶ συμπαθῆ τὰ ἀπ'
αὐτῶν, καὶ ἐξήρτηται αὐτῶν κατὰ φύσιν, καὶ ὀρέγεται τῆς πρὸς 30
αὐτὰ συναφῆς, ὀρεγόμενα τοῦ ἀγαθοῦ καὶ τυγχάνοντα διὰ τῆς
αἰτίας τοῦ ὀρεκτοῦ, δῆλον δὴ ὅτι μᾶλλον ἥνωται τοῖς παράγουσι
τὰ παραγόμενα ἢ διακέκριται ἀπ' αὐτῶν. τὰ δὲ μᾶλλον ἡνωμένα
ὅμοιά ἐστι μᾶλλον ἢ ἀνόμοια τούτοις οἷς μάλιστα ἥνωται. τὰ

27. 7 διά PQW : καὶ διά BCDM   8 πολυπλασιάζον MPQ
28. 12 ἐστὶν ἐξ ἀνάγκης PQ   13 καὶ ἴσα ἁπλῶς καὶ ἴσα M   14 ταῦτα
M   17 πάντη ω (πάντα O¹ edd.)   ἀσύμβατον P   18 οὐδέ] οὐ BCE
θατέρου ω (om. edd.)   20 μετέχοντι PQ   23 ἑκάτερα PQ   26 μᾶλλον
post γεννήσαντος legunt PQ et (ni fallor) W : post ἀλλότριον ΜΕ : post ἂν BCD
27 αὐτό BCD : ἑαυτό MPQW   μᾶλλον post ἀνάρμοστον legunt O edd.   28-9 εἰ
οὖν συγγενῆ τοῖς θείοις PQ   29-30 ἀπ' αὐτῶν ω (ἀφ' αὐτῶν Cr.)   34 μάλιστα
BCDP : μᾶλλον MQ : om. W

brings to existence the secondary principles without movement and without loss, itself being what it is, neither transmuted into the secondaries nor suffering any diminution. For the product is not a parcelling-out of the producer: that is not a character even of physical generation or generative causes. Nor is it a transformation : the producer is not the matter of what proceeds from it, for it remains as it is, and its product is a fresh existence beside it. Thus the engenderer is established beyond alteration or diminution, multiplying itself in virtue of its generative potency and furnishing from itself secondary substances.

PROP. **28**. *Every producing cause brings into existence things like to itself before the unlike.*

For since the producer is necessarily superior to the product (prop. 7), they can never be identical without qualification, or equal in potency. And if they are not identical and equal, but diverse and unequal, either they are altogether distinct from each other or they are at once united and distinguished.

But if they be altogether distinct they will be incapable of association, and there will be no sympathy between effect and cause. Accordingly the one will not participate the other, if they be completely diverse : for the participated bestows upon the participant communion in that which it participates. But it is necessary that the effect should participate the cause, inasmuch as it derives its being from the latter.

Let us suppose, then, that the product is distinguished in one respect from its producing cause, united to it in another. If it were affected in equal degrees by distinction and union, it would in equal degrees participate the cause and fail to participate it, so that it would both derive and in like manner not derive its being from its cause. And if it were distinguished more than united, the engendered would be more alien from the engenderer than akin to it and less adjusted to it than maladjusted ; its capacity for sympathy would be less than its incapacity. Inasmuch, then, as derivative principles are in their very being cognate and sympathetic with their causes, inasmuch as they are by nature dependent from them and desire to be conjoined with them (for they desire the Good, and obtain their desire through the mediation of their cause), it is plain that products are more united to their producing causes than they are distinguished from them. But things which are united to, more than they are distinguished from, those principles with which they are most closely

ὅμοια ἄρα πρὸ τῶν ἀνομοίων ὑφίστησι πᾶν τὸ παρακτικὸν
αἴτιον.

29. Πᾶσα πρόοδος δι' ὁμοιότητος ἀποτελεῖται τῶν δευτέρων
πρὸς τὰ πρῶτα.

εἰ γὰρ τὸ παράγον τὰ ὅμοια πρὸ τῶν ἀνομοίων ὑφίστησιν, 5
ἡ ὁμοιότης ἀπὸ τῶν παραγόντων ὑφίστησι τὰ παραγόμενα·
τὰ γὰρ ὅμοια δι' ὁμοιότητος ὅμοια ἀποτελεῖται, ἀλλ' οὐ δι'
ἀνομοιότητος. εἰ οὖν ἡ πρόοδος ἐν τῇ ὑφέσει σώζει τὸ ταὐτὸν
τοῦ γεννηθέντος πρὸς τὸ γεννῆσαν, καὶ οἷον ἐκεῖνο πρώτως,
τοιοῦτον ἐκφαίνει τὸ μετ' αὐτὸ δευτέρως, δι' ὁμοιότητος ἔχει τὴν 10
ὑπόστασιν.

30. Πᾶν τὸ ἀπό τινος παραγόμενον ἀμέσως μένει τε ἐν τῷ
παράγοντι καὶ πρόεισιν ἀπ' αὐτοῦ.

εἰ γὰρ πᾶσα πρόοδος· μενόντων τε γίνεται τῶν πρώτων καὶ
δι' ὁμοιότητος ἀποτελεῖται, τῶν ὁμοίων πρὸ τῶν ἀνομοίων 15
ὑφισταμένων, μένει πῃ καὶ τὸ παραγόμενον ἐν τῷ παράγοντι.
τὸ γὰρ πάντῃ προϊὸν οὐδὲν ἂν ἔχοι ταὐτὸν πρὸς τὸ μένον, ἀλλ'
ἔστι πάντῃ διακεκριμένον· εἰ δὲ ἕξει τι κοινὸν καὶ ἡνωμένον
πρὸς αὐτό, μένοι ἂν καὶ αὐτὸ ἐν ἐκείνῳ, ὥσπερ κἀκεῖνο ἐφ'
ἑαυτοῦ μένον ἦν. εἰ δὲ μένοι μόνον μὴ προϊόν, οὐδὲν διοίσει 20
τῆς αἰτίας οὐδὲ ἔσται μενούσης ἐκείνης ἄλλο γεγονός· εἰ γὰρ
ἄλλο, διακέκριται καὶ ἔστι χωρίς· εἰ δὲ χωρίς, μένει δὲ ἐκείνη,
προῆλθε τοῦτο ἀπ' αὐτῆς ἵνα διακριθῇ μενούσης. ᾗ μὲν ἄρα
ταὐτόν τι πρὸς τὸ παράγον ἔχει, τὸ παραγόμενον μένει ἐν αὐτῷ·
ᾗ δὲ ἕτερον, πρόεισιν ἀπ' αὐτοῦ. ὅμοιον δὲ ὄν, ταὐτόν πῃ ἅμα 25
καὶ ἕτερόν ἐστι· μένει ἄρα καὶ πρόεισιν ἅμα, καὶ οὐδέτερον
θατέρου χωρίς.

31. Πᾶν τὸ προϊὸν ἀπό τινος κατ' οὐσίαν ἐπιστρέφεται πρὸς
ἐκεῖνο ἀφ' οὗ πρόεισιν.

εἰ γὰρ προέρχοιτο μέν, μὴ ἐπιστρέφοι δὲ πρὸς τὸ αἴτιον τῆς 30
προόδου ταύτης, οὐκ ἂν ὀρέγοιτο τῆς αἰτίας· πᾶν γὰρ τὸ
ὀρεγόμενον ἐπέστραπται πρὸς τὸ ὀρεκτόν. ἀλλὰ μὴν πᾶν τοῦ
ἀγαθοῦ ἐφίεται, καὶ ἡ ἐκείνου τεῦξις διὰ τῆς προσεχοῦς αἰτίας
ἑκάστοις· ὀρέγεται ἄρα καὶ τῆς ἑαυτῶν αἰτίας ἕκαστα. δι' οὗ
γὰρ τὸ εἶναι ἑκάστῳ, διὰ τούτου καὶ τὸ εὖ· δι' οὗ δὲ τὸ εὖ, πρὸς 35

29. 7-8 διὰ ἀνομοιότητος edd.   8-11 ἡ οὖν (omisso εἰ) πρόοδος... ἔχον τὴν
ὑπόστασιν PQ
30. 12 ἀπό τινος MPQ : ὑπό τινος BCD   15 ἀποτελεῖται MPQ : τελεῖται
BCDO   16 καί non agnosc. W   19-20 ὑφ' ἑαυτοῦ μένει (omisso ἦν) PQ, in
seipso manet W   20 μένοι M² : μένει BCDPQW : μένον Arg   22 ἔσται P
31. 28 οὐσίαν ex οὐσίας M   30 ἐπιστρέφει M (ἐπιστρέφοιτο Arg Cr.)
33 τεῦξις BCDM : τάξις PQW   35 δέ] δὲ καί D

united are like them more than they are unlike.   Every productive
cause, therefore, brings into existence like things before unlike.

PROP. **29**. *All procession is accomplished through a likeness of the
secondary to the primary.*

For if the producing cause brings into existence like things before
unlike (prop. 28), it is likeness which generates the product out of
the producer : for like things are made like by likeness, and not by
unlikeness.   The procession, accordingly, since in declension it
preserves an identity betwixt engenderer and engendered, and
manifests by derivation in the consequent that character which the
other has primitively (prop. 18), owes to likeness its substantive
existence.

PROP. **30**. *All that is immediately produced by any principle both
remains in the producing cause and proceeds from it.*

For if in every procession the first terms remain steadfast
(prop. 26), and if the procession is accomplished by means of likeness (prop. 29), like terms coming to existence before unlike
(prop. 28), then the product in some sense remains in the producer.
For a term which proceeded completely would have no identity with
that which remained : such a term is wholly distinct from the prior.
If it is to be united by any common link with its cause, it must
remain in the latter as we saw that the latter remained in itself.   If,
on the other hand, it should remain only, without procession, it will
be indistinguishable from its cause, and will not be a new thing
which has arisen while the cause remains.   For if it is a new thing,
it is distinct and separate ; and if it is separate and the cause
remains steadfast, to render this possible it must have proceeded
from the cause.   In so far, then, as it has an element of identity
with the producer, the product remains in it ; in so far as it differs
it proceeds from it.   But being like it, it is at once identical with it
in some respect and different from it : accordingly it both remains
and proceeds, and the two relations are inseparable.

PROP. **31**. *All that proceeds from any principle reverts in respect of its
being upon that from which it proceeds.*

For if it should proceed yet not revert upon the cause of this
procession, it must be without appetition of that cause, since all that
has appetition is turned towards the object of its appetite.   But all
things desire the Good, and each attains it through the mediation
of its own proximate cause : therefore each has appetition of its own
cause also.   Through that which gives it being it attains its well-being ;

τοῦτο ἡ ὄρεξις πρῶτον· πρὸς ὃ δὲ πρῶτον ἡ ὄρεξις, πρὸς τοῦτο ἡ ἐπιστροφή.

32. Πᾶσα ἐπιστροφὴ δι' ὁμοιότητος ἀποτελεῖται τῶν ἐπιστρεφομένων πρὸς ὃ ἐπιστρέφεται.

τὸ γὰρ ἐπιστρεφόμενον πᾶν πρὸς πᾶν συνάπτεσθαι σπεύδει 5 καὶ ὀρέγεται τῆς πρὸς αὐτὸ κοινωνίας καὶ συνδέσεως. συνδεῖ δὲ πάντα ἡ ὁμοιότης, ὥσπερ διακρίνει ἡ ἀνομοιότης καὶ διίστησιν. εἰ οὖν ἡ ἐπιστροφὴ κοινωνία τίς ἐστι καὶ συναφή, πᾶσα δὲ κοινωνία καὶ συναφὴ πᾶσα δι' ὁμοιότητος, πᾶσα ἄρα ἐπιστροφὴ δι' ὁμοιότητος ἀποτελοῖτο ἄν. 10

33. Πᾶν τὸ προϊὸν ἀπό τινος καὶ ἐπιστρέφον κυκλικὴν ἔχει τὴν ἐνέργειαν.

εἰ γάρ, ἀφ' οὗ πρόεισιν, εἰς τοῦτο ἐπιστρέφει, συνάπτει τῇ ἀρχῇ τὸ τέλος, καὶ ἔστι μία καὶ συνεχὴς ἡ κίνησις, τῆς μὲν ἀπὸ τοῦ μένοντος, τῆς δὲ πρὸς τὸ μεῖναν γινομένης· ὅθεν δὴ 15 πάντα κύκλῳ πρόεισιν ἀπὸ τῶν αἰτίων ἐπὶ τὰ αἴτια. μείζους δὲ κύκλοι καὶ ἐλάττους, τῶν μὲν ἐπιστροφῶν πρὸς τὰ ὑπερκείμενα προσεχῶς γινομένων, τῶν δὲ πρὸς τὰ ἀνωτέρω καὶ μέχρι τῆς πάντων ἀρχῆς· ἀπὸ γὰρ ἐκείνης πάντα καὶ πρὸς ἐκείνην.

34. Πᾶν τὸ κατὰ φύσιν ἐπιστρεφόμενον πρὸς ἐκεῖνο ποιεῖται 20 τὴν ἐπιστροφήν, ἀφ' οὗ καὶ τὴν πρόοδον ἔσχε τῆς οἰκείας ὑποστάσεως.

εἰ γὰρ κατὰ φύσιν ἐπιστρέφεται, τὴν κατ' οὐσίαν ὄρεξιν πρὸς ἐκεῖνο κέκτηται, πρὸς ὃ ἐπιστρέφεται. εἰ δὲ τοῦτο, καὶ τὸ εἶναι αὐτοῦ πᾶν εἰς ἐκεῖνο ἀνήρτηται, πρὸς ὃ τὴν οὐσιώδη 25 ποιεῖται ἐπιστροφήν, καὶ ὅμοιόν ἐστιν ἐκείνῳ κατ' οὐσίαν· διὸ καὶ συμπαθὲς ἐκείνῳ κατὰ φύσιν, ὡς τῇ οὐσίᾳ συγγενές. εἰ δὲ τοῦτο, ἢ ταὐτόν ἐστι τὸ εἶναι ἀμφοτέρων ἢ ἐκ θατέρου θάτερον ἢ ἄμφω ἐξ ἑνὸς ἄλλου τὸ ὅμοιον ἔλαχεν. ἀλλ' εἰ μὲν ταὐτὸν τὸ εἶναι ἀμφοτέρων, πῶς κατὰ φύσιν θάτερον πρὸς θάτερον 30 ἐπέστραπται; εἰ δὲ ἐξ ἑνὸς ἄμφω, πρὸς ἐκεῖνο ἂν εἴη τὸ κατὰ φύσιν ἐπιστρέφειν ἀμφοτέροις. λείπεται ἄρα ἐκ θατέρου θάτερον

32. 8 εἰ] ἡ M   ἡ ante ἐπιστροφή om. CD   9 prius πᾶσα non agnosc. W   10 ἀποτελοῖτο ἄν M, ἀποτελοῖτ' ἄν BCD : ἀποτελεῖται ἄν PQ : efficitur Wγ, om. a¹β, efficietur a²
33. 14 κίνησις sup. lin. M   15 γινομένης BC et suprascr. m. i D : γενομένης DMPQ   16 ἀπὸ γὰρ τῶν M   ἐπὶ τὰ αἰτιατὰ καὶ ἀπὸ τούτων ἐπὶ-τὰ αἴτια Q² in mg.   17 ἐπιστροφῶν τῶν μέν videtur voluisse Q²   18 προσεχῶς ω, proxime W (συνεχῶς edd.)
34. 25 ὃ καὶ τήν M   26 ἐκεῖνο suprascr. PQ   27 ἐκεῖνο PQ   28 τό BCD : τῷ MPQ (ex corr. Q)   29 ἐξ ἑνὸς ἄλλου ω : ex aliquo altero W : ἐξ ἑνὸς τοῦ ἄλλου dett. : ἐξ ἑνός του ἄλλου Cr., fort. recte   32 ἀμφοτέροις ω, ambobus W (ἀμφότερον dett., edd.)

the source of its well-being is the primary object of its appetite; and the primary object of its appetite is that upon which it reverts.

PROP. **32.** *All reversion is accomplished through a likeness of the reverting terms to the goal of reversion.*

For that which reverts endeavours to be conjoined in every part with every part of its cause, and desires to have communion in it and be bound to it. But all things are bound together by likeness, as by unlikeness they are distinguished and severed. If, then, reversion is a communion and conjunction, and all communion and conjunction is through likeness, it follows that all reversion must be accomplished through likeness.

PROP. **33.** *All that proceeds from any principle and reverts upon it has a cyclic activity.*

For if it reverts upon that principle whence it proceeds (prop. 31), it links its end to its beginning, and the movement is one and continuous, originating from the unmoved and to the unmoved again returning. Thus all things proceed in a circuit, from their causes to their causes again. There are greater circuits and lesser, in that some revert upon their immediate priors, others upon the superior causes, even to the beginning of all things. For out of the beginning all things are, and towards it all revert.

PROP. **34.** *Everything whose nature it is to revert reverts upon that from which it derived the procession of its own substance.*

For if it reverts by nature, it has existential appetition of that upon which it reverts. And if so, its being also is wholly dependent on the principle upon which it reverts existentially, and in its existence it resembles this latter: hence it is naturally sympathetic with this principle, since it is akin to it in existence. If so, either the being of the two is identical, or one is derived from the other, or else both have received their like character from a single third principle. But if they be identical, how comes it that one is by nature reverted upon the other? And if the two be from one source, that source must be the goal of natural reversion for both (prop. 31). It remains, therefore, that one has its being from the

τὸ εἶναι ἔχειν. εἰ δὲ τοῦτο, καὶ ἡ πρόοδος ἀπ᾽ ἐκείνου, πρὸς ὃ ἡ κατὰ φύσιν ἐπιστροφή.

ἐκ δὴ τούτων φανερὸν ὅτι καὶ ὀρεκτὸν πᾶσι νοῦς, καὶ πρόεισι πάντα ἀπὸ νοῦ, καὶ πᾶς ὁ κόσμος ἀπὸ νοῦ τὴν οὐσίαν ἔχει, κἂν ἀΐδιος ᾖ. καὶ οὐ διὰ τοῦτο οὐχὶ πρόεισιν ἀπὸ νοῦ, διότι ἀΐδιος· 5 οὐδὲ γὰρ διὰ τοῦτο οὐκ ἐπέστραπται, διότι ἀεὶ τέτακται· ἀλλὰ καὶ πρόεισιν ἀεὶ καὶ ἀΐδιος κατ᾽ οὐσίαν, καὶ ἐπέστραπται ἀεὶ καὶ ἄλυτος κατὰ τὴν τάξιν.

35. Πᾶν τὸ αἰτιατὸν καὶ μένει ἐν τῇ αὑτοῦ αἰτίᾳ καὶ πρόεισιν ἀπ᾽ αὐτῆς καὶ ἐπιστρέφει πρὸς αὐτήν.   10

εἰ γὰρ μένοι μόνον, οὐδὲν διοίσει τῆς αἰτίας, ἀδιάκριτον ὄν· ἅμα γὰρ διακρίσει πρόοδος. εἰ δὲ προΐοι μόνον, ἀσύναπτον ἔσται πρὸς αὐτὴν καὶ ἀσυμπαθές, μηδαμῇ τῇ αἰτίᾳ κοινωνοῦν. εἰ δὲ ἐπιστρέφοιτο μόνον, πῶς τὸ μὴ τὴν οὐσίαν ἀπ᾽ αὐτῆς ἔχον κατ᾽ οὐσίαν ποιεῖται τὴν πρὸς τὸ ἀλλότριον ἐπιστροφήν; εἰ δὲ 15 μένοι μὲν καὶ προΐοι, μὴ ἐπιστρέφοιτο δέ, πῶς ἡ κατὰ φύσιν ὄρεξις ἑκάστῳ πρὸς τὸ εὖ καὶ τὸ ἀγαθὸν καὶ ἡ ἐπὶ τὸ γεννῆσαν ἀνάτασις; εἰ δὲ προΐοι μὲν καὶ ἐπιστρέφοιτο, μὴ μένοι δέ, πῶς ἀποστὰν μὲν τῆς αἰτίας συνάπτεσθαι σπεύδει πρὸς αὐτήν, ἀσύναπτον δὲ ἦν πρὸ τῆς ἀποστάσεως; εἰ γὰρ συνῆπτο, κατ᾽ 20 ἐκεῖνο πάντως ἔμενεν. εἰ δὲ μένοι καὶ ἐπιστρέφοιτο, μὴ προέρχοιτο δέ, πῶς τὸ μὴ διακριθὲν ἐπιστρέφειν δυνατόν; τὸ γὰρ ἐπιστρέφον πᾶν ἀναλύοντι ἔοικεν εἰς ἐκεῖνο, ἀφ᾽ οὗ διῄρηται κατ᾽ οὐσίαν.

ἀνάγκη δὲ ἢ μένειν μόνον ἢ ἐπιστρέφειν μόνον ἢ προϊέναι 25 μόνον ἢ συνδεῖν τὰ ἄκρα μετ᾽ ἀλλήλων ἢ τὸ μεταξὺ μεθ᾽ ἑκατέρου τῶν ἄκρων ἢ τὰ σύμπαντα. λείπεται ἄρα καὶ μένειν πᾶν ἐν τῷ αἰτίῳ καὶ προϊέναι ἀπ᾽ αὐτοῦ καὶ ἐπιστρέφειν πρὸς αὐτό.

36. Πάντων τῶν κατὰ πρόοδον πληθυνομένων τὰ πρῶτα 30 τελειότερα τῶν δευτέρων ἐστί, καὶ τὰ δεύτερα τῶν μετ᾽ αὐτά, καὶ ἐφεξῆς ὡσαύτως.

εἰ γὰρ αἱ πρόοδοι διακρίνουσιν ἀπὸ τῶν αἰτίων τὰ παρ-

(L. 3 δή ω (δέ Cr.)   prius καί om. PQ, neque agnosc. W   πᾶσι] πᾶς PQ
3-4 πρόεισιν ἀπὸ νοῦ πάντα edd.   5 οὐ διὰ τοῦτο BCDW : οὐ om. M, post
οὐχί ins. PQ   6 οὐδὲ γάρ CDMW (ex οὐ γάρ M) : οὐ γάρ B : οὐδέ PQ
35. 9 αὑτοῦ BCDM (cf. p. 104, l. 1, etc.) : αὐτή Q : αὐτῆς P   11 μένοι·
PQ : μένει BCDMW   13 μηδαμῇ MPQ, nullatenus W : καὶ μηδαμῇ BCD
14 ἐπιστρέφοντι [M], convertitur W   15 τό om. PQ   17 ἑκάστου PQW
18 ἀνάτασις M   ἐπιστρέφοι PQ   μένει BCD   20 συνῆπτο ω
(συνῆπτον edd.)   22 μή om. M, non agnosc. W   26 συνδεῖν BCDM² :
συνδύο [M]PQW   τὰς ἄκρας PQ   27 ἑκατέρου ω (ἑκατέρων edd.)
36. 30 τῶν deletum D   31 εἰσίν C   33 εἰ] οἱ M   καὶ διακρίνουσιν PQ

other. And if so, its procession is from that upon which it naturally reverts.

Cor. From this it is apparent that as the Intelligence is an object of appetition to all things, so all things proceed from the Intelligence, and the whole world-order, though eternal, has its being therefrom. The eternity of the world-order affords no ground for denying that it proceeds from the Intelligence; just as it keeps its own station for ever, yet is none the less reverted upon the Intelligence. It proceeds eternally, and is eternal in its being; it is eternally reverted, and is steadfast in its own station.

PROP. 35. *Every effect remains in its cause, proceeds from it, and reverts upon it.*

For if it should remain without procession or reversion, it will be without distinction from, and therefore identical with, its cause, since distinction implies procession. And if it should proceed without reversion or immanence, it will be without conjunction or sympathy with its cause, since it will have no communication with it. And if it should revert without immanence or procession, how can that which has not its being from the higher revert existentially upon a principle thus alien? And if it should remain and proceed, but not revert, how comes it that each thing has a natural appetition of its well-being and of the Good, and an upward tension towards its begetter? And if it should proceed and revert, but not remain, how comes it that being parted from its cause it endeavours to be conjoined with it, although before the severance there was no conjunction (since if it was conjoined with the cause it certainly remained in it)? Finally, if it should remain and revert, but not proceed, how can there be reversion without distinction (since all reversion seems to be the resolution of a principle into something from which its being divides it)?

But the effect must either remain simply, or revert simply, or proceed simply, or combine the extreme terms, or combine the mean term with one of the other two; or else combine all three. By exclusion, then, every effect remains in its cause, proceeds from it, and reverts upon it.

PROP. 36. *In all that multiplies itself by procession, those terms which arise first are more perfect than the second, and these than the next order, and so throughout the series.*

For if procession is that which distinguishes product from cause,

ἀγόμενα, καὶ ὑφέσεις εἰσὶ πρὸς τὰ πρῶτα τῶν δευτέρων, τὰ μὲν πρῶτα προελθόντα συνῆπται μᾶλλον τοῖς αἰτίοις, ἀπ' αὐτῶν ἐκείνων ἐκβλαστάνοντα, τὰ δὲ δεύτερα πορρωτέρω τῶν αἰτίων ἐστί, καὶ ἑξῆς ὁμοίως. τὰ δὲ ἐγγυτέρω καὶ τὰ συγγενέστερα τοῖς αἰτίοις τελειότερα (καὶ γὰρ τὰ αἴτια τῶν αἰτιατῶν)· τὰ δὲ 5 πορρώτερον ἀτελέστερα, ἀνομοιούμενα τοῖς αἰτίοις.

37. Πάντων τῶν κατ' ἐπιστροφὴν ὑφισταμένων τὰ πρῶτα ἀτελέστερα τῶν δευτέρων, καὶ τὰ δεύτερα τῶν ἑξῆς· τὰ δὲ ἔσχατα τελεώτατα.

εἰ γὰρ αἱ ἐπιστροφαὶ γίνονται κατὰ κύκλον, καὶ ἀφ' οὗ ἡ 10 πρόοδος, εἰς τοῦτο ἡ ἐπιστροφή, ἀπὸ δὲ τοῦ τελειοτάτου ἡ πρόοδος, ἡ ἐπιστροφὴ ἄρα εἰς τὸ τελειότατον. καὶ εἰ, ἐφ' ὃ ἡ πρόοδος ἔσχατον, ἀπὸ τούτου πρώτου ἡ ἐπιστροφή, ἡ δὲ πρόοδος εἰς ἔσχατον τὸ ἀτελέστατον, καὶ ἡ ἐπιστροφὴ ἀπὸ τοῦ ἀτελεστάτου. πρῶτα μὲν ἄρα ἐν τοῖς κατ' ἐπιστροφὴν τὰ ἀτελέστατα, 15 ἔσχατα δὲ τὰ τελεώτατα.

38. Πᾶν τὸ προϊὸν ἀπό τινων πλειόνων αἰτίων, δι' ὅσων πρόεισι, διὰ τοσούτων καὶ ἐπιστρέφεται· καὶ πᾶσα ἐπιστροφὴ διὰ τῶν αὐτῶν, δι' ὧν καὶ ἡ πρόοδος.

ἐπεὶ γὰρ δι' ὁμοιότητος ἑκατέρα γίνεται, τὸ μὲν ἀμέσως ἀπό 20 τινος προελθὸν καὶ ἐπέστραπται ἀμέσως πρὸς αὐτό (ἡ γὰρ ὁμοιότης ἄμεσος ἦν)· τὸ δὲ μεσότητος ἐν τῷ προϊέναι δεόμενον μεσότητος δεῖται καὶ κατὰ τὴν ἐπιστροφήν (δεῖ γὰρ πρὸς τὸ αὐτὸ ἑκατέραν γίνεσθαι), ὥστε πρὸς τὸ μέσον ἐπιστραφήσεται πρῶτον, ἔπειτα πρὸς τὸ τοῦ μέσου κρεῖττον. δι' ὅσων ἄρα τὸ 25 εἶναι, διὰ τοσούτων καὶ τὸ εὖ εἶναι ἑκάστοις· καὶ ἔμπαλιν.

39. Πᾶν τὸ ὂν ἢ οὐσιωδῶς ἐπιστρέφει μόνον, ἢ ζωτικῶς, ἢ καὶ γνωστικῶς.

ἢ γὰρ τὸ εἶναι μόνον ἀπὸ τῆς αἰτίας κέκτηται, ἢ τὸ ζῆν μετὰ τοῦ εἶναι, ἢ καὶ γνωστικὴν ἐκεῖθεν ὑπεδέξατο δύναμιν. ᾗ μὲν 30 οὖν ἔστι μόνον, οὐσιώδη ποιεῖται τὴν ἐπιστροφήν· ᾗ δὲ καὶ ζῇ,

---

36. 1 καὶ αἱ ὑφέσεις P   2 παρελθόντα PQ   3 τὰ δὲ ... 4 ὁμοίως om. PQ
4 ἐστί BCDM (εἰσί dett., edd.)   ἐγγυτέρω τε καί BCD   alt. τά om. C[1]
6 πορρώτερα Q   et non similia causis W
37. 9 τελεώτατα MPQ (sed vide ne hic et l. 16 scribendum sit τελειότατα, quam scripturam fere ubique huius opusculi praebent libri): τελεώτερα BCD
10 αἱ ω (om. dett., edd.)   οὗ] οὖ καί D   11 τῆς τελειότητος PQ
12 τὴν τελειότητα PQ   εἰ] ἡ M   13 πρώτου BCDM[2]W : πρώτη [M] : om. PQ
38. 19 καί om. D   20 ἑκατέρα BCM : ἑκάτερα DPQ dett.   21 διελθόν supraser. M[2]   23 τό om. BCD   24 ἑκάτερα BCDM, utramque Wγ : ἑκάτερα P : utruinque Wβ : Q et Wα incerta   ὥστε καὶ πρός P   26 alt. εἶναι om. PQ
39. 27 prius ἢ om. PQ, non agnosc. W   ἢ καὶ ζωτικῶς Arg (nescio an

and there is a declination in secondaries relatively to primals (prop. 28), then the first terms in such processions are more closely conjoined with the causes, since they spring direct from them ; and so throughout. But that which is closer and more akin to the cause is more perfect (for causes are more perfect than effects (prop. 7)) ; and the more remote is less perfect, as it loses the likeness of the cause.

PROP. 37. *In all that is generated by reversion the first terms are less perfect than the second, and these than the next order ; and the last are the most perfect.*

For if reversion is the return of a circuit (prop. 33), and the goal of reversion is the source of procession (prop. 34), then if the procession is from the most perfect term (prop. 36), the reversion is toward the most perfect term. And if the last term of the procession is the first term of the reversion, and the least perfect term of the procession is its last, then the reversion begins from its least perfect term. In the order of reversion, then, the least perfect terms are first and the most perfect last.

PROP. 38. *All that proceeds from a plurality of causes passes through as many terms in its reversion as in its procession ; and all reversion is through the same terms as the corresponding procession.*

For since both procession and reversion are accomplished through likeness (props. 29, 32), that which proceeds immediately from any principle is immediately reverted upon it, the likeness being immediate. But that which requires mediation in its procession requires it also in its reversion, since both moments must be related to the same term (prop. 34) : so that it will revert first to the mean term, then to that superior to the mean. Accordingly the well-being of each thing is derived through as many causes as its being ; and conversely.

PROP. 39. *All that exists reverts either in respect of its existence only, or in respect of its life, or by the way of knowledge also.*

For either it has from its cause existence only, or life together with existence, or else it has received from thence a cognitive faculty also. In so far, then, as it has bare existence, its reversion is existential ; in so far as it also lives, vital ; in so far as it has know-

42 THE ELEMENTS OF THEOLOGY

καὶ ζωτικήν· ᾗ δὲ καὶ γινώσκει, καὶ γνωστικήν. ὡς γὰρ
προῆλθεν, οὕτως ἐπέστραπται, καὶ τὰ μέτρα τῆς ἐπιστροφῆς
ὥρισται τοῖς κατὰ τὴν πρόοδον μέτροις. καὶ ἡ ὄρεξις οὖν τοῖς
μέν ἐστι κατ᾽ αὐτὸ τὸ εἶναι μόνον, ἐπιτηδειότης οὖσα πρὸς τὴν
μέθεξιν τῶν αἰτίων· τοῖς δὲ κατὰ τὴν ζωήν, κίνησις οὖσα πρὸς 5
τὰ κρείττονα· τοῖς δὲ κατὰ τὴν γνῶσιν, συναίσθησις οὖσα τῆς
τῶν αἰτίων ἀγαθότητος.

40. Πάντων τῶν ἀφ᾽ ἑτέρας αἰτίας προϊόντων ἡγεῖται τὰ παρ᾽
ἑαυτῶν ὑφιστάμενα καὶ τὴν οὐσίαν αὐθυπόστατον κεκτημένα.

εἰ γὰρ πᾶν τὸ αὔταρκες ἢ κατ᾽ οὐσίαν ἢ κατ᾽ ἐνέργειαν 10
κρεῖττον τοῦ εἰς ἄλλην αἰτίαν ἀνηρτημένου· τὸ δὲ ἑαυτὸ
παράγον, ἑαυτῷ τοῦ εἶναι παρεκτικὸν ὑπάρχον, αὔταρκες πρὸς
οὐσίαν, τὸ δὲ ἀπ᾽ ἄλλου μόνον παραγόμενον οὐκ αὔταρκες· τῷ
δὲ ἀγαθῷ συγγενέστερον τὸ αὔταρκες· τὰ δὲ συγγενέστερα καὶ
ὁμοιότερα ταῖς αἰτίαις πρὸ τῶν ἀνομοίων ὑφέστηκεν ἐκ τῆς 15
αἰτίας· τὰ ἄρα παρ᾽ ἑαυτῶν παραγόμενα καὶ αὐθυπόστατα
πρεσβύτερά ἐστι τῶν ἀφ᾽ ἑτέρου μόνον εἰς τὸ εἶναι προελθόντων.

ἢ γὰρ οὐδὲν ἔσται αὐθυπόστατον, ἢ τὸ ἀγαθὸν τοιοῦτον, ἢ
τὰ πρῶτα ἐκ τἀγαθοῦ ὑποστάντα. ἀλλ᾽ εἰ μὲν μηδὲν αὐθυπόστατον, ἐν οὐδενὶ τὸ αὔταρκες ἔσται κατ᾽ ἀλήθειαν. οὔτε γὰρ 20
ἐν τἀγαθῷ (κρεῖττον γὰρ αὐταρκείας ἓν ὂν ἐκεῖνο καὶ αὐτοαγαθόν, ἀλλ᾽ οὐχὶ ἔχον τἀγαθόν)· οὔτε ἐν τοῖς μετὰ τἀγαθόν
(πᾶν γὰρ ἐνδεὲς ἄλλου ἔσται, τοῦ πρὸ αὐτοῦ μόνον ⟨ὄν⟩). εἰ δὲ
τἀγαθὸν αὐθυπόστατον, αὐτὸ ἑαυτὸ παράγον οὐχ ἓν ἔσται· τὸ
γὰρ ἀπὸ τοῦ ἑνὸς προϊὸν οὐχ ἕν. ἀφ᾽ ἑαυτοῦ γὰρ πρόεισιν, 25
εἴπερ αὐθυπόστατον· ὥστε ἓν ἅμα καὶ οὐχ ἓν τὸ ἕν. ἀνάγκη
ἄρα τὸ αὐθυπόστατον εἶναι μετὰ τὸ πρῶτον· καὶ δῆλον ὡς πρὸ
τῶν ἀφ᾽ ἑτέρας αἰτίας μόνον προελθόντων· κυριώτερον γὰρ
ἐκείνων καὶ τἀγαθῷ συγγενέστερον, ὡς δέδεικται.

41. Πᾶν μὲν τὸ ἐν ἄλλῳ ὂν ἀπ᾽ ἄλλου μόνον παράγεται· 30
πᾶν δὲ τὸ ἐν ἑαυτῷ ὂν αὐθυπόστατόν ἐστι.

τὸ μὲν γὰρ ἐν ἄλλῳ ὂν καὶ ὑποκειμένου δεόμενον ἑαυτοῦ

---

39. 1 ᾗ] εἰ PQ   3 τήν om. BCD   5 τῶν αἰτ (sic) P, τῆς αἰτίας Q
6 κρείττω C
40. 11 τοῦ] τῆς PQ   ἀνηρτημένου MQ: ἀνηρτημένης P: ἠρτημένου
BCD: cf. p. 10, l. 15   12 ἑαυτῷ] ἑαυτό M   13 ὑπ᾽ ἄλλου PQ   15 ταῖς
αἰτίαις] substantiis (= οὐσίαις?) W   17 εἰς τὸ εἶναι non agnosc. W   παρελ-
θόντων PQ dett.   19 μέν om. BCD   20 ἔσται om. PQ   21 γὰρ ω,
enim W (om. edd.)   21–2 αὐτοαγαθόν BCDM: αὐτὸ ἀγαθόν PQ   22 ἔχον
ἀγαθόν Cr.²   23 πᾶν BCDPQ: πάντα M (omnia ... indigentia W)
ἔσται ἄλλου CPQ   μόνου Arg   ὄν inserui: cf. p. 46, l. 6   24–5 τὸ
γὰρ ... 26 τὸ ἕν om. W   25 ἀφ᾽ ἑαυτοῦ ω (ἑαυτοῦ edd.)   28 ante
κυριώτερον parvam rasuram M
41. 30 ὑπ᾽ ἄλλου edd.   31 ἐν ἑαυτῷ BCD: ἐν αὐτῷ MPQ

ledge likewise, cognitive. For as it proceeds, so it reverts; and the measure of its reversion is determined by the measure of its procession. Some things, accordingly, have appetition in respect of bare existence only, that is, a fitness for the participation of their causes; others have a vital appetition, that is, a movement towards the higher; others, again, a cognitive appetition, which is a consciousness of the goodness of their causes.

E. OF THE SELF-CONSTITUTED.

PROP. 40. *All that proceeds from another cause is subordinate to principles which get their substance from themselves and have a self-constituted existence.*

For if all that is self-sufficient either in its existence or in its activity is superior to that which depends upon another cause (prop. 9); and if that which produces itself, having the power of furnishing its own being, is self-sufficient in respect of its existence, whereas that which is produced entirely by another is not self-sufficient; and if the self-sufficient is nearer akin to the Good (prop. 9); and if terms which have more of kinship and likeness to their causes are generated from the cause before the unlike terms (prop. 28): then terms which are produced by themselves and self-constituted are senior to those which derive their being solely from another.

For either there is nothing self-constituted, or the Good is such, or else the principles which arise first from the Good. But if there be nothing self-constituted, there will be no true self-sufficiency in anything: neither in the Good, which is superior to self-sufficiency (prop. 10), since it is not a possessor of the Good, but is One (prop. 13) and Good-absolute (prop. 8); nor in things posterior to the Good, since each will depend upon another, belonging not to itself but wholly to its prior. And if the Good be self-constituted, producing itself it will lose its unity, inasmuch as that which proceeds from the One is not-one (prop. 2) (for if it be self-constituted it proceeds from itself): accordingly the One will be one and at the same time not-one. It follows, then, that the self-constituted must exist, but posterior to the First Principle. That it is prior to those terms which proceed wholly from another cause, is evident: for it is more autonomous than they, and nearer akin to the Good, as has been shown above.

PROP. 41. *All that has its existence in another is produced entirely from another; but all that exists in itself is self-constituted.*

For that which exists in another and requires a substrate can

γεννητικὸν οὐκ ἄν ποτε εἴη· τὸ γὰρ γεννᾶν ἑαυτὸ πεφυκὸς
ἕδρας ἄλλης οὐ δεῖται, συνεχόμενον ὑφ' ἑαυτοῦ καὶ σωζόμενον
ἐν ἑαυτῷ τοῦ ὑποκειμένου χωρίς. τὸ δὲ ἐν ἑαυτῷ μένειν καὶ
ἰδρῦσθαι δυνάμενον ἑαυτοῦ παρακτικόν ἐστιν, αὐτὸ εἰς ἑαυτὸ
προϊόν, καὶ ἑαυτοῦ συνεκτικὸν ὑπάρχον, καὶ οὕτως ἐν ἑαυτῷ ὄν, 5
ὡς ἐν αἰτίῳ τὸ αἰτιατόν. οὐ γὰρ ὡς ἐν τόπῳ, οὐδὲ ὡς ἐν
ὑποκειμένῳ· καὶ γὰρ ὁ τόπος τοῦ ἐν τόπῳ ἕτερος, καὶ τοῦ
ὑποκειμένου τὸ ἐν ὑποκειμένῳ ὄν· τοῦτο δὲ ἑαυτῷ ταὐτόν.
αὐθυποστάτως ἄρα καὶ ὡς ἐν αἰτίᾳ τὸ ἀπ' αἰτίας, οὕτως ἐν
ἑαυτῷ ἐστιν.   10

42. Πᾶν τὸ αὐθυπόστατον πρὸς ἑαυτό ἐστιν ἐπιστρεπτικόν.

εἰ γὰρ ἀφ' ἑαυτοῦ πρόεισι, καὶ τὴν ἐπιστροφὴν ποιήσεται
πρὸς ἑαυτό· ἀφ' οὗ γὰρ ἡ πρόοδος ἑκάστοις, εἰς τοῦτο καὶ ἡ τῇ
προόδῳ σύστοιχος ἐπιστροφή. εἰ γὰρ πρόεισιν ἀφ' ἑαυτοῦ
μόνον, μὴ ἐπιστρέφοιτο δὲ προϊὸν εἰς ἑαυτό, οὐκ ἄν ποτε τοῦ 15
οἰκείου ἀγαθοῦ ὀρέγοιτο καὶ ὃ δύναται ἑαυτῷ παρέχειν. δύναται
δὲ πᾶν τὸ αἴτιον τῷ ἀπ' αὐτοῦ διδόναι μετὰ τῆς οὐσίας, ἧς
δίδωσι, καὶ τὸ εὖ τῆς οὐσίας, ἧς δίδωσι, συζυγές· ὥστε καὶ αὐτὸ
ἑαυτῷ. τοῦτο ἄρα τὸ οἰκεῖον τῷ αὐθυποστάτῳ ἀγαθόν. τούτου
δὲ οὐκ ὀρέξεται τὸ ἀνεπίστροφον πρὸς ἑαυτό· μὴ ὀρεγόμενον δέ, 20
οὐδ' ἂν τύχοι, καὶ μὴ τυγχάνον, ἀτελὲς ἂν εἴη καὶ οὐκ αὔταρκες.
ἀλλ' εἴπερ τῳ ἄλλῳ, προσήκει καὶ τῷ αὐθυποστάτῳ αὐτάρκει
καὶ τελείῳ εἶναι. καὶ τεύξεται ἄρα τοῦ οἰκείου καὶ ὀρέξεται
καὶ πρὸς ἑαυτὸ στραφήσεται.

43. Πᾶν τὸ πρὸς ἑαυτὸ ἐπιστρεπτικὸν αὐθυπόστατόν ἐστιν. 25

εἰ γὰρ ἐπέστραπται πρὸς ἑαυτὸ κατὰ φύσιν καὶ ἔστι τέλειον
ἐν τῇ πρὸς ἑαυτὸ ἐπιστροφῇ, καὶ τὴν οὐσίαν ἂν παρ' ἑαυτοῦ
ἔχοι· πρὸς ὃ γὰρ ἡ κατὰ φύσιν ἐπιστροφή, ἀπὸ τούτου καὶ ἡ
πρόοδος ἡ κατ' οὐσίαν ἑκάστοις. εἰ οὖν ἑαυτῷ τὸ εὖ εἶναι
παρέχει, καὶ τὸ εἶναι δήπου ἑαυτῷ παρέξει, καὶ ἔσται τῆς 30
ἑαυτοῦ κύριον ὑποστάσεως. αὐθυπόστατον ἄρα ἐστὶ τὸ πρὸς
ἑαυτὸ δυνάμενον ἐπιστρέφειν.

41. 3 alt. ἐν ἑαυτῷ BCD : ἐν αὐτῷ M : ὑπὲρ ἑαυτοῦ (αὐτοῦ Q) PQ   4 ἰδρύεσθαι PQ
8 ἑαυτῷ] ἐν αὐτῷ M²   9 αὐθυπόστατον ?[M], antipostato ... idem W   ἄρα]
γάρ M²   ἐν αἰτίῳ M (fort. ex corr.)   τὸ ὑπ' αἰτίας PQ
42. 15 εἰς αὐτό MQ   17 τῷ ἀπ' αὐτοῦ ω (τὸ ἀπ' αὐτοῦ dett., Port. Cr.¹)
ἧς M¹PQ : ἣν BCDM²   18–19 αὐτὸ αὐτῷ MPQ   19 τοῦτο om. Arg (M¹
incert.)   ἀγαθῷ Arg (Cr.)   20 ὀρέξεται ω, appetet αγ : ὀρέγεται O², appetit β
τὸ ἀνεπίστροφον BCD : τὸ ἐπιστρέφον MPQ, conversum W   21 οὐδ'] οὐκ PQ
τύχῃ BDQ   22 αὐτάρκεια dett., edd.   24 στραφήσεται BCDM : ἐπιστραφήσεται PQ, convertetur W
43. 27 ἐπιστροφῇ BCDPQ, conversione W : στροφῇ M   ἄν ω (om. dett.,
Port. Cr.¹)   29 τὸ εὖ ἔχειν PQ   30 παρέχοι C dett.   τὸ δήπου εἶναι M
καὶ ἔσται καὶ τῆς PQ

never be self-generative, since a principle capable of generating itself needs no alien seat, being contained by itself and conserved in itself without a substrate. On the other hand, that which can remain firmly seated in itself is self-productive, since it proceeds from itself to itself : it has the power of containing itself, and is in itself not spatially, nor as in a substrate, but as the effect is in the cause. For space and substrate are alike distinct from their content, whereas the principles in question are self-identical. Such a term, therefore, exists in itself by self-constitution, and as the consequent exists in the cause.

PROP. **42**. *All that is self-constituted is capable of reversion upon itself.*

For if it proceeds from itself it will also revert upon itself, since the source of the procession of any term is the goal of the corresponding reversion (prop. 31). If, proceeding from itself, it should in proceeding not revert, it could never have appetition of its proper good, a good which it can bestow upon itself. For every cause can bestow upon its product, along with the existence which it gives, the well-being which belongs to that existence : hence it can bestow the latter upon itself also, and this is the proper good of the self-constituted. Of this good it will have no appetition if it be incapable of reversion upon itself ; not desiring, it cannot attain ; and not attaining, it will be incomplete and not self-sufficient. But self-sufficiency and completeness belong to the self-constituted if they belong to anything. Accordingly the self-constituted must attain its proper good ; and must therefore desire it ; and must therefore revert upon itself.

PROP. **43**. *All that is capable of reversion upon itself is self-constituted.*

For if it is by nature reverted upon itself, and is made complete by such reversion, it must derive its existence from itself, since the goal of natural reversion for any term is the source from which its existence proceeds (prop. 34). If, then, it is the source of its own well-being, it will certainly be also the source of its own being and responsible for its own existence as a substance. Thus what is able to revert upon itself is self-constituted.

44. Πᾶν τὸ κατ' ἐνέργειαν πρὸς ἑαυτὸ ἐπιστρεπτικὸν καὶ κατ' οὐσίαν ἐπέστραπται πρὸς ἑαυτό.

εἰ γὰρ τῇ μὲν ἐνεργείᾳ δύναται ἐπιστρέφεσθαι πρὸς ἑαυτό, τῇ δὲ οὐσίᾳ ἀνεπίστροφον ὑπάρχοι, κρεῖττον ἂν εἴη κατὰ τὴν ἐνέργειαν μᾶλλον ἢ κατὰ τὴν οὐσίαν, τῆς μὲν ἐπιστρεπτικῆς 5 οὔσης, τῆς δὲ ἀνεπιστρόφου· τὸ γὰρ ἑαυτοῦ ὂν κρεῖττον ἢ τὸ ἄλλου μόνον, καὶ τὸ ἑαυτοῦ σωστικὸν τελειότερον ἢ τὸ ὑπ' ἄλλου μόνον σωζόμενον. εἰ ἄρα τι κατ' ἐνέργειάν ἐστι τὴν ἀπὸ τῆς οὐσίας πρὸς ἑαυτὸ ἐπιστρεπτικόν, καὶ τὴν οὐσίαν ἐπιστρε-πτικὴν ἔλαχεν, ὡς μὴ ἐνεργεῖν πρὸς ἑαυτὸ μόνον, ἀλλὰ καὶ 10 ἑαυτοῦ εἶναι καὶ ὑφ' ἑαυτοῦ συνέχεσθαι καὶ τελειοῦσθαι.

45. Πᾶν τὸ αὐθυπόστατον ἀγένητόν ἐστιν.

εἰ γὰρ γενητόν, διότι μὲν γενητόν, ἀτελὲς ἔσται καθ' ἑαυτὸ καὶ τῆς ἀπ' ἄλλου τελειώσεως ἐνδεές· διότι δὲ αὐτὸ ἑαυτὸ παράγει, τέλειον καὶ αὔταρκες. πᾶν γὰρ γενητὸν ὑπ' ἄλλου 15 τελειοῦται τοῦ παρέχοντος αὐτῷ γένεσιν οὐκ ὄντι· καὶ γὰρ ἡ γένεσις ὁδός ἐστιν ἐκ τοῦ ἀτελοῦς εἰς τὸ ἐναντίον τέλειον. εἰ δ' ἑαυτό τι παράγει, τέλειον ἀεί ἐστιν, ἀεὶ τῇ ἑαυτοῦ αἰτίᾳ συνόν, μᾶλλον δὲ ἐνυπάρχον, πρὸς τὸ τῆς οὐσίας τελειωτικόν.

46. Πᾶν τὸ αὐθυπόστατον ἄφθαρτόν ἐστιν. 20

εἰ γὰρ φθαρήσεται, ἀπολείψει ἑαυτὸ καὶ ἔσται ἑαυτοῦ χωρίς. ἀλλὰ τοῦτο ἀδύνατον. ἓν γὰρ ὄν, ἅμα καὶ αἴτιόν ἐστι καὶ αἰτιατόν. πᾶν δὲ τὸ φθειρόμενον ἀποστὰν τῆς ἑαυτοῦ αἰτίας φθείρεται· ἐν ὅσῳ γὰρ ἂν ἐξέχηται τοῦ συνέχοντος αὐτὸ καὶ σώζοντος, ἕκαστον συνέχεται καὶ σώζεται. οὐδέποτε δὲ ἀπο- 25 λείπει τὴν αἰτίαν τὸ αὐθυπόστατον, ἅτε ἑαυτὸ οὐκ ἀπολεῖπον· αἴτιον γὰρ αὐτὸ ἑαυτῷ ἐστιν. ἄφθαρτον ἄρα ἐστὶ τὸ αὐθυπό-στατον πᾶν.

47. Πᾶν τὸ αὐθυπόστατον ἀμερές ἐστι καὶ ἁπλοῦν.

εἰ γὰρ μεριστόν, αὐθυπόστατον ὄν, ὑποστήσει μεριστὸν ἑαυτό, 30 καὶ ὅλον αὐτὸ στραφήσεται πρὸς ἑαυτὸ καὶ πᾶν ἐν παντὶ ἑαυτῷ ἔσται. τοῦτο δὲ ἀδύνατον. ἀμερὲς ἄρα τὸ αὐθυπόστατον. ἀλλὰ μὴν καὶ ἁπλοῦν. εἰ γὰρ σύνθετον, τὸ μὲν χεῖρον ἔσται ἐν αὐτῷ, τὸ δὲ βέλτιον, καὶ τό τε βέλτιον ἐκ τοῦ χείρονος ἔσται

44. 3 δύναται BC : δύναιτο DMPQ, posset W   4 ὑπάρχει M et ? C
7 σωματικόν C et ? [M]   11 prius καί] ὡς PQ : non agnosc. W
45. 13 ἔστι PQ   14 ἀπ' ἄλλου ω (ὑπ' ἄλλου edd.)   17–18 δ' ἑαυτό τι
BD : δὲ αὐτό τι CMPQ   18 αἰτίᾳ] οὐσίᾳ [M]
46. 24 γάρ non agnosc. W   ἐξέχεται Ο (edd.)   26 ἅτε ἑαυτό BCD :
ἅτε αὐτό PQ : ἅτε ἑαυτοῦ M   27 αὐτὸ ἑαυτῷ BCDMW : αὐτὸ ἑαυτῶν Q, αὐτὸ
ἑαυτόν P
47. 31 αὐτό om. PQ   στραφήσεται BCDM, vertetur W : ἐπιστραφήσεται PQ
34 τε om. PQ

PROP. **44**. *All that is capable in its activity of reversion upon itself is also reverted upon itself in respect of its existence.*

For if, being capable of reversion upon itself in its activity, it were not reversive in its existence, its activity would be superior to its existence, the former being reversive, the latter not : inasmuch as what belongs to itself is superior to that which belongs wholly to another, and what conserves itself is more complete than that which is conserved wholly by another (prop. 9). If, then, anything is capable of reversion upon itself in respect of the activity which proceeds from its existence, its existence is likewise reversive, so that it not only has an activity directed upon itself but also belongs to itself and is by itself contained and perfected.

PROP. **45**. *All that is self-constituted is without temporal origin.*

For if it have an origin, *qua* originated it will be in itself incomplete and need the perfective operation of another, whereas *qua* self-produced it is complete and self-sufficient. For all that has an origin is perfected by another, which brings into being that which as yet is not, since coming-to-be is a process leading from incompleteness to the opposite completeness. But whatever produces itself is perpetually complete, being perpetually conjoined with—or rather, immanent in—its cause, which is the principle that perfects its being.

PROP. **46**. *All that is self-constituted is imperishable.*

For if it be destined to perish, it will then desert itself and be severed from itself. But this is impossible. For being one, it is at once cause and effect. Now whatever perishes is in perishing severed from its cause : for each thing is held together and conserved so long as it is linked with a principle which contains and conserves it. But the self-constituted, being its own cause, never deserts its cause since it never deserts itself. Therefore all that is self-constituted is imperishable.

PROP. **47**. *All that is self-constituted is without parts and simple.*

For if, being self-constituted, it yet have parts, it will constitute itself as a divisible principle ; and it will be reverted upon itself in its entirety, so that every part will be immanent in every other : which is impossible. The self-constituted is therefore without parts.

Again, it is simple. For if it be composite, there will be a worse and a better part in it ; and the better will be derived from the

καὶ τὸ χεῖρον ἐκ τοῦ βελτίονος, εἴπερ ὅλον ἀφ᾽ ὅλου ἑαυτοῦ
πρόεισιν· ἔτι δὲ οὐκ αὔταρκες, προσδεὲς ὂν τῶν ἑαυτοῦ στοιχείων, ἐξ ὧν ὑφέστηκεν. ἁπλοῦν ἄρα ἐστὶ πᾶν ὅπερ ἂν
αὐθυπόστατον ᾖ.

48. Πᾶν τὸ μὴ ἀΐδιον ἢ σύνθετόν ἐστιν, ἢ ἐν ἄλλῳ ὑφέστη- 5
κεν.

ἢ γὰρ διαλυτόν ἐστιν εἰς ταῦτα ἐξ ὧν ἐστι, καὶ πάντως
σύγκειται ἐξ ἐκείνων εἰς ἃ διαλύεται· ἢ ὑποκειμένου δεόμενον,
καὶ ἀπολεῖπον τὸ ὑποκείμενον οἴχεται εἰς τὸ μὴ ὄν. εἰ δὲ
ἁπλοῦν εἴη καὶ ἐν ἑαυτῷ, ἀδιάλυτον ἔσται καὶ ἀσκέδαστον. 10

49. Πᾶν τὸ αὐθυπόστατον ἀΐδιόν ἐστι.

δύο γάρ εἰσι τρόποι, καθ᾽ οὓς ἀνάγκη τι μὴ ἀΐδιον εἶναι, ὅ τε
ἀπὸ τῆς συνθέσεως καὶ ὁ ἀπὸ τῶν ἐν ἄλλῳ ὄντων. τὸ δὲ αὐθυπόστατον οὔτε σύνθετόν ἐστιν, ἀλλ᾽ ἁπλοῦν· οὔτε ἐν ἄλλῳ, ἀλλ᾽
ἐν ἑαυτῷ. ἀΐδιον ἄρα ἐστίν. 15

50. Πᾶν τὸ χρόνῳ μετρούμενον ἢ κατὰ τὴν οὐσίαν ἢ κατὰ
τὴν ἐνέργειαν γένεσίς ἐστι ταύτῃ, ᾗ μετρεῖται κατὰ χρόνον.

εἰ γὰρ ὑπὸ χρόνου μετρεῖται, προσήκοι ἂν αὐτῷ τὸ κατὰ
χρόνον εἶναι ἢ ἐνεργεῖν, καὶ τὸ ἦν καὶ τὸ ἔσται διαφέροντα
ἀλλήλων· εἰ γὰρ ταὐτὸν κατὰ ἀριθμὸν τὸ ἦν καὶ τὸ ἔσται, 20
οὐδὲν ὑπὸ χρόνου πέπονθε πορευομένου καὶ ἀεὶ ἄλλο τὸ πρότερον
ἔχοντος καὶ τὸ ὕστερον. εἰ οὖν ἄλλο τὸ ἦν καὶ ἄλλο τὸ ἔσται,
γινόμενον ἄρα ἐστὶ καὶ οὐδέποτε ὄν, ἀλλὰ τῷ χρόνῳ συμπορεύε-
ται, ὑφ᾽ οὗ μετρεῖται, ἐν τῷ γίνεσθαι ὂν καὶ οὐχ ἱστάμενον ἐν
τῷ αὐτῷ εἶναι, ἀλλ᾽ ἀεὶ δεχόμενον τὸ εἶναι ἄλλο καὶ ἄλλο, ὡς 25
τὸ νῦν κατὰ τὸν χρόνον ἄλλο ἀεὶ καὶ ἄλλο διὰ τὴν τοῦ χρόνου
πορείαν. οὐχ ἅμα ἄρα ὅλον ἐστίν, ἐν τῷ σκιδναμένῳ τῆς
χρονικῆς παρατάσεως ὄν, καὶ συνεκτεινόμενον· τοῦτο δέ ἐστιν
ἐν τῷ μὴ εἶναι τὸ εἶναι ἔχειν· τὸ γὰρ γινόμενον ὃ γίνεται οὐκ
ἔστι. γένεσις ἄρα ἐστὶ τὸ οὕτως ὄν. 30

47. 2 ἔτι δὲ οὐκ ex corr. M², ἔτι δὲ ἢ Arg 3 ἔσται M ἄν PQ : om. BCDM
48. Tit. περὶ ἀϊδίου, πρὸς τὸ δεῖξαι, ὅτι ἀΐδιος ὁ κόσμος DM 5 πᾶν τὸ μὴ
ἀΐδιον om. W (novum caput non indicat β) : spatium rel. a, quod ita expleverunt,
videlicet e coniectura, βγ :—Omne antipostaton (*lege* authupostaton) indissolubile
(solubile est γ) et indispergibile. Si enim dissolubile vel dispergibile est [erit antipostaton—vel sic : omne antipostaton in se ipso indissolubile et indispergibile
est—] (uncis quadratis inclusa om. γ) : apographa recentiora alia aliter 10 ἐν
αὐτῷ BCD ἀδιάλυτόν τε ἔσται M
49. 12 τι] τίς PQ 13 καὶ ὁ ἀπό BCD, et qui ab W : καὶ ἀπό MPQ
ἄλλῳ] ἄλλων ? [M]
50. Tit. περὶ χρόνου καὶ τῶν κατὰ χρόνον M 16 τό] τῷ [M] 18 ὑπὸ
τοῦ χρόνου P προσήκει [M] τό om. M 22 τὸ ὕστερον PQ, quod
posterius W : ὕστερον BCDM 25 ἄλλο καί] ἄλλοτε PQ 27 οὐκ ἄρα
ἅμα PQ 28 παρατάσεως M 29 ἐν τῷ μὴ εἶναι om. BCD ᾖ] quando
a et suprascr. β : om. γ 29–30 οὐκ ἔστι ex corr. M¹ vel M²

worse as well as the worse from the better, since it proceeds from itself as a whole from a whole. Further, it will not be self-sufficient, since it will need its own elements, out of which it is composed. Therefore all that is self-constituted is simple.

PROP. **48**. *All that is not perpetual either is composite or has its sub-sistence in another.*

For either it is dissoluble into elements (and if so, it is necessarily composite of those elements); or else it needs a substrate, and passes into non-existence by abandoning that substrate. If it were simple and existed in itself, it would be subject neither to dissolution nor to dispersion.

PROP. **49**. *All that is self-constituted is perpetual.*

For anything which is not perpetual must be so in one of two ways, either as being composite or as existing in another (prop. 48). But the self-constituted is simple, not composite (prop. 47), and exists in itself, not in another (prop. 41). It is therefore perpetual.

PROP. **50**. *All that is measured by time either in its existence or in its activity is in process of coming-to-be in that respect in which it is measured by time.*

For if it is measured by time, it must have a temporal existence or activity, and a past and a future which are mutually distinct; since if its past and its future be numerically identical, it is un-affected by the passage of time, which always contains a distinguish-able 'earlier' and 'later'. If, then, its past and its future are distinct, it is something which becomes and never is, but moves with the movement of the time which measures it; it exists in becoming and is not steadfast in its own essence, but continually admits of being one thing and then another, as the temporal 'now' is different in every moment by reason of the passage of time. Accordingly it does not exist as a simultaneous whole; for it has the dispersed existence of temporal duration, and is extended with extending time: that is, it has its being in not-being; for what is coming-to-be is not the thing which it is becoming. Therefore what exists in this way is in process of coming-to-be.

51. Πᾶν τὸ αὐθυπόστατον ἐξῄρηται τῶν ὑπὸ χρόνου μετρουμένων κατὰ τὴν οὐσίαν.

εἰ γὰρ ἀγένητόν ἐστι τὸ αὐθυπόστατον, οὐκ ἂν ὑπὸ χρόνου
κατὰ τὸ εἶναι μετροῖτο· γένεσις γὰρ περὶ τὴν ὑπὸ χρόνου
μετρουμένην φύσιν ἐστίν. οὐδὲν ἄρα τῶν αὐθυποστάτων ἐν 5
χρόνῳ ὑφέστηκεν.

52. Πᾶν τὸ αἰώνιον ὅλον ἅμα ἐστίν· εἴτε τὴν οὐσίαν ἔχει
μόνον αἰώνιον, ὅλην ἅμα παροῦσαν αὐτὴν ἔχον, καὶ οὐ τὸ μὲν
αὐτῆς ὑποστὰν ἤδη, τὸ δὲ εἰσαῦθις ὑποστησόμενον, ὃ μήπω
ἔστιν, ἀλλ' ὁπόσον εἶναι δύναται, τοσοῦτον ὅλον ἤδη κεκτημένον 10
ἀνελαττώτως καὶ ἀνεπιτάτως· εἴτε τὴν ἐνέργειαν πρὸς τῇ
οὐσίᾳ, καὶ ταύτην ἀθρόαν ἔχον καὶ ἐν τῷ αὐτῷ μέτρῳ τῆς
τελειότητος ἑστηκυῖαν καὶ οἷον παγεῖσαν καθ' ἕνα καὶ τὸν αὐτὸν
ὅρον ἀκινήτως καὶ ἀμεταβάτως.

εἰ γὰρ αἰώνιόν ἐστιν (ὡς καὶ τοὔνομα ἐμφαίνει) τὸ ἀεὶ ὄν, τὸ 15
δὲ ποτὲ εἶναι καὶ τὸ γίνεσθαι ἕτερον τοῦ ἀεὶ ὄντος, οὐ δεῖ τὸ
μὲν πρότερον εἶναι, τὸ δὲ ὕστερον· γένεσις γὰρ ἔσται, καὶ οὐκ
ὄν. ὅπου δὲ μήτε τὸ πρότερον καὶ ὕστερον μήτε τὸ ἦν καὶ τὸ
ἔσται, ἀλλὰ τὸ εἶναι μόνον ὅ ἐστιν, ὅλον ἅμα ἐστὶν ἕκαστον ὅ
ἐστι.   τὸ δὲ αὐτὸ καὶ ἐπὶ τοῦ ἐνεργεῖν.   20

ἐκ δὴ τούτου φανερὸν ὅτι τοῦ ὅλοις εἶναι ὁ αἰὼν αἴτιος, εἴπερ
πᾶν τὸ αἰώνιον ἢ κατ' οὐσίαν ἢ κατ' ἐνέργειαν ὅλην ἅμα τὴν
οὐσίαν ἢ τὴν ἐνέργειαν ἔχει παροῦσαν αὐτῷ.

53. Πάντων τῶν αἰωνίων προϋπάρχει ὁ αἰών, καὶ πάντων
τῶν κατὰ χρόνον ὁ χρόνος προϋφέστηκεν.   25

εἰ γὰρ πανταχοῦ πρὸ τῶν μετεχόντων ἔστι τὰ μετεχόμενα
καὶ πρὸ τῶν μετεχομένων τὰ ἀμέθεκτα, δῆλον ὅτι ἄλλο μὲν τὸ
αἰώνιον, ἄλλο δὲ ὁ ἐν τῷ αἰωνίῳ αἰών, ἄλλο δὲ ὁ καθ' αὐτὸν
αἰών, τὸ μὲν ὡς μετέχον, τὸ δὲ ὡς μετεχόμενον, ὁ δὲ ὡς ἀμέθ-
εκτος· καὶ τὸ ἔγχρονον ἄλλο (μετέχον γάρ), καὶ ὁ ἐν τούτῳ 30
χρόνος ἄλλος (μετεχόμενος γάρ), καὶ ὁ πρὸ τούτου χρόνος,

51. 4 περί BCDM : παρά PQ
52. Tit. τί ἐστιν αἰώνιον ; M   7 ἔχοι M, ἔχον Arg   8 μόνον MQW :
μόνην BCDP (ante ἔχει legit C)   10 κεκρατημένον BCD   11 ἀνεπιτάττως
PQM², sine ordine W   εἴτε καί BCD   11-12 πρὸς τὴν οὐσίαν CM²   12 alt.
καί ω (om. O edd.)   13 τελειότητος] ἡλικίας PQ   alt. καί om. MPQ
14 ἀκινήτως] ἀμετακινήτως PQ   16 ποτέ BCD : om. MPQW   prius τό
om. PQ   τοῦ ἀεὶ ὄντος ἑτέρου PQ   18 tert. τό om. PQ   21 τοῦ] τοῖς [M]
22 τό om. PQ   23 ἐν ἑαυτῷ PQ
53. Tit. περὶ αἰῶνος καὶ τῶν αἰωνίων M   28 prius ὁ om. P, post αἰωνίῳ transp. Q
καθ' αὐτό M¹PQ   29 μετασχόν PQ   29-30 τὸ δὲ ὡς ἀμέθεκτον PQ, hoc
autem ut imparticipabile W   30 τὸ ἔγχρονον BCD² : τὸ ἐν χρόνῳ MPQ et
fort. D¹, quod in tempore W   ἐν τούτῳ] τούτου PQ   31 ἄλλο· μετεχόμενον [M]P

PROP. 51. *All that is self-constituted transcends the things which are measured by time in respect of their existence.*

For if the self-constituted is without temporal origin (prop. 45), it cannot be measured by time in respect of its being; for coming-to-be is predicated of everything that is measured by time (prop. 50). Nothing, therefore, which is self-constituted has its subsistence in time.

F. OF TIME AND ETERNITY.

PROP. 52. *All that is eternal is a simultaneous whole.*

If its existence alone be eternal, that existence is simultaneously present in its entirety; there is not one part of it which has already emerged and another which will emerge later, but as yet is not; all that it is capable of being it already possesses in entirety, without diminution and without serial extension. If its activity be eternal in addition to its existence, this too is simultaneously entire, steadfast in an unvarying measure of completeness and as it were frozen in one unchanging outline, without movement or transition.

For if the 'eternal' (*aionion*) means, as the word itself shows, that which always is (*aei on*), as distinct from temporary existence or coming-to-be, then its parts cannot be distinguished as earlier and later; otherwise it will be a process of coming-to-be, not something which is (prop. 50). And where there is neither an earlier nor a later, neither a 'was' nor a 'will be', but only a being what it is, there each thing is simultaneously the whole of what it is. A like argument applies to activity.

Cor. From this it is apparent that eternity is the cause of things existing as wholes, inasmuch as all that is eternal in its existence or in its activity has the whole of its existence or activity simultaneously present to it.

PROP. 53. *Prior to all things eternal there exists Eternity; and prior to all things temporal, Time.*

For if everywhere participated principles exist before the participants, and unparticipated principles before the participated (prop. 23), it is plain that an eternal thing is distinct from its eternity, and both these from Eternity in itself, the first being a participant, the second participated, the third unparticipated; and again that a temporal thing, which is a participant, is distinguished from its time, which is participated, and this in turn from a more primitive unpar-

ἀμέθεκτος ὤν. καὶ τούτων μὲν ἑκάτερος τῶν ἀμεθέκτων πανταχοῦ καὶ ἐν πᾶσιν ὁ αὐτός· ὁ δὲ μετεχόμενος ἐν ἐκείνοις μόνον, ὑφ' ὧν μετέχεται.   πολλὰ γὰρ καὶ τὰ αἰώνια καὶ τὰ ἔγχρονα, ἐν οἷς πᾶσιν αἰών ἐστι κατὰ μέθεξιν καὶ χρόνος διῃρημένος· ὁ δὲ ἀδιαίρετος αἰὼν καὶ ὁ εἷς χρόνος πρὸ τούτων, καὶ ὁ μὲν 5 αἰὼν αἰώνων, ὁ δὲ χρόνων χρόνος, τῶν μετεχομένων ὄντες ὑποστάται.

54. Πᾶς αἰὼν μέτρον ἐστὶ τῶν αἰωνίων, καὶ πᾶς χρόνος τῶν ἐν χρόνῳ· καὶ δύο ταῦτα μέτρα μόνα ἐστὶν ἐν τοῖς οὖσι τῆς ζωῆς καὶ τῆς κινήσεως.   10

πᾶν γὰρ τὸ μετροῦν ἢ κατὰ μέρος μετρεῖ ἢ ὅλον ἅμα ἐφαρμοσθὲν τῷ μετρουμένῳ. τὸ μὲν οὖν καθ' ὅλον μετροῦν αἰών ἐστι, τὸ δὲ κατὰ μέρη χρόνος· δύο ἄρα μόνα τὰ μέτρα, τὸ μὲν τῶν αἰωνίων, τὸ δὲ τῶν ἐν χρόνῳ ὄντων.

55. Πᾶν τὸ κατὰ χρόνον ὑφεστὸς ἢ τὸν ἀεὶ χρόνον ἔστιν ἢ 15 ποτὲ ἐν μέρει χρόνου τὴν ὑπόστασιν κεκτημένον.

εἰ γὰρ αἱ πρόοδοι πᾶσαι δι' ὁμοιότητός εἰσι, καὶ πρὸ τῶν πάντῃ ἀνομοίων συνεχῆ τοῖς πρώτοις ὑφίσταται τὰ ὅμοια πρὸς αὐτὰ μᾶλλον ὄντα ἢ ἀνόμοια, τοῖς δὲ αἰωνίοις συνάπτειν τὰ ἐν μέρει χρόνου γινόμενα ἀδύνατον (καὶ γὰρ ὡς γινόμενα ἐκείνων 20 ὄντων καὶ ὡς ποτὲ τῶν ἀεὶ ὑφεστηκότων διέστηκε), μέσα δὲ τούτων τε καὶ ἐκείνων ἐστὶ τὰ πῇ μὲν ὅμοια ἐκείνοις, πῇ δὲ ἀνόμοια, οὐκοῦν τῶν ποτὲ γινομένων καὶ τῶν ἀεὶ ὄντων μέσον ἢ τὸ ἀεὶ γινόμενον ἢ τὸ ποτὲ ὄν—τοῦτο δέ ἐστιν ἢ τὸ ποτὲ οὐκ ὄντως ὂν ἢ τὸ ποτὲ ὄντως ὄν. ἀλλὰ τὸ ποτὲ ὄντως ὂν ἀδύνατον 25 εἶναι, τὸ δὲ ποτὲ οὐκ ὄντως ὂν τῷ γινομένῳ ταὐτόν· οὐκ ἄρα μέσον τὸ ποτὲ ὄν. λείπεται ἄρα τὸ ἀεὶ γινόμενον εἶναι τὸ μέσον ἀμφοῖν, τῷ μὲν γίνεσθαι συνάπτον τοῖς χείροσι, τῷ δὲ ἀεὶ μιμούμενον τὴν αἰώνιον φύσιν.

ἐκ δὴ τούτων φανερὸν ὅτι διττὴ ἦν ἡ ἀϊδιότης, αἰώνιος μὲν 30 ἄλλη, κατὰ χρόνον δὲ ἄλλη· ἡ μὲν ἑστῶσα ἀϊδιότης, ἡ δὲ γινομένη· καὶ ἡ μὲν ἠθροισμένον ἔχουσα τὸ εἶναι καὶ ὁμοῦ πᾶν,

53. 1 ἑκάτερος ἐκ τῶν M   3 τὰ ἔγχρονα BCDM, temporalia W : τὰ ἐν χρόνῳ PQ   4 πᾶσιν MPQW : πᾶσι καί BCD   διῃρημένως M   5 αἰών] ὤν M²
6 χρόνος χρόνων PQArg, tempus . . . temporum W
54. 8–9 τῶν ἐν χρόνῳ] temporalium W   9 μόνα BCD : μόνον MPQ, solum W   τῆς om. BCD   12 καθόλου M   13 κατὰ μέρος PQ   μόνον PQ
55.¹ 15 ὑφεστός M : ὑφεστώς cett.   22 τε om. BCD   24 ποτὲ ὂν τοῦτο δέ ἐστιν ἢ τό BCD : om. PQ : τοῦτο δέ ἐστιν om. MW   alt. ποτέ PQ : om. BCDMW   25 primum ὄν om. M¹, non agnosc. W   27 post ποτέ ins. οὐκ ὄντως PQ   28 alt. τῷ] τό M   29 αἰωνίαν PQ, eternorum W   30 ἦν om. PQ, non agnosc. W   αἰώνια PQ   31 ἡ ἀϊδιότης M

ticipated Time. Each of these unparticipated terms is identically present everywhere and in all members of its order (prop. 19), while the participated term exists only in those members which participate it. For the eternal things are many, and likewise the temporal: all the former have an eternity by participation, all the latter a time which is parcelled out. But prior to these are the undivided Eternity and the one Time; these are the Eternity of eternities and the Time of times, since they generate the participated terms.

PROP. **54.** *Every eternity is a measure of things eternal, and every time of things in time; and these two are the only measures of life and movement in things.*

For any measure must measure either piecemeal or by simultaneous application of the whole measure to the thing measured. That which measures by the whole is eternity; that which measures by parts, time. There are thus two measures only, one of eternal things, the other of things in time.

PROP. **55.** *Of things which exist in time, some have a perpetual duration, whilst others have a dated existence in a part of time.*

For if all procession is through likeness (prop. 29), and the first term of any series is immediately succeeded by terms which are like it rather than unlike, the wholly unlike having a lower station (prop. 28); and if it is impossible to attach directly to the eternals things which come-to-be in a part of time (since the latter are doubly distinguished from the former, both as things in process from things which are and as dated from perpetual existences), so that there must be an intermediate order which resembles the eternals in one respect but differs from them in the other: then the mean between things which come-to-be for a time and things which perpetually are is either that which perpetually comes-to-be or that which is for a time. Now 'that which is for a time' may refer either to a temporary being which is not fully real or to a temporary true being. But no true being can be temporary; and temporary being which is not fully real is one with coming-to-be. Therefore 'that which is for a time' is not the mean. It remains that the mean is that which perpetually comes-to-be: which in virtue of its coming-to-be is attached to the inferior order, while in its perpetuity it imitates the eternal nature.

Cor. From this it is apparent that the perpetuity we spoke of (props. 48, 49) was of two kinds, the one eternal, the other in time; the one a perpetual steadfastness, the other a perpetual process; the one having its existence concentrated in a simultaneous whole, the

ἡ δὲ ἐκχυθεῖσα καὶ ἐξαπλωθεῖσα κατὰ τὴν χρονικὴν παράτασιν·
καὶ ἡ μὲν ὅλη καθ' αὑτήν, ἡ δὲ ἐκ μερῶν, ὧν ἕκαστον χωρίς
ἐστι κατὰ τὸ πρότερον καὶ ὕστερον.

56. Πᾶν τὸ ὑπὸ τῶν δευτέρων παραγόμενον καὶ ἀπὸ τῶν
προτέρων καὶ αἰτιωτέρων παράγεται μειζόνως, ἀφ' ὧν καὶ τὰ 5
δεύτερα παρήγετο.

εἰ γὰρ τὸ δεύτερον ὅλην ἔχει τὴν οὐσίαν ἀπὸ τοῦ πρὸ αὐτοῦ,
καὶ ἡ δύναμις αὐτῷ τοῦ παράγειν ἐκεῖθεν· καὶ γὰρ αἱ δυνάμεις
αἱ παρακτικαὶ κατ' οὐσίαν εἰσὶν ἐν τοῖς παράγουσι, καὶ συμπλη-
ροῦσιν αὐτῶν τὴν οὐσίαν. εἰ δὲ τὴν τοῦ παράγειν δύναμιν ἀπὸ τῆς 10
ὑπερκειμένης αἰτίας ἔλαχε, παρ' ἐκείνης ἔχει τὸ εἶναι αἴτιον ὧν
ἐστιν αἴτιον, μετρηθὲν ἐκεῖθεν κατὰ τὴν ὑποστατικὴν δύναμιν. εἰ
δὲ τοῦτο, καὶ τὰ ἀπ' αὐτοῦ προϊόντα αἰτιατά ἐστι διὰ τὸ πρὸ αὐτοῦ·
τὸ γὰρ θάτερον ἀποτελέσαν αἴτιον καὶ θάτερον αἰτιατὸν ἀποτελεῖ. εἰ δὲ τοῦτο, καὶ τὸ αἰτιατὸν ἐκεῖθεν ἀποτελεῖται τοιοῦτον. 15
ἀλλὰ μὴν ὅτι καὶ μειζόνως ἐκεῖθεν, δῆλον. εἰ γὰρ τὴν
αἰτίαν τῷ δευτέρῳ τοῦ παράγειν αὐτὸ δέδωκεν, εἶχεν ἄρα
πρώτως ταύτην τὴν αἰτίαν, καὶ διὰ τοῦτο καὶ τὸ δεύτερον γεννᾷ,
τὴν τοῦ δευτέρως γεννᾶν δύναμιν ἐκεῖθεν λαβόν. εἰ δὲ τὸ μὲν
κατὰ μέθεξιν ἐγένετο παρακτικόν, τὸ δὲ κατὰ μετάδοσιν καὶ 20
πρώτως, μειζόνως αἴτιον ἐκεῖνο τὸ καὶ ἄλλῳ τῆς γεννητικῆς τῶν
ἐφεξῆς δυνάμεως μεταδεδωκός.

57. Πᾶν αἴτιον καὶ πρὸ τοῦ αἰτιατοῦ ἐνεργεῖ καὶ μετ' αὐτὸ
πλειόνων ἐστὶν ὑποστατικόν.

εἰ γάρ ἐστιν αἴτιον, τελειότερόν ἐστι καὶ δυνατώτερον τοῦ 25
μετ' αὐτό. καὶ εἰ τοῦτο, πλειόνων αἴτιον· δυνάμεως γὰρ μείζονος
τὸ πλείω παράγειν, ἴσης δὲ τὰ ἴσα, καὶ τῆς ἐλάττονος ἐλάττω·
καὶ ἡ μὲν τὰ μείζονα ἐν τοῖς ὁμοίοις δυναμένη δύναμις καὶ τὰ
ἐλάττονα δύναται, ἡ δὲ τὰ ἐλάττονα δυναμένη οὐκ ἐξ ἀνάγκης
τὰ μείζω δυνήσεται. εἰ οὖν δυνατώτερον τὸ αἴτιον, πλειόνων 30
ἐστὶ παρακτικόν.

ἀλλὰ μὴν καὶ ὅσα δύναται τὸ αἰτιατόν, μειζόνως ἐκεῖνο

55. 3 τό om. M¹
56. 9 αἱ om. M   10 ἑαυτῶν BCD   alt. τήν om. M¹   13 καί
ante τοῦτο ins. M   14 ἀποτελέσαν ω (ἀποτελέσαι edd.)   17 τῷ δευτέρῳ
post αὐτό transp. Arg   αὐτό BDE et ?[M], ipsum W : αὐτῷ CPQM²
18 ταύτην BCDM : αὐτήν PQ, ipsam W   ἐγέννα M¹W   19 δευτέρως DE :
δεύτερον MW : δευτέρου BCPQ   21 ἄλλῳ CDEM : ἄλλο B : τοῖς ἄλλοις Q,
aliis W : τῆς ἄλλης P   τῶν PQ : τῷ BCDMW
57. 23 post ἐνεργεῖ fort. inserendum καὶ σὺν αὐτῷ   μετ' αὐτοῦ PQ
25 εἰ BCD : ἢ MPQW   26 εἰ] εἰς M primitus   27 τὸ πλείω PQ : πλείω
BCDM (sed cf. c. 7, l. 13)   δὲ καὶ τά BCD   30 καὶ τὰ μείζω PQ   32 καί ω
(om. edd.)

other diffused and unfolded in temporal extension; the one entire in itself, the other composed of parts each of which exists separately in an order of succession.

G. OF THE GRADES OF CAUSALITY.

PROP. 56. *All that is produced by secondary beings is in a greater measure produced from those prior and more determinative principles from which the secondary were themselves derived.*

For if the secondary has its whole existence from its prior, thence also it receives its power of further production, since productive powers reside in producers in virtue of their existence and form part of their being. But if it owes to the superior cause its power of production, to that superior it owes its character as a cause in so far as it is a cause, a character meted out to it from thence in proportion to its constitutive capacity. If so, the things which proceed from it are caused in virtue of its prior; for the same principle which makes the one a cause makes the other an effect. If so, the effect owes to the superior cause its character as an effect.

Again, it is evident that the effect is determined by the superior principle in a greater measure. For if the latter has conferred on the secondary being the causality which enabled it to produce, it must itself have possessed this causality primitively (prop. 18), and it is in virtue of this that the secondary being generates, having derived from its prior the capacity of secondary generation. But if the secondary is productive by participation, the primal primitively and by communication, the latter is causative in a greater measure, inasmuch as it has communicated to another the power of generating consequents.

PROP. 57. *Every cause both operates prior to its consequent and gives rise to a greater number of posterior terms.*

For if it is a cause, it is more perfect and more powerful than its consequent (prop. 7). And if so, it must cause a greater number of effects: for greater power produces more effects, equal power, equal effects, and lesser power, fewer; and the power which can produce the greater effects upon a like subject can produce also the lesser, whereas a power capable of the lesser will not necessarily be capable of the greater. If, then, the cause is more powerful than its consequent, it is productive of a greater number of effects.

But again, the powers which are in the consequent are present in a greater measure in the cause. For all that is produced by secondary

δύναται. πᾶν γὰρ τὸ ὑπὸ τῶν δευτέρων παραγόμενον ὑπὸ τῶν
προτέρων καὶ αἰτιωτέρων παράγεται μειζόνως. συνυφίστησιν
ἄρα αὐτῷ πάντα ὅσα πέφυκε παράγειν.

εἰ δὲ καὶ αὐτὸ πρότερον παράγει, δῆλον δήπουθεν ὅτι πρὸ
αὐτοῦ ἐνεργεῖ κατὰ τὴν παρακτικὴν αὐτοῦ ἐνέργειαν. ἅπαν 5
ἄρα αἴτιον καὶ πρὸ τοῦ αἰτιατοῦ ἐνεργεῖ καὶ σὺν αὐτῷ καὶ μετ'
αὐτὸ ἄλλα ὑφίστησιν.

ἐκ δὴ τούτων φανερὸν ὅτι ὅσων μὲν αἰτία ψυχή, καὶ νοῦς
αἴτιος, οὐχ ὅσων δὲ νοῦς, καὶ ψυχὴ αἰτία· ἀλλὰ καὶ πρὸ ψυχῆς
ἐνεργεῖ, καὶ ἃ δίδωσι ψυχὴ τοῖς δευτέροις, δίδωσι καὶ νοῦς μει- 10
ζόνως, καὶ μηκέτι ψυχῆς ἐνεργούσης νοῦς ἐλλάμπει τὰς ἑαυτοῦ
δόσεις, οἷς μὴ δέδωκε ψυχὴ ἑαυτήν· καὶ γὰρ τὸ ἄψυχον, καθόσον
εἴδους μετέσχε, νοῦ μετέχει καὶ τῆς τοῦ νοῦ ποιήσεως.

καὶ δὴ καὶ ὅσων νοῦς αἴτιος, καὶ τὸ ἀγαθὸν αἴτιον· οὐκ
ἔμπαλιν δέ. καὶ γὰρ αἱ στερήσεις τῶν εἰδῶν ἐκεῖθεν (πάντα γὰρ 15
ἐκεῖθεν)· νοῦς δὲ στερήσεως ὑποστάτης οὐκ ἔστιν, εἶδος ὤν.

58. Πᾶν τὸ ὑπὸ πλειόνων αἰτίων παραγόμενον συνθετώτερόν
ἐστι τοῦ ὑπὸ ἐλαττόνων παραγομένου.

εἰ γὰρ πᾶν αἴτιον δίδωσί τι τῷ ἀπ' αὐτοῦ προϊόντι, τὰ μὲν
πλείονα αἴτια πλείονας ποιήσεται τὰς δόσεις, τὰ δὲ ἐλάττονα 20
ἐλάττους. ὥστε καὶ τῶν μετασχόντων τὰ μὲν ἐκ πλειόνων
ἔσται, τὰ δὲ ἐξ ἐλαττόνων, ὧν ἑκάτερα μετέσχε, τὰ μὲν διὰ τὴν
ἐκ πλειόνων αἰτίων πρόοδον, τὰ δὲ διὰ τὴν ἐκ τῶν ἐλαττόνων.
τὰ δὲ ἐκ πλειόνων συνθετώτερα, τὰ δὲ ἐξ ἐλαττόνων τῶν αὐτῶν
ἁπλούστερα. πᾶν ἄρα τὸ ὑπὸ πλειόνων αἰτίων παραγόμενον 25
συνθετώτερον, τὸ δὲ ὑπὸ ἐλαττόνων ἁπλούστερον· ὧν γὰρ θάτερον
μετέχει, καὶ θάτερον· ἀλλ' οὐκ ἔμπαλιν.

59. Πᾶν τὸ ἁπλοῦν κατ' οὐσίαν ἢ κρεῖττόν ἐστι τῶν συνθέτων ἢ χεῖρον.

εἰ γὰρ τὰ ἄκρα τῶν ὄντων ὑπὸ ἐλαττόνων καὶ ἁπλουστέρων 30
παράγεται, τὰ δὲ μέσα ὑπὸ πλειόνων, ταῦτα μὲν ἔσται σύνθετα,
τὰ δὲ ἄκρα τὰ μὲν κατὰ τὸ κρεῖττον ἁπλούστερα, τὰ δὲ κατὰ
τὸ χεῖρον. ἀλλὰ μὴν ὅτι τὰ ἄκρα ὑπὸ ἐλαττόνων παράγεται,
δῆλον· διότι τὰ ἀνωτέρω καὶ ἄρχεται πρὸ τῶν καταδεεστέρων
καὶ ὑπερεκτείνεται αὐτῶν ἐφ' ἃ μὴ πρόεισιν ἐκεῖνα δι' ὕφεσιν 35
δυνάμεως. διὰ γὰρ τοῦτο καὶ τὸ ἔσχατον τῶν ὄντων ἁπλούστατον, ὥσπερ τὸ πρῶτον, ὅτι ἀπὸ μόνου πρόεισι τοῦ πρώτου· ἀλλ'

57. 7 τὰ ἄλλα M primitus ?   14 καί ante ὅσων om. PQ   16 στερήσεων PQ
58. 19 τι om. MW (exceptis apogr. recc. W)   23 alt. ἐκ om. BM
59. 28 τῶν ω (om. Cr.)   34 δηλοῖ PQ   τὰ ἀνώτερα PQ   36 τῶν
ὄντων τὸ ἔσχατον C   τό ex corr. M

beings is produced in a greater measure by prior and more determinative principles (prop. 56). The cause, then, is co-operative in
the production of all that the consequent is capable of producing.

And if it first produces the consequent itself, it is of course plain
that it is operative before the latter in the activity which produces it.
Thus every cause operates both prior to its consequent and in conjunction with it, and likewise gives rise to further effects posterior to it.

Cor. From this it is apparent that what Soul causes is caused also
by Intelligence, but not all that Intelligence causes is caused by
Soul: Intelligence operates prior to Soul; and what Soul bestows
on secondary existences Intelligence bestows in a greater measure;
and at a level where Soul is no longer operative Intelligence irradiates
with its own gifts things on which Soul has not bestowed itself—
for even the inanimate participates Intelligence, or the creative
activity of Intelligence, in so far as it participates Form.

Again, what Intelligence causes is also caused by the Good, but
not conversely. For even privation of Form is from the Good, since
it is the source of all things; but Intelligence, being Form, cannot
give rise to privation.

PROP. 58. *All that is produced by a greater number of causes is more
composite than the product of fewer causes.*

For if every cause gives something to that which proceeds from it,
the more numerous causes will bestow more gifts, the less numerous
fewer. So that of the participants some will be made up of more
participated elements, others of fewer, in virtue of their respective
procession from more or fewer causes. But things made up of
more elements are more composite; things made up of fewer of the
same elements are less so. The product, then, of more causes is
always more composite; of fewer causes, less so. For what the
latter participates is participated by the former; but not conversely.

PROP. 59. *Whatever is simple in its being may be either superior to
composite things or inferior to them.*

For if the extremes of being be produced by fewer and simpler
causes, the intermediate existences by more, the latter will be composite (prop. 58), while of the extreme terms some will be simpler
as being higher, others as being lower. But that the extreme terms
are produced by fewer causes is plain, since the higher principles
both begin to operate before the lower and extend beyond them to
things which the lower by remission of power are precluded from
reaching (prop. 57). For the last being is, like the first, perfectly
simple, for the reason that it proceeds from the first alone; but the

ἡ ἁπλότης ἡ μὲν κατὰ τὸ κρεῖττόν ἐστι πάσης συνθέσεως, ἡ δὲ
κατὰ τὸ χεῖρον. καὶ ἐπὶ πάντων ὁ αὐτός ἐστι λόγος.

60. Πᾶν τὸ πλειόνων αἴτιον κρεῖττόν ἐστι τοῦ πρὸς ἐλάττονα
τὴν δύναμιν λαχόντος καὶ μέρη παράγοντος ὧν θάτερον ὅλων
ὑποστατικόν ἐστιν.   5

εἰ γὰρ τὸ μὲν ἐλαττόνων, τὸ δὲ πλειόνων αἴτιον, μέρη δὲ τὰ
ἔτερα τῶν ἑτέρων, ἃ μὲν ποιεῖ θάτερον, καὶ τὸ λοιπὸν ποιήσει,
τὸ τῶν πλειόνων ὑποστατικόν· ἃ δὲ τοῦτο παράγει, τούτων οὐ
πάντων ἐστὶν ἐκεῖνο παρακτικόν. δυνατώτερον ἄρα καὶ περι-
ληπτικώτερον· ὡς γὰρ τὸ προελθὸν πρὸς τὸ προελθόν, οὕτω τὸ 10
παραγαγὸν πρὸς τὸ παραγαγόν, κατ' ἄλληλα ληφθέντα, τὸ δὲ
πλείω δυνάμενον μείζονα δύναμιν ἔχει καὶ ὁλικωτέραν· τοῦτο δέ,
ἐγγυτέρω τῆς πάντων αἰτίας· τὸ δὲ ἐγγυτέρω ταύτης μειζόνως
ἐστὶν ἀγαθόν, εἴπερ αὕτη τὸ ἀγαθόν. τὸ ἄρα πλειόνων αἴτιον
κατ' οὐσίαν κρεῖττον ὑπάρχει τοῦ ἐλάττονα παράγοντος.   15

61. Πᾶσα δύναμις ἀμέριστος μὲν οὖσα μείζων ἐστί, μεριζομένη δὲ ἐλάττων.

εἰ γὰρ μερίζεται, πρόεισιν εἰς πλῆθος· εἰ δὲ τοῦτο, πορρωτέρω
γίνεται τοῦ ἑνός· εἰ δὲ τοῦτο, ἐλάττω δυνήσεται, τοῦ ἑνὸς καὶ
τοῦ συνέχοντος αὐτὴν ἀφισταμένη· καὶ ἀτελής, εἴπερ τὸ 20
ἑκάστου ἀγαθὸν ὑπάρχει κατὰ τὴν ἕνωσιν.

62. Πᾶν πλῆθος ἐγγυτέρω τοῦ ἑνὸς ὂν ποσῷ μέν ἐστι τῶν
πορρωτέρω ἔλαττον, τῇ δυνάμει δὲ μείζον.

ὅμοιον γὰρ τῷ ἑνὶ μᾶλλον τὸ ἐγγύτερον· τὸ δὲ ἓν πάντων ἦν
ὑποστατικὸν ἀπληθύντως. τὸ ἄρα ὁμοιότερον αὐτῷ, πλειόνων 25
αἴτιον ὑπάρχον, εἴπερ ἐκεῖνο πάντων, ἑνοειδέστερον ἔσται καὶ
ἀμεριστότερον, εἴπερ ἐκεῖνο ἕν. ὡς μὲν οὖν ἑνὶ τὸ ἧττον πεπληθυσμένον μᾶλλον συγγενές, ὡς δὲ πάντων αἰτίῳ τὸ πλειόνων
παρακτικόν—τοῦτο δέ, δυνατώτερον.

ἐκ δὴ τούτων φανερὸν ὅτι πλείους μὲν αἱ σωματικαὶ φύσεις 30
τῶν ψυχῶν, πλείους δὲ αὗται τῶν νόων, οἱ δὲ νόες πλείους τῶν
θείων ἑνάδων· καὶ ἐπὶ πάντων ὁ αὐτὸς λόγος.

59. 2 ὁ αὐτός ἐστι λόγος BCD, est eadem ratio β (cf. *El. Phys.* 44. 13): ὁ αὐτὸς
ἔστω λ. M¹P(Q), eadem fit (γρ. sit ?) ratio αγ: ὁ αὐτὸς ἔσται λ. M²   in P hoc
caput inde a l. 1 ἁπλότης et init. sequentis usque ad l. 10 a tineis mutilata
60. 4 ὅλων CDM : ὅλον BPW (suprascr. D) : εἶλον Q   6 τά om. Arg
9 ἄρα] ἅμα Arg : M¹ incert.   10 primum τό ω (om. Cr.²)   οὕτω καὶ τό PQ dett.
11 παράγον bis PQ (παραγαγόν priore loco D)   post alt. παράγον pergunt PQ
δείκνυσι καὶ ὁ στοιχειωτὸς (sic) εὐκλείδης ὅτι τὰ μέρη τοῖς ὡσαύτως πολλαπλασίοις
τὸν αὐτὸν ἔχει λόγον, quod manifestum scholium est   ληφθέντα κατ' ἄλληλα PQ
13 ταύτης] αὐτῆς PQ, ipsi W   14 αὐτή PQ   15 τοῦ τὰ ἐλάσσονα PQM²
61. 16 μὲν οὖσα] οὖσα P : manens (= μένουσα) W   18 prius εἰ] qua (= ἧ) W
20–1 τὸ ἑκάστου ω (ἑκάστου Port., ἑκάστου τό Cr.)
62. 23 πορρωτέρων P   26 εἴπερ ἐκεῖνο πάντων om. PQ   32 ἐνάδων
om. PQ   λόγος ω (λόγος ἐστί edd.)

one is simple as being above all composition, the other as being beneath it. And the same reasoning applies to all other terms.

PROP. **60**. *Whatever principle is the cause of a greater number of effects is superior to that which has a power limited to fewer objects and which gives rise to parts of those existences constituted by the other as wholes.*

For if the one is cause of fewer effects, the other of more, and the fewer form a part of the more numerous, then whatever is produced by the former cause will be produced also by the latter, but the former is not productive of all that the latter produces. The latter is therefore the more powerful and comprehensive : for as consequent is to consequent, so is cause to cause, considered relatively, and that which can give rise to more effects has greater and more universal power. But this means that it is nearer to the cause of all things ; and what is nearer to the cause is in a greater measure good, the Good being that cause (prop. 12). The cause of more numerous effects is therefore superior in its being to that which produces fewer.

PROP. **61**. *Every power is greater if it be undivided, less if it be divided.*

For if it be divided, it proceeds to a manifold ; and if so, it becomes more remote from the One ; and if so, it will be less powerful, in proportion as it falls away from the One which contains it in unity, and imperfect, inasmuch as the good of each thing consists in its unity (prop. 13).

PROP. **62**. *Every manifold which is nearer to the One has fewer members than those more remote, but is greater in power.*

For that which is nearer to the One is more like to it ; and we saw that the One is constitutive of all things without becoming manifold (prop. 5). Accordingly that which is more like to it, being the cause of more existences, as the One is of all existences, will be more unitary and less divisible, as the first cause is One. The less pluralized is more akin to it *qua* One ; and *qua* universal cause, the more productive—that is to say, the more powerful.

Cor. From this it is apparent that bodily natures are more numerous than souls, and these than intelligences, and the intelligences more numerous than the divine henads. And the same principle applies universally.

63. Πᾶν τὸ ἀμέθεκτον διττὰς ὑφίστησι τῶν μετεχομένων τὰς τάξεις, τὴν μὲν ἐν τοῖς ποτὲ μετέχουσι, τὴν δὲ ἐν τοῖς ἀεὶ καὶ συμφυῶς μετέχουσι.

τῷ γὰρ ἀμεθέκτῳ τὸ ἀεὶ μετεχόμενον ὁμοιότερον ἢ τὸ ποτέ. πρὶν ἄρα ὑποστῇ τὸ ποτὲ μεθεκτόν, τὸ ἀεὶ μεθεκτὸν ὑποστή- 5 σεται, τῷ μὲν μετέχεσθαι τοῦ μετ' αὐτὸ μὴ διενεγκόν, τῷ δὲ ἀεὶ συγγενέστερον ὂν τῷ ἀμεθέκτῳ καὶ ὁμοιότερον. καὶ οὔτε μόνα ἔστι τὰ ποτὲ μετεχόμενα (πρὸ γὰρ τούτων τὰ ἀεὶ μετεχόμενα, δι' ὧν καὶ ταῦτα συνδεῖται κατά τινα πρόοδον εὔτακτον τοῖς ἀμεθέκτοις)· οὔτε μόνα τὰ ἀεὶ μετεχόμενα (καὶ γὰρ ταῦτα, 10 δύναμιν ἔχοντα ἄσβεστον, εἴπερ ἀεὶ ἔστιν, ἄλλων ἐστὶν οἰστικὰ τῶν ποτὲ μετεχομένων· καὶ μέχρι τούτων ἡ ὕφεσις).

ἐκ δὴ τούτων φανερὸν ὅτι καὶ αἱ ἀπὸ τοῦ ἑνὸς ἑνώσεις ἐλλαμπό- μεναι τοῖς οὖσιν αἱ μὲν ἀεὶ μετέχονται, αἱ δὲ ποτέ, καὶ αἱ νοεραὶ μεθέξεις διτταὶ ὡσαύτως, καὶ αἱ τῶν ψυχῶν ψυχώσεις, καὶ αἱ 15 τῶν ἄλλων εἰδῶν ὁμοίως· καὶ γὰρ τὸ κάλλος καὶ ἡ ὁμοιότης καὶ ἡ στάσις καὶ ἡ ταυτότης, ἀμέθεκτα ὄντα, ὑπό τε τῶν ἀεὶ μετ- εχόντων μετέχεται καὶ ὑπὸ τῶν ποτὲ δευτέρως κατὰ τὴν αὐτὴν τάξιν.

64. Πᾶσα ἀρχικὴ μονὰς διττὸν ὑφίστησιν ἀριθμόν, τὸν μὲν 20 αὐτοτελῶν ὑποστάσεων, τὸν δὲ ἐλλάμψεων ἐν ἑτέροις τὴν ὑπόστασιν κεκτημένων.

εἰ γὰρ καθ' ὕφεσιν ἡ πρόοδος διὰ τῶν οἰκείων τοῖς ὑποστα- τικοῖς αἰτίοις, καὶ ἀπὸ τῶν παντελείων τὰ τέλεια καὶ διὰ τούτων μέσων τὰ ἀτελῆ πρόεισιν εὐτάκτως· ὥστε αἱ μὲν ἔσονται αὐτο- 25 τελεῖς ὑποστάσεις, αἱ δὲ ἀτελεῖς. καὶ αὖται μὲν γίνονται ἤδη τῶν μετεχόντων (ἀτελεῖς γὰρ οὖσαι δέονται τῶν ὑποκειμένων εἰς τὴν ἑαυτῶν ὕπαρξιν)· αἱ δὲ ἑαυτῶν ποιοῦσι τὰ μετέχοντα (τέλειαι γὰρ οὖσαι πληροῦσι μὲν ἑαυτῶν ἐκεῖνα καὶ ἑδράζουσιν ἐν ἑαυταῖς, δέονται δὲ οὐδὲν τῶν καταδεεστέρων εἰς τὴν ὑπό- 30 στασιν τὴν ἑαυτῶν). αἱ μὲν οὖν αὐτοτελεῖς ὑποστάσεις, διὰ τὴν εἰς πλῆθος διάκρισιν ἠλαττωμέναι τῆς ἀρχικῆς αὐτῶν μονάδος, διὰ τὴν αὐτοτελῆ ὕπαρξιν ὁμοιοῦνταί πη πρὸς ἐκείνην· αἱ δὲ

63. 4 ὁμοιότερον] ὅμοιόν ἐστιν PQ   5 τὸ ἀεὶ μεθεκτόν om. D¹M
6 μὴ del. M², om. edd.   7 ὁμοιοτέρῳ M (ex corr. ?) PQ   13 δὴ ω) (δέ
Cr.)   αἱ om. PQ
64. 24 αἰτίων C¹D   παντελῶν BCD   25 ὥστε om. PQ, fort. recte
(sed agnoscit W)   26 ἤδη BArg : εἴδη DEMPQW : in C prima syllaba casu
oblitterata.   30 ἐν ἑαυταῖς scripsi (cf. in Remp. I. 178. 21, II. 205. 15):
ἑαυταῖς BCDM, seipsis W : ἐν αὐταῖς PQ   οὐδενός W ut videtur   31 διὰ
μὲν τήν PQ   32 μοναρχικῆς PQ   μονάδος αὐτῶν M primitus   33 διὰ
τήν BCD : διὰ δὲ τήν MPQW, quo recepto scr. l. 32 ἠλάττωνται (sunt mino-
rate W)

PROP. **63.** *Every unparticipated term gives rise to two orders of participated terms, the one in contingent participants, the other in things which participate at all times and in virtue of their nature.*

For what is enduringly participated is more like to the unparticipated than what is participated for a time only. Prior, therefore, to the constitution of the last-named, there will be constituted something enduringly participated (prop. 28), which *qua* participated does not differ from the succeeding term, but *qua* enduring is more akin to the unparticipated and more like to it. Terms participated for a time only are not the sole class of participated terms : for prior to them there exist terms enduringly participated, through which they too are linked with the unparticipated in an ordered sequence of procession. Nor are terms enduringly participated the sole class : for inasmuch as they exist perpetually they have an inextinguishable power, whereby they are productive of further terms (prop. 25), namely those which are participated for a time only ; and this is the limit of declension.

Cor. From this it is apparent that the states of unity with which the One irradiates existents are participated some enduringly, others for a time ; and in like manner intellective participations are of two kinds, and the ensoulments produced by souls, and similarly the participations of Forms also—for beauty and likeness and steadfastness and identity, being unparticipated, are yet participated by certain participants enduringly, and derivatively by others for a time in the same class of existents.

PROP. **64.** *Every original monad gives rise to two series, one consisting of substances complete in themselves, and one of irradiations which have their substantiality in something other than themselves.*

For if the outgoing proceeds by a declension through terms akin to the constitutive causes (prop. 28), from the wholly perfect must arise things complete in their kind, and by these latter the origin of things incomplete must be mediated in due sequence : so that there will be one order of substances complete in themselves, and another of incomplete substances. The latter are upon such a level that they belong to their participants : for being incomplete they require a substrate for their existence. The former make the participants belong to them : for being complete they fill the participants with themselves (prop. 25) and establish them in themselves, and for their substantial existence they have no need of inferior beings. Accordingly those substances which are complete in themselves, while by their discrimination into a manifold they fall short of their original monad, are yet in some wise assimilated to it by their self-

ἀτελεῖς καὶ τῷ ἐν ἄλλοις εἶναι τῆς καθ' αὑτὴν ὑφεστώσης καὶ τῷ ἀτελεῖ τῆς πάντα τελειούσης ἀφεστήκασιν. αἱ δὲ πρόοδοι διὰ τῶν ὁμοίων ἄχρι τῶν πάντη ἀνομοίων. διττὸν ἄρα ὑφίστησιν ἀριθμὸν ἑκάστη τῶν ἀρχικῶν μονάδων.

ἐκ δὴ τούτων φανερὸν ὅτι καὶ ἑνάδες αἱ μὲν αὐτοτελεῖς ἀπὸ 5 τοῦ ἑνὸς προῆλθον, αἱ δὲ ἐλλάμψεις ἑνώσεων· καὶ νόες οἱ μὲν οὐσίαι αὐτοτελεῖς, οἱ δὲ νοεραί τινες τελειότητες· καὶ ψυχαὶ αἱ μὲν ἑαυτῶν οὖσαι, αἱ δὲ τῶν ψυχουμένων, ὡς ἰνδάλματα μόνον οὖσαι ψυχῶν. καὶ οὕτως οὔτε πᾶσα ἕνωσις θεός, ἀλλ' ἡ αὐτοτελὴς ἑνάς, οὔτε πᾶσα νοερὰ ἰδιότης νοῦς, ἀλλ' ἡ οὐσιώδης 10 μόνον, οὔτε πᾶσα ψυχῆς ἔλλαμψις ψυχή, ἀλλ' ἔστι καὶ τὰ εἴδωλα τῶν ψυχῶν.

65. Πᾶν τὸ ὁπωσοῦν ὑφεστὸς ἢ κατ' αἰτίαν ἔστιν ἀρχοειδῶς ἢ καθ' ὕπαρξιν ἢ κατὰ μέθεξιν εἰκονικῶς.

ἢ γὰρ ἐν τῷ παράγοντι τὸ παραγόμενον ὁρᾶται, ὡς ἐν αἰτίᾳ 15 προϋπάρχον, διότι πᾶν τὸ αἴτιον ἐν ἑαυτῷ τὸ αἰτιατὸν προείληφε, πρώτως ὂν ὅπερ ἐκεῖνο δευτέρως· ἢ ἐν τῷ παραγομένῳ τὸ παράγον (καὶ γὰρ τοῦτο, μετέχον τοῦ παράγοντος, ἐν ἑαυτῷ δείκνυσι δευτέρως ὃ τὸ παράγον ὑπάρχει πρώτως)· ἢ κατὰ τὴν ἑαυτοῦ τάξιν ἕκαστον θεωρεῖται, καὶ οὔτε ἐν τῷ αἰτίῳ οὔτε ἐν 20 τῷ ἀποτελέσματι· τὸ μὲν γὰρ ἔστι κρειττόνως ἢ ἔστι, τὸ δὲ χειρόνως ἢ ἔστι, δεῖ δέ που εἶναι καὶ ὅ ἐστιν· ἔστι δὲ καθ' ὕπαρξιν ἐν τῇ ἑαυτοῦ τάξει ἕκαστον.

66. Πάντα τὰ ὄντα πρὸς ἄλληλα ἢ ὅλα ἐστὶν ἢ μέρη ἢ ταὐτὰ ἢ ἕτερα. 25

ἢ γὰρ περιέχει θάτερα, περιέχεται δὲ τὰ λοιπά· ἢ οὔτε περιέχει οὔτε περιέχεται, καὶ ἢ ταὐτόν τι πέπονθεν, ὡς ἑνὸς μετέχοντα, ἢ διακέκριται ἀλλήλων. ἀλλ' εἰ μὲν περιέχει, ὅλα ἂν εἴη· εἰ δὲ περιέχοιτο, μέρη· εἰ δ' ἑνὸς τὰ πολλὰ μετέχοι, ταὐτά ἐστι κατὰ τὸ ἕν· εἰ δὲ πλείω μόνον εἴη, ἕτερα ἀλλήλων 30 ταύτῃ, καθὸ πολλά ἐστιν.

64. 1 prius καί non agnosc. W   τῷ BCQ: τῶν DP: τό M   2 πάντων M²
5 τούτου W ut videtur   καί om. C   καὶ αἱ ἑνάδες αἱ MPQ   6 ἑνώσεως
[M]   νόες BCD: νόος· MW: νόων PQ   6–7 αἱ μὲν ... αἱ δέ M (ex corr. !) W
7 νοεραί ... 8 αἱ δέ om. MW   8 ἐφ' ἑαυτῶν PQ   ὡς ἰνδάλματα Q: ἰνδ. καί
BCD: ἰνδάλματα MW (P incert. propter foedam tinearum lacerationem)   9 πᾶσα
ἕνωσις MQ (P incert.) : πᾶσα ἑνάς BCD, omnis unitas W   10–11 ἡ οὐσιώδης
μόνον BCD: οὐσ. μόνος M¹Q (P incert.) : ὁ οὐσ. μόνος M²W
65. 13 ὑφεστός M: ὑφεστῶς cett.   14 ἢ κατὰ μέθεξιν om. C¹, in mg. M¹
15 alt. ἐν] εἶναι [M]   αἰτίᾳ ω (αἰτίῳ edd.)   18 τὸ παραγαγόν BCD
19 προυπάρχει Q et ! P   20 αὑτοῦ PQ   21 et 22 ἢ bis BCDArgW : ἢ
MPQ   22 δήπου Arg (Cr.)   23 τῇ om. M¹   αὑτοῦ M¹PQ
66. 26 γάρ om. M¹   27 καί non agnosc. W   ταυτότητι (ἡ ex ο)
περιπέπονθεν M   28 διακέκρινται BCD   29 μετέχει C   30 ταῦτα BD dett.

complete existence; whereas the incomplete not only as existing in another fall away from the monad which exists in itself, but also as incomplete from the all-completing monad. But all procession advances through similars until it reaches the wholly dissimilar (prop. 28). Thus each of the original monads gives rise to two series.

Cor. From this it is apparent that of the henads some proceed self-complete from the One, while others are irradiated states of unity; and of the intelligences some are self-complete substances, while others are intellectual perfections; and of souls some belong to themselves, while others belong to ensouled bodies, as being but phantasms of souls. And so not every unity is a god, but only the self-complete henad; not every intellectual property is an intelligence, but only the existential; not every irradiation of Soul is a soul, but there are also reflections of souls.

PROP. **65.** *All that subsists in any fashion has its being either in its cause, as an originative potency; or as a substantial predicate; or by participation, after the manner of an image.*

For either we see the product as pre-existent in the producer which is its cause (for every cause comprehends its effect before its emergence, having primitively that character which the latter has by derivation (prop. 18)); or we see the producer in the product (for the latter participates its producer and reveals in itself by derivation what the producer already is primitively); or else we contemplate each thing in its own station, neither in its cause nor in its resultant (for its cause has a higher, its resultant a lower mode of being than itself, and besides these there must surely be some being which is its own)—and it is as a substantial predicate that each has its being in its own station.

H. OF WHOLES AND PARTS.

PROP. **66.** *Every existent is related to every other either as a whole or as a part or by identity or by difference.*

For either some are comprehensive and the rest comprehended; or else neither of two existents comprehends or is comprehended by the other. In the latter case either they have a common affect, as participating a common principle, or they are mutually diverse. But comprehensive terms must be wholes, and comprehended terms parts; if the many participate one, they are identical in respect of that unity; and if on the other hand they are a mere plurality, in that respect in which they are many they differ one from another.

67. Πᾶσα ὁλότης ἢ πρὸ τῶν μερῶν ἐστιν ἢ ἐκ τῶν μερῶν
ἢ ἐν τῷ μέρει.

ἢ γὰρ ἐν τῇ αἰτίᾳ τὸ ἑκάστου θεωροῦμεν εἶδος, καὶ ὅλον
ἐκεῖνο πρὸ τῶν μερῶν λέγομεν τὸ ἐν τῷ αἰτίῳ προϋποστάν· ἢ
ἐν τοῖς μετέχουσιν αὐτῆς μέρεσι.   καὶ τοῦτο διχῶς· ἢ γὰρ ἐν 5
ἅπασιν ὁμοῦ τοῖς μέρεσι, καὶ ἔστι τοῦτο ἐκ τῶν μερῶν ὅλον, οὗ
καὶ ὁτιοῦν μέρος ἀπὸν ἐλαττοῖ τὸ ὅλον· ἢ ἐν ἑκάστῳ τῶν μερῶν,
ὡς καὶ τοῦ μέρους κατὰ μέθεξιν τοῦ ὅλου (ὅλου) γεγονότος, ὃ καὶ
ποιεῖ τὸ μέρος εἶναι ὅλον μερικῶς.   καθ' ὕπαρξιν μὲν οὖν ὅλον
τὸ ἐκ τῶν μερῶν· κατ' αἰτίαν δὲ τὸ πρὸ τῶν μερῶν· κατὰ 10
μέθεξιν δὲ τὸ ἐν τῷ μέρει.   καὶ γὰρ τοῦτο κατ' ἐσχάτην ὕφεσιν
ὅλον, ᾗ μιμεῖται τὸ ἐκ τῶν μερῶν ὅλον, ὅταν μὴ τὸ τυχὸν ᾖ
μέρος, ἀλλὰ τῷ ὅλῳ δυνάμενον ἀφομοιοῦσθαι οὗ καὶ τὰ μέρη
ὅλα ἐστίν.

68. Πᾶν τὸ ἐν τῷ μέρει ὅλον μέρος ἐστὶ τοῦ ἐκ τῶν μερῶν ὅλου. 15

εἰ γὰρ μέρος ἐστίν, ὅλου τινός ἐστι μέρος· καὶ ἤτοι τοῦ ἐν
αὐτῷ ὅλου, καθ' ὃ λέγεται ἐν τῷ μέρει ὅλον (ἀλλ' οὕτως αὐτὸ
ἑαυτοῦ μέρος, καὶ ἴσον τῷ ὅλῳ τὸ μέρος ἔσται, καὶ ταὐτὸν ἑκάτερον)· ἢ ἄλλου τινὸς ὅλου.   καὶ εἰ ἄλλου, ἢ μόνον ἐστὶν ἐκείνου
μέρος, καὶ οὕτως οὐδὲν ἂν πάλιν τοῦ ὅλου διαφέροι, ἑνὸς ὄντος ἐν 20
ὃν μέρος· ἢ μεθ' ἑτέρου (παντὸς γὰρ ὅλου τὰ μέρη πλείω ἑνός),
κἀκεῖνο ἔσται, ἐκ πλειόνων ὄν, ὅλον ἐκ τῶν μερῶν ἐξ ὧν ἐστι·
καὶ οὕτω τὸ ἐν τῷ μέρει ὅλον τοῦ ἐκ τῶν μερῶν ἐστι μέρος.

69. Πᾶν τὸ ἐκ τῶν μερῶν ὅλον μετέχει τῆς πρὸ τῶν μερῶν
ὁλότητος.
25
εἰ γὰρ ἐκ μερῶν ἐστι, πεπονθός ἐστι τὸ ὅλον (τὰ γὰρ μέρη ἓν
γενόμενα τὸ ὅλον διὰ τὴν ἕνωσιν πέπονθε), καὶ ἔστιν ὅλον ἐν
μὴ ὅλοις τοῖς μέρεσι.   παντὸς δὲ τοῦ μετεχομένου προϋφέστηκε
τὸ ἀμέθεκτον.   ἡ ἄρα ἀμέθεκτος ὁλότης προϋπάρχει τῆς μετεχομένης.   ἔστιν ἄρα τι εἶδος ὁλότητος πρὸ τοῦ ἐκ τῶν μερῶν 30
ὅλου, ὃ οὐ πεπονθός ἐστι τὸ ὅλον, ἀλλ' αὐτοολότης, ἀφ' ἧς ἡ ἐκ
τῶν μερῶν ὁλότης.

ἐπεὶ καὶ τὸ μὲν ἐκ τῶν μερῶν ὅλον πολλαχοῦ καὶ ἐν πολλοῖς

67. 3 θεωρούμενον [M]W·   4 τὸ ... προϋποστάν (ὑποστάν edd.) fort.
secludenda   5 αὐτῆς BDE : αὐτοῖς C : αὐτοῦ MPQ   γάρ om. BCD
6–7 quo et quecunque pars est minor quam totum W (ἔλασσον fort. M¹)   8 τοῦ
ὅλου (ὅλου) scripsi : τοῦ ὅλου PQM² : ὅλου BCD : τὸ ὅλον M¹, totum W   9 μέρος
ὅλον εἶναι PQ   11 κατ' ἐσχάτην ω (κατὰ τὴν ἐσχ. edd.)
68. 15 τῶν] τοῦ M   17 αὐτό om. M¹   19 alt. ἄλλου] ἄλλο M²   20 τοῦ
ὅλου πάλιν PQ   21–2 totius cuius ... secundum illud (= ὅλου οὗ ... κατ'
ἐκεῖνο) W   22 ὄν [M] W : om. cett.
69. 26 εἰ γὰρ καὶ ἐκ P   27 γινόμενα P   ἐν] ἕν D : ἐκ M   29 ἡ
ἄρα] ἢ ὅτι [M]   •   30 τι] τό M¹   33 μέν om. D, non agnosc. W

PROP. **67**. *Every whole is either a whole-before-the-parts, a whole-of-parts, or a whole-in-the-part.*

For either we contemplate the form of each thing in its cause, and to this form pre-existing in the cause we give the name of whole-before-the-parts; or else we contemplate it in the parts which participate the cause, and this after one of two manners. Either we see it in all the parts taken together, and it is then a whole-of-parts, the withdrawal from which of any single part diminishes the whole; or else we see it in each part severally, in the sense that even the part has become a whole by participation of the whole, which causes the part to *be* the whole in such fashion as is proper to a part. The whole-of-parts is the whole as existence; the whole-before-the-parts is the whole in its cause; the whole-in-the-part is the whole by participation (prop. 65). For this last is still the whole, though in its extreme declension, in so far as it imitates the whole-of-parts: which is not true of any and every part, but only of such as can assimilate themselves to a whole whose parts are wholes.

PROP. **68**. *Every whole-in-the-part is a part of a whole-of-parts.*

For if it is a part, it is a part of some whole; and this must be either the whole which it contains, in virtue of which it is called a whole-in-the-part, or else some other whole. But on the former supposition it will be a part of itself, and the part will be equal to the whole, and the two identical. And if it is a part of some other whole, either it is the only part, and if so will again be indistinguishable from the whole, being the one part of a pure unity; or else, since the parts of any whole are at least two, this whole will include a further element and, being composed of a plurality of parts, will be a whole of the parts which compose it. Accordingly, the whole-in-the-part is a part of a whole-of-parts.

PROP. **69**. *Every whole-of-parts participates the whole-before-the-parts.*

For if it is composed of parts, it has wholeness as an affect, since the parts in becoming one acquired the character of wholeness through their unification; and it is a whole immanent in a sum of parts which are not wholes. But prior to every participated term there exists the unparticipated (prop. 23). Therefore the unparticipated whole exists prior to the participated. Prior to the whole-of-parts there is thus a Form of wholeness, which does not possess wholeness as an affect, but is Wholeness-itself, from which is derived the wholeness-of-parts.

For again, wholeness-of-parts exists in many places and in many

ἐστιν, ἐν ἄλλοις καὶ ἐν ἄλλοις ἐκ μερῶν οὖσι, τοῖς μὲν ἄλλων,
τοῖς δὲ ἄλλων· δεῖ δὲ εἶναι τὴν μονάδα πασῶν τῶν ὁλοτήτων
καθ' αὑτήν. οὔτε γὰρ εἰλικρινὲς ἕκαστον τῶν ὅλων τούτων,
ἐπιδεὲς ὂν τῶν μερῶν ἐξ ὧν ἐστιν οὐχ ὅλων ὄντων· οὔτε ἐν τινὶ
γεγονὸς τοῖς ἄλλοις ἅπασιν αἴτιον εἶναι δύναται τοῦ εἶναι ὅλοις. 5
τὸ ἄρα τοῦ ὅλοις εἶναι τοῖς ὅλοις ἅπασιν αἴτιον πρὸ τῶν μερῶν
ἐστιν. εἰ γὰρ καὶ τοῦτο ἐκ τῶν μερῶν, τὶ ὅλον ἔσται καὶ οὐχ
ἁπλῶς ὅλον, καὶ πάλιν τοῦτο ἐξ ἄλλου, καὶ ἢ εἰς ἄπειρον ἢ
ἔσται τὸ πρώτως ὅλον, οὐκ ἐκ μερῶν ὅλον, ἀλλ' ὅ ἐστιν ὁλότης
ὄν.   10

70. Πᾶν τὸ ὁλικώτερον ἐν τοῖς ἀρχηγικοῖς καὶ πρὸ τῶν μερικῶν εἰς τὰ μετέχοντα ἐλλάμπει καὶ δεύτερον ἐκείνων ἀπολείπει
τὸ μετασχόν.

καὶ γὰρ ἄρχεται πρὸ τοῦ μετ' αὐτὸ τῆς ἐνεργείας τῆς εἰς τὰ
δεύτερα, καὶ σὺν τῇ ἐκείνου παρουσίᾳ πάρεστι, καὶ ἐκείνου 15
μηκέτι ἐνεργοῦντος ἔτι πάρεστι καὶ ἐνεργεῖ τὸ αἰτιώτερον· καὶ
οὐκ ἐν διαφόροις μόνον ὑποκειμένοις, ἀλλὰ καὶ ἐν ἑκάστῳ τῶν
ποτὲ μετεχόντων. δεῖ γὰρ (εἰ τύχοι) γενέσθαι πρῶτον ὄν, εἶτα
ζῷον, εἶτα ἄνθρωπον. καὶ ἄνθρωπος οὐκέτι ἔστιν ἀπολιπούσης
τῆς λογικῆς δυνάμεως, ζῷον δὲ ἔστιν ἐμπνέον καὶ αἰσθανόμενον· 20
καὶ τοῦ ζῆν πάλιν ἀπολιπόντος μένει τὸ ὄν (καὶ γὰρ ὅταν μὴ
ζῇ τὸ εἶναι πάρεστι). καὶ ἐπὶ πάντων ὡσαύτως. αἴτιον δέ,
ὅτι δραστικώτερον ὑπάρχον τὸ αἰτιώτερον πρότερον εἰς τὸ
μετέχον ἐνεργεῖ (τὸ γὰρ αὐτὸ ὑπὸ τοῦ δυνατωτέρου πάσχει
προτέρου)· καὶ τοῦ δευτέρου πάλιν ἐνεργοῦντος κἀκεῖνο συνεργεῖ, 25
διότι πᾶν, ὅπερ ἂν ποιῇ τὸ δεύτερον, συναπογεννᾷ τούτῳ καὶ τὸ
αἰτιώτερον· καὶ ἀπολιπόντος ἐκείνου τοῦτο ἔτι πάρεστιν (ἡ γὰρ
τοῦ δυνατωτέρου μετάδοσις, δρῶσα μειζόνως, ὑστέρα τὸ μετασχὸν ἀπολείπει· καὶ γὰρ διὰ τῆς τοῦ δευτέρου μεταδόσεως τὴν
ἑαυτῆς ἔλλαμψιν ἐδυνάμωσεν).   30

71. Πάντα τὰ ἐν τοῖς ἀρχηγικοῖς αἰτίοις ὁλικωτέραν καὶ
ὑπερτέραν τάξιν ἔχοντα ἐν τοῖς ἀποτελέσμασι κατὰ τὰς ἀπ'

69. 1 alt. ἐν om. M¹PQ   2 εἶναι MW : καὶ εἶναι PQ : εἰδέναι BCD   3 καὶ
καθ' αὑτήν BCD   5 τοῦ εἶναι ὅλοις om. BCDM²   6 τὸ ἄρα τοῦ] τούτου [M]
τοῖς ὅλοις] τοῖς ἄλλοις PE   7 ἔσται] ἐστί PQ   8 τοῦτο πάλιν M   prius
ἢ om. PQM²   9 ἔσται] διά MW
70. 11 ἀρχηγικοῖς BQM² : ἀρχικοῖς C (corr. eadem m.) DP : M¹ incert.
12 δεύτερον ω (δευτέρας edd.)   13 τό] τι MW   17 μόνον ω (μόνοις
edd.)   18 εἰ τύχῃ PQ   19 οὐκέτι BCD[M]W : οὐκ PQM²   ἀπολιπούσης
Arg : ἀπολιπούσης ω   21 ἀπολείποντος PQ   καὶ γάρ] εἰ γάρ MW
22 καί] καὶ γάρ MW   24–5 προτέρου πάσχει MPQ, prius patitur W   25 συν-
ενεργεῖ B   26 τούτῳ scripsi, et sic fort. leg. W (huic γ, hoc αβ) : τοῦτο ω
27 ἀπολιπόντος M¹ : ἀπολείποντος cett.   28 δράσασα PQM²   29 τοῦ om.
BCD

diverse wholes composed of diverse parts ; and the monad of all these wholenesses must exist in independence of them. For each of these wholes is impure, since it needs the parts of which it is composed, and these latter are not wholes. And since each resides in a particular group of parts it cannot be the cause of the wholeness of all other wholes. Accordingly that which makes all wholes to be wholes is prior to the parts. For if this too be composed of parts, it will be a particular whole, and not Wholeness unqualified ; thus it in turn will be derived from another, and either there will be infinite regress or there will exist a term which is primitively whole, being not a whole-of-parts but Wholeness in its essence.

PROP. 70. *All those more universal characters which inhere in the originative principles both irradiate their participants before the specific characters and are slower to withdraw from a being which has once shared in them.*

For the higher cause begins its operation upon secondary beings before its consequent, and is present concomitantly with the presence of the latter, and is still present and operative when the consequent has ceased to operate ; and this is true not only in respect of the range of objects affected (prop. 57) but in regard to each several contingent participant. Thus, for example, a thing must exist before it has life, and have life before it is human. And again, when the logical faculty has failed it is no longer human, but it is still a living thing, since it breathes and feels ; and when life in turn has aban. doned it existence remains to it, for even when it ceases to live it still has being. So in every case. The reason is that the higher cause, being more efficacious (prop. 56), operates sooner upon the participant (for where the same thing is affected by two causes it is affected first by the more powerful) ; and in the activity of the secondary the higher is co-operative, because all the effects of the secondary are concomitantly generated by the more determinative cause ; and where the former has withdrawn the latter is still present (for the gift of the more powerful principle is slower to abandon the participant, being more efficacious, and also inasmuch as through the gift of its consequent it has made its own irradiation stronger).

PROP. 71. *All those characters which in the originative causes have higher and more universal rank become in the resultant beings,*

αὐτῶν ἐλλάμψεις ὑποκείμενά πως γίνεται ταῖς τῶν μερικωτέρων
μεταδόσεσι· καὶ αἱ μὲν ἀπὸ τῶν ἀνωτέρων ἐλλάμψεις ὑπο-
δέχονται τὰς ἐκ τῶν δευτέρων προόδους, ἐκεῖναι δὲ ἐπὶ τούτων
ἑδράζονται· καὶ οὕτω προηγοῦνται μεθέξεις ἄλλαι ἄλλων, καὶ
ἐμφάσεις ἄλλαι ἐπ' ἄλλαις ἄνωθεν εἰς τὸ αὐτὸ φοιτῶσιν ὑπο- 5
κείμενον, τῶν ὁλικωτέρων προενεργούντων, τῶν δὲ μερικωτέρων
ἐπὶ ταῖς ἐκείνων ἐνεργείαις τὰς ἑαυτῶν μεταδόσεις χορηγούντων
τοῖς μετέχουσιν.

εἰ γὰρ τὰ αἰτιώτερα πρὸ τῶν δευτέρων ἐνεργεῖ, διὰ περιουσίαν δυνάμεως καὶ τοῖς ἀτελεστέραν ἔχουσι τὴν ἐπιτηδειότητα 10
παρόντα καὶ ἐλλάμποντα κἀκείνοις, τὰ δὲ ὑφειμένα κατὰ τὴν
τάξιν δεύτερα χορηγεῖ τὰ ἀπ' αὐτῶν, δῆλον ὡς αἱ τῶν ὑπερτέρων ἐλλάμψεις, προκαταλαμβάνουσαι τὸ μετέχον ἀμφοτέρων,
ἐπερείδουσι τὰς τῶν ὑφειμένων μεταδόσεις· αἱ δὲ ταῖς ἀπ'
ἐκείνων ἐμφάσεσιν ὑποβάθραις χρῶνται, καὶ δρῶσιν εἰς τὸ 15
μετέχον, προειργασμένον ὑπ' ἐκείνων.

72. Πάντα τὰ ἐν τοῖς μετέχουσιν ὑποκειμένων ἔχοντα λόγον
ἐκ τελειοτέρων πρόεισι καὶ ὁλικωτέρων αἰτίων.

τὰ γὰρ πλειόνων αἴτια δυνατώτερά ἐστι καὶ ὁλικώτερα καὶ
ἐγγυτέρω τοῦ ἑνὸς ἢ τὰ τῶν ἐλαττόνων. τὰ δὲ τῶν προϋπο- 20
κειμένων ἄλλοις ὑποστατικὰ πλειόνων αἴτιά ἐστιν, ὑφιστάντα
καὶ τὰς ἐπιτηδειότητας πρὸ τῆς τῶν εἰδῶν παρουσίας. ὁλικώτερα
ἄρα ταῦτα καὶ τελειότερά ἐστιν ἐν τοῖς αἰτίοις.

ἐκ δὴ τούτων φανερὸν διότι ἡ μὲν ὕλη, ἐκ τοῦ ἑνὸς ὑποστᾶσα,
καθ' αὑτὴν εἴδους ἐστὶν ἄμοιρος· τὸ δὲ σῶμα καθ' αὑτό, εἰ καὶ 25
τοῦ ὄντος μετέσχε, ψυχῆς ἀμέτοχόν ἐστιν. ἡ μὲν γὰρ ὕλη,
ὑποκείμενον οὖσα πάντων, ἐκ τοῦ πάντων αἰτίου προῆλθε· τὸ δὲ
σῶμα, ὑποκείμενον ὂν τῆς ψυχώσεως, ἐκ τοῦ ὁλικωτέρου τῆς
ψυχῆς ὑφέστηκε, τοῦ ὄντος ὁπωσοῦν μετασχόν.

73. Πᾶν μὲν ὅλον ἅμα ὄν τί ἐστι, καὶ μετέχει τοῦ ὄντος· οὐ 30
πᾶν δὲ ὂν ὅλον τυγχάνει ὄν.

ἢ γὰρ ταὐτόν ἐστιν ὂν καὶ ὅλον, ἢ τὸ μὲν πρότερον, τὸ δὲ
ὕστερον. ἀλλ' εἰ καὶ τὸ μέρος, ᾗ μέρος, ὂν μέν ἐστιν (ἐκ γὰρ
μερῶν ὄντων ἐστὶ τὸ ὅλον), οὐ μέντοι καὶ ὅλον καθ' αὑτό, οὐκ

71. 1 μερικῶν PQ   2 ἀνωτέρω PQ   10 ἀτελεστέρως PQ
12 χορηγεῖ τά P : χορηγεῖταί Q : χορηγεῖται cett. W   13 προκαταλαμβάνουσαι
...15 χρῶνται] προκαταλαμβάνουσι αἷς βάθραις χρῶνται τὰ δεύτερα PQ   16 προ-
ειργασμένων C dett.   ὑπ' ω (om. edd.)
72. 17 ὑποκείμενα P, ὑποκείμενον M²   19 πλείονα BCD   20 post δέ ins.
τά BD   20–1 προκειμένων M primitus   21 ὑποτακτικά M   22 ἐπιτηδειότητας ω (ἰδιότητας edd.)   24 διατί [M]   28 ὄν om. M
73. 31 τυγχάνει ὅλον PQ, omisso alt. ὄν   33 ἀλλ' om. [M]W   ᾗ μέρος
μέν, ἔστιν ὂν PQ

through the irradiations which proceed from them, a kind of substra-
tum for the gifts of the more specific principles ; and while the irradia-
tions of the superior principles thus serve as a basis, the characters which
proceed from secondary principles are founded upon them : there is
thus an order of precedence in participation, and successive rays strike
downwards upon the same recipient, the more universal causes
affecting it first, and the more specific supplementing these by the
bestowal of their own gifts upon the participants.

For if the more determinative causes operate before the secondary
(prop. 70), being present through their superfluity of power even to
things which have less perfect capacity of reception, and irradiating
even these (prop. 57), whereas causes subordinate in rank confer
their gifts later, then it is plain that the irradiations of the superior
causes, being the first to occupy the common participant, serve as
a support to the bestowals of their subordinates, which use these
irradiations as a foundation and act upon a participant prepared for
them by the more general principles.

PROP. 72. *All those characters which in the participants have the*
relative position of a basis proceed from more complete and more
universal causes.

For the cause of more numerous effects is more powerful and
universal, and nearer to the One, than the cause of fewer (prop. 60).
And the principles which bring into existence the prerequisite
foundations for other gifts are causes of more effects, since they
generate even the receptivity which is a condition of the presence
of the specific Forms. These characters, therefore, are as they
exist in the causes more universal and more complete than the rest.

Cor. From this it is apparent why Matter, taking its origin from
the One, is in itself devoid of Form ; and why body, even though it
participates Being, is in itself without participation in soul. For
Matter, which is the basis of all things, proceeded from the cause of
all things ; and body, which is the basis of ensouled existence, is
derived from a principle more universal than soul, in that after its
fashion it participates Being.

PROP. 73. *Every whole is at the same time an existent thing, and*
participates Being ; but not every existent is a whole.

For either ' existent ' and ' whole ' mean the same thing, or one of
these terms is prior to the other.

But if even the part *qua* part is an existent (for a whole must be
composed of existent parts), although it is not in itself a whole, then

ἄρα ταὐτόν ἐστιν ὂν καὶ ὅλον. εἴη γὰρ ἂν τὸ μέρος οὐκ ὄν·
εἰ δὲ τὸ μέρος οὐκ ὄν, οὐδὲ τὸ ὅλον ἔστι.   πᾶν γὰρ ὅλον μερῶν
ἐστιν ὅλον, ἢ ὡς πρὸ αὐτῶν ὂν ἢ ὡς ἐν αὐτοῖς· μὴ ὄντος οὖν
τοῦ μέρους, οὐδὲ τὸ ὅλον εἶναι δυνατόν.

εἰ δὲ τὸ ὅλον πρὸ τοῦ ὄντος, ἔσται πᾶν ὂν ὅλον εὐθύς· οὐκ 5
ἄρα ἔσται πάλιν τὸ μέρος μέρος.   ἀλλὰ ἀδύνατον· εἰ γὰρ τὸ
ὅλον ἐστὶν ὅλον, μέρους ὂν ὅλον, καὶ τὸ μέρος ἔσται μέρος, ὅλου
μέρος ὄν.   λείπεται ἄρα πᾶν μὲν εἶναι τὸ ὅλον ὄν, οὐ πᾶν δὲ τὸ
ὂν ὅλον.

ἐκ δὴ τούτων φανερὸν ὅτι τὸ πρώτως ὂν ἐπέκεινα τῆς ὁλό- 10
τητός ἐστιν, εἴπερ τὸ μὲν πλείοσι πάρεστι, τὸ ὄν (καὶ γὰρ τοῖς
μέρεσιν, ᾗ μέρη, τὸ εἶναι ὑπάρχει), τὸ δὲ ἐλάττοσι.   τὸ γὰρ
πλειόνων αἴτιον κρεῖττον, τὸ δὲ ἐλαττόνων καταδεέστερον, ὡς
δέδεικται.

74. Πᾶν μὲν εἶδος ὅλον τί ἐστιν (ἐκ γὰρ πλειόνων ὑφέστηκεν, 15
ὧν ἕκαστον συμπληροῖ τὸ εἶδος)· οὐ πᾶν δὲ ὅλον εἶδος.

καὶ γὰρ τὸ τὶ καὶ ἄτομον ὅλον μέν ἐστιν, ᾗ ἄτομον, εἶδος δὲ
οὐκ ἔστι.   πᾶν γὰρ ὅλον ἐστὶ τὸ ἐκ μερῶν ὑφεστός, εἶδος δὲ
τὸ εἰς πλείω τὰ καθέκαστα ἤδη τεμνόμενον.   ἄλλο ἄρα τὸ ὅλον
καὶ ἄλλο τὸ εἶδος· καὶ τὸ μὲν ὑπάρχει πλείοσι, τὸ δὲ ἐλάττοσιν. 20
ὑπὲρ τὰ εἴδη ἄρα τῶν ὄντων ἐστὶ τὸ ὅλον.

ἐκ δὴ τούτων φανερὸν ὅτι τὸ ὅλον μέσην ἔχει τάξιν τοῦ τε
ὄντος καὶ τῶν εἰδῶν.   ᾧ ἔπεται τὸ καὶ πρὸ τῶν εἰδῶν ὑφεστάναι
τὸ ὄν, καὶ τὰ εἴδη ὄντα εἶναι, μὴ μέντοι πᾶν ὂν εἶδος.   ὅθεν καὶ
ἐν τοῖς ἀποτελέσμασιν αἱ στερήσεις ὄντα μέν πώς εἰσιν, εἴδη δὲ 25
οὔκ εἰσι, διὰ τὴν ἑνιαίαν τοῦ ὄντος δύναμιν καὶ αὐταὶ τοῦ εἶναι
καταδεξάμεναί τινα ἀμυδρὰν ἔμφασιν.

75. Πᾶν τὸ κυρίως αἴτιον λεγόμενον ἐξήρηται τοῦ ἀποτελέσ-
ματος.

ἐν αὐτῷ γὰρ ὄν, ἢ συμπληρωτικὸν αὐτοῦ ὑπάρχον ἢ δεόμενόν 30
πως αὐτοῦ πρὸς τὸ εἶναι, ἀτελέστερον ἂν εἴη ταύτῃ τοῦ αἰτιατοῦ.
τὸ δὲ ἐν τῷ ἀποτελέσματι ὂν συναίτιόν ἐστι μᾶλλον ἢ αἴτιον, ἢ
μέρος ὂν τοῦ γινομένου ἢ ὄργανον τοῦ ποιοῦντος· τό τε γὰρ
μέρος ἐν τῷ γινομένῳ ἐστίν, ἀτελέστερον ὑπάρχον τοῦ ὅλου, καὶ
τὸ ὄργανον τῷ ποιοῦντι πρὸς τὴν γένεσιν δουλεύει, τὰ μέτρα 35

---

73. 1 post οὐκ ὄν ins. εἰ μόνον τὸ ὅλον ἐστὶν ὄν PQ   6 alt. μέρος om.
D¹ dett.   11 τὸ ὄν fort. secludendum
74. 17 τουτὶ καὶ τὸ ἄτομον PQ   18 ὑφεστός M : ὑφεστώς cett.   19 ἤδη
BDE : εἴδη CMPQW   20 post τὸ μέν ins. τὸ ὅλον PQ   22 ἐκ . . . ὅλον
inepte repetunt edd.   23 alt. καί om. PQ, non agnosc. W   26 οὐκ ω
(οὐκέτι edd.)   αὐταί scripsi : αὖται ω   τοῦ εἶναι ω (om. edd.)
75. 35 τῷ ποιοῦντι] τὸ ποιοῦν τι Arg (Cr.²)   δουλεύει PQ : om. cett. W

'existent' and 'whole' cannot be identical. For this would make the part non-existent, and thereby the whole also; since every whole is a whole of parts, either as prior to them or as immanent in them (prop. 67), and if the part do not exist, neither can the whole.

And if Wholeness be prior to Being, all that exists will immediately be a whole, and thus again the part will not exist as a part. But this is impossible: for if the whole is a whole because it includes a part, so also a part will be a part because it belongs to a whole. By exclusion, then, every whole is existent, but not every existent is a whole.

Cor. From this it is apparent that primal Being is beyond Wholeness, inasmuch as the former is present to a greater number of participants (since existence is predicable even of parts *qua* parts), and the latter to fewer; for the cause of more effects is superior, that of fewer, inferior, as has been shown (prop. 60).

PROP. 74. *Every specific Form is a whole, as being composed of a number of individuals each of which goes to make up the Form; but not every whole is a specific Form.*

For even the atomic individual is a whole as being atomic, although it is not a Form; since anything is a whole which is composed of parts, but a Form is that which is actually divided into a plurality of individuals. Wholeness and Form are therefore mutually distinct; and the former is the more extensive predicate. Accordingly Wholeness is above the Forms of Being (prop. 60).

Cor. From this it is apparent that Wholeness occupies a mean station between Being and the Forms. It follows that Being is prior also to the Forms; and that the Forms are existent things, but not every existent is a Form. Hence in the resultants, privations are in some sense existent although they are not Forms; for through the unitary power of Being they too have received some feeble irradiation of existence.

I. OF THE RELATION OF CAUSES TO THEIR EFFECTS; AND OF POTENCY.

PROP. 75. *Every cause properly so called transcends its resultant.*

For if such a cause were immanent in its effect, either it would be a complementary part of the latter or it would in some way need it for its own existence (prop. 64), and it would in this regard be inferior to the effect. That which exists in the resultant is not so much a cause as a by-cause, being either a part of the thing produced or an instrument of the maker: for the several parts of the thing exist within it, but are less perfect than the whole; and the instrument serves the maker for the process of production, but is unable to

τῆς ποιήσεως ἀφορίζειν ἑαυτῷ μὴ δυνάμενον. ἅπαν ἄρα τὸ κυρίως αἴτιον, εἴ γε καὶ τελειότερόν ἐστι τοῦ ἀπ' αὐτοῦ καὶ τὸ μέτρον αὐτὸ τῇ γενέσει παρέχεται, καὶ τῶν ὀργάνων ἐξῄρηται καὶ τῶν στοιχείων καὶ πάντων ἁπλῶς τῶν καλουμένων συναιτίων.

76. Πᾶν μὲν τὸ ἀπὸ ἀκινήτου γινόμενον αἰτίας ἀμετάβλητον ⁵ ἔχει τὴν ὕπαρξιν· πᾶν δὲ τὸ ἀπὸ κινουμένης, μεταβλητήν.

εἰ γὰρ ἀκίνητόν ἐστι πάντῃ τὸ ποιοῦν, οὐ διὰ κινήσεως, ἀλλ' αὐτῷ τῷ εἶναι παράγει τὸ δεύτερον ἀφ' ἑαυτοῦ· εἰ δὲ τοῦτο, σύνδρομον ἔχει τῷ ἑαυτοῦ εἶναι τὸ ἀπ' αὐτοῦ· εἰ δὲ τοῦτο, ἕως ἂν ᾖ, παράγει. ἀεὶ δὲ ἔστιν· ἀεὶ ἄρα ὑφίστησι τὸ μετ' αὐτό· ὥστε ¹⁰ καὶ τοῦτο ἀεὶ γίνεται ἐκεῖθεν καὶ ἀεὶ ἔστι, τῷ ἐκείνου ἀεὶ κατὰ τὴν ἐνέργειαν συνάψαν τὸ ἑαυτοῦ κατὰ τὴν πρόοδον ἀεί.

εἰ δὲ δὴ κινεῖται τὸ αἴτιον, καὶ τὸ ἀπ' αὐτοῦ γινόμενον ἔσται μεταβλητὸν κατ' οὐσίαν· ᾧ γὰρ τὸ εἶναι διὰ κινήσεως, τοῦτο τοῦ κινουμένου μεταβάλλοντος μεταβάλλει τὸ εἶναι. εἰ γὰρ ἐκ ¹⁵ κινήσεως παραγόμενον ἀμετάβλητον αὐτὸ μένοι, κρεῖττον ἔσται τῆς ὑποστησάσης αἰτίας. ἀλλ' ἀδύνατον. οὐκ ἄρα ἀμετάβλητον ἔσται. μεταβαλεῖ ἄρα καὶ κινήσεται κατ' οὐσίαν, τὴν ὑποστήσασαν αὐτὸ κίνησιν μιμούμενον.

77. Πᾶν τὸ δυνάμει ὂν ἐκ τοῦ κατ' ἐνέργειαν ὄντος ὃ τοῦτο ²⁰ δυνάμει ἐστὶν εἰς τὸ ἐνεργείᾳ πρόεισι· τὸ μέν πῃ δυνάμει ἐκ τοῦ πῃ κατ' ἐνέργειαν, ᾗ αὐτὸ δυνάμει· τὸ δὲ πάντῃ δυνάμει ὂν ἐκ τοῦ πάντῃ κατ' ἐνέργειαν ὄντος.

αὐτὸ μὲν γὰρ ἑαυτὸ τὸ δυνάμει προάγειν εἰς ἐνέργειαν οὐ πέφυκεν, ἀτελὲς ὄν· εἰ γὰρ ἀτελὲς ὂν αἴτιον ἑαυτῷ γίνοιτο τοῦ ²⁵ τελείου καὶ κατ' ἐνέργειαν, τὸ αἴτιον ἔσται τοῦ ἀπ' αὐτοῦ γεγονότος ἀτελέστερον. οὐκ ἄρα τὸ δυνάμει, ᾗ δυνάμει, ἑαυτῷ τοῦ κατ' ἐνέργειαν αἴτιον· ἔσται γάρ, ᾗ ἀτελές, τοῦ τελείου αἴτιον, εἴπερ τὸ δυνάμει πᾶν, ᾗ δυνάμει, ἀτελές, τὸ δ' ἐνεργείᾳ πᾶν, ᾗ ἐνεργείᾳ, τέλειον. ³⁰

εἰ ἄρα ἔσται τὸ δυνάμει κατ' ἐνέργειαν, ἀπ' ἄλλου τινὸς ἕξει τὸ τέλειον· καὶ ἤτοι καὶ αὐτὸ δυνάμει (ἀλλ' ἔσται οὕτω πάλιν

75. 1 ἀφορίζει, (omissa virgula ante τά, p. 70, l. 35) BCD 'Aνάπτ. mensuras factionis ᾳ cum virtute determinat seipso non potens W 2 εἴ γε] ἀεί PQ 3 αὐτό BCDM²: αὐτῷ [M]PQW
76. 6 ἀπὸ τῆς κινουμένης BCD 8 τῷ] τό M¹ 11–12 τὸ ἐκείνου ... τῷ ἑαυτοῦ PQ 13 δή om. PQ, non agnosc. W 15 κινουμένου MPQW: κινοῦντος B (ex corr. ?) CD 16 αὐτῷ M¹ ut vid. μένει M¹PQ 18 μετα-. βαλεῖ BCDβγ: μεταβάλλει MPQα
77. 22 et 23 πάντα (bis) MW 24 ἑαυτό] αὐτό M¹ τό ω (om. O¹ edd.) 25 alt. ὄν ω (om. edd.) 25–6 τοῦ τελείου om. M¹ (τοῦ τέλους edd.) 26 et 28 ἔσται] ἄρα (bis) [M] 28 τοῦ τελείου ω (τοῦ τέλους edd.) 30 πᾶν, ᾗ ἐνερ-γείᾳ, ω (om. edd.) 32 τέλειον ω (τέλος O Port. Cr.¹) ἔσται καὶ οὕτω Arg (Cr.) πάλιν οὕτω BCD

determine for itself the limits of creation.   Accordingly every cause properly so called, inasmuch as it both is more perfect than that which proceeds from it (prop. 7) and itself furnishes the limit of its production, transcends the instruments, the elements, and in general all that is described as a by-cause.

PROP. 76. *All that arises from an unmoved cause has an invariable substance ; all that arises from a mobile cause, a variable.*

For if the maker be wholly unmoved, it produces from itself the secondary not through a movement but by its mere existence (prop. 26) ; and if so, concurrently with its own being it contains the being which proceeds from it ; and if this be so, while it continues to exist it continues to produce.   But it exists perpetually : therefore it perpetually produces its consequent, so that the latter arises perpetually from it and perpetually exists, attaching its ceaseless procession to the ceaseless activity of its cause.

If on the other hand the cause be mobile, that which arises from it will be correspondingly variable in its being.   For that which gets its being through a movement varies its being with the variation of the mobile cause.   If being produced by movement it remained itself invariable it would be superior to its originative cause, and this is impossible (prop. 7) : therefore it is not invariable.   It will therefore be variable and mobile in its existence, imitating the movement which gave rise to it.

PROP. 77. *All that exists potentially is advanced to actuality by the agency of something which is actually what the other is potentially : the partially potential by that which is actual in the same partial respect, and the wholly potential by the wholly actual.*

For it is not in the nature of the potential to advance itself to actuality, being imperfect; since if being imperfect it became the cause of its own perfection or actualization the cause would be less perfect than the effect.   Thus the potential *qua* potential is not the cause of its own actualization : for in that respect in which it is imperfect it would be the cause of perfection, inasmuch as everything potential is imperfect *qua* potential, while everything actual is perfect *qua* actual.

If, then, the potential is to exist in actuality, it must derive that perfection from another.   And either this other is itself potential— but if so, the imperfect will again be parent to the perfect—or it

τὸ ἀτελὲς τοῦ τελείου γεννητικόν) ἢ ἐνεργείᾳ, καὶ ἤτοι ἄλλο τι
ἢ τοῦτο ὃ δυνάμει τὸ κατ' ἐνέργειαν γινόμενον. ἦν. ἀλλ' εἰ
μὲν ἄλλο τι ἐνεργείᾳ ὂν ποιεῖ, κατὰ τὴν ἑαυτοῦ ἰδιότητα ποιοῦν
οὐ τὸ δυνάμει τὸ ἐν θατέρῳ ποιήσει ἐνεργείᾳ· οὐδὲ τοῦτο τοίνυν
ἔσται κατ' ἐνέργειαν, εἴπερ μή, ᾗ δυνάμει ἔστι, ταύτῃ γίνοιτο. 5
λείπεται ἄρα ἐκ τοῦ κατ' ἐνέργειαν ὄντος ὃ δυνάμει τί ἐστιν εἰς
τὸ ἐνεργείᾳ μεταβάλλειν.

78. Πᾶσα δύναμις ἢ τελεία ἐστὶν ἢ ἀτελής.

ἡ μὲν γὰρ τῆς ἐνεργείας οἰστικὴ τελεία δύναμις· καὶ γὰρ
ἄλλα ποιεῖ τέλεια διὰ τῶν ἑαυτῆς ἐνεργειῶν, τὸ δὲ τελειωτικὸν 10
ἄλλων μειζόνως αὐτὸ τελειότερον. ἡ δὲ ἄλλου του δεομένη τοῦ
κατ' ἐνέργειαν προϋπάρχοντος, καθ' ἣν δυνάμει τι ἔστιν, ἀτελής·
δεῖται γὰρ τοῦ τελείου ἐν ἄλλῳ ὄντος, ἵνα μετασχοῦσα ἐκείνου
τελεία γένηται· καθ' αὑτὴν ἄρα ἀτελής ἐστιν ἡ τοιαύτη δύναμις.
ὥστε τελεία μὲν ἡ τοῦ κατ' ἐνέργειαν δύναμις, ἐνεργείας οὖσα 15
γόνιμος· ἀτελὴς δὲ ἡ τοῦ δυνάμει, παρ' ἐκείνου κτωμένη τὸ
τέλειον.

79. Πᾶν τὸ γινόμενον ἐκ τῆς διττῆς γίνεται δυνάμεως.

καὶ γὰρ αὐτὸ δεῖ ἐπιτήδειον εἶναι καὶ δύναμιν ἀτελῆ ἔχειν,
καὶ τὸ ποιοῦν, κατ' ἐνέργειαν ὃ τοῦτο δυνάμει ἐστὶν ὑπάρχον, 20
δύναμιν προειληφέναι τελείαν. πᾶσα γὰρ ἐνέργεια ἐκ δυνάμεως τῆς ἐνούσης πρόεισιν· εἴτε γὰρ τὸ ποιοῦν μὴ ἔχοι δύναμιν,
πῶς ἐνεργήσει καὶ ποιήσει εἰς ἄλλο; εἴτε τὸ γινόμενον μὴ ἔχοι
τὴν κατ' ἐπιτηδειότητα δύναμιν, πῶς ἂν γένοιτο; τὸ γὰρ ποιοῦν
εἰς τὸ παθεῖν δυνάμενον ποιεῖ πᾶν, ἀλλ' οὐκ εἰς τὸ τυχὸν καὶ ὃ 25
μὴ πέφυκεν ὑπ' αὐτοῦ πάσχειν.

80. Πᾶν σῶμα πάσχειν καθ' αὑτὸ πέφυκε, πᾶν δὲ ἀσώματον
ποιεῖν, τὸ μὲν ἀδρανὲς ὂν καθ' αὑτό, τὸ δὲ ἀπαθές· πάσχει δὲ
καὶ τὸ ἀσώματον διὰ τὴν πρὸς τὸ σῶμα κοινωνίαν, ὡς δύναται
ποιεῖν καὶ τὰ σώματα διὰ τὴν τῶν ἀσωμάτων μετουσίαν. 30

τὸ μὲν γὰρ σῶμα, ᾗ σῶμα, διαιρετόν ἐστι μόνον, καὶ ταύτῃ
παθητόν, πάντῃ ὂν μεριστόν, καὶ πάντῃ εἰς ἄπειρον. τὸ δὲ
ἀσώματον, ἁπλοῦν ὄν, ἀπαθές ἐστιν· οὔτε γὰρ διαιρεῖσθαι

77. 1 τό om. MP   4 ποιήσειεν M   6 ὅ] ᾗ PQ
78. 11 μειζόνως ὡς [M]W, μειζόνως ὡς M²   του non agnosc. W
13 δεῖται ω (δεῖ O edd.)   post γάρ deficit P (in fine paginae)   τελείου
ω (τέλους edd.)   14 ἀτελής ω (ἀτελές Cr.²)   15 ὥστε ... δύναμις om.
MW   15–16 οὖσα δύναμις γόνιμος [M]W
79. 20 ὃ τοῦτο BDEM : ὃ τοῦ C, ὅτου Arg et ? W, ὃ τό Q   23 πῶς γάρ BC
ἐνεργήσῃ κ. ποιήσῃ edd. contra libros   24 τήν om. BCD
80. 28 ἀδρανές ... ἐμπαθές [M]W   29 alt. τό om. M   30 ποιεῖ M
31 ᾗ σῶμα om. M¹   33 ἁπλοῦν ὄν om. Q : ἁπλοῦν, ὅθεν καί D   33–p. 76,
l. 1 δύναται διαιρεῖσθαι BCD

exists actually, and is actually either some other thing or else that which the thing being actualized was potentially. But the agent will not render actual that which is potential in this latter if it be itself actually some other thing, for it produces according to its own character (prop. 18); nor will the latter be actual unless it be made actual in that respect in which it is already potential. It follows by exclusion that any particular thing passes into actuality through the agency of that in which its potentiality is already actual.

PROP. 78. *There is a perfect and an imperfect potency.*

For the potency which brings to actuality is perfect, since through its own activities it makes others perfect, and that which can perfect others is itself more greatly perfect. But that potency which needs some extraneous presubsistent actuality (prop. 77), the potency in virtue of which a thing exists potentially, is imperfect. For it needs the perfection which resides in another in order to become perfect by participating it: in itself, therefore, such a potency is imperfect. Thus the perfect potency is that which resides in the actual and breeds new actuality; the imperfect is that which resides in the potential and derives its fulfilment from the actual.

PROP. 79. *All that comes to be arises out of the twofold potency.*

For the subject of the process must itself be fitted for it and so possess an imperfect potency; and the agent, being already in actuality what the subject is potentially (prop. 77), must already have a perfect potency. For every actuality proceeds from the in-dwelling potency; if the agent should be without potency, how shall it be operative and act upon another? and if the subject of the process should lack the receptive potency, how shall the process occur? An agent acts always upon something capable of being affected, and not on any chance subject, whose nature may prevent it from responding.

PROP. 80. *The proper nature of all bodies is to be acted upon, and of all incorporeals to be agents, the former being in themselves inactive and the latter impassible; but through association with the body the incorporeal too is acted upon, even as through partnership with incorporeals bodies too can act.*

For body, *qua* body, has no character save divisibility, which renders it capable of being acted upon, being in every part subject to division, and that to infinity in every part. But the incorporeal, being simple, is impassible: for that which is without parts cannot

δύναται τὸ ἀμερὲς οὔτε ἀλλοιοῦσθαι τὸ μὴ σύνθετον. ἢ οὖν οὐδὲν
ἔσται ποιητικὸν ἢ τὸ ἀσώματον, εἴπερ τὸ σῶμα, καθὸ σῶμα,
οὐ ποιεῖ, πρὸς τὸ διαιρεῖσθαι μόνον καὶ πάσχειν ἐκκείμενον.
ἐπεὶ καὶ πᾶν τὸ ποιοῦν δύναμιν ἔχει ποιητικήν· ἄποιον δὲ 5
καὶ ἀδύναμον τὸ σῶμα καθ' αὑτό· ὥστε οὐ καθὸ σῶμα ποιήσει,
ἀλλὰ κατὰ τὴν τοῦ ποιεῖν ἐν αὐτῷ δύναμιν· μεθέξει ἄρα
δυνάμεως ποιεῖ, ὅταν ποιῇ. καὶ μὴν καὶ τὰ ἀσώματα παθῶν
μετέχει ἐν σώματι γενόμενα, συνδιαιρούμενα σώμασι καὶ ἀπο-
λαύοντα τῆς μεριστῆς ἐκείνων φύσεως, ἀμερῆ ὄντα κατὰ τὴν 10
ἑαυτῶν οὐσίαν.

81. Πᾶν τὸ χωριστῶς μετεχόμενον διά τινος ἀχωρίστου
δυνάμεως, ἣν ἐνδίδωσι, τῷ μετέχοντι πάρεστιν.

εἰ γὰρ [καὶ] αὐτὸ χωριστὸν ὑπάρχει τοῦ μετέχοντος καὶ οὐκ
ἔστιν ἐν ἐκείνῳ, ὡς τὴν ὑπόστασιν ἐν ἑαυτῷ κεκτημένον, δεῖ δή 15
τινος αὐτοῖς μεσότητος συνεχούσης θάτερον πρὸς θάτερον, ὁμοιο-
τέρας τῷ μετεχομένῳ καίτοι ἐν αὐτῷ τῷ μετέχοντι οὔσης. εἰ γὰρ
ἐκεῖνο χωριστόν ἐστι, πῶς τοῦτο μετέχει, μήτε αὐτὸ ἐκεῖνο ἔχον
μήτε ἄλλο ἀπ' αὐτοῦ; δύναμις ἄρα ἀπ' ἐκείνου καὶ ἔλλαμψις
εἰς τὸ μετέχον προελθοῦσα συνάψει ἄμφω· καὶ τὸ μὲν ἔσται δι' 20
οὗ ἡ μέθεξις, τὸ δὲ μετεχόμενον, τὸ δὲ μετέχον.

82. Πᾶν ἀσώματον, πρὸς ἑαυτὸ ἐπιστρεπτικὸν ὄν, ὑπ' ἄλλων
μετεχόμενον χωριστῶς μετέχεται.

εἰ γὰρ ἀχωρίστως, ἡ ἐνέργεια αὐτοῦ οὐκ ἔσται χωριστὴ τοῦ
μετέχοντος, ὥσπερ οὐδὲ ἡ οὐσία. εἰ δὲ τοῦτο, οὐκ ἐπιστρέψει 25
πρὸς ἑαυτό· ἐπιστρέψαν γὰρ ἔσται τοῦ μετέχοντος χωρίς,
ἄλλου ὄντος αὐτὸ ἄλλο ὄν. εἰ ἄρα δύναται πρὸς ἑαυτὸ ἐπιστρέφειν, χωριστῶς μετέχεται, ὅταν μετέχηται ὑπ' ἄλλων.

83. Πᾶν τὸ ἑαυτοῦ γνωστικὸν πρὸς ἑαυτὸ πάντῃ ἐπιστρεπτικόν ἐστιν. 30

ὅτι μὲν γὰρ τῇ ἐνεργείᾳ πρὸς ἑαυτὸ ἐπιστρέφει, γινῶσκον
ἑαυτό, δῆλον· ἐν γάρ ἐστι τὸ γινῶσκον καὶ γινωσκόμενον, καὶ
ἡ γνῶσις αὐτοῦ πρὸς ἑαυτὸ ὡς γνωστόν· ὡς μὲν γινώσκοντος,

80. 5-7 ὥστε ... δύναμιν et ἄποιον ... καθ' αὐτό transposui   6 ἀδύνατον M
7 τοῦ om. BCD   8 alt. καί om. B   9 σώματι] σώμασι M   γινόμενα
M primitus   σώμασι] σώματι DE
81. 14 prius καί om. Q : seclusi   alt. καί om. Q   15 ἑαυτῷ] αὐτῷ MQ
16 συνεχούσης] ἐνούσης QM³   17 καίτοι scripsi : καὶ τῆς ω   18 μετέχοι
M   19 καὶ ἔλλαμψις ἀπ' ἐκείνου BCD (O edd.)   20 ante ἄμφω ins. καί
BCD
82. 22 ὄν om. MW, ante ἐπιστρεπτικόν Q   27 αὐτό BCDW : αὐτό, αὐτό M:
αὐτοῦ αὐτό Q (τὸ αὐτό edd.)   28 μετέχηται] μετέχεται M
83. 29 ἑαυτό] ἑαυτοῦ M   32 καὶ τὸ γινωσκόμενον Arg (Cr.)   33 αὐτοῦ]
ἑαυτοῦ Q (O edd.)

be divided, and that which is not composite is not subject to change (prop. 48). Either, then, there is no active principle or the incorporeal is such, since body, *qua* body, is not an agent but is subject only to being divided and acted upon.

Again, every agent has an active potency; but body in itself is without quality and without potency: therefore it cannot act in virtue of being body, but only in virtue of a potency of action residing in it—that is, it acts, when it does act, by participation of potency. Further, even incorporeals participate passive affections when they come to be in a body, because they are then divided along with their bodies and feel the effect of the divisible nature of the latter, although in their own being they are without parts.

PROP. 81. *All that is participated without loss of separateness is present to the participant through an inseparable potency which it implants.*

For if it is itself something separate from the participant and not contained in it, something which subsists in itself, then they need a mean term to connect them, one which more nearly resembles the participated principle than the participant does, and yet actually resides in the latter. For if the former is separate, how can it be participated by that which contains neither it nor any emanation from it? Accordingly a potency or irradiation, proceeding from the participated to the participant, must link the two ; and this medium of participation will be distinct from both.

PROP. 82. *Every incorporeal, if it be capable of reverting upon itself, when participated by other things is participated without loss of separateness.*

For if it be participated inseparably, its activity will no more be separable from the participant than will its existence. And if so, it will not revert upon itself: for if it do so, it will be separate from the participant as one distinct thing over against another (prop. 16). If, then, it be capable of reverting upon itself, when participated by others it is separably participated.

PROP. 83. *All that is capable of self-knowledge is capable of every form of self-reversion.*

For that it is self-reversive in its activity is evident, since it knows itself: knower and known are here one, and its cognition has itself as object ; as the act of a knower this cognition is an activity,

ἐνέργειά τις οὖσα· αὐτοῦ δὲ πρὸς ἑαυτό, διότι ἑαυτοῦ γνωστικόν
ἐστιν. ἀλλὰ μὴν ὅτι καὶ τῇ οὐσίᾳ, εἰ τῇ ἐνεργείᾳ, δέδεικται·
πᾶν γὰρ τὸ τῷ ἐνεργεῖν πρὸς ἑαυτὸ ἐπιστρεπτικὸν καὶ οὐσίαν
ἔχει πρὸς ἑαυτὴν συννεύουσαν καὶ ἐν ἑαυτῇ οὖσαν.

84. Πᾶν τὸ ἀεὶ ὂν ἀπειροδύναμόν ἐστιν.

εἰ γὰρ ἀνέκλειπτός ἐστιν αὐτοῦ ἡ ὑπόστασις, καὶ ἡ δύναμις,
καθ' ἥν ἐστιν ὅ ἐστι καὶ εἶναι δύναται, ἄπειρός ἐστι. πεπερασμένη γὰρ οὖσα ἡ κατὰ τὸ εἶναι δύναμις ἀπολίποι ἄν ποτε·
ἀπολιποῦσα δέ, καὶ τὸ εἶναι τοῦ ἔχοντος αὐτὴν ἀπολίποι καὶ
οὐκέτ' ἂν ἀεὶ ὂν ὑπάρχοι. δεῖ ἄρα τὴν τοῦ ἀεὶ ὄντος δύναμιν, 10
τὴν συνέχουσαν αὐτὸ κατὰ τὴν οὐσίαν, ἄπειρον εἶναι.

85. Πᾶν τὸ ἀεὶ γινόμενον ἄπειρον τοῦ γίνεσθαι δύναμιν ἔχει.

εἰ γὰρ ἀεὶ γίνεται, ἀνέκλειπτός ἐστιν ἡ τῆς γενέσεως ἐν
αὐτῷ δύναμις. πεπερασμένη γὰρ οὖσα, ἐν τῷ ἀπείρῳ χρόνῳ
παύσεται· παυσαμένης δὲ τῆς τοῦ γίνεσθαι δυνάμεως παύσαιτο 15
ἂν καὶ τὸ γινόμενον τὸ κατ' αὐτὴν γινόμενον, καὶ οὐκέτ' ἂν ἀεὶ
γινόμενον εἴη. ἀλλὰ μὴν ἀεὶ ὑπόκειται γινόμενον· ἄπειρον ἄρα
ἔχει τὴν τοῦ γίνεσθαι δύναμιν.

86. Πᾶν τὸ ὄντως ὂν ἄπειρόν ἐστιν οὔτε κατὰ τὸ πλῆθος
οὔτε κατὰ τὸ μέγεθος, ἀλλὰ κατὰ τὴν δύναμιν μόνην. 20

πᾶν [μὲν] γὰρ τὸ ἄπειρον ἢ ἐν ποσῷ ἐστιν ἢ ἐν πηλίκῳ ἢ ἐν
δυνάμει. τὸ δ' ὄντως ὂν ἄπειρον μὲν ὡς ἄσβεστον, ἔχον τὴν
ζωὴν καὶ τὴν ὕπαρξιν ἀνέκλειπτον καὶ τὴν ἐνέργειαν ἀνε-
λάττωτον· οὔτε δὲ διὰ μέγεθός ἐστιν ἄπειρον (ἀμέγεθες γὰρ τὸ
ὄντως ὄν, αὐθυποστάτως ὄν· πᾶν γὰρ τὸ αὐθυποστάτως ὂν 25
ἀμερές ἐστι καὶ ἁπλοῦν), οὔτε διὰ πλῆθος (ἑνοειδέστατον γάρ,
ἅτε ἐγγυτάτω τοῦ ἑνὸς τεταγμένον, καὶ τῷ ἑνὶ συγγενέστατον),
ἀλλὰ κατὰ τὴν δύναμιν ἄπειρον ἐκεῖνο. διὸ κατὰ ταὐτὸν ἀμερὲς
ἐκεῖνο καὶ ἄπειρον· καὶ ὅσῳ δὴ μᾶλλον ἓν καὶ μᾶλλον ἀμερές,
τοσούτῳ καὶ ἄπειρον μᾶλλον. ἡ γὰρ μεριζομένη δύναμις 30
ἀσθενὴς ἤδη καὶ πεπερασμένη, καὶ αἵ γε πάντῃ μερισταὶ
δυνάμεις πεπερασμέναι πάντως εἰσίν· αἱ γὰρ ἔσχαται καὶ

83. 1 αὐτοῦ] ἑαυτοῦ M   πρὸς ἑαυτό D[M]: πρὸς αὐτό BCQM²   2 εἰ BCDM²:
ἐν [M], καί Q, simul cum W   3 καί om. Q   4 ἐν ἑαυτῇ M : ἐν αὐτῇ cett.
84. 6 ἐστιν αὐτοῦ BCDM (αὐτῆς edd.): αὐτοῦ ἐστιν Q   8 post δύναμις
ins. καθ' ἥν ἐστι Q   λείποι Q   9 ἀπολείπουσα Q   ἀπολείποι Q   10 ἀεὶ
ὄντος Q, semper entis W : ὄντος ἀεί BCDM
85. 13 ἐν om. C   16 prius τό om. Q fort. recte   alt. τό om. Arg (Cr.²)
17 ὑπόκειται ἀεί BCD
86. 19 ὄντως ὄν] ὂν τῷ ὄντι Arg   alt. τό om. DQ   20 τό om. DQ   21 μέν
om. Q, non agnosc. W : seclusi   τὸ ἄπειρον ω (ἄπειρον edd.)   22 τὸ
δὲ ἀεὶ ὄν M (corr. in mg. m. rec.) W   25 αὐθυπόστατον bis [M]   27 malim
συγγενέστατον ὄν   28 τήν om. M¹   28–9 διὸ καὶ ταὐτὸν ἀμερὲς ἐκεῖ καί [M]
30 τοσούτῳ] οὕτω [M]   32 πάντως] πως [M]   αἱ γάρ] εἰ δὲ αἱ Q

and it is self-reversive since in it the subject knows itself. But if in activity, then also in existence, as has been shown : for everything whose activity reverts upon itself has also an existence which is self-concentrated and self-contained (prop. 44).

PROP. **84.** *All that perpetually is is infinite in potency.*

For if its subsistence is unfailing, then the potency, in virtue of which it is what it is and is able to exist, is likewise infinite : since this potency of being, if it were finite, would one day fail ; which failing, the existence of its possessor would also fail and that possessor would no longer be perpetual. Accordingly that potency in perpetual Being which maintains it in existence must be infinite.

PROP. **85.** *All that perpetually comes to be has an infinite potency of coming to be.*

For if it perpetually comes to be, the potency of becoming is unfailing in it : since if this be finite, it will cease in the course of infinite time ; and when the potency of becoming ceases, the subject which comes to be in virtue of it must also cease and be no longer a subject of perpetual process. But by hypothesis it is such a subject : therefore its potency of coming to be is infinite.

PROP. **86.** *All true Being is infinite neither in number nor in size, but only in potency.*

For all infinitude is either of quantity or of bulk, or else of potency. Now true Being is infinite as having an unquenchable life, an unfailing subsistence and an undiminished activity (props. 49, 84). But it is not infinite in virtue of its size : for true Being, as self-constituted, is devoid of magnitude, since all that is self-constituted is without parts and simple (prop. 47). Nor is it so in virtue of its number : for it has the utmost unity as standing closest to the One, and is most nearly akin to the latter (prop. 62). Its infinitude is in respect of potency. Accordingly what renders it indivisible makes it also infinite ; and a being is more infinite in proportion as it is more one and indivisible. For as a potency is divided it becomes weak and finite (prop. 61), and potencies completely divided are in every way finite : the last potencies, which are most remote

8o THE ELEMENTS OF THEOLOGY

πορρωτάτω τοῦ ἑνὸς διὰ τὸν μερισμὸν πεπερασμέναι πάντως
εἰσίν, αἱ δὲ πρῶται διὰ τὴν ἀμέρειαν ἄπειροι· ὁ μὲν γὰρ
μερισμὸς διαφορεῖ καὶ ἐκλύει τὴν ἑκάστου δύναμιν, ἡ δὲ ἀμέρεια
σφίγγουσα καὶ συσπειρῶσα ἀνέκλειπτον αὐτὴν καὶ ἀνελάττωτον
ἐν ἑαυτῇ συνέχει. ἀλλὰ μὴν ἡ κατὰ μέγεθος ἀπειρία καὶ ἡ 5
κατὰ πλῆθος στέρησίς ἐστι πάντῃ τῆς ἀμερείας καὶ ἀπόπτωσις·
ἐγγυτάτω μὲν γὰρ τοῦ ἀμεροῦς τὸ πεπερασμένον, πορρωτάτω δὲ
τὸ ἄπειρον, πάντῃ τοῦ ἑνὸς ἐκβεβηκός. οὐκ ἄρα τὸ κατὰ
δύναμιν ἄπειρον ἐν ἀπείρῳ κατὰ πλῆθός ἐστιν ἢ μέγεθος, εἴπερ
ἡ μὲν ἄπειρος δύναμις τῇ ἀμερείᾳ σύνεστι, τὸ δὲ πλήθει ἢ ιc
μεγέθει ἄπειρον πορρωτάτω τοῦ ἀμεροῦς ἐστιν. εἰ οὖν τὸ ὂν
μεγέθει ἦν ἢ πλήθει ἄπειρον, οὐκ ἂν ἀπειροδύναμον ἦν· ἀλλὰ
μὴν ἀπειροδύναμόν ἐστιν· οὐκ ἄρα ἄπειρον κατὰ πλῆθός ἐστιν
ἢ μέγεθος.

87. Πᾶν μὲν τὸ αἰώνιον ὄν ἐστιν, οὐ πᾶν δὲ τὸ ὂν αἰώνιον. 15
καὶ γὰρ τοῖς γενητοῖς ὑπάρχει πως τοῦ ὄντος μέθεξις, καθ'
ὅσον οὐκ ἔστι ταῦτα τὸ μηδαμῶς ὄν, εἰ δὲ μὴ ἔστι τὸ γινόμενον
οὐδαμῶς ὄν, ἔστι πως ὄν. τὸ δὲ αἰώνιον οὐδαμῇ τοῖς γενητοῖς
ὑπάρχει, καὶ μάλισθ' ὅσα μηδὲ τῆς κατὰ χρόνον τὸν ὅλον
ἀϊδιότητος μετείληφεν. ἀλλὰ μὴν πᾶν τὸ αἰώνιον ἀεί ἐστι· 20
μετέχει γὰρ αἰῶνος, ὃς τὸ ἀεὶ εἶναι δίδωσιν ὑφ' ὧν ἂν μετέχηται.
τὸ ἄρα ὂν ὑπὸ πλειόνων μετέχεται ἢ ὁ αἰών. ἐπέκεινα ἄρα τοῦ
αἰῶνος τὸ ὄν· οἷς μὲν γὰρ αἰῶνος μέτεστι, καὶ τοῦ ὄντος· οἷς δὲ
τοῦ ὄντος, οὐ πᾶσι καὶ αἰῶνος.

88. Πᾶν τὸ ὄντως ὂν ἢ πρὸ αἰῶνός ἐστιν ἢ ἐν τῷ αἰῶνι ἢ 25
μετέχον αἰῶνος.

ὅτι μὲν γάρ ἐστι πρὸ αἰῶνος, δέδεικται. ἀλλὰ μὴν καὶ ἐν
τῷ αἰῶνι· ὁ γὰρ αἰὼν τὸ ἀεὶ μετὰ τοῦ ὄντος ἔχει. καὶ μετέχον
αἰῶνος· τὸ γὰρ αἰώνιον πᾶν μεθέξει καὶ τοῦ ἀεὶ καὶ τοῦ ὄντος
αἰώνιον λέγεται. τοῦτο μὲν γὰρ κατὰ μέθεξιν ἄμφω ἔχει, καὶ 30
τὸ ἀεὶ καὶ τὸ ὄν· ὁ δὲ αἰὼν τὸ μὲν ἀεὶ πρώτως, τὸ δὲ ὂν κατὰ
μέθεξιν· τὸ δὲ ὂν αὐτὸ πρώτως ὄν ἐστιν.

86. 1-2 πάντως εἰσίν scripsi : πώς εἰσιν ωW   4 συσφίγγουσα Q   συσπείρουσα
BCQ   6 ἀμερείας MQW : ἀπειρίας BCD   7 μέν om. BCD   9 κατὰ τὸ
πλῆθος C   ἐστιν om. M¹   10 τό] τῷ [M]   11 τὸ ὄντως ὄν Q   13 ἄπειρον
ω (om. edd.)
87. 15 μέν om. M   αἰώνιον καὶ ὄν M   19 τῆς] τοῖς BD   20 ἀεὶ ὄν
ἐστι Q   21 τὸ ἀεί τι εἶναι O (edd.)   δίδωσι πᾶσιν Q fort. recte   23 γὰρ
τοῦ αἰῶνος Arg (Cr.)
88. 25 τοῦ αἰῶνος Q   26 αἰῶνος μετέχον Q   28 μετ' αὐτοῦ ὄντως Q
τὸ μετέχον QM²   29 τὸ γὰρ ... 30 λέγεται ω (om. Port., αἰώνιον λέγεται
om. Arg Cr.)   30 γάρ ω (om. dett., edd.)

from the One, are in every way finite because of their partition, while the first are infinite because they are without parts.   For partition dissipates and dissolves the potency of the individual, but indivisibility, compressing and concentrating it, keeps it self-contained without exhaustion or diminution.   But infinitude of size or number signifies a complete lapse from indivisibility and total privation of it : for the quantitative finite is nearest to the indivisible, and the quantitative infinite, which has completely escaped from unity, is the most remote.   Hence infinitude of potency cannot reside in anything infinite in number or size, since infinite potency accompanies indivisibility, and the infinite of number or size stands furthest from the indivisible.   If, then, Being were infinite in size or number, it would not have infinite potency ; but it has infinite potency (prop. 84) : therefore it is not infinite in number or size.

J. OF BEING, LIMIT, AND INFINITUDE.

PROP. 87. *All that is eternal has Being ; but not all that has Being is eternal.*

For participation of Being is in some sense predicable even of things having temporal origin, inasmuch as they are distinct from the non-existent, and if the thing of process is not non-existent, it in some sense *is*.   But eternity is in no sense a predicate of things originated, and least of all is it a predicate of such as do not participate even temporal perpetuity.   On the other hand all that is eternal perpetually *is* ; for it participates Eternity, which bestows perpetuity of Being upon its participants.   Thus Being is participated by a greater number of terms than Eternity.   Therefore Being is beyond Eternity (prop. 60) : for what shares in Eternity shares also in Being, but not all that shares in Being shares also in Eternity.

PROP. 88. *There is true Being both prior to and in Eternity, and there is also true Being which participates Eternity.*

For that true Being exists prior to Eternity has already been shown (prop. 87).   But it exists also in Eternity : for Eternity has perpetuity combined with Being.   And as a participant of Eternity : for all that is eternal is so called because it participates both perpetuity and Being.   This last grade has both its characters by participation, perpetuity and Being ; Eternity has perpetuity primitively, Being by participation ; while Being itself is primitively Being.

89. Πᾶν τὸ ὄντως ὂν ἐκ πέρατός ἐστι καὶ ἀπείρου.

εἰ γὰρ ἀπειροδύναμόν ἐστι, δῆλον ὅτι ἄπειρόν ἐστι, καὶ ταύτῃ ἐκ τοῦ ἀπείρου ὑφέστηκεν. εἰ δὲ ἀμερὲς καὶ ἑνοειδές, ταύτῃ πέρατος μετείληφε· τὸ γὰρ ἑνὸς μετασχὸν πεπέρασται. ἀλλὰ μὴν ἀμερὲς ἅμα καὶ ἀπειροδύναμόν ἐστιν. ἐκ πέρατος ἄρα ἐστὶ 5 καὶ ἀπείρου πᾶν τὸ ὄντως ὄν.

90. Πάντων τῶν ἐκ πέρατος καὶ ἀπειρίας ὑποστάντων προϋπάρχει καθ᾿ αὑτὰ τὸ πρῶτον πέρας καὶ ἡ πρώτη ἀπειρία.

εἰ γὰρ τῶν τινὸς ὄντων τὰ ἐφ᾿ ἑαυτῶν ὄντα προϋφέστηκεν ὡς κοινὰ πάντων καὶ ἀρχηγικὰ αἴτια καὶ μὴ τινῶν, ἀλλὰ 10 πάντων ἁπλῶς, δεῖ πρὸ τοῦ ἐξ ἀμφοῖν εἶναι τὸ πρῶτον πέρας καὶ τὸ πρώτως ἄπειρον. τὸ γὰρ ἐν τῷ μικτῷ πέρας ἀπειρίας ἐστὶ μετειληφὸς καὶ τὸ ἄπειρον πέρατος· τὸ δὲ πρῶτον ἑκάστου οὐκ ἄλλο ἐστὶν ἢ ὅ ἐστιν· οὐκ ἄρα δεῖ περατοειδὲς εἶναι τὸ πρώτως ἄπειρον καὶ ἀπειροειδὲς τὸ πρῶτον πέρας· πρὸ τοῦ μικτοῦ ἄρα 15 ταῦτα πρώτως.

91. Πᾶσα δύναμις ἢ πεπερασμένη ἐστὶν ἢ ἄπειρος· ἀλλ᾿ ἡ μὲν πεπερασμένη πᾶσα ἐκ τῆς ἀπείρου δυνάμεως ὑφέστηκεν, ἡ δὲ ἄπειρος δύναμις ἐκ τῆς πρώτης ἀπειρίας.

αἱ μὲν γὰρ ποτὲ οὖσαι δυνάμεις πεπερασμέναι εἰσί, τῆς τοῦ 20 ἀεὶ εἶναι ἀπειρίας ἀποπεσοῦσαι· αἱ δὲ τῶν ἀεὶ ὄντων ἄπειροι, μηδέποτε τὴν ἑαυτῶν ἀπολείπουσαι ὕπαρξιν.

92. Πᾶν τὸ πλῆθος τῶν ἀπείρων δυνάμεων μιᾶς ἐξῆπται τῆς πρώτης ἀπειρίας, ἥτις οὐχ ὡς μετεχομένη δύναμίς ἐστιν, οὐδὲ ἐν τοῖς δυναμένοις ὑφέστηκεν, ἀλλὰ καθ᾿ αὑτήν, οὐ τινὸς οὖσα 25 δύναμις τοῦ μετέχοντος, ἀλλὰ πάντων αἰτία τῶν ὄντων.

εἰ γὰρ καὶ τὸ ὂν αὐτὸ τὸ πρῶτον ἔχει δύναμιν, ἀλλ᾿ οὐκ ἔστιν ἡ αὐτοδύναμις. ἔχει γὰρ καὶ πέρας· ἡ δὲ πρώτη δύναμις ἀπειρία ἐστίν. αἱ γὰρ ἄπειροι δυνάμεις διὰ μετουσίαν ἀπειρίας ἄπειροι· ἡ οὖν αὐτοαπειρία πρὸ πασῶν ἔσται δυνάμεων, δι᾿ ἣν 30 καὶ τὸ ὂν ἀπειροδύναμον καὶ πάντα μετέσχεν ἀπειρίας. οὔτε γὰρ τὸ πρῶτον ἡ ἀπειρία (μέτρον γὰρ πάντων ἐκεῖνο, τἀγαθὸν ὑπάρχον καὶ ἕν) οὔτε τὸ ὄν (ἄπειρον γὰρ τοῦτο, ἀλλ᾿ οὐκ ἀπειρία)· μεταξὺ ἄρα τοῦ πρώτου καὶ τοῦ ὄντος ἡ ἀπειρία, πάντων αἰτία τῶν ἀπειροδυνάμων καὶ αἰτία πάσης τῆς ἐν τοῖς οὖσιν ἀπειρίας. 35

89. Tit. περὶ ἀπείρου καὶ πέρατος M   3 ante ἀμερές ins. καὶ BCD   5 ante ἀμερές ins. καὶ B   ἅμα om. Q : ἄρα M²   καὶ τὸ ἀπειροδύναμόν BCD   ἐστὶ om. M¹
90. 9 τινος [M]W : τινων BCDQM²   12 τὸ πρῶτον ἄπειρον Arg(Cr.)   15 καὶ πρὸ τοῦ BCD   μικτοῦ (ω) (μικροῦ Cr.² errore preli)
91. 17 ἢ] εἰ [M]Q   22 ἀπολιποῦσαι M
92. 30 ἐστι Q   32 ἀγαθόν M¹   33 ὑπάρχει Q   34 post αἰτία nescio an exciderit οὖσα   35 τῆς] τοῖς M²

PROP. 89. *All true Being is composed of limit and infinite.*

For if it have infinite potency, it is manifestly infinite, and in this way has the infinite as an element. And if it be indivisible and unitary, in this way it shares in limit; for 'what participates unity is finite. But it is at once indivisible (prop. 47) and of infinite potency (prop. 84). Therefore all true Being is composed of limit and infinite.

PROP. 90. *Prior to all that is composed of limit and infinitude there exist substantially and independently the first Limit and the first Infinity.*

For if prior to the characters of individuals there subsist these characters in themselves as universal and originative causes, belonging not to some but to all without restriction (prop. 23), then before their common product there must exist the first Limit and the primitively Infinite. For the limit contained in the mixture has a share of infinitude, and the infinite of limit; but the first manifestation of any principle is free from alien elements, and hence the primitively Infinite can have no infusion of limit, nor the first Limit of infinitude: therefore these characters exist primitively prior to the mixture.

PROP. 91. *There are both finite and infinite potencies; but all finite potency arises from infinite potency, and this latter from the first Infinity.*

For temporal potencies are finite, having lapsed from the infinitude of perpetual Being; but those of perpetual things are infinite, never abandoning the existence to which they belong (props. 84, 85).

PROP. 92. *The whole multitude of infinite potencies is dependent upon one principle, the first Infinity, which is not potency in the sense that it is participated or exists in things which are potent, but is Potency-in-itself, not the potency of an individual but the cause of all that is.*

For even if primal Being itself possesses potency, yet it is not simple Potency. For it also possesses limit (prop. 89); whereas the first Potency is Infinity. For infinite potencies are such by participation of Infinity; so that prior to all potencies there must be simple Infinity, in virtue of which Being is infinite in potency (prop. 86) and all things have a portion of infinitude. Infinity is not the First Principle; for that is the measure of all things, being the Good (prop. 12) and Unity (prop. 13). Neither is it Being; for Being is infinite and not Infinity. Cause of all things infinite in potency and cause of all infinitude in things, Infinity falls between the First Principle and Being.

93. Πᾶν τὸ ἄπειρον ἐν τοῖς οὖσιν οὔτε τοῖς ὑπερκειμένοις ἄπειρόν ἐστιν οὔτε ἑαυτῷ.

ᾧ γὰρ ἄπειρον ἕκαστον, τούτῳ καὶ ἀπερίγραφον ὑπάρχει. πᾶν δὲ ἐν ἐκείνοις ἑαυτῷ τε ὥρισται καὶ τοῖς πρὸ αὐτοῦ πᾶσι. μόνοις δὴ λείπεται τοῖς καταδεεστέροις ἄπειρον εἶναι τὸ ἐν 5 ἐκείνοις ἄπειρον, ὧν ὑπερήπλωται τῇ δυνάμει τοσοῦτον ὥστε πᾶσιν αὐτοῖς ἀπερίληπτον ὑπάρχειν. κἂν γὰρ ἐφ᾽ ὁσονοῦν ἐκεῖνα πρὸς αὐτὸ ἀνατείνηται, ἀλλ᾽ ἔχει τι πάντως ἀπ᾽ αὐτῶν ἐξῃρημένον· κἂν εἰσίῃ πάντα εἰς αὐτό, ἀλλ᾽ ἔχει τι κρύφιον τοῖς δευτέροις καὶ ἀκατάληπτον· κἂν ἐξελίττῃ τὰς ἐν αὐτῷ 10 δυνάμεις, ἀλλ᾽ ἔχει τι δι᾽ ἕνωσιν ἀνυπέρβλητον, συνεσπειραμένον, ἐκβεβηκὸς τῆς ἐκείνων ἀνελίξεως. ἑαυτὸ δὲ συνέχον καὶ ὁρίζον οὐκ ἂν ἑαυτῷ ἄπειρον ὑπάρχοι· οὐδὲ πολλῷ μᾶλλον τοῖς ὑπερκειμένοις, μοῖραν ἔχον τῆς ἐν ἐκείνοις ἀπειρίας· ἀπειρότεραι γὰρ αἱ τῶν ὁλικωτέρων δυνάμεις, ὁλικώτεραι οὖσαι καὶ ἐγγυτέρω 15 τεταγμέναι τῆς πρωτίστης ἀπειρίας.

94. Πᾶσα μὲν ἀϊδιότης ἀπειρία τίς ἐστιν· οὐ πᾶσα δὲ ἀπειρία ἀϊδιότης.

πολλὰ γὰρ τῶν ἀπείρων οὐ διὰ τὸ ἀεὶ ἔχει τὸ ἄπειρον, ὥσπερ καὶ ἡ κατὰ τὸ ποσὸν ἀπειρία καὶ ἡ κατὰ τὸ πηλίκον 20 καὶ ἡ τῆς ὕλης ἀπειρία καὶ εἴ τι ἄλλο τοιοῦτον, ἢ διὰ τὸ ἀδιεξίτητον ἄπειρον ὑπάρχον ἢ διὰ τὸ ἀόριστον τῆς οὐσίας. ὅτι δὲ ἡ ἀϊδιότης ἀπειρία δῆλον· τὸ γὰρ μηδέποτε ἐπιλεῖπον ἄπειρον· τοῦτο δὲ τὸ ἀεί, τὴν ὑπόστασιν ἀνέκλειπτον ἔχον. ἡ ἄρα ἀπειρία πρὸ τῆς ἀϊδιότητός ἐστι· τὸ γὰρ πλειόνων 25 ὑποστατικὸν καὶ ὁλικώτερον αἰτιώτερόν ἐστιν. ἐπέκεινα ἄρα τοῦ αἰῶνος ἡ πρώτη ἀπειρία [καὶ ἡ αὐτοαπειρία πρὸ αἰῶνος].

95. Πᾶσα δύναμις ἑνικωτέρα οὖσα τῆς πληθυνομένης ἀπειροτέρα.

εἰ γὰρ ἡ πρώτη ἀπειρία τοῦ ἑνὸς ἐγγυτάτω, καὶ τῶν δυνάμεων 30 ἡ τῷ ἑνὶ συγγενεστέρα τῆς ἀφισταμένης ἐκείνου μειζόνως ἄπειρος· πληθυνομένη γὰρ ἀπόλλυσι τὸ ἑνοειδές, ἐν ᾧ μένουσα τὴν πρὸς τὰς ἄλλας εἶχεν ὑπεροχήν, συνεχομένη διὰ τὴν ἀμέρειαν. καὶ γὰρ ἐν τοῖς μεριστοῖς αἱ δυνάμεις συναγόμεναι μὲν πολλαπλασιάζονται, μεριζόμεναι δὲ ἀμυδροῦνται. 35

93. 5 μόνοις] μόνον Q   7 ὑπάρχει Q   καὶ γάρ M   8 ἐκεῖνα· ω (ἐκεῖνο edd.)   ἀνατείνεται QM²   ἐξ αὐτῶν Q   9 πάντα] αᾖ πάντῃ ?   τι] τό [M]   10 ἀνελίττῃ Q   14 ἐν ἐκείνοις BDMW : ἐκείνοις C : ἐκείνων Q   16 πρώτης M¹ ut vid.
94. 22 ὑπάρχον ἄπειρον BCD   διὰ τὸ ἀδιόριστον Q   26 malim ὁλικωτέρων   καὶ ante αἰτιώτερον add. Qβ (non agnosc. αγ)   27 καὶ . . . αἰῶνος seclusi
95. 34 συγγενόμεναι Q

PROP. 93. *All infinitude in things which have Being is infinite neither to the superior orders nor to itself.*

For to whomsoever anything is infinite, to him it is also uncircumscribed. But among things which have Being each is determinate both to itself and to all principles prior to it. It remains, then, that the infinitude in such things is infinite only to inferior principles, above which it is so supereminent in potency as to escape the grasp of any of them. For though they extend themselves toward it with whatsoever reach, yet it has something which altogether transcends them ; though all of them enter into it, yet it has something which for secondary beings is occult and incomprehensible ; though they unfold the potencies contained in it, yet it has something unattainable in its unity, an unexpanded life which evades their explication. But containing and determining itself as it does, it cannot be infinite for itself; and still less for those above it, since it possesses but a parcel of the infinitude which is in them. For the potencies of the more universal terms are more infinite, being themselves more universal and nearer in rank to the primal Infinity.

PROP. 94. *All perpetuity is a kind of infinitude, but not all infinitude is perpetuity.*

For of things infinite many have this attribute in a sense other than that of perpetuity ; as the infinitude of quantity and of bulk, and the infinitude of Matter, and the like, which are infinite either because they cannot be enumerated or traversed or else by the indetermination of their essence. But it is plain that perpetuity is an infinitude ; for that which never fails is infinite, and this is what we mean by perpetuity, which involves an unfailing subsistence. Hence infinitude is prior to perpetuity, since that principle is the more causative which gives rise to the greater number of terms and is the more universal (prop. 60). Thus the first Infinity is prior to Eternity.

PROP. 95. *The more unified potency is always more infinite than one which is passing into plurality.*

For if the first Infinity is nearest to the One (prop. 92), then of two potencies that which is more akin to the One is infinite in a greater degree than that which falls away from it ; since a potency as it becomes manifold loses that likeness to the One which caused it while it abode therein to transcend the rest, concentrated in indivisibility. For even in things subject to division potencies are multiplied by co-ordination, enfeebled by partition.

96. Παντὸς πεπερασμένου σώματος ἡ δύναμις, ἄπειρος οὖσα, ἀσώματός ἐστιν.

εἰ γὰρ σωματική, εἰ μὲν τὸ σῶμα τοῦτο ἄπειρον, ἔσται ἐν πεπερασμένῳ ἄπειρον. εἰ δὲ πεπερασμένον, οὐ καθὸ σῶμα ἄρα, κατὰ τοῦτο δύναμίς ἐστιν· εἰ γάρ, ᾗ σῶμα, πεπέρασται, ᾗ δὲ 5 δύναμις, ἄπειρος, οὐκ ἔσται, καθὸ σῶμα, δύναμις. ἀσώματος ἄρα ἡ ἐν τῷ πεπερασμένῳ σώματι δύναμις ἐνοῦσα ἄπειρος.

97. Πᾶν τὸ καθ' ἑκάστην σειρὰν ἀρχικὸν αἴτιον τῇ σειρᾷ πάσῃ τῆς ἑαυτοῦ μεταδίδωσιν ἰδιότητος· καὶ ὅ ἐστιν ἐκεῖνο πρώτως, τοῦτό ἐστιν αὕτη καθ' ὕφεσιν. 10

εἰ γὰρ ἡγεῖται τῆς ὅλης σειρᾶς, καὶ πάντα τὰ σύστοιχα πρὸς αὐτὸ συντέτακται, δῆλον δὴ ὅτι πᾶσι τὴν μίαν ἰδέαν, καθ' ἣν ὑπὸ τὴν αὐτὴν τέτακται σειράν, ἐκεῖνο δίδωσιν. ἢ γὰρ ἀναιτίως πάντα τῆς πρὸς ἐκεῖνο μετέσχεν ὁμοιότητος ἢ ἀπ' ἐκείνου τὸ ταὐτὸν ἐν πᾶσιν. ἀλλὰ τὸ ἀναιτίως ἀδύνατον· τὸ γὰρ ἀναιτίως 15 καὶ αὐτόματον· τὸ δὲ αὐτόματον ἐν οἷς τάξις ἐστὶ καὶ ἀλληλουχία καὶ τὸ ἀεὶ ὡσαύτως οὐκ ἄν ποτε γένοιτο. ἀπ' ἐκείνου ἄρα τὴν ἰδιότητα τῆς ἐκείνου ὑποστάσεως πᾶσα δέχεται ἡ σειρά.

εἰ δὲ ἀπ' ἐκείνου, φανερὸν ὅτι μετὰ ὑφέσεως καὶ τῆς προσ- 20 ηκούσης τοῖς δευτέροις ὑποβάσεως. ἢ γὰρ ὁμοίως ἔν τε τῷ ἡγουμένῳ καὶ ἐν τοῖς ἄλλοις ἡ ἰδιότης ὑπάρχει—καὶ πῶς ἔτι τὸ μὲν ἡγεῖται, τὰ δὲ μετ' ἐκεῖνο τὴν ὑπόστασιν ἔλαχεν ;—ἢ ἀνομοίως· καὶ εἰ τοῦτο, δῆλον ὡς ἀφ' ἑνὸς τῷ πλήθει τὸ ταὐτόν, ἀλλ' οὐκ ἔμπαλιν, καὶ δευτέρως ἔστιν ἐν τῷ πλήθει τὸ πρώτως 25 ἐν τῷ ἑνὶ προϋπάρχον ἰδίωμα τῆς σειρᾶς ἐξαίρετον.

98. Πᾶν αἴτιον χωριστὸν πανταχοῦ ἐστιν ἅμα καὶ οὐδαμοῦ.

τῇ μὲν γὰρ μεταδόσει τῆς ἑαυτοῦ δυνάμεώς ἐστι πανταχοῦ· τοῦτο γάρ ἐστιν αἴτιον, τὸ πληρωτικὸν τῶν μεταλαγχάνειν αὐτοῦ πεφυκότων καὶ ἀρχικὸν τῶν δευτέρων πάντων καὶ παρὸν πᾶσι 30 ταῖς τῶν ἐλλάμψεων γονίμοις προόδοις. τῇ δὲ ἀμίκτῳ πρὸς τὰ ἐν τόπῳ ὄντα οὐσίᾳ καὶ τῇ ἐξῃρημένῃ καθαρότητι οὐδαμοῦ ἐστιν· εἰ γὰρ χωριστόν ἐστι τῶν ἀποτελεσμάτων, ὑπερίδρυται πάντων ὡσαύτως καὶ ἐν οὐδενί ἐστι τῶν ἑαυτοῦ καταδεεστέρων. εἴτε

96. 3 εἰ γάρ] ἤπερ [M], aut W   7 ἐνοῦσα] ens W
97. 16 καὶ . . . ἐν οἷς] καὶ τὸ αὐτόματον ἐν οἷς M¹W   21 τε ex corr. M²,
om. Arg   22 ἐν om. MQ   ἄλλοις [M]W : δευτέροις BCDQM³ : ἄλλοις
δευτέροις M²   πῶς ω (πως edd.)   ἔτι [M], adhuc W : om. cett.   23 τά]
τό M¹   24 τό om. CD
98. 28 μέν om. BCD   μεταδώσει M   29 αὐτοῦ ω (αὐτοῦ Cr.²)
30 ἁπάντων [M]   33 τῶν ἀποτελεσμάτων ω (om. O edd.)   πάντως
M   34 εἴτε] εἰ BCD

Prop. 96. *If the potency of any finite body be infinite, it is incorporeal.*

For suppose the potency to be itself a body: if this body be infinite, the infinite will be contained in the finite. And if it be finite, the potency is not potency in that respect in which it is a body: for if it be finite *qua* body and infinite *qua* potency, in that respect in which it is body it will not be potency. Therefore infinite potency resident in a finite body must be incorporeal.

K. Supplementary Theorems on Causality, Etc.

Prop. 97. *The originative cause of each series communicates its distinctive property to the entire series; and what the cause is primitively the series is by remission.*

For if it is sovereign over the whole series and all the members are grouped together by their relation to it (prop. 21), it is plain that from it all derive the single form in virtue of which they are ranked under the same series. For either their common likeness to it is uncaused or all derive from their cause this element of identity. But the former supposition is impossible: for the uncaused is spontaneous; and spontaneity can never occur where there is order and continuity and perpetual freedom from variation. From its cause, then, the entire series receives the distinctive character proper to the being of that cause.

If so, it manifestly receives it with remission, that is, with the declension appropriate to secondary existences. For this character belongs either in the same degree to the antecedent term and to the rest—and how then can the one still be antecedent, the others posterior in being?—or in an unequal degree. In the latter case it is plain that the identical element is derived by the manifold from the one, and not reversely; so that the distinctive character peculiar to the series, which pre-exists primitively in the unitary term, exists in the manifold by derivation.

Prop. 98. *Every cause which is separate from its effects exists at once everywhere and nowhere.*

For by the communication of its proper potency (prop. 97) it is everywhere: we mean by 'cause' that which fills all things naturally capable of participating it, which is the source of all secondary existences and by the fecund outpouring of its irradiations is present to them all. But by its mode of being, which has no admixture of the spatial, and by its transcendent purity it is nowhere: for if it is separate from its effects it is enthroned above all alike and resides in no being inferior to itself. If it were merely everywhere, this

γὰρ πανταχοῦ μόνον ἦν, αἴτιον μὲν εἶναι οὐκ ἐκωλύετο καὶ ἐν
πᾶσιν εἶναι τοῖς μετέχουσι, πρὸ πάντων δὲ οὐκ ἂν ἦν χωριστῶς·
εἴτε οὐδαμοῦ, τοῦ πανταχοῦ χωρίς, πρὸ πάντων μὲν εἶναι οὐκ
ἐκωλύετο καὶ μηδενὸς εἶναι τῶν ὑποδεεστέρων, ἐν πᾶσι δὲ οὐκ
ἂν ἦν ὡς τὰ αἴτια πέφυκεν ἐν τοῖς αἰτιατοῖς εἶναι, ταῖς ἑαυτῶν 5
ἀφθόνοις μεταδόσεσιν. ἵν' οὖν καὶ αἴτιον ὑπάρχον ἐν πᾶσιν ᾖ
τοῖς δυναμένοις μετέχειν, καὶ χωριστὸν ὂν ἐφ' ἑαυτοῦ πρὸ
πάντων ᾖ τῶν ἀπ' αὐτοῦ πληρουμένων, πανταχοῦ ἐστιν ἅμα καὶ
οὐδαμοῦ.

καὶ οὐ μέρει μὲν πανταχοῦ, μέρει δὲ οὐδαμοῦ· οὕτως γὰρ ἂν 10
αὐτὸ ἑαυτοῦ διεσπασμένον εἴη καὶ χωρίς, εἴπερ τὸ μὲν αὐτοῦ
πανταχοῦ καὶ ἐν πᾶσι, τὸ δὲ οὐδαμοῦ καὶ πρὸ τῶν πάντων·
ἀλλ' ὅλον πανταχοῦ, καὶ οὐδαμοῦ ὡσαύτως. καὶ γὰρ τὰ
μετέχειν αὐτοῦ δυνάμενα ὅλῳ ἐντυγχάνει καὶ ὅλον ἑαυτοῖς
εὑρίσκει παρόν, κἀκεῖνο ὅλον ἐξῄρηται· τὸ γὰρ μετασχὸν οὐκ 15
ἐκεῖνο ἐν ἑαυτῷ κατέταξεν, ἀλλ' ἀπ' ἐκείνου μετέσχεν ὅσον
χωρῆσαι δεδύνηται. καὶ οὔτε τῷ μεταδιδόναι ἑαυτοῦ στενο-
χωρεῖται ταῖς τῶν πλειόνων μεθέξεσι, χωρὶς ὄν· οὔτε τὰ μετέχοντα ἐλλιπῶς μεταλαγχάνει, πανταχοῦ ὄντος τοῦ μεταδιδόντος.

99. Πᾶν ἀμέθεκτον, ᾗ ἀμέθεκτόν ἐστι, ταύτῃ ἀπ' ἄλλης 20
αἰτίας οὐχ ὑφίσταται, ἀλλ' αὐτὸ ἀρχή ἐστι καὶ αἰτία τῶν
μετεχομένων πάντων· καὶ οὕτως ἀρχὴ πᾶσα καθ' ἑκάστην
σειρὰν ἀγένητος.

εἰ γάρ ἐστιν ἀμέθεκτον, ἐν τῇ οἰκείᾳ σειρᾷ τὸ πρωτεῖον ἔλαχε,
καὶ οὐ πρόεισιν ἀπ' ἄλλων· οὐ γὰρ ἂν εἴη πρῶτον ἔτι, τὴν 25
ἰδιότητα ταύτην, καθ' ἣν ἐστιν ἀμέθεκτον, παρ' ἄλλου τινὸς
ὑποδεχόμενον. εἰ δὲ ἄλλων ἐστὶ καταδεέστερον καὶ ἀπ' ἐκείνων
πρόεισιν, οὐχ ᾗ ἀμέθεκτόν ἐστι, ταύτῃ πρόεισιν, ἀλλ' ᾗ μετέχον.
ἀφ' ὧν γὰρ ὥρμηται, τούτων δήπου μετέχει, καὶ ὧν μετέχει,
ταῦτα οὐκ ἔστι πρώτως· ὃ δὲ ἀμεθέκτως ἐστί, τοῦτο πρώτως 30
ἐστίν· οὐκ ἄρα ᾗ ἀμέθεκτον, ταύτῃ ἀπ' αἰτίας ἐστίν. ᾗ μὲν
γὰρ ἀπ' αἰτίας, μετέχον ἐστὶ καὶ οὐκ ἀμέθεκτον· ᾗ δὲ ἀμέθεκτον,
μετεχομένων αἴτιον, ἀλλ' οὐκ αὐτὸ μετέχον ἄλλων.

98. 5 αἰτιατοῖς] αἰτίοις M²   6 ὑπάρχῃ [M]   8 ὑπ' αὐτοῦ BCD (sed
cf. Porph. ἀφ. 21.12)   11 αὐτοῦ om. Q   12 τῶν del. M²   14 ὅλῳ]
ὅλα M¹   15–16 οὐκ ἐκεῖνο] οὐ κἀκεῖνο M   17 δεδύνηται [M], potuit W : δύναται
BCDQM²   τῷ BCD : τό MQW   αὐτοῦ M   18–19 μετασχόντα M¹
99. 21 ἀρχὴ καὶ αἰτία ἐστί Q   28 ᾗ prius] ὅ Q et fort. M¹   30 ἀμεθέκτως
ἐστί [M]W : ἀμέθεκτόν ἐστι BCDQM²   33 ἀλλ' ω (καὶ O edd.)

would not hinder it from being a cause and present in all the participants; but it would not exist separately prior to them all. Were it nowhere without being everywhere, this would not hinder it from being prior to all and pertaining to no inferior existent; but it would not be omnipresent in that sense in which causes are capable of immanence in their effects, namely by unstinted self-bestowal. In order that as cause it may be present in all that can participate it while as a separate and independent principle it is prior to all the vessels which it fills, it must be at once everywhere and nowhere.

It is not in part everywhere and in some other part nowhere: for thus it would be dismembered and disparted from itself, if one portion of it were everywhere and in all things, another nowhere and prior to all. It is entire everywhere, and likewise nowhere. Whatsoever can participate it at all attains it in its entirety and finds it present as a whole: yet it is also transcendent as a whole; the participant does not absorb it, but derives *from* it so much as it has been able to contain. Because it is separate it is not pinched in its self-bestowal if the number of participants be increased; because it is omnipresent the participants never fail of their due portion.

PROP. 99. *Every unparticipated term arises* qua *unparticipated from no cause other than itself, but is itself the first principle and cause of all the participated terms; thus the first principle of each series is always without origin.*

For if it is unparticipated, in its own series it has primacy (prop. 24), and does not proceed from earlier terms; since if it received from an external source that character in respect of which it is unparticipated, it would no longer be the first term. If there be superior terms from which it is derived, it proceeds from them not *qua* unparticipated but *qua* participant. For those principles from which it has taken its rise are of course participated by it, and the characters which it participates it does not possess primitively; but it has primitively what it has imparticipably: so that *qua* unparticipated it is uncaused. *Qua* caused, it is a participant, not an unparticipated principle; *qua* unparticipated, it is a cause of the participated and not itself a participant.

100. Πᾶσα μὲν σειρὰ τῶν ὅλων εἰς ἀμέθεκτον ἀρχὴν καὶ αἰτίαν ἀνατείνεται, πάντα δὲ τὰ ἀμέθεκτα τῆς μιᾶς ἐξέχεται τῶν πάντων ἀρχῆς.

εἰ γὰρ ἑκάστη σειρὰ ταὐτόν τι πέπονθεν, ἔστι τι ἐν ἑκάστῃ ἡγεμονοῦν τὸ τῆς ταυτότητος αἴτιον· ὡς γὰρ τὰ ὄντα πάντα 5 ἀφ' ἑνός, οὕτω καὶ πᾶσα σειρὰ ἀφ' ἑνός.

πᾶσαι δὲ αὖ αἱ ἀμέθεκτοι μονάδες εἰς τὸ ἓν ἀνάγονται, διότι πᾶσαι τῷ ἑνὶ ἀνάλογον· ᾗ οὖν ταὐτόν τι καὶ αὗται πεπόνθασι, τὴν πρὸς τὸ ἓν ἀναλογίαν, ταύτῃ εἰς τὸ ἓν αὐταῖς ἡ ἀναγωγὴ γίνεται. καὶ ᾗ μὲν ἀπὸ τοῦ ἑνὸς πᾶσαι, οὐδεμία τούτων ἀρχή 10 ἐστιν, ἀλλ' ὡς ἀπ' ἀρχῆς ἐκείνης· ᾗ δὲ ἑκάστη ἀμέθεκτος, ταύτῃ ἀρχὴ ἑκάστη. τινῶν οὖν ἀρχαὶ οὖσαι τῆς πάντων ἀρχῆς ἐξέχονται. πάντων γὰρ ἀρχή ἐστιν ἧς πάντα μετείληφε· μετείληφε δὲ μόνου πάντα τοῦ πρώτου, τῶν δὲ ἄλλων οὐ πάντα, ἀλλά τινά. διὸ καὶ τὸ ἁπλῶς πρῶτον ἐκεῖνο, τὰ δὲ ἄλλα πρὸς 15 τινὰ μὲν τάξιν ἐστὶ πρῶτα, ἁπλῶς δὲ οὐ πρῶτα.

101. Πάντων τῶν νοῦ μετεχόντων ἡγεῖται ὁ ἀμέθεκτος νοῦς, καὶ τῶν τῆς ζωῆς ἡ ζωή, καὶ τῶν τοῦ ὄντος τὸ ὄν· αὐτῶν δὲ τούτων τὸ μὲν ὂν πρὸ τῆς ζωῆς, ἡ δὲ ζωὴ πρὸ τοῦ νοῦ.

διότι μὲν γὰρ ἐν ἑκάστῃ τάξει τῶν ὄντων πρὸ τῶν μετεχομένων 20 ἐστὶ τὰ ἀμέθεκτα, δεῖ πρὸ τῶν νοερῶν εἶναι τὸν νοῦν καὶ πρὸ τῶν ζώντων τὴν ζωὴν καὶ πρὸ τῶν ὄντων τὸ ὄν. διότι δὲ προηγεῖται τὸ τῶν πλειόνων αἴτιον ἢ τὸ τῶν ἐλαττόνων, ἐν ἐκείνοις τὸ μὲν ὂν ἔσται πρώτιστον· πᾶσι γὰρ πάρεστιν, οἷς ζωὴ καὶ νοῦς (ζῶν γὰρ πᾶν καὶ νοήσεως μετέχον ἔστιν ἐξ ἀνάγκης), οὐκ ἔμπαλιν 25 δέ (οὐ γὰρ τὰ ὄντα πάντα ζῇ καὶ νοεῖ). δευτέρα δὲ ἡ ζωή· πᾶσι γάρ, οἷς νοῦ μέτεστι, καὶ ζωῆς μέτεστιν, οὐκ ἔμπαλιν δέ· πολλὰ γὰρ ζῇ μέν, γνώσεως δὲ ἄμοιρα ἀπολείπεται. τρίτος δὲ ὁ νοῦς· πᾶν γὰρ τὸ γνωστικὸν ὁπωσοῦν καὶ ζῇ καὶ ἔστιν. εἰ οὖν πλειόνων αἴτιον τὸ ὄν, ἐλαττόνων δὲ ἡ ζωή, καὶ ἔτι 30 ἐλαττόνων ὁ νοῦς, πρώτιστον τὸ ὄν, εἶτα ζωή, εἶτα νοῦς.

---

100. 1 μέν om. Q, non agnosc. W   1-2 ἀρχὴν καὶ αἰτίαν [M]W (cf. p. 14, ll. 1, 22-3 ; p. 88, l. 21) : αἰτ. κ. ἀρχ. BCDQM²   2 ἐξήρτηται Q (in mg. γρ. ἐξέχεται)   3 τῶν om. M¹   4 alt. τι] τό M¹ ut vid.   8 ἀνάλογοι Q καὶ αὗται πεπόνθασι] πέπονθε Q   11 ante ἑκάστη aliquid habuisse videtur M¹   12 ἑκάστη τινῶν. εἰ ἀρχαί Q   τῆς τῶν πάντων BCD (sed τῶν non agnosc. 'Ανάπτ. 126. 8)   14 μόνου πάντα ω (μ. πάντη Port., πάντα μόνον Arg Cr.)

101. 18 τῶν τῆς ζωῆς BCDM²W : τῆς ζωῆς Q : τῶν ζώων [M]   23 prius τῶν om. M   24 ὄν ἐστι BCD   ζῶν] ζωῆς Q   26 οὐδὲ γάρ [M]W   30 πλείστων [M]

PROP. 100. *Every series of wholes is referable to an unparticipated first principle and cause; and all unparticipated terms are dependent from the one First Principle of all things.*

For if each series is affected throughout by some identical character, there is in each some dominant principle which is the cause of this identity: as all existence proceeds from a single term (prop. 11), so also do all the members of any series (prop. 21).

Again, all the unparticipated monads are referable to the One, because all are analogous to the One (prop. 24): in so far as they too are affected by a common character, namely their analogy to the One, so far we can refer them to the One. In respect of their common origin from the latter none of them is a first principle, but all have as their first principle the One; each, however, is a first principle *qua* unparticipated (prop. 99). As principles of a certain order of things they are dependent from the Principle of all things. For the Principle of all things is that which all participate, and this can only be the primal cause; the rest are participated not by all but by a certain some. Hence also that cause is 'the Primal' without qualification, while the rest are primal relatively to a certain order, but when considered absolutely are not primal.

PROP. 101. *All things which participate intelligence are preceded by the unparticipated Intelligence, those which participate life by Life, and those which participate being by Being; and of these three unparticipated principles Being is prior to Life and Life to Intelligence.*

For in the first place, because in each order of existence unparticipated terms precede the participated (prop. 100), there must be Intelligence prior to things intelligent, Life prior to living things, and Being prior to things which are. And secondly, since the cause of more numerous effects precedes the cause of fewer (prop. 60), among these principles Being will stand foremost; for it is present to all things which have life and intelligence (since whatever lives and shares in intellection necessarily exists), but the converse is not true (since not all that exists lives and exercises intelligence). Life has the second place; for whatever shares in intelligence shares in life, but not conversely, since many things are alive but remain devoid of knowledge. The third principle is Intelligence; for whatever is in any measure capable of knowledge both lives and exists. If, then, Being gives rise to a greater number of effects, Life to fewer, and Intelligence to yet fewer, Being stands foremost, next to it Life, and then Intelligence.

102. Πάντα μὲν τὰ ὁπωσοῦν ὄντα ἐκ πέρατός ἐστι καὶ ἀπείρου διὰ τὸ πρώτως ὄν· πάντα δὲ τὰ ζῶντα ἑαυτῶν κινητικά ἐστι διὰ τὴν ζωὴν τὴν πρώτην· πάντα δὲ τὰ γνωστικὰ γνώσεως μετέχει διὰ τὸν νοῦν τὸν πρῶτον.

εἰ γὰρ τὸ καθ' ἑκάστην σειρὰν ἀμέθεκτον τῆς οἰκείας ἰδιότη- 5 τος πᾶσι τοῖς ὑπὸ τὴν αὐτὴν σειρὰν μεταδίδωσι, δῆλον δὴ ὅτι καὶ τὸ ὂν τὸ πρώτιστον μεταδίδωσι πᾶσι πέρατος ἅμα καὶ ἀπειρίας, μικτὸν ὑπάρχον ἐκ τούτων πρώτως· καὶ ἡ ζωὴ τῆς παρ' ἑαυτῇ κινήσεως (καὶ γὰρ ἡ ζωὴ πρώτη πρόοδός ἐστι καὶ κίνησις ἀπὸ τῆς μονίμου τοῦ ὄντος ὑποστάσεως)· καὶ ὁ νοῦς τῆς 10 γνώσεως (πάσης γὰρ γνώσεως ἡ ἀκρότης ἐστὶν ἐν νῷ, καὶ νοῦς τὸ πρώτως γνωστικόν).

103. Πάντα ἐν πᾶσιν, οἰκείως δὲ ἐν ἑκάστῳ· καὶ γὰρ ἐν τῷ ὄντι καὶ ἡ ζωὴ καὶ ὁ νοῦς, καὶ ἐν τῇ ζωῇ τὸ εἶναι καὶ τὸ νοεῖν, καὶ ἐν τῷ νῷ τὸ εἶναι καὶ τὸ ζῆν, ἀλλ' ὅπου μὲν νοερῶς, ὅπου 15 δὲ ζωτικῶς, ὅπου δὲ ὄντως ὄντα πάντα.

ἐπεὶ γὰρ ἕκαστον ἢ κατ' αἰτίαν ἔστιν ἢ καθ' ὕπαρξιν ἢ κατὰ μέθεξιν, ἔν τε τῷ πρώτῳ τὰ λοιπὰ κατ' αἰτίαν ἔστι, καὶ ἐν τῷ μέσῳ τὸ μὲν πρῶτον κατὰ μέθεξιν τὸ δὲ τρίτον κατ' αἰτίαν, καὶ ἐν τῷ τρίτῳ τὰ πρὸ αὐτοῦ κατὰ μέθεξιν, καὶ ἐν τῷ ὄντι ἄρα ζωὴ 20 προείληπται καὶ νοῦς, ἑκάστου δὲ κατὰ τὴν ὕπαρξιν χαρακτηρι-ζομένου καὶ οὔτε κατὰ τὴν αἰτίαν (ἄλλων γάρ ἐστιν αἴτιον) οὔτε κατὰ τὴν μέθεξιν (ἀλλαχόθεν γὰρ ἔχει τοῦτο, οὗ μετείλη-φεν), ὄντως ἐστὶν ἐκεῖ καὶ τὸ ζῆν καὶ τὸ νοεῖν, ζωὴ οὐσιώδης καὶ νοῦς οὐσιώδης· καὶ ἐν τῇ ζωῇ κατὰ μέθεξιν μὲν τὸ εἶναι, κατ' 25 αἰτίαν δὲ τὸ νοεῖν, ἀλλὰ ζωτικῶς ἑκάτερον (κατὰ τοῦτο γὰρ ἡ ὕπαρξις)· καὶ ἐν τῷ νῷ καὶ ἡ ζωὴ καὶ ἡ οὐσία κατὰ μέθεξιν, καὶ νοερῶς ἑκάτερον (καὶ γὰρ τὸ εἶναι τοῦ νοῦ γνωστικὸν καὶ ἡ ζωὴ γνῶσις).

104. Πᾶν τὸ πρώτως αἰώνιον τήν τε οὐσίαν καὶ τὴν ἐνέργειαν 30 αἰώνιον ἔχει.

εἰ γὰρ πρώτως μεταλαγχάνει τῆς τοῦ αἰῶνος ἰδιότητος, οὐ τῇ μὲν αὐτοῦ μετέχει τῇ δὲ οὔ, ἀλλὰ πάντη μετέχει. ἢ γὰρ κατὰ τὴν ἐνέργειαν μετέχον οὐ μετέχει κατὰ τὴν οὐσίαν (ἀλλ'

102. 1 μὲν τά M¹ ut vid. (τὰ μέν Λrg), quidem W : τά cett.   6 τήν non
agnosc. W   αὐτήν om. C   δή ω (δέ Port.Cr.¹)   7 alt. τό om. Q
8 ἡ om. M   9 παρ' ἑαυτῇ BCDM² : παρ' ἑαυτῶν [M], a seipsis W : om.
Q   12 πρῶτον BCD dett.
103. 16 ante ὄντως rasuram M   18 τε om. Q : autem W   23 οὗ
BCDQ : δ MW   24 ἐκεῖ καί] ἐκεῖνο Q   25 μέθεξιν μὲν τό ex corr. M
26 ἀλλὰ καὶ ζωτικῶς BCD   27 καὶ ἡ οὐσία καὶ ἡ ζωή Q
104. 31 ἔχει αἰώνιον BCD   32 πρώτως om. BCD   τοῦ αἰωνίου M
ἀιδιότητος Q dett.   33 αὐτοῦ om. Q (αὐτῆς edd.)

PROP. 102. *All that in any sense exists is composite of limit and infinite because of the primal Being ; all that lives has self-movement because of the primal Life ; and all that is cognitive participates knowledge because of the primal Intelligence.*

For if the unparticipated term in each series communicates its own distinctive property to all existences which fall under the same series (prop. 97), it is plain that the primal Being communicates to all things limit together with infinitude, being itself the primal compound of these two (prop. 89) ; that Life communicates the movement inherent in it, inasmuch as Life is the first procession or movement away from the steadfast substance of Being ; and that Intelligence communicates knowledge, since the summit of all knowledge is in the Intelligence, which is the first Knower.

PROP. 103. *All things are in all things, but in each according to its proper nature : for in Being there is life and intelligence ; in Life, being and intelligence ; in Intelligence, being and life ; but each of these exists upon one level intellectually, upon another vitally, and on the third existentially.*

For since each character may exist either in its cause or as substantial predicate or by participation (prop. 65), and since in the first term of any triad the other two are embraced as in their cause, while in the mean term the first is present by participation and the third in its cause, and finally the third contains its priors by participation, it follows that in Being there are pre-embraced Life and Intelligence, but because each term is characterized not by what it causes (since this is other than itself) nor by what it participates (since this is extrinsic in origin) but by its substantial predicate, Life and Intelligence are present there after the mode of Being, as existential life and existential intelligence ; and in Life are present Being by participation and Intelligence in its cause, but each of these vitally, Life being the substantial character of the term ; and in Intelligence both Life and Being by participation, and each of them intellectually, for the being of Intelligence is cognitive and its life is cognition.

PROP. 104. *All that is primitively eternal has both eternal existence and eternal activity.*

For if it primitively participates the distinctive character of eternity, it shares in eternity not in one way only, but in all. Suppose the contrary : either it participates in respect of its activity but not of its existence—which is impossible, since activity will then

ἀδύνατον· ἡ γὰρ ἐνέργεια κρείττων ἔσται τῆς οὐσίας)· ἢ κατ'
οὐσίαν μετέχον οὐ μετέχει κατὰ τὴν ἐνέργειαν, καὶ ἔσται
πρώτως αἰώνιον τὸ αὐτὸ καὶ χρόνου μετέχον πρώτως, καὶ χρόνος
μέν τινων μετρήσει τὴν ἐνέργειαν πρώτως, αἰὼν δὲ οὐδενός, ὁ
παντὸς χρόνου κρείττων, εἴπερ τὸ πρώτως αἰώνιον οὐ συνέχεται 5
κατ' ἐνέργειαν ὑπὸ αἰῶνος. ἄπαν ἄρα τὸ πρώτως αἰώνιον
τήν τε οὐσίαν ἔχει καὶ τὴν ἐνέργειαν αἰώνιον.

105. Πᾶν τὸ ἀθάνατον ἀΐδιον· οὐ πᾶν δὲ τὸ ἀΐδιον ἀθάνατον.

εἰ γὰρ ἀθάνατόν ἐστι τὸ ἀεὶ ζωῆς μετέχον, τὸ δὲ ἀεὶ ζωῆς
μετέχον καὶ τοῦ εἶναι μετέχει, καὶ τὸ ἀεὶ ζῶν ἀεὶ ἔστιν· ὥστε τὸ 10
ἀθάνατον πᾶν ἀΐδιον (ἔστι γὰρ τὸ ἀθάνατον τὸ ἄδεκτον θανάτου
καὶ ἀεὶ ζῶν, ἀΐδιον δὲ τὸ ἄδεκτον τοῦ μὴ εἶναι καὶ ἀεὶ ὄν).

εἰ δὲ πολλὰ τῶν ὄντων ἐστὶ καὶ κρείττονα καὶ χείρονα τῆς
ζωῆς, ἄδεκτα ὄντα τοῦ ἀθανάτου, ἀεὶ δὲ ὄντα, οὐ πᾶν ἄρα τὸ
ἀΐδιον ἀθάνατόν ἐστιν. ἀλλὰ μὴν ὅτι πολλὰ ἀεὶ ὄντα οὐκ 15
ἀθάνατά ἐστι, δῆλον· ἔστι γάρ τινα τῶν ὄντων ἄμοιρα μὲν
ζωῆς, ἀεὶ δὲ ὄντα καὶ ἀνώλεθρα. ὡς γὰρ ἔχει τὸ ὂν πρὸς τὴν
ζωήν, οὕτως τὸ ἀΐδιον πρὸς τὸ ἀθάνατον (ἡ γὰρ ἀναφαίρετος
ζωὴ τὸ ἀθάνατόν ἐστι, καὶ τὸ ἀναφαιρέτως ὂν ἀΐδιον)· τὸ δὲ ὂν
τῆς ζωῆς περιληπτικώτερον· καὶ τοῦ ἀθανάτου ἄρα τὸ ἀΐδιον. 20

106. Παντὸς τοῦ πάντῃ αἰωνίου κατά τε οὐσίαν καὶ ἐνέργειαν
καὶ τοῦ τὴν οὐσίαν ἔχοντος ἐν χρόνῳ μέσον ἐστὶ τὸ πῇ μὲν
αἰώνιον, πῇ δὲ χρόνῳ μετρούμενον.

τὸ γὰρ τὴν οὐσίαν ἔχον ὑπὸ χρόνου περιεχομένην κατὰ
πάντα ἐστὶν ἔγχρονον (πολλῷ γὰρ πρότερον τοῦτο καὶ τὴν 25
ἐνέργειαν ἔγχρονον ἔλαχε)· τὸ δὲ κατὰ πάντα ἔγχρονον τῷ
κατὰ πάντα αἰωνίῳ πάντῃ ἀνόμοιον· αἱ δὲ πρόοδοι πᾶσαι διὰ
τῶν ὁμοίων· ἔστιν ἄρα τι μεταξὺ τούτων. ἢ οὖν τῇ οὐσίᾳ αἰώνιον, τῇ ἐνεργείᾳ δὲ ἔγχρονον τὸ μέσον, ἢ ἀνάπαλιν. ἀλλὰ
τοῦτο ἀδύνατον· ἔσται γὰρ τῆς οὐσίας ἡ ἐνέργεια κρείττων. 30
λείπεται δὴ θάτερον εἶναι τὸ μέσον.

107. Πᾶν τὸ πῇ μὲν αἰώνιον, πῇ δὲ ἔγχρονον, ὄν τέ ἐστιν
ἅμα καὶ γένεσις.

καὶ γὰρ τὸ αἰώνιον πᾶν ὄν ἐστι, καὶ τὸ μετρούμενον ὑπὸ

104. 1 ἢ] ἢ [M] dett. : si W (sed codd. recc. 'vel')   2 κατ' ἐνέργειαν B
3 prius πρώτως M¹ et (ut vid.) W : τὸ πρώτως BCDQM²   4 ἐνέργειαν Q : οὐσίαν
cett. W   6 ἐνέργειαν BCDQ : οὐσίαν MW   πρώτως ω (πρῶτον edd.)
105. 11 γάρ ω (δέ edd.)   12 τοῦ] τό M primitus   13 prius καί om. M
14 ἀθανάτου BCQD²M² : θανάτου D¹M¹W   prius ὄντα post (ἀ)θανάτου transp.
O (edd.)   19 τὸ ἀναφαιρέτως ω (τό om. edd.)
106. 21 οὐσίαν ω (αἰτίαν Cr.)   25 τοῦτο καὶ] τοῦ κατά [M]   26 ἔλαχεν
ἔγχρονον B primitus (corr. ead. m.)   30 γάρ] ἄρα M¹
107. 32 ὄν τί ἐστιν D et fort. M¹

be superior to existence—or in respect of existence but not of activity. In the latter case the same thing which primitively participates Time will also be primitively eternal, and while Time will be the primal measure of the activity of certain beings (prop. 54), Eternity, which is superior to all Time, will have none to measure, if the primitively eternal be not contained by Eternity in respect of its activity. Therefore all that is primitively eternal has both eternal existence and eternal activity.

PROP. 105. *All that is immortal is perpetual; but not all that is perpetual is immortal.*

For if the immortal is that which always participates Life, and such participation of Life involves participation of Being (prop. 101), then the ever-living is ever existent: thus whatever is immortal is perpetual, the immortal being that which excludes death and is ever-living, while the perpetual is that which excludes not-being and is ever existent.

But if there exist many things both above life and below it which are ever existent but insusceptible of the predicate 'immortal', then the perpetual is not of necessity immortal. Now it is plain that there are many things ever existent but not immortal: some are devoid of life although ever existent and imperishable. For as Being is to Life, so is the perpetual to the immortal, since immortality is inalienable Life and inalienable Being is perpetuity; but Being is more comprehensive than Life: therefore perpetuity is more comprehensive than immortality.

PROP. 106. *Intermediate between that which is wholly eternal (viz. in respect both of existence and of activity) and that which has its existence in time there is a principle eternal in one regard but in another measured by time.*

For that which has its existence embraced by time is in all respects temporal, since a fortiori it has a temporal activity; and the fully temporal is altogether unlike the fully eternal; but all procession is through like terms (prop. 29): therefore there exists an intermediate principle. This mean term will be either eternal in its existence and temporal in its activity, or conversely. But the•latter is impossible: for activity will then be superior to existence. It remains that the mean must be the former.

PROP. 107. *All that is eternal in one regard and temporal in another is at once a Being and a coming-to-be.*

For all that is eternal has Being (prop. 87), and that which is

χρόνου γένεσις· ὥστ' εἰ τὸ αὐτὸ χρόνου μετέχει καὶ αἰῶνος, οὐ κατὰ τὸ αὐτὸ δέ, καὶ τὸ αὐτὸ ἔσται ὄν τε καὶ γένεσις, οὐ καθ' ἓν ἄμφω.

ἐκ δὴ τούτων φανερὸν ὅτι ἡ μὲν γένεσις, καὶ τὴν οὐσίαν ἔγχρονον ἔχουσα, ἀνήρτηται εἰς τὸ πῇ μὲν ὄντος, πῇ δὲ γενέ- 5 σεως κοινωνοῦν, αἰῶνος ἅμα καὶ χρόνου μετέχον· τοῦτο δὲ εἰς τὸ κατὰ πάντα αἰώνιον· τὸ δὲ κατὰ πάντα αἰώνιον εἰς τὸν αἰῶνα· ὁ δὲ αἰὼν εἰς τὸ ὂν τὸ προαιώνιον.

108. Πᾶν τὸ ἐν ἑκάστῃ τάξει μερικὸν διχῶς μετέχειν δύναται τῆς ἐν τῇ προσεχῶς ὑπερκειμένῃ διακοσμήσει μονάδος· ἢ διὰ 10 τῆς οἰκείας ὁλότητος, ἢ διὰ τοῦ ἐν ἐκείνῃ μερικοῦ καὶ συστοίχου πρὸς αὐτὸ κατὰ τὴν πρὸς ὅλην τὴν σειρὰν ἀναλογίαν.

εἰ γὰρ δι' ὁμοιότητος ἡ ἐπιστροφὴ πᾶσι, καὶ ἔστι τῷ ἐν τῇ ὑπερκειμένῃ τάξει μοναδικῷ καὶ ὅλῳ τὸ ἐν τῇ καταδεεστέρᾳ μερικὸν ἀνόμοιον καὶ ὡς ὅλῳ μερικὸν καὶ ὡς τάξεως ἄλλης καὶ 15 ἄλλης, πρὸς δὲ τὸ ἐκ τῆς αὐτῆς σειρᾶς ὅλον ὅμοιον διὰ τὴν τῆς ἰδιότητος κοινωνίαν καὶ πρὸς τὸ τῆς ὑπερκειμένης προσεχῶς ὁμοταγὲς διὰ τὴν ἀνάλογον ὑπόστασιν, δῆλον δὴ ὅτι διὰ τούτων αὐτῷ μέσων ἡ πρὸς ἐκεῖνο γίνεσθαι πέφυκεν ἐπιστροφὴ ὡς δι' ὁμοίων, ἀνόμοιον ⟨ὄν⟩. τὸ μὲν γὰρ ὡς μερικῷ μερικὸν ὅμοιον, τὸ 20 δὲ ὡς τῆς αὐτῆς ὂν σειρᾶς οἰκεῖον· ἐκεῖνο δὲ τὸ τῆς ὑπερκειμένης ὅλον κατ' ἀμφότερα ἀνόμοιον.

109. Πᾶς μερικὸς νοῦς μετέχει τῆς ὑπὲρ νοῦν καὶ πρωτίστης ἑνάδος διά τε τοῦ ὅλου νοῦ καὶ διὰ τῆς ὁμοταγοῦς αὐτῷ μερικῆς ἑνάδος· καὶ πᾶσα μερικὴ ψυχὴ τοῦ ὅλου μετέχει νοῦ διά τε τῆς 25 ὅλης ψυχῆς καὶ τοῦ μερικοῦ νοῦ· καὶ πᾶσα σώματος μερικὴ φύσις διά τε τῆς ὅλης φύσεως καὶ μερικῆς ψυχῆς μετέχει τῆς ὅλης ψυχῆς.

πᾶν γὰρ μερικὸν μετέχει τῆς ἐν τῇ ὑπερκειμένῃ τάξει μονάδος ἢ διὰ τῆς οἰκείας ὁλότητος ἢ διὰ τοῦ ἐν ἐκείνῃ μερικοῦ καὶ 30 πρὸς αὐτὸ ὁμοταγοῦς.

107. 1 εἰ om. M¹W   7 τὸ δὲ ... αἰώνιον] οὗτοι δέ Q   7-8 εἰς τὸν ... αἰών om. Q, del. M²
108. 13 πᾶσι, καὶ ἔστι BCDMW (D primitus πάσῃ): πᾶσα ἐστί Q: πᾶσίν ἐστι O (edd.)   14 τό] τῷ M¹   15 prius ὡς] ὅλως (sic) M   16 ὅλον ω (ὄν Arg Cr.)   19 αὐτῷ] αὐτῶν B: om. W   20 ὄν addidi   τὸ μέν BM¹Q: τῷ αὐτῷ CDM²W   20-21 τῷ δέ D   21-2 ἐκείνῳ δὲ τῷ ... ὅλῳ BCD, ἐκεῖνο δὲ τῷ ... ὅλῳ W ut vid.
109. 24 ἑνάδος] μονάδος BCD   νοῦ erasum M (om. dett., edd.)   25 νοῦ ω (om. edd.)   27 ante μερικῆς fort. inserendum τῆς

measured by Time is a process of coming-to-be (prop. 50): so that if the same thing participate at once Time and Eternity, though not in the same regard, the same thing will be at once a Being and a coming-to-be, but in different respects.

Cor. From this it is apparent that coming-to-be, which is temporal even in its existence, is dependent upon that which shares partly in Being, partly in coming-to-be, participating at once Eternity and Time; and this latter is dependent upon the fully eternal; and the fully eternal upon Eternity (prop. 53); and Eternity upon Being, which is pre-eternal (prop. 87).

PROP. **108.** *Every particular member of any order can participate the monad of the rank immediately supra-jacent in one of two ways: either through the universal of its own order, or through the particular member of the higher series which is co-ordinate with it in respect of its analogous relation to that series as a whole.*

For if all things achieve reversion through likeness (prop. 32), and if the particular member of the inferior order differs from the monadic universal of the superior both as particular from universal and also by the difference of its order, whereas it resembles the universal of its own series by sharing in the same distinctive character and resembles the corresponding term of the immediately supra-jacent series in virtue of its analogous place in the procession, it is plain that the two latter are the mean terms through which its reversion upon the former can take place, advancing through similars to the dissimilar: for the one resembles it through their common particularity, and the other is closely bound to it as a member of the same series, while the universal of the supra-jacent series is unlike it in both these respects.

PROP. **109.** *Every particular intelligence participates the first Henad, which is above intelligence, both through the universal Intelligence and through the particular henad co-ordinate with it; every particular soul participates the universal Intelligence both through the universal Soul and through its particular intelligence; and every particular corporeal nature participates the universal Soul both through universal Nature and through a particular soul.*

For every particular participates the monad of the supra-jacent order either through its own universal or through that particular in the higher order which is co-ordinate with it (prop. 108).

110. Πάντων τῶν καθ' ἑκάστην σειρὰν διατεταγμένων τὰ μὲν πρῶτα καὶ τῇ ἑαυτῶν μονάδι συνημμένα μετέχειν δύναται τῶν ἐν τῇ ὑπερκειμένῃ σειρᾷ προσεχῶς ἱδρυμένων διὰ τῆς ἀναλογίας, τὰ δὲ ἀτελέστερα καὶ πολλοστὰ ἀπὸ τῆς οἰκείας ἀρχῆς οὐ πέφυκεν ἐκείνων ἀπολαύειν. 5

διότι γὰρ τὰ μέν ἐστι συγγενῆ πρὸς ἐκεῖνα, φύσιν ἐν τῇ σφετέρᾳ τάξει λαχόντα κρείττονα καὶ θειοτέραν, τὰ δὲ πορρώτερον προελήλυθε, δευτέραν καὶ ὑπηρετικὴν ἀλλ' οὐ πρωτουργὸν καὶ ἡγεμονικὴν ἐν τῇ σειρᾷ πάσῃ κεκληρωμένα πρόοδον, ἐξ ἀνάγκης τὰ μὲν ὁμοφυῶς συζεύγνυται τοῖς ἐκ τῆς ὑπερκειμένης 10 τάξεως, τὰ δὲ ἀσύναπτά ἐστι πρὸς ἐκείνην. οὐ γὰρ ἅπαντα τῆς ἴσης ἐστὶν ἀξίας, κἂν ἐκ τῆς αὐτῆς ᾖ διακοσμήσεως· οὐδὲ γὰρ εἷς ὁ λόγος, ἀλλ' ὡς ἀφ' ἑνὸς καὶ πρὸς ἕν [πάντα πρόεισιν ἐκ τῆς οἰκείας μονάδος]. ὥστε οὐδὲ δύναμιν ἔλαχε τὴν αὐτήν, ἀλλὰ τὰ μὲν ὑποδέχεσθαι δύναται τὰς τῶν ὑπερκειμένων προσ- 15 εχῶς μεθέξεις, τὰ δὲ ἀνομοιούμενα ταῖς ἀπὸ τῶν ἀρχῶν ἐπὶ πλεῖστον προόδοις τῆς τοιαύτης παρήρηται δυνάμεως.

111. Πάσης τῆς νοερᾶς σειρᾶς οἱ μέν εἰσι θεῖοι νόες ὑποδεξάμενοι θεῶν μεθέξεις, οἱ δὲ νόες μόνον· καὶ πάσης τῆς ψυχικῆς αἱ μέν εἰσι νοεραὶ ψυχαὶ εἰς νοῦς ἀνηρτημέναι οἰκείους, αἱ δὲ 20 ψυχαὶ μόνον· καὶ πάσης τῆς σωματικῆς φύσεως αἱ μὲν καὶ ψυχὰς ἔχουσιν ἐφεστώσας ἄνωθεν, αἱ δέ εἰσι φύσεις μόνον, τῆς τῶν ψυχῶν ἄμοιροι παρουσίας.

ἑκάστης γὰρ σειρᾶς οὐχ ὅλον τὸ γένος εἰς τὸ πρὸ αὐτοῦ ἀνηρτῆσθαι πέφυκεν, ἀλλὰ τὸ ἐν αὐτῇ τελειότερον καὶ συμ- 25 φύεσθαι τοῖς ὑπερκειμένοις ἱκανόν. οὔτε οὖν πᾶς νοῦς θεοῦ ἐξῆπται, ἀλλ' οἱ ἀκρότατοι καὶ ἑνικώτατοι τῶν νόων (οὗτοι γὰρ ταῖς θείαις ἑνάσι συγγενεῖς)· οὔτε πᾶσαι ψυχαὶ μετέχουσι νοῦ τοῦ μεθεκτοῦ, ἀλλ' ὅσαι νοερώταται· οὔτε πᾶσαι σωματικαὶ φύσεις ἀπολαύουσι ψυχῆς παρούσης καὶ μετεχομένης, ἀλλ' αἱ 30 τελειότεραι καὶ λογοειδέστεραι. καὶ οὗτος ἐπὶ πάντων ὁ λόγος τῆς ἀποδείξεως.

112. Πάσης τάξεως τὰ πρώτιστα μορφὴν ἔχει τῶν πρὸ αὐτῶν.

τὰ γὰρ καθ' ἑκάστην ἀκρότατα γένη διὰ τὴν ὁμοιότητα 35 συνάπτεται τοῖς ὑπερκειμένοις καὶ διὰ τὴν συνέχειαν τῆς προ-

110. 3 τῆς om. MQ   7–8 πορρωτέρω Q   13–14 πάντα . . . μονάδος seclusi   14 οὐδέ Q: οὔτε cett. (B primitus οὐ)   15 ὑποδεδέχθαι Q 17 παρήρηται Q, secus pendent W

111. 19 μέθεξιν Q   20 νοῦς] νόας Q   22 ante ψυχάς ins. πρός Q   28 νοῦ del. M²   31 οὗτος BCDM¹W : οὔτως M¹ : ὁ αὐτός (omisso ὁ ante λόγος) Q

112. 35 ἀκρότατα BCD 'Ανάπτ. : ἀκρότητα MQW   36 ὑποκειμένοις M²

PROP. 110. *The first members of any transverse series, which are closely linked with their own monad, can participate in virtue of their analogous position those members of the supra-jacent series which lie immediately above them ; but the less perfect members of the lower order, which are many degrees removed from their proper originative principle, are incapable of enjoying such participation.*

For because the first members are akin to the higher order in that their natural place in their own order is higher and more divine, whereas the others have proceeded further from their source and have been endowed not with a primitive and dominant but with a secondary and subordinate rank in the series as a whole, it necessarily follows that the former are conjoined by community of nature with the members of the supra-jacent order, while the latter have no contact with it.   For not all things are of equal worth, even though they be of the same cosmic order : such terms are not in fact identical in definition, but are co-ordinate only as proceeding from, and referable to, a single common principle.   Differing in definition, they differ also in potency : some of them are capable of receiving participation in the principles immediately supra-jacent to them, while others are deprived of this kind of power, losing likeness to their origins in proportion to their extreme remoteness from them.

PROP. 111. *The intellective series comprises divine intelligences which have received participation in gods, and also bare intelligences ; the psychical series comprises intellective souls, linked each with its own intelligence, and also bare souls ; corporeal nature comprises natures over which souls preside, and also bare natures destitute of a soul's company.*

For not all the members of any series are capable of being linked with the prior order, but only those more perfect members which are fit to identify themselves with the higher principles (prop. 110). Accordingly not every intelligence is attached to a god, but only the supreme intelligences which have the most unity (these being akin to the divine henads) ; not all souls communicate in the participable intelligence, but only the most intellective ; not all bodily natures enjoy the presence of, and participation in, a soul, but only the more perfect, which have a more rational form.   The same principle of demonstration may be applied universally.

PROP. 112. *The first members of any order have the form of their priors.*

For the highest classes in each order are conjoined with the supra-jacent principles because of their likeness to them (prop. 110)

ὁδοῦ τῶν ὅλων· ὥστε οἷά πέρ ἐστιν ἐκεῖνα πρώτως, τοιαύτην
ἔλαχε καὶ ταῦτα μορφήν, συγγενῆ πρὸς τὴν ἐκείνων φύσιν· καὶ
φαίνεται εἶναι τοιαῦτα κατὰ τὴν ἰδιότητα τῆς ὑποστάσεως, οἷα
τὰ πρὸ αὐτῶν.

113. Πᾶς ὁ θεῖος ἀριθμὸς ἑνιαῖός ἐστιν.

εἰ γὰρ ὁ θεῖος ἀριθμὸς αἰτίαν ἔχει προηγουμένην τὸ ἕν, ὡς ὁ
νοερὸς τὸν νοῦν καὶ ὁ ψυχικὸς τὴν ψυχήν, καὶ ἔστιν ἀνάλογον
τὸ πλῆθος πανταχοῦ πρὸς τὴν αἰτίαν, δῆλον δὴ ὅτι καὶ ὁ θεῖος
ἀριθμὸς ἑνιαῖός ἐστιν, εἴπερ τὸ ἓν θεός· τοῦτο δέ, εἴπερ τἀγαθὸν
καὶ ἓν ταὐτόν· καὶ γὰρ τἀγαθὸν καὶ θεὸς ταὐτόν (οὗ γὰρ μηδέν
ἐστιν ἐπέκεινα καὶ οὗ πάντα ἐφίεται, θεὸς τοῦτο· καὶ ἀφ' οὗ τὰ
πάντα καὶ πρὸς ὅ, τοῦτο δὲ τἀγαθόν). εἰ ἄρα ἔστι πλῆθος
θεῶν, ἑνιαῖόν ἐστι τὸ πλῆθος. ἀλλὰ μὴν ὅτι ἔστι, δῆλον, εἴπερ
πᾶν αἴτιον ἀρχικὸν οἰκείου πλήθους ἡγεῖται καὶ ὁμοίου πρὸς
αὐτὸ καὶ συγγενοῦς.

114. Πᾶς θεὸς ἑνάς ἐστιν αὐτοτελής, καὶ πᾶσα αὐτοτελὴς
ἑνὰς θεός.

εἰ γὰρ τῶν ἑνάδων διττὸς ὁ ἀριθμός, ὡς δέδεικται πρότερον,
καὶ αἱ μὲν αὐτοτελεῖς εἰσιν αἱ δὲ ἐλλάμψεις ἀπ' ἐκείνων, τῷ δὲ
ἑνὶ καὶ τἀγαθῷ συγγενὴς καὶ ὁμοφυὴς ὁ θεῖος ἀριθμός, ἑνάδες
εἰσὶν αὐτοτελεῖς οἱ θεοί.

καὶ ἔμπαλιν, εἰ ἔστιν αὐτοτελὴς ἑνάς, θεός ἐστι. καὶ γὰρ
ὡς ἑνὰς τῷ ἑνὶ καὶ ὡς αὐτοτελὴς τἀγαθῷ συγγενεστάτη διαφερόντως ἐστί, καὶ κατ' ἄμφω τῆς θείας ἰδιότητος μετέχει, καὶ
ἔστι θεός. εἰ δὲ ἦν ἑνὰς μὲν οὐκ αὐτοτελὴς δέ, ἢ αὐτοτελὴς
μὲν ἡ ὑπόστασις οὐκέτι· δὲ ἑνάς, εἰς ἑτέραν ἂν ἐτάττετο τάξιν
διὰ τὴν τῆς ἰδιότητος ἐξαλλαγήν.

115. Πᾶς θεὸς ὑπερούσιός ἐστι καὶ ὑπέρζωος καὶ ὑπέρνους.

εἰ γὰρ ἑνάς ἐστιν ἕκαστος αὐτοτελής, ἕκαστον δὲ τούτων
οὐχὶ ἑνὰς ἀλλ' ἡνωμένον, δῆλον δὴ ὅτι πάντων ἐστὶν ἐπέκεινα
τῶν εἰρημένων ἅπας θεός, οὐσίας καὶ ζωῆς καὶ νοῦ. εἰ γὰρ διέστηκε μὲν ταῦτα ἀλλήλων, πάντα δέ ἐστιν ἐν πᾶσιν, ἕκαστον τὰ
πάντα ὂν ἂν οὐκ ἂν εἴη μόνον.

ἔτι δέ, εἰ τὸ πρῶτον ὑπερούσιον, ἅπας δὲ θεὸς τῆς τοῦ πρώτου
σειρᾶς ἐστιν ᾗ θεός, ὑπερούσιος ἕκαστος ἂν εἴη. ἀλλὰ μὴν ὅτι
τὸ πρῶτον ὑπερούσιον, φανερόν. οὐ γὰρ ταὐτὸν ἑνί τε εἶναι καὶ

112. 1 οἷά πέρ ω (οἷά tacite Cr.)
113. 6–7 τὸ ὄν, ὡς ὁ ἔρως τὸν νοῦν [M]   8 καί om. BCD   10 καὶ τὸ ἕν
Arg   11 τά om. Q   12 τἀγαθόν Q : ἀγαθόν cett.
114. 25 ἦν ω (om. Arg edd.)
115. 28 ὑπέρζως C   30 ἑνάς ἐστιν ἀλλ' W ut vid.   ὅτι καὶ πάντων Q
33 prius ἄν fort. secludendum   35 ᾗ] ἤ M

and because of the continuity of procession in the universe : so that they are endowed with a form akin to the nature of the supra-jacent order and reproducing the attributes proper to it.   The distinctive character of their being thus appears as a reflection of their priors.

L. OF DIVINE HENADS, OR GODS.

PROP. 113. *The whole number of the gods has the character of unity.*

For if the divine series has for antecedent cause the One, as the intellective series has Intelligence and the psychical series Soul (prop. 21 *cor.*), and if at every level the manifold is analogous to its cause (prop. 97), it is plain that the divine series has the character of unity, if the One is God.   Now that the One is God follows from its identity with the Good (prop. 13) : for the Good is identical with God, God being that which is beyond all things and to which all things aspire, and the Good being the 'whence' and the 'whither' of all things.   Thus if a plurality of gods exist they must have the character of unity.   But it is evident that such a plurality in fact exists, inasmuch as every originative cause introduces its proper manifold, which resembles it and is akin to it (props. 21, 97).

PROP. 114. *Every god is a self-complete henad or unit, and every self-complete henad is a god.*

For if there are two orders of henads, as has been shown above (prop. 64 *cor.*), one consisting of self-complete principles, the other of irradiations from them, and the divine series is akin to the One or the Good and of like nature with it (prop. 113), then the gods are self-complete henads.

And conversely, if a henad be self-complete it is a god.   For *qua* henad it is most closely and especially akin to the One, and *qua* self-complete, to the Good ; participating in both these respects the distinctive character of godhead, it is a god.   If, on the other hand, it were a henad but not self-complete, or a self-complete principle but no longer a henad, it would be assigned to another order in virtue of its variation from the divine character.

PROP. 115. *Every god is above Being, above Life, and above Intelligence.*

For if each god is a self-complete henad (prop. 114), whereas Being, Life, and Intelligence are not henads but unified groups, then it is plain that every god transcends all the three principles in question (prop. 5).   For if these three, though mutually distinct, are each implicit in the other two (prop. 103), then no one of them can be a pure unity, since each contains all.

Again, if the First Principle transcend Being, then since every god, *qua* god, is of the order of that Principle (prop. 113), it follows that all of them must transcend Being.   But that the First Principle transcends Being is evident.   For unity and Being are not identical : it is one

οὐσίᾳ εἶναι, οὐδὲ ταὐτὸν τὸ ἔστι καὶ τὸ ἥνωται. εἰ δὲ μὴ
ταὐτόν, ἢ ἄμφω τὸ πρῶτον, καὶ ἔσται οὐχ ἓν μόνον ἀλλά τι
καὶ ἄλλο παρὰ τὸ ἕν, καὶ μετέχον δὴ λοιπὸν ἑνὸς ἀλλ' οὐκ
αὐτοέν· ἢ θάτερον τούτων. ἀλλ' εἰ μὲν οὐσία, ἐνδεὲς ἔσται τοῦ
ἑνός· ὅπερ ἀδύνατον, εἶναι τἀγαθὸν καὶ τὸ πρῶτον ἐνδεές. ἓν 5
ἄρα μόνον ἐκεῖνο· ὥστε ὑπερούσιον. . εἰ δέ, ὃ ἕκαστόν ἐστι
πρώτως, τούτου τὴν ἰδιότητα πάσῃ τῇ σειρᾷ δίδωσι, καὶ ὁ θεῖος
ἀριθμὸς ἅπας ὑπερούσιός ἐστιν. ἐπεὶ καὶ τὰ ὅμοια παράγει πρὸ
τῶν ἀνομοίων ἕκαστον τῶν ἀρχικῶν αἰτίων· εἰ ἄρα ὁ πρώτιστος
θεὸς ὑπερούσιος, καὶ θεοὶ πάντες ὑπερούσιοι (ταύτῃ γὰρ ὅμοιοι 10
ἔσονται)· οὐσίαι δὲ ὄντες, ἀπὸ οὐσίας ἂν παράγοιντο τῆς πρώτης,
ὡς μονάδος τῶν οὐσιῶν.

116. Πᾶς θεὸς μεθεκτός ἐστι, πλὴν τοῦ ἑνός. .

ὅτι μὲν γὰρ ἐκεῖνο ἀμέθεκτον, δῆλον, ἵνα μὴ μετεχόμενον καὶ
τινὸς διὰ τοῦτο γενόμενον μηκέτι πάντων ὁμοίως ᾖ τῶν τε 15
προόντων καὶ τῶν ὄντων αἴτιον.

ὅτι δὲ αἱ ἄλλαι ἑνάδες μετέχονται ἤδη, δείξομεν οὕτως. εἰ
γὰρ ἔστιν ἄλλη μετὰ τὸ πρῶτον ἀμέθεκτος ἐνάς, τί διοίσει τοῦ
ἑνός; ἢ γὰρ ὡσαύτως ἕν ἐστιν ὥσπερ ἐκεῖνο—καὶ πῶς τὸ μὲν
δεύτερον, τὸ δὲ πρῶτον ;—ἢ οὐχ ὡσαύτως, καὶ τὸ μὲν αὐτοέν, τὸ 20
δὲ ἕν τε καὶ οὐχ ἕν. ἀλλὰ τὸ οὐχ ἓν τοῦτο εἰ μὲν μηδεμία ὑπόστασις, ἔσται μόνον ἕν· εἰ δὲ ὑπόστασίς τις ἄλλη παρὰ τὸ ἕν,
μετεχόμενον ἔσται τὸ ἓν ὑπὸ τοῦ οὐχ ἑνός· καὶ τὸ μὲν αὐτοτελὲς
τὸ ἕν, ᾧ συνάπτει πρὸς τὸ αὐτοέν, ὥστε τοῦτο πάλιν ὁ θεός, ᾗ
θεός· τὸ δὲ οὐχ ἓν ὑποστὰν ἐν μεθέξει τοῦ ἑνὸς ὑφέστηκε. 25
μεθεκτὴ ἄρα ἐστὶ πᾶσα ἑνὰς μετὰ τὸ ἓν ὑποστᾶσα, καὶ πᾶς
θεὸς μεθεκτός.

117. Πᾶς θεὸς μέτρον ἐστὶ τῶν ὄντων.

εἰ γάρ ἐστιν ἑνιαῖος ἅπας θεός, τὰ πλήθη πάντα τῶν ὄντων
ἀφορίζει καὶ μετρεῖ. πάντα μὲν γὰρ τὰ πλήθη, τῇ ἑαυτῶν 30
φύσει ἀόριστα ὄντα, διὰ τὸ ἓν ὁρίζεται· τὸ δὲ ἑνιαῖον μετρεῖν
καὶ περατοῦν, οἷς ἂν παρῇ, βούλεται, καὶ περιάγειν εἰς
ὅρον τὸ μὴ τοιοῦτον κατὰ τὴν αὑτοῦ δύναμιν. γίνεται γὰρ

115. 1 τὸ ἕν ἐστι καὶ τὸ ἡνῶσθαι Q (ἡνῶσθαι etiam M²)   9 πρῶτος Q
10 ὑπερούσιος om. Q   ταύτῃ ω (πάντῃ edd.)   11 οὐσίαι] ὑπερούσιοι Q
12 ὡς om. Q   μονάδος Q : μονάδες BCDMW
116. 14 ἀμέθεκτόν ἐστι Q   15 τινὸς διὰ τοῦτο BCDW : διὰ τοῦτο τινὸς
MQ   γινόμενον Q   ὁμοίων ap. Cr.² error preli   17 ἑνάδες]
μονάδες [M]   δείξωμεν BC   19 ἕν om. BCDM²   20 καὶ ω
(om. Cr.²)   24 ᾧ CDMQW : ὃ BArg et suprascr. pr. m. D   25 ἕν ante.
μεθ. scripsi : ἐν ῷ
117. 29 πάντα] πάντων Q   31 ἑνιαῖον [M]W : ἓν ὄν cett.   μετρεῖν
[M]W : μετροῦν cett.   32 alt. καί ω (om. O edd.)   περιάγειν] παράγειν
Q, educere W   33 αὑτοῦ Cr. tacite   γίνεται] κύεται BC

thing to say 'it exists', another to say 'it has unity'. Now if they
are not identical, either both must be attributes of the First
Principle—on which hypothesis, it will be not merely one but also
something other than one, and we are left with a principle participating unity, in place of Unity itself (prop. 4)—or it has one of these
attributes only.   If it have Being only, it will lack unity.   But it is
impossible to ascribe deficiency to the First Principle, which is the
Good (props. 10, 12).   Therefore it has unity only, which implies that
it transcends Being.   And if every principle bestows upon the whole
of its order the distinctive character which belongs primitively to
itself (prop. 97), then the whole number of the gods transcends
Being.   Or again, every originative cause produces like terms before
unlike (prop. 28): if, then, the primal Godhead transcends Being,
all the other gods will resemble it in this respect.   Were they
existences, they would owe their origin to the primal Being, since
this is the monad of all existences.

PROP. 116. *Every god is participable, except the One.*

For in the first place it is clear that the One is imparticipable :
were it participated, it would thereby become the unity of a particular
and cease to be the cause both of existent things and of the principles
prior to existence (prop. 24).

That with the other henads we reach the participable, we shall
prove as follows.   If after the First Principle there be another
imparticipable henad, how will it differ from the One ?   If it be one
in the same degree as the latter, why should we call it secondary
and the One primal ?   And if in a different degree, then relatively
to simple Unity it will be one and not-one.   If that element of
'not-one' be nothing substantive, the henad will be pure unity (and
identical with the One); but if it be a substantive character other
than unity, then the unity in the henad will be participated by the
non-unity.   What is self-complete will then be this unity whereby it
is linked to the One itself, so that once more the god, *qua* god, will
be this component (prop. 114), while that which came into existence
as not-one exists as one by participation in the unity.   Therefore
every henad posterior to the One is participable ; and every god is
thus participable.

PROP. 117. *Every god is a measure of things existent.*

For if every god has the character of unity (prop. 113), he defines
and measures all the manifolds of existent things.   For all manifolds
are in their own nature indeterminate, but receive determination
through unity (prop. 1) ; and that which has the character of unity
tends to measure and delimit the subjects in which it is present and
by its virtue to bring the indefinite to definition.   By participation

κἀκεῖνο ἐνοειδὲς τῇ μεθέξει· τοῦτο δέ, τῆς ἀοριστίας τε καὶ
ἀπειρίας ἀφίσταται· καὶ ὅσῳ μᾶλλον ἐνοειδές, τοσούτῳ ἧττον
ἀόριστον καὶ ἄμετρον. μετρεῖται ἄρα πᾶν πλῆθος τῶν ὄντων
ὑπὸ τῶν θείων ἑνάδων.

118. Πᾶν ὅ τι περ ἂν ἐν τοῖς θεοῖς ᾖ, κατὰ τὴν αὐτῶν ἰδιό- 5
τητα προϋφέστηκεν ἐν αὐτοῖς, καὶ ἔστιν ἡ ἰδιότης αὐτῶν ἐνιαία
καὶ ὑπερούσιος· ἐνιαίως ἄρα καὶ ὑπερουσίως πάντα ἐν αὐτοῖς.

καὶ γὰρ εἰ τριχῶς ἕκαστον ὑφέστηκεν, ἢ κατ᾽ αἰτίαν ἢ καθ᾽
ὕπαρξιν ἢ κατὰ μέθεξιν, πρῶτος δὲ πάντων ἀριθμὸς ὁ θεῖος
ἀριθμός, οὐδὲν ἐν αὐτοῖς ἔσται κατὰ μέθεξιν, ἀλλὰ πάντα καθ᾽ 10
ὕπαρξιν ἢ κατ᾽ αἰτίαν. ἀλλὰ καὶ ὅσα ὡς αἴτιοι πάντων προει-
λήφασιν, οἰκείως τῇ ἑαυτῶν ἑνώσει προειλήφασι· καὶ γὰρ πᾶν
τὸ κατ᾽ αἰτίαν τῶν δευτέρων ἡγεμονοῦν, ὡς αὐτὸ πέφυκεν, οὕτως
ἔχει τὴν αἰτίαν τῶν καταδεεστέρων. πάντα ἄρα ἔστιν ἐν τοῖς
θεοῖς ἐνιαίως καὶ ὑπερουσίως. 15

119. Πᾶς θεὸς κατὰ τὴν ὑπερούσιον ἀγαθότητα ὑφέστηκε,
καὶ ἔστιν ἀγαθὸς οὔτε καθ᾽ ἕξιν οὔτε κατ᾽ οὐσίαν (καὶ γὰρ αἱ
ἕξεις καὶ αἱ οὐσίαι δευτέραν καὶ πολλοστὴν ἔλαχον τάξιν ἀπὸ
τῶν θεῶν), ἀλλ᾽ ὑπερουσίως.

εἰ γὰρ τὸ πρῶτον ἓν καὶ τἀγαθόν, καὶ ᾗ ἕν, τἀγαθόν, καὶ ᾗ 20
τἀγαθόν, ἕν, καὶ πᾶσα ἡ σειρὰ τῶν θεῶν ἐνοειδής τέ ἐστι καὶ
ἀγαθοειδὴς κατὰ μίαν ἰδιότητα, καὶ οὐ κατ᾽ ἄλλο ἕκαστος ἑνὰς
καὶ ἀγαθότης, ἀλλ᾽ ᾗ ἑνάς, ταύτῃ ἀγαθότης, καὶ ᾗ ἀγαθότης,
ἑνάς· καὶ ὡς μὲν ἀπὸ τοῦ πρώτου προελθόντες, οἱ μετὰ
τὸ πρῶτον ἀγαθοειδεῖς καὶ ἐνοειδεῖς, εἴπερ ἐκεῖνο ἓν καὶ τἀγα- 25
θόν· ὡς δὲ θεοί, πάντες ἑνάδες καὶ ἀγαθότητες. ὡς οὖν τὸ
ἓν τὸ τῶν θεῶν ὑπερούσιον, οὕτω καὶ τὸ ἀγαθὸν αὐτῶν ὑπερούσιον, οὐκ ἄλλο τι ὂν παρὰ τὸ ἕν· οὐ γὰρ ἄλλο ἕκαστος, εἶτα
ἀγαθόν, ἀλλὰ μόνον ἀγαθόν, ὥσπερ οὐδὲ ἄλλο, εἶτα ἕν, ἀλλὰ
μόνον ἕν. 30

120. Πᾶς θεὸς ἐν τῇ ἑαυτοῦ ὑπάρξει τὸ προνοεῖν τῶν ὅλων
κέκτηται· καὶ τὸ πρώτως προνοεῖν ἐν τοῖς θεοῖς.

τὰ μὲν γὰρ ἄλλα πάντα μετὰ θεοὺς ὄντα διὰ τὴν ἐκείνων
μετουσίαν προνοεῖ, τοῖς δὲ θεοῖς ἡ πρόνοια συμφυής ἐστιν. εἰ
γὰρ τὸ τῶν ἀγαθῶν μεταδιδόναι τοῖς προνοουμένοις ἐξαίρετόν 35

117. 1-2 τῆς ἀοριστίας καὶ τῆς ἀπειρίας Q   2 τοσοῦτον M
118. 5 αὐτῶν] αὐτήν M   9 ἀριθμῶν CDE   10 ἀριθμός om. Q
14-15 ἐν τοῖς θεοῖς ἐστιν Q
119. 17 καθ᾽ ἕξιν BCDM²: καθ᾽ ἕξιν νοῦ W: κατὰ μέθεξιν [M]Q   22 κατὰ
τὴν μίαν C   23 alt. ᾗ] ἢ M   24 ante ἑνάς ins. ταύτῃ καί Q   προσελ-
θόντες M   26 θεοί ω (οἱ θεοί O edd.)   29 μόνον αὐτὸ τἀγαθόν [M]W
120. 31 ἐν τῇ ὑπάρξει ἑαυτοῦ Q   34 ἐστιν om. M¹

in it even the indefinite acquires a unitary form (that is to say, it loses its indetermination or infinitude); and the more it has of unitary form, the less is it indeterminate or measureless. Thus every manifold of existent things is measured by the divine henads.

PROP. 118. *Every attribute of the gods pre-subsists in them in a manner consonant with their distinctive character as gods, and since this character is unitary (prop. 113) and above Being (prop. 115), they have all their attributes in a unitary and supra-existential mode.*

For if all attributes subsist in one of three ways, by implication in their cause, or as substantial predicates, or by participation (prop. 65), and the divine order is the first order of all, the gods will have no attribute by participation, but all as substantial predicates or as implicit in their causality. Now besides their substantial predicates, those attributes which the gods pre-embrace as causes of all things are pre-embraced by them in a manner conformable to their unity ; for every sovereign principle which is related as cause to secondary existences contains the cause of the inferior order in the mode which is proper to its own nature (prop. 18). Thus the gods have all their attributes in a unitary and supra-existential mode.

PROP. 119. *The substance of every god is a supra-existential excellence ; he has goodness neither as a state nor as part of his essence (for both states and essences have a secondary and remote rank relatively to the gods), but is supra-existentially good.*

For if the First Principle is One and the Good, and *qua* One is the Good, and *qua* the Good is One (prop. 13), then likewise the entire series of gods has the form of unity and the form of goodness as a single character : they are not henads in one respect, excellences in another, but each is an excellence *qua* henad and a henad *qua* excellence. As derivative terms proceeding from the First Principle, they have the form of goodness and unity, inasmuch as that Principle is One and the Good ; as gods, all are henads and excellences. Now the unity of the gods being supra-existential (prop. 115), so also is their goodness, which is indistinguishable from their unity. Neither their goodness nor their unity is a quality superadded upon other qualities ; they are pure goodness, as they are pure unity.

PROP. 120. *Every god embraces in his substance the function of exercising providence towards the universe ; and the primary providence resides in the gods.*

For all things else, being posterior to the gods, exercise providence in virtue of divine compresence, whereas the gods do so by their very nature. For if the office distinctive of the providential character is the bestowal of good things upon the beings which are its objects,

ἐστι τῆς προνοητικῆς ἰδιότητος, οἱ δὲ θεοὶ πάντες ἀγαθότητές
εἰσιν, ἢ οὐδενὶ μεταδώσουσιν ἑαυτῶν, καὶ οὐδὲν ἔσται ἀγαθὸν ἐν
τοῖς δευτέροις (πόθεν γὰρ τὸ κατὰ μέθεξιν ἢ ἀπὸ τῶν πρώτως
τὰς ἰδιότητας ἐχόντων;)· ἢ μεταδιδόντες ἀγαθῶν μεταδιδοῦσι,
καὶ ταύτῃ προνοήσουσι τῶν πάντων. ἐν θεοῖς οὖν ἡ πρόνοια 5
πρώτως. καὶ ποῦ γὰρ ἡ πρὸ νοῦ ἐνέργεια ἢ ἐν τοῖς ὑπερουσίοις ;
ἡ δὲ πρόνοια, ὡς τοὔνομα ἐμφαίνει, ἐνέργειά ἐστι πρὸ νοῦ. τῷ
εἶναι ἄρα θεοὶ καὶ τῷ ἀγαθότητες εἶναι πάντων προνοοῦσι,
πάντα τῆς πρὸ νοῦ πληροῦντες ἀγαθότητος.

121. Πᾶν τὸ θεῖον ὕπαρξιν μὲν ἔχει τὴν ἀγαθότητα, δύναμιν 10
δὲ ἑνιαίαν καὶ γνῶσιν κρύφιον καὶ ἄληπτον πᾶσιν ὁμοῦ τοῖς
δευτέροις.

εἰ γάρ ἐστι προνοητικὸν τῶν ὅλων, ἔστιν ἐν αὐτῷ δύναμις
κρατητικὴ τῶν προνοουμένων, δι᾽ ἥν, ἀκράτητον καὶ ἀπερίγραφον τοῖς πᾶσιν ὑπάρχουσαν, πάντα πεπληρώκασιν ἑαυτῶν, 15
πάντα ὑποστρώσαντες ἑαυτοῖς· πᾶν γὰρ τὸ ἀρχικὸν ἄλλων
αἴτιον καὶ κρατητικὸν διὰ δυνάμεως περιουσίαν ἄρχει καὶ κρατεῖ
κατὰ φύσιν. ἔστι δὴ ὖν ἡ πρωτίστη δύναμις ἐν τοῖς θεοῖς, οὐ
τῶν μὲν κρατοῦσα τῶν δὲ οὔ, πάντων δὲ ἐξ ἴσου προλαβοῦσα
τὰς δυνάμεις ἐν ἑαυτῇ τῶν ὄντων, οὔτε οὐσιώδης οὖσα δύναμις 20
οὔτε πολλῷ πλέον ἀνούσιος, ἀλλὰ τῇ ὑπάρξει τῶν θεῶν συμφυὴς
καὶ ὑπερούσιος.

ἀλλὰ μὴν καὶ τὰ πέρατα πασῶν τῶν γνώσεων ἑνοειδῶς ἐν
τοῖς θεοῖς προϋφέστηκε· διὰ γὰρ τὴν θείαν γνῶσιν τὴν ἐξῃρημένην τῶν ὅλων καὶ αἱ ἄλλαι πᾶσαι γνώσεις ὑπέστησαν, οὔτε 25
νοερὰν οὖσαν οὔτε ἔτι μᾶλλον τῶν μετὰ νοῦν τινα γνώσεων,
ἀλλὰ κατὰ τὴν ἰδιότητα τὴν θείαν ὑπὲρ νοῦν ἱδρυμένην.

εἴτε ἄρα γνῶσίς ἐστι θεία, κρύφιός ἐστιν αὕτη καὶ ἑνοειδὴς ἡ
γνῶσις· εἴτε δύναμις, ἀπερίγραφος πᾶσι καὶ περιληπτικὴ
πάντων ὡσαύτως· εἴτε ἀγαθότης, τὴν ὕπαρξιν αὐτῶν ἀφορί- 30
ζουσα. καὶ γὰρ εἰ πάντα ἐστὶν ἐν αὐτοῖς, γνῶσις δύναμις
ἀγαθότης, ἀλλ᾽ ἡ ὕπαρξις τῷ ἀρίστῳ χαρακτηρίζεται καὶ ἡ
ὑπόστασις κατὰ τὸ ἄριστον· τοῦτο δὲ ἡ ἀγαθότης.

120. 6 ἐνέργεια λέγεται ἢ Q   7 et 8 τῷ] τό (bis) M primitus
121. 11 καὶ ἄληπτον ω (καί om. Arg Cr.)   14 τῶν προνοουμένων κρατη-
τική Q   21 ἀνούσιος] νοερὰ οὖσα Q   23 πασῶν BCD : πάντων MQ (unde
πάντων τῶν γνωστῶν male Cr.)   32 τῷ ἀορίστῳ Q   33 τὸ ἀόριστον Q,
indeterminatum W (sed superiore loco ‘optimo’)

and if every god is an excellence (prop. 119), then either the gods will communicate themselves to no recipient, and there will thus be nothing good in the secondary existences (whence should they procure participation of things good, if not from the principles which have these characters primitively?); or, if they communicate anything, what they communicate is good, and in this way they will exercise providence towards all things. Providence, then, resides primitively in the gods. For indeed, where should an activity prior to Intelligence be found, if not in the principles above Being? And providence, as its name (*pronoia*) shows, is an activity prior to Intelligence (*pro nou*). In virtue of their being, then, and in virtue of being excellences, the gods exercise providence towards all things, filling all with a goodness which is prior to Intelligence.

PROP. 121. *All that is divine has a substance which is goodness (prop. 119), a potency which has the character of unity, and a mode of knowledge which is secret and incomprehensible to all secondary beings alike.*

For if it has the function of exercising providence towards the universe (prop. 120), then it has a potency which dominates the objects of its providence, a potency past all resisting and without all circumscription, in virtue of which the gods have filled all things with themselves; all things are subjected to them, since every cause which originates and dominates other existences by superfluity of potency is naturally originative and dominative. Thus the primary potency resides in the gods, not dominant over a part only, but pre-embracing in itself the potencies of all existent things alike; it is not an existential potency, and still less a non-existential, but congruent with the substance of the gods, that is, supra-existential (prop. 118).

Again, the determinative principles of all forms of knowledge pre-subsist in the gods after the mode of unity. For all other forms of knowledge came into existence in virtue of the divine knowledge, which transcends the sum of things; it is not intellective, and still less is it any of the modes of cognition posterior to Intelligence, but it is enthroned above Intelligence according to the distinctive character of godhead (prop. 118).

Thus if there is a divine knowledge, this knowledge is secret and unitary; if a divine potency, it is without all circumscription and embraces all alike; if a divine goodness, it defines the substance of the gods—for notwithstanding they have all three attributes, knowledge, potency, and goodness, yet their substance is characterized and their proper nature determined by that which is best, namely, their goodness.

122. Πᾶν τὸ θεῖον καὶ προνοεῖ τῶν δευτέρων καὶ ἐξῄρηται τῶν προνοουμένων, μήτε τῆς προνοίας χαλώσης τὴν ἄμικτον αὐτοῦ καὶ ἑνιαίαν ὑπεροχὴν μήτε τῆς χωριστῆς ἑνώσεως τὴν πρόνοιαν ἀφανιζούσης.

μένοντες γὰρ ἐν τῷ ἑνιαίῳ τῷ ἑαυτῶν καὶ ἐν τῇ ὑπάρξει τὰ 5 πάντα πεπληρώκασι τῆς ἑαυτῶν δυνάμεως· καὶ πᾶν τὸ δυνά-μενον αὐτῶν μεταλαγχάνειν ἀπολαύει τῶν ἀγαθῶν ὧν δέχεσθαι δύναται κατὰ τὰ μέτρα τῆς οἰκείας ὑποστάσεως, ἐκείνων αὐτῷ τῷ εἶναι, μᾶλλον δὲ προεῖναι, τἀγαθὰ τοῖς οὖσιν ἐπιλαμπόντων. ὄντες γὰρ οὐδὲν ἄλλο ἢ ἀγαθότητες, αὐτῷ τῷ εἶναι τοῖς πᾶσιν 10 ἀφθόνως τἀγαθὰ χορηγοῦσιν, οὐ κατὰ λογισμὸν ποιούμενοι τὴν διανομήν, ἀλλὰ τούτων μὲν κατὰ τὴν αὐτῶν ἀξίαν δεχομένων, ἐκείνων δὲ κατὰ τὴν αὐτῶν ὕπαρξιν διδόντων. οὔτε οὖν προ-νοοῦντες σχέσιν ἀναδέχονται πρὸς τὰ προνοούμενα· τῷ γὰρ εἶναι ὅ εἰσι πάντα ἀγαθύνουσιν, πᾶν δὲ τὸ τῷ εἶναι ποιοῦν 15 ἀσχέτως ποιεῖ (ἡ γὰρ σχέσις πρόσθεσίς ἐστι τοῦ εἶναι· διὸ καὶ παρὰ φύσιν)· οὔτε χωριστοὶ ὄντες ἀναιροῦσι τὴν πρόνοιαν· οὕτω γὰρ ἂν ἀναιροῖεν (ὃ μηδὲ θέμις εἰπεῖν) τὴν ὕπαρξιν τὴν ἑαυτῶν, ἧς ἰδιότης ἡ ἀγαθότης ἐστίν. ἀγαθοῦ γὰρ ἡ μετάδοσις εἰς πᾶν τὸ μετέχειν δυνάμενον, καὶ τὸ μέγιστόν ἐστιν οὐ τὸ 20 ἀγαθοειδές, ἀλλὰ τὸ ἀγαθουργόν. τοῦτο τοίνυν ἢ οὐδὲν ἕξει τῶν ὄντων ἢ θεοὶ πρὸ τῶν ὄντων· οὐ γὰρ ἄν που τοῖς μὲν κατὰ μέθεξιν ἀγαθοῖς ὑπάρχοι τὸ μεῖζον ἀγαθόν, τοῖς δὲ πρώτως ἀγαθοῖς τὸ ἔλαττον.

123. Πᾶν τὸ θεῖον αὐτὸ μὲν διὰ τὴν ὑπερούσιον ἕνωσιν ἄρρητόν 25 ἐστι καὶ ἄγνωστον πᾶσι τοῖς δευτέροις, ἀπὸ δὲ τῶν μετεχόντων ληπτόν ἐστι καὶ γνωστόν· διὸ μόνον τὸ πρῶτον παντελῶς ἄγνωστον, ἅτε ἀμέθεκτον ὄν.

πᾶσα γὰρ ἡ διὰ λόγου γνῶσις τῶν ὄντων ἐστὶ καὶ ἐν τοῖς οὖσιν ἔχει τὸ τῆς ἀληθείας καταληπτικόν (καὶ γὰρ νοημάτων 30 ἐφάπτεται καὶ ἐν νοήσεσιν ὑφέστηκεν)· οἱ δὲ θεοὶ πάντων εἰσὶν ἐπέκεινα τῶν ὄντων. οὔτε οὖν δοξαστὸν τὸ θεῖον οὔτε διανοη-τὸν οὔτε νοητόν. πᾶν γὰρ τὸ ὂν ἢ αἰσθητόν ἐστι, καὶ διὰ τοῦτο δοξαστόν· ἢ ὄντως ὄν, καὶ διὰ τοῦτο νοητόν· ἢ μεταξὺ

122. 5 ἐν τῇ ὑπάρξει ω (ἐν om. edd.)   7 αὐτῶν om. BCD   10 ἀγαθότητες ω (ἀγαθότης Ο edd.)   10–11 τὰ ἀγαθὰ τοῖς πᾶσιν χορηγοῦσιν (omisso ἀφθόνως) Arg, M¹ incert.   12 αὐτῶν BDQM² : ἑαυτῶν C : om. M¹W   14 ἀναδέχον-ται Q   16 πρόθεσίς ἐστι BCD (corr. B)   18 ἄν ω (om. Ο edd.)   μηδέ] μή M   19 ἰδιότης ἡ ἀγαθότης M¹Q : ἡ ἰδιότης ἀγαθότης BCDM²   20 ἐστιν om. Q   22 ἢ θεοὶ πρὸ τῶν ὄντων in mg. M¹, om. Q   23 ἀγαθοῖς ex corr. M²   ὑπάρχει M   24 πρώτως BC et 'Ανάπτ. 151. 4, prime W : πρώτοις DMQ   123. 25 θεῖον] ens W   29 ἡ om. M¹   30 καταληπτόν BCD   33 et 34 νοητόν bis ex corr. M   33 καί] ἥ M, aut αβ (aut et γ)

PROP. **122.** *All that is divine both exercises providence towards secondary existences and transcends the beings for which it provides: its providence involves no remission of its pure and unitary transcendence, neither does its separate unity annul its providence.*

For without declension from the unity which is their substance the gods have filled all things with their power (prop. 121); and whatsoever is able to participate them enjoys such good things as it is capable of receiving according to the limitations of its own nature, whilst they radiate good to all existents in virtue of their very being, or rather their priority to Being. For being pure excellences, by their very being they furnish to all things good without stint; they make no calculated apportionment, but the participants receive according to their deserts what the gods bestow according to their own substance. Thus in exercising providence they assume no relation to those for whom they provide, since it is in virtue of being what they are that they make all things good, and what acts in virtue of its being acts without relation (for relation is a qualification of its being, and therefore contrary to its nature). Nor, again, does their separateness annul their providence; for it would at the same time annul—a thing unlawful even to suggest—their substance, whose distinctive character is goodness (prop. 119). For it is the mark of goodness to bestow on all that can receive, and the highest is not that which has the form of goodness but that which does good. If the latter character belongs to any being it must belong to the gods prior to Being: for the greater goodness cannot be a character of principles good by participation and the lesser of those whose goodness is primal.

PROP. **123.** *All that is divine is itself ineffable and unknowable by any secondary being because of its supra-existential unity, but it may be apprehended and known from the existents which participate it: wherefore only the First Principle is completely unknowable, as being unparticipated.*

For all rational knowledge, inasmuch as it grasps intelligible notions and consists in acts of intellection, is knowledge of real existents and apprehends truth by an organ which is itself a real existent; but the gods are beyond all existents (prop. 115). Accordingly the divine is an object neither of opinion nor of discursive reason nor yet of intellection: for all that exists is either sensible, and therefore an object of opinion; or true Being, and therefore an object of intellection; or of intermediate rank, at once Being and

τούτων, ὃν ἅμα καὶ γενητόν, καὶ διὰ τοῦτο διανοητόν. εἰ οὖν
οἱ θεοὶ ὑπερούσιοι καὶ πρὸ τῶν ὄντων ὑφεστήκασιν, οὔτε δόξα
ἔστιν αὐτῶν οὔτε ἐπιστήμη καὶ διάνοια οὔτε νόησις.
ἀλλ᾽ ἀπὸ τῶν ἐξηρτημένων οἷαί πέρ εἰσιν αὐτῶν αἱ ἰδιότητες
γνωρίζονται, καὶ τοῦτο ἀναγκαίως. κατὰ γὰρ τὰς τῶν μετ- 5
εχομένων ἰδιότητας καὶ αἱ τῶν μετεχόντων συνδιαιροῦνται διαφορότητες, καὶ οὔτε πᾶν μετέχει παντός (οὐ γὰρ ἔστι σύνταξις
τῶν πάντῃ ἀνομοίων) οὔτε τὸ τυχὸν τοῦ τυχόντος μετέχει, ἀλλὰ
τὸ συγγενὲς ἑκάστῳ συνῆπται καὶ ἀφ᾽ ἑκάστου πρόεισιν.

124. Πᾶς θεὸς ἀμερίστως μὲν τὰ μεριστὰ γινώσκει, ἀχρόνως 10
δὲ τὰ ἔγχρονα, τὰ δὲ μὴ ἀναγκαῖα ἀναγκαίως, καὶ τὰ μεταβλητὰ
ἀμεταβλήτως, καὶ ὅλως πάντα κρειττόνως ἢ κατὰ τὴν αὐτῶν
τάξιν.

εἰ γὰρ ἅπαν, ὅ τι περ ἂν ᾖ παρὰ τοῖς θεοῖς, κατὰ τὴν αὐτῶν
ἔστιν ἰδιότητα, δῆλον δήπουθεν ὡς οὐχὶ κατὰ τὴν τῶν χειρόνων 15
φύσιν ἐν τοῖς θεοῖς οὖσα ἡ γνῶσις αὐτῶν ἔσται, ἀλλὰ κατὰ τὴν
αὐτῶν ἐκείνων ἐξῃρημένην ὑπεροχήν. ἐνοειδὴς ἄρα καὶ ἀπαθὴς
ἡ γνῶσις ἔσται τῶν πεπληθυσμένων καὶ παθητῶν. εἰ ἄρα καὶ
τὸ γνωστὸν εἴη μεριστόν, ἀλλ᾽ ἡ θεία γνῶσις ἀμέριστος καὶ ἡ
τῶν μεριστῶν· καὶ εἰ μεταβλητόν, ἀμετάβλητος· καὶ εἰ ἐνδεχό- 20
μενον, ἀναγκαία· καὶ εἰ ἀόριστον, ὡρισμένη. οὐ γὰρ ἀπὸ τῶν
χειρόνων εἰσδέχεται τὸ θεῖον τὴν γνῶσιν, ἵνα οὕτως ἡ γνῶσις
ἔχῃ, ὡς τὸ γνωστὸν ἔχει φύσεως. ἀλλὰ τὰ χείρονα περὶ τὸ
ὡρισμένον τῶν θεῶν ἀοριστταίνει, καὶ περὶ τὸ ἀμετάβλητον
μεταβάλλει, καὶ τὸ ἀπαθὲς παθητικῶς ὑποδέχεται καὶ τὸ 25
ἄχρονον ἐγχρόνως. τοῖς μὲν γὰρ χείροσιν ἀπὸ τῶν κρειττόνων
παρεκβαίνειν δυνατόν, τοῖς δὲ θεοῖς εἰσδέχεσθαί τι παρὰ τῶν
χειρόνων οὐ θέμις.

125. Πᾶς θεός, ἀφ᾽ ἧς ἂν ἄρξηται τάξεως ἐκφαίνειν ἑαυτόν,
πρόεισι διὰ πάντων τῶν δευτέρων, ἀεὶ μὲν πληθύνων τὰς ἑαυτοῦ 30
μεταδόσεις καὶ μερίζων, φυλάττων δὲ τὴν ἰδιότητα τῆς οἰκείας
ὑποστάσεως.

αἱ μὲν γὰρ πρόοδοι δι᾽ ὑφέσεως γινόμεναι τὰ πρῶτα πανταχοῦ
πληθύνουσιν εἰς τὰς τῶν δευτέρων ὑποβάσεις, τὰ δὲ προϊόντα

123. 2 πρὸ τῶν ὄντων] primo W   4 αὐτῶν] αὗται B   ἀιδιότητες M primitus
(et sim. saepius)   5 ἀναγκαῖον Q
124. 12 αὐτοῦ B, αὐτὴν D   14 ἅπαν] πᾶν Q   15 οὐχί] οὐ CD
(O edd.)   τῶν om. Q   20 prius εἰ] ἡ DArg   μεταβλητόν] μεταβλητῶν
D et primitus Q, τῶν μεταβλητῶν Arg   20–1 καὶ ἡ τῶν ἐνδεχομένων ... καὶ ἡ
τῶν ἀορίστων dett., edd.   23 ἔχῃ] ἔχοι B fort. recte (cf. in Tim. I. 138. 6; 226.
22)
125. 33 πανταχοῦ ω (πανταχοῦ πως edd.)

thing of process (prop. 107), and therefore object of discursive reason. If, then, the gods are supra-existential, or have a substance prior to existents, we can have neither opinion concerning them nor scientific knowledge by discourse of reason, nor yet intellection of them.

Nevertheless from the beings dependent upon them the character of their distinctive properties may be inferred, and with cogency. For differences within a participant order are determined by the distinctive properties of the principles participated ; participation is not of all by all, since there can be no conjunction of the wholly disparate (prop. 29), neither is it a random connexion, but to each cause is attached, and from each proceeds, that effect which is akin to it.

PROP. 124. *Every god has an undivided knowledge of things divided and a timeless knowledge of things temporal ; he knows the contingent without contingency, the mutable immutably, and in general all things in a higher mode than belongs to their station.*

For if the gods have all their attributes in a mode consonant with their character as gods (prop. 118), it is surely manifest that their knowledge, being a divine property, will be determined not by the nature of the inferior beings which are its object but by their own transcendent majesty. Accordingly their knowledge of things pluralized and passible will be unitary and impassive: though its object be a thing of parts, yet even of such the divine knowledge will be undivided; though its object be mutable, itself will be immutable ; though contingent, necessary; and though undetermined, determinate. For the divine does not get knowledge extraneously, from its inferiors: why then should its knowledge be restricted by the nature of its object? Those inferiors, on the other hand, have an indeterminate thought of the determinate divine nature, and changing concepts of the immutable; its impassibility they conceive in terms of passion, its timelessness in terms of time. For the lower can fall away from the higher ; but that the gods should receive aught from their inferiors is a thing which may not be.

PROP. 125. *From that station wherein he first reveals himself every god proceeds through all the secondary orders, continually multiplying and particularizing his bestowals, yet preserving the distinctive character of his proper nature.*

For all procession, operating through remission, multiplies its first characters in declining to derivative terms (prop. 62) ; but these

κατὰ τὴν πρὸς τὰ παράγοντα ὁμοιότητα τὴν ἑαυτῶν ὑποδέχεται διάταξιν, ὥστε τὸ ὅλον ταὐτόν πως εἶναι, καὶ ἕτερον τὸ προϊὸν τῷ μένοντι, διὰ μὲν τὴν ὕφεσιν ἀλλοῖον φαινόμενον, διὰ δὲ τὴν συνέχειαν τὴν πρὸς ἐκεῖνο τῆς ταυτότητος οὐκ ἐξιστάμενον, οἷον δέ ἐστιν ἐκεῖνο ἐν τοῖς πρώτοις, τοιοῦτον ἐν τοῖς 5 δευτέροις ὑφιστάμενον αὐτό, καὶ τῆς σειρᾶς τὴν ἀδιάλυτον κοινωνίαν διαφυλάττον. ἐκφαίνεται μὲν οὖν ἕκαστος τῶν θεῶν οἰκείως ταῖς τάξεσιν, ἐν αἷς ποιεῖται τὴν ἔκφανσιν, πρόεισι δὲ ἐντεῦθεν ἄχρι τῶν ἐσχάτων διὰ τὴν γεννητικὴν τῶν πρώτων δύναμιν· πληθύνεται δὲ ἀεὶ διὰ τὴν πρόοδον ἀφ᾽ ἑνὸς εἰς πλῆθος 10 γινομένην, φυλάττει δὲ τὸ ταὐτὸν ἐν τῇ προόδῳ διὰ τὴν ὁμοιότητα τῶν προϊόντων πρὸς τὸ ἑκάστης σειρᾶς ἡγεμονοῦν καὶ πρωτουργὸν αἴτιον.

126. Πᾶς θεὸς ὁλικώτερος μέν ἐστιν ὁ τοῦ ἑνὸς ἐγγυτέρω, μερικώτερος δὲ ὁ πορρώτερον. 15

τοῦ γὰρ πάντα παράγοντος ὁ πλειόνων αἴτιος ἐγγυτέρω, ὁ δὲ ἐλαττόνων πορρωτέρω· καὶ ὁ μὲν πλειόνων αἴτιος ὁλικώτερος, ὁ δὲ ἐλαττόνων μερικώτερος. καὶ ἑκάτερος μὲν ἑνάς ἐστιν· ἀλλ᾽ ὁ μὲν δυνάμει μείζων, ὁ δὲ ἐλάττων κατὰ τὴν δύναμιν. καὶ οἱ μερικώτεροι γεννῶνται ἐκ τῶν ὁλικωτέρων οὔτε μεριζομένων 20 ἐκείνων (ἑνάδες γάρ) οὔτε ἀλλοιουμένων (ἀκίνητοι γάρ) οὔτε σχέσει πληθυνομένων (ἀμιγεῖς γάρ), ἀλλ᾽ ἀφ᾽ ἑαυτῶν δευτέρας ἀπογεννώντων προόδους διὰ δυνάμεως περιουσίαν, ὑφειμένας τῶν πρὸ αὐτῶν.

127. Πᾶν τὸ θεῖον ἁπλοῦν πρώτως ἐστὶ καὶ μάλιστα, καὶ 25 διὰ τοῦτο αὐταρκέστατον.

ὅτι μὲν γὰρ ἁπλοῦν, ἐκ τῆς ἑνώσεως φανερόν· ἑνικώτατον γάρ ἐστι πᾶν, τὸ δὲ τοιοῦτον διαφερόντως ἁπλοῦν. ὅτι δὲ αὐταρκέστατον, μάθοι τις ἂν ἐννοήσας ὅτι τὸ μὲν σύνθετον ἐνδεές ἐστιν, εἰ καὶ μὴ τῶν ἄλλων, ὧν ἐστιν ἔξω, ἀλλ᾽ ἐκείνων 30 γε, ἐξ ὧν συνετέθη· τὸ δὲ ἁπλούστατον καὶ ἑνιαῖον καὶ τὸ ἓν τῷ ἀγαθῷ ταὐτὸν προστησάμενον αὐταρκέστατον· τοιοῦτον δὲ τὸ θεῖον πᾶν. οὔτε οὖν τῶν ἄλλων δεῖται, αὐτοαγαθότης ὑπάρχον, οὔτε ἐξ ὧν ὑφέστηκεν, ἑνιαῖον ὑπάρχον.

125. 2 εἶναι] ἔσται [M]   3 φαινόμενον] γενόμενον vel γινόμενον [M] (utramque Arg), factum αβ (intellectum γ)   8 ἔκφασιν M   10 πληθύνεται B et suprascr. C   διά om. M
126. 14 ἐγγύτερον Q   16 τοῦ γὰρ ... 17 πορρωτέρω om. BC   16 ἐγγυτέρω ... 17 αἴτιος om. M¹   20 μεριζομένων ω (μεριζομένον Cr.² errore preli)
127. 25 prius καί ω (om. edd.)   31 τὸ ἕν BCE : τὸ ἐν DMQW   32 προστησόμενον M   33 αὐταγαθότης BCD

latter receive a rank in their own order determined by their likeness
to their producing causes (prop. 28). So that the entire procession
is in a sense one and identical, although that part which proceeds is
distinct from that which remains steadfast, appearing to differ from
it in kind because of the remission, but continuous with it and
therefore not losing its identity with it, existing as its analogue in
the derivative order and so maintaining the unbroken bond of
common quality which links the series.   Each of the gods reveals
himself in the modes proper to those orders in which he makes the
revelation, and thence proceeds even to the last regions of being—
such is the generative power of first principles.   Because the procession is from unity to a manifold, his character is continually
multiplied ; yet in the procession identity is preserved, because of
the likeness of the successive terms of each series to its sovereign
primordial cause.

PROP. 126. *A god is more universal as he is nearer to the One, more
specific in proportion to his remoteness from it.*

For the god who causes more numerous effects is nearer to the
universal cause ; he that causes fewer, more remote (prop. 60).
And the cause of more numerous effects is more universal ; the
cause of fewer, more specific (*ibid.*).   Each is a henad, but the
former has the greater potency (prop. 61).   The more universal
gods generate the more specific, not by division (since they are
henads) nor by alteration (since they are unmoved), nor yet being
multiplied by way of relation (since they transcend all relation), but
generating from themselves through superfluity of potency (prop. 27)
derivative emanations which are less than the prior gods.

PROP. 127. *All that is divine is primordially and supremely simple,
and for this reason completely self-sufficient.*

That it is simple, is apparent from its unity : all deity is perfectly
unitary (prop. 113), and as such is simple in an especial degree.
That it is completely self-sufficient, may be learned from the reflection that whereas the composite is dependent, if not upon things
external to it, at least upon its own elements, the perfectly simple
and unitary, being a manifestation of that Unity which is identical
with the Good (prop. 13), is wholly self-sufficient ; and perfect
simplicity is the character of deity.   Being a pure excellence
(prop. 119), deity needs nothing extraneous ; being unitary, it is not
dependent upon its own elements.

128. Πᾶς θεός, ὑπὸ μὲν τῶν ἐγγυτέρω μετεχόμενος, ἀμέσως μετέχεται· ὑπὸ δὲ τῶν πορρωτέρω, διὰ μέσων ἢ ἐλαττόνων ἢ πλειόνων τινῶν.

τὰ μὲν γάρ, διὰ συγγένειαν ἑνοειδῆ καὶ αὐτὰ ὄντα, μετέχειν αὐτόθεν δύναται τῶν θείων ἑνάδων· τὰ δὲ δι' ὕφεσιν καὶ τὴν εἰς 5 πλῆθος ἔκτασιν ἄλλων δεῖται τῶν μᾶλλον ἡνωμένων ἵνα μετάσχῃ τῶν αὐτοενάδων οὐσῶν, ἀλλ' οὐχ ἡνωμένων. τῆς γὰρ ἑνάδος μεταξὺ καὶ τοῦ διῃρημένου πλήθους ἐστὶ τὸ ἡνωμένον πλῆθος, συμφύεσθαι μὲν τῇ ἑνάδι δυνάμενον διὰ τὴν ἕνωσιν, συγγενὲς δέ πως ὂν καὶ τῷ διῃρημένῳ πλήθει διὰ τὴν τοῦ 10 πλήθους ἔμφασιν.

129. Πᾶν μὲν σῶμα θεῖον διὰ ψυχῆς ἐστι θεῖον τῆς ἐκθεουμένης, πᾶσα δὲ ψυχὴ θεία διὰ τοῦ θείου νοῦ, πᾶς δὲ νοῦς [θεῖος] κατὰ μέθεξιν τῆς θείας ἑνάδος· καὶ ἡ μὲν ἑνὰς αὐτόθεν θεός, ὁ δὲ νοῦς θειότατον, ἡ δὲ ψυχὴ θεία, τὸ δὲ σῶμα θεοειδές. 15

εἰ γὰρ ὑπὲρ νοῦν ἐστιν ἅπας ὁ τῶν θεῶν ἀριθμός, αἱ δὲ μεθέξεις διὰ τῶν συγγενῶν καὶ τῶν ὁμοίων ἐπιτελοῦνται, ἡ μὲν ἀμέριστος οὐσία μεθέξει πρώτως τῶν ὑπερουσίων ἑνάδων, δευτέρως δὲ ἡ γενέσεως ἐφαπτομένη, τρίτως δὲ ἡ γένεσις· καὶ ἕκαστα διὰ τῶν προσεχῶς ὑπερκειμένων. καὶ φοιτᾷ μὲν ἄχρι τῶν 20 ἐσχάτων ἐν τοῖς μετέχουσιν ἡ τῶν θεῶν ἰδιότης, διὰ μέσων δὲ τῶν πρὸς ἑαυτὴν συγγενῶν. ἡ γὰρ ἑνὰς πρώτῳ μὲν τῷ νῷ δίδωσι τὴν ἑαυτῆς ἐξαίρετον ἐν τοῖς θείοις δύναμιν, καὶ ἀποτελεῖ κἀκεῖνον τοιοῦτον νοῦν, οἷα ἐστὶ καὶ αὐτὴ κατὰ τὸ ἑνιαῖον πλῆθος. διὰ δὲ νοῦ καὶ ψυχῇ πάρεστι, συνεξάπτουσα κἀκείνην τῷ 25 νῷ καὶ συνεκπυροῦσα, εἰ ὁ νοῦς οὗτος εἴη μεθεκτός. διὰ δὲ ψυχῆς ἀπήχημα τῆς οἰκείας ἰδιότητος καὶ τῷ σώματι δίδωσιν, εἰ μετέχοι τι σῶμα ψυχῆς· καὶ οὕτω γίνεται τὸ σῶμα οὐ μόνον ἔμψυχον καὶ νοερόν, ἀλλὰ καὶ θεῖον, ζωὴν μὲν καὶ κίνησιν λαβὸν παρὰ ψυχῆς, διαμονὴν δὲ ἄλυτον ἀπὸ νοῦ, ἕνωσιν δὲ 30 θείαν ἀπὸ τῆς μετεχομένης ἑνάδος· ἕκαστον γὰρ τῆς ἑαυτοῦ ὑπάρξεως μεταδίδωσι τοῖς ἐφεξῆς.

128. 4 καὶ αὐτοόντα M¹W   5 αὐτόθι Q   6 ἔκτασιν MW : ἔκστασιν BCDQ   τῶν om. M¹   8 ἑνάδος [M]QW : αὐτοενάδος BCDM²

129. 13 διά om. BC   τοῦ θείου νοῦ scripsi : τὸν θεῖον νοῦν ω   θεῖος [M]W : om. BCDQM², seclusi   14 ἡ μέν] siquidem W   16 εἰ γὰρ καί edd. contra libros   αἱ δέ] ἀλλ' αἱ Q   23 θεοῖς Arg fort. recte   24 κἀκεῖνον] illum W   οἷα ἐστὶν αὕτη Q   25 ψυχῇ BDQ : ψυχὴ CW : ψυχῆς M 26 συνεκπυροῦσα] condervans αβ, conterminans γ   οὗτος ω (οὕτως Arg Cr., om. O Port.)   28 μετέχει [M]W   τι om. M¹

PROP. 128. *Every god, when participated by beings of an order rela-tively near to him, is participated directly; when by those more remote, indirectly through a varying number of intermediate principles.*

For the higher orders, having themselves the character of unity through their kinship to the divine (prop. 62), can participate the divine henads without mediation ; whereas the rest, because of their declension and their extension into multiplicity, require the media-tion of principles more unified than themselves if they are/to partici-pate what is not a unified group, but a pure henad.   Between the henad and the discrete manifold lies the unified manifold, which in virtue of its unification is capable of identifying itself with the henad, but in virtue of its implicit plurality is in some fashion akin also to the discrete manifold.

PROP. 129. *All divine bodies are such through the mediation of a divinized soul, all divine souls through a divine intelligence, and all divine intelligences by participation in a divine henad : the henad is immediate deity, the intelligence most divine, the soul divine, the body deisimilar.*

For if the whole order of gods is above the Intelligence (prop. 115), and if all participation is accomplished through kinship and likeness (prop. 32), the primary participant of the supra-existential henads will be undivided Being, the next, that Being which touches process, and third, the world of process ; and each will participate through the order immediately supra-jacent to it.   The divine character penetrates even to the last terms of the participant series (prop. 125), but always through the mediation of terms akin to itself.   Thus the henad bestows first on an intelligence that power among the divine attributes which is peculiarly its own, and causes this intelligence to be in the intellectual order what itself is in the order of unities.   If this intelligence be participable, through it the henad is present also to a soul, and is co-operative (prop. 56) in linking the soul to the intelligence and inflaming it.   Through this soul again, if it be participated by a body, the henad communicates even to the body an echo of its own quality : in this way the body becomes not only animate and intellective but also divine, in the sense that it has received from a soul life and movement, from an intelligence indis-soluble permanence, and from the henad which it participates a divine unification, each successive principle communicating to the consequent terms something of its own substance (prop. 18).

130. Πάσης θείας τάξεως τὰ πρῶτα μειζόνως ἐξῄρηται τῶν προσεχῶς ὑπ' αὐτὰ τεταγμένων ἢ ταῦτα τῶν ἐφεξῆς, καὶ μειζόνως ἐξέχεται τὰ δεύτερα τῶν προσεχῶς ὑπερκειμένων ἢ τούτων τὰ μετὰ ταῦτα.

ὅσῳ γὰρ ἂν ἐνικώτερον ᾖ τι καὶ ὁλικώτερον, τοσούτῳ καὶ 5 τὴν ὑπεροχὴν ἔλαχε μείζονα πρὸς τὰ ἐφεξῆς, ὅσῳ δ' ἂν ὑφειμένον κατὰ τὴν δύναμιν, τοσούτῳ μᾶλλόν ἐστι τοῖς μετ' αὐτὸ συμφυέστερον· καὶ τὰ μὲν ὑψηλότερα μᾶλλον ἐνίζεται τοῖς ἑαυτῶν αἰτιωτέροις, τὰ δὲ καταδεέστερα ἧττον. δυνάμεως γάρ ἐστι μείζονος τὸ μᾶλλον ἐξῃρῆσθαι τῶν ὑφειμένων καὶ μᾶλλον 10 ἡνῶσθαι τοῖς κρείττοσιν· ὥσπερ αὖ ἔμπαλιν τὸ τῶν μὲν ἀφίστασθαι μᾶλλον, τοῖς δὲ συμπάσχειν, ἐλάττωσίς ἐστι δυνάμεως, ὃ δὴ συμβαίνει τοῖς δευτέροις καθ' ἑκάστην τάξιν, ἀλλ' οὐ τοῖς πρώτοις.

131. Πᾶς θεὸς ἀφ' ἑαυτοῦ τῆς οἰκείας ἐνεργείας ἄρχεται. 15

τὴν γὰρ ἰδιότητα τῆς εἰς τὰ δεύτερα παρουσίας ἐν ἑαυτῷ πρῶτον ἐπιδείκνυσι· διότι δὴ καὶ τοῖς ἄλλοις ἑαυτοῦ μεταδίδωσι, κατὰ τὸ ὑπέρπληρες ἑαυτοῦ. οὔτε γὰρ τὸ ἐλλεῖπον οἰκεῖον τοῖς θεοῖς οὔτε τὸ πλῆρες μόνον. τὸ μὲν γὰρ ἐλλεῖπον πᾶν ἀτελὲς ὑπάρχει, καὶ ἄλλο τέλειον ποιεῖν, αὐτὸ μὴ τέλειον ὑπάρχον, 20 ἀμήχανον· τὸ δὲ πλῆρες αὔταρκες μόνον, οὔπω δὲ εἰς μετάδοσιν ἕτοιμον. ὑπέρπληρες ἄρα εἶναι δεῖ τὸ πληρωτικὸν ἄλλων καὶ εἰς ἄλλα διατεῖνον τὰς ἑαυτοῦ χορηγίας. εἰ οὖν τὸ θεῖον ἅπαντα ἀφ' ἑαυτοῦ πληροῖ τῶν ἀγαθῶν τῶν ἐν αὐτῷ, ἕκαστον ὑπέρπληρές ἐστιν· εἰ δὲ τοῦτο, ἐν ἑαυτῷ πρώτῳ τὴν ἰδιότητα 25 ἱδρυσάμενον ὧν δίδωσι τοῖς ἄλλοις, οὕτω δὴ κἀκείνοις ἐπορέγει τὰς μεταδόσεις τῆς ὑπερπλήρους ἀγαθότητος.

132. Πᾶσαι τῶν θεῶν αἱ τάξεις μεσότητι συνδέδενται.

καὶ γὰρ πᾶσαι τῶν ὄντων αἱ πρόοδοι διὰ τῶν ὁμοίων ἀποτελοῦνται· καὶ πολλῷ δὴ μᾶλλον αἱ τῶν θεῶν διακοσμήσεις ἀδιά- 30 λυτον κέκτηνται τὴν συνέχειαν, ἅτε ἑνοειδῶς ὑφεστηκυῖαι καὶ κατὰ τὸ ἓν ἀφωρισμέναι τὸ ἀρχηγικὸν αὐτῶν αἴτιον. ἡνωμένως οὖν αἱ ὑφέσεις γίνονται καὶ μειζόνως ἢ κατὰ τὴν ἐν τοῖς οὖσι τῶν δευτέρων πρὸς τὰ πρῶτα ὁμοιότητα, ὅσῳ δὴ καὶ ἡ τῶν

130. 1 τάξεως θείας BCD   ἐξήρτηται M   4 τά] τῶν M   5 ὅσον [M]?
γὰρ ω (μὲν γὰρ dett., edd.)   ἄν om. Q et? [M]   τι om. BCD
131. 15 οἰκείας] ἰδίας Q et fort. W   17 διότι] an διό?   21 μόνον
BCDQM²: μέν [M]W   21-2 εἰς μετάδοσιν ἐστιν ἕτοιμον Q   22 δεῖ] δή
M primitus   ἄλλου CQ   23 ἄλλο QM²W   24 ἅπαντα BCQM²: ἅπαν
τά DE: om. M¹W (transposita virgula post ἕκαστον)   τῶν ἐν αὐτῷ om. M¹, τῶν
ἐν ἑαυτῷ M²   26 ἱδρῦσαν [M]   ὧν [M], de quibus W : ἢν BCD : ἢ QM²
132. 30 δὴ non agnosc. W   33 μειζόνως ἢ [M]W : μόνως BCDQM²

PROP. 130. *In any divine order the highest terms more completely transcend those immediately subordinate to them than do these latter the subsequent terms ; and the second order of terms are more closely linked with their immediate superiors than are their consequents with them.*

For in proportion as any principle is more unitary and more universal, its degree of superiority to later terms is correspondingly enhanced ; while the declension of power which such a principle exhibits is the measure of its natural community with its consequents. And, again, the higher terms are more closely united to causes more fundamental than themselves, the lower less so. For a more complete transcendence of the inferior and a more complete union with the superior are marks of greater power ; as on the other hand a wider separation from the latter and a closer sympathy with the former signify a diminution of power, such as we find in the later members of every order but not in the earlier.

PROP. 131. *Every god begins his characteristic activity with himself.*

For the quality which marks his presence in secondary beings is displayed first in himself, and it is indeed for this reason that he communicates himself to others, in virtue of the superabundance of his own nature. Neither deficiency nor a mere fullness is proper to the gods. Whatever is deficient is imperfect ; and being itself incomplete, it is impossible that it should bestow completion on another. And that which is full is sufficient merely to itself, and still unripe for communication. Hence that which fulfils others and extends to others its free bestowals must itself be more than full. If, then, the divine from its own substance fulfils all things with the good which it contains (prop. 120), each divinity is filled to overflowing ; and if so, it has established first in its own nature the character distinctive of its bestowals, and in virtue of this extends to others also communications of its superabundant goodness.

PROP. 132. *All orders of gods are bound together by mean terms.*

For all procession of things existent is accomplished through like terms (prop. 29) : much more do the ranks of the gods possess unbroken continuity, inasmuch as their substance is unitary and they take their definition from the One which is their originative cause (prop. 113). In the divine orders remission of power is introduced without loss of unity, and as the gods are more essentially unified than existents, so the likeness of the derivative to the primary

θεῶν ὕπαρξις ἐν τῷ ἡνῶσθαι τῶν ὄντων μᾶλλον ὑφέστηκε.

πάντα οὖν τὰ θεῖα γένη συνδέδεται ταῖς οἰκείαις μεσότησι, καὶ οὐκ ἀμέσως ἐπὶ τὰς διαφερούσας πάντη προόδους χωρεῖ τὰ πρῶτα, ἀλλὰ διὰ τῶν ἑκατέροις κοινῶν γενῶν, ἀφ' ὧν τε πρόεισι καὶ ὧν ἐστιν ἀμέσως αἴτια· ταῦτα γὰρ συνάγει τὰ ἄκρα κατὰ 5 μίαν ἕνωσιν, τοῖς μὲν ὑπεστρωμένα συμφυῶς, τῶν δὲ ἐξῃρημένα προσεχῶς, καὶ τὴν εὔτακτον διαφυλάττει τῶν θείων ἀπογέννησιν.

133. Πᾶς μὲν θεὸς ἑνάς ἐστιν ἀγαθουργὸς ἢ ἀγαθότης ἐνοποιός, καὶ ταύτην ἔχει τὴν ὕπαρξιν καθόσον ἕκαστος θεός· ἀλλ' ὁ μὲν πρώτιστος ἁπλῶς τἀγαθὸν καὶ ἁπλῶς ἕν, τῶν δὲ 10 μετὰ τὸν πρῶτον ἕκαστος τὶς ἀγαθότης ἐστὶ καὶ τὶς ἑνάς.

ἡ γὰρ ἰδιότης ἡ θεία διέστησε τὰς ἑνάδας καὶ τὰς ἀγαθότητας τῶν θεῶν, ὥστε ἕκαστον κατά τι τῆς ἀγαθότητος ἰδίωμα πάντα ἀγαθύνειν, οἷον τελεσιουργεῖν ἢ συνέχειν ἢ φρουρεῖν· τούτων γὰρ ἕκαστον τὶ ἀγαθόν ἐστιν, ἀλλ' οὐ πᾶν τὸ ἀγαθόν, 15 οὗ τὴν ἑνιαίαν αἰτίαν τὸ πρῶτον προεστήσατο· διὸ καὶ τἀγαθόν ἐστιν ἐκεῖνο, ὡς πάσης ἀγαθότητος ὑποστατικόν. οὐδὲ γὰρ αἱ πᾶσαι τῶν θεῶν ὑπάρξεις ἅμα παρισοῦνται τῷ ἑνί· τοσαύτην ἐκεῖνο πρὸς τὸ πλῆθος τῶν θεῶν ἔλαχεν ὑπερβολήν.

134. Πᾶς θεῖος νοῦς νοεῖ μὲν ὡς νοῦς, προνοεῖ δὲ ὡς θεός. 20 τοῦ μὲν γὰρ νοῦ τὸ γινώσκειν τὰ ὄντα καὶ ἐν νοήσεσιν ἔχειν τὸ τέλειον ἐξαίρετόν ἐστι· τοῦ δὲ θεοῦ τὸ προνοεῖν καὶ ἀγαθῶν πάντα πληροῦν. ἡ δὲ μετάδοσις αὕτη καὶ ἡ πλήρωσις δι' ἕνωσιν γίνεται τῶν πληρουμένων πρὸς τὰ πρὸ αὐτῶν· ἣν καὶ ὁ νοῦς μιμούμενος εἰς ταὐτὸν ἔρχεται τοῖς νοητοῖς. ᾗ οὖν προ- 25 νοεῖ, θεός, ἐν τῇ πρὸ νοῦ ἐνεργείᾳ τῆς προνοίας ἱσταμένης. διὸ καὶ πᾶσι μὲν ἑαυτοῦ μεταδίδωσιν ὡς θεοῦ, οὐ πᾶσι δὲ πάρεστιν ὡς νοῦς· καὶ γὰρ ἐφ' ἃ τὸ νοερὸν ἰδίωμα μὴ πρόεισιν, ἐπὶ ταῦτα φθάνει τὸ θεῖον. καὶ γὰρ τὰ μὴ νοοῦντα προνοεῖσθαι βούλεται καὶ ἀγαθοῦ τινος μεταλαγχάνειν· τοῦτο δὲ διότι νοῦ 30 μὲν οὐ πάντα ἐφίεται, οὐδὲ οἷς μετασχεῖν δυνατόν, τοῦ δὲ ἀγαθοῦ πάντα ἐφίεται καὶ σπεύδει τυχεῖν.

132. 3 χωρεῖ προόδους Q   4 πρόεισι ex corr. M   6 ὑπεστραμμένα Q
133. 8 μέν non agnosc. W   11 ἕκαστος ex corr. M   12–13 τὰς
ἀγαθότητας Q : ἀγαθότητας cett.   16 οὐ τὴν ἑνιαίαν Arg et ? M¹ : τὴν δὲ
(δ' Q) ἑνιαίαν cett. : cuius unialem W, unde οὗ τὴν ἑνιαίαν scripsi   17 οὐδέ
ω (οὐ dett., edd.)   19 ἔλαχε τὴν ὑπερβολήν Q
134. 21 τοῦ μὲν γὰρ νοῦ] νοῦ μὲν γάρ Q   22 ἀγαθὸν M primitus   24 πληρουμένων BCD : πληρούντων MQW   δ om. Q   27 οὐ om. BC et primitus
D   32 ἐπιτυχεῖν C

is greater than in the existential orders. Accordingly all the classes of gods are bound together by the appropriate mean terms, and the first principles do not pass immediately into emanations wholly diverse from themselves; there are intermediate classes, having characters in common both with their causes and with their immediate effects. These intermediate principles link the extreme terms in one unified structure; by community of nature susceptible of influence from their neighbours above, transcending without interval their neighbours below, they preserve an ordered sequence in the generation of deities.

PROP. 133. *Every god is a beneficent henad or a unifying excellence, and has this substantive character* qua *god* (*prop. 119*); *but the primal God is the Good unqualified and Unity unqualified, whilst each of those posterior to him is a particular excellence and a particular henad.*

For the several henads and the excellences of the several gods are distinguished by their several divine functions, so that each in respect of some especial individuation of goodness renders all things good, perfecting or preserving in unity or shielding from harm. Each of these functions is a particular good, but not the sum of good: the unitary cause of the latter is pre-established in the First Principle, which for this reason is called the Good, as being constitutive of all excellence (prop. 8). For not all the gods together may be matched with the One, so far does it overpass the divine multitude.

PROP. 134. *Every divine intelligence exercises intellection* qua *intelligence, but providence* qua *god.*

For it is the peculiar mark of an intelligence to know the real existents and to have its perfection in intellective acts; but of a god to exercise providence and fulfil all things with good (prop. 120). This communication and fulfilment takes place in virtue of a union between the things fulfilled and the principles prior to them; which union the Intelligence imitates in identifying itself with its objects. In so far, then, as it exercises providence, which is a pre-intellectual activity, the Intelligence is a god. Hence it communicates itself *qua* god to all things; but it is not present to all *qua* intelligence. For deity extends even to those things which the distinctive character of intelligence cannot reach (prop. 57 *cor.*). Even things devoid of intelligence have appetition of providential care and seek to receive some portion of good; for whereas even of the beings fitted to participate intelligence not all desire it, towards the Good all things have desire and all endeavour its attainment.

135. Πᾶσα θεία ἑνὰς ὑφ' ἑνός τινος μετέχεται τῶν ὄντων ἀμέσως, καὶ πᾶν τὸ ἐκθεούμενον εἰς μίαν ἑνάδα θείαν ἀνατείνεται· καὶ ὅσαι αἱ μετεχόμεναι ἑνάδες, τοσαῦτα καὶ τὰ μετέχοντα γένη τῶν ὄντων.

οὔτε γὰρ δύο ἢ πλείους ἑνάδες ὑφ' ἑνὸς μετέχονται (πῶς 5 γάρ, τῶν ἐν αὐταῖς ἰδιοτήτων ἐξηλλαγμένων, οὐχὶ καὶ τὸ ἑκάστῃ συμφυόμενον ἐξήλλακται, δι' ὁμοιότητος τῆς συναφῆς γινομένης ;) οὔτε μία ἑνὰς ὑπὸ πλειόνων μετέχεται διῃρημένως. ἀσύναπτα γὰρ τὰ πολλὰ ὄντα τῇ ἑνάδι, καὶ ὡς ὄντα τῇ πρὸ τῶν ὄντων καὶ ὡς πολλὰ ἑνάδι· δεῖ δὲ τὸ μετέχον πῇ μὲν 10 ὅμοιον εἶναι τῷ μετεχομένῳ, πῇ δὲ ἕτερον καὶ ἀνόμοιον. ἐπεὶ οὖν τὸ μετέχον τῶν ὄντων τί ἐστιν, ἡ δὲ ἑνὰς ὑπερούσιος, καὶ κατὰ τοῦτο ἀνωμοίωνται, ἐν ἄρα εἶναι χρὴ τὸ μετέχον, ἵνα [καὶ] κατὰ τοῦτο ὅμοιον ᾖ τῷ μετεχομένῳ ἑνί, εἰ καὶ τὸ μὲν οὕτως ἓν ὡς ἑνάς, τὸ δὲ ὡς πεπονθὸς τὸ ἓν καὶ ἡνωμένον διὰ τὴν ἐκείνης 15 μέθεξιν.

136. Πᾶς θεὸς ὁλικώτερος μὲν ὑπάρχων καὶ ἐγγυτέρω τοῦ πρώτου τεταγμένος ὑπὸ ὁλικωτέρου γένους τῶν ὄντων μετέχεται, μερικώτερος δὲ καὶ πορρώτερον, ὑπὸ μερικωτέρου· καὶ ὡς τὸ ὂν πρὸς τὸ ὄν, οὕτως ἡ ἑνὰς πρὸς τὴν ἑνάδα τὴν θείαν. 20

εἰ γὰρ ὅσα τὰ ὄντα, τοσαῦται καὶ αἱ ἑνάδες, καὶ ἔμπαλιν, μιᾶς ὑφ' ἑνὸς μετεχομένης, δῆλον δὴ ὅτι κατὰ τὴν τῶν ἑνάδων τάξιν ἡ τῶν ὄντων πρόεισι τάξις, ὁμοιουμένη τῇ πρὸ αὐτῆς, καὶ ταῖς μὲν ὁλικωτέραις τὰ ὁλικώτερα συμφύεται, ταῖς δὲ μερικωτέραις ἑνάσι τὰ μερικώτερα ὄντα. εἰ γὰρ μή, πάλιν τὰ 25 ἀνόμοια τοῖς ἀνομοίοις συνάψει, καὶ ἡ κατ' ἀξίαν διανομὴ οὐκ ἔσται. ταῦτα δὲ ἀδύνατα, εἴπερ καὶ τοῖς ἄλλοις ἅπασι τὸ ἓν καὶ τὸ οἰκεῖον μέτρον ἐκεῖθεν ἐπιλάμπεται καὶ ἀπ' ἐκείνων ἐφήκει· πολλῷ δὴ οὖν μᾶλλον ἐν αὐτοῖς τάξις ἔσται τῆς μεθέξεως, τὰ ὅμοια κατὰ τὴν δύναμιν τῶν ὁμοίων ἐξάπτουσα. 30

137. Πᾶσα ἑνὰς συνυφίστησι τῷ ἑνὶ τὸ μετέχον αὐτῆς ὄν.

τὸ μὲν γὰρ ἕν, ὡς πάντων ἐστὶν ὑποστατικόν, οὕτω καὶ τῶν ἑνάδων τῶν μετεχομένων καὶ τῶν ὄντων τῶν εἰς τὰς ἑνάδας ἀνηρτημένων αἴτιον, τὸ δὲ ἑκάστης ἐξημμένον ἡ ἑνὰς ἢ εἰς αὐτὸ ἐλλάμπουσα παράγει· ἁπλῶς μὲν εἶναι τοῦ ἑνὸς ποιοῦντος, τὸ 35

135. 1 τινος om. BCD, neque agnosc. W   3 alt. καί om. M¹, neque agnosc. W   6 ἐν αὐταῖς] ἑαυταῖς M   7 δι' ὁμοιότητα Q   τῆς om. Q   8 γενομένης Q dett.   10 μέν Q : om. cett., non agnosc. W   11 post ἕτερον ins εἴ B¹, εἶναι B²CE   12 τί in rasura M²   13 μετέχον] μετεχόμενον [M]W   καί om. B : seclusi   14 κατά om. W et fort. primitus M
136. 20 οὕτως MQ : οὕτω BC, οὕτω καί DE (καί non agnosc. W)
137. 31 ὄν om. M¹W   34 ἐξ ἑκάστης M

PROP. 135.   *Every divine henad is participated without mediation by some one real-existent, and whatever is divinized is linked by an upward tension to one divine henad: thus the participant genera of existents are identical in number with the participated henads.*

For there cannot be two or more henads participated by one existent: as the distinctive characters of the henads vary, so the existents whose nature is identified with theirs cannot but vary also, since conjunction comes by likeness (prop. 29).   Nor, again, can one henad be independently participated by several existents.   For a plurality of existents is doubly discontinuous with the henad, as existent with that which is prior to existents (prop. 115) and as plurality with a henad; whereas the participant must be like the participated in one respect though distinct and dissimilar in another. Since, then, the participant is an existent while the henad is above Being, and this is their dissimilarity, it follows that the participant must be one, in order that in this respect it may resemble the participated unity, even though the latter is the unity of a henad while the former is unified through participation in this henad and has unity only as an affect.

PROP. 136.   *Of any two gods the more universal, who stands nearer to the First Principle (prop. 126), is participated by a more universal genus of existents, the more particular and more remote by a more particular genus: and as existent to existent, so is henad to divine henad.*

For if for every real-existent there is a henad and for every henad a real-existent, one existent only participating one henad only (prop. 135), it is evident that the order of real-existents reflects its prior and corresponds in its sequence with the order of henads, so that the more universal existents are united by their nature to the more universal henads and the more particular to the more particular. Otherwise, the unlike will here again be conjoined with the unlike, and apportionment will cease to bear any relation to desert.   These consequences are impossible: all other things receive from the real-existents their unity and their appropriate measure, as an irradiation from that source; much more, then, must the real-existents themselves be governed by the law of participation which attaches to each principle a consequent of similar potency.

PROP. 137.   *Every henad is co-operative with the One in producing the real-existent which participates it.*

For as the One is constitutive of all things (props. 12, 13), so it is the cause both of the participated henads and of the real-existents dependent upon them; at the same time the dependent existents are severally produced by the henads which irradiate them (prop. 125). To the One they owe simply their existence; their community of

δὲ συμφυὲς εἶναι τῆς ἑνάδος ἀπεργαζομένης, ᾗ ἐστι συμφυές.
αὕτη οὖν ἐστιν ἡ καθ' ἑαυτὴν ἀφορίζουσα τὸ μετέχον αὐτῆς ὂν
καὶ τὴν ἰδιότητα τὴν ὑπερούσιον ἐν αὐτῷ δεικνύουσα οὐσιωδῶς·
ἐκ γὰρ τοῦ πρώτως πανταχοῦ τῷ δευτέρως ὑπάρχει τὸ εἶναι
τοῦτο, ὅ ἐστιν. ἥτις οὖν ἐστι τῆς θεότητος ὑπερούσιος ἰδιότης, 5
αὕτη καὶ τοῦ ὄντος ἐστί, τοῦ μετέχοντος αὐτῆς, οὐσιωδῶς.

138. Πάντων τῶν μετεχόντων τῆς θείας ἰδιότητος καὶ ἐκ-
θεουμένων πρώτιστόν ἐστι καὶ ἀκρότατον τὸ ὄν.

εἰ γὰρ καὶ τοῦ νοῦ καὶ τῆς ζωῆς ἐπέκεινα τὸ ὄν, ὡς δέδεικται,
εἴπερ πλείστων τοῦτο μετὰ τὸ ἓν αἴτιον, ἀκρότατον ἂν εἴη τὸ 10
ὄν. τούτων μὲν γὰρ ἑνικώτερον, καὶ διὰ τοῦτο πάντως σεμνό-
τερον· ἄλλο δὲ πρὸ αὐτοῦ οὐκ ἔστι πλὴν τοῦ ἑνός. πρὸ γὰρ
τοῦ ἑνιαίου πλήθους τί ἄλλο ἢ τὸ ἕν; πλῆθος δὲ ἑνιαῖον τὸ ὄν,
ὡς ἐκ πέρατος ὂν καὶ ἀπείρου. καὶ ὅλως πρὸ τῆς οὐσίας τὸ
ὑπερούσιον μόνον· ἐπεὶ καὶ ἐν ταῖς εἰς τὰ δεύτερα ἐλλάμψεσι 15
μόνον τὸ ἓν ἐπέκεινα φθάνει τοῦ ὄντος, τὸ δὲ ὂν εὐθὺς μετὰ τὸ
ἕν. τὸ γὰρ δυνάμει ὄν, οὔπω δὲ ὄν, ἕν ἐστι κατὰ τὴν ἑαυτοῦ
φύσιν· καὶ τὸ μετὰ τοῦτο ἤδη ἐνεργείᾳ ὄν. καὶ ἐν ταῖς ἀρχαῖς
ἄρα τοῦ ὄντος ἐπέκεινα εὐθὺς τὸ μὴ ὂν ὡς κρεῖττον τοῦ ὄντος
καὶ ἕν. 20

139. Πάντα τὰ μετέχοντα τῶν θείων ἑνάδων, ἀρχόμενα ἀπὸ
τοῦ ὄντος, εἰς τὴν σωματικὴν τελευτᾷ φύσιν· τὸ γὰρ πρῶτόν
ἐστι τῶν μετεχόντων τὸ ὄν, ἔσχατον δὲ τὸ σῶμα (καὶ γὰρ
σώματα θεῖα εἶναί φαμεν).

πάντων γὰρ τῶν γενῶν τὰ ἀκρότατα τοῖς θεοῖς ἀνεῖται, 25
σωμάτων, ψυχῶν, νόων, ἵνα ἐν πάσῃ τάξει τὰ τοῖς θεοῖς ἀναλογοῦντα συνεκτικὰ καὶ σωστικὰ τῶν δευτέρων ὑπάρχῃ, καὶ
ἕκαστος ἀριθμὸς ὅλος ᾖ κατὰ τὸ ἓν τῷ μέρει ὅλον, ἔχων ἐν
ἑαυτῷ πάντα καὶ πρὸ τῶν ἄλλων τὴν θείαν ἰδιότητα. ἔστιν
οὖν καὶ σωματικῶς καὶ ψυχικῶς καὶ νοερῶς τὸ θεῖον γένος. καὶ 30
δῆλον ὅτι πάντα ταῦτα θεῖα κατὰ μέθεξιν· τὸ γὰρ πρώτως θεῖον
ἐν ταῖς ἑνάσιν ὑφέστηκε. τὰ ἄρα μετέχοντα τῶν θείων ἑνάδων
ἄρχεται μὲν ἀπὸ τοῦ ὄντος, λήγει δὲ εἰς τὴν σωματικὴν φύσιν.

137. 1 ἥ ἐστι M   alt. συμφυές] συμφυὴς Q   3 ἐν αὐτῇ QM²   4 τῷ B
CDQ : τό MW   5 ἥτις] εἴτις M   6 αὕτη] αὐτή Q   οὐσιωδὴς B et
suprascr. C
138. 7 καί ω (om. edd.)   9 εἰ γάρ MQW : εἴγε BCD   10 εἴπερ
[M]QW : εἰ γάρ καί B, εἰ γάρ CDM²   πλεῖστον M   15 μόνον scripsi : ὂν ω :
ἓν ci. T. Taylor   16 μετά ω (κατά Cr. errore preli)   17 ἑαυτοῦ [M],
suam W : αὐτοῦ BCDQM²   19 ἄρα ex corr. M   19-20 tanquam dignius
ente sit unum W
139. 27 ὑπάρχῃ QM² : ὑπάρχοι BCD : ὑπάρχει [M] !   28 prius ἐν] ἓν M
τῷ] τό M¹ (om. Ō edd.)   31 πάντα ταῦτα BCDW : πάντα τά M : ταῦτα πάντα Q

nature with a particular henad is due to the activity of that henad. Thus it is the henad which imposes its own character upon the participating existent and displays existentially in the latter the quality which itself possesses supra-existentially : for it is always by derivation from the primal that the secondary is what it is (prop. 18). Hence whatever supra-existential character is proper to a particular divinity appears existentially in the real-existent which participates it.

PROP. 138. *Of all the principles which participate the divine character and are thereby divinized the first and highest is Being.*

For if, as has been shown (prop. 101), Being is beyond both Intelligence and Life, since next to the One it is the most universal cause, it must be the highest participant. It has more of unity than Intelligence or Life, and is therefore necessarily more august (prop. 62). And prior to it there is no further principle save the One. For what else save unity can precede the unitary manifold? And Being, as composite of limit and infinite (prop. 89), is a unitary manifold. To use a more general argument, there can be nothing prior to the principle of Existence unless it be the supra-existential. For again, in the irradiation of secondary things Unity alone has a longer reach than Being (prop. 72 *cor.*), and Being stands immediately next to it. That which as yet is not, but exists only potentially, has already a natural unity ; all that lies above this level has actual existence. So in the first principles there must be a corresponding order : immediately beyond Being must stand a not-Being which is Unity and superior to Being.

PROP. 139. *The sequence of principles which participate the divine henads extends from Being to the bodily nature, since Being is the first (prop. 138) and body (inasmuch as we speak of heavenly or divine bodies) the last participant.*

For in each class of existents—bodies, souls, intelligences—the highest members belong to the gods, in order that in every rank there may be terms analogous to the gods, to maintain the secondaries in unity and preserve them in being ; and that each series may have the completeness of a whole-in-the-part (prop. 67), embracing in itself all things (prop. 103) and before all else the character of deity. Thus deity exists on the corporeal, the psychical, and the intellective level—evidently by participation in each case, since deity in the primary sense is proper to the henads. The sequence, then, of principles which participate the divine henads begins with Being and ends with the bodily nature.

140. Πᾶσαι τῶν θεῶν αἱ δυνάμεις ἄνωθεν ἀρχόμεναι καὶ διὰ τῶν οἰκείων προϊοῦσαι μεσοτήτων μέχρι τῶν ἐσχάτων καθήκουσι καὶ τῶν περὶ γῆν τόπων.

οὔτε γὰρ ἐκείνας διείργει τι καὶ ἀποκωλύει τῆς εἰς πάντα παρουσίας (οὐδὲ γὰρ δέονται τόπων καὶ διαστάσεων, διὰ τὴν 5 ἄσχετον πρὸς πάντα ὑπεροχὴν καὶ τὴν ἄμικτον πανταχοῦ παρουσίαν), οὔτε· τὸ μετέχειν αὐτῶν ἐπιτήδειον κωλύεται τῆς μεθέξεως, ἀλλ' ἅμα τέ τι πρὸς τὴν μετουσίαν ἕτοιμον γίνεται κἀκεῖναι πάρεισιν, οὔτε τότε παραγενόμεναι οὔτε πρότερον ἀποῦσαι, ἀλλ' ἀεὶ ὡσαύτως ἔχουσαι. ἐὰν οὖν τι τῶν περὶ γῆν 10 ἐπιτήδειον ᾖ μετέχειν, καὶ τούτῳ πάρεισι· καὶ πάντα πεπληρώκασιν ἑαυτῶν, καὶ τοῖς μὲν ὑπερτέροις μειζόνως πάρεισι, τοῖς δὲ μέσοις κατὰ τὴν αὐτῶν τάξιν, τοῖς δὲ ἐσχάτοις ἐσχάτως. ἄνωθεν οὖν μέχρι τῶν τελευταίων ἐκτείνουσιν ἑαυτάς· ὅθεν καὶ ἐν τούτοις εἰσὶ τῶν πρώτων ἐμφάσεις, καὶ συμπαθῆ πάντα πᾶσιν, ἐν μὲν 15 τοῖς πρώτοις τῶν δευτέρων προϋπαρχόντων, ἐν δὲ τοῖς δευτέροις τῶν πρώτων ἐμφαινομένων· τριχῶς γὰρ ἦν ἕκαστον, ἢ κατ' αἰτίαν ἢ καθ' ὕπαρξιν ἢ κατὰ μέθεξιν.

141. Πᾶσα πρόνοια θείων ἡ μὲν ἐξῃρημένη τῶν προνοουμένων ἐστίν, ἡ δὲ συντεταγμένη.

20

τὰ μὲν γὰρ κατὰ τὴν ὕπαρξιν καὶ τὴν τῆς τάξεως ἰδιότητα παντελῶς ὑπερήπλωται τῶν ἐλλαμπομένων· τὰ δὲ τῆς αὐτῆς ὄντα διακοσμήσεως προνοεῖ τῶν ὑφειμένων τῆς αὐτῆς συστοιχίας, μιμούμενα καὶ ταῦτα τὴν τῶν ἐξῃρημένων θεῶν προνοητικὴν ἐνέργειαν καὶ πληροῦν ἐφιέμενα τὰ δεύτερα τῶν ἀγαθῶν, ὧν 25 δύνανται.

142. Πᾶσι μὲν οἱ θεοὶ πάρεισιν ὡσαύτως· οὐ πάντα δὲ ὡσαύτως τοῖς θεοῖς πάρεστιν, ἀλλ' ἕκαστα κατὰ τὴν αὐτῶν τάξιν τε καὶ δύναμιν μεταλαγχάνει τῆς ἐκείνων παρουσίας, τὰ μὲν ἑνοειδῶς, τὰ δὲ πεπληθυσμένως, καὶ τὰ μὲν ἀϊδίως, τὰ δὲ 30 κατὰ χρόνον, καὶ τὰ μὲν ἀσωμάτως, τὰ δὲ σωματικῶς.

ἀνάγκη γὰρ τὴν διάφορον μέθεξιν τῶν αὐτῶν ἢ παρὰ τὸ μετέχον γίνεσθαι διάφορον ἢ παρὰ τὸ μετεχόμενον. ἀλλὰ τὸ θεῖον πᾶν ἀεὶ τὴν αὐτὴν ἔχει τάξιν, καὶ ἄσχετόν ἐστι πρὸς

140. 1 θεῶν [M]W : θείων BCDQM²   3 τόπων in rasura M   5 οὐδέ QW, οὐδέ vel οὐ M¹ : οὐδέν BCDM²   6 πάντας M   τὴν om. M   9 πάρεισιν] προίασιν Q   11 ἐπιτηδείων (?) μετέχει M¹   τοῦτο CM¹   πάρεστι Q   14 οὖν] quidem igitur (= μὲν οὖν ?) W   17 ἐκφαινομένων Q   τριττῶς Q   γὰρ ω (tacite om. Cr.)
141. 19 θείων scripsi : θεῶν ω   26 δύναται Q
142. 28 αὐτῶν BDEM (cf. c. 117, l. 33, etc.): αὐτοῖς C : ἑαυτῶν Q   30 πληθυσμένως M¹   32 ἤ οιφ. Q, in M deletum

PROP. 140. *All the powers of the gods, taking their origin above and proceeding through the appropriate intermediaries, descend even to the last existents and the terrestrial regions.*

For on the one hand there is nothing to exclude these powers or hinder them from reaching all things; they do not require space at all or spatial intervals, since they transcend all things without relation and are everywhere present without admixture (prop. 98). Nor, again, is the fit participant baulked of its participation; so soon as a thing is ready for communion with them, straightway they are present—not that in this moment they approached, or till then were absent, for their activity is eternally unvarying. If, then, any terrestrial thing be fit to participate them, they are present even to it : they have fulfilled all things with themselves, and though present more mightily to the higher principles they reveal themselves also to the intermediate orders in a manner consonant with such a station, and for the meanest orders there is a meanest mode of presence. Thus they extend downwards even to the uttermost existents ; and hence it is that even in these appear reflections of the first principles, and there is sympathy between all things, the derivative pre-existing in the primal, the primal reflected in the derivative—for we saw that all characters have three modes of existence, in their causes, substantially, and by participation (prop. 65).

PROP. 141. *There is one divine providence which transcends its objects and one which is co-ordinate with them.*

For some divine principles in virtue of their substance and the especial character of their station are completely exalted in their simplicity above the beings which they irradiate (prop. 122) ; whilst others, belonging to the same cosmic order as their objects, exercise providence towards the inferior members of their own series, imitating in their degree the providential activity of the transcendent gods and desiring to fulfil secondary existences with such good things as they can.

PROP. 142. *The gods are present alike to all things ; not all things, however, are present alike to the gods, but each order has a share in their presence proportioned to its station and capacity, some things receiving them as unities and others as manifolds, some perpetually and others for a time, some incorporeally and others through the body.*

For differences in the participation of the same principles must be due to a difference either in the participant or in that which is participated. But whatever is divine keeps the same station for ever,

πάντα καὶ ἄμικτον. παρὰ τὸ μετέχον ἄρα μόνον λείπεται τὴν
ἐξαλλαγὴν ὑφίστασθαι, καὶ τὸ οὐχ ὡσαύτως ἐν τούτοις εἶναι, καὶ
ταῦτα ἄλλοτε ἄλλως, καὶ ἄλλα ἄλλως παρεῖναι τοῖς θεοῖς· ὥστε
πᾶσιν ἐκείνων ὡσαύτως παρόντων, τὰ πάντα οὐχ ὡσαύτως
πάρεστιν ἐκείνοις, ἀλλ᾽ ὡς ἕκαστα δύναται, πάρεστι, καὶ ὡς 5
πάρεστιν, οὕτως ἐκείνων ἀπολαύει· κατὰ γὰρ τὸ μέτρον τῆς
τούτων παρουσίας ἡ μέθεξις.

143. Πάντα τὰ καταδεέστερα τῇ παρουσίᾳ τῶν θεῶν ὑπεξ-
ίσταται· κἂν ἐπιτήδειον ᾖ τὸ μετέχον, πᾶν μὲν τὸ ἀλλότριον
τοῦ θείου φωτὸς ἐκποδὼν γίνεται, καταλάμπεται δὲ πάντα ιο
ἀθρόως ὑπὸ τῶν θεῶν.

ἀεὶ μὲν γὰρ τὰ θεῖα περιληπτικώτερα καὶ δυνατώτερα τῶν
ἀπ᾽ αὐτῶν προελθόντων ἐστίν, ἡ δὲ τῶν μετεχόντων ἀνεπιτηδειό-
της τῆς ἐλλείψεως τοῦ θείου φωτὸς αἰτία γίνεται· ἀμυδροῖ γὰρ
κἀκεῖνο τῇ ἑαυτῆς ἀσθενείᾳ. ἐκείνου δὲ ἀμυδρουμένου ἄλλο τι 15
δοκεῖ τὴν ἐπικράτειαν μεταλαμβάνειν, οὐ κατὰ τὴν αὐτοῦ
δύναμιν, ἀλλὰ κατὰ τὴν τοῦ μετέχοντος ἀδυναμίαν κατεξανίστασθαι δοκοῦν τοῦ θείου τῆς ἐλλάμψεως εἴδους.

144. Πάντα τὰ ὄντα καὶ πᾶσαι τῶν ὄντων αἱ διακοσμήσεις
ἐπὶ τοσοῦτον προεληλύθασιν, ἐφ᾽ ὅσον καὶ αἱ τῶν θεῶν διατάξεις. 20
καὶ γὰρ ἑαυτοῖς οἱ θεοὶ τὰ ὄντα συμπαρήγαγον, καὶ οὐδὲν
οἷόν τε ἦν ὑποστῆναι καὶ μέτρου καὶ τάξεως τυχεῖν ἔξω τῶν
θεῶν· καὶ γὰρ τελειοῦνται πάντα κατὰ τὴν αὐτῶν δύναμιν, καὶ
τάττεται καὶ μετρεῖται παρὰ τῶν θεῶν. καὶ πρὸ τῶν ἐσχάτων
οὖν ἐν τοῖς οὖσι γενῶν προϋπάρχουσιν οἱ καὶ ταῦτα κοσμοῦντες 25
θεοὶ καὶ διδόντες καὶ τούτοις ζωὴν καὶ εἰδοποιίαν καὶ τελειότητα
καὶ ἐπιστρέφοντες καὶ ταῦτα πρὸς τὸ ἀγαθόν, καὶ πρὸ τῶν
μέσων ὡσαύτως, καὶ πρὸ τῶν πρώτων. καὶ πάντα ἐνδέδεται καὶ
ἐνερρίζωται τοῖς θεοῖς, καὶ σώζεται διὰ ταύτην τὴν αἰτίαν·
ἀποστὰν δέ τι τῶν θεῶν, καὶ ἔρημον γενόμενον παντελῶς, εἰς 30
τὸ μὴ ὂν ὑπεξίσταται καὶ ἀφανίζεται, τῶν συνεχόντων αὐτὸ
πάντῃ στερούμενον.

142. 1 μόνον MW : om. BCDQ dett.   2 τούτοις] τοῖς οὖσιν [M]   3 alt.
ἄλλως] ἄλλοις [M]W   4 ἐκείνων παρόντων ὡσαύτως M, eodem modo illis
praesentibus W   5-6 ὡς πάρεστιν MW: ὡς ἔστιν BCD : ὡς πάρεστι καὶ ὡς ἔστιν
Q, καὶ ὡς ἔστιν suprascr. M²   6 κατά MQW : καί BCD
143. 8 τῇ ἐξουσίᾳ Q   8-9 ὑπεξίστανται C   13 ἐστίν om. M¹   13-14 ἀν-
επιτηδειότης] ydoneitas W   14 ἐλλείψεως BCD : ἐλλάμψεως MQW   φωτός ω
(om. edd.)   15 κάκεῖνο ... ἐκείνου δὲ ἀμυδρουμένου BCD : κάκεῖνην ...
ἐκείνης δὲ ἀμυδρουμένης MQW   16 αὐτοῦ] αὐτὴν M¹
144. 20 περιεληλύθασιν M   23 τελειοῦται Q   27 τὸ ἀγαθόν ω
(τἀγαθόν edd.)   29 ἐρρίζωται Q, radicantur W, ita fort. etiam Nic. (cf. Ἀνάπτ.
166. 19)   31 αὐτό M (ult. syll. ex corr.) QW : om. BCD   32 στερόμενον Q
dett.

and is free from all relation to the lower and all admixture with it
(prop. 98). It follows by exclusion that the variation can be due
only to the participants; in them must lie the lack of uniformity,
and it is they that are present to the gods diversely at different times
and diversely one from another. Thus, while the gods are present
alike to all things, not all things are present alike to them; each
order is present in the degree of its capacity, and enjoys them in the
degree of its presence, which is the measure of its participation.

PROP. 143. *All inferior principles retreat before the presence of the
gods ; and provided the participant be fit for its reception, whatever
is alien makes way for the divine light and all things are continuously
illuminated by the gods.*

For the divine principles are always more comprehensive and
more potent than those which proceed from them (prop. 57), and
it is the unfitness of the participants which occasions the failure of
the divine light (prop. 142), obscuring by its weakness even that
radiance. When the light is obscured, another principle appears to
assume dominion ; yet it is not by its own potency, but through the
impotence of the participant, that it has the appearance of revolting
against the divine form of illumination.

PROP. 144. *The procession of all things existent and all cosmic orders
of existents extends as far as do the orders of gods.*

For in producing themselves the gods produced the existents, and
without the gods nothing could come into being and attain to
measure and order ; since it is by the gods' power that all things reach
completeness, and it is from the gods that they receive order and
measure. Thus even the last kinds in the realm of existence are
consequent upon gods who regulate even these, who bestow even on
these life and formative power and completeness of being, who
convert even these upon their good ; and so also are the intermediate
and the primal kinds. All things are bound up in the gods and
deeply rooted in them, and through this cause they are preserved in
being; if anything fall away from the gods and become utterly
isolated from them, it retreats into non-being and is obliterated,
since it is wholly bereft of the principles which maintained its unity.

145. Πάσης θείας τάξεως ⟨ἡ⟩ ἰδιότης διὰ πάντων φοιτᾷ τῶν δευτέρων, καὶ δίδωσιν ἑαυτὴν ἅπασι τοῖς καταδεεστέροις γένεσιν.

εἰ γὰρ ἄχρι τοσούτου τὰ ὄντα πρόεισιν, ἕως οὗ καὶ τῶν θεῶν οἱ διάκοσμοι προεληλύθασιν, ἐν ἑκάστοις γένεσίν ἐστιν ἡ τῶν θείων δυνάμεων ἰδιότης, ἄνωθεν ἐλλαμπομένη· κομίζεται γὰρ 5 ἕκαστον ἀπὸ τῆς οἰκείας προσεχοῦς αἰτίας τὴν ἰδιότητα, καθ' ἣν ἐκείνη τὴν ὑπόστασιν ἔλαχε. λέγω δὲ οἷον εἴ τις ἔστι θεότης καθαρτική, καὶ ἐν ψυχαῖς ἔστι κάθαρσις καὶ ἐν ζώοις καὶ ἐν φυτοῖς καὶ ἐν λίθοις· καὶ εἴ τις φρουρητική, ὡσαύτως, καὶ εἴ τις ἐπιστρεπτική, καὶ εἰ τελεσιουργός, καὶ εἰ 10 ζωοποιός, ὁμοίως. καὶ ὁ μὲν λίθος μετέχει τῆς καθαρτικῆς δυνάμεως σωματικῶς μόνον, τὸ δὲ φυτὸν ἔτι τρανέστερον κατὰ τὴν ζωήν, τὸ δὲ ζῷον ἔχει καὶ κατὰ τὴν ὁρμὴν τὸ εἶδος τοῦτο, ψυχὴ δὲ λογικὴ λογικῶς, νοῦς δὲ νοερῶς, οἱ δὲ θεοὶ ὑπερουσίως καὶ ἑνιαίως· καὶ πᾶσα ἡ σειρὰ τὴν αὐτὴν ἔχει δύναμιν ἀπὸ 15 μιᾶς τῆς θείας αἰτίας. καὶ ἐπὶ τῶν λοιπῶν ὁ αὐτὸς λόγος. πάντα γὰρ ἐξῆπται τῶν θεῶν, καὶ τὰ μὲν ἐξ ἄλλων, τὰ δὲ ἐξ ἄλλων προλάμπεται, καὶ αἱ σειραὶ μέχρι τῶν ἐσχάτων καθή- κουσι· καὶ τὰ μὲν ἀμέσως, τὰ δὲ διὰ μέσων πλειόνων ἢ ἐλαττό- νων εἰς ἐκείνους ἀνήρτηται· " μεστὰ δὲ πάντα θεῶν ", καὶ ὃ 20 ἕκαστον ἔχει κατὰ φύσιν, ἐκεῖθεν ἔχει.

146. Πασῶν τῶν θείων προόδων τὰ τέλη πρὸς τὰς ἑαυτῶν ἀρχὰς ὁμοιοῦται, κύκλον ἄναρχον καὶ ἀτελεύτητον σώζοντα διὰ τῆς πρὸς τὰς ἀρχὰς ἐπιστροφῆς.

εἰ γὰρ καὶ ἕκαστον τῶν προελθόντων ἐπιστρέφεται πρὸς τὴν 25 οἰκείαν ἀρχήν, ἀφ' ἧς προελήλυθε, πολλῷ δήπου μᾶλλον αἱ ὅλαι τάξεις, ἀπὸ τῆς ἑαυτῶν ἀκρότητος προελθοῦσαι, πάλιν ἐπιστρέφονται πρὸς ἐκείνην. ἡ δὲ ἐπιστροφὴ τοῦ τέλους εἰς τὴν ἀρχὴν μίαν ἀπεργάζεται πᾶσαν καὶ ὡρισμένην καὶ εἰς ἑαυτὴν συννεύουσαν καὶ ἐν τῷ πλήθει τὸ ἐνοειδὲς ἐπιδεικνυμένην διὰ 30 τῆς συννεύσεως.

147. Πάντων τῶν θείων διακόσμων τὰ ἀκρότατα τοῖς πέρασιν ὁμοιοῦται τῶν ὑπερκειμένων.

εἰ γὰρ δεῖ συνέχειαν εἶναι τῆς θείας προόδου καὶ ταῖς οἰκείαις ἑκάστην τάξιν συνδεδέσθαι μεσότησιν, ἀνάγκη τὰς 35

---

145. 1 ἡ supplevi   6 προσεχῶς Q   9 τοῖς ζώοις M   9 et 10 εἴ τις] ἥτις (bis) QW   10 καὶ εἰ τελεσιουργός MW : καὶ εἴ τις τ. BCD : καὶ τελεσιουργός Q   14 λογικὴ om. M¹W   18 ἀλλήλων M   προλάμπεται ω (ἐλλάμπεται O edd.)   20 μετὰ δὲ πάντα θεόν BCD dett.   21 ἕκαστον ἔχει] ἔχει ἕκαστον C
146. 25 καί ω (om. edd.)   29 ἐργάζεται Q   31 τῆς om. B
147. 33 ὁμοιοῦνται M primitus   35–p. 130, l. 1 τὴν ἀκρότητα [M]?

PROP. **145.** *The distinctive character of any divine order travels through all the derivative existents and bestows itself upon all the inferior kinds.*

For if the procession of existents extends as far as do the orders of gods (prop. 144), the distinctive character of the divine powers, radiating downwards, is found in every kind, since each thing obtains from its own immediate cause the distinctive character in virtue of which that cause received its being. I intend that if, for example, there be a purifying deity, then purgation is to be found in souls, in animals, in vegetables, and in minerals ; so also if there be a protective deity, and the same if there be one charged with the conversion or the perfection or the vitalizing of things existent. The mineral participates the purifying power only as bodies can ; the vegetable in a clearer manner also, that is, vitally ; the animal possesses this form in an additional mode, that of appetition ; a rational soul, rationally ; an intelligence, intellectually or intuitively ; the gods, supra-existentially and after the mode of unity : and the entire series possesses the same power as the result of a single divine cause. The same account applies to the other characters. For all things are dependent from the gods, some being irradiated by one god, some by another, and the series extend downwards to the last orders of being. Some are linked with the gods immediately, others through a varying number of intermediate terms (prop. 128); but 'all things are full of gods', and from the gods each derives its natural attribute.

PROP. **146.** *In any divine procession the end is assimilated to the beginning, maintaining by its reversion thither a circle without beginning and without end.*

For if each single processive term reverts upon its proper initial principle, from which it proceeded (prop. 31), much more, surely, do entire orders proceed from their highest point and revert again upon it. This reversion of the end upon the beginning makes the whole order one and determinate, convergent upon itself and by its convergence revealing unity in multiplicity.

PROP. **147.** *In any divine rank the highest term is assimilated to the last term of the supra-jacent rank.*

For if there must be continuity in the divine procession and each order must be bound together by the appropriate mean terms (prop. 132), the highest terms of the secondary rank are of necessity

ἀκρότητας τῶν δευτέρων συνάπτειν ταῖς ἀποπερατώσεσι τῶν
πρώτων· ἡ δὲ συναφὴ δι' ὁμοιότητος. ὁμοιότης ἄρα ἔσται τῶν
ἀρχῶν τῆς ὑφειμένης τάξεως πρὸς τὰ τέλη τῆς ὑπεριδρυμένης.

148. Πᾶσα θεία τάξις ἑαυτῇ συνήνωται τριχῶς, ἀπό τε τῆς
ἀκρότητος τῆς ἐν αὐτῇ καὶ ἀπὸ τῆς μεσότητος καὶ ἀπὸ τοῦ τέλους. 5

ἡ μὲν γάρ, ἐνικωτάτην ἔχουσα δύναμιν, εἰς πᾶσαν αὐτὴν
διαπέμπει τὴν ἔνωσιν καὶ ἑνοῖ πᾶσαν ἄνωθεν, μένουσα ἐφ'
ἑαυτῆς. ἡ δὲ μεσότης, ἐπ' ἄμφω τὰ ἄκρα διατείνουσα, συνδεῖ
πᾶσαν περὶ ἑαυτήν, τῶν μὲν πρώτων διαπορθμεύουσα τὰς
δόσεις, τῶν δὲ τελευταίων ἀνατείνουσα τὰς δυνάμεις, καὶ πᾶσι 10
κοινωνίαν ἐντιθεῖσα καὶ σύνδεσιν πρὸς ἄλληλα· μία γὰρ οὕτως
ἡ ὅλη γίνεται διάταξις ἔκ τε τῶν πληρούντων καὶ τῶν πληρουμένων, ὥσπερ εἴς τι κέντρον εἰς τὴν μεσότητα συννευόντων.
ἡ δὲ ἀποπεράτωσις, ἐπιστρέφουσα πάλιν εἰς τὴν ἀρχὴν καὶ
τὰς προελθούσας ἐπανάγουσα δυνάμεις, ὁμοιότητα καὶ σύννευσιν 15
τῇ ὅλῃ τάξει παρέχεται. καὶ οὕτως ὁ σύμπας διάκοσμος εἷς
ἐστι διὰ τῆς ἑνοποιοῦ τῶν πρώτων δυνάμεως ⟨καὶ⟩ διὰ τῆς ἐν
τῇ μεσότητι συνοχῆς καὶ διὰ τῆς τοῦ τέλους εἰς τὴν ἀρχὴν
τῶν προόδων ἐπιστροφῆς.

149. Πᾶν τὸ πλῆθος τῶν θείων ἑνάδων πεπερασμένον ἐστὶ 20
κατὰ ἀριθμόν.

εἰ γὰρ ἐγγυτάτω τοῦ ἑνός ἐστιν, οὐκ ἂν ἄπειρον ὑπάρχοι· οὐ
γὰρ συμφυὲς τῷ ἑνὶ τὸ ἄπειρον, ἀλλὰ ἀλλότριον. εἰ γὰρ καὶ τὸ
πλῆθος καθ' αὑτὸ ἀφίσταται τοῦ ἑνός, τὸ ἄπειρον πλῆθος
δῆλον ὡς παντελῶς ἔρημον ἐκείνου· διὸ καὶ ἀδύναμον καὶ 25
ἀδρανές. οὐκ ἄρα ἄπειρον τὸ τῶν θεῶν πλῆθος. ἑνοειδὲς ἄρα
καὶ πεπερασμένον, καὶ παντὸς ἄλλου πλήθους μᾶλλον πεπε-
ρασμένον· παντὸς γὰρ ἄλλου πλήθους μᾶλλον τῷ ἑνὶ συγγενές.
εἰ μὲν οὖν ἡ ἀρχὴ πλῆθος, ἔδει τὸ ἐγγυτέρω τῆς ἀρχῆς τοῦ
πορρώτερον μᾶλλον εἶναι πλῆθος (ὁμοιότερον γὰρ τὸ ἐγγύτερον)· 30
ἐπεὶ δὲ ἕν ἐστι τὸ πρῶτον, τὸ ἐκείνῳ συναφὲς πλῆθος ἧττον
πλῆθος τοῦ πορρώτερον· τὸ δὲ ἄπειρον οὐχ ἧττον πλῆθος, ἀλλὰ
μάλιστα πλῆθος.

147. 2 δέ MQW : γάρ BCD
148. 5 ἐν αὐτῇ BCDQM² : ἑαυτῇ M¹ ut videtur, ἑαυτῆς ArgW   7 μένουσα
M¹QW : μένουσαν BCM², μέλλουσαν DE   9 περὶ αὐτήν M   10 πᾶσαν Q
13 ἐν τῇ μεσότητι Q et in mg. M   τῶν συννευόντων M   14 εἰς] πρός Q
17 δυνάμεως BCD   καὶ addidi W secutus   18 καί MW : om. BCDQ
149. 22 οὐκ ἂν ... ὑπάρχοι M¹ (ὑπάρχει M², suprascr. ὑπάρχῃ M³), non utique
... existet W : οὐκ ... ὑπάρχει BCDQ   24 καθ' αὑτό om. M¹W   29 ἢ om. B
τό BCArg : τῷ DEMQ   30 εἶναι μᾶλλον MQ (sed 'magis esse' W)   31 ἧττον]
minus est W

conjoined with the limiting terms of the primal. Now conjunction is effected through likeness (props. 29, 32). Therefore there will be likeness between the initial principles of the lower order and the last members of the higher.

PROP. 148. *Every divine order has an internal unity of threefold origin, from its highest, its mean, and its last term.*

For the highest term, having the most unitary potency of the three, communicates its unity to the entire order and unifies the whole from above while remaining independent of it (prop. 125). Secondly, the mean term, reaching out toward both the extremes, links the whole together with itself as mediator (prop. 132); it transmits the bestowals of the first members of its order, draws upward the potentialities of the last, and implants in all a common character and mutual nexus—for in this sense also givers and receivers constitute a single complete order, in that they converge upon the mean term as on a centre. Thirdly, the limiting term produces a likeness and convergence in the whole order by reverting again upon its initial principle and carrying back to it the potencies which have emerged from it (prop. 146). Thus the entire rank is one through the unifying potency of its first terms, through the connective function of the mean term, and through the reversion of the end upon the initial principle of procession.

PROP. 149. *The entire manifold of divine henads is finite in number.*

For if it stands nearest to the One (prop. 113), it cannot be infinite, since the infinite is not cognate with the One but alien from it: for if the manifold as such is already a departure from the One, it is plain that an infinite manifold is completely bereft of its influence (and for this reason bereft also of potency and activity). The manifold of gods is therefore not infinite, but marked by unity and limit; and this in a higher degree than any other, since of all manifolds it is nearest akin to the One. Were the first Principle a manifold, then each should be more manifold in proportion as it stood nearer to that Principle, likeness being proportionate to nearness; but since the Primal is One (prop. 5), a manifold which is conjoined with it will be less manifold than one more remote; and the infinite, far from being less manifold, is the extreme manifold.

150. Πᾶν τὸ προϊὸν ἐν ταῖς θείαις τάξεσι πάσας ὑποδέχεσθαι τὰς τοῦ παράγοντος δυνάμεις οὐ πέφυκεν, οὐδὲ ὅλως τὰ δεύτερα πάσας τὰς τῶν πρὸ αὐτῶν, ἀλλ᾽ ἔχει τινὰς ἐκεῖνα τῶν καταδεεστέρων ἐξῃρημένας δυνάμεις καὶ ἀπεριλήπτους τοῖς μετ᾽ αὐτά.

εἰ γὰρ αἱ τῶν θεῶν ἰδιότητες διαφέρουσιν, αἱ μὲν τῶν ὑφειμένων ἐν τοῖς ὑπερτέροις προϋπάρχουσιν, αἱ δὲ τῶν ὑπερτέρων, ὁλικωτέρων ὄντων, ἐν τοῖς ὑφειμένοις οὔκ εἰσιν, ἀλλὰ τὰς μὲν ἐνδίδωσι τὰ κρείττονα τοῖς ἀπ᾽ αὐτῶν παραγομένοις, τὰς δὲ ἐν αὐτοῖς προείληφεν ἐξῃρημένως. δέδεικται γὰρ 10 ὅτι ὁλικώτεροι μέν εἰσιν οἱ ἐγγυτέρω τοῦ ἑνός, μερικώτεροι δὲ οἱ πορρώτερον· οἱ δὲ ὁλικώτεροι τῶν μερικωτέρων περιληπτικωτέρας ἔχουσι δυνάμεις· οὐκ ἄρα τὴν ἐκείνων δύναμιν οἱ δευτέραν ἔχοντες τάξιν καὶ μερικωτέραν περιλήψονται. ἔστιν ἄρα ἐν τοῖς ὑπερτέροις ἀπερίληπτόν τι καὶ ἀπερίγραφον τοῖς ὑφειμένοις. 15 καὶ γὰρ ἄπειρον ἕκαστον τῶν θείων οὕτως οὔτε ἑαυτῷ δέδεικται ὂν οὔτε τοῖς ὑπὲρ αὐτὸ πολλῷ πρότερον, ἀλλὰ τοῖς μεθ᾽ ἑαυτὸ πᾶσιν· ἡ δὲ ἀπειρία κατὰ τὴν δύναμιν ἐν ἐκείνοις· τὸ δὲ ἄπειρον ἀπερίληπτον, οἷς ἐστιν ἄπειρον· οὐκ ἄρα πασῶν μετέχει τῶν δυνάμεων τὰ καταδεέστερα, ὧν ἐν ἑαυτοῖς τὰ 20 κρείττονα προείληφεν (ἦν γὰρ ἂν ἐκεῖνα περιληπτὰ τοῖς δευτέροις, ὥσπερ δὴ καὶ αὐτοῖς τὰ δεύτερα). οὔτε οὖν πάσας ἔχει ταῦτα τὰς ἐκείνων, διὰ τὸ μερικώτερον· οὔτε ἃς ἔχει, τὸν αὐτὸν ἐκείνοις ἔχει τρόπον, διὰ τὴν ἀπειρίαν τὴν ἐκεῖνα ὑπερφέρειν τῶν καταδεεστέρων ποιοῦσαν. 25

151. Πᾶν τὸ πατρικὸν ἐν τοῖς θεοῖς πρωτουργόν ἐστι καὶ ἐν τἀγαθοῦ τάξει προϊστάμενον κατὰ πάσας τὰς θείας διακοσμήσεις.

τὰς γὰρ ὑπάρξεις τῶν δευτέρων καὶ τὰς δυνάμεις ὅλας καὶ τὰς οὐσίας αὐτὸ παράγει κατὰ μίαν ἄρρητον ὑπεροχήν· διὸ καὶ πατρικὸν ἐπονομάζεται, τὴν ἡνωμένην καὶ ἀγαθοειδῆ τοῦ 30 ἑνὸς δύναμιν ἐμφαῖνον καὶ τὴν ὑποστατικὴν τῶν δευτέρων αἰτίαν. καὶ καθ᾽ ἑκάστην τῶν θεῶν τάξιν τὸ πατρικὸν ἡγεῖται γένος, παράγον ἀφ᾽ ἑαυτοῦ πάντα καὶ κοσμοῦν, ἅτε τῷ ἀγαθῷ τεταγμένον ἀνάλογον. καὶ πατέρες οἱ μὲν ὁλικώτεροι, οἱ δὲ μερικώτεροι, καθάπερ καὶ αὐταὶ τῶν θεῶν αἱ τάξεις τῷ ὁλικωτέρῳ 35

150. 3 prius τῶν om. M   4-5 τοῖς μετ᾽ αὐτά] τῶν μετὰ ταῦτα Q   7 ὑπάρχουσιν M¹W   9 ὑπ᾽ αὐτῶν C   12 alt. οἱ (ʘ) (εἰ dett., edd.)   13 τὰς δυνάμεις Q   14 καὶ μερικωτέραν ἔχοντες τάξιν Q   16 γάρ MW : γοῦν BCD : om. Q   οὕτως M¹QW : ὄντως BCDM² : fort. secludendum   18 ἐν om. BC(Arg edd.)   20 τῶν δυνάμεων μετέχει Q   21 ἂν om. BCD   περιληπτά Q : ἀπερίληπτα cett. W   22 αὐτοῖς τὰ δεύτερα MQW :

PROP. 150. *Any processive term in the divine orders is incapable of receiving all the potencies of its producer, as are secondary principles in general of receiving all the potencies of their priors; the prior principles possess certain powers which transcend their inferiors and are incomprehensible to subsequent grades of deity.*

For if the gods differ in their distinctive properties, the characters of the lower pre-subsist in the higher, whereas those of the higher and more universal are not found in the lower ; the superior deities implant in their products some of their own characters, but others they pre-embrace as transcendent attributes. For it has been shown (prop. 126) that the gods nearer to the One are more universal, whilst the more remote are more specific ; and since the former have more comprehensive potencies than the latter, it follows that gods of secondary and more specific rank will not comprehend the power of the primal. Thus in the higher gods there is something which for the lower is incomprehensible and uncircumscribed.

It has in fact been shown (prop. 93) that each divine principle is in this sense infinite, not for itself, and still less for its priors, but for all its consequents. Now the divine infinitude is an infinitude of potency (prop. 86) ; and the infinite is incomprehensible to those for whom it is infinite. Hence the inferior principles do not participate all the potencies which are pre-embraced by the superior : otherwise the latter would be no less comprehensible to the secondaries than the secondaries to them. Thus the lower, being more specific, possess only certain of the potencies of the higher ; and even these they possess in an altered fashion, because of the infinitude which causes the higher to overpass them.

PROP. 151. *All that is paternal in the gods is of primal operation and stands in the position of the Good at the head of the several divine ranks.*

For by itself it produces the substantive existence of the secondary principles, the totality of their powers, and their being, in virtue of a single unspeakable transcendence : whence indeed it is named 'paternal', as manifesting the unified and boniform potency of the One and the constitutive cause of all secondaries. In each order of gods the paternal kind is sovereign, producing from itself the whole and regulating it, as being analogous in station to the Good. Fathers differ in degree of universality, as do the divine

αὐτὰ τοῖς καταδεεστέροις BCD   23 ταῦτα τάς] ταύτας M, suprascr. τάς M²
24 ἐκεῖνα BCD : ἐκείνας M primitus (in ἐκείνους mutatum) QW
    151. 26 alt. ἐν om. Q

καὶ μερικωτέρῳ διαφέρουσι, κατὰ τὸν τῆς αἰτίας λόγον· ὅσαι
οὖν αἱ ἕλαι τῶν θεῶν πρόοδοι, τοσαῦται καὶ αἱ τῶν πατέρων
διαφορότητες. εἰ γὰρ ἔστι τι κατὰ πᾶσαν τάξιν ἀνάλογον
τἀγαθῷ, δεῖ τὸ πατρικὸν ἐν πάσαις εἶναι, καὶ προϊέναι ἀπὸ τῆς
πατρικῆς ἐνώσεως ἑκάστην.   5

152. Πᾶν τὸ γεννητικὸν τῶν θεῶν κατὰ τὴν ἀπειρίαν τῆς
θείας δυνάμεως πρόεισι, πολλαπλασιάζον ἑαυτὸ καὶ διὰ πάντων
χωροῦν, καὶ τὸ ἀνέκλειπτον ἐν ταῖς τῶν δευτέρων προόδοις
διαφερόντως ἐπιδεικνύμενον.

τὸ γὰρ πληθύνειν τὰ προϊόντα καὶ ἀπὸ τῆς ἐν ταῖς αἰτίαις 10
κρυφίας περιοχῆς προάγειν εἰς ἀπογεννήσεις τίνος ἐξαίρετόν
ἐστιν ἢ τῆς ἀπείρου τῶν θεῶν δυνάμεως, δι' ἣν πάντα γονίμων
ἀγαθῶν πεπλήρωται τὰ θεῖα, παντὸς τοῦ πλήρους ἀλλ' ἀφ'
ἑαυτοῦ παράγοντος κατὰ τὴν ὑπερπλήρη δύναμιν; γεννητικῆς
οὖν θεότητος ἴδιον ἡ τῆς δυνάμεως ἐπικράτεια, πολλαπλα- 15
σιάζουσα τὰς τῶν γεννωμένων δυνάμεις καὶ γονίμους ἀπεργα-
ζομένη καὶ ἀνεγείρουσα πρὸς τὸ γεννᾶν ἄλλα καὶ ὑφιστάνειν.
εἰ γὰρ ἕκαστον τῆς οἰκείας ἰδιότητος, ἣν ἔχει πρώτως, τοῖς
ἄλλοις μεταδίδωσι, πᾶν δήπου τὸ γόνιμον καὶ τοῖς μεθ' ἑαυτὸ
τὴν γόνιμον ἐνδίδωσι πρόοδον καὶ τὴν ἀπειρίαν ἐνεικονίζεται τὴν 20
τῶν ὅλων ἀρχέγονον, ἀφ' ἧς πᾶσα γεννητικὴ προῆλθε δύναμις,
τὰς ἀεννάους τῶν θείων προόδους ἐξῃρημένως ἀπορρέουσα.

153. Πᾶν τὸ τέλειον ἐν τοῖς θεοῖς τῆς θείας ἐστὶ τελειότητος
αἴτιον.

ὡς γὰρ ἄλλαι τῶν ὄντων εἰσὶν ὑποστάσεις, ἄλλαι τῶν ὑπερ- 25
ουσίων, οὕτω δὴ καὶ τελειότητες ἄλλαι μὲν αἱ τῶν θεῶν αὐτῶν
κατὰ τὴν ὕπαρξιν, ἄλλαι δὲ αἱ τῶν ὄντων δεύτεραι μετ' ἐκείνας·
καὶ αἱ μὲν αὐτοτελεῖς καὶ πρωτουργοί, διότι καὶ τὸ ἀγαθὸν ἐν
ἐκείνοις πρώτως, αἱ δὲ κατὰ μέθεξιν ἔχουσαι τὸ τέλειον. ἄλλη
μὲν οὖν διὰ ταῦτα ἡ τῶν θεῶν τελειότης καὶ ἄλλη τῶν ἐκθεου- 30
μένων. τὸ δὲ ἐν τοῖς θεοῖς πρώτως τέλειον οὐ μόνον τοῖς
ἐκθεουμένοις τῆς τελειότητος αἴτιον, ἀλλὰ καὶ τοῖς θεοῖς αὐτοῖς.
εἰ γάρ, ᾗ τέλειον ἕκαστον, ἐπέστραπται πρὸς τὴν οἰκείαν
ἀρχήν, τὸ πάσης τῆς θείας ἐπιστροφῆς αἴτιον τελεσιουργόν
ἐστι τοῦ τῶν θεῶν γένους.   35

151. ι αἱ ὅλαι ω (αἱ om. Arg Cr., ὅλαι om. Port)   3 τι om. BCD
152. 11 περιοχῆς] eminentia (= ὑπεροχῆς?) W   εἰς om. B   13 παντός]
οὐκ ἀπό Q   ἀλλ' [M], ἄλλα BC : ἀλλ' DQM²W   15 ἴδιον θεότητος CD,
ἰδιότητος B   17 ἀλλά M   20 ἐκδίδωσι M primitus (dat W)
153. 23 ἐστί om. M¹   26 αἱ ω (om. edd.)   28 tert. καί om. M primitus
29 ἔχουσι Q   ἄλλη] ἀλλ' ἤ M primitus   30-31 θεουμένων BCD   35 τοῦ
τῶν θεῶν γένους BCD : τῶν θεῶν γένος MQW

orders themselves (prop. 136), in proportion to their causal efficacy ; there are thus as many diverse fathers as there are entire processive orders of gods. For if in every order there is something analogous to the Good, the paternal must exist in all of them and each must proceed from a paternal unity.

PROP. 152. *All that is generative in the gods proceeds in virtue of the infinitude of divine potency, multiplying itself and penetrating all things, and manifesting especially the character of unfailing perpetuity in the processive orders of secondary principles.*

For to increase the number of processive terms by drawing them from their secret embracement in their causes and advancing them to generation is surely the peculiar office of the gods' infinite potency, through which all divine principles are filled with fertile excellencies, each in its fulness giving rise to some further principle (prop. 25) in virtue of that superabundant potency (prop. 27). Thus the especial office of generative divinity is the governance of potency, a governance which multiplies and renders fertile the potencies of the generated and spurs them to beget or constitute still other existences. For if each principle communicates to the remaining terms its own distinctive character which it possesses primitively (prop. 97), then assuredly the fertile always implants in its consequents the succession of fertility, and so mirrors that Infinitude which is the primordial parent of the universe, whence proceeded all the generative potency (prop. 92) whose transcendent prerogative it is to diffuse the divine gifts in their unfailing succession.

PROP. 153. *All that is perfect in the gods is the cause of divine perfection.*

For as existents and the principles superior to existence differ in their mode of substance, so also do the perfections proper to the gods themselves differ in nature from the secondary perfections of existents: the former are self-complete and of primal operation, because the gods are the primal possessors of the Good (prop. 119), whereas the latter are perfect by participation. For this reason the perfection of the gods is distinct from that of things divinized. But the primal perfection which resides in the gods is the cause of being perfect not only to things divinized, but also to the gods themselves. For if every principle, in so far as it is perfect, is reverted upon its proper origin (prop. 31), then the cause of all the divine reversion has the office of making perfect the order of gods.

154. Πᾶν τὸ φρουρητικὸν ἐν τοῖς θεοῖς ἕκαστον ἐν τῇ οἰκείᾳ τάξει διαφυλάττει τῶν δευτέρων ἐνοειδῶς ἐξῃρημένον καὶ τοῖς πρώτοις ἐνιδρυμένον.

εἰ γὰρ ἡ φρουρὰ τὸ τῆς ἑκάστου τάξεως μέτρον ἀτρέπτως διασώζει καὶ συνέχει πάντα τὰ φρουρούμενα ἐν τῇ οἰκείᾳ 5 τελειότητι, πᾶσιν ἐνδίδωσι τὴν ἀπὸ τῶν καταδεεστέρων ὑπεροχήν, καὶ ἄμικτον ἕκαστον ἵστησιν ἐφ' ἑαυτοῦ μονίμως, καθαρότητος ἀχράντου τοῖς φρουρουμένοις αἴτιον ὑπάρχον, καὶ ἐνιδρύει τοῖς ὑπερτέροις. τέλειον γὰρ πᾶν ἐστι τῶν μὲν πρώτων ἀντεχόμενον, ἐν ἑαυτῷ δὲ μένον, καὶ τῶν καταδεεστέρων 10 ὑπερηπλωμένον.

155. Πᾶν μὲν τὸ ζωογόνον ἐν τοῖς θείοις γένεσιν αἴτιον γεννητικόν ἐστιν, οὐ πᾶσα δὲ ἡ γόνιμος τάξις ζωογόνος ἐστίν· ὁλικωτέρα γὰρ ἡ γεννητικὴ τῆς ζωογονικῆς καὶ ἐγγυτέρω τῆς ἀρχῆς.   15

ἡ μὲν γὰρ γέννησις τὴν εἰς πλῆθος τὰ ὄντα προάγουσαν αἰτίαν δηλοῖ, ἡ δὲ ζωογονία τὴν χορηγὸν ἁπάσης ζωῆς θεότητα παρίστησιν. εἰ οὖν ἡ μὲν τῶν ὄντων πολλαπλασιάζει τὰς ὑποστάσεις, ἡ δὲ τὰς τῆς ζωῆς προόδους ὑφίστησιν, ὡς ἔχει τὸ ὂν πρὸς τὴν ζωήν, οὕτως ἡ γεννητικὴ τάξις ἕξει πρὸς τὴν 20 ζωογόνον σειράν. ὁλικωτέρα δὴ οὖν ἔσται καὶ πλειόνων αἰτία, καὶ διὰ τοῦτο ἐγγυτέρω τῆς ἀρχῆς.

156. Πᾶν μὲν τὸ τῆς καθαρότητος αἴτιον ἐν τῇ φρουρητικῇ περιέχεται τάξει, οὐκ ἔμπαλιν δὲ πᾶν τὸ φρουρητικὸν τῷ καθαρτικῷ γένει ταὐτόν.   25

ἡ μὲν γὰρ καθαρότης τὸ ἀμιγὲς ἐνδίδωσι πρὸς τὰ χείρονα πᾶσι τοῖς θεοῖς καὶ τὸ ἄχραντον ἐν τῇ προνοίᾳ τῶν δευτέρων, ἡ δὲ φρουρὰ καὶ τοῦτο ἀπεργάζεται καὶ ἐν ἑαυτοῖς πάντα συνέχει καὶ σταθερῶς ἐντίθησι τοῖς ὑπερτέροις. ὁλικώτερον ἄρα τοῦ καθαρτικοῦ τὸ φρουρητικόν ἐστιν· ἴδιον γὰρ ἁπλῶς φρουρᾶς 30 μὲν τὸ τὴν αὐτὴν ἑκάστου τάξιν διατηρεῖν πρός τε ἑαυτὸ καὶ τὰ πρὸ αὐτοῦ καὶ τὰ μετ' αὐτό, καθαρότητος δὲ τὸ ἐξαιρεῖν τῶν καταδεεστέρων τὰ κρείττονα. ταῦτα δέ ἐστι πρώτως ἐν τοῖς θεοῖς. τοῦ γὰρ ἐν πᾶσιν ὄντος δεῖ μίαν αἰτίαν προηγεῖσθαι· καὶ ὅλως

154. 2 φυλάσσει Q   2–3 ἐξηρημένων . . . ἐνιδρυμένων BM   4 εἰ] ἡ M
ἡ ω (om. edd.)   5 ἐν τῇ om. M¹   6 ἀπό om. Q   7 ἀφ' ἑαυτοῦ
CD   10 ἀντεχόμενον MQW : ἀμέσως (μέσως B) ἐχόμενον BCD   μόνον
DE (dett., edd.)
155. 14 γάρ ἐστιν ἡ Q   ἐγγυτέρα Q   16 προσάγουσαν DQ
20 ἔχει [M]
156. 30 ἐστὶ τὸ φρουρητικόν Q   31 ἑκάστῳ Arg   32 ἐξαιρεῖν
scripsi : ἐξαίρειν ω   τῶν ω (om. O edd.)

PROP. **154.** *All that is protective in the gods preserves each principle in its proper station, so that by its unitary character it transcends derivative existences and is founded upon the primals.*

For if the divine protection immutably maintains the measure of the station assigned to each, and conserves in their proper perfection all the objects of its care, then it implants in all a superiority to lower principles, sets each in steadfast independence without alien admixture (for it has the property of causing in its objects an un-contaminated purity), and lastly founds the being of each upon the principles superior to it. For the perfection of any existent consists in its laying fast hold of the primals, remaining steadfast in its own being, and preserving the simplicity by which it transcends the lower.

PROP. **155.** *All that is zoogonic or life-giving in the divine kinds is a generative cause, but not all the generative order is zoogonic ; for the generative is the more universal, and nearer to the First Principle.*

For 'generation' signifies that cause which advances existents to plurality, but 'zoogony' describes the divinity which bestows all life. If, then, the former of these multiplies the number of substantive existences whilst the latter constitutes the successive orders of life, the generative order will be related to the zoogonic series as Being to Life. It will therefore be the more universal (prop. 101) and productive of more numerous effects ; and for this reason it will be nearer to the First Principle (prop. 60).

PROP. **156.** *All that is the cause of purity is embraced in the protective order, but not all the protective is conversely identical with the purificatory.*

For the divine purity isolates all the gods from inferior existences, and enables them to exercise providence toward secondary beings without contamination; whilst divine protection has, besides, the further task of maintaining all things in their proper being and of founding them securely upon the higher principles (prop. 154). Thus the protective is more universal than the purificatory : the distinctive office of protection, as such, is to keep each thing in the same station relatively to itself and its priors no less than to its consequents ; that of purity, to liberate the higher from the lower. And these offices belong primitively to the gods. For any general character must have a single antecedent cause (prop. 21) ; and it is true universally

πάντων τῶν ἀγαθῶν τὰ ἑνοειδῆ μέτρα παρ' ἐκείνοις προείληπται,
καὶ οὐδέν ἐστιν ἐν τοῖς δευτέροις ἀγαθόν, ὃ μὴ προϋφέστηκεν ἐν
τοῖς θεοῖς (πόθεν γὰρ ἔσται τοῦτο, καὶ τίνα ἕξει τὴν αἰτίαν ;).
ἐν ἐκείνοις ἄρα καὶ ἡ καθαρότης πρώτως, ἀγαθὸν οὖσα, καὶ ἡ
φρουρὰ καὶ πᾶν ὅ τι τοιοῦτον.   5

157. Πᾶν μὲν τὸ πατρικὸν αἴτιον τοῦ εἶναι πᾶσίν ἐστι χορηγὸν καὶ τὰς ὑπάρξεις τῶν ὄντων ὑφίστησι· πᾶν δὲ τὸ δημιουργικὸν τῆς εἰδοποιίας τῶν συνθέτων προέστηκε καὶ τῆς τάξεως καὶ
τῆς κατ' ἀριθμὸν αὐτῶν διαιρέσεως, καὶ ἔστι τῆς αὐτῆς τῷ πα-
τρικῷ συστοιχίας ἐν μερικωτέροις γένεσιν.   10
ἑκάτερον γὰρ τῆς τοῦ πέρατός ἐστι τάξεως, ἐπεὶ καὶ ἡ ὕπαρξις καὶ ὁ ἀριθμὸς καὶ τὸ εἶδος περατοειδῆ πάντα ἐστίν· ὥστε
ταύτῃ σύστοιχα ἀλλήλοις. ἀλλὰ τὸ μὲν δημιουργικὸν εἰς πλῆθος
προάγει τὴν ποίησιν, τὸ δὲ ἑνοειδῶς παρέχεται τὰς τῶν ὄντων
προόδους· καὶ τὸ μὲν εἰδοποιόν ἐστι, τὸ δὲ οὐσιοποιόν. ᾗ οὖν 15
ταῦτα διέστηκεν ἀλλήλων, τό τε εἶδος καὶ τὸ ὄν, ταύτῃ τοῦ
δημιουργικοῦ τὸ πατρικὸν διέστηκεν. ἔστι δέ τι ὂν τὸ εἶδος.
ὁλικώτερον ἄρα καὶ αἰτιώτερον ⟨ὄν,⟩ τὸ πατρικόν ἐστιν ἐπέκεινα
τοῦ δημιουργικοῦ γένους, ὡς τὸ ὂν τοῦ εἴδους.

158. Πᾶν τὸ ἀναγωγὸν αἴτιον ἐν τοῖς θεοῖς καὶ τοῦ καθαρ- 20
τικοῦ διαφέρει καὶ τῶν ἐπιστρεπτικῶν γενῶν.
ὅτι μὲν γὰρ εἶναι δεῖ καὶ τοῦτο πρώτως ἐν ἐκείνοις δῆλον,
ἐπειδὴ τῶν ὅλων ἀγαθῶν ἐκεῖ τὰ αἴτια πάντα προϋφέστηκεν.
ἀλλὰ τοῦ μὲν καθαρτικοῦ προϋπάρχει, διότι τὸ μὲν ἀπολύει τῶν
χειρόνων, τοῦτο δὲ συνάπτει τοῖς κρείττοσι· τοῦ δὲ ἐπιστρεπ- 25
τικοῦ μερικωτέραν ἔχει τάξιν, διότι πᾶν τὸ ἐπιστρέφον ἢ πρὸς
ἑαυτὸ ἐπιστρέφει ἢ πρὸς τὸ κρεῖττον, τοῦ δὲ ἀναγωγοῦ τὸ
ἐνέργημα κατὰ τὴν πρὸς τὸ κρεῖττον ἐπιστροφὴν χαρακτηρίζεται, ὡς εἰς τὸ ἄνω καὶ τὸ θειότερον ἄγον τὸ ἐπιστρεφόμενον.

159. Πᾶσα τάξις θεῶν ἐκ τῶν πρώτων ἐστὶν ἀρχῶν, πέρατος 30
καὶ ἀπειρίας· ἀλλ' ἡ μὲν πρὸς τῆς τοῦ πέρατος αἰτίας μᾶλλον,
ἡ δὲ πρὸς τῆς ἀπειρίας.
πᾶσα μὲν γὰρ ἐξ ἀμφοτέρων πρόεισι, διότι τῶν πρώτων
αἰτίων αἱ μεταδόσεις διήκουσι διὰ πάντων τῶν δευτέρων. ἀλλ'

156. 3 τοῖς om. M   πόθεν ... αἰτίαν] κατ' αἰτίαν BCD : πόθεν ... τὴν post
μέτρα (l. 1) habent O Port., omissis 3 αἰτίαν ... 5 τοιοῦτον   τὴν om. Q
4 prius καί ω (om. Arg Cr.)   alt. ἡ om. BCD
157. 8 συνθέτων ap. Cr. error preli   προέστηκε ω (προϋφέστηκε O edd.)
9 αὐτῶν BDMW : αὐτόν CQ   διατηρήσεως Q   14 προάγει ω (παράγει
O edd.)   ἑνοειδῶς scripsi : ἑνοειδὲς ω   παρέχει M   17 ἔστι δέ τι ὄν
T. Taylor: ἔστι δέ τι ἐν BCDM² : ἔστι δ' αἴτιον [M]W : ἔστι δὲ ἑνοειδές (omisso
τὸ εἶδος) Q   18 ὄν inserui
158. 23 ἐπειδή] ἐπεί Q   πάντα om. BCD   25 τοῦτο δέ BCDM² : τὸ δέ

that in the gods the unitary measures of all things good are pre-embraced, and nothing good is found in secondary existences which does not pre-subsist in the gods (what other source or cause could it have ?). Purity, then, being a good, belongs primitively to the gods ; and so also protection and other like offices.

PROP. 157. *Whereas it is the function of all paternal causes to bestow being on all things and originate the substantive existence of all that is, it is the office of all demiurgic or formal causes to preside over the bestowal of Form upon things composite, the assignment of their stations, and their numerical distinction as individuals : the demiurgic is thus in the same succession as the paternal, but is found in the more specific orders of gods.*

For both these causes are ranked under the principle of Limit, since existence has, like number and Form, a limitative character : in this respect the two are in the same succession.   But the demiurgic advances the creative office into plurality, whilst the other without departure from unity originates the processive orders of things existent (prop. 151).   Again, the one creates Form, the other existence.   As Being, then, differs from Form, so does the paternal from the demiurgic.   Now Form is a particular kind of Being (prop. 74 cor.).   Accordingly the paternal, being the more universal and more comprehensive cause, transcends the demiurgic order, as Being transcends Form.

PROP. 158. *All elevative causes among the gods differ both from the purificatory causes and from the conversive kinds.*

For it is evident that this cause also must be found primitively in the gods, since all causes of all goods pre-subsist there.   But it is prior to the purificatory, which liberates from the lower principles (prop. 156), whereas the elevative effects conjunction with the higher ; on the other hand it has a more specific rank than the conversive, since anything which reverts may revert either upon itself or upon the higher principle, whereas the function of the elevative cause, which draws the reverting existence upwards to what is more divine, is characterized only by the latter mode of reversion.

PROP. 159. *Every order of gods is derived from the two initial principles, Limit and Infinity ; but some manifest predominantly the causality of Limit, others that of Infinity.*

For every order must proceed from both, because the communications of the primal causes extend through all derivative ranks

ὅπου μὲν τὸ πέρας ἐνδυναστεύει κατὰ τὴν μῖξιν, ὅπου δὲ τὸ
ἄπειρον· καὶ οὕτω δὴ τὸ μὲν περατοειδὲς ἀποτελεῖται γένος, ἐν
ᾧ τὰ τοῦ πέρατος κρατεῖ· τὸ δὲ ἀπειροειδές, ἐν ᾧ τὰ τῆς ἀπειρίας.

160. Πᾶς ὁ θεῖος νοῦς ἐνοειδής ἐστι καὶ τέλειος καὶ πρώτως 5
νοῦς, ἀφ᾽ ἑαυτοῦ καὶ τοὺς ἄλλους νόας παράγων.

εἰ γὰρ θεῖός ἐστι, πεπλήρωται τῶν θείων ἑνάδων καὶ ἔστιν·
ἐνοειδής· εἰ δὲ τοῦτο, καὶ τέλειος, τῆς ἀγαθότητος τῆς θείας
πλήρης ὑπάρχων. εἰ δὲ ταῦτα, καὶ πρώτως ἐστὶ νοῦς, ἅτε τοῖς
θεοῖς ἡνωμένος· παντὸς γὰρ νοῦ κρείττων ὁ ἐκθεούμενος νοῦς. 10
πρώτως δὲ ὢν νοῦς, καὶ τοῖς ἄλλοις αὐτὸς δίδωσι τὴν ὑπόστασιν·
ἀπὸ γὰρ τῶν πρώτως ὄντων πάντα τὰ δευτέρως ὄντα τὴν
ὕπαρξιν κέκτηται.

161. Πᾶν τὸ ὄντως ὂν τὸ τῶν θεῶν ἐξημμένον θεῖόν ἐστι
νοητὸν καὶ ἀμέθεκτον.   15

ἐπεὶ γὰρ πρῶτόν ἐστι τῶν τῆς θείας ἑνώσεως μετεχόντων τὸ
ὄντως ὄν, ὡς δέδεικται, καὶ πληροῖ τὸν νοῦν ἀφ᾽ ἑαυτοῦ (καὶ γὰρ
ὁ νοῦς ὄν ἐστιν, ὡς τοῦ ὄντος πληρούμενος), θεῖόν ἐστι δήπου
νοητόν· ὡς μὲν ἐκθεούμενον, θεῖον, ὡς δὲ πληρωτικὸν τοῦ νοῦ
καὶ ὑπ᾽ αὐτοῦ μετεχόμενον, νοητόν.   20

καὶ ὁ μὲν νοῦς ὂν διὰ τὸ πρώτως ὄν, αὐτὸ δὲ τὸ πρώτως ὂν
χωριστόν ἐστιν ἀπὸ τοῦ νοῦ, διότι μετὰ τὸ ὄν ἐστιν ὁ νοῦς. τὰ
δὲ ἀμέθεκτα πρὸ τῶν μετεχομένων ὑφέστηκεν· ὥστε καὶ τοῦ
συζύγου πρὸς τὸν νοῦν ὄντος προϋπάρχει τὸ καθ᾽ αὐτὸ καὶ
ἀμεθέκτως ὄν. νοητὸν γάρ ἐστιν οὐχ ὡς τῷ νῷ συντεταγμένον, 25
ἀλλ᾽ ὡς τελειοῦν ἐξῃρημένως τὸν νοῦν, διότι κἀκείνῳ τοῦ εἶναι
μεταδίδωσι καὶ πληροῖ κἀκεῖνον τῆς ὄντως οὔσης οὐσίας.

162. Πᾶν τὸ καταλάμπον τὸ ὄντως ὂν πλῆθος τῶν ἑνάδων
κρύφιον καὶ νοητόν ἐστι· κρύφιον μὲν ὡς τῷ ἑνὶ συνημμένον,
νοητὸν δὲ ὡς ὑπὸ τοῦ ὄντος μετεχόμενον.   30

ἀπὸ γὰρ τῶν ἐξημμένων πάντες οἱ θεοὶ καλοῦνται, διότι καὶ
τὰς ὑποστάσεις αὐτῶν τὰς διαφόρους ἀπὸ τούτων, ἀγνώστους
ὑπαρχούσας, γνῶναι δυνατόν. ἄρρητον γὰρ καθ᾽ αὐτὸ πᾶν τὸ

159. 2 καί om. Q
160. Tit. περὶ νοῦ M : om. cett.   5 πρῶτος D[M]O   6 καὶ πρὸς τοὺς
ἄλλους M²   7 θεῖός ἐστι [M]W : θεός ἐστι BCDQM²   9 πρῶτος
DM¹   12 ἀπὸ ... 13 κέκτηται om. Q   12 δευτέρως ω (δεύτερα O edd.)
161. 15 νοητόν ω (om. O¹ edd.)   16 τῆς om. Q   μετεχόντων ω
(μετασχόντων edd.)   18 πληρούμενος τοῦ θείου, ἔστι Q   20 ἀπ᾽ αὐτοῦ M
primitus?   21 αὐτὸ δὲ τὸ πρώτως ὄν om. M primitus   22 alt. ἐστιν] ἐστι
καί Q   25 ἀμεθέκτως ω (ἀμέθεκτον edd.)
162. 29 συνηνωμένον QM² (corr. in mg. M³)   31 ἐξηρτημένων Q
32 alt. τάς om. M¹   διαφέρουσας M

(prop. 97). But at some points Limit is dominant in the mixture, at others Infinity : accordingly there results one group of a determinative character, that in which the influence of Limit prevails ; and another characterized by infinitude, in which the element of Infinity preponderates.

PROP. 160. *All divine intelligence is perfect and has the character of unity ; it is the primal Intelligence, and produces the others from its own being.*

For if it is divine, it is filled with divine henads (prop. 129) and has the character of unity ; and if this is so, it is also perfect, being full of the divine goodness (prop. 133). But if it has these properties, it is also primal, as being united with the gods : for the highest intelligence is divinized intelligence (prop. 112). And being the primal Intelligence, it bestows by its own act substantiality upon the rest : for all that has secondary existence derives its substance from a principle which exists primitively (prop. 18).

PROP. 161. *All the true Being which is attached to the gods is a divine Intelligible, and unparticipated.*

For since true Being is, as has been shown (prop. 138), the first of the principles which participate divine unification, and since it makes the content of the Intelligence (for the Intelligence too is an existent, because filled with Being), it surely results that true Being is a divine Intelligible—divine as being divinized, intelligible as the principle which gives content to the Intelligence and is participated by it.

And while the Intelligence is an existent because of primal Being, this primal Being is itself separate from the Intelligence, because Intelligence is posterior to Being (prop. 101). Again, unparticipated terms subsist prior to the participated (prop. 23) : so that prior to the Being which is consubstantial with the Intelligence there must be a form of Being which exists in itself and beyond participation. For true Being is intelligible not as co-ordinate with the Intelligence, but as perfecting it without loss of transcendence, in that it communicates to the Intelligence the gift of being and fills it with a truly existent essence.

PROP. 162. *All those henads which illuminate true Being are secret and intelligible : secret as conjoined with the One, intelligible as participated by Being.*

For all the gods are named from the principles which are attached to them, because their diverse natures, otherwise unknowable, may be known from these dependent principles : all deity is in itself

θεῖον καὶ ἄγνωστον, ὡς τῷ ἑνὶ τῷ ἀρρήτῳ συμφυές· ἀπὸ δὲ τῆς
τῶν μετεχόντων ἐξαλλαγῆς καὶ τὰς ἐκείνων ἰδιότητας γνωρίζε-
σθαι συμβαίνει. νοητοὶ δὴ οὖν εἰσιν οἱ τὸ ὄντως ὂν καταλάμ-
ποντες, διότι δὴ τὸ ὄντως ὂν νοητόν ἐστι θεῖον καὶ ἀμέθεκτον,
τοῦ νοῦ προϋφεστηκός. οὐ γὰρ ἂν τοῦτο τῶν πρωτίστων ἐξῆπτο 5
θεῶν, εἰ μὴ κἀκεῖνοι πρωτουργὸν εἶχον ὑπόστασιν καὶ δύναμιν
τελειωτικὴν τῶν ἄλλων θεῶν, εἴπερ ὡς τὰ μετέχοντα πρὸς
ἄλληλα, οὕτω καὶ αἱ τῶν μετεχομένων ἔχουσιν ὑπάρξεις.
163. Πᾶν τὸ πλῆθος τῶν ἑνάδων τὸ μετεχόμενον ὑπὸ τοῦ
ἀμεθέκτου νοῦ νοερόν ἐστιν.   10
ὡς γὰρ ἔχει νοῦς πρὸς τὸ ὄντως ὄν, οὕτως αἱ ἑνάδες αὗται
πρὸς τὰς ἑνάδας τὰς νοητὰς ἔχουσιν. ἧπερ οὖν καὶ ἐκεῖναι,
καταλάμπουσαι τὸ ὄν, νοηταί εἰσι, ταύτῃ καὶ αὗται, καταλάμπουσαι τὸν θεῖον καὶ ἀμέθεκτον νοῦν, νοεραί εἰσιν, ἀλλ' οὐχ
οὕτω νοεραὶ ὡς ἐν νῷ ὑφεστηκυῖαι, ἀλλ' ὡς κατ᾽ αἰτίαν τοῦ νοῦ 15
προϋπάρχουσαι καὶ ἀπογεννῶσαι τὸν νοῦν.
164. Πᾶν τὸ πλῆθος τῶν ἑνάδων τὸ μετεχόμενον ὑπὸ τῆς
ἀμεθέκτου πάσης ψυχῆς ὑπερκόσμιόν ἐστι.
διότι γὰρ ἡ ἀμέθεκτος ψυχὴ πρώτως ὑπὲρ τὸν κόσμον ἐστί,
καὶ οἱ μετεχόμενοι ὑπ' αὐτῆς θεοὶ ὑπερκόσμιοί εἰσιν, ἀνὰ λόγον 20
ὄντες πρὸς τοὺς νοεροὺς καὶ νοητούς, ὃν ἔχει ψυχὴ πρὸς νοῦν
καὶ νοῦς πρὸς τὸ ὄντως ὄν. ὡς οὖν ψυχὴ πᾶσα εἰς νοῦς ἀνήρτηται καὶ νοῦς εἰς τὸ νοητὸν ἐπέστραπται, οὕτω δὴ καὶ οἱ ὑπερκόσμιοι θεοὶ τῶν νοερῶν ἐξέχονται, καθάπερ δὴ καὶ οὗτοι τῶν
νοητῶν.   25
165. Πᾶν τὸ πλῆθος τῶν ἑνάδων τῶν μετεχομένων ὑπό
τινος αἰσθητοῦ σώματος ἐγκόσμιόν ἐστιν.
ἐλλάμπει γὰρ εἴς τι τῶν τοῦ κόσμου μερῶν διὰ μέσων τοῦ
νοῦ καὶ τῆς ψυχῆς. οὔτε γὰρ νοῦς ἄνευ ψυχῆς πάρεστί τινι
τῶν ἐγκοσμίων σωμάτων οὔτε θεότης ἀμέσως συνάπτεται ψυχῇ 30
(διὰ γὰρ τῶν ὁμοίων αἱ μεθέξεις)· καὶ αὐτὸς ὁ νοῦς κατὰ τὸ
νοητὸν τὸ ἑαυτοῦ καὶ τὸ ἀκρότατον μετέχει τῆς ἑνάδος. ἐγκόσ-

162. 3 δὴ ω (om. edd.)   τό om. M¹   4 ἀμέθεκτον ἐστί (sic) Q
5 ἐξῆπτο BD : ἐξῆπται C : ἐξήπτετο MQ
163. hoc totum caput om. B   10 μεθεκτοῦ QM²   12 ἧπερ CDQ : εἴπερ
MW   καί CD : om. MQ, neque agnoscit W   13 τὸ ὄν CDW : τὸν νοῦν M :
τὸ ἔν Q   13–14 ἐκλάμπουσαι Q   16 ἀπογεννῶσαι CD[M] : ἀπογεννήσασαι QM²
164. 18 πάσης fort. secludendum   20 ἀνὰ λόγον scripsi : ἀνάλογον ω
21 post ψυχή ins. λόγος B, λόγον CDE   22 εἰς MQ : πρός BCD   alt.
νοῦς] νοῦν Q dett.   23 εἰς BCDM : πρός Q
165. 28 εἴς τι] ἐπί M   διά] καί M, suprascr. διά M³ (unde καὶ διά O edd.)
μέσων ω (μέσου Arg Cr.)   30 συνάπτεται M¹QW : συνάπτεται καί BCDM²
(ita etiam Ἀνάπτ. 182. 14)   ψυχῇ [M] ut videtur, animae W : τῇ ψυχῇ Q :
ψυχή BCDM² et Ἀνάπτ. l.c.

unspeakable and unknowable, being of like nature with the unspeakable One ; yet from the diversities of the participants may be inferred the peculiar attributes of the participated (prop. 123). Thus the gods who illuminate true Being are intelligible, because true Being is a divine and unparticipated Intelligible which subsists prior to the Intelligence (prop. 161). For inasmuch as participated terms stand in the same mutual relation as their participants, it follows that true Being would not have been attached to the first order of gods did not that order possess a nature primal in its operation and a power of perfecting the remaining gods.

PROP. 163. *All those henads are intellectual whereof the unparticipated Intelligence enjoys participation.*

For as Intelligence is to true Being, so are these henads to the intelligible henads. As, therefore, the latter, illuminating Being, are themselves intelligible (prop. 162), so these, illuminating the divine and unparticipated Intelligence, are themselves intellectual—not as subsisting in the Intelligence, but in the causative sense (prop. 65), as subsisting prior to the Intelligence and bringing it to birth.

PROP. 164. *All those henads are supra-mundane whereof all the unparticipated Soul enjoys participation.*

For since the unparticipated Soul occupies the next station above the world-order, the gods whom it participates are also supra-mundane, and are related to the intellectual and the intelligible gods as Soul is to Intelligence and Intelligence to true Being. As, then, all Soul is dependent upon intelligences (prop. 20) and Intelligence is converted upon the Intelligible (prop. 161), so the supra-mundane gods depend from the intellectual in the same manner as these from the intelligible.

PROP. 165. *All those henads are intra-mundane which any sensible body participates.*

For through the mediation of Intelligence and Soul such henads irradiate certain parts of the world-order. Intelligence is not present without Soul to any intra-mundane body, neither is Deity directly conjoined with Soul, since participation is through like terms (prop. 32) ; and Intelligence itself participates the henad in virtue of its own highest element, which is intelligible. These henads, then,

μιοι οὖν αἱ ἑνάδες ὡς συμπληροῦσαι τὸν ὅλον κόσμον καὶ ὡς
ἐκθεωτικαὶ τῶν ἐμφανῶν σωμάτων. θεῖον γὰρ καὶ τούτων
ἕκαστόν ἐστιν, οὐ διὰ τὴν ψυχήν (οὐ γὰρ πρώτως αὕτη θεός),
οὐδὲ διὰ τὸν νοῦν (οὐδὲ γὰρ οὗτος τῷ ἑνὶ ὁ αὐτός), ἀλλ' ἔμψυχον
μὲν καὶ ἐξ ἑαυτοῦ κινούμενον διὰ ψυχήν, ἀεὶ δὲ ὡσαύτως ἔχον 5
καὶ τάξει τῇ ἀρίστῃ φερόμενον διὰ τὸν νοῦν, θεῖον δὲ διὰ τὴν
ἕνωσιν· καὶ εἰ δύναμιν ἔχει προνοητικήν, διὰ ταύτην ἐστὶ τὴν
αἰτίαν τοιοῦτον.

166. Πᾶς νοῦς ἢ ἀμέθεκτός ἐστιν ἢ μεθεκτός· καὶ εἰ μεθεκτός, ἢ ὑπὸ τῶν ὑπερκοσμίων ψυχῶν μετεχόμενος ἢ ὑπὸ τῶν 10
ἐγκοσμίων.

παντὸς μὲν γὰρ τοῦ πλήθους τῶν νόων ὁ ἀμέθεκτος ἡγεῖται,
πρωτίστην ἔχων ὕπαρξιν· τῶν δὲ μετεχομένων οἱ μὲν τὴν ὑπερκόσμιον καὶ ἀμέθεκτον ἐλλάμπουσι ψυχήν, οἱ δὲ τὴν ἐγκόσμιον.
οὔτε γὰρ ἀπὸ τοῦ ἀμεθέκτου τὸ πλῆθος εὐθὺς τὸ ἐγκόσμιον, 15
εἴπερ αἱ πρόοδοι διὰ τῶν ὁμοίων, ὁμοιότερον δὲ τῷ ἀμεθέκτῳ τὸ
χωριστὸν τοῦ κόσμου μᾶλλον ἢ τὸ διῃρημένον περὶ αὐτόν· οὔτε
μόνον τὸ ὑπερκόσμιον ὑπέστη πλῆθος, ἀλλ' εἰσὶ καὶ ἐγκόσμιοι,
εἴπερ καὶ θεῶν ἐγκοσμίων πλῆθος, καὶ αὐτὸς ὁ κόσμος ἔμψυχος
ἅμα καὶ ἔννους ἐστί, καὶ ἡ μέθεξις ταῖς ἐγκοσμίοις ψυχαῖς τῶν 20
ὑπερκοσμίων νόων διὰ μέσων ἐστὶ τῶν ἐγκοσμίων νόων.

167. Πᾶς νοῦς ἑαυτὸν νοεῖ· ἀλλ' ὁ μὲν πρώτιστος ἑαυτὸν
μόνον, καὶ ἐν κατ' ἀριθμὸν ἐν τούτῳ νοῦς καὶ νοητόν· ἕκαστος
δὲ τῶν ἐφεξῆς ἑαυτὸν ἅμα καὶ τὰ πρὸ αὐτοῦ, καὶ νοητόν ἐστι
τούτῳ τὸ μὲν ὅ ἐστι, τὸ δὲ ἀφ' οὗ ἐστιν.   25

ἢ γὰρ ἑαυτὸν νοεῖ πᾶς νοῦς ἢ τὸ ὑπὲρ ἑαυτὸν ἢ τὸ μεθ'
ἑαυτόν.

ἀλλ' εἰ μὲν τὸ μεθ' ἑαυτόν, πρὸς τὸ χεῖρον ἐπιστρέψει νοῦς
ὤν. καὶ οὐδὲ οὕτως ἐκεῖνο αὐτὸ γνώσεται, πρὸς ὃ ἐπέστρεψεν,
ἅτε οὐκ ὢν ἐν αὐτῷ, ἀλλ' ἔξω αὐτοῦ, τὸν δὲ ἀπ' αὐτοῦ τύπον 30
μόνον, ὃς ἐν αὐτῷ γέγονεν ἀπ' ἐκείνου· ὃ γὰρ ἔχει, οἶδε, καὶ ὃ
πέπονθεν, οὐχ ὃ μὴ ἔχει καὶ ἀφ' οὗ [οὐ] πέπονθεν.

165. 2 ἐκθε ῶ τι καί M (sic : accentus ex corr.), unde ἐκ θεῶν τι καί dett.,
edd. τούτων in τοῦτον mutatum M 3 αὕτη πρώτως BCD dett. 4 οὐδὲ
γάρ] οὐ γάρ B 5 καί om. M¹Q αὐτοῦ MQ ἔχον om. BCD
166. 9 prius ἤ om. Q 10 ὑπερκοσμίων] ἐγκοσμίων M¹ 14 ἐλλάμ-
πουσιν· καὶ ἀμέθεκτον Q 19 ἐγκόσμιον M² 21 prius νόων MQW : θεῶν
BCDO μέσων (ω) (μέσον edd.)
167. 22 post πρώτιστος ins. νοῦς Q 24 ὑφεξῆς ap. Cr. error preli
25 τούτῳ BCDQW : τούτων [M], τοῦτο M² 26 primum ἤ] εἰ CM² 28 convertitur W 29 ἐκεῖνο M¹W : ἐκεῖνος BCDQM² ἐπέστρεφεν BCD 31 ὅς]
ὡς Q dett. ἐν ἑαυτῷ Q dett. 32 οὐ om. M primitus, add. sup. lin.
M¹ ut vid., seclusi : μή Q

are intra-mundane in the sense that they give fulfilment to the entire world-order, and that they render certain visible bodies divine. For any such body is divine not because of Soul, which is not primally divine, nor because of Intelligence—for not even the Intelligence is identical with the One—but while it owes to Soul its life and its power of self-movement, and to Intelligence its perpetual freedom from variation and the perfection of its ordered motion, it is divine not through these things but because it is unified (prop. 129); and if it has a providential office, this character is due to the same cause (prop. 120).

M. Of Intelligences.

PROP. 166. *There is both unparticipated and participated intelligence; and the latter is participated either by supra-mundane or by intra-mundane souls.*

For of the whole number of intelligences the unparticipated is sovereign, having primal existence (props. 23, 24). And of the participated intelligences some irradiate the supra-mundane and unparticipated soul, others the intra-mundane. For the intra-mundane class cannot proceed without mediation from the unparticipated Intelligence, since all procession is through like terms (prop. 29), and a class which is independent of the world-order bears more likeness to the unparticipated than one which is locally distributed. Nor, again, is the supra-mundane class the only one : but there must be intra-mundane intelligences, first, because there are intra-mundane gods (prop. 165) ; secondly, because the world-order itself is possessed of intelligence as well as of soul ; third, because intra-mundane souls must participate supra-mundane intelligences through the mediation of intelligences which are intra-mundane (prop. 109).

PROP. 167. *Every intelligence has intuitive knowledge of itself: but the primal Intelligence knows itself only, and intelligence and its object are here numerically one; whereas each subsequent intelligence knows simultaneously itself and its priors, so that its object is in part itself but in part its source.*

For any intelligence must know either itself or that which is above it or that which is consequent upon it.

If the last be true, this will mean that intelligence reverts upon its inferior. And even so it will not know the object itself, upon which it has reverted, since it is not within the object but is extraneous to it ; it can know only the impress produced upon it by the object. For it knows its own, not what is alien ; its affects, not their extraneous source.

εἰ δὲ τὸ ὑπὲρ αὐτόν, εἰ μὲν διὰ τῆς ἑαυτοῦ γνώσεως, ἑαυτὸν
ἄμα κἀκεῖνο γνώσεται· εἰ δὲ ἐκεῖνο μόνον, ἑαυτὸν ἀγνοήσει νοῦς
ὤν. ὅλως δέ, τὸ πρὸ αὐτοῦ γινώσκων, οἶδεν ἄρα ὅτι καὶ αἴτιόν
ἐστιν ἐκεῖνο, καὶ ὧν αἴτιον· εἰ γὰρ ταῦτα ἀγνοήσει, κἀκεῖνο
ἀγνοήσει τὸ τῷ εἶναι παράγον, [ἃ παράγει, καὶ] ἃ παράγει μὴ 5
γινώσκων. ὃ δὲ ὑφίστησι καὶ ὧν αἴτιον τὸ πρὸ αὐτοῦ γινώσκων,
καὶ ἑαυτὸν ἐκεῖθεν ὑποστάντα γνώσεται. πάντως ἄρα τὸ πρὸ
αὐτοῦ γινώσκων γνώσεται καὶ ἑαυτόν.

εἰ οὖν τις ἔστι νοῦς νοητός, ἐκεῖνος ἑαυτὸν εἰδὼς καὶ τὸ νοητὸν
οἶδε, νοητὸς ὤν, ὅ ἐστιν αὐτός· ἕκαστος δὲ τῶν μετ' ἐκεῖνον τὸ 10
ἐν αὐτῷ νοητὸν νοεῖ ἄμα καὶ τὸ πρὸ αὐτοῦ. ἔστιν ἄρα καὶ ἐν
τῷ νῷ νοητὸν καὶ ἐν τῷ νοητῷ νοῦς· ἀλλ' ὁ μὲν τῷ νοητῷ ὁ
αὐτός, ὁ δὲ [τῷ νοοῦντι] τῷ μὲν ἐν αὐτῷ ὁ αὐτός, τῷ πρὸ αὐτοῦ
δὲ οὐχ ὁ αὐτός· ἄλλο γάρ τὸ ἁπλῶς νοητὸν καὶ ἄλλο τὸ ἐν τῷ
νοοῦντι νοητόν. 15

168. Πᾶς νοῦς κατ' ἐνέργειαν οἶδεν ὅτι νοεῖ· καὶ οὐκ ἄλλου
μὲν ἴδιον τὸ νοεῖν, ἄλλου δὲ τὸ νοεῖν ὅτι νοεῖ.

εἰ γάρ ἐστι κατ' ἐνέργειαν νοῦς καὶ νοεῖ ἑαυτὸν οὐκ ἄλλον
ὄντα παρὰ τὸ νοούμενον, οἶδεν ἑαυτὸν καὶ ὁρᾷ ἑαυτόν. ὁρῶν δὲ
νοοῦντα καὶ ὁρῶντα γινώσκων, οἶδεν ὅτι νοῦς ἐστι κατ' ἐνέργειαν· 20
τοῦτο δὲ εἰδώς, οἶδεν ὅτι νοεῖ, καὶ οὐχ ἃ νοεῖ μόνον. ἄμα ἄρα
ἄμφω οἶδε, καὶ τὸ νοητὸν καὶ ὅτι νοεῖ ἐκεῖνο καὶ νοεῖται ὑφ'
ἑαυτοῦ νοοῦντος.

169. Πᾶς νοῦς ἐν αἰῶνι τήν τε οὐσίαν ἔχει καὶ τὴν δύναμιν
καὶ τὴν ἐνέργειαν. 25

εἰ γὰρ ἑαυτὸν νοεῖ καὶ ταὐτὸν νοῦς καὶ νοητόν, καὶ ἡ νόησις
τῷ νῷ ταὐτὸν καὶ τῷ νοητῷ· μέση γὰρ οὖσα τοῦ τε νοοῦντος καὶ
τοῦ νοουμένου, τῶν αὐτῶν ἐκείνων ὄντων, ἔσται δήπου καὶ ἡ
νόησις ἡ αὐτὴ πρὸς ἄμφω. ἀλλὰ μὴν ὅτι ἡ οὐσία τοῦ νοῦ
αἰώνιος, ⟨δῆλον⟩· ὅλη γὰρ ἄμα ἐστί. καὶ ἡ νόησις ὡσαύτως, 30

167. 3 ἄρα om. M¹QW   5 τῷ τὸ εἶναι M   prius ἃ παράγει om. M¹QW :
seclusi   καί om. Q : seclusi   μὴ om. BCD   6 prius γινώσκων] γινώσκον Q   ὃ δέ M (suprascr. τις M², unde ὃ δέ τις O Port.) QW : οἶδε τίνα BCD
alt. γινώσκων BCDMW : γινῶσκον QArg (suprascr. γινώσκων)   7 ἑαυτόν
... 8 γινώσκων om. BCD   9 τὸ νοητόν BCDArgW : τὸν νοητόν MQ
10 αὐτός M¹W : οὗτος BCDQM²   ἕκαστος ω (ἕκαστον Cr. tacite)   μετ'
ἐκεῖνον M()W : μετεχόντων BCD   13 τῷ νοοῦντι om. BCDQ : seclusi   τὸ
μέν M primitus
168. 16 ὅτι νοεῖ M¹ (ut videtur) Q, quod intelligit W : ὃ νοεῖ καὶ ὅτι νοεῖ BCD :
ὃ νοεῖ M²   17 prius τό ω (τί Cr.² errore preli)   18 ἄλλον] aliud W
19 τὸν νοούμενον M²   21 ἃ MQ : ὃ BCD : simul (= ἄμα) W   alt. νοεῖ ω
(ἐννοεῖ edd.)
169. 26–7 ταὐτόν bis ω (ταὐτό Arg Cr.)   26 ἡ om. MQ   29 ὅτι καὶ ἡ Q
τοῦ νοῦ MW : τούτου BCDQ dett.   30 δῆλον add. T. Taylor

Suppose next that it knows what is above it. If it know this through knowing itself, it will have simultaneous knowledge of the two; but if it know the higher only, it will be an intelligence ignorant of itself. There is also the general consideration, that if it know its prior it must know that this prior is a cause, and must know the effects whereof it is a cause: for if it know not these effects, its ignorance of them will involve ignorance of their cause, which produces them in virtue of its being (prop. 18). But if it know what its prior constitutes or causes, it will know itself, since it is constituted thence. Thus if it know its prior it will necessarily know itself also.

If, then, there is an intelligible Intelligence, in knowing itself, being intelligible, it knows the intelligible which is its own being; whilst each subsequent intelligence knows simultaneously the intelligible which is its own content and the prior intelligible. There is thus an intelligible in the Intelligence and an intelligence in the Intelligible; but the higher Intelligence is identical with its object, whereas the lower is identical with its own content but not with the prior Intelligible—for the unconditioned Intelligible is distinct from the intelligible in the knower.

PROP. 168. *Every intelligence in the act of intellection knows that it knows: the cognitive intelligence is not distinct from that which is conscious of the cognitive act.*

For if it is an intelligence in action and knows itself as indistinguishable from its object (prop. 167), it is aware of itself and sees itself. Further, seeing itself in the act of knowing and knowing itself in the act of seeing, it is aware of itself as an active intelligence: and being aware of this, it knows not merely *what* it knows but also *that* it knows. Thus it is simultaneously aware of the thing known, of itself as the knower, and of itself as the object of its own intellective act.

PROP. 169. *Every intelligence has its existence, its potency and its activity in eternity.*

For if it knows itself, and intelligence and its object are identical (prop. 167), then also the intellective act is identical with the intellectual subject and the intelligible object. For being intermediate between the knower and the known, if these are identical, the intellective act will naturally be identical with both. Now it is plain that the existence of intelligence is eternal, since it is a simultaneous whole (prop. 52). So also is the intellective act,

εἴπερ τῇ οὐσίᾳ ταὐτόν· εἰ γὰρ ἀκίνητος ὁ νοῦς, οὐκ ἂν ὑπὸ
χρόνου μετροῖτο οὔτε κατὰ τὸ εἶναι οὔτε κατὰ τὴν ἐνέργειαν.
τούτων δὲ ὡσαύτως ἐχόντων, καὶ ἡ δύναμις αἰώνιος.

170. Πᾶς νοῦς πάντα ἅμα νοεῖ· ἀλλ' ὁ μὲν ἀμέθεκτος ἁπλῶς
πάντα, τῶν δὲ μετ' ἐκεῖνον ἕκαστος καθ' ἓν πάντα.   5

εἰ γὰρ ἅπας νοῦς ἐν αἰῶνι τήν τε οὐσίαν ἰδρύσατο τὴν ἑαυτοῦ
καὶ ἅμα τῇ οὐσίᾳ τὴν ἐνέργειαν, πάντα ἅμα νοήσει πᾶς. εἰ
γὰρ κατὰ μέρος καὶ ἄλλο καὶ ἄλλο τῶν ἐφεξῆς, οὐκ ἐν αἰῶνι·
τὸ γὰρ ἐφεξῆς ἐν χρόνῳ πᾶν· πρότερον γὰρ καὶ ὕστερον τὸ
ἐφεξῆς, ἀλλ' οὐχ ὁμοῦ πᾶν.   10

εἰ μὲν οὖν ὁμοίως πάντα νοήσουσι πάντες, οὐ διοίσουσιν
ἀλλήλων. εἰ γὰρ ὁμοίως πάντα νοοῦσιν, ὁμοίως πάντα εἰσίν, ἃ
νοοῦσιν ὄντες· ὁμοίως δὲ πάντα ὄντες, οὐχ ὁ μὲν ἀμέθεκτος, ὁ
δὲ οὔ. ὧν γὰρ αἱ νοήσεις αἱ αὐταί, καὶ αἱ οὐσίαι, εἴπερ ἡ
νόησις ἡ ἑκάστου ταὐτὸν τῷ ἑκάστῳ εἶναι, καὶ ἕκαστος ἄμφω, 15
καὶ ἡ νόησις καὶ τὸ εἶναι.

λείπεται δὴ οὖν, εἰ μὴ ὁμοίως, ἢ ⟨μὴ⟩ πάντα νοεῖν ἕκαστον, ἀλλ'
ἕν· ἢ πλείω, μὴ πάντα δὲ ὅμως· ἢ πάντα καθ' ἕν. ἀλλὰ τὸ μὲν
μὴ πάντα νοεῖν λέγειν νοῦν ἐστι ποιεῖν ἀγνοοῦντά τι τῶν ὄντων·
οὐδὲ γὰρ μεταβήσεται καὶ νοήσει ἃ μὴ πρότερον, ἀκίνητος ὤν· 20
καὶ ἔσται ψυχῆς χείρων τῆς ἐν τῷ κινεῖσθαι πάντα νοούσης,
διὰ τὸ μένειν ἓν μόνον νοῶν.

πάντα ἄρα νοήσει καθ' ἕν (ἢ γὰρ πάντα ἢ ἓν ἢ πάντα καθ'
ἕν), τῆς νοήσεως ἀεὶ μὲν καὶ ἐν πᾶσι πάντων οὔσης, τὰ δὲ
πάντα ἑνὶ τῶν πάντων ὁριζούσης· ὥστε εἶναί τι κρατοῦν ἐν τῇ 25
νοήσει καὶ τοῖς νοουμένοις ἕν, πάντων ἅμα κατὰ τὸ ἓν νοουμέ-
νων, καὶ τοῦ ἑνὸς αὐτῷ τὰ πάντα χαρακτηρίζοντος.

169. ι εἴπερ] καὶ γάρ Q
170. 5 alt. πάντα ω (ἅπαντα Arg Cr.)   7 πᾶς. εἰ scripsi : πᾶσι MW : πάντα
BCD : τό Q   8 prius καί ω (om. edd.)   ἄλλο καί MQW : ἄλοτε BCD
τῶν] τό Q   11 οὖν] νοῦν M   πάντα [M]W : om. BCDQM²
12 πάντα (πάντες Q) νοοῦσιν, ὁμοίως ω (om. dett., edd.)   14 αἱ νοήσεις ω (αἱ om.
Arg Cr.)   αἱ οὐσίαι M¹Q: αἱ om. BCDM²   14 εἴπερ... 16 τὸ εἶναι om. D
15 τῷ ἑκάστῳ MW : τῷ ἑκάστου BC dett. : τῷ ἐκείνου Q   17 εἰ μή scripsi : ἢ
μή ω   ἢ [M]W : om. BCDQM²   μή ante πάντα inserui
18 ὅμως BCDW, in ὁμῶς mutatum M : ἅμα Q et suprascr. M   μέν om.
BC   20 οὐδὲ γὰρ μεταβήσεται καὶ νοήσει ἃ μὴ πρότερον QW et fort. [M]:
καὶ (εἰ M²) γὰρ μεταβήσεται εἰ (καὶ M²) νοεῖ οὐχ ἅμα, ἀλλὰ πρότερον καὶ ὕστερον
BCDM²   22 μένειν BCDMW : μὴ μεταβαίνειν Q : νοεῖν in mg. M² et M³
23 intelligit W   23-4 καθ' ἓν πάντα M primitus   25 εἶναι τὸ κρατοῦν
[M]W   26 κατά] καί M primitus

inasmuch as it is identical with the existence; for if intelligence is unmoved, it cannot be measured by time in respect either of its being or of its activity. (prop. 50). And if the existence and the activity of intelligence are invariable, so likewise is its potency.

PROP. 170. *Every intelligence has simultaneous, intellection of all things: but while the unparticipated Intelligence knows all unconditionally, each subsequent intelligence knows all in one especial aspect.*

For if every intelligence has its existence established in eternity, and with its existence its activity (prop. 169), each one will know all things simultaneously. For if it knew them by parts and in a distinguishable succession, it would not be in eternity : all that is successive is in time, since it involves an earlier and a later and is not a simultaneous whole (prop. 52).

If, however, all intelligences are to be alike in their manner of knowing all things, there will be no distinction between them. For what they know is themselves (prop. 167); and if they be alike in their universal knowledge they are alike in their universal being, and there could thus be no distinction between unparticipated and participated intelligence : identity of intellection comports identity of existence, inasmuch as the intellection of each is the same as its being and each intelligence is identical both with its intellection and with its being.

It remains, then, if they are not alike in their knowledge, that each knows not all things but one thing; or more than one, yet not all ; or else all things in one especial aspect. But to deny that they have intellection of all things is to assume an intelligence which is ignorant of a part of existence. For being unmoved, it cannot pass from point to point and gain knowledge of what before it did not know ; and knowing one thing alone by reason of its steadfastness, it will be inferior to Soul, which in its movement gets knowledge of all things.

Since, then, it must know all things or one or else all in one especial aspect, we shall conclude that the last is the truth : intellection embraces all things perpetually, and in all intelligences, but in each it delimits all its objects by a particular character. So that in the act of cognition and in the content known there must be some one dominant aspect, under which all things are simultaneously known and by which all are characterized for the knower.

171. Πᾶς νοῦς ἀμέριστός ἐστιν οὐσία.

εἰ γὰρ ἀμεγέθης καὶ ἀσώματος καὶ ἀκίνητος, ἀμέριστός
ἐστι. πᾶν γὰρ τὸ ὁπωσοῦν μεριστὸν ἢ κατὰ πλῆθος ἢ κατὰ
μέγεθος ἢ κατὰ τὰς ἐνεργείας ἐστὶ μεριστὸν ἐν χρόνῳ φερομέναις·
ὁ δὲ νοῦς κατὰ πάντα αἰώνιος, καὶ ἐπέκεινα σωμάτων, καὶ 5
ἥνωται τὸ ἐν αὐτῷ πλῆθος· ἀμέριστος ἄρα ἐστίν.

ὅτι μὲν οὖν ἀσώματος ὁ νοῦς, ἡ πρὸς ἑαυτὸν ἐπιστροφὴ δηλοῖ·
τῶν γὰρ σωμάτων οὐδὲν πρὸς ἑαυτὸ ἐπιστρέφεται. ὅτι δὲ
αἰώνιος, ἡ τῆς ἐνεργείας πρὸς τὴν οὐσίαν ταυτότης· οὕτω γὰρ
δέδεικται πρότερον. ὅτι δὲ ἥνωται τὸ πλῆθος, ἡ πρὸς τὰς 10
ἑνάδας τὰς θείας τοῦ νοεροῦ πλήθους συνέχεια· αἱ μὲν γάρ εἰσι
πρῶτον πλῆθος, οἱ δὲ νόες μετ᾽ ἐκείνας. εἰ οὖν καὶ πλῆθος ἅπας
νοῦς, ἀλλ᾽ ἡνωμένον πλῆθος· πρὸ γὰρ τοῦ διῃρημένου τὸ συν-
επτυγμένον καὶ ἐγγυτέρω τοῦ ἑνός.

172. Πᾶς νοῦς ἀιδίων ἐστὶ προσεχῶς καὶ ἀμεταβλήτων κατ᾽ 15
οὐσίαν ὑποστάτης.

τὸ γὰρ ἀπὸ ἀκινήτου παραγόμενον αἰτίας ἅπαν ἀμετάβλητόν
ἐστι κατὰ τὴν οὐσίαν· νοῦς δὲ ἀκίνητος, αἰώνιος πάντῃ ὢν καὶ
ἐν αἰῶνι μένων. καὶ τῷ εἶναι παράγει ἃ ἂν παράγῃ· εἰ δὲ ἀεὶ
ἔστι καὶ ὡσαύτως ἔστιν, ἀεὶ παράγει καὶ ὡσαύτως· οὐκ ἄρα 20
ποτὲ μὲν ὄντων, ποτὲ δὲ μὴ ὄντων αἴτιος, ἀλλὰ τῶν ἀεὶ ὄντων.

173. Πᾶς νοῦς νοερῶς ἐστι καὶ τὰ πρὸ αὐτοῦ καὶ τὰ μετ᾽
αὐτόν· τὰ μὲν γάρ ἐστι κατ᾽ αἰτίαν, ὅσα μετ᾽ αὐτόν, τὰ δὲ κατὰ
μέθεξιν, ὅσα πρὸ αὐτοῦ· νοῦς δὲ αὐτός ἐστι καὶ νοερὰν ἔλαχεν
οὐσίαν· κατὰ τὴν ἑαυτοῦ ἄρα ὕπαρξιν ἀφορίζει πάντα, καὶ ἃ 25
κατ᾽ αἰτίαν ἐστὶ καὶ ἃ κατὰ μέθεξιν.

καὶ γὰρ ἕκαστον, ὡς πέφυκεν, οὕτω μετέχει τῶν κρειττόνων,
ἀλλ᾽ οὐχ ὡς ἐκεῖνα ἔστιν. ἤδη γὰρ ἂν ὡσαύτως ὑπὸ πάντων
μετείχετο· μετέχει δὲ ἄλλα ἄλλως· κατὰ τὴν ἰδιότητα ἄρα τῶν
μετεχόντων καὶ δύναμιν αἱ μεθέξεις. νοερῶς ἄρα ἐν τῷ νῷ τὰ 30
πρὸ αὐτοῦ.

---

171. 1 οὐσίᾳ M   2 εἰ] ἡ D   ἀμέριστος ω (ἀμέριστον Arg Cr.)
3-4 ἢ κατὰ πλῆθος ἢ κατὰ μέγεθος ω (ἢ κ. μέγ. ἢ κ. πλ. dett., edd.)   7 ἀσώματός
ἐστιν QW   9 πρὸς τὴν οὐσίαν ταυτότης ω (ταυτότης π. τ. οὐσίαν dett.,
edd.)   11 τάς ex τῆς M   12 καί om. B   πλῆθος ἅπας] τὸ πλῆθος ἅπαν
[M]W   13 τό ω (om. dett., edd.)
172. 18 ἐστι om. M¹   αἰώνιος scripsi : αἰωνίως ω   πάντῃ B :
πάντα cett.   19 ἐν om. M   ἃ ἂν παράγῃ [M]Q, quecunque producit W :
ἃ ἂν παράγοι M² : ἃ παράγει BCD
173. 22 νοερῶς DEMW : νοερὸς BCQ dett.   24 ὅσα τὰ πρό [M]
αὐτός MQ, et ipse W : ὁ αὐτός BCD dett.   25 ἑαυτοῦ ω (αὐτοῦ Cr².)
26 καὶ ἅ ω (ὡς τά Arg Cr.)   28 ὡς ἐκεῖνα ἔστιν ω (ὡς ἐκεῖνα ἐκεῖνά ἐστιν edd.)
ἤδη scripsi : ἢ BCE : ἦ DQ : ἦ MW   30 ἄρα om. [M]   τῷ
om. [M]

PROP. 171.   *Every intelligence is an indivisible existence.*

For if it be without magnitude, body or movement, it is indivisible. ·
For whatever is in any sense divisible is so either as a manifold or
as a magnitude or else in respect of the temporal course of its
activities; but intelligence is in all respects eternal, it transcends
bodies, and its manifold content is unified : therefore intelligence is
indivisible.

That intelligence is incorporeal is shown by its reversion upon
itself (prop. 167); for bodies are incapable of such reversion
(prop. 15).   That it is eternal is shown by the identity of its activity
with its existence, as has been proved above (prop. 169).   That its
multiplicity is unified is shown by the continuity of the intellectual
manifold with the divine henads (prop. 160); for these are the first
manifold (prop. 113), upon which the intelligences are consequent,
and therefore every intelligence, though a manifold, is a unified
manifold, since the implicit exists prior to the discrete and is nearer
to the One (prop. 62).

PROP. 172.   *Every intelligence is directly constitutive of things which
are perpetual and as regards their existence invariable.*

For all products of an unmoved cause are invariable in their
existence (prop. 76); and intelligence is unmoved, being eternal in
every sense and steadfast in eternity (prop. 169).   Again, it is in
virtue of its being that intelligence gives rise to its products (prop. 26);
and if its being is perpetual and unchanging, so also is its productive
activity: therefore its effects exist not at certain times only, but
perpetually.

PROP. 173.   *Every intelligence is intellectually identical both with its
priors and with its consequents—with the latter as their cause, with
the former by participation.   But since it is itself an intelligence and
its essence is intellectual, it defines everything, both what it is as
cause and what it is by participation, according to its own substantive
character.*

For each principle participates its superiors in the measure of its
natural capacity, and not in the measure of their being.   On the
latter supposition they must be participated in the same manner by
all things, which is not the case : therefore participation varies with
the distinctive character and capacity of the participants.   In the
Intelligence, accordingly, its priors are contained intellectually.

152 THE ELEMENTS OF THEOLOGY

ἀλλὰ μὴν καὶ τὰ μετ' αὐτὸν νοερῶς ἐστιν. οὐ γὰρ ἐκ τῶν ἀποτελεσμάτων ἐστίν, οὐδὲ ἐκεῖνα ἔχει ἐν ἑαυτῷ, ἀλλὰ τὰς αἰτίας τὰς ἐκείνων· ἔστι δὲ πάντων τῷ εἶναι αἴτιος· τὸ δὲ εἶναι αὐτοῦ νοερόν· καὶ τὰ αἴτια ἄρα νοερῶς ἔχει τῶν πάντων. ὥστε πάντα νοερῶς ἐστι πᾶς νοῦς, καὶ τὰ πρὸ αὐτοῦ καὶ τὰ 5 μετ' αὐτόν. ὡς οὖν τὰ νοητὰ νοερῶς ἔχει πᾶς, οὕτω καὶ τὰ αἰσθητὰ νοερῶς.

174. Πᾶς νοῦς τῷ νοεῖν ὑφίστησι τὰ μετ' αὐτόν, καὶ ἡ ποίησις ἐν τῷ νοεῖν, καὶ ἡ νόησις ἐν τῷ ποιεῖν.

εἰ γὰρ νοητόν ἐστι καὶ νοῦς ταὐτὸν καὶ τὸ εἶναι ἑκάστου τῇ 10 νοήσει τῇ ἐν ἑαυτῷ [ταὐτόν], ποιεῖ δὲ ἃ ποιεῖ τῷ εἶναι, καὶ παράγει κατὰ τὸ εἶναι ὅ ἐστι, καὶ τῷ νοεῖν ἂν παράγοι τὰ παραγόμενα. τὸ γὰρ εἶναι καὶ τὸ νοεῖν ἐν ἄμφω· καὶ γὰρ ὁ νοῦς καὶ [πᾶν] τὸ ὂν τὸ ἐν αὐτῷ ταὐτόν. εἰ οὖν ποιεῖ τῷ εἶναι, τὸ δὲ εἶναι νοεῖν ἐστι, ποιεῖ τῷ νοεῖν. 15

καὶ ἡ νόησις ἡ κατ' ἐνέργειαν ἐν τῷ νοεῖν· τοῦτο δὲ τῷ εἶναι ταὐτόν· τὸ δὲ εἶναι ἐν τῷ ποιεῖν (τὸ γὰρ ἀκινήτως ποιοῦν τὸ εἶναι ἐν τῷ ποιεῖν ἀεὶ ἔχει)· καὶ ἡ νόησις ἄρα ἐν τῷ ποιεῖν.

175. Πᾶς νοῦς ὑπὸ τῶν κατ' οὐσίαν ἅμα καὶ ἐνέργειαν νοερῶν μετέχεται πρώτως. 20

ἀνάγκη γὰρ ἢ ὑπὸ τούτων ἢ ὑπ' ἄλλων τῶν νοερὰν μὲν ἐχόντων τὴν οὐσίαν, μὴ ἀεὶ δὲ νοούντων. ἀλλ' ὑπ' ἐκείνων ἀδύνατον. καὶ γὰρ ἡ ἐνέργεια τοῦ νοῦ ἀκίνητος· καὶ ὑφ' ὧν ἄρα μετέχεται, ταῦτα ἀεὶ νοοῦντα ἀεὶ μετέχει, τῆς νοερᾶς ἐνεργείας ἀεὶ νοερὰ τὰ μετέχοντα ποιούσης. τῷ γὰρ αἰωνίῳ 25 τῆς ἐνεργείας τὸ ἐν μέρει τινὶ τοῦ χρόνου τὴν ἐνέργειαν ἔχον ἀσύναπτον· μεταξὺ δέ, ὥσπερ ἐν ταῖς οὐσίαις, οὕτω δὴ καὶ ἐν ταῖς τῶν ἐνεργειῶν ἐξαλλαγαῖς τῆς αἰωνίου πάσης ἐνεργείας καὶ τῆς ἐν τινὶ χρόνῳ τελείας ἡ κατὰ πάντα τὸν χρόνον ἔχουσα τὸ τέλειον. οὐδαμοῦ γὰρ αἱ πρόοδοι γίνονται ἀμέσως, ἀλλὰ 30 διὰ τῶν συγγενῶν καὶ ὁμοίων κατά τε τὰς ὑποστάσεις καὶ τὰς τῶν ἐνεργειῶν τελειότητας ὡσαύτως. πᾶς ἄρα νοῦς ὑπ' ἐκείνων μετέχεται πρώτως τῶν κατὰ πάντα χρόνον νοεῖν δυναμένων καὶ ἀεὶ νοούντων, εἰ καὶ κατὰ χρόνον ἀλλὰ μὴ αἰωνίως ἡ νόησις. 35

173. 4-5 τῶν ... ἐστι om. Q   5 ἐστι [M]W : ἔχει BCDM²   6 πᾶς ω (πᾶς νοῦς ArgCr.)
174. 9 ποιεῖν] νοεῖν M primitus   10 ἑκάστου ex ἕκαστον M   11 ἐν αὐτῷ Q   ταὐτόν [M]W : om. BCDQM² : seclusi   12 κατὰ τὸ εἶναι] τῷ εἶναι Q   τῷ] τό C primitus, DQ   14 πᾶν om. M¹W : seclusi   alt. τό om Q (τῷ dett., edd.)   18 prius ποιεῖν ω (νοεῖν dett. Cr.)   ἡ om. M

But again, it is also intellectually identical with its consequents. For it is not composite of its resultants: what it contains is not the resultants but their causes. Now it is in virtue of its being that it causes all things (prop. 26); and its being is intellectual: hence it contains intellectually the causes of all things.

Thus every intelligence is all things intellectually, both its priors and its consequents: that is to say, as it contains the intelligible world intellectually, so also it contains the sensible world in the same mode.

PROP. 174. *Every intelligence gives rise to its consequents by the act of intellection: its creative activity is thinking, and its thought is creation.*

For if intelligence is identical with its object (prop. 167) and the existence of each intelligence with its thought (prop. 169), and if further it creates by existing all that it creates, and produces by virtue of being what it is (prop. 26), then it must constitute its products by the act of thought. For its existence and its intellection are one thing, since intelligence is identical with the being which is its content. If, then, it creates by existing, and its existence is thought, it creates by the act of thinking.

Again, its thought is actualized in the act of thinking, which is identical with its existence; and its existence is creation (for that which creates without movement has its existence perpetually in the creative act): therefore its thought too is creation.

PROP. 175. *Every intelligence is primarily participated by principles which are intellectual at once in their existence and in their activity.*

For if not by these, then by principles which have an intellectual existence but do not at all times exercise intellection. But this is impossible. For the activity of intelligence is without movement (prop. 169), and consequently those principles which participate it do so at all times, enjoying a perpetual intellection whereof the activity of the intelligence perpetually makes them capable. For a being which has its activity in some certain part of time is discontinuous with one whose activity is eternal: as with existences (prop. 55), so in the gradations of activity there is an intermediate degree between any activity which is eternal and one which is complete in a certain time, namely the activity which has its completion in the whole of time. For nowhere does procession take place without mediation, but always through terms which are akin and alike (prop. 29); and this holds for the grades of completeness in activities no less than for substances. Accordingly every intelligence is primarily participated by principles which are at all times capable of intellection and enjoy it perpetually, notwithstanding that they exercise it in time and not in eternity.

---

175. 24 post ὧν ins. ἡ ἐνέργεια φασίν [M]W   ἀεὶ νοοῦντα [M]QW : om.
BCDM²   25 post ἐνεργείας ins. δυνάμεις Q   29-30 τὸ τέλειον ἔχουσα Q
33 νοεῖν om. [M]

ἐκ δὴ τούτου φανερὸν ὅτι ψυχὴν ποτὲ νοοῦσαν, ποτὲ δὲ μή,
νοῦ προσεχῶς μετέχειν ἀδύνατον.

176. Πάντα τὰ νοερὰ εἴδη καὶ ἐν ἀλλήλοις εἰσὶ καὶ καθ᾽
αὐτὸ ἕκαστον.

εἰ γὰρ ἀμέριστος πᾶς νοῦς καὶ ἡνωμένον διὰ τὴν νοερὰν 5
ἀμέρειαν καὶ τὸ ἐν αὐτῷ πλῆθος, ἐν ἑνὶ πάντα ὄντα καὶ ἀμερεῖ
ἥνωται ἀλλήλοις, καὶ φοιτᾷ πάντα διὰ πάντων· εἰ δὲ ἀΰλως
ἔστι πάντα καὶ ἀσωμάτως, ἀσύγχυτά ἐστι πρὸς ἄλληλα, καὶ
χωρὶς ἕκαστον φυλάττον τὴν ἑαυτοῦ καθαρότητα μένει ὅ ἐστι.

δηλοῖ δὲ τὸ μὲν ἀσύγχυτον τῶν νοερῶν εἰδῶν ἡ τῶν ἑκάστου 10
διακεκριμένως μετεχόντων ἰδιάζουσα μέθεξις. εἰ μὴ γὰρ τὰ
μετεχόμενα διεκέκριτο καὶ ἦν χωρὶς ἀλλήλων, οὐδ᾽ ἂν τὰ μετέχοντα αὐτῶν ἑκάστου μετεῖχε διακεκριμένως, ἀλλ᾽ ἦν ἂν πολλῷ
μᾶλλον ἐν τοῖς καταδεεστέροις ἀδιάκριτος σύγχυσις, χείροσιν
οὖσι κατὰ τὴν τάξιν· πόθεν γὰρ ἂν ἐγίνετο διάκρισις, τῶν 15
ὑφιστάντων αὐτὰ καὶ τελειούντων ἀδιακρίτων ὄντων καὶ συγ-
κεχυμένων;

τὸ δὲ αὖ ἡνωμένον τῶν εἰδῶν ἡ τοῦ περιέχοντος ἀμερὴς
ὑπόστασις τεκμηριοῦται καὶ ἡ ἐνοειδὴς οὐσία. τὰ γὰρ ἐν
ἀμερεῖ καὶ ἐνοειδεῖ τὴν ὕπαρξιν ἔχοντα, ἐν τῷ αὐτῷ ἀμερίστως 20
ὄντα (πῶς γὰρ ἂν μερίσαις τὸ ἀμερὲς καὶ τὸ ἕν;), ὁμοῦ ἐστι
καὶ ἐν ἀλλήλοις, ὅλα δι᾽ ὅλων φοιτῶντα ἀδιαστάτως. οὐ γὰρ
διαστατὸν τὸ περιέχον, καὶ ὡς ἐν διαστατῷ τὸ μὲν ἐν τῳδί, τὸ δὲ
ἀλλαχοῦ, ἀλλ᾽ ἅμα ἐν τῷ ἀμερεῖ καὶ ἑνὶ πᾶν· ὥστε καὶ ἐν
ἀλλήλοις. 25

πάντα ἄρα τὰ νοερὰ εἴδη καὶ ἐν ἀλλήλοις ἐστὶν ἡνωμένως
καὶ χωρὶς ἕκαστον διακεκριμένως. εἰ δέ τις ἐπὶ ταῖσδε ταῖς
ἀποδείξεσι καὶ παραδειγμάτων δέοιτο, τὰ θεωρήματα νοείτω τὰ
ἐν μιᾷ ψυχῇ· ἃ δὴ πάντα ἐν τῇ αὐτῇ ὄντα ἀμεγέθει οὐσίᾳ καὶ
ἥνωται ἀλλήλοις (τὸ γὰρ ἀμέγεθες οὐ τοπικῶς ἔχει τὰ ἐν αὐτῷ, 30
ἀλλ᾽ ἀμερίστως καὶ ἀδιαστάτως) [καὶ ἥνωται] καὶ διακέκριται·
πάντα γὰρ εἰλικρινῶς ἡ ψυχὴ προάγει καὶ χωρὶς ἕκαστον,
μηδὲν ἐφέλκουσα ἀπὸ τῶν λοιπῶν, ἃ εἰ μὴ διεκέκριτο ἀεὶ κατὰ
τὴν ἕξιν οὐδ᾽ ἂν ἡ ἐνέργεια διέκρινε τῆς ψυχῆς.

176. 3 ἐστί Q   6 prius καί MW : om. cett.   ὄντα ω (om. edd.)
ἀμερῆ MW   7 πάντα om. BCD   8 ἐστι πάντα ω (om. O Port. : πάντα
τὰ νοερὰ εἴδη ex coni. suppl. Cr.)   ἀσύγχυτα ἔσται MW   11 εἰ μὴ γάρ
M : εἰ γὰρ μή BCDQ   15 ἐγίνετο M (ex ἐγίνετο), Q   18-19 ὑπόστασις ἀμερή
Q   19 τεκμηριοῦται BCDQM² : τεκμηριοῦνται [M]W : τεκμηριοῖ O³ in mg.,
quod malim.   20 ἐνοειδῆ B primitus, D, M primitus   21 alt. τό om. Q
23 alt. ἐν om. M¹   26 ἐστίν BCD[M]W : ἐστὶ καί QM²   27 ταῖσδε ταῖς
BD (et sic voluit M²) : ταῖς διτταῖς C : ταῖς M¹QW   31 καὶ ἥνωται om. [M]W :

Cor. From this it is apparent that a soul which exercises intellection only at certain times cannot directly participate an intelligence.

PROP. 176. *All the intellectual Forms are both implicit each in other and severally existent.*

For if every intelligence is indivisible, and through this intellectual indivisibility its manifold content is also unified (prop. 171), then all the Forms, being contained in a single intelligence devoid of parts, are united with one another, and all interpenetrate all; but if all exist immaterially and without bodies, there is no confusion among them, but each remains itself, keeping its pure distinctness uncontaminated.

That the intellectual Forms are unconfused is shown in the specific participations enjoyed by the lower principles, which may participate any Form in independence of the others. For were not the participated terms mutually distinct and separate, the participants could not enjoy each of them discriminately, but the indiscriminate confusion would exist *a fortiori* in the later principles, since they are inferior in rank : from what source could they derive discrimination, if the Forms which constitute and perfect them were indistinguishable and confused ?

On the other hand, the unity of the Forms is evidenced by the undivided substance and unitary existence of the intelligence which embraces them. For things which have their being in a unitary principle devoid of parts, existing in one same mind without division (how should you divide that which is one and without parts ?), must be together and mutually implicit, interpenetrating one another in their entirety without spatial interval. For that which contains them is not spatially extended : it does not like extended things embrace a 'here' and an 'elsewhere', but exists all together in an undivided unity. So that the Forms are also implicit each in other.

Thus all the intellectual Forms exist both in one another as a unity and also each apart in its distinctness. If in addition to the above proofs anyone should feel the need of examples, let him consider the theorems which are contained in a single soul. All these, existing in the same unextended substance, are united one to another, since the unextended embraces its content not spatially but without partition or interval. At the same time they are mutually distinct : for the soul can produce them all in their purity, bringing out each by itself and drawing forth nothing of the rest in its company ; and the soul's activity could not thus discriminate them were they not permanently discriminated in their passive state.

seclusi διακέκριται BCDQM²: διακεκριμένως [M]W   33 ἐφέλκουσα BCD dett., attrahens W : ἀφέλκουσα M : ὑφέλκουσα Q   34 ἕξιν BCDM²: μέθεξιν [M]QW

177. Πᾶς νοῦς πλήρωμα ὢν εἰδῶν, ὁ μὲν ὁλικωτέρων, ὁ δὲ μερικωτέρων ἐστὶ περιεκτικὸς εἰδῶν· καὶ οἱ μὲν ἀνωτέρω νόες ὁλικώτερον ἔχουσιν ὅσα μερικώτερον οἱ μετ᾽ αὐτούς, οἱ δὲ κατωτέρω μερικώτερον ὅσα ὁλικώτερον οἱ πρὸ αὐτῶν.

οἱ μὲν γὰρ ἀνωτέρω δυνάμεσι χρῶνται μείζοσιν, ἐνοειδέστεροι 5 τῶν δευτέρων ὄντες· οἱ δὲ κατωτέρω, πληθυνόμενοι μᾶλλον, ἐλαττοῦσι τὰς δυνάμεις ἃς ἔχουσι. τὰ γὰρ τῷ ἑνὶ συγγενέστερα, τῷ ποσῷ συνεσταλμένα, τῇ δυνάμει τὰ μετ᾽ αὐτὰ ὑπεραίρει· καὶ τὰ τοῦ ἑνὸς πορρώτερον ἔμπαλιν. δύναμιν οὖν οἱ ἀνωτέρω προστησάμενοι μείζονα, πλῆθος δὲ ἔλαττον, δι᾽ 10 ἐλαττόνων κατὰ τὸ ποσὸν εἰδῶν πλείω παράγουσι διὰ τὴν δύναμιν· οἱ δὲ μετ᾽ ἐκείνους διὰ πλειόνων ἐλάττω κατὰ τὴν τῆς δυνάμεως ἔλλειψιν. εἰ οὖν ἐκεῖνοι δι᾽ ἐλαττόνων πλείονα παράγουσιν, ὁλικώτερα τὰ ἐν αὐτοῖς εἴδη· καὶ εἰ οἵδε διὰ πλειόνων ἐλάττονα, μερικώτερα τὰ ἐν τούτοις. 15

ἐξ ὧν δὴ συμβαίνει τὰ καθ᾽ ἓν εἶδος ἐκ τῶν ὑπερτέρων ἀπογεννώμενα κατὰ πλείους ἰδέας ἐκ τῶν δευτέρων διῃρημένως παράγεσθαι, καὶ ἔμπαλιν τὰ διὰ πολλῶν καὶ διακεκριμένων ἰδεῶν ὑπὸ τῶν καταδεεστέρων παραγόμενα δι᾽ ἐλαττόνων. καὶ ὁλικωτέρων ὑπὸ τῶν ἀνωτέρω παράγεσθαι· καὶ τὸ μὲν ὅλον καὶ 20 κοινὸν πᾶσι τοῖς μετέχουσιν ἄνωθεν παραγίνεσθαι, τὸ δὲ μεμερισμένον καὶ τὸ ἴδιον ἐκ τῶν δευτέρων. ὅθεν οἱ δεύτεροι νόες ταῖς τῶν εἰδῶν μερικωτέραις διακρίσεσιν ἐπιδιαρθροῦσί πως καὶ λεπτουργοῦσι τὰς τῶν πρώτων εἰδοποιίας.

178. Πᾶν νοερὸν εἶδος ἀιδίων ἐστὶν ὑποστατικόν. 25

εἰ γὰρ αἰώνιόν ἐστι καὶ ἀκίνητον πᾶν, ἀμεταβλήτων ἐστὶ κατ᾽ οὐσίαν αἴτιον καὶ ἀιδίων ὑποστάσεων, ἀλλ᾽ οὐ γινομένων καὶ φθειρομένων· ὥστε πᾶν τὸ κατ᾽ εἶδος νοερὸν ὑποστὰν [νοερὸν] ἀίδιόν ἐστι.

καὶ γὰρ εἰ αὐτῷ τῷ εἶναι πάντα τὰ εἴδη παράγει τὰ μετ᾽ 30 αὐτά, τὸ δὲ εἶναι αὐτῶν ἀεὶ ὡσαύτως ἔχει, καὶ τὰ [παραγόμενα] ἀπ᾽ αὐτῶν ὡσαύτως ἕξει καὶ ἀίδια ἔσται. οὔτε ἄρα τὰ γενητὰ κατά τινα χρόνον ἀπ᾽ αἰτίας ὑφέστηκεν εἰδητικῆς οὔτε τὰ φθαρτά,

177. 3 ὅσα CDQM² : ὅσῳ B[M]W   4 ὅσα BCDQM² : ὅσῳ [M]W
5 ἀνώτεροι MQ   8 μετ᾽ αὐτά QArg(M¹ incert.)W : μετὰ ταῦτα BCDM²
13 ἔλλειψιν ω (ἔλλαμψιν dett., edd.)   πλείω Q   17 διῃρημένως BCDMW :
διῃρημένας Q (διῃρημένων AigCr.)   18 τά . . . διακεκριμένων] τὰ διακεκριμένα
M   19 ἰδεῶν C ex corr., QW, ἰδῶν (sic) BD : εἰδέων M   19–20 καὶ ὁλικωτέρων
ὑπὸ τῶν ω (καί et ὑπὸ τῶν om. edd.)   23 εἰδῶν [M]W : ἰδῶν BD, ἰδεῶν ex
εἰδῶν C, ἰδίων QM²
178. 29 νοερὸν om. M¹QW : seclusi   30–1 μετ᾽ αὐτά QW : μετὰ ταῦτα
cett.   31 αὐτῶν BCDQM² : αὐτό M¹ : ipso autem esse (= τῷ δὲ εἶναι αὐτῷ ?)
W   παραγόμενα QM² : om. BCDM¹W : seclusi   32 γενητά scripsi :
γεννητά BCDQ (generabilia W) : γένη τά M   33 εἰδικῆς C

PROP. 177. *Every intelligence is a complete sum of Forms, but certain of them embrace more universal and others more specific Forms ; and while the higher intelligences possess in a more universal manner all that their consequents possess more specifically, the lower also possess more specifically all that their priors have more universally.*

For the higher intelligences, being more unitary than the derivative, exercise greater powers, whereas the lower, being more advanced in plurality, thereby restrict the powers which they possess. For those principles which are more akin to the One, while their number is relatively contracted, excel their consequents in power; and of those more remote the opposite is true (prop. 62). Accordingly the higher intelligences, manifesting greater power with smaller numbers, produce in virtue of their power more effects by means of fewer Forms, while their consequents through defect of power produce fewer effects by more Forms. Now if this is so, the Forms embraced in the higher intelligences are more universal, those in the lower more specific.

From which it follows that things generated out of the superior intelligences in virtue of a single Form are produced parcelwise from the derivative intelligences in virtue of a number of Forms ; and conversely, things produced by the inferior intelligences through many distinct Forms are produced through fewer and more universal by the higher : what is general and common to all the participants comes to them from above, but the particular and peculiar quality of each species from secondary intelligences. Hence the secondary intelligences by their more specific discrimination of the Forms as it were articulate and elaborate in detail the formative work of the primals.

PROP. 178. *Every intellectual Form is constitutive of things perpetual.*

For if every such Form is eternal and unmoved, it is the cause of substances invariable in their existence and perpetual, not of things which come-to-be and perish (prop. 76): thus all that has its subsistence in virtue of an intellectual Form is perpetual.

For again, if all Forms produce their consequents in virtue of their mere existence (prop. 26), and their existence is perpetually free from variation, their products likewise will be unchanging and perpetual. Accordingly, things which have come-to-be at some point of time cannot take their subsistence from a Form as cause, nor can

ἢ φθαρτά, εἶδος ἔχει νοερὸν προϋπάρχον· ἦν γὰρ ἂν ἄφθαρτα
καὶ ἀγένητα, πρὸς ἐκεῖνα τὴν ὑπόστασιν ἔχοντα.

179. Πᾶς ὁ νοερὸς ἀριθμὸς πεπέρασται.

εἰ γὰρ ἔστι μετ' αὐτὸν ἄλλο πλῆθος κατ' οὐσίαν ὑφειμένον,
καὶ οὗτος ἐγγυτέρω τοῦ ἑνός, ἐκεῖνο δὲ πορρώτερον, τὸ δὲ ἐγγυ- 5
τέρω τοῦ ἑνὸς ἔλαττον κατὰ τὸ ποσόν, πλεῖον δὲ τὸ πορρώτερον, καὶ ὁ νοερὸς ἀριθμὸς ἐλάττων ἂν εἴη παντὸς τοῦ μετ'
αὐτὸν πλήθους. οὐκ ἄρα ἄπειρός ἐστι· πεπέρασται ἄρα τὸ
πλῆθος τῶν νόων. τὸ γὰρ τινὸς ἔλαττον οὐκ ἄπειρον, διότι τὸ
ἄπειρον οὐδενὸς ἔλαττον, ἢ ἄπειρον. 10

180. Πᾶς νοῦς ὅλος ἐστίν, ⟨οὐχ⟩ ὡς ἐκ μερῶν ὑποστάς
[ἕκαστος καὶ ἥνωται τοῖς ἄλλοις καὶ διακέκριται ἀπ' αὐτῶν],
ἀλλ' ὁ μὲν ἀμέθεκτος νοῦς ἁπλῶς ὅλος, ὡς καὶ τὰ μέρη πάντα
ὁλικῶς ἔχων ἐν ἑαυτῷ, τῶν δὲ μερικῶν ἕκαστος ὡς ἐν μέρει τὸ
ὅλον ἔχει, καὶ οὕτως πάντα ἐστὶ μερικῶς. 15

εἰ γὰρ καθ' ἓν πάντα, τὸ δὲ καθ' ἓν οὐδὲν ἄλλο ἐστὶν ἢ
μερικῶς, τὸ ἄρα ὅλον οὕτως ἐστὶν ἐν ἑκάστῳ τούτων μερικῶς,
καθ' ἕν τι τῶν μερικῶν ἐπικρατοῦν ἐν τοῖς πᾶσιν ἀφοριζόμενον.

181. Πᾶς ὁ μετεχόμενος νοῦς ἢ θεῖός ἐστιν, ὡς θεῶν ἐξημ-
μένος, ἢ νοερὸς μόνον. 20

εἰ γὰρ ἔστιν ὁ θεῖος καὶ ἀμέθεκτος νοῦς πρώτως, τούτῳ
δήπου συγγενής ἐστιν οὐχ ὁ κατ' ἀμφότερα διαφέρων, καὶ τῷ
μὴ εἶναι θεῖος καὶ τῷ μὴ ἀμέθεκτος εἶναι· τὰ γὰρ κατ' ἄμφω
ἀνόμοια ἀσύναπτα ἀλλήλοις. δῆλον δὴ οὖν ὅτι τῇ μὲν ὅμοιόν
ἐστι τῷ πρώτως ὄντι νῷ τὸ μέσον, τῇ δὲ ἀνόμοιον. ἢ οὖν ἀμέθ- 25
εκτόν ἐστι καὶ οὐ θεῖον ἢ μετεχόμενον καὶ θεῖον. ἀλλὰ πᾶν
τὸ ἀμέθεκτον θεῖον, ὡς τῷ ἑνὶ τὴν ἀνάλογον τάξιν ἐν τῷ πλήθει
λαχόν. ἔσται ἄρα τις νοῦς θεῖος ἅμα καὶ μετεχόμενος.

ἀλλὰ μὴν εἶναι δεῖ νοῦν καὶ μὴ μετέχοντα τῶν θείων ἑνάδων,
ἀλλὰ νοοῦντα μόνον· καθ' ἑκάστην γὰρ σειρὰν τὰ μὲν πρῶτα 30
καὶ τῇ ἑαυτῶν μονάδι συνημμένα μετέχειν δύναται τῶν ἐν τῇ
ὑπερκειμένῃ προσεχῶς τάξει, τὰ δὲ πολλοστὰ ἀπὸ τῆς ἀρχικῆς
μονάδος οὐχ οἷά τέ ἐστιν ἐκείνων ἐξῆφθαι.

179. 3 ὁ non agnoscit 'Ανάπτ. 196. 15   πεπέρασθαι M   4 αὐτόν (ω)
(αὐτό tacite Cr.)   5 οὗτος BCDQ: οὕτως MW unde oitus totum locum
iniuria refinxit Cr.   5-6 ἐγγύτερον Q dett.

180. 11 οὐχ inserui   11-12 ἕκαστος ὑποστάς Q   12 ἕκαστος ... αὐτῶν
seclusi   13 καί om. Q dett.   14 ὡς om. M¹W   15 ἔχει] ἄγει C
18 ἐν τοῖς πᾶσιν] ἐν τῶν πάντων Q

181. 21 τοῦτο M   22 et 23 τῷ bis M : τό cett.   25 τῷ]τό M² (om. ArgCr.)
ἦ] εἴ (sic) B, εἰ M²   25-6 ἀμέθεκτον ἔσται Q   27 τήν ω (om. Cr. tacite)
29 δεῖ ... μετέχοντα ω (om. O Port., καί om. Cr.)   30 νοοῦντα] νοῦν ὄντα
Q   31 μονάδι MQW : ἑνάδι BCD   32 τάξει προσεχῶς BCDO

things perishable, *qua* perishable, have a pre-existent intellectual
Form : for were their subsistence related to such Forms they would
be imperishable and without temporal origin.

PROP. **179**. *The entire intellectual series is finite.*

For if posterior to it there is another manifold, inferior in its mode
of being, and if the intellectual series is nearer to the One, the other
more remote, and if again that which is nearer to the One is quanti-
tatively less, the more remote greater (prop. 62), then the intellectual
series must be less in number than any subsequent manifold. It
follows that it is not infinite : that is, the number of intelligences is
limited. For that which is exceeded by another is not infinite, since
the infinite is unexceeded in that respect in which it is infinite.

PROP. **180**. *Every intelligence is a whole, though not one composite of
parts (prop. 171): whilst the unparticipated Intelligence is without
qualification a whole, as having all its parts implicit in its totality,
each of the specific intelligences contains the whole as a whole-in-the-
part, and is thus all things specifically.*

For if each is all things in one aspect (prop. 170), and 'in one
aspect' means the same thing as 'specifically', then the whole is in
this sense contained in each specifically, being delimited by some
one specific aspect which dominates the entire content of a specific
intelligence.

PROP. **181**. *Every participated intelligence is either divine, as being
linked to gods, or purely intellectual.*

For if the primal Intelligence is divine (prop. 160) and unparticipated (prop. 166), its closest kin is evidently not an intelligence
which differs from it in both regards, being neither divine nor unparticipated : for principles dissimilar in both regards are disjunct
(prop. 28). It is plain, then, that the mean term resembles the
primal Intelligence in one of these respects while differing from it
in the other : either it is unparticipated but not divine, or it is divine
but participated. But all that is unparticipated is divine, as being
endowed with that rank in its own order which is analogous to the
One (prop. 24). Accordingly there must be an intelligence which
is at once divine and participated.

But again, there must also be an intelligence which does not
participate the divine henads but merely exercises intellection : for
while the first members of any series, which are closely linked with
their own monad, can participate the corresponding members of the
immediately supra-jacent order, those which are many degrees
removed from their originative monad are incapable of being attached
to that order (prop. 110).

ἔστιν ἄρα καὶ νοῦς θεῖος καὶ νοῦς τις νοερὸς μόνον, ὁ μὲν
κατὰ τὴν ἰδιότητα τὴν νοερὰν ἱστάμενος, ἣν ἀπὸ τῆς ἑαυτοῦ
μονάδος ἔχει [καὶ τοῦ ἀμεθέκτου]· ὁ δὲ κατὰ τὴν ἕνωσιν, ἣν ἀπὸ
τῆς μετεχομένης ἑνάδος ὑπεδέξατο.

182. Πᾶς θεῖος νοῦς μετεχόμενος ὑπὸ ψυχῶν μετέχεται 5
θείων.

εἰ γὰρ ἡ μέθεξις ἐξομοιοῖ τῷ μετεχομένῳ τὸ μετέχον καὶ
συμφυὲς ἀποτελεῖ, δῆλον δὴ ὅτι θείαν εἶναι ψυχὴν ἀνάγκη τὴν
τοῦ θείου νοῦ μετέχουσαν καὶ εἰς θεῖον νοῦν ἀνηρτημένην, καὶ
διὰ μέσου τοῦ νοῦ τῆς ἐν αὐτῷ θεότητος μετέχειν. ἡ γὰρ θεότης 10
συνεξάπτει τῷ νῷ τὴν μετέχουσαν αὐτοῦ ψυχὴν καὶ συνδεῖ τῷ
θείῳ τὸ θεῖον.

183. Πᾶς νοῦς μετεχόμενος μέν, νοερὸς δὲ μόνον ὤν, μετέχεται ὑπὸ ψυχῶν οὔτε θείων οὔτε νοῦ καὶ ἀνοίας ἐν μεταβολῇ
γινομένων. 15

οὔτε γὰρ θεῖαι ψυχαί εἰσιν αἱ τοιαῦται, οὐδὲ νοῦ μετέχουσαι
⟨θείου⟩· θεῶν γὰρ αἱ ψυχαὶ διὰ νοῦ μετέχουσιν, ὡς δέδεικται
πρότερον· οὔτε [αἱ] μεταβολῆς δεκτικαί· πᾶς γὰρ νοῦς ὑπὸ τῶν
κατ' οὐσίαν ἀεὶ καὶ κατ' ἐνέργειαν νοερῶν μετέχεται (καὶ γὰρ
τοῦτο δῆλον ἐκ τῶν ἔμπροσθεν). 20

184. Πᾶσα ψυχὴ ἢ θεία ἐστίν, ἢ μεταβάλλουσα ἀπὸ νοῦ
εἰς ἄνοιαν, ἢ μεταξὺ τούτων ἀεὶ μὲν νοοῦσα, καταδεεστέρα δὲ
τῶν θείων ψυχῶν.

εἰ γὰρ ὁ μὲν θεῖος νοῦς ὑπὸ θείων μετέχεται ψυχῶν, ὁ δὲ
νοερὸς μόνον ὑπὸ τῶν μήτε θείων μήτε μεταβολῆς δεκτικῶν ἀπὸ 25
νοήσεως εἰς ἄνοιαν, εἰσὶ δὲ καὶ αἱ τοῦτο πάσχουσαι καὶ ποτὲ
μὲν νοοῦσαι, ποτὲ δὲ μή, φανερὸν ὅτι τρία γένη τῶν ψυχῶν
εἰσιν· καὶ πρῶται μὲν αἱ θεῖαι, δεύτεραι δὲ τῶν μὴ θείων αἱ
ἀεὶ νοῦ μετέχουσαι, τρίται δὲ αἱ ποτὲ μὲν εἰς νοῦν, ποτὲ δὲ εἰς
ἄνοιαν μεταβάλλουσαι. 30

181. 1 καὶ νοῦς θεῖος BCD : om. MQW   τις [M]W : om. BCDQM²
2 ἀϊδιότητα M   ἱστάμενος] an ὑφιστάμενος?   3 καὶ τοῦ ἀμεθέκτου seclusi (καί
om. Cr².)   4 ἑνάδος [M]QW : μονάδος BCDM²
182. 7 εἰ ex ἢ M   9 νοῦ om. M¹   10 θειότητος et θειότης BCD
11 αὐτοῦ] αὐτῷ CD   συνδεσμεῖ B   12 θείῳ BCDM² : θεῷ [M]QW   τὸν
θεῖον M²
183. 13 νοερῶς M primitus?   ὤν om. M¹W   17 θείου addidi ex
Nicolai coniectura   18 αἱ om. BCDM¹ : seclusi
184. Titulum περὶ ψυχῆς praebent CDEM   22 εἰς MQ : πρός BCD   μὲν
νοοῦσα QW : μένουσα cett.   28 εἰσιν om. Q   μή om. Q

Thus there is both a divine intelligence and a kind which is purely intellectual, the latter arising in virtue of the distinctive power of intellection which it derives from its own monad, the former in virtue of the unity imposed by the henad which it participates.

PROP. 182. *Every participated divine intelligence is participated by divine souls.*

For if participation assimilates the participant to the participated principle and causes it to have the same nature, it is plain that a soul which participates and is annexed to a divine intelligence is itself divine, participating through the mediation of the intelligence the divinity immanent therein. For that divinity is co-operative in linking the participant soul to the intelligence and thus binding the divine to the divine (prop. 56).

PROP. 183. *Every intelligence which is participated but purely intellectual is participated by souls which are neither divine nor yet subject to the alternation of intelligence with unintelligence.*

For this order of souls cannot be divine, since they do not participate a divine intelligence, and it is through an intelligence that souls participate the gods, as has been shown above (prop. 129). Nor, on the other hand, can they admit of change: for every intelligence is participated by principles perpetually intellectual both in their existence and in their activity—this again is plain from what has been said earlier (prop. 175).

N. OF SOULS.

PROP. 184. *Every soul is either divine, or subject to change from intelligence to unintelligence, or else intermediate between these orders, enjoying perpetual intellection although inferior to the divine souls.*

For if the divine intelligence is participated by divine souls (prop. 182), and the purely intellectual by souls which are not divine yet do not admit of change from intellection to unintelligence (prop. 183), and if there are also souls subject to such change and exercising intellection intermittently (prop. 63), it is apparent that there are three orders of souls: first the divine, then such of the remainder as perpetually participate intelligence, and third those which change now to intelligence and again to unintelligence.

162   THE ELEMENTS OF THEOLOGY

185. Πᾶσαι μὲν αἱ θεῖαι ψυχαὶ θεοί εἰσι ψυχικῶς, πᾶσαι δὲ
αἱ τοῦ νοεροῦ μετέχουσαι νοῦ θεῶν ὀπαδοὶ ἀεί, πᾶσαι δὲ αἱ
μεταβολῆς δεκτικαὶ θεῶν ὀπαδοὶ ποτέ.

εἰ γὰρ αἱ μὲν ἔχουσι τὸ θεῖον φῶς ἄνωθεν ἐπιλάμπον, αἱ δὲ
ἀεὶ νοοῦσιν, αἱ δὲ ποτὲ ταύτης μεταλαγχάνουσι τῆς τελειότητος, 5
αἱ μὲν ἐν τῷ πλήθει τῶν ψυχῶν ἀνάλογον ἵστανται θεοῖς· αἱ
δὲ ἀεὶ συνέπονται θεοῖς, κατὰ νοῦν ἐνεργοῦσαι ἀεί, καὶ τῶν θείων
ἐξήρτηνται ψυχῶν, τοῦτον ἔχουσαι πρὸς αὐτὰς λόγον, ὃν τὸ
νοερὸν πρὸς τὸ θεῖον· αἱ δὲ ποτὲ νοοῦσαι καὶ ἕπονται ποτὲ θεοῖς,
οὔτε νοῦ μετέχειν ἀεὶ ὡσαύτως οὔτε ταῖς θείαις συνεπιστρέφεσθαι 10
ψυχαῖς ἀεὶ δυνάμεναι (τὸ γὰρ ποτὲ νοῦ μεταλαγχάνον οὐδεμία
μηχανὴ τοῖς θεοῖς ἀεὶ συνάπτεσθαι).

186. Πᾶσα ψυχὴ ἀσώματός ἐστιν οὐσία καὶ χωριστὴ
σώματος.

εἰ γὰρ γινώσκει ἑαυτήν, πᾶν δὲ τὸ ἑαυτὸ γινῶσκον πρὸς 15
ἑαυτὸ ἐπιστρέφεται, τὸ δὲ πρὸς ἑαυτὸ ἐπιστρέφον οὔτε σῶμά
ἐστι (πᾶν γὰρ σῶμα πρὸς ἑαυτὸ ἀνεπίστροφον) οὔτε σώματος
ἀχώριστον (καὶ γὰρ τὸ σώματος ἀχώριστον οὐ πέφυκε πρὸς
ἑαυτὸ ἐπιστρέφειν· χωρίζοιτο γὰρ ἂν ταύτῃ σώματος), ἡ ἄρα
ψυχὴ οὔτε σωματική ἐστιν οὐσία οὔτε σώματος ἀχώριστος. 20
ἀλλὰ μὴν ὅτι γινώσκει ἑαυτήν, φανερόν· εἰ γὰρ καὶ τὰ ὑπὲρ
αὐτὴν γινώσκει, καὶ ἑαυτὴν πέφυκε γινώσκειν πολλῷ μειζόνως,
ἀπ' αἰτίων τῶν πρὸ αὐτῆς γινώσκουσα ἑαυτήν.

187. Πᾶσα ψυχὴ ἀνώλεθρός ἐστι καὶ ἄφθαρτος.

πᾶν γὰρ τὸ ὁπωσοῦν διαλύεσθαι καὶ ἀπόλλυσθαι δυνάμενον 25
ἢ σωματικόν ἐστι καὶ σύνθετον ἢ ἐν ὑποκειμένῳ τὴν ὑπόστασιν
ἔλαχε· καὶ τὸ μὲν διαλυόμενον, ὡς ἐκ πολλῶν ὑπάρχον, φθεί-
ρεται· τὸ δὲ ἐν ἑτέρῳ εἶναι πεφυκὸς τοῦ ὑποκειμένου χωριζό-
μενον ἀφανίζεται εἰς τὸ μὴ ὄν. ἀλλὰ μὴν ἡ ψυχὴ καὶ ἀσώματός ἐστι καὶ ἔξω παντὸς ὑποκειμένου, ἐν ἑαυτῇ οὖσα καὶ 30
πρὸς ἑαυτὴν ἐπιστρέφουσα. ἀνώλεθρος ἄρα ἐστὶ καὶ ἄφθαρτος.

185. 1 αἱ θεῖαι ψυχαί M¹QW : ψυχαὶ θεῖαι BCD, ψυχαί M²   2 μετέχουσαι
νοῦ om. BCD   2 et 3 ὀπαδοί bis DQ   2 δέ om. M primitus   5 ante
ταύτης in M parva rasura   8 ante λόγον in M parva rasura, ubi fort. scriptum
erat τόν   9 νοοῦσαι] ἐνεργοῦσαι Q ex corr.   alt. ποτέ ω (om. Port. Cr¹.)
τοῖς θεοῖς Q   12 τοῖς ω (om. edd.)   θείοις C
186. 16 σῶμα] σώματος M²   17 ἀνεπίστροφον πρὸς ἑαυτό BCDO   18-19
πρὸς αὐτό M¹   19 ἡ [M]QW : πᾶσα BCDM²   21-2 τὰ ὑπὲρ ἑαυτήν M
23 ante ἀπ' αἰτίων fort. inserendum ὡς (tanquam W)   πρὸ ἑαυτῆς Q
187. 31 ἀνώλεθρός ἐστιν ἄρα BCDO

PROP. 185. *All divine souls are gods upon the psychic level; all those which participate the intellectual intelligence are perpetually attendant upon gods; all those which admit of change are at certain times attendant upon gods.*

For if some souls have the divine light illuminating them from above, while others have perpetual intellection, and others again participate this perfection at certain times (prop. 184), then the first order occupy a station in the psychic series analogous to that of gods; the second, having an intellectual activity at all times, are at all times in the company of gods, and are linked to the divine souls, bearing that relation to them which the intellectual has to the divine; and those which enjoy intermittent intellection are intermittently in the company of gods, being unable perpetually and without change to participate intelligence or perpetually to consort with the divine souls—for that which shares in intelligence at certain times only has no means to be conjoined perpetually with the gods.

PROP. 186. *Every soul is an incorporeal substance and separable from body.*

For if it know itself, and if whatever knows itself reverts upon itself (prop. 83), and what reverts upon itself is neither body (since no body is capable of this activity [prop. 15]) nor inseparable from body (since, again, what is inseparable from body is incapable of reversion upon itself, which would involve separation [prop. 16]), it will follow that soul is neither a corporeal substance nor inseparable from body. But that it knows itself is apparent: for if it has knowledge of principles superior to itself, it is capable *a fortiori* of knowing itself, deriving self-knowledge from its knowledge of the causes prior to it.

PROP. 187. *Every soul is indestructible and imperishable*

For all that is capable of being in any way dissolved or destroyed either is corporeal and composite or has its being in a substrate: the former kind, being made up of a plurality of elements, perishes by dissolution, while the latter, being capable of existence only in something other than itself, vanishes into non-existence when severed from its substrate (prop. 48). But the soul is both incorporeal and independent of any substrate, existing in itself and reverting upon itself (prop. 186). It is therefore indestructible and imperishable.

188. Πᾶσα ψυχὴ καὶ ζωή ἐστι καὶ ζῶν.

ᾧ γὰρ ἂν παραγένηται ψυχή, τοῦτο ζῇ ἐξ ἀνάγκης· καὶ τὸ ψυχῆς ἐστερημένον ζωῆς εὐθὺς ἄμοιρον ἀπολείπεται. ἢ οὖν διὰ ψυχὴν ζῇ, ἢ δι' ἄλλο τι καὶ οὐ διὰ ψυχήν. ἀλλὰ δι' ἄλλο τι μόνον, ἀδύνατον. πᾶν γὰρ τὸ μετεχόμενον ἢ ἑαυτὸ ἢ ἑαυτοῦ 5 τι τῷ μετέχοντι δίδωσι, μηδέτερον δὲ παρέχον, οὐδ' ἂν μετέχοιτο· ψυχὴ δὲ μετέχεται ὑπ' ἐκείνου, ᾧ ἂν παρῇ, καὶ ἔμψυχον ἐκεῖνο λέγεται τὸ ψυχῆς μετέχον.

εἰ οὖν ζωὴν ἐπιφέρει τοῖς ἐμψύχοις, ἢ ζωή ἐστιν ἢ ζῶν μόνον ἢ τὸ συνάμφω, ζωὴ ἅμα καὶ ζῶν. ἀλλ' εἰ μὲν ζῶν μόνον, 10 οὐκέτι δὲ ζωή, ἔσται ἐκ ζωῆς καὶ μὴ ζωῆς· οὐκ ἄρα γινώσκει ἑαυτὴν οὐδὲ ἐπιστρέφεται πρὸς ἑαυτήν· ζωὴ γὰρ ἡ γνῶσις, καὶ τὸ γνωστικόν, ᾗ τοιοῦτον, ζῇ· εἰ οὖν τι ἐν αὐτῇ ἄζων ἐστί, τοῦτο οὐκ ἔχει καθ' αὑτὸ τὴν τοῦ γινώσκειν δύναμιν.

εἰ δὲ ζωὴ μόνον ἐστίν, οὐκέτι μεθέξει τῆς νοερᾶς ζωῆς. τὸ 15 γὰρ ζωῆς μετέχον ζῶν ἐστι καὶ οὐ ζωὴ μόνον· ζωὴ γὰρ μόνον ἡ πρώτη καὶ ἀμέθεκτος, ἡ δὲ μετ' ἐκείνην ζῶν ἅμα καὶ ζωή· ψυχὴ δὲ οὐκ ἔστιν ἡ ἀμέθεκτος ζωή. ἅμα ἄρα ζωή ἐστι καὶ ζῶν ἡ ψυχή.

189. Πᾶσα ψυχὴ αὐτόζως ἐστίν.   20

εἰ γὰρ ἐπιστρεπτικὴ πρὸς ἑαυτήν, τὸ δὲ πρὸς ἑαυτὸ ἐπι-στρεπτικὸν πᾶν αὐθυπόστατον, καὶ ἡ ψυχὴ ἄρα αὐθυπόστατος καὶ ἑαυτὴν ὑφίστησιν. ἀλλὰ μὴν καὶ ζωή ἐστι καὶ ζῶν, καὶ ἡ ὕπαρξις αὐτῆς κατὰ τὸ ζωτικόν· καὶ γὰρ οἷς ἂν παρῇ ζωῆς μεταδίδωσιν αὐτῷ τῷ εἶναι, κἂν ᾖ τὸ μετέχον ἐπιτήδειον, εὐθὺς 25 ἔμψυχον γίνεται καὶ ζῶν, οὐ λογισαμένης τῆς ψυχῆς καὶ προελο-μένης, οὐδὲ λογισμῷ καὶ κρίσει ζωοποιούσης, ἀλλ' αὐτῷ τῷ εἶναι ὅ ἐστι τὴν ζωὴν τῷ μεθεκτικῷ χορηγούσης. τὸ ἄρα εἶναι αὐτῆς ταὐτὸν τῷ ζῆν. εἰ οὖν τὸ εἶναι παρ' ἑαυτῆς ἔχει, τοῦτο δὲ τῷ ζῆν ταὐτὸν καὶ ἔχει κατ' οὐσίαν τὸ ζῆν, καὶ τὴν ζωὴν ἂν ἑαυτῇ 30 παρέχοι καὶ παρ' ἑαυτῆς ἔχοι. εἰ δὲ τοῦτο, αὐτόζως ἂν εἴη ἡ ψυχή.

188. 2–3 τὸ τῆς ψυχῆς Q et fort. M¹   4 post ἢ ins. οὐ Q et fort. M¹
6 παρέχον Q : πάσχον cett. W   8 τὸ ψυχῆς μετέχον M¹ : τὸ τῆς ψ.
μετέχον BCDM² : τῷ ψ. μετέχειν Q   9 εἰ QW : ἢ BCD : ἦ M   12 οὐδέ
M¹ : οὔτε cett.   13 ζῇ BCDMW : ζωή Q (ζῶν edd.)   16 οὐ om. B
primitus, D   ζωὴ γὰρ μόνον om. M (γάρ post prius ζωή ins. M²)   17 μετ'
ἐκείνη (sic) M   ζωὴ ἅμα καὶ ζῶν Q
189. 20 αὐτόζως hic et ubique BCD : αὐτόζωος saepius M¹, ubique Q   ἐστίν
om. Q   23 καὶ ἡ ζωή [M]   24 αὐτοῦ [M]   25 εὐθύς om. Q
26 γίνεται] ἐστί Q   28 μεθεκτικῷ BCDM² : μεθεκτῷ [M]Q   τὸ ἄρα] τοῦ
[M]   29 τό] τῷ MD   alt. τῷ] τό CM   31 καὶ παρ' ἑαυτῆς ἔχοι om. Q,
idem voluisse videtur M²

PROP. **188.** *Every soul is at once a principle of life and a living thing.*

For that into which soul enters necessarily lives, and when a body is deprived of soul it is thereupon left lifeless. Now its life is due either to soul or to some other cause and not to soul. But that it should be wholly due to some other cause is impossible. For any participated principle gives to the participant either itself or some part of itself: unless it furnished one or the other, it would not be participated. Now soul is participated by that in which it is present, and we call 'ensouled' or animate that which participates a soul.

If, then, it bestows life upon animate bodies, soul is either a principle of life or simply a living thing or else both together, at once a principle of life and a living thing. But if it be simply a living thing and fall short of being a principle of life, it will be composite of life and not-life: upon which supposition it cannot know itself or revert upon itself. For cognition is a kind of life, and the cognitive is as such alive. If, therefore, soul contain a lifeless element, this element has in itself no cognitive faculty.

And if it be purely a principle of life, it will no longer participate the life of intelligence. For that which participates life is a living thing, and not purely a principle of life: the pure principle is the first and unparticipated Life (prop. 101), while that which is consequent upon it is not only a principle of life but a living thing. Now the unparticipated Life is not a soul. Therefore soul is at once a principle of life and a living thing.

PROP. **189.** *Every soul is self-animated (or has life in its own right).*

For if it is capable of reversion upon itself (prop. 186), and all that is capable of such reversion is self-constituted (prop. 43), then soul is self-constituted and the cause of its own being. But again, soul is both a principle of life and a living thing (prop. 188), and its essential character is vitality; for where it is present it communicates life by its mere being, and the participant, if it be fit for the reception, straightway becomes ensouled and alive; the soul does not calculate or choose, nor is it in consequence of any calculation or judgement that it animates the body, but simply through being what it is it endows with life that which is adapted to participate it (prop. 26). Its being, therefore, is being alive. If, then, its being is self-derived, and this being is the being alive which is its essential character, its life too must be self-furnished and self-derived. That is, soul must be self-animated.

190. Πᾶσα ψυχὴ μέση τῶν ἀμερίστων ἐστὶ καὶ τῶν περὶ τοῖς σώμασι μεριστῶν.

εἰ γὰρ αὐτόζως ἐστὶ καὶ αὐθυπόστατος καὶ χωριστὴν ἔχει σωμάτων τὴν ὕπαρξιν, ἐξήρηται κρείττων οὖσα τῶν μεριστῶν πάντων περὶ τοῖς σώμασιν· ἐκεῖνα γὰρ ἀχώριστα πάντῃ τῶν 5 ὑποκειμένων ἐστί, συμμερισθέντα τοῖς μεριστοῖς ὄγκοις, καὶ ἑαυτῶν μὲν ἐκστάντα καὶ τῆς ἑαυτῶν ἀμερείας συνδιαστάντα δὲ τοῖς σώμασι, κἂν ἐν ζωαῖς ὑφεστήκῃ, οὐχ ἑαυτῶν ζωαὶ ὄντα, ἀλλὰ τῶν μετασχόντων, κἂν ἐν οὐσίᾳ καὶ ἐν εἴδεσιν ὑπάρχῃ, οὐχ ἑαυτῶν ὄντα εἴδη, ἀλλὰ τῶν εἰδοπεποιημένων. 10

εἰ δὲ μὴ ταῦτα μόνον ἐστὶν ἡ ψυχή, οὐσία αὐθυπόστατος καὶ ζωὴ αὐτόζως καὶ γνῶσις ἑαυτῆς γνωστική, καὶ χωριστὴ κατὰ πάντα ταῦτα σωμάτων, ἀλλὰ καὶ μετέχον ζωῆς, εἰ δὲ τοῦτο, καὶ οὐσίας μετέχον, μετέχει δὲ καὶ γνώσεως ἀπ' ἄλλων αἰτίων, δῆλον δὴ ὅτι καταδεεστέρα τῶν ἀμερίστων ἐστίν. ὅτι μὲν οὖν 15 ζωῆς ἀλλαχόθεν πληροῦται (ἀλλὰ καὶ οὐσίας, εἴπερ καὶ ζωῆς), δῆλον· πρὸ γὰρ ψυχῆς καὶ ἡ ἀμέθεκτος ζωὴ καὶ ἡ ἀμέθεκτος οὐσία. ὅτι δὲ καὶ τὸ πρώτως γνωστικὸν οὐκ ἔστι, φανερόν, εἴπερ καθὸ μὲν ψυχή, πᾶσα ζῇ, οὐ καθὸ δὲ ψυχή, πᾶσα γνῶσιν ἔχει· καὶ γὰρ ἀγνοεῖ τὰ ὄντα ψυχή τις μένουσα ψυχή. οὐκ 20 ἄρα πρώτως ἐστὶ γνωστικόν, οὐδὲ αὐτῷ τῷ εἶναι γνῶσίς ἐστι. δευτέραν ἄρα τὴν οὐσίαν ἔχει τῶν πρώτως καὶ αὐτῷ τῷ εἶναι γνωστικῶν. ἐπεὶ δὲ ταύτης τὸ εἶναι διῄρηται τῆς γνώσεως, οὐκ ἄρα τῶν ἀμερίστων ἐστὶν ἡ ψυχή. δέδεικται δὲ ὅτι οὐδὲ τῶν περὶ τοῖς σώμασι μεριστῶν. μέση ἄρα ἀμφοτέρων ἐστίν. 25

191. Πᾶσα ψυχὴ μεθεκτὴ τὴν μὲν οὐσίαν αἰώνιον ἔχει, τὴν δὲ ἐνέργειαν κατὰ χρόνον.

ἢ γὰρ ἄμφω αἰωνίως ἕξει, ἢ ἄμφω κατὰ χρόνον, ἢ τὸ μὲν αἰωνίως, τὸ δὲ κατὰ χρόνον. ἀλλ' οὔτε ἄμφω αἰωνίως (ἔσται γὰρ ἀμέριστος οὐσία, καὶ οὐδὲν διοίσει τῆς νοερᾶς ὑποστάσεως 30 ἡ ψυχῆς φύσις, τῆς ἀκινήτου ἢ αὐτοκίνητος) οὔτε ἄμφω κατὰ

190. 1-2 περὶ τὰ σώματα Arg (item ll. 5, 25) cum Platone, sed cf. in Tim. II. 255. 6, Th. Pl. p. 33 etc.   5 πάντῃ] πάντα M primitus   6 μεριστοῖς om. BCD 7 μέν om. M primitus   συνδιαστάντα τὰ δέ M   8 σώμασι] ἀσωμάτοις [M] ὑφεστήκῃ M⁴: ὑφεστήκοι BCD[M]: ὑφεστήκει QM²   ἑαυτῶν] αἱ αὐτῶν B primitus, C   9 μετεχόντων Q   ἐν οὐσίᾳ BCDQM²: οὐσίαι M¹W   καὶ MQW: κἂν BCD   ὑπάρχῃ BCD: ὑπάρξεις [M]W, ὑπάρξῃ QM²   10 ὄντα εἴδη ex corr. M²   12 alt. καί ω (om. Cr².)   13 ταῦτα om. Q   μετέχει Q   14 μετέχον] μετέχοι Q   ὑπ' ἄλλων Q   15 οὖν om. CM 16 ἀλλά om. MW   καί ante ζωῆς om. BCD dett.   17 ψυχῆς] ζωῆς M prius καί ω (om. Cr.)   18 τό om. Q   γνωστικόν BCDQ: ζωτικόν MW 19 ζῇ W et fort. M¹: ζωή BCDQM²   20 γάρ om. BCD   23 τὸ εἶναι om. M (τῷ εἶναι O edd.)   24 οὐδὲ τῶν BCDM, neque eorum W: μηδὲ τῶν Q (οὐδέπω edd.)   25 ἐστὶν ἀμφοτέρων Q 191. 30 οὐδέν] οὐ [M]   31 καὶ τῆς ἀκινήτου W ut videtur

PROP. 190. *Every soul is intermediate between the indivisible principles and those which are divided in association with bodies.*

For if it is self-animated and self-constituted (prop. 189) and has an existence separable from bodies (prop. 186), it is superior to all principles which are divided in association with bodies, and transcends them. For such principles are wholly inseparable from their substrates: they are partitioned together with the partitioned bulk, and falling away from their own nature, which is without parts, they are infected by corporeal extension; if they be of the order of vital principles, they belong as life-principles not to themselves but to their participants; if they be of the order of Being and the Forms, they belong as forms not to themselves but to that which they inform.

But on the other hand, if besides being these things, a self-constituted substance, a self-animated life, a self-cognitive knowledge, and on all these grounds separable from bodies, the soul be also something which has life, and consequently being, by participation, and knowledge too by participation of causes distinct from itself, it will then plainly be inferior to the indivisible principles. Now it is evident that it draws its life, and consequently its being, from a source other than itself; for prior to soul there is both an unparticipated Life and an unparticipated Being (prop. 101). Again, that it is not the first cognitive principle is apparent, since whereas every soul *qua* soul is alive (prop. 189), not every soul *qua* soul has knowledge: there are souls ignorant of reality which yet remain souls. Soul, then, is not the first cognitive principle, nor is it by its mere existence knowledge. Its existence, therefore, is secondary to those principles which are cognitive primally and in virtue of their being. And since in soul existence is distinct from knowledge, it cannot rank with the indivisible principles. But it has been shown that equally it does not rank with those which are divided in association with bodies. Therefore it is betwixt the two.

PROP. 191. *Every participated soul has an eternal existence but a temporal activity.*

For either it will have both its existence and its activity in eternity, or both in time, or else one in eternity and the other in time. But it cannot have both in eternity: otherwise it will be undivided Being, and there will be nothing to distinguish the psychic nature from intellectual substance, the self-moved principle from the unmoved (prop. 20). Nor can it have both in time: otherwise it will be

χρόνον· εἴη γὰρ ἂν γενητὴ μόνον καὶ οὔτε αὐτόζως οὔτε αὐθ-
υπόστατος· οὐδὲν γὰρ τῶν ὑπὸ χρόνου κατ᾽ οὐσίαν μετρουμένων
αὐθυπόστατον. ἡ δὲ ψυχὴ αὐθυπόστατος· τὸ γὰρ κατ᾽ ἐνέργειαν πρὸς ἑαυτὸ ἐπιστρέφον καὶ κατ᾽. οὐσίαν ἐπιστρεπτικόν
ἐστι πρὸς ἑαυτὸ καὶ ἀφ᾽ ἑαυτοῦ προϊόν.   5
λείπεται ἄρα τῇ μὲν αἰώνιον εἶναι ψυχὴν πᾶσαν, τῇ δὲ
χρόνου μετέχουσαν. ἢ οὖν κατ᾽ οὐσίαν αἰώνιός ἐστι, κατ᾽ ἐνέργειαν δὲ χρόνου μέτοχος· ἢ ἔμπαλιν. ἀλλὰ τοῦτο ἀδύνατον.
πᾶσα ἄρα ψυχὴ μεθεκτὴ τὴν μὲν οὐσίαν αἰώνιον ἔλαχε, τὴν δὲ
ἐνέργειαν κατὰ χρόνον.   10

192. Πᾶσα ψυχὴ μεθεκτὴ τῶν τε ἀεὶ ὄντων ἐστὶ καὶ πρώτη
τῶν γενητῶν.

εἰ γὰρ αἰώνιός ἐστι κατ᾽ οὐσίαν, ὄντως ὄν ἐστι κατὰ τὴν
ὕπαρξιν καὶ ἀεὶ ὄν· τὸ γὰρ αἰῶνος μετέχον τοῦ ἀεὶ εἶναι μετείληφεν. εἰ δὲ κατὰ τὴν ἐνέργειάν ἐστιν ἐν χρόνῳ, γενητή ἐστι· 15
πᾶν γὰρ τὸ χρόνου μετέχον, γινόμενον ἀεὶ κατὰ τὸ πρότερον καὶ
ὕστερον τοῦ χρόνου καὶ οὐχὶ ἅμα ὅ ἐστιν ὂν ὅλον, γενητόν ἐστιν.
εἰ δέ πῃ γενητή ἐστι πᾶσα ψυχή, κατ᾽ ἐνέργειαν, πρώτη ἂν εἴη
τῶν γενητῶν· τὸ γὰρ πάντῃ γενητὸν πορρωτέρω τῶν αἰωνίων.

193. Πᾶσα ψυχὴ προσεχῶς ἀπὸ νοῦ ὑφέστηκεν.   20

εἰ γὰρ ἀμετάβλητον ἔχει τὴν οὐσίαν καὶ αἰώνιον, ἀπὸ
ἀκινήτου πρόεισιν αἰτίας· τὸ γὰρ ἀπὸ κινουμένης προϊὸν αἰτίας
πᾶν μεταβάλλει κατὰ τὴν οὐσίαν. ἀκίνητον ἄρα τὸ τῆς ψυχῆς
πάσης αἴτιον. εἰ δὲ προσεχῶς ὑπὸ νοῦ τελειοῦται, καὶ ἐπιστρέφεται πρὸς νοῦν· καὶ εἰ μετέχει τῆς γνώσεως, ἣν ὁ νοῦς 25
δίδωσι τοῖς μετέχειν δυναμένοις (πᾶσα γὰρ γνῶσις ἀπὸ νοῦ
πᾶσίν ἐστιν, οἷς ἐστιν), εἰς ὃ δὲ πάντα ἐπιστρέφεται κατὰ
φύσιν, ἀπὸ τούτου καὶ τὴν πρόοδον ἔχει κατ᾽ οὐσίαν, πᾶσα
ἄρα ψυχὴ ἀπὸ νοῦ πρόεισιν.

194. Πᾶσα ψυχὴ πάντα ἔχει τὰ εἴδη, ἃ ὁ νοῦς πρώτως ἔχει. 30

εἰ γὰρ ἀπὸ νοῦ πρόεισι καὶ νοῦς ὑποστάτης ψυχῆς, καὶ
αὐτῷ τῷ εἶναι ἀκίνητος ὢν πάντα ὁ νοῦς παράγει, δώσει καὶ τῇ
ψυχῇ τῇ ὑφισταμένῃ τῶν ἐν αὐτῷ πάντων οὐσιώδεις λόγους·

191. 1 τὸν χρόνον Q   2 μετρουμένων κατ᾽ οὐσίαν BCD dett.   9 μεθεκτή om. MW
192. 11 τε M¹ : om. cett.   ἀεὶ ω (om. O Port. : post ἀεὶ ex Taylori
versione sine libris intulit καὶ ὄντως Cr¹., καὶ Cr².)   πρώτη BCDM² cf.
infra l. 18 : πρῶτον M¹ : προτέρα Q, ante W   14 ὄν om. W   ὄν· τὸ γὰρ
αἰῶνος] ὄντων αἰωνίως [M]   15 τὴν ω (om. edd.)   18 κατ᾽ ἐνέργειαν fort.
secludendum   πρώτη] προτέρα Q (sed 'prima' W)
193. 22 prius αἰτίας [M]QW : οὐσίας BCDM²   προιών BD   alt. αἰτίας
[M]W : οὐσίας BCDQM²   23 πᾶν scripsi : πάντα ω (cf. p. 42, l. 23)   τῆς ω (om.
edd.)   24-5 καὶ ἐπιστρέφεται] ἐπιστρέφει Q   27 alt. ἐστιν M¹ ut videtur, W:

purely a thing of process, and neither self-animated nor self-constituted; for nothing which is measured by time in respect of its
existence is self-constituted (prop. 51). But the soul is self-constituted; for that which reverts upon itself in its activity is also self-
reversive in respect of its existence (prop. 44), that is, it proceeds
from itself as cause (prop. 43).

Accordingly it remains that every soul must be eternal in one
regard and participate time in the other. Either, then, it is eternal
in respect of its existence and participates time in respect of its
activity, or the reverse. But the latter is impossible. Therefore
every participated soul is endowed with an eternal existence but
a temporal activity.

PROP. 192. *Every participated soul is of the order of things which
perpetually are and is also the first of the things of process.*

For if it is eternal in its existence (prop. 191), its substance is true
Being (prop. 87), and is perpetually; for that which participates
eternity shares in perpetuity of being. And if it is in time as regards
its activity (prop. 191), it is a thing of temporal process; for whatever
participates time, perpetually coming-to-be in a temporal order of
events and not being simultaneously the whole of what it is, is a
thing of process (prop. 50). But if every soul is a thing of process
in one aspect only, namely its activity, it must have primacy among
such things; for that which belongs wholly to the temporal process
is more remote from the eternal principles.

PROP. 193. *Every soul takes its proximate origin from an intelligence.*

For if it has an invariable and eternal existence (prop. 191), it
proceeds from an unmoved cause, since all that proceeds from
a mobile cause is variable in its existence (prop. 76). The cause of
all soul, then, is unmoved. And if the proximate source of its
perfection is an intelligence, it reverts upon an intelligence. Now if
it participates the cognitive faculty which intelligence gives to
principles capable of participating it (for all cognitive faculty is
derived by its possessors from an intelligence), and if all things
proceed in respect of their existence from that upon which they
naturally revert (prop. 34), it follows that every soul proceeds from
an intelligence.

PROP. 194. *Every soul possesses all the Forms which intelligence
possesses primitively.*

For if soul proceeds from intelligence and has intelligence as its
originative principle (prop. 193), and intelligence being unmoved
produces all things by its mere existence (prop. 26), then it will give
to the soul which arises from it, as part of that soul's being, rational

ἐστι νοῦς BCDQM² (ἐστι, καί edd.)

194. 30 καὶ ἃ BD (C incert. propter lituram fortuitam)   ὁ om. Q   alt.
ἔχει om. Q   31 ὁ ὑποστάτης M   32 πάντη Q   καί MW : om. BCDQ

πᾶν γὰρ τὸ τῷ εἶναι ποιοῦν, ὅ ἐστι πρώτως, τοῦτο τῷ γινομένῳ
δευτέρως ἐνδίδωσι. τῶν νοερῶν ἄρα εἰδῶν ψυχὴ δευτέρως ἔχει
τὰς ἐμφάσεις.

195. Πᾶσα ψυχὴ πάντα ἐστὶ τὰ πράγματα, παραδειγματικῶς μὲν τὰ αἰσθητά, εἰκονικῶς δὲ τὰ νοητά.   5

μέση γὰρ οὖσα τῶν ἀμερίστων καὶ τῶν περὶ τὸ σῶμα
μεριστῶν, τὰ μὲν παράγει καὶ ὑφίστησι, τὰ δὲ αἴτια προεστήσατο ἑαυτῆς, ἀφ' ὧν προελήλυθεν. ὧν μὲν οὖν αἰτία προϋπάρχει, ταῦτα προείληφε παραδειγματικῶς· ἀφ' ὧν δὲ ὑπέστη,
ταῦτα κατὰ μέθεξιν ἔχει καὶ ὡς γεννήματα τῶν πρώτων. τὰ 10
μὲν ἄρα αἰσθητὰ πάντα κατ' αἰτίαν προείληφε, καὶ τοὺς λόγους
τῶν ἐνύλων ἀύλως καὶ τῶν σωματικῶν ἀσωμάτως καὶ τῶν
διαστατῶν ἀδιαστάτως ἔχει· τὰ δὲ νοητὰ εἰκονικῶς, καὶ τὰ
εἴδη τὰ ἐκείνων μεριστῶς μὲν τῶν ἀμερίστων, πεπληθυσμένως
δὲ τῶν ἑνιαίων, αὐτοκινήτως δὲ τῶν ἀκινήτων ὑπεδέξατο. πάντα 15
ἄρα ἐστὶ τὰ ὄντα, τὰ μὲν κατὰ μέθεξιν, τὰ πρῶτα· τὰ δὲ
παραδειγματικῶς, τὰ μετ' αὐτήν.

196. Πᾶσα ψυχὴ μεθεκτὴ σώματι χρῆται πρώτῳ ἀϊδίῳ καὶ
ἀγένητον ἔχοντι τὴν ὑπόστασιν καὶ ἄφθαρτον.

εἰ γὰρ πᾶσα ψυχὴ κατ' οὐσίαν ἐστὶν ἀΐδιος καὶ αὐτῷ τῷ 20
εἶναι πρώτως ψυχοῖ τι τῶν σωμάτων, ἀεὶ αὐτὸ ψυχοῖ· τὸ γὰρ
εἶναι πάσης ψυχῆς ἀμετάβλητον. εἰ δὲ τοῦτο, καὶ τὸ ψυχού-
μενον ἀεὶ ψυχοῦται καὶ ἀεὶ μετέχει ζωῆς· τὸ δὲ ἀεὶ ζῶν πολλῷ
πρότερον ἀεὶ ἔστι· τὸ δὲ ἀεὶ ὂν ἀΐδιον· τὸ ἄρα πρώτως ἔμψυχον
σῶμα καὶ πρώτως ἐξημμένον [ἑκάστης] πάσης ψυχῆς ἀΐδιόν ἐστιν. 25
ἀλλὰ μὴν πᾶσα μεθεκτὴ ψυχὴ ὑπὸ σώματός τινος μετέχεται
πρώτως, εἴπερ καὶ μεθεκτή ἐστιν, ἀλλ' οὐκ ἀμέθεκτος, καὶ αὐτῷ
τῷ εἶναι ψυχοῖ τὸ μετέχον. πᾶσα ἄρα ψυχὴ μετεχομένη
σώματι χρῆται πρώτῳ ἀϊδίῳ καὶ ἀγενήτῳ καὶ ἀφθάρτῳ κατὰ
τὴν οὐσίαν.   30

194. 1 τοῦτο ω (tacite om. Cr.)   2 ἐνδίδωσι M, dat W : μεταδίδωσι BCDQ
ἡ ψυχή QM³
195. 4 πράγματα] ὄντα Q   5 νοητά D¹[M]W : νοερά BCQD²M²
6 τό om. Q   12, 13 ἀύλους ... ἀσωμάτους ... ἀδιαστάτους BCDQM²
13 καὶ τά] τὰ δέ Q   14 τὰ ἐκείνων] τῶν ἐκείνων BC
196. 18 πρώτως Q   22 καί] πρός M (om. edd.)   23 ἀεὶ μετέχει
BCD), semper participat W : ἀεὶ μετέχοι M : μετέχει ἀεί Q   24–5 πρώτως
ἔμψυχον σῶμα καί ω (om. Port., πρώτως om. Cr.)   25 ἑκάστης seclusi :
πάσης om. Q dett.   26 μήν ω (μέν edd.)   μεθεκτική M   μετέχεται
τινός BCD   27 prius καί om. M   29 πρώτῳ ω (πρώτως Arg Cr.)

notions of all that it contains; for whatever creates by existing implants by derivation in its product that which itself is primitively (prop. 18). Soul, therefore, possesses by derivation the irradiations of the intellectual Forms.

PROP. 195. *Every soul is all things, the things of sense after the manner of an exemplar and the intelligible things after the manner of an image.*

For being intermediate between the indivisible principles and those which are divided in association with body (prop. 190), it produces and originates the latter and likewise manifests its own causes, from which it has proceeded. Now those things whereof it is the pre-existent cause it pre-embraces in the exemplary mode, and those from which it took its origin it possesses by participation as generated products of the primal orders. Accordingly it pre-embraces all sensible things after the manner of a cause, possessing the rational notions of material things immaterially, of bodily things incorporeally, of extended things without extension ; on the other hand it possesses as images the intelligible principles, and has received their Forms— the Forms of undivided existents parcelwise, of unitary existents as a manifold, of unmoved existents as self-moved. Thus every soul is all that is, the primal orders by participation and those posterior to it in the exemplary mode.

PROP. 196. *Every participated soul makes use of a first body which is perpetual and has a constitution without temporal origin and exempt from decay.*

For if every soul is perpetual in respect of its existence (prop. 192), and if further by its very being it directly ensoul some body, it must ensoul it at all times, since the being of every soul is invariable (prop. 191). And if so, that which it ensouls is on its part ensouled at all times, and at all times participates life ; and what lives at all times *a fortiori* exists at all times ; and what exists at all times is perpetual : therefore a body directly ensouled and directly attached to any soul is perpetual. But every participated soul is directly participated by some body, inasmuch as it is participated and not unparticipated and by its very being ensouls the participant. Accordingly every participated soul makes use of a first body which is perpetual and in respect of its existence is without temporal origin or decay.

197. Πᾶσα ψυχὴ οὐσία ἐστὶ ζωτικὴ καὶ γνωστική, καὶ ζωὴ οὐσιώδης καὶ γνωστική, καὶ γνῶσις ὡς οὐσία καὶ ζωή· καὶ ἅμα ἐν αὐτῇ πάντα, τὸ οὐσιῶδες, τὸ ζωτικόν, τὸ γνωστικόν, καὶ πάντα ἐν πᾶσι καὶ χωρὶς ἕκαστον.

εἰ γὰρ μέση τῶν ἀμερίστων ἐστὶ καὶ τῶν περὶ σῶμα μερι- 5 ζομένων εἰδῶν, οὔτε οὕτως ἀμέριστός ἐστιν ὡς τὰ νοερὰ πάντα οὔτε οὕτω μεριστὴ ὡς τὰ σωματοειδῆ. διῃρημένων οὖν ἐν τοῖς σωματικοῖς τῶν οὐσιῶν καὶ ζωῶν καὶ γνώσεων, ἀμερίστως ἐστὶν ἐν ψυχαῖς ταῦτα καὶ ἡνωμένως καὶ ἀσωμάτως, καὶ ὁμοῦ πάντα διὰ τὴν ἀϋλίαν καὶ τὴν ἀμέρειαν· καὶ ἐν τοῖς νοεροῖς πάντων 10 καθ' ἕνωσιν ὄντων, διακέκριται ἐν ψυχαῖς καὶ μεμέρισται. πάντα ἄρα καὶ ὁμοῦ καὶ χωρίς. εἰ δὲ ὁμοῦ καὶ ἐν ἑνὶ πάντα ἀμερεῖ, δι' ἀλλήλων πεφοίτηκε· καὶ εἰ χωρίς, διῄρηται πάλιν ἀσυγχύτως· ὥστε καὶ ἐφ' ἑαυτοῦ ἕκαστον καὶ πάντα ἐν πᾶσι.

καὶ γὰρ ἐν τῇ οὐσίᾳ ἡ ζωὴ καὶ ἡ γνῶσις· εἰ γὰρ μή, οὐ 15 γνώσεται πᾶσα ἑαυτήν, εἴπερ ἡ οὐσία ἡ ἄζως καὶ γνώσεως ἐστέρηται καθ' αὐτήν. καὶ ἐν τῇ ζωῇ ἥ τε οὐσία καὶ ἡ γνῶσις· ἡ γὰρ ἀνούσιος ζωὴ καὶ ἡ ἄνευ γνώσεως ταῖς ἐνύλοις προσήκει ζωαῖς, αἳ μήτε γινώσκειν ἑαυτὰς δύνανται μήτε οὐσίαι εἰσὶν εἰλικρινεῖς. καὶ ἡ γνῶσις ἡ ἀνούσιος καὶ ἄζως ἀνυπόστατος· 20 πᾶσα γὰρ γνῶσις καὶ ζῶντός ἐστι καὶ οὐσίαν καθ' αὐτὸ λαχόντος.

198. Πᾶν τὸ χρόνου μετέχον, ἀεὶ δὲ κινούμενον, περιόδοις μετρεῖται.

διότι μὲν γὰρ χρόνου μετέχει, μέτρου καὶ ὅρου μετείληφεν ἡ 25 κίνησις, καὶ κατ' ἀριθμὸν πορεύεται· διότι δὲ ἀεὶ κινεῖται, καὶ τὸ ἀεὶ τοῦτο οὐκ αἰώνιόν ἐστιν, ἀλλὰ χρονικόν, ἀνάγκη χρῆσθαι περιόδοις. ἡ μὲν γὰρ κίνησις μεταβολή τίς ἐστιν ἀφ' ἑτέρων εἰς ἕτερα· τὰ δὲ ὄντα ὥρισται καὶ τοῖς πλήθεσι καὶ τοῖς μεγέθεσι· τούτων δὲ ὡρισμένων, οὔτε κατ' εὐθεῖαν ἄπειρον ἡ 30 μετάβασίς ἐστιν οὔτε τὸ ἀεὶ κινούμενον πεπερασμένως μεταβαίνειν δυνατόν. ἀπὸ τῶν αὐτῶν ἄρα ἐπὶ τὰ αὐτὰ πάλιν ἥξει τὸ ἀεὶ κινούμενον, ὥστε ποιῆσαι περίοδον.

197. 1 alt. καί om. M   2 γνῶσις ὡς ω (ὡς γνῶσις edd.)   8 ἐστίν om. BCD   12 καὶ ὁμοῦ καὶ χωρίς BCDQW : κ. χωρὶς κ. ὁμοῦ M   δέ MQW : γάρ BCD   13 ἀμερεῖ MQW : ἀμερῆ BCD dett.   15 εἰ γὰρ μή ω (om. dett., edd., unde proxime οὐ γάρ Cr. Taylorum secutus)   16 ἡ ἄζως BCD. ἄζωος Q : ζωῆς MW (καὶ ζωῆς O edd.)   18 ἀνούσιος [M]QW : ἄνους BCDM² alt. ἤ om. M   19-20 εἰσὶν εἰλικρινεῖς] εἰλικρινεῖς εἶναι Q
198. 25 γάρ om. M   χρόνου μετέχει MQW : χρόνῳ μετρεῖται BCD   μέτρου καὶ ὅρου MW (μετ. κ. ὅρ. χρόνου AτgCr.) : καὶ μέτρου καὶ ὅρου BCQ, καὶ ὅρου D   27 ἀνάγκη χρήσεται M   29 prius καί om. M   30 ἄπειρος Q   33 ποιήσει Q
In c. 198 fin. desinunt BCE : in D excipit manus recentior (d), cuius lectiones nonnisi rarius adhibui utpote ex M depromptas

PROP. 197. *Every soul is a vital and cognitive substance, a substantial and cognitive principle of life, and a principle of knowledge as being a substance and a life-principle ; and all these characters coexist in it, the substantial, the vital and the cognitive, all in all and each severally.*

For if it is intermediate between the indivisible Forms and those which are divided in association with a body (prop. 190), it is neither indivisible in the same sense as all the intellectual kinds nor divided in the same sense as those assimilated to body. Accordingly whereas the substantial, vital, and cognitive principles are in corporeal things disjoined one from another, in souls they exist as a unity, without division and without body ; all are together because soul is immaterial (prop. 186) and has no parts. And again whereas in the intellectual kinds all exist as a unity (prop. 176), in souls they are distinguished and divided. Thus all exist both together and severally. But if all are together in one being devoid of parts, they interpenetrate one another ; and if they exist severally, they are on the other hand distinct and unconfused : so that each exists by itself, yet all in all.

For in the substance of soul life and knowledge are implicit : otherwise not every soul will know itself, inasmuch as a lifeless substance is in itself bereft of knowledge. And in its life are implicit substance and knowledge : for a non-substantial life and one devoid of knowledge are proper only to lives involved in Matter, which cannot know themselves and are not pure substances. Finally, a knowledge without substance or life is non-existent : for all knowledge implies a living knower which is in itself possessed of substance.

PROP. 198. *All that participates time but has perpetuity of movement is measured by periods.*

For because it participates time, its movement has the character of measure and finitude (prop. 54) and its path is determined by a numerical principle ; and because it moves perpetually, with a perpetuity not eternal but temporal, it must move in periods. For movement is a change from one set of conditions to another ; and the sum of things is finite both in number and in magnitude ; and the sum being finite, it is not possible that change should proceed in an infinite straight line, neither can anything perpetually in motion pass through a finite number of changes. Therefore what moves perpetually will return to its starting-point, so as to constitute a period.

199. Πᾶσα ψυχὴ ἐγκόσμιος περιόδοις χρῆται τῆς οἰκείας ζωῆς καὶ ἀποκαταστάσεσιν.

εἰ γὰρ ὑπὸ χρόνου μετρεῖται καὶ μεταβατικῶς ἐνεργεῖ, καὶ ἔστιν αὐτῆς ἰδία κίνησις, πᾶν δὲ τὸ κινούμενον καὶ χρόνου μετέχον, ἀΐδιον ὄν, χρῆται περιόδοις καὶ περιοδικῶς ἀνακυκλεῖται ₅ καὶ ἀποκαθίσταται ἀπὸ τῶν αὐτῶν ἐπὶ τὰ αὐτά, δῆλον ὅτι καὶ πᾶσα ψυχὴ ἐγκόσμιος, κίνησιν ἔχουσα καὶ ἐνεργοῦσα κατὰ χρόνον, περιόδους τε τῶν κινήσεων ἕξει καὶ ἀποκαταστάσεις· πᾶσα γὰρ περίοδος τῶν ἀϊδίων ἀποκαταστατική ἐστιν.

200. Πᾶσα ψυχῆς περίοδος χρόνῳ μετρεῖται· ἀλλ' ἡ μὲν ₁₀ τῶν ἄλλων ψυχῶν περίοδος τινὶ χρόνῳ μετρεῖται, ἡ δὲ τῆς πρώτης ὑπὸ χρόνου μετρουμένης τῷ σύμπαντι χρόνῳ.

εἰ γὰρ καὶ πᾶσαι αἱ κινήσεις τὸ πρότερον ἔχουσι καὶ ὕστερον, καὶ αἱ περίοδοι ἄρα· καὶ διὰ τοῦτο χρόνου μετέχουσι, καὶ τὸ μετροῦν ἁπάσας τὰς περιόδους τῶν ψυχῶν χρόνος ἐστίν. ἀλλ' εἰ ₁₅ μὲν αἱ αὐταὶ πασῶν ἦσαν περίοδοι καὶ περὶ τὰ αὐτά, καὶ χρόνος ἂν ἦν πασῶν ὁ αὐτός· εἰ δὲ ἄλλαι ἄλλων ἀποκαταστάσεις, καὶ χρόνος περιοδικὸς ἄλλος ἄλλων καὶ ἀποκαταστατικός.

ὅτι μὲν οὖν ἡ πρώτως ὑπὸ χρόνου μετρουμένη ψυχὴ τῷ σύμπαντι χρόνῳ μετρεῖται, δῆλον. εἰ γὰρ μέτρον ὁ χρόνος ₂₀ κινήσεως ἁπάσης, τὸ πρώτως κινούμενον ἔσται παντὸς τοῦ χρόνου μετέχον καὶ ὑπὸ παντὸς μεμετρημένον· μὴ γὰρ τὸ πρώτως μετέχον μετρήσας ὁ σύμπας χρόνος οὐδὲ ἄλλο μετρήσει καθ' ὅλον ἑαυτὸν οὐδέν.

ὅτι δὲ καὶ πᾶσαι αἱ ἄλλαι ψυχαὶ μερικωτέροις τοῦ σύμπαντος ₂₅ χρόνου μετροῦνταί τισι μέτροις, φανερὸν ἐκ τούτων. εἰ γὰρ μερικώτεραι τῆς ψυχῆς εἰσι τῆς πρώτως χρόνου μετεχούσης, οὐδὲ χρόνῳ τῷ σύμπαντι τὰς ἑαυτῶν ἐφαρμόσουσι περιόδους, ἀλλ' αἱ πολλαὶ αὐτῶν ἀποκαταστάσεις μέρη ἔσονται μιᾶς περιόδου καὶ ἀποκαταστάσεως, ἣν ἡ χρόνου μετέχουσα πρώτως ₃₀ ἀποκαθίσταται· τῆς γὰρ ἐλάττονος δυνάμεως ἡ μερικωτέρα μέθεξις, τῆς δὲ μείζονος ἡ ὁλικωτέρα. ὅλον οὖν τὸ χρονικὸν μέτρον κατὰ μίαν ζωὴν αἱ ἄλλαι ψυχαὶ δέχεσθαι οὐ πεφύκασι, τῆς πρώτως ⟨ὑπὸ⟩ χρόνου μετρουμένης ὑφειμένην λαχοῦσαι τάξιν. ₃₅

199. 2 ἀποκαταστάσεως Q   4 αὐτῆς M² vel M³: αὕτη M¹QW   ἰδία M¹Q : ἡ ἰδία M² vel M³
200. 13 prius καί om. Q neque agnoscit W   ὕστερον MQ (τὸ ὕστ. O edd.) 15 τῶν ψυχῶν QM²W : τῷ χρόνῳ [M]   17 αἱ ἀποκαταστάσεις Q   25 αἱ ἄλλαι ψυχαί πᾶσαι Q   26 τισι om. QW   29 αὐτῶν M : τούτων Q   34 ὑπὸ addidi   χρόνου μετρουμένης M : χρόνου μετεχούσης Q : χρόνῳ με-τρουμένης dett., quae . . . tempore mensuratur W

PROP. 199. *Every intra-mundane soul has in its proper life periods and cyclic reinstatements.*

For if it is measured by time and has a transitive activity (prop. 191), and movement is its distinctive character (prop. 20), and all that moves and participates time, if it be perpetual, moves in periods and periodically returns in a circle and is restored to its starting-point (prop. 198), then it is evident that every intra-mundane soul, having movement and exercising a temporal activity, will have a periodic motion, and also cyclic reinstatements (since in the case of things perpetual every period ends in a reinstatement of the original condition).

PROP. 200. *Every psychic period is measured by time ; but while the periods of the other souls are measured by some particular time, that of the first soul measured by time has the whole of time for measure.*

For if all movements involve an earlier and a later, then periodic movements do so; hence they participate time, and time is the measure of all psychic periods (prop. 54). If all souls had the same period and traversed the same course, all would occupy the same time ; but if their reinstatements do not coincide, they vary also in the periodic times which bring about the reinstatements.

Now it is evident that the soul with which temporal measurement begins has the whole of time for measure. For if time is the measure of all movement (prop. 50), the first mobile principle will participate the whole of time and be measured by time in its entirety, since if the sum total of time do not measure its primal participant it cannot as a whole measure any other.

And that all other souls are measured by certain measures less universal than the whole of time is apparent from the above. For if they are less universal than the soul which primitively participates time, it follows that they cannot make their periods coextensive with time in its entirety : their many cyclic reinstatements will be parts of the single period or reinstatement wherein that soul is reinstated which is the primal participant of time. For the more specific participation is proper to the lesser potency, the more universal to the greater. Thus the other souls lack the capacity to receive the whole of the temporal measure within the limits of a single life, since they have been allotted a station subordinate to that of the soul with which temporal measurement begins.

201. Πᾶσαι αἱ θεῖαι ψυχαὶ τριπλᾶς ἔχουσιν ἐνεργείας, τὰς μὲν ὡς ψυχαί, τὰς δὲ ὡς νοῦν ὑποδεξάμεναι θεῖον, τὰς δὲ ὡς θεῶν ἐξηρτημέναι· καὶ προνοοῦσι μὲν τῶν ὅλων ὡς θεοί, γινώσκουσι δὲ τὰ πάντα κατὰ τὴν νοερὰν ζωήν, κινοῦσι δὲ τὰ σώματα κατὰ τὴν αὐτοκίνητον ὕπαρξιν. 5

διότι γὰρ συμφυῶς μετέχουσι τῶν ὑπερκειμένων καί εἰσιν οὐ ψυχαὶ ἁπλῶς, ἀλλὰ θεῖαι ψυχαί, τὴν ἀνάλογον τοῖς θεοῖς ἐν τῷ ψυχικῷ πλάτει προστησάμεναι τάξιν, ἐνεργοῦσιν οὐ ψυχικῶς μόνον, ἀλλὰ καὶ θείως, τὴν ἀκρότητα τῆς ἑαυτῶν οὐσίας ἔνθεον λαχοῦσαι. καὶ διότι νοερὰν ὑπόστασιν ἔχουσι, δι᾽ ἣν καὶ 10 ὑπεστρωμέναι ταῖς νοεραῖς οὐσίαις τυγχάνουσιν, ἐνεργοῦσιν οὖν οὐ θείως μόνον, ἀλλὰ καὶ νοερῶς, τὴν μὲν κατὰ τὸ ἓν τὸ ἐν αὐταῖς, τὴν δὲ κατὰ τὸν νοῦν ἱδρύσασαι ἐνέργειαν. τρίτη δὲ αὐταῖς πάρεστιν ἡ κατὰ τὴν ἰδίαν ὕπαρξιν ἐνέργεια, κινητικὴ μὲν ὑπάρχουσα τῶν φύσει ἑτεροκινήτων, ζωοποιὸς δὲ τῶν ἐπείσακτον 15 ἐχόντων τὴν ζωήν· πάσης γὰρ ψυχῆς τοῦτό ἐστι τὸ ἴδιον ἐνέργημα, τὰ δὲ ἄλλα κατὰ μέθεξιν, ὡς τὸ νοεῖν καὶ προνοεῖν.

202. Πᾶσαι ψυχαὶ θεῶν ὀπαδοὶ καὶ ἀεὶ ἑπόμεναι θεοῖς καταδεέστεραι μέν εἰσι τῶν θείων, ὑπερήπλωνται δὲ τῶν μερικῶν ψυχῶν. 20

αἱ μὲν γὰρ θεῖαι καὶ νοῦ μετέχουσι καὶ θεότητος (διὸ νοεραί τέ εἰσιν ἅμα καὶ θεῖαι) καὶ τῶν ἄλλων ψυχῶν ἡγεμονοῦσι, καθόσον καὶ οἱ θεοὶ τῶν ὄντων ἁπάντων· αἱ δὲ μερικαὶ ψυχαὶ καὶ τῆς εἰς νοῦν ἀναρτήσεως παρήρηνται, μὴ δυνάμεναι προσεχῶς τῆς νοερᾶς οὐσίας μετέχειν· οὐδὲ γὰρ ἂν τῆς νοερᾶς 25 ἐνεργείας ἀπέπιπτον κατ᾽ οὐσίαν μετέχουσαι τοῦ νοῦ, καθάπερ δέδεικται πρότερον. μέσαι ἄρα εἰσὶν αἱ ἀεὶ θεοῖς ἑπόμεναι ψυχαί, νοῦν μὲν ὑποδεξάμεναι τέλειον καὶ ταύτῃ τῶν μερικῶν ὑπερφέρουσαι, οὐκέτι δὲ καὶ θείων ἑνάδων ἐξημμέναι· οὐ γὰρ θεῖος ἦν ὁ μετεχόμενος ὑπ᾽ αὐτῶν νοῦς. 30

203. Παντὸς τοῦ ψυχικοῦ πλήθους αἱ μὲν θεῖαι ψυχαί, τῇ δυνάμει μείζους οὖσαι τῶν ἄλλων, συνήρηνται κατὰ τὸν ἀριθμόν· αἱ δὲ ἀεὶ αὐταῖς ἑπόμεναι καὶ τῇ δυνάμει καὶ τῷ ποσῷ μέσην ἔχουσιν ἐν πάσαις τάξιν· αἱ δὲ μερικαὶ τῇ μὲν δυνάμει καταδεέστεραι τῶν ἄλλων εἰσίν, εἰς ἀριθμὸν δὲ πλείονα προεληλύ- 35 θασιν.

αἱ μὲν γάρ εἰσι τῷ ἑνὶ συγγενέστεραι διὰ τὴν ὕπαρξιν θείαν

PROP. 201. *All divine souls have a threefold activity, in their threefold capacity as souls, as recipients of a divine intelligence, and as derived from gods : as gods they exercise providence towards the universe, in virtue of their intellectual life they know all things, and in virtue of the self-movement proper to their being they impart motion to bodies.*

For because it belongs to their nature to participate the suprajacent principles, because they are not souls merely but divine souls, manifesting on the psychic plane a rank analogous to the gods (prop. 185), it follows that they exercise not only a psychic but also a divine activity, in that the summit of their being is possessed by a god. And because they have an intellectual substance which renders them susceptible of influence from the intellectual essences (prop. 182), they use not only a divine but also an intellectual activity, the former based upon the unity within them, the latter upon their immanent intelligence. Their third activity is that proper to their especial mode of being, whose function it is to move what is naturally moved *ab extra* (prop. 20) and to bestow life upon principles whose life is adventitious (prop. 188) ; for this is the distinctive operation of every soul, whereas its other activities, such as intellection and providence, are derived through participation.

PROP. 202. *All souls which are attendant upon gods and perpetually in their company are inferior to the divine grade, but are exalted above the particular souls.*

For the divine souls participate both intelligence and deity (prop. 129)—hence it is that they are at once intellectual and divine (prop. 201)—and they have sovereignty over the other souls, as the gods are sovereign over all that is (prop. 144). On the other hand the particular souls are deprived even of attachment to an intelligence, being unable directly to participate intellectual existence—for if in respect of their existence they participated intelligence, they would not fall away from intellectual activity, as has been proved above (prop. 175). Intermediate, therefore, between these two classes stand those souls which are perpetually in the company of gods ; which are recipients of a perfect intelligence and in this regard overpass the particular souls, but fall short of connexion with divine henads, since the intelligence they participate was not divine (prop. 185).

PROP. 203. *In the entire psychic manifold the divine souls, which are greater in power than the rest, are restricted in number ; those which are perpetually in their company have in the order as a whole a middle station in respect both of power and of multitude ; while the particular souls are inferior in power to the others but are advanced to a greater number.*

For the first class are nearer akin to the One because of their

οὖσαν, αἱ δὲ μέσαι διὰ τὴν νοῦ μετουσίαν, αἱ δὲ ἔσχαται κατὰ
τὴν τάξιν, ἀνομοιώδεις κατὰ τὴν οὐσίαν ταῖς τε μέσαις καὶ ταῖς
πρώταις. τὰ δὲ ἐγγυτέρω τοῦ ἑνὸς ἐν τοῖς ἀϊδίοις τῶν πορρωτέρων ἀριθμῷ ἑνικώτερά ἐστι καὶ συνήρηται κατὰ τὸ πλῆθος, τὰ
δὲ πορρωτέρω μᾶλλον πληθύνεται. αἵ τε οὖν δυνάμεις τῶν 5
ἀνωτέρω μείζους, καὶ τοῦτον ἔχουσι τὸν λόγον πρὸς τὰς δευτέρας,
ὃν τὸ θεῖον πρὸς τὸ νοερὸν καὶ τοῦτο πρὸς τὸ ψυχικόν· καὶ αἱ
ποσότητες τῶν κατωτέρω πλείους· τὸ γὰρ πορρώτερον τοῦ ἑνὸς
πλῆθος μᾶλλόν ἐστι καὶ τὸ ἐγγύτερον ἧττον.

204. Πᾶσα θεία ψυχὴ πολλῶν μὲν ἡγεῖται ψυχῶν ἀεὶ 10
θεοῖς ἑπομένων, πλειόνων δὲ ἔτι τῶν ποτὲ ταύτην τὴν τάξιν
δεχομένων.

θείαν μὲν γὰρ οὖσαν, πάντων ἡγεμονικὴν τάξιν εἰληχέναι
δεῖ καὶ πρωτουργὸν ἐν ταῖς ψυχαῖς (καὶ γὰρ τὸ θεῖον ἐν πᾶσι
τοῖς οὖσιν ἡγεῖται τῶν ὅλων)· οὔτε δὲ τῶν ἀεὶ ἑπομένων μόνον 15
ἑκάστην ἄρχειν οὔτε τῶν ποτὲ μόνον. εἰ μὲν γὰρ τῶν ποτὲ
ἑπομένων ἡγοῖτό τις μόνων, πῶς ἡ συναφὴ ταύταις ἔσται πρὸς
τὴν θείαν ψυχήν, πάντη διαφερούσαις καὶ μήτε νοῦ προσεχῶς
μετεχούσαις μήτε πολλῷ πλέον θεῶν; εἰ δὲ τῶν ἀεὶ ἑπομένων,
πῶς μέχρις ἐκείνων ἡ σειρὰ προῆλθεν; ἔσται γὰρ οὕτως ἔσχατα 20
τὰ νοερὰ καὶ ἄγονα, καὶ τελειοῦν ἄλλα καὶ ἀνάγειν οὐ πεφυκότα.
ἀνάγκη ἄρα πάσης ψυχῆς θείας πρώτως μὲν ἐξηρτῆσθαι τὰς
ἀεὶ ἑπομένας ψυχὰς καὶ κατὰ νοῦν ἐνεργούσας καὶ εἰς νόας
ἀνηγμένας μερικωτέρους τῶν θείων νόων, δευτέρας δὲ τὰς
μερικὰς καὶ διὰ τούτων μέσων νοῦ μετέχειν καὶ τῆς θείας 25
ζωῆς δυναμένας· διὰ γὰρ τῶν ἀεὶ μετεχόντων τῆς κρείττονος
μοίρας τὰ ποτὲ μετέχοντα τελειοῦται.

καὶ αὖ πάλιν πλείους εἶναι περὶ ἑκάστην ψυχὴν θείαν τὰς
ποτὲ ἑπομένας ψυχὰς τῶν ἀεὶ ἑπομένων· ἡ γὰρ τῆς μονάδος
δύναμις κατὰ τὴν ὕφεσιν εἰς πλῆθος ἀεὶ πρόεισι, τῇ μὲν δυνάμει 30
λειπόμενον, τῷ δὲ ἀριθμῷ πλεονάζον. ἐπεὶ καὶ ἑκάστη ψυχὴ
τῶν ἀεὶ θεοῖς ἑπομένων πλειόνων ἡγεῖται μερικῶν ψυχῶν,
μιμουμένη τὴν θείαν ψυχήν, καὶ πλείους ἀνέλκει ψυχὰς εἰς τὴν

203. 1 μετουσίαν] μεσιτείαν d, in mg. Arg   post μετουσίαν in M excipit
altera manus eiusdem fere aetatis   3 δέ MW : γάρ Q   3-4 πορρωτέρω Arg
nescio an recte   4 ἀριθμῶν Q   κατὰ πλῆθος Q   τά MQW (τό dett.,
edd.)   5 πορρώτερα Q   πληθύεται Q   9 post ἐστι ins. πλῆθος Q
204. 10 Πᾶσα] ἆσα M rubricatoris delicto ; ita etiam in reliquis ab altera
manu scriptis capitibus   ψυχῶν ἡγεῖται Q   11 θείοις Q   17 ἡγοῖτό
τις dett.: ἡγεῖτό τις M, εἱγεῖτό τις (sic) Q   μόνον Q primitus, dett.
19 πλέω M   21 post τὰ νοερά ins. κατ' οὐσίαν Q   ἀλλὰ M   23 ἀεί Q :
om. MW   24 an δευτέρως?   26 ἀεί om. Q   30 ἀεί om. Q

divine mode of being (prop. 113), the second are intermediate because they participate intelligence, the third are last in rank, differing in their existence both from the intermediate and from the primal (prop. 202). Now among perpetual principles those nearer to the One are more unified in number than the more remote, that is, they are restricted in respect of multitude, while the more remote are more numerous (prop. 62). Thus on the one hand the powers of the higher souls are greater, and bear that relation to the secondary powers which the divine has to the intellectual and this latter to the psychic (props. 201, 202); on the other hand the members of the lower grades are more numerous, since that which is more remote from the One is more manifold, the nearer less so.

PROP. 204. *Every divine soul is sovereign over many souls which are perpetually in the divine company, and over yet more which are at certain times admitted to that station.*

For being divine, it must be endowed with a rank of universal sovereignty and primal operation in the order of souls, since in all orders of being the divine is sovereign over the whole (prop. 144). And each must govern not merely souls which perpetually enjoy its company nor merely such as enjoy it intermittently. For were one of them sovereign over these latter only, how should these be conjoined with the divine soul, being wholly disparate and participating not even an intelligence directly, still less any of the gods? And were it sovereign over the former only, how came the series to progress to the lower terms? On this supposition the intellectual principles will be the lowest, sterile and incapable of perfecting and exalting further beings. Of necessity, therefore, to every divine soul are attached directly those souls which at all times accompany it and use an intellectual activity and are linked by an upward tension to intelligences more specific than the divine intelligences (prop. 183); and in a secondary grade the particular souls, which through these intermediaries are able to participate intelligence and divine life—for through principles which perpetually participate the higher destiny the contingent participants are made perfect.

Again, each divine soul must have about it a greater number of souls which intermittently enjoy its company than of souls perpetually attendant; for as the power of the monad declines it proceeds ever further into plurality, making up in numbers what it loses in power. And moreover each of the souls perpetually attendant upon gods, imitating its divine soul, is sovereign over a number of particular souls, and thus draws upward a number of souls to the primal monad

πρωτουργὸν μονάδα τῆς ὅλης σειρᾶς. πᾶσα ἄρα θεία ψυχὴ
πολλῶν μὲν ἡγεῖται ψυχῶν τῶν ἀεὶ θεοῖς ἑπομένων, πλειόνων
δὲ ἔτι τῶν ποτὲ τὴν τάξιν ταύτην δεχομένων.

205. Πᾶσα ψυχὴ μερικὴ τοῦτον ἔχει τὸν λόγον πρὸς τὴν
θείαν ψυχήν, ὑφ᾽ ἣν τέτακται κατ᾽ οὐσίαν, ὃν τὸ ὄχημα αὐτῆς 5
πρὸς τὸ ἐκείνης ὄχημα.

εἰ γὰρ κατὰ φύσιν ἡ διανομὴ τῶν ὀχημάτων ἑκάσταις,
ἀνάγκη πάσης μερικῆς ψυχῆς ὀχήματι τοῦτον εἶναι τὸν λόγον
πρὸς τὸ ὄχημα τῆς ὅλης, ὅς ἐστιν αὐτῆς πρὸς ἐκείνην. ἀλλὰ
μὴν ἡ διανομὴ κατὰ φύσιν· τὰ γὰρ πρώτως μετέχοντα αὐτοφυῶς 10
συνῆπται τοῖς μετεχομένοις. εἰ οὖν ὡς ἡ θεία πρὸς τὸ θεῖον
σῶμα, οὕτως ἡ μερικὴ πρὸς τὸ μερικόν, αὐτῷ τῷ εἶναι μετεχομένης ἑκατέρας, καὶ τὸ ἐξ ἀρχῆς ἀληθές, ὅτι καὶ τὰ ὀχήματα
ταῖς ψυχαῖς τὸν αὐτὸν ἔχει πρὸς ἄλληλα λόγον.

206. Πᾶσα ψυχὴ μερικὴ κατιέναι τε εἰς γένεσιν ἐπ᾽ ἄπειρον 15
καὶ ἀνιέναι δύναται ἀπὸ γενέσεως εἰς τὸ ὄν.

εἰ γὰρ ποτὲ μὲν ἕπεται θεοῖς, ποτὲ δὲ ἀποπίπτει τῆς πρὸς
τὸ θεῖον ἀνατάσεως, νοῦ τε καὶ ἀνοίας μετέχει, δῆλον δὴ ὅτι
παρὰ μέρος ἔν τε τῇ γενέσει γίνεται καὶ ἐν τοῖς θεοῖς ἔστιν.
οὐδὲ γὰρ ⟨τὸν ἄπειρον οὖσα χρόνον ἐν σώμασιν ἐνύλοις ἔπειτα 20
ἕτερον τοιοῦτον χρόνον ἔσται ἐν τοῖς θεοῖς, οὐδὲ⟩ τὸν ἄπειρον
οὖσα χρόνον ἐν τοῖς θεοῖς αὖθις ὅλον τὸν ἐφεξῆς χρόνον ἔσται
ἐν τοῖς σώμασι· τὸ γὰρ ἀρχὴν χρονικὴν μὴ ἔχον οὐδὲ τελευτήν
ποτε ἕξει, καὶ τὸ μηδεμίαν ἔχον τελευτὴν ἀνάγκη μηδὲ ἀρχὴν
ἔχειν. λείπεται ἄρα περιόδους ἑκάστην ποιεῖσθαι ἀνόδων τε ἐκ 25
τῆς γενέσεως καὶ τῶν εἰς γένεσιν καθόδων, καὶ τοῦτο ἄπαυστον
εἶναι διὰ τὸν ἄπειρον χρόνον. ἑκάστη ἄρα ψυχὴ ·μερικὴ
κατιέναι τε ἐπ᾽ ἄπειρον δύναται καὶ ἀνιέναι, καὶ τοῦτο οὐ μὴ
παύσεται περὶ ἁπάσας τὸ πάθημα γινόμενον.

207. Πάσης μερικῆς ψυχῆς τὸ ὄχημα ἀπὸ αἰτίας ἀκινήτου 30
δεδημιούργηται.

εἰ γὰρ ἀϊδίως ἐξήρτηται τῆς χρωμένης αὐτῷ ψυχῆς καὶ
συμφυῶς, ἀμετάβλητον ὂν κατ᾽ οὐσίαν, ἀπ᾽ αἰτίας ἀκινήτου τὴν
ὑπόστασιν ἔλαχε· τὸ γὰρ ἐκ κινουμένων αἰτίων γεγονὸς μεταβάλλει πᾶν κατὰ τὴν οὐσίαν. ἀλλὰ μὴν πᾶσα ψυχὴ ἀΐδιον 35

205. 4 ψυχὴ μερικὴ Q, anima partialis W : μερικὴ ψυχή M   5 θείαν om.
M   7 εἰ QW : ἡ M   9 ὅς MQ (ὃ O eddd.)   13 prius καί om. Q
206. 19 τε MQ (tacite om. Cr.)   20–1 lacunam statui et exempli gratia
explevi   21 τὸ ἄπειρον M primitus   22 ὅλον om. Q   24–5 ἀρχὴν ποτε ἔχειν
Q   27 an τοῦ ἀπείρου χρόνου?   29 παύσηται Q   πάθος Q   γενόμενον M
207. 30 Πάσης QW : ης M (unde Τῆς O, Πάσης τῆς Port.), ασης M⁴ (cf. ad c.
204, l. 10)

of the entire series. Therefore every divine soul is sovereign over many souls which are perpetually in the divine company, and over yet more which at certain times are admitted to that station.

PROP. 205. *Every particular soul bears to the divine soul under which it is ranked in respect of its being the same relation as its vehicle bears to the vehicle of that divine soul.*

For if the apportionment of vehicles to the several classes of souls be determined by their nature, the vehicle of every particular soul must bear that relation to the vehicle of a universal soul which the particular soul itself itself bears to the universal. But the apportionment must be so determined, since direct participants are conjoined by their very nature with the principles they participate (prop. 63). If, then, the particular soul is to the particular body as the divine soul to the divine body, each soul being participated in virtue of its very existence, the proposition we have enunciated is also true, namely that the vehicles bear the same mutual relation as the souls.

PROP. 206. *Every particular soul can descend into temporal process and ascend from process to Being an infinite number of times.*

For if at certain times it is in the company of gods and at others falls away from its upward tension towards the divine, and if it participates both intelligence and unintelligence (prop. 202), it is plain that by turns it comes-to-be in the world of process and has true Being among the gods. For it cannot ⟨have been for an infinite time in material bodies and thereafter pass a second infinite time among the gods, neither can it⟩ have spent an infinite time among the gods and again be embodied for the whole time thereafter, since that which has no temporal beginning will never have an end, and what has no end cannot have had a beginning. It remains, then, that each soul has a periodic alternation of ascents out of process and descents into process, and that this movement is unceasing by reason of the infinitude of time. Therefore each particular soul can descend and ascend an infinite number of times, and this shall never cease to befall every such soul.

PROP. 207. *The vehicle of every particular soul has been created by an unmoved cause.*

For if it be perpetually and congenitally attached to the soul which uses it, being invariable in respect of its existence it must have received its being from an unmoved cause, since all that arises from mobile causes is variable in its existence (prop. 76). But

ἔχει σῶμα, τὸ πρώτως αὐτῆς μετέχον· ὥστε καὶ ἡ μερικὴ ψυχή.
καὶ τὸ αἴτιον ἄρα τοῦ ὀχήματος αὐτῆς ἀκίνητόν ἐστι, καὶ διὰ
τοῦτο ὑπερκόσμιον.

208. Πάσης μερικῆς ψυχῆς τὸ ὄχημα ἄϋλόν ἐστι καὶ
ἀδιαίρετον κατ' οὐσίαν καὶ ἀπαθές.   5

εἰ γὰρ ἐξ ἀκινήτου προῆλθε δημιουργίας καὶ ἔστιν ἀίδιον,
ἄϋλον ὑπόστασιν ἔχει καὶ ἀπαθῆ. τὰ γὰρ πάσχειν κατὰ τὴν
οὐσίαν πεφυκότα καὶ μεταβάλλει καὶ ἔνυλα πάντα ἐστί, καὶ
ἄλλοτε ἄλλως ἔχοντα τῶν κινουμένων αἰτίων ἐξήρτηται· διὸ
καὶ μεταβολὴν ἐπιδέχεται παντοίαν, συγκινούμενα ταῖς ἑαυτῶν 10
ἀρχικαῖς αἰτίαις.

ἀλλὰ μὴν ὅτι καὶ ἀδιαίρετον, δῆλον. τὸ γὰρ διαιρούμενον
πᾶν ταύτῃ φθείρεται, ᾗ διαιρεῖται, τοῦ τε ὅλου καὶ τῆς
συνεχείας ἀφιστάμενον· εἰ οὖν ἀμετάβλητον κατὰ τὴν οὐσίαν
καὶ ἀπαθές, ἀδιαίρετον ἂν εἴη.   15

209. Πάσης μερικῆς ψυχῆς τὸ ὄχημα κάτεισι μὲν προσθέσει
χιτώνων ἐνυλοτέρων, συ⟨να⟩νάγεται δὲ τῇ ψυχῇ δι' ἀφαιρέσεως
παντὸς τοῦ ἐνύλου καὶ τῆς εἰς τὸ οἰκεῖον εἶδος ἀναδρομῆς,
ἀνάλογον τῇ χρωμένῃ ψυχῇ· καὶ γὰρ ἐκείνη κάτεισι μὲν
ἀλόγους προσλαβοῦσα ζωάς, ἄνεισι δὲ ἀποσκευασαμένη πάσας 20
τὰς γενεσιουργοὺς δυνάμεις, ἃς ἐν τῇ καθόδῳ περιεβάλλετο,
καὶ γενομένη καθαρὰ καὶ γυμνὴ τῶν τοιούτων πασῶν δυνάμεων
ὅσαι πρὸς τὴν τῆς γενέσεως χρείαν ὑπηρετοῦσι.

τὰ γὰρ συμφυῆ ὀχήματα μιμεῖται τὰς ζωὰς τῶν χρωμένων
ψυχῶν, καὶ συγκινεῖται κινουμέναις αὐταῖς πανταχοῦ· καὶ τῶν 25
μὲν τὰς νοήσεις ἀπεικονίζεται ταῖς ἑαυτῶν περιφοραῖς, τῶν δὲ τὰς
ἀποπτώσεις ταῖς εἰς τὴν γένεσιν ῥοπαῖς, τῶν δὲ τὰς καθάρσεις
ταῖς εἰς τὸ ἄϋλον περιαγωγαῖς. διότι γὰρ αὐτῷ τῷ εἶναι τὰς
ψυχὰς ζωοποιεῖται παρ' αὐτῶν καὶ ἔστι συμφυῆ ἐκείναις,
παντοίως συμμεταβάλλει ταῖς ἐκείνων ἐνεργείαις καὶ συνέπεται 30
πάντῃ, παθαινομέναις τε συμπάσχει καὶ κεκαθαρμέναις συν-
αποκαθίσταται καὶ ἀναγομέναις συνεπαίρεται, τῆς ἑαυτῶν
ἐφιέμενα τελειότητος· πᾶν γὰρ τελειοῦται τῆς οἰκείας ὁλότητος
τυχόν.

207. 3 ὑπερκείμενον Q
208. 8 μεταβάλλει καί QW: μεταβάλλει· τά M (unde μεταβάλλειν τά dO²
Port., μεταβάλλειν Cr².)   πάντα] πάντῃ Q primitus   11 ἀρχηγικαῖς Q
12 τὸ γὰρ διαιρούμενον M : διαιρούμενον γάρ Q   14 κατ' οὐσίαν Q
209. 16-17 προσθέσει χιτώνων Q dett.: πρόσθεὶς χιτόνων (sic) M, om. W
17 συ⟨να⟩νάγεται scripsi collato l. 32 infra et Th. Pl. p. 192 : συνάγεται M·W :
συνάπτεται Q   20 ἀλόγους QW: ἀλόγως M   ἀποσκευασαμένη (sic) M
21 περιεβάλλετο MQ (περιεβάλλετον Port., περιεβάλετο Cr.)   22 καθαρά...
24 συμφυῆ om. M, suppl. M⁴ (καθαρὰ...ὀχήματα om. O edd.)   23 χρείαν

every soul has a perpetual body which participates it directly (prop. 196). Accordingly the particular soul has such a body. Therefore the cause of its vehicle is unmoved, and for that reason supra-mundane.

PROP. 208. *The vehicle of every particular soul is immaterial, indiscerptible in respect of its existence, and impassible.*

For if it proceeds from an immobile act of creation (prop. 207) and is perpetual (prop. 196), it has an immaterial and impassible being. For all things capable of being acted upon in respect of their existence are both mutable and material (prop. 80), and since their states vary they are attached to mobile causes (prop. 76) : hence it is that they admit all manner of change, sharing in the movement of their originative principles.

But again, it is clearly indiscerptible. For if anything be discerpted it perishes in that respect in which it is discerpted, since it loses its integrity and continuity. If, therefore, the vehicle is invariable in respect of its existence and impassible, it must be indiscerptible.

PROP. 209. *The vehicle of every particular soul descends by the addition of vestures increasingly material; and ascends in company with the soul through divestment of all that is material and recovery of its proper form, after the analogy of the soul which makes use of it : for the soul descends by the acquisition of irrational principles of life ; and ascends by putting off all those faculties tending to temporal process with which it was invested in its descent, and becoming clean and bare of all such faculties as serve the uses of the process.*

For the congenital vehicles imitate the lives of the souls which use them, and move everywhere with their movements : the intellectual activity of certain souls they reflect by circular revolutions, the declension of others by a subsidence into process, the purgation of yet others by a conversion towards the immaterial. For because in virtue of the very existence of the souls these vehicles are animated by them and are congenital to them (prop. 196), they undergo all manner of changes in sympathy with the souls' activities and accompany them everywhere : when the souls suffer passion, they suffer with them ; when they have been purified, they are restored with them ; when they are led upwards, they rise with them, craving their own perfection—for all things are perfected when they attain to their proper integrity.

QW : πορείαν M⁴   26 ἀπεικονίζονται M   28–9 ταῖς ψυχαῖς M primitus 29 συμφυῆ Q : συμφυής MW   30 παντοίων M   συμμεταβάλλει MQ, transmutantur W (συμβάλλει edd.)   33 ἐφιέμενα QW : ἐφιέμεναι M

210. Πᾶν ψυχῆς ὄχημα συμφυὲς καὶ σχῆμα τὸ αὐτὸ ἀεὶ καὶ μέγεθος ἔχει, μεῖζον δὲ καὶ ἔλαττον ὁρᾶται καὶ ἀνομοιόσχημον δι' ἄλλων σωμάτων προσθέσεις καὶ ἀφαιρέσεις.

εἰ γὰρ ἐξ αἰτίας ἀκινήτου τὴν οὐσίαν ἔχει, δῆλον δὴ ὅτι καὶ τὸ σχῆμα καὶ τὸ μέγεθος αὐτῷ παρὰ τῆς αἰτίας ἀφώρισται, 5 καὶ ἔστιν ἀμετάβλητον καὶ ἀνεξάλλακτον ἑκάτερον. ἀλλὰ μὴν ἄλλοτε ἀλλοῖον φαντάζεται καὶ μεῖζον καὶ ἔλαττον. δι' ἄλλα ἄρα σώματα ἀπὸ τῶν ὑλικῶν στοιχείων προστιθέμενα καὶ αὖθις ἀφαιρούμενα τοιόνδε ἢ τοιόνδε καὶ τοσόνδε ἢ τοσόνδε φαίνεται.

211. Πᾶσα μερικὴ ψυχὴ κατιοῦσα εἰς γένεσιν ὅλη κάτεισι, 10 καὶ οὐ τὸ μὲν αὐτῆς ἄνω μένει, τὸ δὲ κάτεισιν.

εἰ γάρ τι μένοι τῆς ψυχῆς ἐν τῷ νοητῷ, ἢ ἀμεταβάτως νοήσει ἀεὶ ἢ μεταβατικῶς. ἀλλ' εἰ μὲν ἀμεταβάτως, νοῦς ἔσται καὶ οὐ μέρος ψυχῆς, καὶ ἔσται ἡ ψυχὴ προσεχῶς νοῦ μετέχουσα· τοῦτο δὲ ἀδύνατον. εἰ δὲ μεταβατικῶς, ἐκ τοῦ ἀεὶ νοοῦντος καὶ 15 ⟨τοῦ⟩ ποτὲ νοοῦντος μία οὐσία ἔσται. ἀλλ' ἀδύνατον· ταῦτα γὰρ εἴδει διαφέρει, ὡς δέδεικται, πρὸς τῷ καὶ ἄτοπον εἶναι τὸ τῆς ψυχῆς ἀκρότατον, ἀεὶ τέλειον ὄν, μὴ κρατεῖν τῶν ἄλλων δυνάμεων κἀκείνας τελείας ποιεῖν. πᾶσα ἄρα ψυχὴ ⟨μερικὴ ὅλη⟩ κάτεισιν. 20

210. 9 ἢ τοσόνδε MQW (om. edd.)
211. 10 ψυχὴ μερικὴ Q 12 μένει Q 15-16 καὶ ποτὲ νοοῦντος QW : om. M (suppl. M⁴): τοῦ add. T. Taylor 17 εἴδει Q : ἀεί MW τῷ ex corr. Q : τό M, Q primitus καί om. Q 19 κἀκείνας τελείας coni. Port. : κἀκεῖνα τέλεια MQW 19-20 ψυχὴ ⟨μερικὴ ὅλη⟩ scripsi (μερικὴ ψυχὴ ὅλη Cr.), anima partialis tota W : ψυχή M : ἡ ψυχή Q
Subscriptionem τέλος τῶν σια' κεφαλαίων τῶν περὶ θεολογίας πρόκλου praebet M

PROP. 210. *Every congenital psychic vehicle keeps the same shape and size perpetually, but is seen as greater or smaller and in varying shapes by reason of the addition or removal of other bodies.*

For if it has its being from an unmoved cause (prop. 207), it is plain that both its shape and its size are determined for it by its cause, and both are immutable and invariable.   Yet its appearances at different times are diverse, and it seems now greater, now smaller. Therefore it is by reason of other bodies, which are added to it from the material elements and again removed (prop. 209), that it appears of such and such a shape and magnitude.

PROP. 211. *Every particular soul, when it descends into temporal process, descends entire: there is not a part of it which remains above and a part which descends.*

For suppose that some part of the soul remains in the intelligible. It will exercise perpetual intellection, either without transition from object to object or transitively.   But if without transition, it will be an intelligence and not a fragment of a soul, and the soul in question will be one which directly participates an intelligence ; and this is impossible (prop. 202).   And if transitively, the part which has perpetual intellection and that which has intermittent intellection will be one substance.   But this is impossible, for they differ in kind, as has been shown (prop. 184); and it is, moreover, unaccountable that the highest part of the soul, if it be perpetually perfect, does not master the other faculties and render them also perfect.   Therefore every particular soul descends entire.

COMMENTARY

ΣΤΟΙΧΕΙΩΣΙΣ ΘΕΟΛΟΓΙΚΗ : the term στοιχείωσις ('ABC', 'elementary handbook') seems to occur first in Epicurus, who called his *Letter to Herodotus* ἐπιτομὴ καὶ στοιχείωσις τῶν ὅλων δοξῶν (*Ep.* I. 37), and also composed a work with the title Δώδεκα Στοιχειώσεις (Diog. Laert. X. 44). Cf. also the Ἠθικὴ Στοιχείωσις attributed to the Stoic Eudromus (*ibid.* VII. 39), the Μετεωρολογικὴ Στοιχείωσις of Poseidonius, and the (probably imaginary) Θεολογικαὶ Στοιχειώσεις ascribed by ps.-Dion. (*Div. Nom.* 2. 9 ; 3. 2) to his teacher Hierotheus.

'Theology' is used here in its Aristotelian sense, as a synonym of 'first philosophy' or metaphysic in contrast with 'physics' (Arist. *Metaph.* 1026 a 18 τρεῖς ἂν εἶεν φιλοσοφίαι θεωρητικαί, μαθηματική, φυσική, θεολογική).[1] As 'natural science' had been dealt with in the Στοιχείωσις Φυσική, so 'divine science' will be dealt with here. But since all things are for the Neoplatonist in some measure divine (*El. Th.* 145), the boundary between θεολογική and φυσική or φυσιολογία is not a rigid one : the latter may be called 'a kind of theology' (*in Tim.* I. 217. 25). Psellus *de omnif. doct.* cap. 73 quotes the *El. Th.* simply as τὰ κεφάλαια.

A. Of the One and the Many [2] (props. 1–6).

The order of exposition of the *Elements of Theology* is an order of progression from the simpler to the more complex. Proclus begins, therefore, with the bare opposition of the One and the Many as elements in the world of experience, an opposition which had been

---

[1] Similarly θεολογία appears as the last of the six parts into which Cleanthes divided philosophy, the others being Dialectic, Rhetoric, Ethics, Politics, Physics (*Stoic. Vet. Fragm.* I. 482). Plutarch *def. orac.* 2 συνῆγεν ἱστορίαν οἷον· ὕλην φιλοσοφίας, θεολογίαν, ὥσπερ αὐτὸς ἐκάλει, τέλος ἐχούσης is often quoted as an anticipation of the medieval doctrine that philosophy is *ancilla fidei* ; but here again θεολογία is to be equated with metaphysic and not with 'faith'.

[2] I have thought it convenient to indicate in my translation by means of headings the natural grouping of the propositions. In doing so I have followed no manuscript authority. The headings to propositions or groups of propositions which appear in certain MSS. and in the printed texts of Portus and Creuzer are relegated to the *apparatus criticus*. My reasons for rejecting them are (1) that they do not occur in PQ or in William de Morbecca's Latin version ; (2) that they are inserted quite arbitrarily and sporadically (before propositions 6, 7, 8, 9, 11, 14, 15, 21, 23, 25, 48, 53, 160, 184) ; (3) that some of them clearly betray the hand of a medieval reader, either by their inappropriateness (e.g. the heading to prop. 21, ὅτι οὐ πρῶτον αἴτιον ὁ νοῦς, misrepresents the point of the proposition) or by their form (e.g. the heading to prop. 48, περὶ ἀϊδίου, πρὸς τὸ δεῖξαι ὅτι ἀΐδιος ὁ κόσμος).

fundamental in Greek philosophy for about 1,000 years. In the *in Parm.* (696. 32 ff.) he distinguishes four possible solutions of this problem : the ἀρχή or underlying determinant of the universe may be (*a*) pure plurality, (*b*) explicit plurality having an implicit unity, (*c*) explicit unity having an implicit plurality, (*d*) pure unity. The last was, of course, the accepted view of Neoplatonic orthodoxy, its ultimate source being the 'first hypothesis' of Plato's *Parmenides* (137 C ff.).[1] The props. of the present group are directed to establishing this view by exclusion of the other alternatives. That pure plurality does not exist is shown in prop. 1 ; props. 2–4 distinguish pure from partial unity, and show that our experience of the latter involves the existence of the former ; prop. 5 establishes that no partial unity can be an *ultimate* ἀρχή ; prop. 6 distinguishes two grades of partial unity, corresponding to (*b*) and (*c*) above, and assigns to them their respective positions as subordinate ἀρχαί, thus leading up to the doctrine of the hierarchy of causes, which forms the subject of the next group of propositions.

Nicolaus of Methone (Ἀνάπτ. 5. 18 ff.) suggests that in putting τὸ ἕν in the forefront of his exposition Pr. was deliberately challenging the Christian doctrine of a Trinity worshipped ὡς πλῆθος πρὸ τοῦ ἑνὸς ἢ καὶ σὺν τῷ ἑνί. But the *El. Th.* betrays no preoccupation with Christianity ; and that this part of Pr.'s doctrine was not felt to be incompatible with Christian theology is shown by ps.-Dion.'s enthusiastic acceptance of it (e.g. *Div. Nom.* 13. 2. οὐδὲ γάρ ἐστι πλῆθος ἀμέτοχόν πη τοῦ ἑνός . . . 3 εἰ ἀνέλοις τὸ ἕν, οὔτε ὁλότης οὔτε μόριον οὔτε ἄλλο οὐδὲν τῶν ὄντων ἔσται).

PROP. 1. This prop. is placed at the head of Pr.'s system in order to exclude the assumption of a world of pure quantitative plurality devoid of that qualitative shaping which Neoplatonism attributed to the operation of a transcendent unity and which we call individuality. Pr. found his authority for this exclusion in Plato *Parm.* 157 C ff., where it is shown that every manifold τοῦ ἑνὸς μετέχει πη, both as a whole and in each of its parts. The thesis that whatever is has unity in some degree is a favourite one with Plotinus, e.g. *Enn.* VI. ix. 1, V. vi. 3. But the formal argument by which it is here established does not occur in Plato, nor, I think, in Plotinus. It is directed against the concept of infinite actual (as distinct from potential)[2]

[1] In *Class. Qu.* 22, 1928, I have tried to trace back the affiliation of the doctrine through Neopythagoreanism and (less certainly) the Old Academy to the *Parmenides.*
[2] Cf. Arist. *Phys.* 204 a 20, and *infra* prop. 94 n.

divisibility, and turns on the impossibility of conceiving a sum
of numerical infinites, which must itself be numerically greater than
infinity.

The proof given in the text is elaborated at length in *Th. Pl.* II. i,
where two other proofs are added, viz. (1) that a pure plurality would
be ἄπειρον, and so unknowable (cf. *infra*, prop. 11, l. 26), and
therefore on Platonic principles unreal; (2) that in a universe of
pure plurality the very basis of knowledge would be destroyed, since
all unity between the mind and its objects would *ex hypothesi* be
excluded. Cf. also *in Parm.* 1100. 24 ff.

3. ἐκείνων. This reading is confirmed by *Th. Pl.* II. i. 74 ἐξ ὧν
τοῦτό ἐστιν, ἀπείρων ὄντων, καὶ τούτων ἕκαστον ἄπειρον.

10. ταῦτα δὲ ἀδύνατα. Compare the argument of Zeno that if
things are infinitely divisible they are infinitely great (assuming their
parts to have size), or else infinitely small (assuming their parts to be
without magnitude, like mathematical points).

PROP. 2. Having shown that the universe consists of 'ones', Pr.
next shows that these 'ones' are not pure unities. Their relation
to 'One' or Unity¹ is precisely the same relation as subsists between
any group of particulars and the Form in which they share. If any
particular beautiful thing were ὅπερ καλόν, if it were definable by no
quality except its beauty, it would not have beauty as a predicate
(μετέχειν καλοῦ) but would be indistinguishable from the Form of
Beauty: it must therefore contain something other, in virtue of
which it is not-beautiful (except in so far as this 'other' is transmuted
into beauty by the Form). The same argument holds for the One
and the ones, despite the fact that the One is not a Form: every
unit contains an 'other' as well as a 'one' (although the 'other'
may in certain conditions be almost completely transmuted²). This
analysis had already been made by Plato, *Parm.* 142 B ff. and *Soph.*
245 A. Cf. *in Tim.* II. 304. 19; *in Parm.* 697. 2; 1078. 13;
1197. 19; and *Enn.* V. iii. 12 *fin.*

16. εἰ γὰρ . . . 17. παρὰ τὸ ἕν. Cf. Plato, *Parm.* 158 A μετέχοι δέ
γε ἂν τοῦ ἑνὸς δῆλον ὅτι ἄλλο ὂν ἢ ἕν· οὐ γὰρ ἂν μετεῖχεν, ἀλλ᾽ ἦν ἂν αὐτὸ ἕν.

20-1. [τὸ μετέχον . . . ὡς μετέχον τοῦ ἑνός]. These words appear
to have been originally written in the margin as a summary of the
argument and then erroneously incorporated in the text, where they

¹ It will be observed that the formal proof of the *existence* of such a pure unity
is reserved for prop. 4.
² Cf. Damasc. I. 24. 18 τὸ ἡνωμένον ἐνδείκνυται ἐν ἑαυτῷ ἔχον τό τε ἑνιζόμενον (εἰ
καὶ ἐπ᾽ ἔσχατον εἴη καταπεπομένον τὸ ἑνιζόμενον ὑπὸ τοῦ ἑνίζοντος· ὅμως γὰρ ἡνωμένον ὑπόκειται) καὶ αὐτὸ τὸ ἕν.

not only are otiose, but hopelessly confuse the proof by anticipating the conclusion. If I am right in rejecting them, the corruption of the following τούτῳ is explained : it was changed to τοῦτο after the intrusion of the marginal note had obscured its meaning.

22. ὅπερ ἕν: 'what "one" is', i.e. definable by the term 'unity', or having unity as its essence. See Ross on Arist. *Metaph.* 1001 a 26.

PROP. 3. Having analysed each of the 'ones' of experience into a unity and something which is unified, Pr. proceeds to prove (or rather, to assert under the form of proof) that the former element cannot be evolved from the latter but must be introduced *ab extra* : thus every 'one' implies a purer 'one' from which it derives its unity. The nerve of the 'proof' is the tacit assumption of the Aristotelian principle that the potential does not pass into actuality without the operation of the already actual—a principle which is itself 'proved' in prop. 77. τὸ γινόμενον ἕν is at the beginning of the process δυνάμει ἕν : it cannot become ἐνεργείᾳ ἕν unless there be something which is already ἐνεργείᾳ ἕν. Cf. Syrian. *in Metaph.* 45. 30 ; 59. 8.

7–8. ἐκ τοῦ μὴ ἑνός. Though the MSS. of the Ἀνάπτυξις have ἐκ τοῦ μὴ ἓν εἶναι, yet Nicolaus in his discussion of this prop. writes (Ἀνάπτ. 10. 21) ἐκ τοῦ μὴ ἑνὸς γινομένη ἕν—which looks as if he had before him the passage as read in MPQW. The words ἐκ τῆς στερήσεως, written above the line in a late hand in M, and inserted in the text by Portus, are due to some reader of Aristotle, who had in mind passages like *Metaph.* 1033 a 8 ff.

PROP. 4. This proposition is not directed so much to distinguishing the 'ones' from the One (this has already been done in prop. 2) as to establishing the actual existence of the latter by showing that the analysis already made must lead to infinite regress, unless a term is put to it by positing an unanalysable unity : the existence of an Absolute is inferred (as how often since !) from the simple fact of relativity—in the language of the *Parmenides*, there cannot be a ἓν ὄν unless there be a (transcendent) ἕν. So also for ps.-Dion. God is the ὑπερηνωμένη ἑνάς (*Div. Nom.* 2. 1).

11. εἰ γὰρ καὶ τοῦτο κτλ. Cf. *Enn.* VI. vii. 17 *fin.* (II. 448. 13) ἔδει δὲ τὸ πρῶτον μὴ πολὺ μηδαμῶς εἶναι· ἀνήρτητο γὰρ ἂν τὸ πολὺ αὐτοῦ εἰς ἕτερον αὖ πρὸ αὐτοῦ : and *in Parm.* 1100. 35 ff.

17. πλῆθος ἄπειρον ἔσται: by indefinitely repeating the division into a 'one' and a 'not-one'. Cf. Plato, *Parm.* 142 D ff., esp. 144 E

τὸ ἓν ἄρα αὐτὸ κεκερματισμένον ὑπὸ τῆς οὐσίας πολλά τε καὶ ἄπειρα τὸ
πλῆθός ἐστιν. So also *Enn.* V. iii. 15 *fin.* (II. 199. 12 ff.).

PROP. 5. This proposition demonstrates that the Absolute Unity
whose existence was established in prop. 4 is at once completely
transcendent, in the sense of being uninfected by plurality, and completely immanent, in the sense that all plurality 'participates' it or is
determined by it. The argument proceeds by excluding in turn all
the possible alternatives, viz. (*a*) the view that unity participates
plurality, but not *vice versa*, i.e. that unity is not an ultimate ἀρχή at
all (p. 4, ll. 20–6) ; (*b*) the view that neither principle participates the
other, i.e. that unity is transcendent without being immanent (p. 4,
l. 27–p. 6, l. 3) ; (*c*) the view that each principle participates the
other, i.e. that unity is immanent without being transcendent (p. 6,
ll. 7–21). The only other possible view, viz. that plurality participates unity, but not *vice versa*, i.e. that unity is at once transcendent
and immanent (p. 6, ll. 4–6), is thus left in possession of the field.
Alternatives (*a*) and (*b*) have in reality been disposed of in prop. 1 ;
but they are here formally reconsidered. The substance of the
proposition lies in the exclusion of (*c*) by an argument similar in
principle to the 'third man' difficulty (Plato, *Parm.* 132 D ; Arist.
Metaph. 990 b 17, with Alexander *ad loc.*), that if the Forms are
related to particulars by ὁμοιότης we must posit a cause of this
relation, and then a cause which will relate this cause to the Forms,
and so *ad infinitum*. Pr. sees that the only way out of this (short of
rejecting substantive Forms altogether, as Aristotle did) is to regard
the relation as one of ὁμοίωσις and not of ὁμοιότης, i.e. to insist that
it qualifies only *one* of the related terms. We must say that the
Form is *not* 'like' the particulars, but belongs to a different order of
existence ; at the same time, unless the Form is to be inoperative
(ἀργόν), we must say that the particulars are 'like' the Form, in the
sense that they are caused by it (*in Parm.* 906 ff.). So here the
many 'participate' the One which causes them ; but the One is not
thereby infected with any element of plurality. Proclus rejects not
only immanentism of the Stoic type, but the opinion of those
Neoplatonists who regarded the One as containing the Many in a
seminal mode.[1] The argument of this proposition is worked out
more fully in *Th. Pl.* II. i. 78–9. Its conclusion is adopted by
ps.-Dion., *Div. Nom.* 2. 1 ἄνευ μὲν τοῦ ἑνὸς οὐκ ἔσται πλῆθος, ἄνευ δὲ
τοῦ πλήθους ἔσται τὸ ἕν.

---

[1] *in Parm.* 1107. 9 ff. : cf. anon. *in Parm.* p. 9 (*Rhein. Mus.* N. F. 47, 1892).

22. πρὶν γένηται. The subjunctive (without ἄν) is in Pr. the normal construction of πρίν in primary sequence, whether the meaning be 'until' or 'before'.

27. εἰ δὲ δὴ ... 30. ὕστερον. I have adopted in l. 28 πολλά ἐστιν, which is certainly the original reading in M as well as in BCD, and is therefore likely to have stood in the archetype. χρόνῳ is contrasted (as often in Aristotle) with φύσει, and σύστοιχα εἶναι ἀλλήλοις is to be supplied with κωλύει.[1] Pr. holds that unity is *not* temporally prior to plurality: both are found in pure Being (prop. 89), which is not merely eternal but 'superior to Eternity' (prop. 87).

2. πάντῃ: i.e. both as a whole and in each of its parts. The formal discrepancy between this statement and prop. 1 (πᾶν πλῆθος μετέχει πῃ τοῦ ἑνός) is correctly explained by Nicolaus (13. 23 ff.) : τὸ μὲν ἓν οὐ πάντῃ μετέχεται (μᾶλλον γὰρ ἀμέθεκτόν ἐστι), τὸ δὲ πλῆθος πάντῃ (ἀντὶ τοῦ καθ' ὅλον ἑαυτό) μετέχει τοῦ ἑνός. Particulars can only participate the One indirectly and imperfectly; but they do so in every fraction of their being. Cf. prop. 23 n.

13. ἀντικείμενα γὰρ οὐ σπεύδει εἰς ἄλληλα. Cf. Arist. *Metaph.* 1069 b 6 οὐ γὰρ τὰ ἐναντία μεταβάλλει. In *Th. Pl.* II. i. the hypothesis of a voluntary union between the One and the many is rejected on this ground; and that of an accidental conjunction on the ground that it would admit of an equally accidental severance (and so reintroduce the possibility of a πλῆθος ἀμέτοχον ἑνός). There is indeed a ἓν πολλά such as is here posited (the unity of the Forms in the divine Intellect); but this, like all mixtures of πέρας and ἄπειρον, implies the existence of an αἰτία τῆς μίξεως.

PROP. 6. The argument of this proposition is simple and seemingly unimportant; but Pr. has tacitly imported into it a metaphysical interpretation which has far-reaching consequences for his system. He begins by pointing out that no manifold can be indefinitely divisible, for the reasons given in prop. 1. Every manifold must therefore be composed of constituents which 'participate the One' both as wholes and in their parts (if any): i.e. it must consist either (*a*) of indivisible units, or (*b*) of unified groups ultimately analysable into such units.[2] Pr. then goes on to describe the manifold of type (*a*) as the 'first' unified group, and to identify this with τὸ πρώτως μετέχον τοῦ ἑνός. The identification rests (as does, at bottom, the whole Neoplatonic system) on the identification of logical with

---

[1] I owe this explanation to the kindness of Mr. W. D. Ross.
[2] Prof. Taylor compares the Leibnizian doctrine that all complexes must be complexes of individuals.

metaphysical priority. Type (*a*) is simpler than type (*b*), and independent of it. Any manifold of type (*b*) will evidently contain
a number of manifolds of type (*a*), as the genus contains a number
of *infimae species*: without type (*a*), type (*b*) would be infinitely
divisible and so unreal (ll. 28–9). But type (*a*) can exist without
type (*b*). Type (*a*) is therefore 'prior' to type (*b*); and for Pr. this
means that it is nearer to the One and occurs on a higher level of
reality. We shall find later that the group whose members are
unanalysable units is exemplified not only in the *infima species* but
also at the other end of the scale, in a system of 'divine units' or
gods (props. 113 ff.). The way is here prepared for this development,
though the term ἑνάς means in the present prop. simply 'indivisible
unit' (*in Parm.* 1220. 3 ἑκάστη γὰρ ἑνὰς ἀδιαίρετος). On the history
of the term, and on the conception of 'divine units', see introductory
note to Section L.

26. ἐξ ὧν τὸ πρώτως ἡνωμένον: '(one of the parts) of which the first
unified group (is composed)'. Failure to realize the ellipse seems to
be accountable for the corruption of ἑνάς to ἑνάδες here and in l. 25.

29. εἰς ἄπειρον. This is true only on the assumption that indivisible units do not occur *anywhere* in the series. The possibility
that they may occur at the *end* of the series without occurring also at
the beginning is ignored by Pr.

30. τὸ ἐξ ἀρχῆς. Cf. prop. 205, l. 13, and *Th. Pl.* II. i. 79.

B. *Of Causes* (props. 7–13).

1. The cause is superior to the effect (7).
2. Unity and transcendence of the Good or Final Cause (8): it is
distinct from the goodness both of dependent and of self-sufficient
principles (9–10).
3. Unity and transcendence of the Efficient Cause (11).
4. Identity of the Good with the Efficient Cause (12).
5. Identity of the Good with the One (13).

PROP. 7. This is the principle on which the whole structure of
Neoplatonism is really founded. If it is accepted, any emergence
of the higher from the lower must be attributed to the causative
operation of a higher which already exists ἐνεργείᾳ. That such
emergence is characteristic of the phenomenal order is fully recognized by the Neoplatonists (cf. prop. 37 n. and *in Tim.* III. 322. 1 ff.),
but it is for them incomprehensible save as a return (ἐπιστροφή) of
power to its source, a return which would be impossible were not

that source eternally and unchangeably active in the real order. It is in virtue of this law that from the sequence of temporal evolution [1] out of the unconscious life of Nature through successive grades of animal and human consciousness, and thence through the synoptic intuition of the philosopher towards an all-embracing spiritual unity, the Neoplatonists believed themselves entitled to infer an inverse sequence of timeless dependence, an 'involution' of spiritual force from the One through a divine Intelligence, a divine Soul, a universal Nature, towards the minimal reality of bare Matter.   Though Plotinus was the first to apply systematically the principle that the cause has always a higher and fuller reality than the effect, it is not peculiar to Neoplatonism, but is already implicit in Plato's doctrine of Being and Becoming.   Indeed, in the *Philebus* the Neoplatonists thought that they found an explicit statement of it: 27 B ἡγεῖται μὲν τὸ ποιοῦν ἀεὶ κατὰ φύσιν, τὸ δὲ ποιούμενον ἐπακολουθεῖ γιγνόμενον ἐκείνῳ (cf. *Enn.* V. v. 13 [II. 222. 18]; *in Tim.* I. 259. 27). Plato's ἡγεῖται, it is true, hardly carries all the metaphysical significance which Plot. and his successors read into it.   We do, however, find the doctrine quite clearly formulated in Cic. *N. D.* II. 33. 86, 'ea quae efferant aliquid ex sese perfectiores habere naturas quam ea quae ex his efferantur'—a passage which may reflect the teaching of Antiochus (Reinhardt).   With the Neoplatonists it is fundamental: cf. e.g. *Enn.* V. iv. 1 (II. 204. 2); Porph. ἀφ. xiii: Iamb. *de myst.* III. 20 (148. 9).   But Pr. is, so far as I know, the only writer who offers a formal 'proof' of it.

1. παρακτικόν.   Proclus prefers this term to ποιητικόν because, as Nicolaus remarks ('Ανάπτ. 102. 16), he wishes to exclude the idea of volition.   γεννητικόν, which he sometimes uses, has the disadvantage of suggesting too strongly a beginning in time.   παράγειν in this technical sense seems to occur first in Plotinus (e.g. II. 505. 19).

19. εἰ δὲ αὐτὸ κτλ.   For this argument cf. *Th. Pl.* II. iii. 88; and Descartes' third proof of the existence of God, in the *Reply to the Second Objections* : ' God, having the power of conserving me, should have, *a fortiori*, the power of conferring these perfections on himself '.

23. πάντα γὰρ τοῦ ἀγαθοῦ ὀρέγεται κατὰ φύσιν: Arist. *E. N.* 1094 a 1.

PROP. 8.   As props. 4 and 5 established the existence of a transcendent One, so Pr. now argues to the existence of a transcendent Good.   This result is readily elicited from the ordinary Greek

---

[1] Not of course in the Darwinian sense, since the Neoplatonists, like Aristotle, believed in fixed species, but in the sense of a *scala naturae* wherein each grade achieves its perfection by self-identification with that immediately above it.

assumptions that 'good' means object of desire,[1] and that everything
which has existence has some conscious or unconscious *nisus*
towards 'good' (cf. Plato, *Phil.* 20 D, Arist. *E.N.* 1094 a 1). Nothing
which has such a *nisus* can *be* completely good : for desire is, like
causality, a transitive relation between substantives—τὸ ἐφιέμενον can
never be identical with τὸ ἐφετόν (ll. 33 ff.). Particular things do
indeed on occasion attain, in a sense, the goal of their desire : but
what they attain becomes, by being attained, part of themselves, and
is thereby distinguished from τὸ κοινὸν ἐφετόν. They 'participate
good' or have 'good' as a predicate : we can say of them that they
are good, but not that they are *the* Good, just as we can say of any
object that it is one, but not that it is *the* One (ll. 4-8). This is
confirmed (ll. 9–13) by the Plotinian form of the same argument :
goodness, being the highest universal of ethics, becomes not more
but less perfect by the addition to it of any other character—for this
'addition' can only emphasize some part or aspect of what is already
contained in goodness at the expense of some other part or aspect.
Pr., like Spinoza, sees that all definition involves a denial : goodness
is indefinable because it is the fundamental character of *all* reality
as such ; and because it is indefinable it is, with the usual Neoplatonic leap from logic to ontology, affirmed to be transcendent.—
With the whole proposition cf. Plot., *Enn.* V. v. 13. The Platonic
source for the transcendence of the Good is *Rep.* 509 B. On the
general subject of 'negative theology' in the Neoplatonists see
Appendix I. The doctrine is taken over by ps.-Dion.: e.g. *Div.
Nom.* 5. 8. πάντα αὐτοῦ (sc. τοῦ θεοῦ) καὶ ἅμα κατηγορεῖται, καὶ οὐδέν
ἐστι τῶν πάντων.

2. [ἕτερον καὶ] ἀπεξενωμένον. The readings of our MSS. here are
most easily accounted for if we suppose the archetype to have had
ἀπεξενωμένον with a gloss ἕτερον written above it. That both words
stood in the MS. used by Nicolaus is confirmed by Ἀνάπτ. 18. 2
οὔκουν ἕτερον οὐδ' ἀπεξενωμένον τοῦ ἀγαθοῦ τὸ ὄν.

3. τὸ ὄν and τὸ ἀγαθόν may well be a reader's explanatory additions ;
but I hesitate to eject them, for Pr. is often his own *glossator*.
Similar instances are *Th. Pl.* VI. xv. 387 τῶν μὲν ἥνωνται μᾶλλον, τῶν
ὑποδεεστέρων, τῶν δὲ πληθύονται μᾶλλον : *in Tim.* I. 231. 32 ff. : and
infra prop. 73, l. 11.

10. ἠλάττωσας τῇ προσθέσει. The epigram is Plotinus's (*Enn.* III.
viii. 11 [I. 345. 12] ; III. ix. 3 [I. 350. 30] ; V. v. 13 [II. 221. 18] ;

---

[1] Plotinus, however, denies that the Good is good *because* it is ἐφετόν : on the
contrary, it is ἐφετόν because it is good (*Enn.* VI. vii. 25). In ethics, as in
ontology, the Neoplatonists are careful to steer clear of subjectivism.

and, with a different application, VI. v. 12 [II. 397. 23]). In *Th. Pl.*
(II. vii. 101) Pr. says the same thing about 'the gods' in general :
αἱ γὰρ προσθέσεις ἐν τοῖς θεοῖς ἀφαιρέσεις εἰσί. Platonic 'authority'
was found· for this in *Ep.* II. 312 E τὸ δὴ μετὰ τοῦτο ἡ ψυχή φησιν,
Ἀλλὰ ποῖόν τι μήν; τοῦτ' ἐστίν … τὸ ἐρώτημα ὃ πάντων αἴτιόν ἐστιν κακῶν:
which is explained by Pr. as meaning that ἡ προσθήκη τοῦ ποίου …
ἀφίστησι (τὴν ψυχὴν) τῆς ἐξῃρημένης τῶν ὅλων ἀγαθότητος (*Th. Pl.* II.
104 : cf. *in Parm.* 1107. 22 ff.).

PROPS. 9 and 10. The self-sufficient is a ' mean term ' (see Introd.
p. xxii) between the Good, which is (*a*) the source of its own goodness, (*b*) nothing else but good, and the 'good things' of sense-
experience, whose goodness is (*a*) derivative and (*b*) impure.   Mid-
way between this pair of doubly contra-distinguished terms stands
the self-sufficient, which resembles the Good in that its goodness is
self-derived, the 'good things' in that its goodness inheres in the
not-good or less-good.   To put the doctrine in another way, the
Good is purely ἐφετόν and the individual is purely ἐφιέμενον : between
them must come a class of things which are at once ἐφετά and
ἐφιέμενα, i.e. contain their good within their own nature—otherwise
the gap between desire and its object, or between the world and
God, can never be bridged.   This intermediate class includes the
whole range of spiritual reality, as is made clear by a passage in
Th. Pl. : νοῦς μὲν γὰρ κατὰ μέθεξιν, ψυχὴ δὲ κατ' ἔλλαμψιν, τὸ δὲ πᾶν
τοῦτο κατὰ τὴν πρὸς τὸ θεῖον ὁμοιότητα αὐταρκές· αὐτοὶ δὲ οἱ θεοὶ δι'
ἑαυτοὺς καὶ παρ' ἑαυτῶν αὐτάρκεις, ἑαυτοὺς πεπληρωκότες, μᾶλλον δὲ
πληρώματα τῶν ὅλων ἀγαθῶν ὑπάρχοντες (I. xix. 50). For the αὐτάρκεια
of the gods, cf. prop. 127.—It is natural to ask, as Nicolaus does
(Ἀνάπτ. 19. 19 ff.), how any but the supreme principle can in
a monistic system be 'self-sufficient' in the sense defined in prop. 10,
τὸ παρ' ἑαυτοῦ καὶ ἐν ἑαυτῷ τὸ ἀγαθὸν κεκτημένον. Pr. (*in Tim.* II. 90.
8 ff.) answers this question in discussing the αὐτάρκεια which Plato in
the *Timaeus* (33 D) ascribes to the κόσμος. The substance of his
reply is that ' self-sufficiency ' does not exclude a timeless causal
dependence on a higher principle.   The self-sufficient does indeed
eternally *possess* its good in virtue of its own nature :[1] but its nature
is what it is only because of the existence of something higher. This
is a particular application of the general doctrine that immanence is
unintelligible without transcendence : the logically analysable is the
ontologically derivative.   Cf. note on prop. 40.

[1] Cf. *Enn.* I. i. 2 (I. 40. 16) αὔταρκες τό γε ἁπλοῦν ἐν οὐσίᾳ, οἷόν ἐστι μένον ἐν
οὐσίᾳ τῇ αὐτοῦ.

As to Pr.'s sources here, that God is not ἐνδεής is traditional Greek teaching : cf. e.g. Plato, *Rep.* 381 C, *Phil.* 67 A ; Arist. *Metaph.* 1091 b 16 ; 'Euryphamus' *ap.* Stob. V. 914. 7 ; Philo V. 268. 17 C.W., &c. ; Plut. *def. orac.* 8 (413 E) ; *Corp. Herm.* VI. *init.* The distinction of two grades of divine independence comes from Plot., *Enn.* V. iii. 13 (II. 196. 21) ; *ibid.* 17 (201. 19). In the latter passage the One is said to be ἐπέκεινα αὐταρκείας. Syrian., however, speaks of the Good in the traditional way as αὐταρκέστατον (*in Metaph.* 183. 10).

14. ἢ κατ' οὐσίαν ἢ κατ' ἐνέργειαν. We are told in *Th. Pl.* I. xix. 50 that θεῖαι ψυχαί are αὐτάρκεις κατ' οὐσίαν but not κατ' ἐνέργειαν, since their ἐνέργεια is temporal. Cf. prop. 191.

15. οὐσίαν. For the confusion of this word with αἰτίαν cf. prop. 11, l. 11 ; prop. 39, l. 29 ; prop. 45, l. 18 ; prop. 193, l. 22. A trace of the true reading is perhaps preserved in the meaningless αἰτίου, which seems to have been the original reading of M ; it may well have arisen from αἰτίαν.

18. καὶ τὸ μὲν κτλ. The insertion of καί (with PQ) seems essential to the sense, for τὸ μὲν ... χωρὶς οὖσαν is not an inference from τὸ μὲν ... ἐπιδεὲς ἄλλου (as it must be if καί is omitted), but another way of saying the same thing.

23. ἐπεὶ οὖν [ὅτι καὶ ὅμοιον καὶ ἠλαττωμένον]. The bracketed words are a reader's marginal note, similar in form to a number of *marginalia* in M. Their introduction into the text threw it into hopeless confusion, and gave rise in the renaissance copies to a whole crop of further corruptions, most of which are duly reproduced by Port. and Cr.

PROP. 11. Having affirmed in prop. 8 the unity and transcendence of the final cause, Pr. now assigns a similar character to the efficient cause, thus preparing the way for the identification of the two. The argument proceeds by rejecting (*a*) views which deny efficient causality (excluded as involving agnosticism), ll. 12–17 ; (*b*) doctrines of bi-lateral causality (excluded by prop. 7), ll. 18–24 ; (*c*) the assumption of an infinite chain of unilateral causation (excluded on the same grounds as (*a*)), ll. 25–8 ; (*d*) pluralism of the Empedoclean type, which posits a finite number of mutually independent causes (excluded by prop. 5), ll. 32–4. View (*d*) is apparently only mentioned as an afterthought. Cf. *Th. Pl.* II. ii. 80 (substantially the same argument as this) ; and II. iii. 86 ff. (a more elaborate proof that the universe contains both a first cause and a last consequent, the causal series being thus finite, and limited at each end

by an irreducible unity). Pr. has a similar argument for the existence of τὸ ἀεὶ ὄν as efficient cause of γιγνόμενα, *in Tim.* I. 228. 11 ff., *in Parm.* 798. 27 ff.

15. ἡ γὰρ τῶν αἰτίων γνῶσις ἐπιστήμης ἐστὶν ἔργον. So in substance Plato, *Meno* 98 A οὐ πολλοῦ ἄξιαί εἰσιν (αἱ ἀληθεῖς δόξαι) ἕως ἄν τις αὐτὰς δήσῃ αἰτίας λογισμῷ . . . ἐπειδὰν δὲ δεθῶσιν . . . ἐπιστῆμαι γίγνονται. The formulation, however, is Aristotelian (*Phys.* 184 a 12, &c.), as is noted in the margin of M. Cf. Plot., *Enn.* VI. vii. 2, where essence is identified with cause : ὃ γάρ ἐστιν ἕκαστον, διὰ τοῦτο ἔστι· λέγω δὲ οὐχ ὅτι τὸ εἶδος ἑκάστῳ αἴτιον τοῦ εἶναι—τοῦτο μὲν γὰρ ἀληθές—ἀλλ᾽ ὅτι, εἰ καὶ αὐτὸ τὸ εἶδος ἕκαστον πρὸς αὐτὸ ἀναπτύσσοις, εὑρήσεις ἐν αὐτῷ τὸ διὰ τί (II. 426. 31).—γνῶσις in Pr., as in Plot., is a general term for cognition: it has no specifically religious connotation.

21. συνάπτειν: here simply of causal dependence. For the religious implications of the word see Nock, *Sallustius*, p. xcviii.

26. τῶν γὰρ ἀπείρων οὐδενός ἐστι γνῶσις : so *Th. Pl.* II. i. 76. This argument against an infinite chain of causes is Aristotle's (*Metaph.* 994 a 1 οὐκ ἄπειρα τὰ αἴτια τῶν ὄντων . . . b 20 τὸ ἐπίστασθαι ἀναιροῦσιν οἱ οὕτως λέγοντες) : cf. also Plat. *Phil.* 17 E.

31. οἷον ἐκ ῥίζης. Cf. prop. 144, ll. 28–9 πάντα . . . ἐνερρίζωται τοῖς θεοῖς : *in Parm.* 1116. 16 τῷ πρώτῳ . . . ἐνερριζωμένα. The comparison of the universe to a tree having its life-source in the root is a favourite one with the Stoics, e.g. Cic. *N.D.* II. 32. 82 (probably after Posei-donius) ; and with Plotinus (III. iii. 7, viii. 10 ; IV. iii. 4, iv. 11 ; VI. viii. 15 *fin.*). Plotinus protests, however, against its deter-ministic implications (III. i. 4 *init.*). The analogous comparison of *Man* to a tree whose roots are in Heaven is as old as Plato (*Tim.* 90 A).

PROP. 12 follows *Rep.* 509 B in identifying the efficient with the final cause of the universe : the ἀρχὴ τῆς προόδου is also the τέλος τῆς ἐπιστροφῆς. It is Pr.'s prime quarrel with Aristotle that on this cardinal point he lapsed from the Platonic teaching : the Aristotelian system affirms the upward tension towards a God who κινεῖ ὡς ἐρώμενον without tracing the downward chain of causal dependence. Pr. urges that the conception of deity as goal of desire is unintelligible when divorced from its counterpart, the conception of deity as source of being—εἰ γὰρ ἐρᾷ ὁ κόσμος, ὥς φησι καὶ Ἀριστοτέλης, τοῦ νοῦ καὶ κινεῖται πρὸς αὐτόν, πόθεν ἔχει ταύτην τὴν ἔφεσιν; (*in Tim.* I. 267. 4). The formal 'proof' attempted in the present prop. has to the modern mind a decidedly question-begging flavour, hinging as it does on the ambiguous word κρεῖττον. If κρεῖττον *means* ' morally better ',

as is asserted in l. 15, it is at once evident that there can be nothing
τἀγαθοῦ κρεῖττον : but Pr. understands the latter statement in the
sense that there can be nothing higher than the Good in the chain
of causes.   Similarly in the commentary on the *Parmenides* (1143.
39 ff.) he proves that there can be nothing higher than the One with
the help of the assumption that *κρεῖττον means* 'more unified' (αὐτὸ
τὸ κρεῖττον ἑνὸς μετουσίᾳ κρεῖττον).   Flagrant as this may seem, it is
doubtless no more consciously dishonest than is the famous argument
in the *Phaedo* from the inherent meaning of the word ψυχή.   It is
not for nothing that the Greeks described thought and its verbal
clothing by the single term λόγος : even more than modern philosophers they were liable to become the victims of their vocabulary.—
In ll. 18-23 two supplementary arguments are advanced, the first
resting on the assumption that every efficient cause is desired by its
effects (which again begs the question), the second on the traditional
definition of the Good, as οὗ πάντα ἐξήρτηται (cf. Arist. *Metaph.*
1072 b 13).—It is noteworthy that Pr. expresses here none of the
scruples about making the supreme principle a link in the chain of
causation which he elsewhere suggests, e.g. *Th. Pl.* II. 106 οὔτε γὰρ
εἰ αἴτιον ἐκεῖνο τῶν ὄντων οὔτε εἰ γεννητικόν, ἢ γνῶναι τοῖς δευτέροις
θεμιτὸν ἢ λόγῳ διελθεῖν, ἀλλὰ σιγῇ τὸ ἄρρητον αὐτοῦ καὶ πρὸ τῶν αἰτίων
πάντως (γρ. πάντων?) ἀναιτίως αἴτιον ἀνυμνεῖν : cf. *Enn.* VI. viii. 18 [II.
503. 19] αἴτιον δὲ ἐκεῖνο (sc. τὸ ἕν) τοῦ αἰτίου.

12. οὐ γὰρ ... 14. δίδωσι: cf. props. 56, 57.

PROP. 13 completes the account of the First Cause by linking it
with the doctrine of props. 1-6.: the One, which has hitherto
appeared as a metaphysical abstraction, is now identified with the
summum bonum in virtue of its character as σωστικὸν ἑκάστου, the
ground of individuality.   We are justified, I think, in regarding this
Plotinian identification as genuinely Platonic, though it is not made
anywhere in the dialogues.   That it formed part of Plato's oral
teaching is explicitly stated by Aristoxenus, *Harm. El.* II, p. 30 Meib.
(RP 327 A) : cf. also Arist. *Metaph.* 1091 b 13 τῶν δὲ τὰς ἀκινήτους
οὐσίας εἶναι λεγόντων οἱ μέν φασιν αὐτὸ τὸ ἓν τὸ ἀγαθὸν αὐτὸ εἶναι· οὐσίαν
μέντοι τὸ ἓν αὐτοῦ ᾤοντο εἶναι μάλιστα, where it is generally agreed that
οἱ μέν refers primarily to Plato; *ibid.* 988 a 14; *Eth. Eudem.* 1218 a 24.
Furthermore, the assumptions on which Pr. bases his identification do
occur in the dialogues.   For the Good as συνεκτικόν cf. *Phaedo* 99 C 5
(which is quoted by Pr. in support of the identity, *in Parm.* 1097. 14).
That the One is συνεκτικόν is negatively shown in the last hypothesis
of the *Parmenides*, which yields the conclusion μὴ ἐνόντος ἑνὸς ἐν τοῖς

ἄλλοις, οὔτε πολλὰ οὔτε ἕν ἐστι τἆλλα (165 E): cf. *Th. Pl.* I. (xii). 31. See also prop. 20 n.

According to *Th. Pl.* II. (vi). 95 deity *qua* One is the cause of procession ; *qua* Good, of reversion. This view, with its hint of dualism, is not suggested in the present passage, where the One and the Good are treated simply as two names for one principle, not as two aspects or functions of that principle. Deity in the Neoplatonists really transcends the distinction of procession and reversion (or in modern terminology, of existence and value): cf. *Th. Pl.* V. xvi. 277 ὁ πρῶτος θεὸς . . . οὔτε τἀγαθὸν οὔτε ἕν λέγεται κυρίως, διὰ τὴν ἄρρητον ἑαυτοῦ καὶ ἄγνωστον ὑπεροχήν: and *Enn.* VI. ix. 6.

26. τὸ ἀγαθόν ἐστι σωστικὸν τῶν ὄντων ἁπάντων. This is the first definition of the Good in the Platonic Ὅροι: cf. also Arist. *Pol.* 1261 b 9.

28. τῷ γὰρ ἑνὶ σώζεται πάντα. Cf. Arnim, *Stoic. Vet. Fragm.* II. 448 ἕν τι συνέχει τὸν σύνολον κόσμον ἅμα τοῖς ἐν αὐτῷ: *Enn.* V. iii. 15 (II. 198. 15) πᾶν γὰρ τὸ μὴ ἓν τῷ ἓν σώζεται καὶ ἔστιν ὅπερ ἐστὶ τούτῳ: Syrian. *in Metaph.* 60. 7 πάντα τῷ ἑνὶ καὶ ἔστι καὶ σώζεται. σωτηρία in the religious sense of 'salvation' (on which see Reitzenstein *H. M.-R².* 39 ; Nock in Rawlinson's *Essays on the Trinity and the Incarnation,* 88 ff.) is not in question here, though Pr. uses the word in this sense elsewhere, e.g. *in Alc.* 521. 8.

32. τὸ ἓν συναγωγόν ἐστι . . . 33. κατὰ τὴν ἑαυτοῦ παρουσίαν. Cf. ps.-Dion. *Div. Nom.* 4. 6 ἡ τοῦ νοητοῦ φωτὸς παρουσία συναγωγὸς καὶ ἑνωτικὴ τῶν φωτιζομένων ἐστί.

3. ὅθεν δὴ κτλ. : on the correspondence between degrees of unity and degrees of goodness cf. *Enn.* VI. ix. 1, which develops the implications of the Stoic axiom 'nullum bonum ex distantibus' (Arnim, *Stoic. Vet. Fragm.* III. 98 ; Sen. *Ep.* 102. 6–7 (= Arnim III. 160)).

C. *Of the Grades of Reality* (props. 14–24).

  (a) Vertical stratification of reality :

    1. There is an Unmoved and a Self-moved (14).

    2. The Self-moved has reflexive consciousness (17), and is therefore incorporeal (15) and independent of Body (16).

    3. There is nothing in the effect that is not primitively in the cause (18). Therefore Soul, being the source of self-movement in bodies, is primitively self-moved (20).

    4. The primitive character of any grade is permanent and universal (19). Hence Intelligence does not belong primitively to Soul (20).

5. There are thus four grades, Body, Soul, Intelligence, and the One (20).

(*b*) General structure of reality in each stratum:

1. As a One and Many (21-2).
2. As a triad of Unparticipated, Participated, Participant (23-4).

PROP. 14. This is not simply concerned (as the enunciation might suggest) with a formal dichotomous classification of things as moved or unmoved, and of the former class as self-moved or not self-moved. It aims at establishing the actual, and not merely logical, existence of the Aristotelian unmoved mover (*Phys.* Θ. 5) and the Platonic 'self-moving motion' (*Phdr.* 245 C-D; *Legg.* X. 894 B-895 B). The identification of the former with νοῦς and the latter with ψυχή is reserved for prop. 20. The argument of ll. 20-4 is taken from the passage in the *Laws* (895 A 6-B 2); while that of ll. 15-19 seems to be adapted from Aristotle, *Phys.* 256 a 13 ff. The triadic arrangement, κινοῦν μόνον—κινοῦν τε ἅμα καὶ κινούμενον—κινούμενον μόνον (ll. 24-6), comes from the Peripatetic school tradition (Plut. *Symp.* VII. vi. 3).

That τῶν κινούντων καὶ κινουμένων ἡγεῖται τὸ ἀκίνητον is also shown in *El. Phys.* II. 19, by a proof similar to that of ll. 15-19, but rather more fully worked out. From the absence in *El. Phys.* of any reference to the αὐτοκίνητον, Ritzenfeld, in his introduction to the Teubner edition of *El. Phys.*, argues that that work was composed at a very early period of Pr.'s development, 'cum auctor nondum in philosophia Platonica vigebat vel suam sententiam proferre audebat'. I cannot accept this argument: for (1) the existence of τὸ ἀκίνητον is similarly established in the *in Tim.*, III. 9. 7 ff., without any direct mention of τὸ αὐτοκίνητον, and the *in Tim.* cannot date from a 'pre-Platonic' period of Pr.'s thought; (2) τὸ αὐτοκίνητον is in fact indirectly recognized in both passages under another name, as τὸ ἀιδίως κινούμενον. Cf. Introd., p. xvii f.

In *Th. Pl.* I. (xiv). 32 ff. a rather more elaborate classification is offered, again on the basis of the *Laws*. According to this, things are (*a*) κινούμενα μόνον (σώματα); or (*b*) κινούμενα καὶ κινοῦντα (ποιότητες, ἔνυλα εἴδη and ζῷα); or (*c*) αὐτοκίνητα (ψυχαί); or (*d*) ἀκίνητα (νοῦς θεῖος). The inclusion of (*d*) is justified by quoting *Legg.* X. 897 B νοῦν μὲν προσλαβοῦσα ἀεὶ θεῖον (ἡ ψυχή) ... ὀρθὰ καὶ εὐδαίμονα παιδαγωγεῖ πάντά.

9. πᾶν τὸ ὄν κτλ. The cumbrous form of the enunciation is due

to a desire to observe the rule of dichotomous division, as prescribed in the *Sophistes*.

15. κινουμένου. This word is essential to the sense of the passage, since the argument proceeds, as usual, by exclusion of the alternative; κινούμενον, the vulgate reading, is quite otiose.

17. τὸ κινοῦν τοῦ κινουμένου κρεῖττον. The communication of motion is a kind of causation, and therefore falls under the general law laid down in prop. 7.

20. εἰ γὰρ σταίη τὰ πάντα: from *Legg.* 895 A 6 εἰ σταίη πως τὰ πάντα ὁμοῦ γενόμενα, where Plato has in mind the ὁμοῦ πάντα ἦν of Anaxagoras (cf. *Phaedo* 72 C 4).

PROPS. 15–17. These three propositions logically prepare the way for the proof that the soul is incorporeal and independent of the body, and therefore imperishable (props. 186, 187). But they are placed thus early in the book because they are of general application to all spiritual reality, and because they are designed to refute the Stoic psychology from its own premises. Stoicism held at once that the soul is corporeal, and that it finds its good in an introverted contemplation or withdrawal into itself.[1] Pr.'s thesis is that these two tenets are incompatible (props. 15, 16); and that we must choose the second because the soul's power of originating thought involves an activity directed towards itself (prop. 17).[2] With the proof given cf. Porph. ἀφ. xli. The connexion between self-knowledge and separability appears already in Arist. *de an.* 430 b 24 εἰ δέ τινι μή ἐστιν ἐναντίον τῶν αἰτίων, αὐτὸ ἑαυτὸ γινώσκει καὶ ἐνεργείᾳ ἐστὶ καὶ χωριστόν.—In this argument there is no need to attach a mystical meaning to the soul's ' introversion '. ἐπιστροφή means simply ' a turning towards '; and as applied to a mental act, ' a turning or direction of consciousness '. It is a necessary accompaniment of any activity (πρὸς ὃ δὲ ἐνεργεῖ, πρὸς τοῦτο ἐπέστραπται, prop. 17, l. 1), and is the first step towards that identification with the object which for the Neoplatonist is the condition of knowledge (καὶ γὰρ ἔοικε πᾶσα γνῶσις εἶναι οὐδὲν ἄλλο ἢ ἐπιστροφὴ πρὸς τὸ γνωστὸν καὶ οἰκείωσις καὶ ἐφάρμοσις πρὸς αὐτό, *in Tim.* II. 287. 1). The soul is thus πρὸς

[1] Epict. *Diss.* III. 22. 38–9 εἰ γὰρ ἠθέλετε, εὕρετε ἂν αὐτὸ (sc. τὸ ἀγαθὸν) ἐν ὑμῖν ὄν, οὐδ' ἂν ἔξω ἐπλάζεσθε οὐδ' ἂν ἐζητεῖτε τὰ ἀλλότρια ὡς ἴδια. ἐπιστρέψατε αὐτοὶ ἐφ' ἑαυτούς. Cf. *Manual.* 10: M. Aur. vii. 28 εἰς σαυτὸν συνειλοῦ : Sen. *ep.* 7. 8 ' recede in te ipsum '.
[2] Professor A. E. Taylor makes the interesting suggestion that both Leibniz's distinction between ' bare ' monads and souls, and much of Locke's language about ' ideas of reflection ', are influenced by the Neoplatonic doctrine of ἐπιστροφὴ πρὸς ἑαυτόν (*Phil. of Pr.* 631).

ἑαυτὴν ἐπιστρεπτική, in the sense that it can be an object of consciousness to itself: ἡ πρὸς ἑαυτὴν ἐπιστροφὴ γνῶσίς ἐστιν ἑαυτῆς
(in Tim. II. 286. 32: cf. infra, prop. 83). This is also the usual
meaning of 'introversion' in the Stoics: Epictetus notes the power
of self-contemplation as the distinguishing character of the λογιστικόν
(Diss. I. 20. 1–5). Introversion does, however, acquire a deeper
significance in Neoplatonism (and to some extent already in the
later Stoics [1]) because the 'self' which is thus known is not an
isolated individual, but contains in potentia the whole range of reality.
Thus after defining introversion as self-knowledge, in the passage
last quoted, Pr. adds 'and knowledge of all things, whether within
the soul, prior to it, or posterior to it.' [2] Even the Good itself is
within us, as both Epictetus (Diss. III. 22. 38) and Seneca (Ep. 41. 1),
and with a more definite metaphysical implication Plotinus (Enn.
VI. v. 1 [II. 384. 29]), affirm ; and to know the self truly is to know
it as actually one though potentially all things, and thus as divine
(cf. Damasc. I. 170. 16 ff.), so that 'we go inwards to God'. But
this passage through self-knowledge to the knowledge of God is not
directly involved in the present group of propositions.

35. ὅταν ἓν γένηται ἄμφω. Nicolaus takes this to mean that prior to
the act of self-contemplation the soul is not a unity : τὸ τοίνυν γινόμενον ἕν, ὃ πάντως οὐκ ἦν πρὸ τοῦ γενέσθαι, καὶ τὸ ἐπιστρεφόμενον ὡς
ἄλλο τι ὂν παρὰ τὸ πρὸς ὃ ἐπιστρέφεται, πῶς λέγεται πρὸς ἑαυτὸ καὶ οὐχὶ
πρὸς ἄλλο μᾶλλον ἐπιστρέφειν ; (p. 30). But the thought may be that
self-knowledge is the limiting case where subject and object, which
in all types of knowledge tend to identity, actually 'become'
identical.

9. σώματος οὑτινοσοῦν. The intention is to exclude not only the
material and corruptible body, but also (as is recognized in the
scholion preserved by PQ) the 'first body', the ὄχημα. Every soul
except the ἀμέθεκτος ψυχή has in fact an ὄχημα permanently attached
to it (prop. 196); but it is metaphysically prior to the ὄχημα, and
therefore independent of it.

10. ἀδύνατον . . . 12. χωριστήν. Cf. Plot. Enn. IV. vii. 8 (II. 129. 8)

[1] Bréhier, La Philosophie de Plotin 108–9, finds it 'impossible to understand'
how the Stoic conception of self-knowledge could have developed into the
Plotinian conception (which he would derive from Indian sources); but he seems
to me to underestimate the rational element in Neoplatonism and to ignore the
mystical element in the later Stoicism. Seneca's 'prope est a te deus, tecum est,
intus est ' surely points forward to Plotinus's στραφεῖσα οὐδὲν μεταξὺ ἔχει.
[2] Cf. also Prov. et Fat. 160. 36 ff.; Th. Pl. I. iii. 7. Similarly ps.-Dion. Div.
Nom. 4. 9. In Th. Pl. II (viii). 104–5, the idea of introversion is linked with the
magical doctrine of σύμβολα or συνθήματα : ἕκαστον εἰς τὸ τῆς ἑαυτοῦ φύσεως
ἄρρητον εἰσδυόμενον εὑρίσκει τὸ σύμβολον τοῦ πάντων πατρός. This is a post-
Plotinian development (cf. prop. 39 n.).

εἰ οὖν τὸ νοεῖν ἐστι τὸ ἄνευ σώματος ἀντιλαμβάνεσθαι, πολὺ πρότερον δεῖ μὴ σῶμα αὐτὸ τὸ νοῆσον εἶναι: Pr. *Prov. et. Fat.* 158. 23 ff. Pr.'s proof that, if ἐνέργεια is separable, so is οὐσία reappears in Philoponus (*de anima* 15. 11 ff.) and Psellus (*de anima* 1048 D Migne). They are hardly right in claiming Aristotle's authority for the doctrine: Aristotle only says that in so far as any part of the soul has an activity independent of the body it *may* be separable: εἰ ἐστί τι τῶν τῆς ψυχῆς ἔργων ἢ παθημάτων ἴδιον, ἐνδέχοιτ' ἂν αὐτὴν χωρίζεσθαι (*de an.* 403 a 10: cf. 413 a 4, b 28).

21. **τὸ ἑαυτὸ κινοῦν πρώτως.** τὸ πρὸς ἑαυτὸ ἐπιστρεπτικόν, whose existence has so far been treated as hypothetical (prop. 15, l. 5), is now identified with the middle term of the triad established in prop. 14. Nicolaus complains that this amounts to identifying ἐπιστροφή with κίνησις. But by the qualifying word πρώτως Pr. indicates that the identification is restricted to true spontaneous movement: the body has the power of self-movement δευτέρως (prop. 20), but this does not constitute ἐπιστροφὴ πρὸς ἑαυτό (prop. 15); nor can φύσις revert upon itself.[1]

26. **οὐκ ἔσται καθ' ἑαυτὸ αὐτοκίνητον.** Cf. Plotinus's argument to show that self-knowledge cannot be merely knowledge of one part of a composite by another part, *Enn.* V. iii. 1.

PROP. 18. It has been shown in props. 15–17 that what is *proprie* self-moving has reflexive consciousness, and that what has reflexive consciousness is neither body nor a function of body. To complete the refutation of materialism it remains to be shown that soul is *proprie* self-moving. But the self-movement of soul cannot be directly observed; observation tells us only that some *bodies* appear to move themselves, and that this apparent self-movement is conditional upon the *presence* of life or 'soul'. Hence at this point in his argument Pr. introduces the general proposition that what by its mere presence bestows a quality or power on things other than itself must itself possess that quality or power *proprie*. This is a necessary consequence from the transitive conception of causality; and, once established, it enables him to argue from the dependence of bodily self-movement on life to the primitive self-movement of ψυχή (prop. 20, ll. 8–10). The doctrine is in substance Plotinian, though Plotinus in one passage (VI. vii. 17 [II. 447. 1]) objects to this particular way of formulating it.—When causation occurs αὐτῷ τῷ εἶναι it involves no act of will and no change of any sort in the

---

[1] *in Tim.* I. 10. 19, where read εἰς ἑαυτήν (εἰς αὐτήν MSS. and Diehl).

cause. Some interesting examples of such causation are cited from
Porphyry by Pr. *in Tim.* I. 395. 10 ff. Cf. props. 26, 27.

3. πᾶν τὸ τῷ εἶναι χορηγοῦν. This is, I think, a necessary correction. πᾶν τὸ τὸ εἶναι χορ. (M and Creuzer) looks right on a first
view, and the reference to τὸ ὑποστατικόν in l. 8 might be held to
confirm it. But (*a*) the dative is certain in ll. 5 (see next note) and
17 (τῷ εἶναι θάτερον), as well as in later citations (props. 20, l. 10 ;
194, l. 1), and therefore cannot be dispensed with in the enunciation.
(*b*) The dative, not the accusative, is required if the proposition is
to be applicable to the case of soul and body. Soul does not communicate existence (τὸ εἶναι) to body, but only life or self-movement,
and it does this in virtue of its own existence (τῷ εἶναι), as fire by
existing creates heat. Hence ὑποστατικόν τινος (l. 8) must be understood as covering the creation of qualities or faculties (such as
θερμότης and αὐτοκινησία) as well as of substances ; and M's αὐτῷ τῷ
εἶναι (l. 20) must also be accepted.

5. εἰ γὰρ . . . 6. μετάδοσιν. Cf. *in Parm.* 787. 24 ff. εἰ τοίνυν ἐστὶν
αἰτία τοῦ παντὸς αὐτῷ τῷ εἶναι ποιοῦσα, τὸ δὲ αὐτῷ τῷ εἶναι ποιοῦν ἀπὸ
τῆς ἑαυτοῦ ποιεῖ οὐσίας, τοῦτό ἐστι πρώτως ὅπερ τὸ ποιούμενον δευτέρως,
καὶ ὅ ἐστι πρώτως δίδωσι τῷ ποιουμένῳ δευτέρως, οἷον τὸ πῦρ καὶ δίδωσι
θερμότητα ἄλλῳ καὶ ἔστι θερμόν, ἡ ψυχὴ δίδωσι ζωὴν καὶ ἔχει ζωήν· καὶ
ἐπὶ πάντων ἴδοις ἂν ἀληθῆ τὸν λόγον ὅσα αὐτῷ τῷ εἶναι ποιεῖ. This
makes it certain that αὐτῷ τῷ εἶναι is the true reading here.

11. ἀνάγκη . . . 14. δευτέρως : i.e. the two must be either (*a*) synonymous (in the sense of having a common definition), or (*b*) homonymous (in the sense of having only the name in common), or else
(*c*) must differ not in kind but in degree of intensity, the difference
corresponding to their respective places in the causal series. (The
possibility of their being co-ordinate species in the same genus is
excluded on the same grounds as (*a*)).

15. ἀποτέλεσμα : a Stoic term for 'result' (Epict. *Diss.* I. iv. 13 ;
M. Aur. vi. 42 ; Albinus, *Didasc.* 14).

18. λείπεται . . . 20. χορηγεῖται. Cf. the passage from *in Parm.*
quoted on l. 5. Plotinus expresses this by saying that the recipient
is *potentially* identical with the giver (VI. vii. 17 [II. 447. 5]).

PROP. 19. This lays down a second general principle ancillary to
the determination of the status of Soul, viz. that the characteristic
quality of any grade of reality is distinguished by its permanent and
universal presence within that grade. Pr. is thus enabled in the
next proposition to distinguish Soul, which is capable of intuitive
thinking but capable of it only spasmodically, from Intellect, which

has this character permanently and universally. Nicolaus, or more probably one of his readers, remarks that prop. 18 παρὰ πόδας εὐθὺς ὑπὸ τοῦ μετ' αὐτὸ ἀνατρέπεται. But this is a mere misunderstanding : prop. 18 determines the sense in which the same character can exist at two distinct levels of reality (e.g. αὐτοκινησία in ψυχή and σῶμα, or νόησις in νοῦς and ψυχή), while prop. 19 is concerned with the presence of a character in co-ordinate subjects on the same level (e.g. of αὐτοκινησία in ψυχαί, or νόησις in νόες). In the latter case the character is present καθ' ἕνα λόγον καὶ ὡσαύτως : in the former it is not. Cf. Plot. Enn. VI. i. 25 (II. 292. 15) ἐν μὲν γὰρ τοῖς ἐν οἷς τὸ πρότερον καὶ τὸ ὕστερον, τὸ ὕστερον παρὰ τοῦ προτέρου λαμβάνει τὸ εἶναι· ἐν δὲ τοῖς ὑπὸ τὸ αὐτὸ γένος τὸ ἴσον εἰς τὸ εἶναι ἕκαστον ἔχει παρὰ τοῦ γένους.

PROP. 20. Pr. is now in a position to establish by means of a regressive dialectic the three hypostases which constitute the Neoplatonic 'trinity of subordination', Soul, Intelligence,[1] and the One. The Neoplatonists discovered this trinity in Plato (Porphyry, *Hist. Phil.* fr. 16), combining the One of the *Parmenides* (identified with the Form of the Good), the demiurge of the *Timaeus* (identified with Aristotle's νοῦς), and the world-soul of the *Timaeus* and *Laws* X. The combination was doubtless, as Bréhier remarks,[2] already a commonplace of the school before Plotinus. The crucial steps were the identification of the demiurge with the Aristotelian νοῦς (leading to a changed view of his relation to the Forms) and the equation of τὸ ἕν and τὸ ἓν ὄν in the *Parmenides* with the transcendent Good and the other Forms respectively. The former step had certainly been taken before the time of Albinus (Alcinous),[3] and probably much earlier,[4] whether by Poseidonius, by Antiochus, or, as Nebel thinks,[5] in the Old Academy ; the latter as early as Moderatus (first

---

[1] Several modern scholars prefer ' spirit ' (*esprit*, *Geist*) as an equivalent for the Neoplatonic νοῦς. But this rendering seems to break the link with Aristotle (a link which is particularly close and important in Pr.). I see no real objection to ' Intelligence ', so long as it is understood that ' Intelligence ' is a substance or spiritual force, not a faculty of soul, and that its activity is always intuitive, never discursive.

[2] *Philosophie de Plotin*, p. xi.

[3] Cf. *Didasc.* c. 10.

[4] Seneca (*ep.* 65. 7) cites, apparently as accepted Platonic doctrine, the view that *exemplaria rerum omnium deus intra se habet* ; and the same doctrine occurs in Philo (*de opif. mundi* 20, etc.). Such a view could hardly be elicited from the *Timaeus* except under the influence of the Aristotelian teaching about νοῦς. Cf. also Aetius, *Plac.* I. iii. 21 (p. 288 Diels), Atticus *apud* Euseb. *Prep. Ev.* xv. 13 (815 D), and *infra* prop. 167 n.

[5] *Plotins Kategorien* 22 f. The weakness of the case for ascribing the doctrine to Poseidonius is exposed by R. M. Jones in *Class. Philol.* 21 (1926), 318 ff. The

century A.D.).[1] Plutarch (*de gen. Socr.* 22, 591 B) knows of a divine triad μονάς—νοῦς—φύσις, the last of these being the principle which governs the domain of soul. But it was Plotinus who gave the doctrine permanent shape and structural cohesion.

4. **πᾶν γὰρ σῶμα κτλ.** The substance of this argument comes from Plato, *Laws* 895 C–896 C ; but an attempt is made to give it formal cogency by using as a major premiss the general law established in prop. 18. ψυχή was traditionally defined in the Academy as τὸ αὐτὸ κινοῦν ("Ὅροι 411 C, cf. *Phaedr.* 246 A).

14. **καὶ κατ' ἐνέργειαν ἀκινήτου:** because νοῦς is *wholly ἐν αἰῶνι* (prop. 169), whereas Soul τὴν μὲν οὐσίαν αἰώνιον ἔχει, τὴν δὲ ἐνέργειαν κατὰ χρόνον (prop. 191).

18. **νοῦς δὲ κινεῖ ἀκίνητος ὤν:** Arist. *Metaph.* Λ. c. 7. The acceptance of this Aristotelian doctrine involved the Neoplatonists in considerable difficulties, for Plato had associated νοῦς with movement (*Soph.* 248 E ff. ; *Legg.* 898 A). Plotinus in an early essay (III. ix. 1) toys with the opinion held by Numenius [2] and certain Gnostics,[3] that there is a higher νοῦς which is ἀκίνητος and a lower νοῦς which moves. When he came to write *Enn.* II. ix he had definitely rejected this compromise : νοῦς is ἀεὶ ὡσαύτως ἐνεργείᾳ κείμενος ἑστώσῃ (I. 185. 6). Pr. in the commentary on the *Timaeus* takes the same view : νοῦς μὲν γάρ, εἴ τις αὐτῷ διδοίη κίνησιν, ἀμετάβατον ἔχει ταύτην τὴν ἐνέργειαν· ὅλον γὰρ ὁμοῦ θεᾶται τὸ νοητόν (II. 243. 19) ; it is thus a κίνησις ἀκίνητος (II. 251. 5, where he is following Iamblichus). But in later life he evolved refinements on the lines of the Numenian theory : πᾶς νοῦς ἢ ἔστηκε, καὶ ἔστιν νοητὸς τότε ὡς κρείττων κινήσεως, ἢ κινεῖται, καὶ ἔστιν νοερὸς τότε, ἢ ἀμφότερα, καὶ ἔστιν τότε νοητὸς ἅμα καὶ νοερός (*in Crat.* cviii). Finally, in the *Th. Pl.* (III. (xxiv). 164) he makes the highest νοῦς transcend motion and rest (like the ἕν of the *Parmenides*), while the lower νοῦς has both attributes simultaneously (like the ἓν ὄν).

24. **πρὸ τοῦ νοῦ τὸ ἕν.** νοῦς is inferior to the One (*a*) as containing in itself the duality of subject and object inseparable from all cognition (cf. *Enn.* III. viii. 9 ; V. iii. 10–12) ; (*b*) as a less universal causative force (cf. *infra*, props. 57, 59).

28. **ἡ νοερὰ γνῶσις κτλ.**: Aristotelian (*Anal. Post.* 85 a 1, &c.).

attribution to Antiochus (Theiler, *Vorbereitung des Neuplatonismus* 40) is a plausible guess, but at present hardly more.
[1] Cf. *Class. Qu.* 22 (1928), 136 ff. 'Archytas', another Neopythagorean, teaches that God must be νόῳ τι κρέσσον (Stob. I. 280. 16 [716 H]) : so also *Corp. Herm.* II. 13.
[2] *ap.* Euseb. *Prep. Ev.* XI. 18, 20.
[3] Cf. *Enn.* II. ix. 1 [I. 185. 2].

30. οὐκέτι τοῦ ἑνὸς ἄλλο ἐπέκεινα : perhaps directed against Iamblichus, who is said to have posited a πάντῃ ἄρρητος ἀρχή transcending even the Plotinian ἐν-τἀγαθόν (Damasc. I. 86. 3, &c.).

PROP. 21. The last proposition gave us a fourfold stratification of reality : this one gives the general formula which governs the structure of each stratum. The formula is based on the Pythagorean conception of the arithmetical series : cf. Moderatus' definition of number as προποδισμὸς πλήθους ἀπὸ μονάδος ἀρχόμενος καὶ ἀναποδισμὸς εἰς μονάδα καταλήγων (ap. Stob. Ecl. I. 21. 8 [18 H]). Each member of the series evolves from, or is generated by, the preceding members, and the series as a whole is thus generated by the unit or ' monad ' which is its first member. We may either start from this monad and trace the emergence of the series from it (προποδισμός), or follow the series in the reverse direction until it ends in the monad (ἀναποδισμός) : in the former case we move from cause to effect, in the latter from effect to cause. Such a series furnishes the simplest type of one-sided causal relation : hence its significance for the Neoplatonist. Pr., as usual, transfers the relation from the order of thought to the order of reality : προποδισμός is equated with πρόοδος (l. 10), ἀναποδισμός with ἐπιστροφή (l. 29). But the meaning of this ' outgoing ' and ' return ' is not fully explained until we reach props. 25-39.

Of the transverse series or 'strata' enumerated in the corollary, the first three are Plotinian : for φύσις and φύσεις cf. esp. Enn. IV. iv. 11 (II. 57. 9) πάσας γὰρ τὰς φύσεις κρατεῖ μία, αἱ δὲ ἕπονται [ἀνηρτημέναι καὶ]¹ ἐξηρτημέναι καὶ οἷον ἐκφῦσαι, ὡς αἱ² ἐν κλάδοις τῇ² τοῦ ὅλου φυτοῦ : for disembodied ψυχαί and νόες, Enn. IV. iii. 5. On ἑνάδες see below, pp. 257 ff. ; they complete the symmetry of the schematism. Similar enumerations in Parm. 703. 12 ff., 1069. 23 ff.

1. πᾶσα τάξις κτλ. Cf. de myst. VIII. 3 ἡ περὶ τῶν ἀρχῶν Αἰγυπτίοις πραγματεία ἀφ᾽ ἑνὸς ἄρχεται καὶ πρόεισιν εἰς πλῆθος, τῶν πολλῶν αὖθις ὑφ᾽ ἑνὸς διακυβερνωμένων : Sallust. 10. 14 παντὸς γὰρ πλήθους ἡγεῖται μονάς : Pr. in Parm. 620. 5 ff.

4. ἀρχῆς ἔχουσα λόγον : i.e. the monad of a transverse series is analogous to the One. Cf. Th. Pl. II. (v). 93 καθ᾽ ἑκάστην τῶν ὄντων τάξιν ἀνάλογον ὑπέστη τῷ ἀγαθῷ μονάς, τοῦτο οὖσα πρὸς ὅλον τὸν σύζυγον αὐτῆς ⟨εἱρμὸν⟩ ὃ πρὸς ἁπάσας ἐστὶ τὰς θεῶν διακοσμήσεις τἀγαθόν.

5. διὸ καὶ μία σειρὰ καὶ μία τάξις : sc. ἐστί : μία is predicative. Both σειρά (a term derived ultimately, via Orphism, from Homer Θ,

---

¹ lectio duplex.   ²⁻² I retain the MS. reading.

19–20) and τάξις here refer to transverse series or strata of reality : for the vertical series, consisting of a single principle repeated at different levels of reality, develops not from a monad but from a henad. Bréhier says that σειρά in Pr. refers properly to the transverse, τάξις to the vertical series : but in the *El. Th.*, at any rate, both terms are used indifferently for either type.

10. πρόοδον. Pr. *in Parm.* 746. 10 ff. says that πρόοδος is properly applied only to *vertical* derivation, ὑπόβασις being the correct term for derivation within the transverse series. But even in his latest work, the *Th. Pl.*, he occasionally violates this rule.

12. ἐπεὶ οὖν κτλ. : cf. the fuller argument, prop. 97.

16. τάξιν καὶ εἱρμόν. The reading of PQ is confirmed by the frequent conjunction of the two words elsewhere, e.g. *in Tim.* II. 26. 11, III. 272. 25 ; *in Remp.* II. 343. 24. The MSS. here and in most other passages of Pr. give εἱρμός the *spiritus asper* : no doubt rightly, for, like Philo, Sallustius, the *de mundo* and the Neopythagorean of Photius cod. 249, Pr. plays on the supposed connexion with εἱμαρμένη (e.g. *in Remp.* II. 29. 14).

20. μὴ ὡς τόδε τι ἕκαστον ἀλλ' ὡς τῆσδε τῆς τάξεως ὑπάρχον. The generic attributes, being more fundamental, come from a more primitive cause than the specific (props. 71–2).

22. τῇ φύσει τοῦ σώματος : not = τῷ σώματι (as I wrongly took it in my *Select Passages*), but = τῇ ἐν τῷ σώματι φύσει, the vital element in body. So also prop. 62 αἱ σωματικαὶ φύσεις, prop. 109 σώματος μερικὴ φύσις. Cf. *in Tim.* III. 295. 12 ἡ γὰρ θήρειος φύσις οὐκ ἔστι τὸ σῶμα τὸ θήρειον ἀλλ' ἡ ζωὴ τοῦ θηρίου. The universal φύσις (mentioned in *El. Th.* only here and in prop. 111) κατευθύνει τὸ σωματοειδὲς καὶ οὔτε ὡς θεός ἐστιν οὔτε ἔξω τῆς θείας ἰδιότητος (*in Tim.* I. 8. 7) ; it is the link between soul and matter, the last incorporeal principle (*ibid.* 11. 11) ; it embraces the λόγοι of all material things, both those in the οὐρανός and those below the moon [*Th. Pl.* III. (i). 119]. The particular φύσεις include the immanent forms of the various material substances, earth, fire, &c. (*Th. Pl.*.l. c.), as well as the organic consciousness in men and animals [*ibid.* I. (xv). 42].

30. τὴν ... ἀνάτασιν. The grammatically indefensible accusative (for nominative) is due to the influence of μονάδα in l. 27.

PROP. 22. This is a negative confirmation of the preceding proposition, showing that within any stratum of the real there cannot be a plurality of independent ἀρχαί. Thus the structure of each level of reality mirrors that of reality as a whole.—The argument,

which has suffered badly from textual corruption and mispunctuation
in the renaissance copies and in Creuzer, is in principle the same as
that of props. 2 and 3: it can best be made clear in a concrete
instance. Assume that two souls are claimed as ' being primitively
what they are called ', i.e. as being ἀρχαί of the soul-order. If they
are mutually dependent (so that they do not constitute an ἀρχή except
in combination), or if one is dependent on the other, the claim
obviously fails. And if they are independent, they must be distinguishable by some quality other than their common quality of
being souls (without which they would not be assigned to a common
order): but this means that each possesses a specific character in
addition to the generic one, or, in Platonic language, that it ' participates' Soul and therefore cannot be an ἀρχή of Soul. The force of
the contention depends on an abstract notion of the genus as
excluding the specific characters.—Anselm has a similar argument
to establish the uniqueness of God, *Monologium*, c.4, clviii. 148 C ff.
Migne.

2. μονογενές: cf. Plato, *Tim.* 31 B εἷς ὅδε μονογενὴς οὐρανός. On
the Gnostic and Hermetic use of this word see J. Kroll, *Lehren des
Hermes*[1], 10; 58. 1; E. Böklen in *Theol. Stud. und Krit.* ci. 55 ff.
But Plato is the obvious source here.

13. The insertion of καί before οὐκ ἄμφω in PQ seems to be
a mistaken attempt to mend the sense, which had been destroyed by
the false punctuation perpetuated in Creuzer's edition.

16. τὸ πρώτως ὄν. This cannot refer simply to existence in general,
since it is parallel to the specific hypostases νοῦς and ψυχή: nor can
it refer to the One, which is ὑπερούσιον (prop. 115), and whose
uniqueness has already been independently established. We must
therefore suppose that Pr. introduces here for the first time τὸ ὄν as
a separate principle, anticipating the distinction between ὄν, ζωή and
νοῦς which is drawn in prop. 101 (where see note).

PROP. 23. This has been described as 'le théorème fondamental
du traité, que l'on pourrait appeler théorème de la transcendence'.[1]
It is at the same time the theorem of immanence. It embodies in
its clearest shape the Neoplatonic solution of the problem first raised
in Plato's *Parmenides*, the problem of reconciling the necessary
immanence of the Forms with their necessary transcendence. If
participation is to be real, the Form must be immanent, and therefore divided; if it is to be participation of one undivided principle,

[1] Bréhier, *Hist. de Philosophie*, I. 477.

the Form must be transcendent, and therefore not directly participated. Pr. accepts both necessities ; he also (following the Aristotelian
use of ' Form ' and ' Matter ') extends the meaning of ' participation '
so as to make it a general formula for the relation between the
higher universal (whether a Platonic Form or a Hypostasis) and the
lower particular (whether a material or a spiritual individual). What
is directly participated is an immanent universal—an ἔνυλον εἶδος, a
ψυχὴ ἐν σώματι, a νοῦς ἐν ψυχῇ, a νοητὸν ἐν νῷ, a νοητὴ ἑνάς (in Parm.
1069. 23 ff.).[1] The transcendent (ἐξῃρημένον) universal must exist,
in order to give unity to the many immanent universals (ll. 1–4),
and must be distinct from any of them (ll. 4–5). It is related to
them as the monad to the other members of the σειρά (l. 25). Being
transcendent, it can affect the particulars only ὡς ἐφετόν, like
Aristotle's God (Th. Pl. V. xii. 270), or at most ὡς ἐλλάμπον (in Tim.
I. 406. 8): that is, it is strictly 'unparticipated' (ἀμέθεκτον). If we
substitute logical for metaphysical terms we may say, with Bréhier,[2]
that the ἀμέθεκτον is the intension of the concept, the μετέχοντα
are its extension, and the μετεχόμενα are that which links intension with extension.—The solution of the antinomy by a
multiplication of entities is typical of Pr.'s method. An approach
to it is already discernible in some passages of Plotinus ;[3] but
Plotinus characteristically shrinks from calling the transcendent term
ἀμέθεκτον (cf. esp. Enn. VI. v. 3), though it is ἀμέριστον and ἀπαθές—
his mystical sense of the universe as the expression of a single
divine force made the sharper distinction impossible for him. Pr.
carries the thought to its logical conclusion.[4] But in doing so he
lays himself open to charges of inconsistency : τὸ ἕν is ἀμέθεκτον, yet
we have already been told (prop. 1) that πᾶν πλῆθος μετέχει πῃ τοῦ
ἑνός: and cf. l. 6 of the present proposition. Nicolaus (5. 17 ff., 44.
14 ff.) makes great play with this difficulty ; but the answer is that
a term which is proprie ἀμέθεκτον is yet indirectly μεθεκτόν through
the μετεχόμενα which it generates (cf. prop. 56).[5] Hence ps.-Diony-
sius can speak of ἀμεθέκτως μετεχόμενα (Div. Nom. 2. 5). Nicolaus
himself holds that God is both μεθεκτός and ἀμέθεκτος.

[1] The situation is further complicated by the interpolation, between the transcendent ἀμέθεκτον and the immanent μετεχόμενα, of χωρισ τῶς μετεχόμενα which
are immanent yet transcendent : see props. 64, 81, 82 nn.
[2] l.c.
[3] For transcendent and immanent εἴδη in Plotinus see Enn. IV. ii. 1 ; VI. iv–v;
transcendent and immanent ψυχή, IV. viii. 2–4; transcendent νοῦς and immanent
νόες, VI. ii. 20; the One καὶ καθ' αὑτὸ καὶ ἐν τοῖς μετέχουσιν, VI. ii. 12.
[4] Following Iamblichus, as appears from in Tim. II. 313. 15 ff.
[5] This is the explanation offered by Psellus : εἰ γὰρ καὶ ἀμέθεκτος, ἀλλ' ἐμφάσεις
τινὰς δίδωσι τοῖς μετ' αὐτὸν τῆς ἰδίας ὑπάρξεως (de omnif. doct. cap. 24).

28. οὐδὲν ἂν ἔχοι τίμιον: cf. *in Tim.* I. 373. 2 τοῦ δὲ χείρονος οὐκ ὄντος οὐκ ἔχει χώραν τὸ κρεῖττον.
29. μετέσχε, ὑπέστη : instantaneous aorists.
34. ἢ γὰρ ἐν πᾶσιν κτλ. : cf. prop. 67.

PROP. 24. This supplements the preceding proposition by determining formally the order of priority within the triad ἀμέθεκτον, μετεχόμενα, μετέχοντα, with the help of the principles already invoked in props. 7 and 8. The μετέχον is inferior to the μετεχόμενον because causally determined or 'perfected' by it : in using the question-begging term 'perfected' Pr. is no doubt thinking especially of soul, whose perfection it is to participate νοῦς: cf. *Enn.* V. ix. 4 and Sallust. 28. 27 οἰκεία τελειότης ἑκάστῳ ἡ πρὸς τὴν ἑαυτοῦ αἰτίαν συναφή. The μετεχόμενον is inferior to the ἀμέθεκτον because it is less universal and therefore more remote from the First Cause (cf. the argument of prop. 8).
18. τὸ μέν ἐστιν ἐν πρὸ τῶν πολλῶν κτλ. Cf. the rather different equation of grades of unity with grades of reality in *Enn.* IV. ii. 2 *ad fin.* (II. 8. 25–8) ἔστιν οὖν ψυχὴ ἐν καὶ πολλὰ οὕτως· τὰ δὲ ἐν τοῖς σώμασιν εἴδη πολλὰ καὶ ἕν· τὰ δὲ σώματα πολλὰ μόνον· τὸ δὲ ὑπέρτατον ἐν μόνον. *Th. Pl.* I. xi. 25 gives as traditional equations τὸ πρῶτον = ἕν, νοῦς = ἐν πολλά, ψυχή = ἐν καὶ πολλά, σῶμα = πολλὰ καὶ ἕν.

D. *Of Procession and Reversion* (props. 25–39).

(a) Procession.
1. Law of Emanation (25).
2. Law of Undiminished Giving (26, 27).
3. Law of Continuity (28, 29).
4. Law of Immanence (30).

(b) Reversion.
1. Reversion retraces the movement of Procession (31–4, 38).
2. Triad of Immanence, Procession, Reversion (35).
3. Reversion is recovery of value lost in Procession (36, 37).
4. Three grades of reversion (39).

PROP. 25. This is a formal statement of the Plotinian law of emanation, which seeks to account for the existence of a universe outside the One by the principle that everything which is 'complete' (i.e. has realized the full potentialities of its nature) tends to reproduce itself (*Enn.* V. i. 6 [II. 168. 30] πάντα ὅσα ἤδη τέλεια γεννᾷ). The law is obviously based on the facts of animal reproduction ; the

panzoism of Plotinus makes it easy for him to extend it to the hierarchy of cosmic principles.[1] But it should be noticed (*a*) that cosmic reproduction is timeless (τὸ ἀεὶ τέλειον ἀεὶ καὶ ἀίδιον γεννᾷ, Plotinus l. c.); (*b*) that in cosmic reproduction the product is always inferior to the producer (ἔλαττον δὲ ἑαυτοῦ γεννᾷ, Plotinus l. c.), although, as Nicolaus points out in his comment on the present proposition, men beget men, not pigs.—Authority was found for the doctrine in Plato's account of the Creator's motives, *Tim.* 29 E ἀγαθὸς ἦν, ἀγαθῷ δὲ οὐδεὶς περὶ οὐδενὸς οὐδέποτε ἐγγίγνεται φθόνος. This was interpreted as meaning that 'giving'' or creation is an essential part of the Good: cf. *Enn.* IV. viii. 6 [II. 150. 13] οὐκ ἔδει στῆσαι οἷον περιγράψαντα φθόνῳ: V. iv. 1 [II. 203. 29] πῶς ἂν οὖν τὸ τελειότατον καὶ τὸ πρῶτον ἀγαθὸν ἐν αὐτῷ σταίη ὥσπερ φθονῆσαν ἑαυτοῦ; II. ix. 17, &c.[2] The correlation between degrees of goodness and degrees of creative power in the present proposition follows naturally from this.

22. μιμούμενον τὴν μίαν τῶν ὅλων ἀρχήν: suggested by the address of the demiurge to the young gods, Plato, *Tim.* 41 C, τρέπεσθε κατὰ φύσιν (cf. *infra*, l. 30) ὑμεῖς ἐπὶ τὴν τῶν ζῴων δημιουργίαν, μιμούμενοι τὴν ἐμὴν δύναμιν. The structure of the whole is thus reflected in the structure of the parts. Cf. prop. 26, ll. 18 ff.

35. μᾶλλον ἐλαττόνων: for the double comparative, cf. prop. 44, l. 4 f.; prop. 78, l. 11; *in Tim.* I. 107. 8, &c.

2. ὑφιστάνειν ἢ κοσμεῖν κτλ. With this list of divine activities cf. props. 151–8, and the parallels quoted there.

5. τὸ πορρώτατον τῆς ἀρχῆς: sc. ὕλη: cf. *Enn.* III. vi. 19.

9. ὅτι here = ὁτιοῦν, as in Plato, *Hipp. ma.* 282 D. ὁ ἔτι or ὃ ἔτι in the inferior MSS. of the first family points to a conjecture ἔτι with ὁ suprascript to indicate that the archetype had ὅτι: Mon. 547 has τι, another obvious emendation.

PROPS. **26–7.** Taken by itself, the principle of emanation tends to exhaust the cause by dissipation among the effects, and so to rob it of substantial reality: for this reason many writers[3] refuse to call the Neoplatonic system 'emanationist', despite Plotinus' constant use of such images as the sun and its rays, the source and the river, the root and the sap, to express the relation between God and the

---

[1] Cf. *in Parm.* 922. 1 ff., where Pr. argues from the existence of creative power in the universe, and the fact that it is found in a higher degree in the higher beings, that the Good must be creative κατ' ἐξοχήν, and thus be the efficient cause of all things and not merely, as Aristotle held, their final cause.
[2] On the same idea in Philo and the *Hermetica* see J. Kroll, *Lehren des Hermes*[1], 35, n. 3.
[3] e.g. Zeller III[4]. ii. 560; H. F. Müller, *Hermes* 48. 409; Arnou 151 ff.

world. The law of emanation is, however, qualified in Neoplatonism by a further law, viz. that in giving rise to the effect the cause remains undiminished and unaltered. This doctrine is older than Plotinus. The Platonic 'text' on which Plot. (*Enn.* V. iv. 2) and Pr. (*Th. Pl.* V. xviii. 283) base it is *Tim.* 42 E καὶ ὁ μὲν δὴ (δημιουργὸς) ἅπαντα ταῦτα διατάξας ἔμενεν ἐν τῷ ἑαυτοῦ κατὰ τρόπον ἤθει κτλ.[1] But it seems to be in fact a product of the Middle Stoa, and to have originated in the attempt to give God a real place in the Stoic system over against the cosmos. The earliest passage where I have found it is *Sophia Salomonis* vii. 27 μία δὲ οὖσα πάντα δύναται, καὶ μένουσα ἐν αὑτῇ τὰ πάντα καινίζει (written under Stoic influence in the second half of the first century B.C.). It is stated with varying degrees of clearness in Philo (*Leg. Alleg.* I. 5), Seneca (*Ep.* 41. 5), [Arist.] *de mundo* (6. 7 and 13), M. Aurelius (viii. 57; vii. 59); and quite explicitly by Numenius (*ap.* Euseb. *Prep. Ev.* XI. 18). In the Neoplatonists it is cardinal and of constant recurrence: cf. e.g. Plot. *Enn.* III. viii. 10; IV. viii. 6; V. i. 3 and 6; V. ii. 1 (where creation by ψυχή is said to be the first that involves κίνησις); Porph. ἀφ. xxiv; Sallust. ix; Syrian. *in Metaph.* 187, 6 ff.; Pr. *in Tim.* I. 390. 9 ff.; *in Crat.* civ. It reappears in Christian Neoplatonism, e.g. Clem. *Strom.* VII. 47. 6; Augustine *Conf.* I. 3 'cum effunderis super nos, non tu dissiparis, sed colligis nos': ps.-Dion. *Div. Nom.* 4. 1; Athanasius *expos. fid.* 2 ('the Godhead communicates itself from the Father to the Son without exhaustion or division').[2] Cf. also Shelley's 'True Love in this differs from gold or clay, That to divide is not to take away'; and Bridges' 'Immortal happiness . . . a gift Whose wealth is amplified by spending.'

14 ff. εἰ γὰρ διὰ κινήσεως κτλ. The argument is that the movement cannot occur *within* the One, since any movement would destroy its unity; and if it be external to the One it must itself be derived from the One either by another external movement (which leads to infinite regress) or without movement (which amounts to admitting Pr.'s thesis). Cf. Plot. II. 168. 13 εἰ γὰρ κινηθέντος αὐτοῦ τι γίνοιτο, τρίτον ἀπ' ἐκείνου τὸ γινόμενον μετὰ τὴν κίνησιν ἂν γίνοιτο καὶ οὐ δεύτερον: and *in Parm.* 1168. 19 ff.

16. ἐκ τοῦ ἕν. For the indecl. form cf. Plot. II. 198. 32, 211. 27; anon. *in Parm.* 11. 31. The only exx. I have noted in Pr. occur in

---

[1] Plato clearly held that *participation* of a *Form* does not diminish or alter it: this is expressly stated of the Form of Beauty, *Symp.* 211 B. But difficulties had already been raised about this in his lifetime, as we see from *Parm.* 131 A ff.

[2] Further references will be found in R. E. Witt, 'The Hellenism of Clement of Alexandria', *Class. Qu.* 25 (1931), 200.

Th. Pl., e.g. II. ii. 85 : they seem too numerous there to be due to corruption.

ἢ εἰ μετ' αὐτὸ κτλ. The true reading here is doubtful, though the meaning is clear. οὐκ ἐν αὐτῷ, the reading of BCD, is perhaps most easily explained as a gloss on μετ' αὐτό : and if this is so the insertion of αὐτή, which the third family has preserved (or conjecturally restored), is essential to the sense.

25. διὰ . . . δυνάμεως περιουσίαν. The representation of reality as a chain of spiritual forces is characteristic of Neoplatonism from Plotinus onwards, and is especially prominent in Syrianus and Pr. For Plotinus οὐσία is essentially dynamic : *Enn.* VI. iv. 9 [II. 374. 5] οὐχ οἷόν τε, ὥσπερ οὐσίαν ἄνευ δυνάμεως, οὕτως οὐδὲ δύναμιν ἄνευ οὐσίας. ἡ γὰρ δύναμις ἐκεῖ ὑπόστασις καὶ οὐσία ἢ μεῖζον οὐσίας. The divine Intelligence is full of μέγισται καὶ οἷον σφριγῶσαι δυνάμεις (II. 322. 31); and each Form is a δύναμις ἰδία (II. 254. 1). A remarkable passage in Plato's *Sophistes* already points in this direction (247 E τίθεμαι γὰρ ὅρον τὰ ὄντα ὡς ἔστιν οὐκ ἄλλο τι πλὴν δύναμις, cf. 248 Bff.); and when the Forms came to be regarded as the thoughts of a divine thinker and identified with the content of νοῦς (see prop. 167 n.), they naturally tended to lose their purely paradeigmatic character and become forces.[1] The influence of the later Stoa, with its seminal λόγοι conceived as δυνάμεις γόνιμοι,[2] must also be taken into account : these creative forces in Nature became for Neoplatonism the intermediaries between the Forms and the material world, and as Pr. says (*in Parm.* 908. 36), 'it would be strange if the λόγοι had creative force, yet the intelligible Forms were deprived of efficient causality.' For the Procline conception of the Forms as at once paradeigmatic and creative cf. *in Parm.* 841. 26 ff. τὰ δὲ θεῖα εἴδη παραδείγματά ἐστιν ὁμοῦ καὶ δημιουργικὰ τῶν ὁμοιωμάτων· οὐ γὰρ τοῖς κηροπλαστικοῖς ἔοικε τύποις, ἀλλ' ἔχει δραστήριον τὴν οὐσίαν καὶ ἀφομοιωτικὴν πρὸς αὐτὰ τῶν δευτέρων δύναμιν. See also props. 78–9 n.—For superfluity of δύναμις as the direct cause of creation cf. Plot. II. 150. 15 αἰτίᾳ δυνάμεως ἀπλέτου: *de myst.* 232. 12 ἡ περιουσία τῆς δυνάμεως: Sallust. 8. 13 δυνάμεις γονίμους : Syrian. *in Metaph.* 187. 6 τὰ δὲ θεῖα πάντα . . . πρόεισιν αὐτογόνως διὰ . . . τὴν τῆς γονίμου δυνάμεως τῶν πρωτουργῶν αἰτίων περιουσίαν : ps.-Dion. *Div. Nom.* 8. 6, God creates κατὰ περιουσίαν δυνάμεως.

---

[1] See Nebel, *Plotins Kategorien*, 10 ff., 26 ff., with whom I agree in substance, though he objects to calling the Plotinian Forms dynamic, on the ground that this obscures the distinction between them and the Philonic Forms, which act *directly* upon Matter.

[2] M. Aur. ix. 1. On δύναμις in Poseidonius, see Reinhardt, *Poseidonios*, 239 ff.

216 COMMENTARY

4. οὐδὲ γὰρ γενέσει : cf. *in Tim.* I. 390. 14 εἰ μὲν οὖν κατὰ ἀπο-
μερισμόν, ἄτοπον· οὐδὲ γὰρ ἡ φύσις ἐλαττοῦται ποιοῦσα τρίχας ἢ ὀδόντας
ἢ ἄλλο τι τῶν μορίων· πολλῷ δὴ πλέον τὴν ἐξῃρημένην οὐσίαν καὶ ἑαυτὴν
ὑφιστάνουσαν ἀνελάττωτον προσήκει φυλάττειν: also *Enn.* IV. ix. 4.

PROP. 28. To the laws of Emanation and of Undiminished
Giving Pr. here adds a third principle governing the procession, that
of Continuity. As there is no void in the physical universe, so there
is none in the spiritual : *Prov. et Fat.* 163. 31 'processus entium
nihil relinquunt vacuum, multo magis quam corporum situs '; cf.
Th. Pl. III. i. 118. But spiritual beings are separated not by spatial
but by qualitative intervals : *Enn.* VI. ix. 8 [II. 519. 30] τὰ ἀσώματα
σώμασιν οὐ διείργεται· οὐδ' ἀφέστηκε τοίνυν ἀλλήλων τόπῳ, ἑτερότητι δὲ
καὶ διαφορᾷ.[1] Spiritual continuity means that the qualitative interval
between any term of the procession and its immediate consequent is
the minimum difference compatible with distinctness ; there are thus
no gaps in the divine devolution.[2]—This principle, like the other two,
had already been stated by Plotinus (cf. e.g. *Enn.* II. ix. 3 [I. 187. 14]
ἀνάγκη ἐφεξῆς εἶναι πάντα ἀλλήλοις), but it received later a more precise and clear-cut formulation. Cf. Sallust. 28. 31 οὐδὲν γὰρ τῶν πλεῖστον
διεστώτων ἀμέσως συνάπτεται· ἡ δὲ μεσότης ὁμοία εἶναι τοῖς συναπτο-
μένοις ὀφείλει, with Nock's note ; Syrian. *in Metaph.* 109. 34 πᾶς ὁ αὑτῷ
τῷ εἶναι ποιῶν[3] ὁμοίωμα ἑαυτοῦ ποιεῖ, where the doctrine is ascribed
to the Pythagoreans ; *Th. Pl.* VI. ii. 345. It provides the justification for the Iamblicho-Procline method of mean terms (see Introd.,
p. xxii).—Whittaker[2], 288, makes the interesting suggestion that
Leibniz owes the idea of his *continuum* of monads to Neoplatonism *.
Cf. also Boehme's saying, 'Eternity bringeth to birth nothing but
that which is like itself'; and Aquinas, *Summa c. Gent.* I. 29, 'de
natura agentis est ut agens sibi simile agat.'

18. συμπαθές : i.e. 'attuned' to the higher term by a spiritual
correspondence : cf. prop. 39 n. συμπάθεια depends on likeness
(*Enn.* IV. iv. 32 [II. 84. 20] τῇ ὁμοιότητι συμπασχόντων). For the
history of the word, and its meaning in Plotinus, see Reinhardt,
Kosmos u. Sympathie ; Heinemann, *Plotin* 284–5.

20. ἀνάγκη τὸ αἰτιατὸν τοῦ αἰτίου μετέχειν. This becomes intelligible if we remember that in Neoplatonism ' the cause or producer

---

[1] So also Augustine, *Civ. Dei*, ix. 17 'si ergo Deo quanto similior, tanto fit
quisque propinquior, nulla est ab illo alia longinquitas quam eius dissimilitudo '.
[2] See, however, the qualification of this principle in prop. 130.
[3] As distinct from voluntary creation, which may produce something quite
different in quality from the creator.

is always an agent or the activity of an agent ; the effect produced may be the existence of an individual or a quality of an individual, or both ' (A. E. Taylor, *Phil. of Pr.* 616). Hence the possibility of the 'analogical' argument from the effect to the cause.

34. τούτοις must be taken both with ἡνωμένα and with ὅμοια.

οἷς μάλιστα ἥνωται : i.e. their immediate priors, to which they approach nearest. μάλιστα (BCDP) is more likely to have been corrupted into μᾶλλον (MQ) than *vice versa*.

PROP. 29. This rather superfluous corollary is evidently designed to emphasize the importance of ὁμοιότης as a cosmogonic principle : it is probably inspired by the Platonic texts νομίσας μυρίῳ κάλλιον ὅμοιον ἀνομοίου (*Tim.* 33 B: cf. *in Tim.* II. 78. 12 ff.) and πάντα ὅτι μάλιστα ἐβουλήθη γενέσθαι παραπλήσια ἑαυτῷ (*Tim.* 29 E: cf. *in Parm.* 738. 40). Similarly Porphyry says that real Being τὴν πᾶσαν ἑτερότητα διὰ τῆς ταυτότητος ὑπέστησεν (ἀφ. xxxvi). Cf. prop. 32.

PROP. 30. This paradox is a necessary consequence of the attempt to reconcile transcendence with immanence by the Neoplatonic theory of causation. If the procession is to be timeless, and if reversion is to be possible, the lower can never be cut off from the higher ; but if individuality is to be real, and if the higher is not to be infected with plurality, the lower must be actualized as a separate being, not simply a part of the higher: cf. *Enn.* V. ii. 2 [II. 178. 3] πάντα δὲ ταῦτα ἐκεῖνος καὶ οὐκ ἐκεῖνος· ἐκεῖνος μέν, ὅτι ἐξ ἐκείνου· οὐκ ἐκεῖνος δέ, ὅτι ἐκεῖνος ἐφ' ἑαυτοῦ μένων ἔδωκεν. Thus each hypostasis is said to be 'in' that immediately above it, though it is not a part of the higher hypostasis : ψυχὴ μὲν ἐν νῷ, σῶμα δὲ ἐν ψυχῇ, νοῦς δὲ ἐν ἄλλῳ· τούτου δὲ οὐκέτι ἄλλο, ἵν' ἂν ἦν ἐν αὐτῷ· οὐκ ἐν ὁτῳοῦν ἄρα (*Enn.* V. v. 9).—It will be noticed that Pr. does not in the present passage attempt to determine *in what sense* the lower is 'in' the higher, and in what sense outside it ; but elsewhere (*in Tim.* I. 210. 2) he has the interesting phrase ἑαυτοῖς μὲν προελήλυθε, μένει δὲ τοῖς θεοῖς. If this be pressed, it must mean that the separateness of the lower is an illusion resulting from a partial point of view, and it follows that the sensible and the intelligible cosmos are both of them appearance, and only the One fully real. This doctrine was never accepted by the Neoplatonists, but they often seem to be on the verge of falling into it.—The theory that the effect remains in the cause was found convenient by Christian theologians. Aquinas is thus enabled to prove that God knows not himself only (like

Aristotle's God) but his creatures also (*Summa c. Gent.* I. 49) ; and that he has the active as well as the contemplative virtues (*ibid.* I. 93). Psellus can explain that Christ οὐκ ἀποστὰς θρόνων ἐπὶ τὴν γῆν καταβέβηκε, and that the Virgin ὅλη τε ἄνω ἐστὶ καὶ ὅλη πρὸς ἡμᾶς κάτεισι (*C. M. A. G.* VI. 192). Cf. also prop. 124 n.

12. ἀμέσως. If *a*, *b*, *c*, are three terms in sequence, *b* both proceeds from *a* and remains in it, while *c* proceeds from *a* and *b*, but remains only in *b* : thus Soul both remains in Intelligence and proceeds from it, while Nature has wholly detached itself from Intelligence (*in Tim.* I. 12. 19). Accordingly we have the triadic arrangement (*a*) μονή, (*b*) μονὴ καὶ πρόοδος, (*c*) πρόοδος (*in Tim.* III. 185. 20). Hence Pr. can say (l. 17 f.) that τὸ πάντῃ προϊόν ἐστι (not ἔσται or ἂν εἴη) πάντῃ διακεκριμένον.

PROP. 31. Pr. now turns from the downward to the upward movement, which reunites effect to cause. Notice that (1) ἐπιστροφή is a necessary accompaniment of ὄρεξις, i.e. it is a direction of the will (cf. Plot. II. 147. 6).; (2) as the presuppositions of ὄρεξις are lack of the thing desired and awareness of it, so the conditions of ἐπιστροφή are the distinctness of the effect from the cause and its potential identity with it, in virtue of which it is συμπαθές (cf. *in Parm.* 922. 3 ff.); (3) the cause gives existence to the effect by πρόοδος, value by ἐπιστροφή (δι' οὗ τὸ εἶναι ἑκάστῳ, διὰ τούτου καὶ τὸ εὖ: cf. props. 36, 37, and n.).—The history of the words στροφή and ἐπιστροφή[1] shows a progressive development from a general to a technical meaning : noteworthy are (1) Plato's language about the 'turning' of the eye of the soul (*Rep.* 519 B); (2) the use of ἐπιστροφή, ἐπιστρέφειν for a religious 'turning' or conversion (e.g. *Ev. Luc.* 22. 32 ; *Act. Apost.* 15. 3) ; (3) Albinus ('Alcinous') *Didasc.* 10 (ὁ πρῶτος θεὸς) τὴν ψυχὴν τοῦ κόσμου ἐπεγείρας καὶ εἰς ἑαυτὸν ἐπιστρέψας. Comparing this last with the terms in which Seneca speaks of the return of the soul to its source (*Ep.* 65. 16 *explicari cupit et reverti ad illa, quorum fuit ; Ep.* 79. 12 *sursum illum vocant initia sua* ; cf. 92. 30-1), and with Maximus of Tyre xi. 10, we may fairly conclude that the Neoplatonic concept of reversion has its roots in Middle Platonism, and perhaps in Poseidonius: it is at once an interpretation of Plato and a philosophical counterpart to the Hellenistic religious teaching about the 'Himmelfahrt'.—On ἐπιστροφὴ πρὸς ἑαυτό see props. 15-17 and nn.

28. κατ' οὐσίαν: see prop. 39.

---

[1] Cf. Witt in *Class. Qu.* 25 (1931), 202 f.

COMMENTARY 219

Prop. 32. As likeness is the condition of procession (prop. 29),
so also it is the condition of reversion : cf. Sallust. 26. 22 ἡμεῖς δὲ
ἀγαθοὶ μὲν ὄντες δι' ὁμοιότητα θεοῖς συναπτόμεθα, κακοὶ δὲ γενόμενοι δι'
ἀνομοιότητα χωριζόμεθα. Pr. no doubt has in mind *Theaet.* 176 B
φυγὴ δὲ ὁμοίωσις θεῷ κατὰ τὸ δυνατόν,[1] φυγή being interpreted as
reversion (cf. *Enn.* I. vi. 8). Moreover, likeness is the condition of
all knowledge (*Enn.* I. viii. 1 [I. 99. 14] τῆς γνώσεως ἑκάστων δι'
ὁμοιότητος γιγνομένης : *in Tim.* II. 298. 27, III. 160. 18) ; and knowledge is a kind of reversion (*in Tim.* II. 287. 1, cf. prop. 39). Finally,
likeness is the principle on which theurgy depends for its theoretical
possibility : cf. Pr. *fragm.* in *C. M. A. G.* VI. 148 ff., esp. 148. 21
οἱ πάλαι σοφοί . . . ἐπήγοντο θείας δυνάμεις εἰς τὸν θνητὸν τόπον καὶ διὰ
τῆς ὁμοιότητος ἐφειλκύσαντο· ἱκανὴ γὰρ ἡ ὁμοιότης συνάπτειν τὰ ὄντα
ἀλλήλοις.—The doctrine of this proposition reappears in ps.-Dion.
Div. Nom. 9. 6 καὶ ἔστιν ἡ τῆς θείας ὁμοιότητος δύναμις ἡ τὰ παραγόμενα
πάντα πρὸς τὸ αἴτιον ἐπιστρέφουσα.

4. πρὸς ὅ = πρὸς τὸ πρὸς ὅ : cf. prop. 18, l. 19, ἐν οἷς.

5. πᾶν πρὸς πᾶν : cf. prop. 15, l. 33 πάντα πρὸς πάντα συνάψει.

Prop. 33. Procession and reversion together constitute a single
movement,[2] the diastole-systole which is the life of the universe : cf.
infra prop. 146 ; *in Tim.* I. 210. 10 ; Porph. ἀφ. xxx. § 1.

13. συνάπτει τῇ ἀρχῇ τὸ τέλος : cf. *Enn.* III. viii. 7 [I. 339. 23]
τέλος ἅπασιν ἡ ἀρχή ; V. viii. 7 *fin.* [II. 240. 20] ; *de myst.* 31. 16 ;
Syrian. *in Metaph.* 38. 3. Alcmaeon of Croton had said that man
dies ὅτι οὐ δύναται τὴν ἀρχὴν τῷ τέλει προσάψαι (Arist. *Probl.* 916 a
34) : reversion is thus, as Arnou observes, the guarantee of immortality.

18. τῶν δὲ πρὸς τὰ ἀνωτέρω : i.e. the reversion *may* be carried
beyond the proximate cause to the remoter : cf. prop. 38. So
ps.-Dion. says that he who strives upward passes κατὰ βραχὺ διὰ τῶν
αὐτοῦ πρώτων ἐπὶ τὰ ἔτι πρότερα, καὶ δι' ἐκείνων ἐπὶ τὰ πρώτιστα, καὶ
τελειωθεὶς ἐπὶ τὴν ἀκρότητα τὴν θεαρχικήν (*Eccl. Hier.* 2. 3, 4).

Prop. 34. This is the converse of prop. 31. We saw there that,
given the metaphysical ἀρχή, we can argue to the ethical τέλος : here
we argue from the ethical τέλος to the metaphysical ἀρχή. Both
arguments depend ultimately on the identity of the efficient with the

[1] On the historical importance of this passage see K. Praechter in *Hermes,* 51
(1916), 510-29.
[2] In the case of the higher realities not a movement, strictly speaking, but
a timeless relation. Cf. prop. 34, ll. 5 ff.

final cause (prop. 12), which implies that ethics must retrace in an upward direction the downward path of metaphysics.—In the corollary Pr. infers the creative role of the Intelligence from its character as ὀρεκτόν (which is assumed without proof, cf. prop. 8 n.). This creative role is a necessary consequence from the identification of the Aristotelian νοῦς with the Platonic demiurge.[1] But Pr. is careful to point out that the 'creation' of the world-order, like the 'reversion' of the world-order upon its cause, is timeless, and therefore consistent with the infinite duration of that order in time: cf. *Enn.* III. ii. 1 [I. 226. 23] νοῦν πρὸ αὐτοῦ (τοῦ κόσμου) εἶναι οὐχ ὡς χρόνῳ πρότερον ὄντα, ἀλλ' ὅτι παρὰ νοῦ ἐστι καὶ φύσει πρότερος ἐκεῖνος καὶ αἴτιος τούτου . . . δι' ἐκεῖνον ὄντος καὶ ὑποστάντος ἀεί, and Inge[2] I. 143 ff. The infinite duration of the κόσμος is not formally proved in *El. Th.*; but it was the subject of a separate work, now lost, which provoked the extant reply of Philoponus, *de aeternitate mundi contra Proclum*.

23. τὴν κατ' οὐσίαν ὄρεξιν: see prop. 39.

5. οὐ διὰ τοῦτο οὐχὶ πρόεισιν. The omission of the first negative in M and the printed editions reduces the whole passage to confusion. In PQ it is restored to the text but in the wrong place, obviously by conjecture.

PROP. 35. Combining the results reached in the preceding group of props. Pr. now affirms as a trinity-in-unity the three moments of the Neoplatonic world-process, immanence in the cause, ·procession from the cause, and reversion to the cause—or identity, difference, and the overcoming of difference by identity. This triad is one of the governing principles of Pr.'s dialectic; but Zeller[2] is scarcely justified in regarding it as Pr.'s special contribution to the architecture of the Neoplatonic system. Not only is it applied by Plotinus (as we have seen, and as Z. of course recognizes) to the relation between each hypostasis and its immediate prior; but its further application to the relations *within* a hypostasis, which Z. regards as especially Procline, occurs already in the anonymous fragment on the *Parmenides*, where in the second hypostasis ἡ κατὰ τὴν ὕπαρξιν ἐνέργεια is said to be ἑστῶσα, while ἡ κατὰ τὴν νόησιν is εἰς αὐτὴν στραφεῖσα, and ἡ κατὰ τὴν ζωήν is ἐκ τῆς ὑπάρξεως ἐκνεύσασα.[3] Moreover, Pr. himself says (*in Tim.* II. 215. 5) that Iamblichus called the monad

---

[1] On the difference between Proclus and Plotinus in this matter see prop. 174 n.
[2] III⁴. ii. 847 ff.
[3] p. 14. On the authorship of this work see now P. Hadot, *R.E.G.* 74 (1961), 410 ff., who makes a strong case for assigning it to Porphyry.

the cause of identity, the dyad the introducer of procession and difference, and the triad the origin of reversion: this implies that for Iamblichus identity, procession and reversion were general cosmogonic principles, and we shall probably not be wrong in regarding him as Pr.'s main source in all this part of his doctrine *.— According to Bréhier [1] the difference between Plotinus and the later school in this matter is that the former makes immanence, procession and reversion different aspects of a single reality, such as Soul or Intelligence, while the later writers hypostatize them in three *separate* realities, such as Being, Life and (intellective) Intelligence, thus spoiling the Plotinian world-scheme. Much of Pr.'s language certainly lays him open to this charge ; but the present proposition, with its explicit insistence that the three aspects are inseparable, warns us against assuming that the triadic moments within each stratum of reality are themselves 'hypostases'. Cf. Damasc. I. 171. 26 ἐν παντὶ νῷ τὰ τρία ἐστί, and *infra* prop. 103 n.—The triad immanence —procession—reversion had a considerable history. Ps.-Dion. applies it to the divine love (*Div. Nom.* 4. 14) ; Psellus to the Christian Trinity (*C.M.A.G.* VI. 165. 36 ff.). For Erigena God is 'principium, quia ex se sunt omnia quae essentiam participant ; medium autem, quia in ipso et per ipsum subsistunt atque moventur ; finis vero, quia ad ipsum moventur' (*de div. nat.* 152 A). Dietrich of Freiberg holds that 'sicut omnia ab ipso (deo) intellectualiter procedunt, ita omnia in ipsum conversa sunt' (*de intellectu et intelligibili* 130 Krebs).

PROPS. 36, 37. Procession is a passage from better to worse (cf. *Enn.* V. viii. 1 [II. 231. 25]) ; reversion, a passage from worse to better (cf. *Enn.* VI. ix. 9 [II. 520. 28]). Reversion may be said to restore to reality the value which was lost in the procession, without annihilating the individuality which procession creates. We may trace here the influence of the Aristotelian doctrine that τὸ ἀτελές is γενέσει πρότερον but τῇ οὐσίᾳ ὕστερον (*Metaph.* 1077 a 18, &c.) ; but Pr.'s ἐπιστροφή is not to be equated with Aristotle's γένεσις, since the reversion of the higher realities is timeless (prop. 34, l. 7). Cf. props. 77–9 nn.—It is natural to ask what it is that is 'generated by reversion' (prop. 37, l. 7) ; for while procession is a creative process, reversion has so far appeared as a relation or a state of the will. The answer appears to be that reversion generates the progressive perfection of the lower principle: cf. *Enn.* III. iv. 1 [I. 261. 5]

[1] *Hist. de Philos.* I. 475 f.

ἀμόρφωτον ἐγεννᾶτο, εἰδοποιεῖτο δὲ τῷ ἐπιστρέφεσθαι πρὸς τὸ γεννῆσαν οἷον ἐκτρεφόμενον : *in Tim.* III. 143. 4 ff. Thus the cosmos receives life by reversion to Soul (*in Tim.* II. 284. 6); and Being, which becomes Life by procession, becomes Intelligence by reversion (*Th. Pl.* III. xiv. 143). Cf. props. 71, 72.

12. ἐφ' ὃ ἡ πρόοδος ἔσχατον, ἀπὸ τούτου πρώτου ἡ ἐπιστροφή. Psellus applies this principle to the population of the Christian Heaven— ἐσχάτη τέτακται ἡ ἀγγελική (τάξις), ἣ δὴ πρώτη τοῖς ἀνιοῦσίν ἐστι (*C.M.A.G.* VI. 182. 31).

PROP. 38. The stages of the return repeat those of the procession, but in the reverse order: thus, e.g. body proceeds from the One through Intelligence and Soul, and reverts to it through Soul and Intelligence : cf. props. 128, 129.

23. δεῖ γὰρ πρὸς τὸ αὐτὸ ἑκατέραν γίνεσθαι. ἑκατέραν (sc. πρόοδον καὶ ἐπιστροφήν) is confirmed by l. 20 ἑκατέρα γίνεται (where ἑκάτερα cannot be right). Unless, then, Pr. is using his words here with unaccustomed looseness, πρὸς τὸ αὐτό must mean either ' towards the same *mean* term' (which is the intermediate stage in both movements) ; or '*in relation to* the same highest term' (not 'towards', for this would be true only of the reversion).

PROP. 39. The three grades of reversion here described correspond respectively to σῶμα, ζῷον, and ψυχή in the sensible world ; and to ὄν, ζωή, and νοῦς in the intelligible (cf. prop. 101). When Plot. speaks of reversion, the reference is commonly to the *conscious* reversion of Soul upon Intelligence or of Intelligence upon the One. But (1) if reversion is to be an exact analogue of procession it must be equally universal ; and (2) it had been an accepted commonplace since Eudoxus that *all* things have some *nisus* towards the Good, conscious or unconscious (cf. prop. 8 n.). In the case of organic beings this *nisus* is shown in their tendency to achieve, as they develop, the perfections proper to their kind ; Plato himself had said that the Good Life was choiceworthy even for φυτά (*Phil.* 22 B). This is Pr.'s ζωτικὴ ἐπιστροφή, which is still an ἐνέργεια, though a blind one. It is less easy to see what is meant by the 'existential reversion' of inanimate things, which have no ἐνέργεια,[1] and whose appetition is a mere ἐπιτηδειότης πρὸς μέθεξιν. The explanation is to be found in the theory of συμπάθεια and the actual practice of theurgic magic. The ἐπιτηδειότης is not a generalized capacity for the reception of

_____
[1] *Th. Pl.* II. vi. 96 τὰ πάσης ἐνεργείας ἐστερημένα μετέχει κατὰ τὴν αὐτῶν τάξιν τῆς πρὸς αὐτὸ (τὸ ἕν) συναφῆς.

any and every form, such as bare Matter possesses, nor, indeed, a capacity for the reception of form (in the ordinary sense) at all *, but for the reception of a σύνθημα or σύμβολον, a magical correspondence which links each material thing ἐνταῦθα with a particular spiritual principle or group of principles ἐκεῖ: cf. *in Tim.* I. 210. 20 ἡ φύσις ... ἐντίθησι καὶ τοῖς σώμασι τῆς πρὸς θεοὺς αὐτῶν οἰκειότητος συνθήματα, τοῖς μὲν Ἡλιακά, τοῖς δὲ Σεληνιακά, τοῖς δὲ ἄλλου τινὸς θεῶν, καὶ ἐπιστρέφει καὶ ταῦτα πρὸς θεούς, κτλ. According to *Th. Pl.* II. (viii). 104–5, reversion consists in the desire for identification with this σύνθημα, and through it with the cause : σέβεται πάντα κατὰ φύσιν ἐκεῖνον καὶ διὰ τοῦ προσήκοντος αὐτῷ μυστικοῦ συνθήματος ἐνίζεται, τὴν οἰκείαν φύσιν ἀποδυόμενα καὶ μόνον εἶναι τὸ ἐκείνου σύνθημα σπεύδοντα καὶ μόνου μετέχειν ἐκείνου, πόθῳ τῆς ἀγνώστου φύσεως καὶ τῆς τοῦ ἀγαθοῦ πηγῆς.[1] Certain of these συνθήματα were known to the theurgists, and were used by them as a means to union with the gods (*de myst.* 97. 4, &c.; Pr. in *C. M. A. G.* VI. 148 ff.; Hopfner, *Gr.-Äg. Offenbarungszauber* I. §§ 389 ff.). See also prop. 145 n., and Introd. pp. xx, xxii.—The three types of reversion reappear in Damascius (I. 173 ff.), who expends much useless subtlety in elaborating the doctrine ; and in ps.-Dion. (*Div. Nom.* 4. 4), who, however, intercalates a 'perceptual' reversion between the vital and the cognitive.

E. *Of the Self-constituted* (props. 40–51) :

1. The self-constituted exists (40).
2. It is identical with τὸ ἐν ἑαυτῷ (41).
3. It is that which is capable of reflexive consciousness (42, 43).
4. It is everlasting (first proof, 45, 46 ; second proof, 47–9).
5. It is timeless in its existence, but not necessarily in its activity (50, 51).

Prop. 44 is not logically in place in this group, but seems to be introduced because of the close connexion of the group as a whole with the proof of the immortality of the soul, for which prop. 44 supplies one of the steps.

PROP. 40. The system as so far expounded appears to be a rigid monistic determinism : the higher entity as formal-efficient cause determines completely the procession of the lower, and as final cause its reversion. It was impossible to make a breach in the continuity of this scheme by the introduction of genuinely self-determining

---

[1] Even the inorganic is here credited with something analogous to will. Cf. *Enn.* IV. iv. 36.

principles other than the One; at the same time it was necessary to make some provision for the freedom of the human will, which Hellenistic philosophy in general regarded as a necessary ethical postulate. Hence the concept of the αὐθυπόστατον or 'self-constituted', which is not 'self-caused' in the sense of being an independent ἀρχή, but 'hypostatizes itself' or determines the particular potentiality which shall be actualized in it.[1] Such principles have a double origin καὶ παρὰ τῶν ἀρχηγικῶν αἰτίων καὶ παρ᾽ ἑαυτῶν (*in Tim.* III. 39. 4: cf. *ibid.* 210. 30; Syrian. *in Metaph.* 116. 6, 187. 6); and are thus intermediate between the One which transcends causality and the lower existences which are purely *causata*, just as the αὐτοκίνητα are intermediate between the ἀκίνητον and the ἑτεροκίνητα (prop. 14: cf. *in Parm.* 1145. 34 ff.).—The starting-point of this doctrine of double determination is perhaps to be found in the Platonic conception of Soul as that which has life in its own right : cf. Porph. ἀφ. xvii, ἡ ψυχὴ ... ἐν ζωῇ παρ᾽ ἑαυτῆς ἐχούσῃ τὸ ζῆν κεκτημένη τὸ εἶναι, and xix, τὰ μὲν καθ᾽ ἑαυτὰ ὑφεστηκότα, τὰ δὲ ἄλλων εἰς τὸ εἶναι δεόμενα : also prop. 189 *infra*. But I cannot trace the term αὐθυπόστατον further back than Iamblichus (*ap.* Stob. II. 174. 22 [400 H]); and to him probably is due the elaboration of the doctrine and its extension to all θεῖα: it is already fully developed in Syrianus *.—The 'proof' given here for the existence of the αὐθυπόστατον depends on its identity with the αὔταρκες, whose existence is assumed without proof both here and in props. 9–10.

24. αὐτὸ ἑαυτὸ παράγον οὐχ ἓν ἔσται. Plot. raises a like objection against the doctrine that God is self-created, but meets it by saying that God is altogether *maker*, nothing in him is *made*— he is ἐνέργεια ἄνευ οὐσίας (*Enn.* VI. viii. 20). When, however, τὸ αὐθυπόστατον became a formal attribute of the lower θεῖα, it was necessary that the supreme principle should transcend it, just as it is already ἐπέκεινα αὐταρκείας in Plot. (V. iii. 17). Cf. *in Parm.* 1149. 32 ff.

PROP. 41. There is a close correlation in Neoplatonism between the notions of ὑπ᾽ ἄλλου (ἀπ᾽ ἄλλου, παρ᾽ ἄλλου) and ἐν ἄλλῳ :[2] cf. *Enn.* II. ix. 1 (I. 184. 12) πᾶν τὸ ἐν ἄλλῳ καὶ παρ᾽ ἄλλου : V. v. 9 *init.* : Porph. ἀφ. xxxix : Pr. *in Parm.* 1146. 18. Hence the αὐθυπόστατον is identified with τὸ ἐν ἑαυτῷ,[3] i.e. with that which can exist in its

---

[1] Cf. props. 99, 100 n. In one passage Pr. distinguishes two grades of αὐθ-υπόστατα, placing the human soul in the lower (*in Tim.* I. 232. 12).

[2] Arnou, 162 *.

[3] Pr. sometimes, however, makes τὸ ἐν ἑαυτῷ the equivalent of τὸ ἀμέθεκτον, thus restricting its application to the monad of each transverse series and excluding from its scope the individual souls and intelligences (*in Parm.* 707. 18);

own right without inhering in a substrate, as soul can exist without body, and intelligence without soul. Such a principle is its own substrate in so far as it is its own cause : it is ἐν ἑνὶ τὴν αἰτίαν καὶ τὸ ἀπ' αἰτίας συνῃρηκός (*Th. Pl.* III. (vi). 126). So Plot. says that in the intelligible world 'none walks upon an alien earth : for each the environment is its own essence . . . since the substrate is Intelligence and he is himself Intelligence' (*Enn.* V. viii. 4).—Notice that in *El. Th.* ἐν ἄλλῳ always means 'in something lower', though elsewhere it is sometimes applied to a principle which has identified itself with its cause by reversion : cf. *in Parm.* 1136. 29, where the two senses of the term are contrasted.

PROPS. **42, 43**. On self-reversion or introversion see props. 15–17 n. It appears here as the form of reversion characteristic of the self-constituted ; but it does not, of course, exclude an eventual reversion to a higher principle, any more than the notion of the self-constituted excludes an ultimate procession from such a principle. For the doctrine cf. Porph. ἀφ. xli, where νοῦς is cited as an example of a faculty which is capable of introversion or self-knowledge and is therefore ἐν ἑαυτῷ, in contrast with αἴσθησις, whose objects are external to it and whose being is dependent on these objects and on the bodily organs.[1]

18. ὥστε καὶ αὐτὸ ἑαυτῷ : cf. prop. 7, ll. 19 ff.

24. στραφήσεται. PQ have the usual ἐπιστραφήσεται, but I have thought it unsafe to introduce this into the text here or in prop. 47, l. 31, in view of *in Tim.* I. 210. 4 and *in Crat.* 6. 7, where the MSS. agree in giving the uncompounded forms στροφή, στρέφεσθαι : the latter are frequent in Plot. and Porph.

PROP. **44**. The argument from introverted activity to introverted (i.e. independent) existence is an essential step in the proof of immortality which Pr. has in mind in this and the following props. Cf. Plat. *Phaedo* 79 D ; and for the relation of ἐνέργεια to οὐσία, *supra*, prop. 16.

3. δύναται. The indicative is more in accordance with Pr.'s usage, since this part of the supposition is true. For the indicative of fact in conjunction with the optative of false supposition cf. prop. 42, l. 14 f.

4. κρεῖττον . . . 5. μᾶλλον : cf. prop. 25, l. 35 n.

whereas in *El. Th.* even the μερικὴ ψυχή, being αὐθυπόστατος (prop. 189), is ἐν ἑαυτῇ.

[1] διάνοια is intermediate in this as in other respects between νοῦς and αἴσθησις (*Enn.* V. iii. 3–4).

PROPS. 45, 46. This argument for the eternity of spiritual substances is in principle traditional, and does not depend on the formal concept of the ' self-constituted '. Its real basis is the general theory that the phenomenal order is not self-explanatory (see prop. 7 n.): if spiritual substances were part of the phenomenal order we should have to posit other spiritual substances in order to account for them, and so *ad infinitum*—for γένεσις can be explained only by the operation of οὐσία, and φθορά by its ceasing to operate. Cf. Plat. *Phdr.* 245 C–E : Arist. *de mot. anim.* 700 a 35 γενέσεως καὶ φθορᾶς οὐδαμῶς οἷόν τε αὐτὸ αὑτῷ αἴτιον εἶναι οὐδέν : Plot. *Enn.* IV. vii. 9 (14): Pr. *in Tim.* I. 281. 6 ff., 296. 29 ff.; *Th. Pl.* III. (vi). 126.

16. ἡ γένεσις ὁδός ἐστιν ἐκ τοῦ ἀτελοῦς εἰς τὸ ἐναντίον τέλειον. Cf. Arist. *de gen. et corr.* 331 a 14 ἡ γένεσις εἰς ἐναντία καὶ ἐξ ἐναντίων : *Phys.* 193 b 13 ἡ γένεσις ὁδὸς εἰς φύσιν, 225 a 13 ἡ οὐκ ἐξ ὑποκειμένου εἰς ὑποκείμενον· μεταβολὴ κατ' ἀντίφασιν γένεσίς ἐστιν. Pr. contrasts this evolution of the perfect from the imperfect with the ' involution ' which is characteristic of οὐσία, *in Tim.* III. 322. 1 ff.

19. πρὸς τὸ τῆς οὐσίας τελειωτικόν. I have noticed no other example of συνεῖναι, or ἐνυπάρχειν, πρός τι in Pr. ; but συνουσία πρός occurs in Plot. (Seidel, *de usu praepositionum Plotiniano* 48), and Iamb. (*de myst.* 176. 18). In Plot. II. 417. 32, which Seidel quotes, πρός should not be construed with συνῇ.

26. ἅτε ἑαυτὸ οὐκ ἀπολεῖπον : Plat. *Phdr.* 245 C μόνον δὴ τὸ αὐτὸ κινοῦν, ἅτε οὐκ ἀπολεῖπον ἑαυτό, οὔποτε λήγει κινούμενον.

PROPS. 47–9. These propositions constitute a second argument for the eternity of spiritual substances, independent of the first and, like it, traditional. Its starting point is Plato *Phaedo* 78 C ff., which it combines with the *Phaedrus* passage. Cf. Arist. *Metaph.* 1088 b 14 ff. ; Plot. *Enn.* IV. vii. 12 (17) [II. 140. 11 ff.]; Porph. ἀφ. xiv ; Pr. *in Tim.* I. 285. 11–15 ; Psell. *de anima* 1049 B Migne.

32. τοῦτο δὲ ἀδύνατον : cf. prop. 15, and *in Parm.* 785. 10 ff.

33. τὸ μὲν χεῖρον ἔσται ἐν αὐτῷ, τὸ δὲ βέλτιον. Nicolaus objects that a composite need not be composed of a better and a worse ; but Pr. is following Aristotle, who held that the σύνθετον necessarily includes an element of ὕλη (*Metaph.* 1088 b 15).

10. ἀδιάλυτον (*Phaedo* 80 B) is opposed to resolution into elements ; ἀσκέδαστον (cf. *Phaedo* 77 E), to withdrawal from the substrate.

PROPS. 50, 51. The self-constituted is without beginning or end in time ; but this must not exclude the possibility of its having a

temporal history—otherwise the human soul, which enters into the time-series, will not be self-constituted, and the proof of immortality will be *manqué*. Accordingly Pr. introduces here the distinction between temporal existence and temporal activity : the concept of the self-constituted excludes the former, but not necessarily the latter. As we shall see later (prop. 191), the human soul combines an eternal essence with activity in time (a view suggested by *Legg.* X. 904 A, and held also by Plotinus) ; the same is true of ἡ τοῦ παντὸς φύσις (*in Tim.* I. 257. 8, cf. *Enn.* II. i. and prop. 34 n.) ; and of time itself, which Plato and the *Chaldaean Oracles* had called αἰώνιος (*in Tim.* III. 26. 2). The distinction reappears in ps.-Dion. (*Div. Nom.* 10. 3) and Psellus (*de omnif. doct.* cap. 80). It is, moreover, the source of the scholastic doctrine of *aevum*, which is the mode of being of created intelligences and is intermediate between eternity and time : *aevum* comports change of thought and volition without change of substance.[1]

20. ταὐτὸν κατὰ ἀριθμόν : i.e. identical in material as well as in species (Arist. *Metaph.* 1016 b 31, &c.).

24. ἐν τῷ αὐτῷ εἶναι. Port. and Cr. translate 'in eodem Esse' ; but I can find no parallel in Pr. for this barbarism. τῷ αὐτῷ εἶναι, if sound, must be the dative of τὸ αὐτῷ εἶναι : cf. prop. 170, l. 15 ταὐτὸν τῷ ἑκάστῳ εἶναι.

28. τοῦτο δέ ἐστιν ἐν τῷ μὴ εἶναι τὸ εἶναι ἔχειν. Cf. Arist. *Phys.* 263 b 26 εἰ δ᾽ ἂν ᾖ πρότερον μὴ ὄν, ἀνάγκη γίγνεσθαι ὂν καὶ ὅτε γίγνεται μή ἐστιν, οὐχ οἷόν τε εἰς ἀτόμους χρόνους διαιρεῖσθαι τὸν χρόνον. Nazzari[2] well compares Hegel's saying that time is 'the form of unrest, . . . of that which comes-to-be and passes away : so that its being is not-being' (*Encyclopädie* § 448).

F. *Of Time and Eternity* (props. 52–5).

    1. Nature of eternal existence and eternal activity (52).

    2. Eternity and Time as transcendent hypostases (53).

    3. Eternity and Time as 'measures' (54).

    4. Everlasting duration in time distinguished from eternal existence (55).

PROP. 52. Pr.'s account of eternal existence goes back to Plato *Tim.* 37 E ff. and ultimately to Parmenides (v. 66 οὐδέποτ᾽ ἦν οὐδ᾽

---

[1] Cf. Aquinas, *Summa Theologiae*, Pars. I, qu. x, art. 5, quoted by A. E. Taylor, *Comm. on Plato's Timaeus*, 679 ; Inge[3], II. 99 ff. Inge seems to confuse the doctrine of ψυχή as mediator between time and eternity with that of ἀϊδιότης κατὰ χρόνον (see prop. 55 n.) ; the latter cannot be the prototype of *aevum*, since it involves an 'earlier' and a 'later' not merely in its activity but in its essence.

[2] *La Dialettica di Proclo e il Sopravvento della Filosofia Cristiana* 291.

ἔσται, ἐπεὶ νῦν ἐστιν ὁμοῦ πᾶν). His account of eternal activity is derived from Aristotle's conception of the divine life as an ἐνέργεια ἀκινησίας (*E.N.* 1154 b 27) which is complete in each moment. Cf. Plot. III. vii. 4 *fin.*, where the two concepts are already combined. From Neoplatonism the notion of eternity as a *totum simul* passed into Christian theology : cf. Augustine *Conf.* XI. 11 non praeterire quicquam in aeterno, sed totum esse praesens ; *de Trinitate* XII. 14 ; Boethius *de consol.* V. Prosa 6 interminabilis vitae tota simul et perfecta possessio ; Aquinas, *Summa Theologiae*, Pars I, qu. x, art. 5.

15. ὡς καὶ τοὔνομα ἐμφαίνει : this etymology is as old as Aristotle (*de caelo* 279 a 17 ff.). Cf. Plot. III. vii. 4 *fin.* To Pr. names are significant as being ἀγάλματα τῶν πραγμάτων λογικά (*in Parm.* 851. 8).

PROP. 53. Time and eternity are here treated not as modes of the spirit but as substantive principles having, like other spiritual substances, both an immanent and a transcendent existence. In this Pr. deserts the sober and penetrating analysis of Plotinus, who regards eternity as a διάθεσις of the Real (III. vii. 4 *fin.*), and time as the formal aspect of the activity of Soul (*ibid.* 11–12), 'the form of willed change' (Inge). This unfortunate development may be merely the result of a 'critique simpliste' [1] applying the same formula to all concepts indifferently ; but I suspect that Pr. had a special reason for hypostatizing αἰών and χρόνος, namely their importance in late Hellenistic cultus and contemporary magic. A deified Αἰών [2] (probably in origin a Hellenized form of the Persian God Zervan) has a prominent place not only in Gnostic and Hermetic speculation and in the magical papyri, but in the sacred book of later Neoplatonism, the *Oracula Chaldaica* (cf. *in Tim.* III. 14. 3) ; and Pr. accordingly calls αἰών 'an intelligible god' (*ibid.* III. 13. 22). For the divinity of χρόνος, again, Pr. quotes the authority of 'the best theurgists, such as Julianus' (the author or compiler of the *Orac. Chald.*), *in Tim.* III. 27. 8 ; and he mentions a recipe for evoking χρόνος in bodily form, *ibid.* 20. 22. It is clear from the discussion in *in Tim.* III that the immediate source of much of what Pr. has to say about time and eternity is Iamblichus ; but the blending of the Greek philosophical concept with the oriental religious phantasy is already observable in *Corp. Herm.* xi. It may have been facilitated, as Zepf [3] suggests, by

[1] Bréhier, *Hist. de Philos.* I. 473.
[2] See especially Reitzenstein, *Das iranische Erlösungsmysterium*, 188 ff. ; J. Kroll, *Lehren des Hermes*[1], 67 ff. Plot. himself says that αἰών ' might well be called a god ' (III. vii. 5).
[3] *Archiv f. Religionswissenschaft*, 25 (1927), 247 ff.

Aristotle's description of αἰών as θεῖος in the first book of the *de caelo*, where also we find the contrast between a supreme αἰών and individual αἰῶνες in its original form, as a contrast between the measure of the life of the whole οὐρανός and the measures of the individual lives contained in it.

PROP. 54. The traditional Academic definition of Time was ' the measure of movement ' (Ὄροι 411 B : cf. Arist. *Phys.* 220 b 25). This description was riddled with criticism by Plotinus (III. vii. 9, 12, 13), whose fundamental objection to it is that it tells us what time is used for without bringing us any nearer to understanding what time is. But it serves Pr. as a way of stressing the reality of time as something independent of and higher than its content, against the Aristotelian view which made it a πάθος κινήσεως (*Phys.* 251 b 28) and an ἀριθμητόν, something itself counted or measured (*Phys.* 220 b 8, cf. Pr. *in Tim.* III. 4. 23 ff.). From the same motive Pr. calls αἰών the measure of αἰώνια (following Iamblichus, as appears from *in Tim.* III. 33. 1 ff.). The doctrine reappears in Aquinas (*Summa Theologiae* l.c.).

8. πᾶς αἰών: why '*every* eternity ', asks Nicolaus, when there is only one? But each of the immanent eternities is the measure of its participant eternal, as it in turn is measured by the transcendent Eternity. Cf. Aristotle's αἰῶνες; and the conception of ' relative infinity ', prop. 93.

PROP. 55. The temporal perpetuity (ἀιδιότης κατὰ χρόνον) of the κόσμος was stubbornly maintained by the Neoplatonists against Stoics, Gnostics and Catholics (cf. prop. 34 n.). The purpose of the present prop. is to affirm the necessary existence of a class of things having such perpetuity, and to distinguish this from eternity proper (αἰών), which belongs only to immaterial principles. The conception of temporal perpetuity as a ' mean term ' (see Introd., p. xxii) was suggested by *Tim.* 37 D τοῦτο (the eternal nature of τὸ ὃ ἔστι ζῷον) μὲν δὴ τῷ γενητῷ παντελῶς προσάπτειν οὐκ ἦν δυνατόν. Cf. Plot. I. v. 7 ; Porph. ἀφ. xliv. § 3 ; Pr. *in Tim.* I. 233. 18 ff. ; 235. 21 ff. ; 278. 3 ff. In the last passage two kinds of ἀίδια κατὰ χρόνον are distinguished (after Aristotle), those which are perpetual only as wholes (e.g. the sublunar elements) and those whose parts also are perpetual (the οὐρανός).

23. οὐκοῦν . . . 25. τὸ ποτὲ ὄντως ὄν. Omissions have played havoc with this sentence in the MSS. and printed editions ; but the earlier part of it is fortunately preserved intact in BCD, and the missing

ποτέ before οὐκ ὄντως (ll. 24–5) is supplied by PQ, perhaps from conjecture.

G. *Of the degrees of causality* (props. 56–65).

  1. The earlier members of the causal series have the greater efficacy (56–7).
  2. Relation of multiplicity to causal efficacy (58–62).
  3. Distinction of participated principles as enduringly or contingently participated (63).
  4. Distinction of substances as self-complete or incomplete (64).
  5. Distinction of three modes of existence (65).

PROP. 56. When the principle of transcendence is pressed too hard the world of experience tends to break loose from its ultimate causes.   This and the following proposition are designed to obviate this danger by showing that the ultimate causes are actively present in the whole causal series.   Every cause is responsible not only for the existence of its effects but also for the whole of the causative activity of those effects—a view which seems logically to issue in a rigid deterministic monism, and is difficult to reconcile with the doctrine of αὐθυπόστατα (prop. 40).   For an illustration cf. *in Tim.* III. 222. 7 ff.—This theorem was found very useful by some of the later scholastics as a means of reconciling the emanationism taught by Avicenna with the orthodox ' creationist' view : it is cited for this purpose by Dietrich of Freiberg, *de intellectu et intelligibili*, II. i. 134 Krebs, 'quicquid fiat ab inferiori et secunda causa, illud idem fit a prima causa, sed eminentiori modo, scilicet per modum creationis';[1] cf. also Albert. Magn. X. 413 a Borgnet.

  18. γεννᾷ. ἐγέννα, which Cr. adopts, seems to have been introduced by a scribe who took τὸ δεύτερον as accus.

  19. δευτέρως. δευτέρου, which the edd. keep, is grammatically impossible ; and δεύτερον (M) is at least very awkward, since it has a different reference from τὸ δεύτερον in the preceding clause.   The archetype presumably had β'.

PROP. 57. The last prop. made it clear that any spiritual principle is more potent than its consequent in the sense that it produces all the effects of the consequent and also the consequent itself.   But there is always more in the cause than in the consequent : neither

---

[1] Ueberweg-Geyer[11], 557, is clearly in error in describing this as ' a modification derived from Christian circles '.

its being nor its activity is exhausted in the consequent and its effects. Hence the doctrine that its causal efficacy extends farther down the *scala naturae* than that of its consequent. This is a post-Plotinian development, at least in its explicit formulation. But it is older than Pr.: Syrianus formally applies it to the relation of the One and Being—τὸ γὰρ ἓν καὶ ὑπὲρ τὸ ὂν καὶ σὺν τῷ ὄντι καὶ ἐπὶ τάδε τοῦ ὄντος, ὡς ἐπὶ τῆς ὕλης καὶ τῆς στερήσεως (*in Metaph.* 59. 17). Zeller[1] considers it an undigested borrowing from Aristotle, due to Pr.'s confusion of the causal relation with that of genus and species, and inconsistent with the structure of the Neoplatonic system: e.g. in Aristotle the inanimate is a species of τὸ ὂν co-ordinate with the animate, whereas a Neoplatonist, says Zeller, should only derive it from τὸ ὂν indirectly through the mediation of the animate. But Pr. does not regard the inanimate as co-ordinate with the animate, though both are caused by τὸ ὄν—any more than he regards Matter as co-ordinate with τὸ ὄν, though both are caused by the One (see table below). What he is anxious to vindicate is the direct presence of the divine everywhere, even in Matter. Cf. *in Tim.* I. 209. 13 ff. πάντα τὰ ὄντα θεῶν ἐστιν ἔκγονα καὶ παράγεται ὑπ' αὐτῶν ἀμέσως πάντα καὶ ἱδρύεται ἐν αὐτοῖς. οὐ γὰρ μόνον ἡ κατὰ συν-έχειαν ἐπιτελεῖται τῶν πραγμάτων πρόοδος, ἀεὶ τῶν ἑξῆς ἀπὸ τῶν προσεχῶς αἰτίων ὑφισταμένων, ἀλλὰ καὶ αὐτόθεν ἀπὸ τῶν θεῶν ἐστιν ὅπῃ γεννᾶται τὰ πάντα, κἂν πορρωτάτω τῶν θεῶν εἶναι λέγηται, κἂν αὐτὴν εἴπῃς τὴν ὕλην· οὐδενὸς γὰρ ἀφέστηκε τὸ θεῖον, ἀλλὰ πᾶσιν ἐξ ἴσου πάρεστι. The direct ascription of στερήσεις to the causal agency of the One, bold as it is, was the only possible view if they were not to be attributed (as both Aristotle and Plotinus[2] sometimes seem to attribute them) to an active power of resistance resident in Matter: for as Aristotle had pointed out (*Metaph.* 990 a 13), and as Syrianus agrees (110. 18 ff.), they cannot be accounted for by the theory of Forms—there are no Forms of negations (cf. prop. 74 *fin.* and *in Parm.* 832. 21 ff.). Pr.'s view of στερήσεις is accepted by ps.-Dion. (*Div. Nom.* 4. 18 ff.) and by Nicolaus.—Pr. ingeniously finds confirmation of this theorem in the fact that the greatest teachers have also the widest popular appeal (*in Parm.* 691); while Psellus uses it to account for manifestations of the Virgin to humble people lacking in intelligence (*C. M. A. G.* VI. 193. 32). Aquinas reads it into Aristotle in order to make the Aristotelian πρώτη ὕλη a creation of God: cf. *Summa c. Gentiles* III. 74 'quanto aliqua causa est superior (sc. causato) tanto est majoris virtutis, unde ejus causalitas ad plura se extendit.

[1] 111⁴. ii. 851.   [2] Cf. Inge³, I. 134 ff.

23. πᾶν αἴτιον κτλ. The absence from the enunciation of the words καὶ σὺν αὐτῷ, which appear in the conclusion, may be due to faulty transmission ; but it is possible that the conclusion is intended to summarize the results of props. 56 and 57 taken together. μετ' αὐτοῦ (PQ) is an attempt to mend the text ; but μετ' αὐτό cannot be dispensed with.

13. καὶ τῆς τοῦ νοῦ ποιήσεως : added to explain in what sense the inanimate 'participates Intelligence'. The Intelligence is here the Plotinian hypostasis, identified with τὸ ὄν or the world of Forms : it is first distinguished from τὸ ὄν (which in the stricter Procline theory is the cause of τὸ ἄψυχον, see table below) in prop. 101.

PROPS. **58, 59.** The Platonic-Plotinian One and the Aristotelian-Plotinian Matter are alike simple, because each of them is a last result of abstraction. This (to a Neoplatonist) paradoxical meeting of extremes is noted by Plotinus (VI. vii. 13 [II. 441. 22]) ; but it was, so far as I know, reserved for Pr. to furnish a theoretical explanation of it by means of the principle of prop. 57. This principle also served to explain other troublesome facts, e.g. that the heavenly bodies, which are superior to earthly animals, and inanimate things, which are inferior, have both of them a simpler type of motion than that of animals (*in Tim.* III. 328. 18 ff.). The systematic working out of the theory is illustrated by the following table, which is based on *Th. Pl.* III. (vi). 127-9 (cf. also *in Tim.* I. 386. 25 ff. ; 437. 2 ff.) :

ὄντα {
τὸ ἕν, which is uncaused, has maximal unity.
τὸ ὄν, which is caused by τὸ ἕν, has unity and maximal being.
ζωή, which is caused by τὸ ἕν and τὸ ὄν, has unity, being and maximal life.
νοῦς, which is caused by τὸ ἕν, τὸ ὄν and ζωή, has unity, being, life and maximal intelligence.
ψυχή, which is caused by τὸ ἕν, τὸ ὄν, ζωή and νοῦς, has unity, being, life, intelligence, and discursive reason.
}

γινόμενα {
ζῷα, which are caused by τὸ ἕν, τὸ ὄν, ζωή and νοῦς, have unity, being, life, and minimal intelligence.
φυτά, which are caused by τὸ ἕν, τὸ ὄν and ζωή, have unity, being and minimal life.
νεκρὰ σώματα (τὸ ἄψυχον), which are caused by τὸ ἕν and τὸ ὄν, have unity and minimal being.
}
ὕλη, which is caused by τὸ ἕν, has minimal unity.

It is worth noticing that (1) the spiritual principles, being αὐθ-

ὑπόστατα, add each a quality of its own to those bestowed upon it by its causes, while the corporeal things have no qualities but those of their causes, and have the quality of their last cause only in a minimal degree ; (2) ψυχή does not appear as a cause in this table, its natural place being usurped by ζωή ; (3) νεκρὰ σώματα and φυτά are separated from the One by fewer stages of procession, and therefore also of reversion (prop. 38), than ψυχαί—a conclusion consistent with the importance attached to them in theurgic magic.

PROP. 60. This is the converse of prop. 57: as there Pr. argues from higher status in the causal series to wider causative range, so here from wider range to higher status. Cf. *Th. Pl.* 120.

PROPS. 61, 62. The correlation of degrees of power with degrees of unity is a natural consequence from making pure unity the first cause. The pyramidal picture of reality which is thus arrived at is indeed already implicit in the Platonic method of διαίρεσις :[1] and the development of the doctrine was probably influenced by the treatment of definite number in *Philebus* 16 C ff. as the link between τὸ ἕν and τὸ ἄπειρον (cf. Plot. VI. ii. 22 [II. 325. 11 ff.]). Its growth may be traced in Plot. II. ix. 6 (I. 191. 9 ff.), VI. vii. 8 (II. 435. 5); Porph. ἀφ. xi ; Iamb. *comm. math. sci.* 35. 7 Festa ; Syrian. *in Metaph.* 108. 19 ff. (where the explicit formulation of the theory is implied) ; Pr. *in Parm.* 1174. 7 (where it forms part of an argument ascribed to certain unspecified Neoplatonists earlier than Syrianus). Cf. also props. 86, 95, 110, 149, 179, 203.

PROP. 63. The purpose of this theorem will be best understood by considering the relation between intelligences and souls. Every intelligence is 'participated', i.e. immanent, except the first (prop. 166). But every intelligence is eternally existent and eternally active (prop. 169). Hence it might seem that the immanent intelligences must be immanent in subjects which perpetually enjoy intuitive thought. Now the human consciousness does enjoy intuitive thought, but it does so only intermittently. Accordingly both perpetual and (as a subordinate grade) temporary or contingent immanence must be recognized ; and a class of beings must be postulated for whom the former is possible. Plotinus met the difficulty by holding that the highest part of the human soul enjoys perpetual intuition, even

---

[1] Nebel, *Plotins Kategorien*, 8. The Neoplatonic doctrine also owes a good deal, as Theiler has recently shown, to Poseidonius' conception of the *physical* world as an organic unity.

when 'we' are not aware of it (IV. viii. 8). But Pr. rejects the Plotinian view (*in Tim.* III. 333. 28 ff.: cf. prop. 211 n.), and falls back on a theory of superhuman souls (prop. 184). Similarly, the henads or gods are participated perpetually by 'divine' intelligences, and through these by 'divine' souls and 'divine' bodies (prop. 129), intermittently by all other things; the Forms are participated perpetually by intelligences (prop. 173 n.) and through these by souls (prop. 194), intermittently by γενητά; souls are participated perpetually by their indestructible 'vehicles' (prop. 196), intermittently by mortal bodies (prop. 206). Evil consists in intermittence of participation (*de mal. subsist.* 203. 39 ff., where 'in aliis' may refer to the present prop.).—Both this and the following theorem are 'proved' by the principle of mean terms.

5. πρὶν ἄρα ὑποστῇ: cf. prop. 5, l. 22 n.

16. τῶν ἄλλων εἰδῶν. This may be the redundant use of ἄλλος, or εἰδῶν may be a gloss, as ψυχαί and νόες are not in the technical sense εἴδη.

17. ἀμέθεκτα ὄντα . . . 18. μετέχεται : cf. prop. 23 n.

PROP. 64. This is based on the Plotinian doctrine of the twofold activity of intelligibles, intrinsic and extrinsic (which again has its roots in the Stoic antithesis of ἐνδιάθετος and προφορικὸς λόγος). Cf. esp. *Enn.* VI. ii. 22 *fin.* (II. 325. 24 ff.) ὅτε μὲν γὰρ ἐν αὐτῷ ἐνεργεῖ (ὁ νοῦς), τὰ ἐνεργούμενα οἱ ἄλλοι νοῖ, ὅτε δὲ ἐξ αὐτοῦ, ψυχή· ψυχῆς δὲ ἐνεργούσης ὡς γένους ἢ εἴδους αἱ ἄλλαι ψυχαὶ ὡς εἴδη . . . καὶ τὸ κάτω λεγόμενον αὐτῆς ἴνδαλμά ἐστιν αὐτῆς, οὐκ ἀποτετμημένον δέ. So also νοῦς is a μίμημα or εἴδωλον (V. iv. 2) or an ἴχνος (VI. vii. 17) of τὸ ἕν. Similarly Pr. says (*in Tim.* I. 360. 28) that what gives life to organisms is an ἴνδαλμα of Soul ; what makes souls capable of intellection is an ἔλλαμψις of Intelligence ; what renders Intelligence and Being divine is a πρόλαμψις of the First Principle.—How is this theorem related to the preceding? The ἀμέθεκτον of prop. 63 is evidently a monad or analogous to the monad (μονάδος ἔχον λόγον, prop. 23, l. 25). And the lowest terms of the two triads appear to coincide: for the human soul is ποτὲ νοῦ μετέχουσα (prop. 184 n.), and what it possesses is an ἔλλαμψις νοῦ (*in Crat.* 28. 23 : cf. prop. 175 *cor.*). Hence it would seem that the middle terms must also be equated, and that prop. 64 restates prop. 63 in a different form. If so, it follows that the difference between the αὐτοτελεῖς ὑποστάσεις and the ἐλλάμψεις is merely a difference in degree of immanence: as the ἐλλάμψεις of νοῦς are temporarily in human souls, so the αὐτοτελεῖς νόες are permanently 'in' certain non-human souls, although they 'make them their own'

(l. 28); the αὐτοτελεῖς ἑνάδες, or gods, are in the same sense ' in ' the intelligences, while their ἐλλάμψεις penetrate to the world of experience and appear as τὸ ἐν τῆς ψυχῆς (*in Alc.* 519. 17 ff.). On the other hand it is a mark of the αὐτοτελῆ that they ' have no need of inferior beings for their substantial existence ' (l. 30); and they are called χωριστά, *in Parm.* 1062. 22 ff. Cf. props. 81, 82, where it is shown that all substantive spiritual existences χωριστῶς μετέχεται. Such substantive principles have thus a transcendent-immanent existence intermediate between the pure transcendence of the μονάς or ἀμέθεκτον and the pure immanence of the ἐλλάμψεις.

21. αὐτοτελῶν : an Aristotelian and Stoic term, which Neopythagoreans and Hermetists used as an epithet of various divine principles (Stob. I. 176. 7 [430 H], 82. 3 [188 H]; *Theol. Arithm.* 3. 18). Albinus applies it both to the First God and to the Forms. In Pr. its meaning seems to coincide with that of αὐτάρκης and αὐθυπόστατος.

24. ἀπὸ τῶν παντελείων κτλ. : cf. the triad ὑπερτελές, τέλειον, ἀτελές, *Theol. Arithm.* 18. 17.

25. The omission of ὥστε in PQ is probably a deliberate emendation; but the sentence certainly runs better without it, and its presence in other MSS. may be due to dittography of the last syllable of εὐτάκτως.

6. καὶ νόες κτλ. The omission of a line in the archetype of MW has led to further corruption, so that this sentence as printed by Port. and Cr. is a meaningless jumble. The other families fortunately preserve the true text.

8. ὡς ἰνδάλματα : I accept ὡς (Q) as accounting for the reading of BCD, ἰνδάλματα καί : the tachygrams for ὡς and καί are constantly confused.—For ἰνδάλματα (i.q. εἴδωλα) cf. Plot. I. iv. 3 (I. 66. 28).

PROP. 65. The characters of the effect pre-exist in the cause, or (to express the same thing in another way) the characters of the cause persist in the effect (prop. 18). But, says Pr., these characters must at some stage of the procession appear neither as pre-existent seminal potentialities (κατ᾽ αἰτίαν) nor as persistent echoes or reflexions (κατὰ μέθεξιν), but as fully developed characters inhering essentially in some class of beings (καθ᾽ ὕπαρξιν).[1] This involves the assumption of a triadic structure of Reality parallel to the triadic division of prop. 23. Thus, e.g., beauty is attributable κατ᾽ αἰτίαν to

[1] Prof. Taylor rightly compares the Aristotelian use of ὑπάρχειν τινί for ' to be predicable of something '. But for Pr. a predicate inheres καθ᾽ ὕπαρξιν in its subject only when it is part of the essence of that subject.

τὸ ἀμέθεκτον καλόν, which is the seminal possibility of beauty without internal differentiation ; it inheres καθ' ὕπαρξιν in τὰ μετεχόμενα καλά, which are the various types of beauty actualized in their individuality, though without admixture of matter; it is present κατὰ μέθεξιν in the concrete things which for all time or for a moment ' participate ' or exemplify the individual types of beauty. Characters exist κατ' αἰτίαν at that point in the procession where they are first implicit ; καθ' ὕπαρξιν where they are first explicit ; and κατὰ μέθεξιν in their subsequent manifestations. For illustrations cf. props. 67, 103, 118, 173, 195 ; *in Tim.* I. 8. 17 ff., 234. 23 ff.—The conception of the universe as penetrated by the same forces at successive levels is characteristic of Iamblichus ;[1] but the triadic formulation of this law is possibly Pr.'s own. The terms κατ' αἰτίαν, καθ' ὕπαρξιν, κατὰ μέθεξιν, reappear in ps.-Dion. (e.g. *Ep.* 9. 2). The first two correspond respectively to the medieval ' eminenter ' and ' formaliter '.

H. *Of Wholes and Parts* (props. 66–74).

1. Four types of relation (66).
2. The three kinds of whole (67–9).
3. Relation of universal to specific characters (70–2).
4. Relation of wholeness to Being and Form (73–4).

PROP. 66. Cf. Plato, *Parm.* 146 B πᾶν που πρὸς ἄπαν ὧδε ἔχει, ἢ ταὐτόν ἐστιν ἢ ἕτερον· ἢ ἐὰν μὴ ταὐτὸν ᾖ μηδ' ἕτερον, μέρος ἂν εἴη τούτου πρὸς ὃ οὕτως ἔχει, ἢ ὡς πρὸς μέρος ὅλον ἂν εἴη. Strictly speaking, of course, there are no relations of *pure* identity or (since all things participate unity) of *pure* difference ; and Pr. is careful to indicate this by his wording. Things identical from one point of view (κατὰ τὸ ἕν) are different from another (καθὸ πολλά ἐστιν).

PROPS. 67–9. The antithesis between ὅλον ἐκ τῶν μερῶν and ὅλον πρὸ τῶν μερῶν has its starting-point in Plato *Theaet.* 204 A–205 C, where the notion of a whole as the sum of its parts (ἐκ τῶν μερῶν γεγονός) is distinguished from that of a whole as μία τις ἰδέα ἀμέριστος, a true unity not analysable into its constituents. This distinction, if we can trust Porphyry (*ap.* Stob. *Ecl.* I. 353. 12 ff. [844 H]), was used by one Nicolaus (the Peripatetic philosopher of Damascus ?) to discriminate the unity of a soul or a τέχνη, which belongs to the latter type, from the unity of quantitative things, which ἐκ τῶν μερῶν συμπληροῦται. To these two types of whole Pr. adds a third, viz. the whole as implicit in the existence of *each* of its parts severally (ὅλον ἐν τῷ μέρει). The

[1] Praechter, *Richtungen* 131 ff.

history of this concept is given as follows by Iamblichus (?) *ap.* Stob. *Ecl.* I. 365. 7 [866 H] εἰσὶ δή τινες, οἳ πᾶσαν τὴν τοιαύτην (sc. ἀσώματον) οὐσίαν ὁμοιομερῆ καὶ τὴν αὐτὴν καὶ μίαν ἀποφαίνονται, ὡς καὶ ἐν ὁτῳοῦν αὐτῆς μέρει εἶναι τὰ ὅλα . . . καὶ ταύτης τῆς δόξης ἀναμφισβητήτως μέν ἐστι Νουμήνιος, οὐ πάντῃ δὲ ὁμολογουμένως Πλωτῖνος, ἀστάτως δὲ ἐν αὐτῇ φέρεται Ἀμέλιος· Πορφύριος δὲ ἐνδοιάζει περὶ αὐτήν. With this doxography cf. the passages cited below on prop. 103 ; also Plot. V. viii. 4 (II. 236. 4 ff.), Porph. *ap.* Pr. *in Tim.* I. 422. 14 ff. The representation of the three modes of wholeness as a triad of subordination seems to be due to Theodore of Asine, a pupil of Porphyry and Iamblichus, who was τῶν Νουμηνείων λόγων ἐμφορηθείς (*in Tim.* II. 274. 10): cf. *in Tim.* II. 215. 30 ff. ; III. 173. 24 ff., 178. 7. This triad is clearly parallel to those formulated in props. 23 and 65 * Thus :

whole-before-the-parts : wholes-of-parts : wholes-in-the-part : :

ἀμέθεκτον : μετεχόμενα : μετέχοντα : :

κατ᾽ αἰτίαν : καθ᾽ ὕπαρξιν : κατὰ μέθεξιν.

It is difficult, however, to acquit Pr. of a certain looseness in his application of these formulae. In the *Th. Pl.* (III. xxv. 165) he seems to identify the relation of whole-before-the-parts to wholes-of-parts with that of genus to species (the genus being regarded not as immanent in, but as transcending, the species). On the other hand the intelligible world is said to be the whole-before-the-parts corresponding to the whole-of-parts which is the sensible world (*in Tim.* I. 429. 23), although the sensible can hardly be a 'species' of the intelligible.—Of wholes-of-parts there seem to be two kinds (prop. 67, ll. 11 ff.)—organic unities 'participated' (prop. 69) by their parts (which thereby become wholes-in-the-part), and mechanical unities whose parts are merely parts, as a sheep is part of a flock.

5. αὐτῆς, the *lectio difficilior*, refers to αἰτίᾳ in l. 3. Are the words τὸ ἐν τῷ αἰτίῳ προϋποστάν (l. 4) a gloss on ἐκεῖνο?

6. οὗ καὶ ὁτιοῦν κτλ. : cf. Plato *Parm.* 137 C οὐχὶ οὗ ἂν μέρος μηδὲν ἀπῇ ὅλον ἂν εἴη ;

8. ὡς καὶ τοῦ μέρους κατὰ μέθεξιν τοῦ ὅλου ⟨ὅλου⟩ γεγονότος. Both τοῦ ὅλου and ὅλου seem to be required. The emphasis is on the dependence of the wholeness of the part upon the wholeness of the whole : if τοῦ ὅλου is omitted, this is weakened and the clause becomes a mere anticipation of ὃ καὶ ποιεῖ κτλ. On the other hand the omission of ὅλου would make it difficult to give any meaning to καί before τοῦ μέρους.

29. ἡ ἄρα κτλ. : if the original ἢ ὅτι in M be anything but a misreading based on the similarity of the tachygraphic signs for ἄρα and ὅτι, it must point to a marginal note ὅτι ἀμέθεκτος ὁλότης προϋπάρχει τῆς μετεχομένης having been first mistaken for a variant and introduced into the text, then adapted to the context by the substitution of ἡ ἄρα for ἢ ὅτι. There are parallels in our MSS. for such a history, and the sentence could be omitted without much loss ; but the other explanation is simpler.—On 'participation' of 'unparticipated' terms see prop. 23 n.

PROP. 70. This supplements the conclusion of prop. 57 : not only do the effects of the higher causes extend further down the scale of being, but they emerge earlier[1] in the γένεσις of the empirical individual and survive longer in his φθορά. A child exists in the womb before it can breathe or feel ; it breathes and feels as a ζῷον before the emergence of rationality stamps it as an ἄνθρωπος. Reversely, in old age the human functions tend to disappear before the animal ones ; and when even the latter have failed, the body still has existence for a time as a corpse. That is because the generic qualities come from a higher source than the specific : in the Procline pyramid of abstractions ὁλικώτερον is synonymous with αἰτιώτερον, and the potency of a Form varies directly as its extension, inversely as its intension. Unity, which is the crown of the pyramid, ἔσχατον ἀπέλιπε τὰ ὄντα (Th. Pl. II. iii. 86) : that is why we call sheer nothingness οὐδέν, 'not-even-one'. Cf. in Parm. 904. 18 ff. ; 1081. 18 ff.

21. καὶ γάρ . . . 22. καί. The confusion here in MW and the printed texts is due to a scribe's writing εἰ γάρ for καὶ γάρ in l. 21. This was corrected in the margin, and the correction subsequently introduced in the wrong place.

24. τὸ γὰρ αὐτό : nominative : sc. ὑπὸ δυοῖν πάσχον.

26. τούτῳ : for this reading cf. in Tim. III. 233. 24 συναπογεννᾷ καὶ ἄλλα αἴτια τῷ δημιουργῷ τὴν ψυχήν.

29. καὶ γὰρ διὰ κτλ. I take this to be an additional reason for the persistence of the generic effect, viz. that it is reinforced by the specific—a man is not only more human than an ape, but also more fully alive.

PROPS. 71-2. The generic characters of an individual or a class are involved in, but do not involve, its specific characters (hence their earlier emergence and longer persistence): Pr. expresses this

---

[1] It seems clear that temporal and not merely logical priority is meant, since this priority is associated with temporal persistence. Cf. Arist. de gen. anim. 736 a 35 ff.

by calling them the 'basis' or 'matrix' (ὑποκείμενον, ὑποδοχή) of the latter. The presence of such generic characters is a prerequisite before the individual can be fit (ἐπιτήδειος) to receive the specific form. Pr. is thus enabled to explain away the seeming dualism of the famous passage in the *Timaeus* where the visible world is represented as having had a 'faulty and disordered motion' of its own before the demiurge took it in hand.[1] This motion came not from any evil principle resident in Matter, but from the direct influence of the higher Forms, which are metaphysically prior to the demiurge: it represents the first stirrings in the physical world of the impulse to perfection, and is only called 'faulty' because creation was as yet incomplete until the demiurge introduced measure and proportion into the blindly surging ὑποδοχή (*in Tim.* I. 387. 30 ff.: cf. *in Parm.* 845. 8 ff.).—The doctrine of these props. appears in Syrianus, *in Metaph.* 29. 4 ff. It has an interesting parallel in Origen's theory that souls derive their existence from God the Father, their rational nature from God the Son, and their holiness from the Holy Ghost (*de princip.* I. iii. 8).

5. ἐμφάσεις: i.q. ἐλλάμψεις: cf. prop. 128, l. 11 n.

9. διὰ περιουσίαν δυνάμεως: cf. prop. 27, l. 25 n., and *Th. Pl.* V. xvii. 281.

12. χορηγεῖ τά (P) is a certain correction for χορηγεῖται, which yields an irrelevant sense. But just below PQ seem to be merely patching up by conjecture an accidental lacuna in the archetype of the third family.

24. φανερὸν διότι. διότι = 'quamobrem' (as in *Hyp. Astron.* 8. 12, *Th. Pl.* VI. viii. 362), not as Portus has it 'quod' (for which Pr. always uses ὅτι in this particular formula). That Matter as such excludes Form needed no proof.

ἐκ τοῦ ἑνὸς ὑποστᾶσα: Pr. differs from Plot. in deriving Matter *directly* from the One: cf. prop. 57 n.

PROPS. **73–4.** Wholeness is intermediate in the logical order of universality, and therefore for Pr. in the metaphysical order also, between Being and Form: cf. *in Parm.* 970. 27 ff., 1101. 2 ff. It is associated with eternity (prop. **52** *cor.*), which occupies a similar intermediate position between Being and the eternals (prop. 87). The first discussion of the relation between the concepts of Wholeness and Being occurs in Plato *Soph.* 244 D ff., a passage which in

---

[1] *Tim.* 30 A. On the difficulty which this passage caused Plotinus see Inge², I. 144 f.

the hands of Iamblichus became one of the corner-stones of Neo-platonic scholasticism (*in Tim.* I. 230. 5 ff.).

34. καθ' αὑτό. The part may be a whole κατὰ μέθεξιν (prop. 67), but not καθ' ὕπαρξιν.

7. μέρους ὂν ὅλον. We expect μερῶν as in l. 2 ; but the meaning may be that the *term* 'whole' is relative to the *term* 'part'. In the latter part of this sentence the correct punctuation is preserved by BCD (ἔσται μέρος ὅλου, μέρος ὂν edd.).

19. ἤδη τεμνόμενον: 'actually divided', in distinction from the whole-before-the-parts on the one hand and the concrete individual on the other, both of which are only potentially divisible. For the corruption of ἤδη into εἴδη cf. prop. 64, l. 26 ; the reverse corruption has occurred in 'Ανάπτ. p. 193, l. 19 and in Plato *Parm.* 135 E 3. Pr. is speaking here of the *immanent* Form which exists as a whole-of-parts ; he of course recognizes also transcendent Forms which are wholes-before-the-parts.

24. ὅθεν καὶ κτλ. : cf. prop. 57 *fin.* and note.

I. *Of the Relation of Causes to their Effects ; and of Potency* (props. 75–86).

1. Causes transcend their effects (75).
2. Variability in the effect correlated with mobility in the cause (76).
3. Relation of the potential to the actual (77).
4. Two meanings of 'potency' (78, 79).
5. Application to the relationship of bodies to incorporeals (80–3).
6. Doctrine of infinite potencies (84–6).

PROP. 75. The distinction between true causes and accessory or 'by-'causes (*causae* and *concausae*) appears first in the *Phaedo* (99 A ff.): for the term συναίτιον cf. *Polit.* 281 D, *Tim.* 46 D. It is not apparent why Pr. chooses to introduce it at this point: he might well have taken an earlier opportunity of explaining the restricted sense in which he uses the term 'cause' in *El. Th.* At the beginning of the Timaeus commentary and elsewhere (e.g. *in Parm.* 1059. 11 ff.) he enumerates three κύριαι or ἀρχικαὶ αἰτίαι, viz. the final, the paradeigmatic and the efficient, and two συναίτια, the formal and the material. The addition of the paradeigmatic [1] to Aristotle's

---

[1] Already recognized by Seneca, *Ep.* 65. 8. See Theiler, *Vorbereitung des Neuplatonismus*, 16 ff.

COMMENTARY 241

four was required by the Neoplatonic view which admitted transcendent Forms side by side with ἔνυλα εἴδη. The classification of the two lowest causes as συναίτια served to confine true causality to the intelligible world, in which the three κύριαι αἰτίαι are identified respectively with the three Plotinian hypostases. In some passages (e.g. *in Tim.* I. 261. 15), following Porphyry,[1] Pr. mentions a third type of συναίτιον, the instrumental (ὀργανικόν), suggested by *Polit.* 281 E. In the present proposition ὄργανον τοῦ ποιοῦντος refers to the instrumental cause, while μέρος τοῦ γινομένου covers the formal and the material.

35. τὸ ὄργανον κτλ. That PQ are right in inserting δουλεύει after γένεσιν is rendered certain by a comparison of Plato *Phil.* 27 A οὐ ταὐτὸν αἰτία τ' ἐστὶ καὶ τὸ δουλεῦον εἰς γένεσιν αἰτία—a text much quoted by the Neoplatonists. τὸ ποιοῦν τι (Arg. Cr².) and (p. 72, l. 1) ἀφορίζει (BCD) are merely attempts to cover the gap left by the loss of δουλεύει. W's Latin has been corrupted in transmission, but it looks as if his Gk. MS. had τῇ ἑαυτοῦ δυνάμει after ποιήσεως (l. 1).

PROP. 76. Pr. *in Tim.* I. 294. 12 claims Aristotle as his authority for this doctrine: he probably had in mind *Metaph.* Λ. 6. 1072 a 9 ff., where it is said that permanence requires us to assume an unvarying activity in the cause, change a variable one *. Pr. interprets the 'young gods', who in the *Timaeus* are the creators of things mortal, as symbolizing the mobile causes (*in Tim.* I. 443. 8 ff.). The unmoved causes are the One, the transcendent Forms and the intelligences; Soul is mobile κατ' ἐνέργειαν (*in Parm.* 796. 7), and its effects are accordingly, as Plato taught (*Legg.* 904 C), variable. This accounts for the transitoriness of animal organisms as compared with e.g. the heavenly bodies (which are caused and controlled by νόες); but the animal *species* are permanent as being the temporal expression of unmoved Forms (*in Tim.* III. 225. 12; *in Crat.* lv). Cf. also Syrian. *in Metaph.* 12. 21 ff., 42. 34, 107. 12; and *infra* prop. 172. The theory is echoed by Erigena, 903 C, 960 A, &c. Migne, and later by Dante (*Paradiso* xiii. 52-84).

PROP. 77. This familiar Aristotelian thesis (*Metaph.* Θ. 8) was seized on with eagerness by the Neoplatonists and not only employed against the Stoics (as in *Enn.* VI. i. 26 and similar passages) but turned against its originator (e.g. *in Parm.* 979. 1 ff., where it is used as an argument for transcendent Forms): it is, in fact, the logical

[1] See Simp. *in Phys.* 11. 3, Diels.

242 COMMENTARY

basis of the Neoplatonic theory of 'involution'. The 'proof' offered here depends on the principle of prop. 7, that the cause is always superior to the effect; but that principle in turn really depends on the priority of the actual.

25. ἀτελὲς ὄν: cf. Arist. *Metaph.* 1050 a 7 ἅπαν ἐπ' ἀρχὴν βαδίζει τὸ γιγνόμενον καὶ τέλος (ἀρχὴ γὰρ τὸ οὗ ἕνεκα, τοῦ τέλους δὲ ἕνεκα ἡ γένεσις), τέλος δ' ἡ ἐνέργεια, καὶ τούτου χάριν ἡ δύναμις λαμβάνεται: 1077 a 18 τὸ γὰρ ἀτελὲς μέγεθος γενέσει μὲν πρότερόν ἐστι, τῇ οὐσίᾳ δ' ὕστερον, οἷον ἄψυχον ἐμψύχου.

PROPS. **78, 79.** The distinction between δύναμις as active power (Pr.'s 'perfect potency') and δύναμις as potentiality (Pr.'s 'imperfect potency') was clearly recognized by Aristotle, though he does not always succeed in maintaining it.[1] But in Neoplatonism, which ascribed δύναμις in the active sense not only to God but to all intelligibles (cf. prop. 27, l. 25 n.) while also adopting the Aristotelian doctrine of potentiality, the antithesis between the two meanings of the term became sharper as well as philosophically more important: cf. e.g. *Enn.* V. iii. 15 (II. 199. 7), where the creative potency of the One is contrasted with the passive potency of Matter. Passive potency can, however, be regarded as the last and lowest expression of the divine potency, differing from it ultimately in degree rather than in kind (*Th. Pl.* 133–4). That both potencies are prerequisites to the production of change is still substantially Aristotelian doctrine, though Aristotle does not in this context apply the term δύναμις to the efficient power of τὸ ἐνεργείᾳ ὄν.

11. μειζόνως αὐτὸ τελειότερον: the double comparative (for which cf. prop. 25, l. 35 n.) led to a 'correction' μειζόνων. The archetype of M had μειζόνων̇ (with ως above): hence the intrusive ὡς perpetuated in the printed editions.

PROP. **80.** That Soul is characterized by activity, Body by passivity, is Platonic doctrine (*Legg.* 896); and what is true of Soul must be true *a fortiori* of the higher incorporeal principles.[2] But the question whether the embodied soul could be regarded as entirely and at all times impassible (ἀπαθής) was one which greatly exercised the Neoplatonists. Such a doctrine seemed to render otiose the process of 'separation' or 'purgation' which is the central feature of

---

[1] See Ross's note on *Metaph.* 1045 b 35–46 a 4.
[2] Cf. the Stoic antithesis of τὸ ποιοῦν (λόγος) and τὸ πάσχον (ὕλη), Diog. Laert. vii. 134 etc.

Neoplatonic ethics (cf. *Enn.* III. vi. 5). In two early essays (V. ix and IV. viii) Plot. appears to accept the view that the incarnate human soul is not impassible (II. 251. 22, 145. 7); but in his later and fuller discussions of the subject (IV. iv. 18 ff. and III. vi. 1–5), recognizing no doubt that immortality is bound up with impassibility, he attempts to show that πάθη belong to the ζῷον (organic consciousness), not to the soul proper, though they are perceived by the latter and may produce in it a condition of ταραχή.[1] Porphyry admitted in the περὶ ψυχῆς that the soul is not impassible (Stob. I. xlix. 60 [1048 H]); but when he came to write the ἀφορμαί he had accepted the later Plotinian position (ἀφ. xviii). Iamblichus characteristically distinguished different degrees of impassibility : the gods transcend the antithesis of πάσχειν and ποιεῖν ; the individual soul is κρείττων κατ᾽ οὐσίαν τοῦ πάσχειν, and even its λόγοι in the body are impassible, but it is αἰτία τῷ συνθέτῳ τοῦ πάσχειν (*de myst.* I. 10). Proclus's view is far from clear. In the *Timaeus* commentary he says, like Plotinus, that the πάθη arising from the vegetative and perceptual functions are attributed by the soul to itself only through an illusion, the soul mistakenly identifying itself with those functions (III. 330); yet on page 333 he objects to the view of Plotinus and Theodore of Asine, ἀπαθές τι φυλάττοντας ἐν ἡμῖν καὶ ἀεὶ νοοῦν (cf. *in Alc.* 504. 4 ff. and *infra* prop. 211). Perhaps, as Mr. Whittaker[2] suggests, the point where Pr. differs from Plot. is in admitting that the illusion of πάθος can affect the soul *in its entirety* and not merely the empirical part of it. The qualification made in the present prop. seems to apply not to the soul proper (which is χωριστῶς μετεχόμενον, prop. 82), but to the organic functions and the ἔνυλα εἴδη, which are συνδιαιρούμενα σώμασι (l. 9: cf. prop. 190). See, however, prop. 209, l. 31, where human souls are said παθαίνεσθαι.

31–2. σῶμα ... μεριστὸν ... εἰς ἄπειρον. This seems to conflict with prop. 1 ; but Pr. held with Aristotle (*Phys.* Γ. 6) that magnitudes are *potentially* though not actually divisible to infinity, i.e. they can be divided at any point, but not at every point simultaneously (cf. *in Tim.* I. 453. 19).

33. ἁπλοῦν ὄν. That the incorporeal is simple has not been formally proved, but cf. props. 15, 42, 47.

5–7. ἄποιον δὲ κτλ. The transposition which I have made here

---

[1] The apparent inconsistency between the early and the later essays may be due to the ambiguity of the terms ψυχή and πάθος, and not to any real change in Plot.'s standpoint : cf. Kristeller, *Begriff der Seele in der Ethik des Plotin* 40 ff.

[2] *Neoplatonists*[2], 295.

appears essential to the argument. As the words stand in the MSS., the conclusion (ὥστε ... δύναμιν) precedes the minor premiss (ἄποιον ... καθ' αὑτό); it is difficult, moreover, to supply σῶμα as subject to ποιήσει.—-The edd. translate ἄποιον here *actionis expers* (as if from a-ποιέω), but there is no need to ascribe this unexampled meaning to the word : we have been told above that body *qua* body (i.e. apart from the ἔνυλα εἴδη manifested in it) has no attribute save divisibility. Cf. *in Tim.* III. 337. 29, where ἀδύναμα are contrasted with δύναμις, ἄποια with εἶδος.—For the argument compare *Enn.* IV. vii. 8 (9) [II. 130. 22 ff.].

PROPS. 81-3. These propositions are primarily directed to eluci- dating further the problem of the relation of soul to body, which was raised by prop. 80. The reciprocal interaction of physical and psychical elements in the organism is a fact which Neoplatonists do not attempt to deny. But is not this fact fatal to the conception of the soul as in any sense ἀπαθής? The solution lies in interpolating between soul and body a *tertium quid* which acts at once as a link (like Descartes's pineal gland) and as a buffer. This *tertium quid* is the organic or animal consciousness which Plotinus called the ζῷον or συναμφότερον, and which is here called an ἀχώριστος δύναμις.[1] It is a psychical entity, but is physically conditioned and therefore subject to πάθη; it is related to soul proper as an ἔλλαμψις to an αὐτοτελὴς ὑπόστασις (prop. 64); through it the soul is said to be present to the body 'as its providence' while transcending it by essence (*in Parm.* 1004). A similar relation holds between all self- conscious principles and the entities which 'participate' them : thus the Forms are transcendent, but we know them through their images, the λόγοι in the soul (*in Parm.* 930. 32 ff.), which represent the Forms on the level of discursive reason as the organic consciousness represents soul on the level of sensation.

14. εἰ γὰρ [καὶ] αὐτό. καί seems to have been inserted by a scribe who took αὐτό to refer to the ἀχώριστος δύναμις—wrongly, since, not to speak of the abrupt change of gender, Pr. does not use the present indicative in false suppositions.

15. ἐν ἑαυτῷ is preferable to ἐν αὐτῷ : with the latter reading we should expect κεκτῆσθαι.

22. πρὸς ἑαυτὸ ἐπιστρεπτικὸν ὄν. This is a limiting condition ; the lower incorporeals (ζῷα and ἔνυλα εἴδη) are not capable of reflexive consciousness.

[1] Similarly Porphyry speaks of it as δευτέραν τινὰ δύναμιν προσεχῆ τοῖς σώμασιν (ἀφ. iv). In *Prov. et Fat.* (149. 24) Pr. calls it a second *soul*.

PROPS. **84, 85.** These propositions illustrate the intimate connexion in Neoplatonism between the notions of substance and potency (cf. prop. 27, l. 25 n.): the former is dependent for its continued existence upon the latter, which is indeed at bottom the stuff of which it is constituted.[1] The relationship is comparable to that of matter and energy in some modern physical theories.—For the distinction between τὸ ἀεὶ ὄν and τὸ ἀεὶ γινόμενον cf. prop. 55. ἀεὶ ὄντα have 'perfect potency' (hence eternity is said to be 'no other than potency',[2] in *Parm.* 1120. 20); while ἀεὶ γινόμενα have 'imperfect potency'. Cf. Plot. VI. v. 11 (II. 396. 12 ff.). Porphyry calls the soul ἀπειροδύναμος, ἀφ. 32. 8.

8. ἡ κατὰ τὸ εἶναι δύναμις. The words καθ᾽ ἥν ἐστι, added in Q, are either an accidental repetition from the previous line or more probably a gloss on κατὰ τὸ εἶναι.

9. ἀπολιποῦσα. The anacoluthic assimilation to πεπερασμένη is very likely due to a copyist, but in face of the unanimous testimony of the MSS. I have not ventured to alter it.

PROP. **86.** That the One is infinite[3] not in size or number but in potency was expressly stated by Plotinus (VI. ix. 6 [II. 515. 31]); and it seems clear that he in fact took the same view of all intelligibles (cf. IV. iii. 8). This theory, which confines numerical infinity to the world of appearance, was not unchallenged in later antiquity. Syrianus (*in Metaph.* 147. 1 ff.) ascribes to the school of Amelius the interesting doctrine that there is an infinity of Forms, whose successive mirroring in our finite cosmos will require an infinity of time—a theory exceptional among Greek rationalist cosmologies in that it provides the world with a future different from its past.[4] But Syrianus himself holds, like Proclus, that the number of τὰ θεῖα is finite, though what precisely that number is οὐκ ἂν εἴποι μερικὴ ψυχή (145. 24: cf. Pr. *in Tim.* III. 102. 23 ff. and prop. 62 *supra*).

---

[1] τοῦτο γάρ ἐστι τὸ εἶναι αὐτῶν, τὸ τοιάνδε ἐνέργειαν ἀποδιδόναι, Plot. III. i. 1 [I. 215. 14].

[2] Cf. *Corp. Herm.* XI. 3 δύναμις δὲ τοῦ θεοῦ ὁ αἰών.

[3] More strictly, the One is the *source* of infinitude (II. iv. 15 [I. 165. 2]). Similarly Pr. prefers not to ascribe ἀπειρία to the One except in the sense that it is not limited by any principle external to itself (*in Parm.* 1124).

[4] In *Enn.* V. vii, an early essay which F. Heinemann on inadequate grounds regards as spurious, an echo of this theory seems to survive, though it is only put forward as a possible alternative to the doctrine of world-periods. Elsewhere Plotinus assumes that the Forms must be finite in number, e.g. VI. v. 8 (II. 391. 23). Seneca, on the other hand, calls them 'innumerable' (*Ep.* 58. 18); and this view was known to Chalcidius (303. 2 ff. Wrobel).

22. τὸ δ' ὄντως ὄν. ἀεί (MW edd.) seems to have been a gloss on ὄντως, which in l. 19 was similarly glossed by τῷ ὄντι.

30. ἄπειρον μᾶλλον: cf. props. 90, 93.

J. *Of Being, Limit, and Infinitude* (props. 87-96).

1. Relation of Being to Eternity (87-8).
2. Limit and Infinitude as constituents of Being, and as substantive principles (89-93).
3. Relation of (*a*) perpetuity, (*b*) unity, (*c*) corporeality to infinitude (94-6).

PROPS. **87, 88**. The relation of Being to Eternity is like its relation to Wholeness (prop. 73) and Life (prop. 101): in each case Being is shown to be the more comprehensive term of the pair, and therefore metaphysically 'earlier'. On the conception of Eternity as a substance see prop. 53 n. As 'the first Life' it occupies a middle place in Pr.'s triadic division of the second Plotinian hypostasis,[1] lower than 'the first Being' (which is eternal κατ' αἰτίαν) but higher than 'the first Intelligence' (which is eternal κατὰ μέθεξιν): cf. *Th. Pl.* III. xvi. 146-7, *in Tim.* I. 231. 32, also prop. 101 n. Platonic 'authority' was found in *Tim.* 37 D ἡ μὲν οὖν τοῦ ζῴου φύσις ἐτύγχανεν οὖσα αἰώνιος ... μένοντος αἰῶνος ἐν ἑνί, from which it was inferred that τὸ ὅ ἐστι ζῷον 'participates' Eternity and the latter 'participates' the ἐν ὄν or first Being.

29. **μεθέξει καὶ τοῦ ἀεὶ καὶ τοῦ ὄντος αἰώνιον λέγεται.** Pr. alludes to the supposed derivation of αἰώνιος from ἀεί and ὄν (cf. prop. 52, l. 15).

PROPS. **89-92**. The increased importance assigned to the Limit and the Infinite as cosmogonic principles is one of the distinguishing characteristics of the Athenian school. The fullest expositions of the topic are Syrian. *in Metaph.* 112. 14 ff., Pr. *in Tim.* I. 176, *in Parm.* 1119 ff., and esp. *Th. Pl.* III. vii-ix. The primary source of these speculations is, of course, the *Philebus* of Plato. The Neoplatonists held (as do some of the best recent interpreters) that the Limit and the Infinite are regarded in that dialogue as the ultimate elements not only of phenomenal things but also of the Forms (cf. *Parm.* 144 E ff.). But in what sense can infinitude enter into pure Form, which is in itself a principle of limit? Plotinus replies that infinitude in the intelligible world is the recipient of

---

[1] So Porphyry is said to have recognized a προαιώνιον within the second hypostasis, *Th. Pl.* I. xi. 27.

formal diversity; as such it is analogous to Matter, and it is called by him 'intelligible Matter' (*Enn.* II. iv. 15). Proclus rejects this way of putting it: it is misleading to call Limit 'the Form of Infinitude' or the Infinite 'the Matter of Limit'—rather Limit is related to Infinitude as substance to potency (*Th. Pl.* 137-8). For him the essential character of Infinitude is δύναμις, grading down from the infinite active potency of the intelligibles, through the infinite potency of becoming which in various senses belongs to the soul, the heavens and the animal species, to the infinite variability of τὸ μᾶλλον καὶ ἧττον (seen in such qualities as heat and cold), the infinite divisibility of body, and finally the pure passive potentiality, indefinite rather than infinite, of pure Matter; similarly the essential character of the Limit is uniformity or measure, which appears in diminishing degrees in Eternity (the measure of Being), in the Intelligence, in the soul, in the heavens with their law of periodicity, in body with its finite extension (*ibid.* 133, *in Parm.* 1119 ff.). As usual, Pr. proceeds from analysis to hypostatization. Not only does he find within each hypostasis a triad πέρας—ἄπειρον—μικτόν (analogous to, or identical with, the triad μονή, πρόοδος, ἐπιστροφή); but at the head of his two συστοιχίαι he places respectively τὸ αὐτόπερας and ἡ αὐτοαπειρία, which rank as ἀρχαί immediately after the One, transcending even the henads (prop. 159). In this he is following Neopythagorean[1] tradition (as is shown by *in Tim.* I. 176. 9, 28 and Syrian. *in Metaph.* 165. 33 ff.), with the hope of bridging the gulf which Plotinus left between the One and the world of Forms. In the emergence of Being from the One, and in each subsequent emergence of a new principle, Plotinus notices two distinct logical moments: one in which the the new form of consciousness is still indeterminate (ἀόριστος), being characterized solely by novelty (ἑτερότης); and a second in which it receives definite content from the contemplation of its prior (II. iv. 5 [I. 154. 20], cf. VI. vii. 17). These two moments are representative respectively of the centrifugal and the centripetal force, whose tension makes the Neoplatonic universe; but it was left for later formalism to hypostatize them as ἡ αὐτοαπειρία and τὸ αὐτόπερας. τὸ αὐτόπερας is the 'higher' of the pair, as being more akin to the One (*in Parm.* 1124. 1): it is, indeed, the true causative unity, the supreme principle being in strictness above causality and above unity (*Th. Pl.* 132).[2] ἡ αὐτο-

---

[1] Perhaps mediated by Iamblichus (cf. *comm. math. sci.* 12. 22 ff. Festa).— πέρας and ἀπειρία are also identified with the cosmogonic principles of Orphism, Αἰθήρ and Χάος, *in Parm.* 1121. 26, *in Tim.* I. 176. 12.

[2] It is odd that in *El. Th.* there is no precise account of the status and function

ἀπειρία, on the other hand, is the transcendental ground of all plurality, and in this sense πάντων αἰτία τῶν ὄντων (prop. 92).—The two ἀρχαί survive in an attenuated form in ps.-Dion.: *Div. Nom.* 5. 10 ὁ προὼν (θεός) ... πέρας πάντων καὶ ἀπειρία, πάσης ἀπειρίας καὶ πέρατος ὑπερ-οχικῶς ἐξηρημένος τῶν ὡς ἀντικειμένων.

13. τὸ δὲ πρῶτον ἑκάστου οὐκ ἄλλο ἐστὶν ἢ ὅ ἐστιν: cf. prop. 22, l. 9 : the 'primitive' is the unmixed, which is logically and therefore metaphysically prior.

18. ἡ δὲ ἄπειρος δύναμις ἐκ τῆς πρώτης ἀπειρίας. The proof of this is held over for the next proposition.

32. μέτρον γὰρ πάντων ἐκεῖνο. The One is the measure of measures, which comprehends both time and eternity. Cf. Plato, *Legg.* 716 C ὁ δὴ θεὸς ἡμῖν πάντων χρημάτων μέτρον ἂν εἴη μάλιστα : Plot. V. v. 4 (II. 210. 26).

34. πάντων αἰτία. I suspect that οὖσα has fallen out here owing to its similarity to αἰτία : cf. prop. 9, l. 15 n.

PROP. 93. Quantitative infinitude is of course a character which does not admit of degrees (*dec. dub.* 88. 26 : cf. *supra*, prop. 1, l. 11 f.). But the qualitative infinitude proper to spiritual reality is regarded by Pr. as relative to an exploring consciousness, just as unknowable-ness is relative to a knower. Each grade of such reality is 'infinite in potency', not in the sense that it has no 'limit'—everything has 'limit' except the One which is above limitation and Matter which is below it—but in the sense that its content can never be exhausted in or by any subsequent principle or the sum-total of such principles. It cannot be infinite for its own consciousness, since it is ἐν ἑαυτῷ (prop. 41), i.e. self-defined, and what is infinite is as such unknow-able (prop. 11, l. 26).[1] And it cannot be infinite for higher grades of Being, since its potency is included in theirs (prop. 56). The only infinitude which is absolute is that of Infinity itself.—This doctrine was not invented by Pr. : it occurs in Syrianus (*in Metaph.* 147. 14), and the germ of it is perhaps to be recognized in Porph. ἀφ. xxxi, where the *relative* 'everywhere and nowhere' of the lower νοητά corresponds to Pr.'s relative infinitude.

6. ὑπερήπλωται : a favourite word with Pr. and ps.-Dion., practi-cally synonymous with ἐξήρηται. Properly ὑπερηπλωμένον means

of τὸ πέρας parallel to that of τὸ ἄπειρον. Have some propositions been lost ? Or are the functions of τὸ πρῶτον πέρας considered as subsumed in those of the One ? Its identification with the latter is prohibited by the *Philebus*—if the One is πέρας, what is the αἰτία τῆς μίξεως ?—but it is hard to distinguish the two logically.

[1] So Nicolaus (117. 6) denies that even God can be infinite for his own consciousness, since God has self-knowledge.

COMMENTARY 249

'super-simplified' or 'transcendent in simplicity', not 'extended above' as L. S⁸.: this is certain from *Div. Nom.* 7. 4 πάσης ἁπλότητος ὑπερήπλωται (and cf. ὑπερηνωμένον). Like so much of Pr.'s technical language, it seems to be a legacy from Iamblichus (*de myst.* 251. 13 ff.); cf. also the use of ἁπλωθῆναι, ἐξαπλωθῆναι, by Philo (*Leg. Alleg.* III. 13) and Plot. (VI. vii. 35, &c.), of the simplification of the soul in ecstasy.

8. ἀπ' αὐτῶν ἐξῃρημένον. This verb is commonly used by Pr. with the simple genitive; cf. however *in Crat.* 50. 1.

PROP. 94. With regard to spatial and numerical infinity Pr. adopts the Aristotelian view (*Phys.* Γ. 6). All sensible bodies are finite (*El. Phys.* II. 15). Spatial infinity exists only in the sense that any finite body may be divided at any point, and is therefore 'potentially' divisible *ad infinitum* (prop. 80, l. 31, *in Tim.* I. 453. 19) and in this way ἀδιεξίτητον. The numerical series is infinite, but is only actualized in successive finite parts, as in the infinite succession of individual animals which maintains the perpetuity of the species (*in Tim.* l. c.). For the 'infinity' of Matter, which consists in its complete indetermination or infinite *passive* potency, cf. Arist. *Phys.* Γ. 7. 207 b 35 φανερὸν ὅτι ὡς ὕλη τὸ ἄπειρόν ἐστιν αἴτιον : Plot. II. iv. 15 [I. 164. 22] ἀνάγκη τοίνυν τὴν ὕλην τὸ ἄπειρον εἶναι, οὐχ οὕτω δὲ ἄπειρον, ὡς κατὰ συμβεβηκός. Plot., unlike Pr., regards Matter as the fullest manifestation of infinity (ἀληθεστέρως ἄπειρον, I. 165. 12), though he recognizes in the same passage that the Form of Infinity (τὸ ἀπείρῳ εἶναι) has its place among the intelligibles.

26. ὁλικώτερον. ὁλικωτέρων would agree better with the enunciation of prop. 60: cf. however prop. 60, l. 11 f. τὸ δὲ πλείω δυνάμενον . . . δύναμιν ἔχει . . . ὁλικωτέραν.

27. [καὶ ἡ αὐτοαπειρία πρὸ αἰῶνος]: probably a marginal note made by a reader and (as the καὶ indicates) mistaken by a copyist for a variant. A number of notes of this type occur in the margin of M.

PROP. 95. This is virtually a restatement of prop. 62 in terms of the 'relative infinity' doctrine. In the last sentence Pr. adds one of his rare *a posteriori* arguments : it is an observed fact that at the level of human psychology the 'drawing together' or co-ordination of faculties increases their collective efficiency.

34. συναγόμεναι μὲν πολλαπλασιάζονται, μεριζόμεναι δὲ ἀμυδροῦνται. πολλαπλασιασμός is commonly used of increase in *number*, which is accompanied by decrease in efficacy. Hence T. Taylor's drastic

emendation συναγόμεναι μὲν ἐνίζονται, μεριζόμεναι δὲ πολλαπλασιάζονται καὶ ἀμυδροῦνται, which Cr. adopted in his second edition. But the 'multiplication' of a *potency*, though in one passage (*in Crat.* 54. 1) it does mean subdivision, may quite as naturally signify an increase in intensity or efficacy.

PROP. 98. This theorem is a free adaptation of Aristotle's proof that the Prime Mover is not an extended body (*Phys.* Θ. 10). It is true that in the manner of its enunciation it conflicts with Aristotle's principle, viz. that the potency of a finite body is never infinite; whereas in *El. Phys.* II. 8 Pr. maintains the rule in its Aristotelian form. The discrepancy perhaps furnishes some support to Ritzenfeld's view (see Introd., p. xvii f.) that *El. Phys.* was composed at a much earlier period in Pr.'s life than *El. Th.* The present theorem is, however, a modification rather than a contradiction of Aristotle's: Aristotle regards the infinite incorporeal potency of the Prime Mover as something external to the finite heavens which are moved by it, while Pr. thinks of it as existing both outside and in the heavens, as a transcendent and as a derivative or immanent potency (prop. 81). He argues elsewhere (*in Tim.* I. 267. 12 ff., 295. 3 ff.) that the corporeal universe must have an infinite potency, or it will one day perish; but by Aristotle's principle it cannot have such a potency in its own right (παρ' ἑαυτοῦ): therefore its infinite potency must be incorporeal, i.e. derived from an immaterial cause external to it, and must come to it piecemeal, not as a *totum simul*. The same argument is used by Syrianus, *in Metaph.* 117. 32 ff.: cf. also Pr. *in Parm.* 1119. 26, *Th. Pl.* II. ii. 82.

K. *Supplementary theorems on causality, &c.* (props. 97-112).

1. Relation of first or 'unparticipated' terms to the series which they generate (97, 99-100).
2. True causes are 'everywhere and nowhere' (98).
3. Triad of Being, Life, and Intelligence (101-3).
4. There is an intermediate term between the eternal and the temporal (104, 106-7).
5. The perpetual distinguished from the immortal (105).
6. Principles governing the relation between higher and lower orders of existence (108-12).

This miscellaneous group of theorems completes the first part of the treatise, and is ancillary to the second.

PROP. 97. This combines the results of props. 18 and 21, and prepares the way for the study of the individual σειραί which begins at prop. 113 : thus e.g. the properties of souls expounded in props. 186 ff. all exist *eminentius* in the divine Soul. Cf. *in Parm.* 1109. 14 ff.

16. τὸ δὲ αὐτόματον κτλ. Spontaneity, on which modern thought tends to set so high a value, is by the Greek rationalists either banished from the universe or admitted only to the sublunary world ; for them the existing world-order is the best possible, and spontaneity is not an expression of it but an interference with it. It is not the same thing as freedom, which for the Neoplatonists consists in acceptance of the world-order.— ἀλληλουχία, defined by ps.-Dion. as ἡ τοῦ κόσμου παντὸς συνάφεια καὶ συμπάθεια (*Div. Nom.* 4. 7), is a favourite word from Iamblichus onwards.

22. ἐν τοῖς ἄλλοις. δευτέροις (BCDQ) seems to be a gloss. In the next clause the edd. make nonsense by reading πως. Cf. prop. 116, l. 19 ; and for ἔτι (om. BCDQ), prop. 99, l. 25.

PROP. 98. This solution of the immanence-transcendence antinomy, though characteristically Neoplatonic in its simultaneous affirmation of thesis and antithesis, is in fact older than Neoplatonism. Plotinus speaks of it as an accepted doctrine (VI. viii. 16 *init.*) ; and Porphyry ascribes it to οἱ παλαιοί (ἀφ. xxxviii). It was first proposed, though perhaps not seriously, by Plato himself. When Parmenides asks Socrates how a Form can be present in its entirety in each of the participants, Socrates suggests that it might be like the daylight, ' which is one and the same daylight in many places at once, and yet keeps its undivided unity ' ; but his questioner ignores the suggestion (*Parm.* 131 B). Like the principle of undiminished bestowal, with which it is closely associated, it seems to have been given currency in the school of Poseidonius : cf. Philo, *Conf. Ling.* 27. § 136 (ὁ θεὸς ᾧ πανταχοῦ τε καὶ οὐδαμοῦ συμβέβηκεν εἶναι μόνῳ, *Post. Cain* 5. § 14 ; [Arist.] *de mundo* c. 6. § 7 ; Seneca, *N.Q.* I *praef.* 13 *fin.* ; also *Corp. Herm.* XI. 6. Plotinus offers a proof of it on the same lines as Proclus (III. ix. 3 *init.* : cf. VI. v. 4). From Plotinus it passed into Christian thought through Augustine (*Conf.* VI. 3 *ubique totus es et nusquam locorum es, Epist.* 187. 14), to be echoed by theologians like Athanasius (*de incarnat.* 17 ἐκτὸς μέν ἐστι τοῦ παντὸς κατ' οὐσίαν, ἐν πᾶσι δέ ἐστι ταῖς ἑαυτοῦ δυνάμεσι) and mystics like Suso (*Exempl.* 54 e), as well as Christian Neoplatonists like Erigena (681 A ff. Migne) and Psellus (*C.M.A.G.* VI. 193. 15). The Christian writers apply the doctrine to God, the Logos, or the Virgin

Plot. applies it chiefly to the One, but also to the intelligibles generally (VI. iv, v), as do Porphyry (ἀφ. iii) and Pr. In Pr. it is accommodated to the more rigid theory of 'unparticipated' and 'participated' Forms (prop. 23) : the unparticipated Form is 'everywhere' only through the mediation of the participated Form which is its projected potency.

11. αὐτὸ ἑαυτοῦ . . . χωρίς : cf. Plato, *Parm.* 131 B ὅλον ἅμα ἐνέσται, καὶ οὕτως αὐτὸ αὑτοῦ χωρὶς ἂν εἴη.

13. τὰ μετέχειν αὐτοῦ δυνάμενα ὅλῳ ἐντυγχάνει κτλ. : cf. Plot. VI. iv. 3 (II. 365. 19) οὐκ ἀποτέτμηται ἐκεῖνο τῆς δυνάμεως αὐτοῦ, ἣν ἔδωκεν ἐκείνῳ· ἀλλ' ὁ λαβὼν τοσοῦτον ἐδυνήθη λαβεῖν παντὸς παρόντος. The transcendent Form (in Pr.'s language, the unparticipated term) is present in entirety in the immanent (participated) form or potency ; but the material object which participates the latter never ' contains ' or expresses it adequately—if it did, the transcendent Form would no longer be transcendent.

PROPS. 99, 100 complete the doctrine of ' unparticipated ' principles (props. 23, 24) by showing in what sense they are αὐθυπόστατα (prop. 40). They are self-constituted in so far as their emergence marks a genuinely new stage in the outgoing of individuality from the One—in so far, that is, as they are true ' novelties ' and not merely the more developed expression of characters already present at an earlier level (prop. 99). But they are not independent ἀρχαί ; for they have a common character, that of being monads, and this common character is derived from the archetype of all unity, the One (prop. 100). We may perhaps interpret this to mean that their causality *as such* is derived from the First Cause, while the particular form which it assumes in each is self-determined.

PROPS. 101, 102. In the system of Plotinus the second God or Hypostasis is the duality-in-unity of Being and the divine Intelligence, the transcendental object and the transcendental subject. The elaboration within this hypostasis of a subordinate triad, τὸ ὄν (ὕπαρξις)—ζωή (δύναμις, αἰών)—νοῦς, is in the main the work of his successors, though a tendency in this direction is already observable in one or two passages of the *Enneads*—cf. V. iv. 2 *init.* and esp. VI. vi. 8 (II. 407. 5) εἰ δὴ τὸ ὂν πρῶτον δεῖ λαβεῖν πρῶτον ὄν, εἶτα νοῦν, εἶτα τὸ ζῷον· τοῦτο γὰρ ἤδη πάντα δοκεῖ περιέχειν, ὁ δὲ νοῦς δεύτερος (ἐνέργεια γὰρ τῆς οὐσίας) *. The motives governing this development seem to have been (*a*) the recognition that reality is logically prior to thought (τὸ ὂν τοῦ νοῦ προεπινοεῖν ἀνάγκη, Plot. V. ix. 8 [II. 255. 21]),

since the thinker, in order to think, must first exist;[1] (b) the desire to arrange causes in an ontological order corresponding to their degree of universality (cf. props. 56–62 and nn.); (c) the post-Plotinian theory that all intelligibles have a triadic structure, mirroring at every level the fundamental triad μονή—πρόοδος—ἐπιστροφή (prop. 35 n.) or πέρας—ἄπειρον—μικτόν (props. 89–90 n.). The choice of ζωή as a description for the middle term of the triad, the movement of thought which links object to subject, is determined by Plato, Soph. 248 E ff., where ζωή and νοῦς are said to be characters of τὸ ὄν. Under the influence of this passage Plot. several times[2] mentions ζωή as co-ordinate with τὸ ὄν and νοῦς, though not as a link between them nor as in any sense a separate hypostasis. Later Neoplatonists may possibly have been influenced in the direction of hypostatizing ζωή by the part which it played as a divine principle in the Hermetic and Gnostic systems;[3] cf. the hypostatized Αἰών (prop. 53), which Pr. identifies with ἡ πρώτη ζωή[4] (Th. Pl. III. vi). Authority was also found in the Chaldaean Oracles: from the line ἡ μὲν γὰρ δύναμις σὺν ἐκείνῳ, νοῦς δ' ἐν ἐκείνῳ (Th. Pl. 365. 1) Pr. and Damasc. elicited a triad ὕπαρξις—δύναμις—νοῦς, which they equated with ὄν—ζωή—νοῦς (in Tim. I. 17. 23, &c.). The ὄν—ζωή—νοῦς triad seems to have played a part in the theology of Porphyry (Pr. in Tim. III. 64. 8 ff.),[5] Iamblichus (ibid. 45. 5 ff.), Theodore of Asine (ibid. II. 274. 23, III. 64. 8), the unknown author of Kroll's Parmenides commentary (14. 15), and Syrianus (in Metaph. 46. 37). From Pr. ps.-Dion took over the doctrine. He is at pains to explain that the terms of the triad are not separate θεότητες but separate channels of the divine πρόοδος (Div. Nom. 5. 2, 3); and so also Erigena teaches that God is Being, Wisdom and Life (455 C, 621 B Migne), although he possesses these characters only in an especial transcendent sense (459 D).

8. τῆς παρ' ἑαυτῇ κινήσεως : I retain this reading, though with some hesitation, on the ground that 'self-movement' seems to be every-

---

[1] Cf. J. Wahl, Étude sur le Parménide, 230. But Plotinus in the passage cited warns us against interpreting this logical distinction as an ontological separation.

[2] I. vi. 7 ; V. iv. 2 fin.; V. vi. 6. Cf. also III. viii. 8.

[3] Cf. Corp. Herm. I. 9, 12 ; XIII. 9 ; de myst. 267. 4. The ultimate source of all this may be Iranian (Reitzenstein, H.M-R³. 13), or Egyptian (Scott, ii 289) ; but the thought of Life as an aspect of the divine is so natural that coincidence can hardly be considered a certain proof of indebtedness.

[4] On the scanty authority of Plato, Phaedo 106 D, αὐτὸ τὸ τῆς ζωῆς εἶδος . . . ἀθάνατόν ἐστιν. His real authority is Plotinus, who had defined αἰών as ζωὴ ἄπειρος (III. vii. 5).

[5] W. Kroll suggests that Pr. may here be reading back into Porphyry a doctrine which really belongs only to Theodore ; but in view of Plot.'s language in Enn. VI. vi. 8 there seems to be no good reason for scepticism about Porphyry. Cf. also Th. Pl. I. xi. 27; Damasc. i. 86. 8 ff.

where else expressed by ἡ ὑπὸ (or ἐξ) ἑαυτοῦ κίνησις, not by παρά. παρ' ἑαυτῶν may be due to someone who desired to bring the expression into closer conformity with the enunciation.

PROP. 103. Are Being, Life and Intelligence to be regarded as three aspects of a single reality or as three successive stages in the unfolding of the cosmos from the One? Pr. characteristically answers that both views are true : they are aspects, for each of them implies the others as cause or as consequent; they are successive, not co-ordinate, for each is predominant (though not to the exclusion of the others) at a certain stage of the πρόοδος. This may be expressed by saying that the triad is mirrored within each of its terms, so that while e.g. the first term has Being as its predominant character, it is at the same time Life and Intelligence *sub specie entitatis*. The scheme is elaborately worked out in *Th. Pl.* IV. i–iii ; its purpose, as we there learn, is to reconcile distinctness with continuity.

The general principle of which this is a particular application, viz. that 'all things are in all things, but in each after its own fashion', is ascribed by Syrianus (*in Metaph.* 82. 1 ff.) to 'the Pythagoreans', and by Iamblichus (*ap.* Stob. *Ecl.* I. xlix. 31 [866 H]) to Numenius *. Plot. applies it to the relations of intelligibles in general;[1] it is explicitly laid down by Porphyry[2] (ἀφ. x), and from Iamblichus[3] onwards is much resorted to. The later school saw in it a convenient means of covering all the gaps left by Plotinus in his derivation of the world of experience, and thus assuring the unity of the system : it bridged oppositions without destroying them., Pr. uses it not only to explain the Platonic κοινωνία εἰδῶν (*in Parm.* 751 ff.) and to solve Parmenides' difficulties about transcendent Forms (*ibid.* 928 ff.), but also to link together the four material elements (*in Tim.* II. 26. 23 ff.) ; he even adduces it to justify the community of women and children in the *Republic* (*ibid.* I. 48. 24 ff.) ; and it enables him to evade such a question as 'Where does sphericity begin?' by replying that it exists 'intellectively' in the demiurge, 'intelligibly' in the αὐτοζῷον, and on still higher planes 'secretly' (*ibid.* II. 77 : cf. 83, 161. 26, III. 285. 30, *in Parm.* 812. 10).—The formula was taken over by ps.-Dion. (e.g. *Div. Nom.* 4. 7 αἱ πάντων ἐν πᾶσιν οἰκείως ἑκάστῳ κοινωνίαι), to be echoed at the Renaissance by Bruno,[4] and later given a new significance by Leibniz.[5]

[1] V. viii. 4 (II. 235. 23) ἐξέχει δ' ἐν ἑκάστῳ ἄλλο, ἐμφαίνει δὲ καὶ πάντα.
[2] Though Iamblichus (*l.c.*) says that he elsewhere emphatically rejected it.
[3] Cf. Pr. *in Tim.* I. 426. 20.
[4] Cf. Whittaker², 277.
[5] *Principles of Nature and Grace*, 3: 'Chaque monade est un miroir vivant, représentatif de l'univers suivant son point de vue.'

Props. **104, 106, 107** carry a stage further the argument of props. 50 and 51, and prepare the way for the proof that embodied souls combine a temporal activity with an eternal existence (prop. 191) and are thus at once γενητά and ὄντα (prop. 192). For the history of this doctrine, and its relation to the medieval theory of *aevum*, see note on props. 50, 51.—Prop. **105** distinguishes immortality from perpetuity. We may feel that the distinction scarcely needed to be formally established ; but the two terms were often loosely used as synonyms. Immortality is predicable in varying senses of θεῖα σώματα,[1] μερικαὶ ψυχαί, δαίμονες and θεῖαι ψυχαί (*Th. Pl.* I. xxvii. 65).

1. ἀδύνατον : cf. prop. 16, ll. 10–12 n.

2. ἔσται πρώτως αἰώνιον τὸ αὐτὸ καὶ χρόνου μετέχον πρώτως : i.e. the distinction between soul (which is πρώτη τῶν γενητῶν, prop. 192) and intelligence will disappear.

4. ἐνέργειαν, 6. κατ᾽ ἐνέργειαν. οὐσίαν cannot be right in either of these places, but in l. 4 it probably stood in the archetype, whose text was faithfully preserved by the first family, wrongly corrected by the second and rightly corrected by the third.

14. ἄδεκτα ὄντα τοῦ ἀθανάτου. Neither the highest Being, which transcends the life-principle, nor Matter, which is lifeless, can be called ‘immortal’. Cr. spoiled the sense by adopting θανάτου from Portus's conjecture.

Props. **108, 109** and the two following may be illustrated diagrammatically thus :

$$A \leftarrow a^1 \leftarrow a^2 \leftarrow a^3 \ldots \ldots a^n$$
$$B \leftarrow b^1 \leftarrow b^2 \leftarrow b^3 \ldots \ldots b^n \ldots \ldots b^{n+x}$$

Here $a^1 a^2$, &c. and $b^1 b^2$, &c. represent two successive transverse series or strata of reality proceeding from their respective ‘ monads ’ or universal terms A and B : Pr.'s point is that b^n may obtain knowledge of or contact with A either through B or through a^n. This double reversion reflects a double causation : b^n derives its generic character from B, its specific character from a^n. Thus e.g. the stars reflect in their circular shape and motion the shape and motion of the cosmos which is their ‘ monad ’, but each has also an individual character derived from its immaterial exemplar (*in Tim.* III. 115. 19 ff.). Cf. also *in Tim.* I. 405. 13 ff. ; III. 232. 4 ff. ; *Th. Pl.* 121.

13. καὶ ἔστι τῷ κτλ. The edd., omitting καί, ruin the logic by

---

[1] So Aristotle speaks of the ἀθανασία οὐρανοῦ, *de caelo*, 284 a 1.

making τῷ ἐν τῇ ὑπερκειμένῃ ... ἄλλης καὶ ἄλλης the apodosis to εἰ γὰρ ... πᾶσίν ἐστι.

20. ἀνόμοιον ⟨ὄν⟩ agrees with ἐκεῖνο (the alternative is to read ⟨πρὸς⟩ ἀνόμοιον).

23. τῆς ὑπὲρ νοῦν καὶ πρωτίστης ἑνάδος. BCD read μονάδος, which is probably a mistaken assimilation to the enunciation of prop. 108. With either reading the reference seems, from the analogy with ὁ ὅλος νοῦς and ἡ ὅλη ψυχή, to be to the One, although in the more elaborate scheme required by props. 162 ff. the One is not a member of the same vertical συστοιχία as the Intelligence (see diagram ad loc.). In the simpler system which appears to be assumed here, the One is conceived as the first member both of the first transverse series (ἑνάδες) and of the first vertical series (μονάδες); and the distinctions within the second hypostasis are ignored.—On the contradiction between the ' participation ' and the ' imparticipability ' of the first member of a transverse series see prop. 23 n.

26. σώματος μερικὴ φύσις: cf. prop. 21, l. 22 n.

PROPS. 110, 111. This qualification of the principle last enunciated is required to make it consistent with prop. 62 cor. If the lower order is always more numerous than the higher, a one-one correspondence between the two series, such as Pr. postulates, obviously cannot extend to the whole of the lower series : at its further extremity there will be terms which have no analogue in the superior order and are therefore not directly attached to that order. This is clearly true of the relation of φύσις (in the sense defined in my note on prop. 21, l. 22) and ψυχή. The application of the principle on the next higher level involves the conclusion that there are some ψυχαί which have no νοῦς οἰκεῖος. Pr. places the human soul in this category (prop. 204 : cf. in Tim. I. 245. 18 ff.) on the ground that it enjoys νόησις only intermittently (prop. 184). Finally, authority for the assumption of a similar relation between νόες and θεοί was discovered in Plato's use of the expression θεῖος νοῦς (Phil. 22 C, Legg. 897 B).

11. οὐ γὰρ ἅπαντα κτλ.: cf. Plot. VI. vii. 6 (II. 433. 1) οὐ γὰρ λέγεται θεός, εἰς ὃν ὁ ἄνθρωπος. ἔχει γὰρ διαφοράν, ἣν ἔχουσι ψυχαὶ πρὸς ἀλλήλας, κἂν ἐκ τοῦ αὐτοῦ ὦσι στοίχου. So ps.-Dion. says that there are differences of value even between the ὁμοταγεῖς (Cael. Hier. 4. 3).

13. ὡς ἀφ' ἑνὸς καὶ πρὸς ἕν : i.e. definable by their relationship to a common term—a mode of resemblance intermediate between synonymity and mere homonymity (Arist. Metaph. 1003 a 33, E.N.

1096 b 27 ; Pr. *in Parm.* 709. 8). The words are added here to make the statement consistent with prop. 21, ll. 15 ff., where we are told that the monad of any order gives its members a common λόγος (relation) to each other and to the whole order.—πάντα . . . μονάδος I take to be either a gloss on ἀφ' ἑνός or the inept supplement of a reader unfamiliar with the technical expression ἀφ' ἑνὸς καὶ πρὸς ἕν.

PROP. 112. This principle is one of Pr.'s devices for reconciling the individuality of the successive levels of being with the continuity of the procession as a whole (cf. prop. 28 n.). There is no sudden and sharp transition from gods to intelligences (not here distinguished from νοητά) or from intelligences to souls : the highest intelligence is not only an intelligence but a god (*in Alc.* 381. 10), the two higher classes of souls enjoy perpetual intellection (prop. 184). So also the moon, which is the frontier between heaven and earth, shares the characteristics of both (*in Tim.* III. 142. 8). For further illustrations cf. *Th. Pl.* III. xxi. 158, IV. ii. 183 ; *in Parm.* 1156. 18. The doctrine is echoed by ps.-Dion., *Div. Nom.* 7. 3 *fin.*

3. κατὰ τὴν ἰδιότητα τῆς ὑποστάσεως. Cf. prop. 145, which seems to show that the ἰδιότης referred to here is not that of the lower σειρά or transverse series, but a special power such as κάθαρσις or φρουρά which is transmitted in the vertical succession from certain members of the divine order to the corresponding members of the lower orders of being.

L. *Of the divine henads or gods.*
    1. General characters of the henads (props. 113–27).
    2. Relation of the henads to the universe of Being (props. 128–50).
    3. Specific characters of particular series of henads (props. 151–9).
    4. Classification of henads according to the principles which can participate them (props. 160–5).

The doctrine of divine henads is the most striking of the modifications introduced by later Neoplatonism into the Plotinian world-scheme, and its purpose has been the subject of considerable discussion. It is generally assumed (e.g. by Zeller, Ueberweg-Praechter, Mr. Whittaker and Prof. Taylor) to be the invention of Proclus. But (*a*) if Pr. had really been its originator, Marinus would surely have cited it as the most convincing proof of his hero's originality instead of the relatively unimportant innovation which he does cite for this purpose (*vit. Proc.* 23) ; (*b*) Syrianus in his com-

mentary on the *Metaphysics* has at least one definite allusion to
'henads' which are identical with gods [1]; (c) Pr. himself seems
to attribute the doctrine to τινὲς τῶν ἡμῖν αἰδοίων, a phrase which
usually covers a reference to his teacher, Syrianus.[2] *

While the identification of the 'henads' with the gods may thus
be ascribed to Syrianus,[3] the henads as metaphysical entities have a
much longer history. The term comes from Plato *Phil.* 15 A ὅταν
δέ τις ἕνα ἄνθρωπον ἐπιχειρῇ τίθεσθαι καὶ βοῦν ἕνα καὶ τὸ καλὸν ἓν καὶ
τὸ ἀγαθὸν ἕν, περὶ τούτων τῶν ἐνάδων καὶ τῶν τοιούτων ἡ πολλὴ †σπουδὴ†
μετὰ διαιρέσεως ἀμφισβήτησις γίγνεται. Here ἐνάδες are simply units
or 'examples of ones' : they are called μονάδες just below. But Pr.
(*in Parm.* 880. 30) interprets the passage as referring to the Forms,
which are called μονάδες as belonging to the world of Being, but
ἐνάδες in respect of their transcendent unity. Now we learn from
Plotinus (VI. vi. 9 [II. 408. 18]) that the Neopythagoreans called the
Forms ἐνάδες [4]; and a passage in Theon of Smyrna suggests that
these ἐνάδες were sometimes thought of as co-ordinate with the One.[5]
If this is so, Syrianus' doctrine will on this side be an example of
that harking back to pre-Plotinian sources of which we have some
evidence elsewhere in later Neoplatonism.[6]

The motive of the innovation lay no doubt partly in the desire for
logical completeness and symmetry. Beside Intelligence there were

[1] 183. 24 αἱ μονάδες ἢ ἐνάδες αἱ ἀπὸ τῆς πρωτίστης αἰτίας προελθοῦσαι· ἐκεῖναι γὰρ
οὐ μόνον θεοὶ ἀλλὰ καὶ συνοχαί τινες θεῶν. The terminology is not yet precise:
'monad' is used as a synonym of 'henad'. 'Henads' derived from the One are
also mentioned in another passage, 141. 1 ff. ; but here the reference might be to
what Pr. calls 'monads', the one Intelligence, the one Soul, etc.

[2] *in Parm.* 1066. 16 ἀνάγκη τοίνυν . . . ἢ περὶ τοῦ πρώτου θεοῦ μόνον εἶναι τὸν
παρόντα λόγον (viz. the first hypothesis of the *Parmenides*) . . . ἢ περὶ πάντων θεῶν
καὶ τῶν μετ' ἐκεῖνον, ὥσπερ ἀξιοῦσί τινες τῶν ἡμῖν αἰδοίων. ἐπειδὴ γὰρ πᾶς θεός,
καθὸ θεός, ἑνάς ἐστι . . . διὰ δὴ τοῦτο συνάπτειν ἀξιοῦσι τῇ περὶ θεοῦ τοῦ πρώτου
θεωρίᾳ τὴν περὶ θεῶν ἁπάντων ὑφήγησιν· πάντες γάρ εἰσιν ἐνάδες ὑπερούσιοι.

[3] There is a passage in Damascius (I. 257. 20), noticed by Zeller, which
appears to imply that the identification was made by Iamblichus. It runs τοὺς
θεοὺς οὕτως ὑποτίθενται τοὺς πολλοὺς οἱ πρὸ Ἰαμβλίχου σχεδόν τι πάντες φιλόσοφοι,
ἕνα μὲν εἶναι τὸν ὑπερούσιον θεὸν λέγοντες, τοὺς ἄλλους οὐσιώδεις εἶναι ταῖς ἀπὸ τοῦ
ἑνὸς ἐλλάμψεσιν ἐκθεουμένους, καὶ εἶναι τὸ τῶν ὑπερουσίων πλῆθος ἐνάδων οὐκ
αὐτοτελῶν ὑποστάσεων, ἀλλὰ τῶν ἐλλαμπομένων ἀπὸ τοῦ μόνου θεοῦ καὶ ταῖς οὐσίαις
ἐνδιδομένων θεώσεων. But if the henads played any important part in Iamb.'s
system it is rather strange that we should have no other evidence of it than this.

[4] These Neopythagorean 'henads' may have been, as the Damascius passage
quoted in n. 3 suggests, not the Forms themselves, but the principles of unity im-
planted in them by the One. Cf. note on props. 135, 136.

[5] *Expos. rer. math.* 21. 14 Hiller καὶ γὰρ εἰ παρὰ Πλάτωνι ἐνάδες εἴρηνται ἐν
Φιλήβῳ, οὐ παρὰ τὸ ἓν ἐλέχθησαν, ἀλλὰ παρὰ τὴν ἐνάδα. ἥτις ἐστὶ μονὰς μετοχῇ τοῦ
ἑνός : i.e. ἐνάδες is the plural not of *the* One but of *a* one. Here Theon seems to be
defending the reasonable interpretation of the Platonic passage against persons who
used it as evidence for a theory of transcendent unities akin to that of Proclus.

[6] It is suggestive in this connexion that for Syrianus Plato is ὁ κράτιστος τῶν
Πυθαγορείων (*in Metaph.* 190. 35).

intelligences, beside Soul souls, beside Nature natures : why not also
'ones' beside the One ? 'When the theory had been thought out
for the case of Mind and Soul, it was a mere exigence of logic to
extend it to the first member of the supreme triad' (Taylor, *Phil. of
Pr.* 625). The wording of props. 21 and 113 might be cited in support
of this interpretation. But the henads are not merely a piece of
ornament without structural significance in the system. They are,
like πέρας and ἀπειρία, and like the second 'One' of Iamblichus, an
attempt to bridge the yawning gulf which Plotinus had left between
the One and reality. Of the existence of this gulf no one was more
acutely aware than Plotinus himself: especially significant are such
passages as VI. v. 9 (II. 393. 3 ff.), where he practically confesses that
plurality cannot be got out of unity unless it is first put into it.
The One cannot be, in Plotinian language, δύναμις πάντων without
being also δυνάμει πάντα : but to admit this is to infect the One with
at least the seeds of plurality. The doctrine of henads represents an
attempt to account for the existence of individuality by importing
plurality into the first hypostasis, yet in such a manner as to leave
intact the perfect unity of the One. They are the transcendent
sources of individuality : in them the whole Plotinian κόσμος νοητός
already exists κατ' αἰτίαν, or in a seminal form. On their relationship to the One see props. 133 n. and 151-9 n., where I have stated
my reason for rejecting Professor Taylor's view that 'what Proclus
has in mind is a doctrine of the attributes of God like that of Philo,
or again, of the great scholastics'.

There remains the theological side of the doctrine, which Zeller
and others regard as the really significant part of it. It is certainly
a singular example of the survival of an obsolete creed in mummy
form—a mode of preservation which becomes possible only when
the creed is already dead. The 'gods' with whom the henads are
identified are, as we learn in detail from *Th. Pl.*, the gods of
traditional Greek mythology, and the identification is no doubt to
be understood as a last desperate attempt to carry out the policy of
Iamblichus and maintain the united front of Hellenic philosophy
and Hellenic religion against the inroads of Christianity. This
explains why Pr. holds that 'piety about the gods is the sum total of
virtue' (*in Tim.* I. 212. 5), and that the special task of the Platonic
philosopher is the exact classification of deities (*ibid.* III. 10. 7).
Earlier attempts to relate the gods of popular belief to the First Cause
had not been lacking, as we may see from Sallustius c. 2,[1] and from

___
[1] According to Sallustius οὐδὲ τῆς πρώτης αἰτίας ἢ ἀλλήλων χωρίζονται, ὥσπερ
οὐδὲ νοῦ αἱ νοήσεις οὐδὲ ψυχῆς αἱ ἐπιστῆμαι οὐδὲ ζῴου αἱ αἰσθήσεις. This, if

the very striking letter of the fourth-century pagan Maximus of Madaura (Augustine, *Epist.* XVI. 1), who would interpret them, without obliterating their individuality, as aspects or virtues of one supreme god whose name we do not know.[1] But the doctrine of henads afforded the most convenient means of giving the gods that assured place in the Plotinian world-order which Plotinus had neglected to provide.[2] Unfortunately this ἐπιστημονικὴ θεολογία resulted in depriving the gods of all personality,[3] and even of all identity: for the principle of continuity in the vertical procession involved the splitting of each god into a series of gradually weakening forces, so that Zeus, for example, appears as five different gods each of whom symbolizes the 'jovial' principle on a different plane of reality (*in Tim.* III. 190. 19 ff.). That Homer's Olympians, the most vividly conceived anthropomorphic beings in all literature, should have ended their career on the dusty shelves of this museum of metaphysical abstractions is one of time's strangest ironies.

PROP. 113. The divine series is ἑνιαῖος both in the sense that perfect internal unity is the fundamental character (κυριώτατον τῶν συμπληρούντων) of every god (*in Parm.* 1069. 8); and in the sense that the gods are bound together by a closer collective unity than any subsequent order of existence (*ibid.* 1048. 11).—Noteworthy are (1) the strictly impersonal definition of God, as the transcendent goal of desire; (2) the formal character of the argument for polytheism, which appears here as, in Mr. Whittaker's words, a piece of 'pure deductive metaphysics'.

PROP. 114. On the term 'self-complete' (i.e. independent of extraneous relations) see prop. 64, l. 21 n. There are self-complete principles (intelligences and souls) which are not henads (prop. 64

---

pressed, associates the gods with the One even more closely than Pr.'s scheme, and resembles rather the relation of God to his 'powers' in Philo.

[1] That the philosophical background of Maximus is Stoic or Middle Platonist rather than Neoplatonic has been shown by G. Beyerhaus in *Rhein. Mus.* N. F. 75 (1926), 32 ff. Cf. also Nock in *Rev. des Études anciennes*, 1928, 286 f.

[2] Plot. handles the gods of mythology in a very casual fashion, allegorizing them as it suits him, but without any attempt at consistency: cf. Arnou, Appendix A. This is no doubt to be connected with his personal indifference to cult practices (Porph. *vit. Plot.* 10 *fin.*).

[3] How far Pr is from treating his 'gods' as persons may be seen from such a passage as *in Tim.* III. 184. 21, where he accepts *both* the statement of Hesiod that Oceanos, Tethys, Kronos and Rhea were all of them begotten by Ouranos upon Ge, *and* the statement of the *Timaeus* that Oceanos and Tethys were the parents of Kronos and Rhea. So abstract is the conception that pseudo-Dionysius has no difficulty in substituting his 'thrones, Cherubim and Seraphim' for Pr.'s gods without disturbing the architecture of the system.

cor.); and there are henads which are not self-complete, such as those which are immanent in human souls (τὸ ἐν τῆς ψυχῆς *in Alc.* 519. 27, cf. *dec. dub.* 142. 23 ff. &c.). From prop. 6 it would appear that any unit insusceptible of further analysis may be called a 'henad'. —Nicolaus asks how the gods can be self-complete when they owe their divine character to participation (l. 24). A similar question arises about all 'self-sufficient' and 'self-constituted' principles: see props. 9 and 40 nn., and prop. 118, l. 10 n.

PROP. 115. That the Good which is the final cause of all Being is itself beyond Being is, of course, Platonic and Plotinian doctrine. From Neoplatonism it was taken over by ps.-Dionysius, mediated by whom it reappears in the East in the teaching of John Damascene, and in the West in that of Erigena. Cf. notes on props. 2 and 4.— The present proposition seems to make it plain that whereas Plotinus puts 'all the gods' within νοῦς (V. i. 4), the divine henads are to be placed in the *first* of the three traditional 'hypostases' and not (as Vacherot, Simon and others assume) in the second. But it must be admitted that Pr. is himself responsible for a good deal of the confusion which exists on the subject, in that he frequently speaks of such entities as Eternity, Time, the αὐτοζῷον, and even the sensible world as 'gods', and of gods as 'intelligible', 'intellectual' or 'intra-mundane'. In an important passage of *Th. Pl.* (I. xxvii. 63 ff.) he justifies his loose usage of the term θεός by the example of Plato,[1] while insisting that only the henads are ἁπλῶς or πρώτως θεοί; and explains that the divine nature is 'intelligible' only in a Pickwickian sense, ὡς ἐφετὸν τῷ νῷ καὶ ὡς τελεσιουργὸν καὶ ὡς συνεκτικὸν τοῦ νοῦ (but not as directly knowable by νοῦς, cf. prop. 123). The forced character of the identification θεός = αὐτοτελὴς ἑνάς is evident here: the gods of traditional cultus and their classification in traditional theology (see props. 162–5 n.) cannot be squared with the metaphysical doctrine save by a glaringly artificial application of the convenient principle πάντα ἐν πᾶσιν, οἰκείως δὲ ἐν ἑκάστῳ (cf. prop. 118). Again, Pr. identifies his henads with the ἓν ὄν of the *Parmenides* (*in Parm.* 1068. 34 ff.), which is hardly compatible with their ὑπερουσιότης; but a place had to be found for them somewhere in the hypotheses of that dialogue, and being 'participable' (prop. 116) they could not be identified with the abstract unity of the first hypothesis, although some earlier writer seems to have discovered them there.

---

[1] Cf. props. 128–9 n.

33. ἐν ἂν οὐκ ἂν εἴη μόνον, if sound, is perhaps a reminiscence of Plato, *Tim.* 38 B, where Pr. read (if the MSS. of *in Tim.* are to be trusted) τάχ᾽ ἂν οὐκ ἂν εἴη καιρός, a phrase of closely similar rhythm.

11. οὐσίαι δὲ ὄντες … 12 ὡς μονάδος τῶν οὐσιῶν. Q's ὑπερούσιοι for οὐσίαι is a deliberate and disastrous 'correction'; on the other hand μονάδος, whether due to conjecture or not, is certainly right—the term 'monad' applies only to the first member of a transverse series (prop. 21).

PROP. 116. The henads are 'participable' in accordance with the general law enunciated in prop. 23, which requires that in each order there shall be an intermediate class of predicable terms linking the non-predicable substantative principle with the concrete subjects : the 'unities' link the non-predicable substantive Unity with the concrete ἡνωμένα. How this 'participability' is to be reconciled with the ὑπερουσιότης of the henads we are not told, but it is evidently not to be understood as implying immanence in the ordinary sense — they are not only χωριστῶς μετεχόμενα (like all αὐθυπόστατα, prop. 82) but transcendent in an especial degree (prop. 130). Nor is Pr. always consistent about their participability; in the *in Tim.* it is both affirmed of all henads other than the One (I. 226. 18) and denied of the supra-mundane gods (III. 204. 16 ff.).—The proof given here turns on showing that an imparticipable henad could only be distinguished from the One by ascribing to it (falsely) a lower degree of unity, and that such a lower unity can always be analysed into a *participable* henad and a participant.

15. τῶν τε προόντων: equivalent to τῶν τε πρὸ τῶν ὄντων. Plot. does not, I think, use the term in this sense ; but it was applied by the Valentinian Gnostics to their supreme god (Iren. *c. haer.* I. i), and was also used by Hermetists (Stob. I. 293. 12 [750 H]). Iamblichus (*de myst.* VIII. 2) seems to have introduced it into Neoplatonic, and the author of the *Pastor Hermae* (*sim.* V. vi. 5) into Christian theology.

24. ᾧ συνάπτει πρὸς τὸ αὐτοέν : for συνάπτειν intrans. see prop. 15, l. 34 ; prop. 55, l. 28.

PROP. 117. As time and eternity are the 'measures' of ἐνέργεια (prop. 54), so the henads are the 'measures' of οὐσία, i.e. the principles to which it owes its articulated structure (similarly the 'measures' of γένεσις are the Forms, which determine and delimit the infinitude of Matter, *Th. Pl.* III. x. 138). Pr. has in mind Plato, *Legg.* 716 C ὁ δὴ θεὸς ἡμῖν πάντων χρημάτων μέτρον ἂν εἴη

μάλιστα (cf. also *Politicus* 283–4). So, too, Plot. (V. v. 4) and Syrian. (*in Metaph.* 168. 4 ff.) apply the term μέτρον to the One, and finally ps.-Dion. (*Div. Nom.* 2. 10) applies it to Christ.

PROPS. 118, 119. Like the One, the henads are without internal differentiation, and this undifferentiated character, which is their essential predicate (ὕπαρξις), may be called indifferently their unity or their goodness (cf. prop. 13 n.). Other attributes can only be ascribed to them κατ᾽ αἰτίαν, as implicit in their unity and goodness. Cf. *in Parm.* 811. 4 ff.

10. οὐδὲν ἐν αὐτοῖς ἔσται κατὰ μέθεξιν. This must be understood as meaning that they have none of their characters by *vertical* derivation. They are said to 'participate godhead' (prop. 114, l. 24); but characters derived transversely from the monad by its co-ordinate μετεχόμενα are treated by Pr. as primary predicates of the latter (prop. 19), and so are not in the technical sense κατὰ μέθεξιν.

17. καθ᾽ ἕξιν is confirmed by *in Tim.* III. 364. 13 οὐδὲ ἕξις (ἡ πρὸ τοῦ νοῦ ἀγαθότης) ... οὐδὲ ὅλως οὐσιώδης τις ὑπόστασις: cf. also II. 313. 1 ff., where ὁ καθ᾽ ἕξιν νοῦς is distinguished from ὁ οὐσιώδης and ὁ θεῖος. The variant κατὰ μέθεξιν arose from a mistaken assimilation to the preceding prop.

PROP. 120. To deny that the gods exercise providence was for Plato a blasphemy meriting the severest punishment (*Legg.* 899 D ff.). Partly for this reason, and partly because Stoicism and the Hellenistic religions had raised in an acute form the question of the relation between providence and fate (εἱμαρμένη), the topic of πρόνοια bulks almost as large in Neoplatonism as does that of predestination and grace in the Christian theology of the period. The main lines of the Neoplatonic doctrine, which makes fate distinct from and subordinate to providence, seem to have been already laid down by the second century A.D.[1] Pr. devoted two special treatises to the subject—the *de decem dubitationibus circa providentiam* and the *de providentia et fato*. With the present prop. cf. also *Th. Pl.* I. (xv.) 38 ff.

7. ὡς τοὔνομα ἐμφαίνει: cf. Plot. V. iii. 10 (II. 192. 24). The etymology fits the Plotinian system better than that of Pr.: for, as Nicolaus remarks, it would if pressed require us to ascribe providence to Being and Life also, since they also are πρὸ νοῦ. But it is only

---

[1] See Gercke in *Rhein. Mus.* N. F. 41 (1886). Theiler, *Vorbereitung des Neuplat.* 50, n. 1, finds the starting-point of the theory in Antiochus of Ascalon.

subsidiary to the real contention, viz. that belief in the goodness of the gods involves belief in their providence.

PROP. 121. As all action involves, in addition to the will to act, a power to carry out the will and a knowledge on which the will is based, so the conception of divine providence involves ascribing to the gods not only goodness but also omnipotence and omniscience. But this omnipotence and omniscience has for Pr. to be somehow distinguished from the ἄπειρος δύναμις of ἡ πρώτη ζωή and the ἀκρότης πάσης γνώσεως which belongs to ὁ πρῶτος νοῦς: accordingly these characters are said to 'pre-subsist' in the· gods in a transcendent manner. Goodness, Power and Knowledge constitute the primary divine triad (*Th. Pl.* I. xvi. 44), which prefigures in a seminal form the triad of the second hypostasis, Being, Life and Intelligence (prop. 101).—δύναμις πάντων is already a standing definition of the One in Plot. (e.g. V. iii. 15); and there is in some passages of the *Enneads* an inclination to ascribe to the One some form of consciousness analogous to but transcending νόησις, in order to account for the emergence of the latter: V. iv. 2 ἡ κατανόησις αὐτοῦ αὐτὸ οἱονεὶ συναισθήσει οὖσα . . . ἑτέρως ἡ κατὰ· τὴν νοῦ νόησιν: VI. viii. 16 ὑπερνόησις, 18 τὸν οἷον ἐν ἑνὶ νοῦν οὐ νοῦν ὄντα. On the nature of this divine consciousness see further prop. 124 n.—The Procline doctrine reappears in ps.-Dion., who devotes separate chapters of the *Div. Nom.* to the praise of God as προών, as αἰώνιος ζωή and as κρυφία γνῶσις.

32. τῷ ἀρίστῳ χαρακτηρίζεται : cf. Plot. VI. viii. 10 (II. 491. 25).

PROP. 122. This is the Platonist answer to the Epicurean[1] objection against the doctrine of providence, viz. that it credits the gods with an interest in an infinity of petty problems and so abolishes their transcendence and makes their life πραγματειώδη καὶ ἐπίπονον.[2] The Platonists reply that the law of providence operates automatically, and that the individual unconsciously co-operates towards its fulfilment: 'die Weltgeschichte ist das Weltgericht.' Both objection and answer are already in substance stated by Plato, *Legg.* 903 E ff. ; but the subtlest exponent of the Platonist doctrine is Plotinus, in such passages as IV. iii. 13 and 24. Cf. also [Arist.] *de mundo* c. 6 § 13 (a cruder solution, ascribing providence not to God himself but to his hypostatized 'powers'); Sallust. ix, with Nock *ad loc.* Pr.

---

[1] Contained in the first of Epicurus' κύριαι δόξαι (p. 94 Bailey) : cf. Sall. 16. 30.
[2] *Th. Pl.* 41.

regards the reconciliation of providence with transcendence as the especial glory of Platonism,[1] Aristotle having maintained the second without the first, the Stoics the first without the second.—The formula of the present prop. reappears in ps.-Dion. *Div. Nom.* 2.

10 : Christ is οὐσία πᾶσιν ἐπιβατεύουσα τῇ προνοίᾳ καὶ πάλιν ἐξῃρημένη ἁπάσης οὐσίας τῇ φύσει.

12. διανομὴν . . . κατὰ τὴν αὐτῶν ἀξίαν. Justice was defined in the Academy as ἕξις διανεμητικὴ τοῦ κατ' ἀξίαν ἑκάστῳ ([Plat.] *Def.* 411 E). The phrase is duly reproduced by ps.-Dion. (*Div. Nom.* 9. 10, &c.).

15. τὸ τῷ εἶναι ποιοῦν ἀσχέτως ποιεῖ : cf. prop. 18 n. It is on this assumption of the possibility of *one-sided* causal relations that the whole Neoplatonic system hinges.

20. τὸ μέγιστόν ἐστιν οὐ τὸ ἀγαθοειδές, ἀλλὰ τὸ ἀγαθουργόν. This is not, as has been suggested, an assertion of the superiority of πρᾶξις to θεωρία. For Neoplatonism divine πρᾶξις *is* θεωρία, or rather perhaps its incidental accompaniment (παρακολούθημα, Plot. III. viii. 4 [I. 336. 4]).

PROP. 123. On the general subject of the 'unknown god' in Neoplatonism, see Appendix I. Pr.'s teaching here differs from that of Plotinus (*a*) in the absence of any explicit reference to *unio mystica* ;[2] (*b*) in excluding the One from the possibility of being known by analogy (ἀπὸ τῶν μετεχόντων).[3] The latter is a necessary consequence from Pr.'s doctrine of the ἀμέθεκτον (prop. 23 n.) : even the universal Intelligence has only an *indirect* connexion with the One. Both these departures from Plot. illustrate the growth of agnosticism in Neoplatonic theory, a development which is parallel with the increasing importance attached by Plot.'s successors to theurgic practice (cf. Introd., pp. xx–xxiii).

32. οὔτε οὖν δοξαστὸν κτλ. : the Platonic grades of knowledge. Cf. *in Parm.* 1081. 7 ὡς γὰρ δόξῃ τὰ δοξαστὰ γινώσκομεν καὶ ὡς διανοίᾳ τὰ διανοητὰ καὶ ὡς τῷ νοερῷ τῷ ἐν ἡμῖν τὸ νοητόν, οὕτω καὶ τῷ ἑνὶ τὸ ἕν· τοῦτο δὲ ταὐτὸν τῷ ⟨τῷ⟩ μὴ ὄντι τὸ ἕν· τοῦτο δὲ ταὐτὸν τῷ τῇ ἀποφάσει τὸ ἕν. In the present passage the *via negativa* is not mentioned, but cf. prop. 8.

5. καὶ τοῦτο ἀναγκαίως. The validity of such inferences depends

---

[1] μάλιστα τῆς Πλατωνικῆς θεολογίας ἐξαίρετον, *ibid.* 42.
[2] The possibility of it is not, however, excluded : it is only ἡ διὰ λόγου γνῶσις that is explicitly confined to the realm of ὄντα.
[3] Cf. Numenius *ap.* Euseb. *Prep. Ev.* XI. 22. Hopfner is, I think, mistaken in finding in the doctrine of knowledge ἀπὸ τῶν μετεχόντων a *direct* reference to the Iamblichean theory of σύμβολα (*Offenbarungszauber*, I, § 389). The symbol theory is only a particular development of the much older 'way of analogy'.

on Pr.'s law of continuity (prop. 28 n.). It is this principle that enables him in the *Th. Pl.* to write some 400 folio pages about his 'unknown' gods. But there is always more in the cause than in the effect, so that the method of analogy can never exhaust the content of the divine or fully express its essence. Cf. Plot. V. iii. 14 (II. 197. 18) οὕτως ἔχομεν ὥστε περὶ αὐτοῦ [τοῦ ἑνός] μὲν λέγειν, αὐτὸ δὲ μὴ λέγειν. Pr. says the same of the gods in general, *in Tim.* I. 303. 18.

PROP. 124 embodies Pr.'s answer to the objection raised by the Platonic Parmenides (*Parm.* 134 C ff.) that on the theory of correlation between degrees of cognitive faculty and degrees of reality in its object God, who has perfect intelligence, cannot know our imperfectly real world. Pr.'s doctrine is more fully expounded in *Th. Pl.* I. xxi. 54 ff. and *in Tim.* I. 351. 20 ff. His contention is that (1) only knowledge extraneously acquired (ἐπίκτητος) involves a relation to its object, but the gods' knowledge is given with their being and is therefore in this respect absolute; (2) all knowledge is relative to the knowing subject, so that the gods know all things *sub specie aeternitatis* or 'in their cause', just as all our knowledge is *sub specie temporis*. The divine knowledge is a mode of cognition which we cannot hope to grasp: being a completely unitary ἐνέργεια, it surpasses even νόησις, in which there is still a formal duality. It does not, like νόησις, know the particular in the universal and the unreal in the real: it knows all things as one, yet in the full articulation of their detail,[1] 'even the infinitude of the possible, and Matter itself'. This attempt to picture a grade of intellectual knowledge higher than νόησις is in the main post-Plotinian;[2] its emptiness is shown by the fact that Pr. is obliged to ascribe to it many of the characters which Plot. and Porphyry (ἀφ. xxxiii § 2) had ascribed to νόησις. It has, however, a considerable historical importance: closely imitated by ps.-Dion. (*Div. Nom.* 7. 2), it reappears in Aquinas' teaching that 'God sees all things not in themselves but in himself, in so far as he contains in his essence the likeness of all other things that come from him';[3] and it is probable that it indirectly influenced Spinoza.

11. τὰ δὲ μὴ ἀναγκαῖα ἀναγκαίως: this convenient formula is utilized by Pr. and his medieval successors to reconcile divine fore-

---

[1] This explains why oracles often give answers to the most trifling questions (*Th. Pl., l c.*).

[2] Cf. however the passages from the *Enneads* quoted on prop. 121.

[3] Quoted by Inge[3], II. 115.

knowledge with freewill (*prov. et fat.* 193 ff.: cf. Psellus, *de omnif. doct.* 16; Aquinas, *Summa Theol.* I. 14. 13, *Summa c. Gent.* I. 67).

25. τὸ ἀπαθὲς παθητικῶς ὑποδέχεται καὶ τὸ ἄχρονον ἐγχρόνως : Pr. probably has Christianity in mind. The Christian ascription of changes of heart to the deity and the Christian belief in the temporal origin of the cosmos were two points on which Neoplatonist criticism especially fastened.

PROP. 125. The σειραί of this proposition are *vertical* series, in which the distinctive property of a particular god or henad is successively mirrored at different levels of reality (here called τάξεις) : cf. *in Tim.* I. 36. 7 ff.; III. 81. 31 ff. This doctrine was found useful by Pr. in more ways than one : it enabled him to reconcile irreconcilable texts about Zeus (*in Tim.* III. 190. 19 ff.) and other gods by assuming them to refer to different stages of the πρόοδος ; it helped him to explain away archaic myths about divine intercourse with men by the assumption that they referred not to the henads but to homonymous δαίμονες belonging to their respective σειραί (*in Crat.* cxviii) ; it justified the ascription of divinity to the stars and furnished a rationale of astrology (cf. prop. 129) ; and it accounted for the magical properties attributed by theurgy to stones, herbs and other objects which for the Platonist are ἔσχατα (cf. prop. 145). Authority was discovered for it in Plato *Legg.* X. 903 B. Its systematic development was probably the work of Iamblichus,[1] but the notion that there may be daemons bearing the same names as the gods is older : cf. Plut. *def. orac.* 21, 421 E, " εἰ δὲ τοῖς νενομισμένοις τῶν θεῶν ὀνόμασι δαίμονάς τινας καλοῦμεν, οὐ θαυμαστέον ", εἶπεν ὁ ξένος· " ᾧ γὰρ ἕκαστος θεῷ συντέτακται καὶ οὗ τῆς δυνάμεως καὶ τιμῆς μετείληχεν, ἀπὸ τούτου φιλεῖ καλεῖσθαι " : Plot. VI. vii. 6 (II. 432. 31) ἔστι μίμημα θεοῦ δαίμων εἰς θεὸν ἀνηρτημένος.

8. ταῖς τάξεσιν, ἐν αἷς ποιεῖται τὴν ἔκφανσιν. These vary with the different classes of gods, props. 162–5.

PROP. 126 applies to the henads the general law governing transverse series, and illustrates clearly the reduction. of the 'gods' to hypostatized logical counters.

PROP. 127. This insistence that deity is 'simple', i.e. homogeneous and without parts, is suggested by Plato *Rep.* II. 380 D [cf. *Th. Pl.* I. (xx.) 52], though the term is used there in a different

---

[1] Cf. Praechter, *Richtungen*, 121 ff.

sense.—On αὐτάρκεια see note on props. 9 and 10. The gods have a higher αὐτάρκεια than Intelligence or Soul : they are δι' ἑαυτοὺς καὶ παρ' ἑαυτῶν αὐτάρκεις (*Th. Pl.* I. xix. 50). But they are not, like the One, ὑπὲρ αὐτάρκειαν, since they are not the Good but only individual 'goodnesses'.

31. τὸ ἐν τῷ ἀγαθῷ ταὐτὸν προστησάμενον. The editors and translators, reading ἐν for ἕν, fail to make any sense of this clause. προστήσασθαι means in Pr. (1) to put before (πρὸ τῶν ἄλλων τὰς μονάδας προεστησάμεθα, *Th. Pl.* 272), or pre-establish (δυνάμεις ἐν ἑαυτῷ προεστήσατο τῆς ἀπογεννήσεως ὁ δημιουργός, *in Tim.* III. 270. 29) ; (2) to bring forward in the sense of manifesting or reproducing (τὴν αὐτὴν προεστήσατο τῇ ἑαυτῆς αἰτίᾳ δύναμιν, *Th. Pl.* 197). The last meaning suits all the passages in *El. Th.*, except perhaps prop. 133, l. 16.

PROPS. **128, 129.** The terms θεός and (still more) θεῖος were used by the Greeks at all periods in a wide and loose sense, often without any implication of cult worship.[1] Plato himself.had spoken of a θεῖος νοῦς (*Phil.* 22 C); of soul as θεοειδές (*Phaedo* 95 C) and as μετὰ θεοὺς θειότατον (*Legg.* V. 726); of the sun and the cosmos as gods (*ibid.* XII. 950 D, *Tim.* 92 C). Plotinus defines θεός as τὸ τῷ ἑνὶ συνημμένον, VI. ix. 8 (II. 519. 6), and can apply the name not only to νοῦς and the universal soul but also to the human soul (IV. viii. 5 [II. 149. 18], VI. ix. 9 [II. 522. 17]) and to the stars (V. i. 4 [II. 165. 13]). Later Neoplatonists found this too unsystematic. Porphyry was puzzled as to how the stars can be gods, if all gods are completely incorporeal (Iamb. *de myst.* I. 17 *init.*). Hence the doctrine of θεῖα which directly or indirectly 'participate' the henads or gods proper, and in this sense may themselves be described loosely as θεοί (*in Tim.* II. 213. 18, III. 72. 27, 109. 14 ; *Th. Pl.* I. (xiv.) 36 f.). On θεῖος νοῦς and θεία ψυχή see props. 181 ff., on θεῖα σώματα prop. 139, l. 24 n. ; and for the scheme of participation in henads, props. 162–5 n.—It is noteworthy that in prop. 129 νοῦς is identified with ἡ ἀμέριστος οὐσία : i.e. Pr. here reverts to the Plotinian use of the term, in which it covers the whole of the second hypostasis.—The distinction between mediate and immediate communion in God is reproduced by ps.-Dion. *Cael. Hier.* 6. 2, 7. 2, the thrones, cherubim and seraphim taking the place of the henads, and the remaining orders representing νοῦς and ψυχή.

5. τὴν εἰς πλῆθος ἔκτασιν. This reading is supported by *in Tim.* I.

---

[1] Cf. Burnet, *Thales to Plato*, 28 ff.

446. 14 τὰς εἰς πλῆθος ἐκτάσεις τῶν εἰδῶν. ἔκστασις is, indeed, associated with μερισμός by Syrianus, *in Metaph.* 174. 14, and occurs as
a variant for ἔκτασις in *in Tim.* I. 178. 26 and several other places in
Pr. ; but probably the less familiar and less ambiguous word ἔκτασις
is the true reading in all the Proclus passages.

11. ἔμφασιν: 'implicit trace' or 'foreshowing'. Pr. commonly
applies this term, like Plot. and Philo, to the reflection of the higher
principle in the lower (prop. 71, l. 5, &c.); but occasionally, as
in Tim. I. 399. 31 and here, to a seminal trace of the lower principle
pre-existing in the higher.

13. διὰ τοῦ θείου νοῦ. The accusative would flatly contradict
prop. 165, l. 4.

26. συνεκπυροῦσα: metaphorical, but perhaps suggested by the
fact that θεῖαι ψυχαί are the souls of stars (*in Tim.* III. 255. 10 ff.).
Cf. also *Hymn.* V. 2 ἀναγώγιον ἀψάμενοι πῦρ, and *Th. Pl.* III. i. 118.
Neither of the renderings in the MSS. of W can represent συνεκπυροῦσα. Possibly he read συνεκπερατοῦσα ('conterminans'); but it
seems more likely that the Latin text is corrupt in all MSS.

26. εἴη, 28. μετέχοι: for the syntax cf. Syrian. *in Metaph.* 163. 28
εἰ . . . δημιουργοίη, τὴν αἰτίαν ἔχει.

PROP. 130. This apparently self-contradictory proposition is explained by the double sense in which Neoplatonism can speak of
'immanence'—as immanence of the cause in the effect, or as
immanence of the effect in the cause. The former arises by procession, and is most strikingly exemplified in the world of γένεσις:
the soul is more definitely 'in' the body, i.e. conditioned by it, than
intelligence is 'in' the soul. The latter arises by reversion, and is
characteristic of οὐσία: body cannot identify itself fully with soul
in the manner in which soul can identify itself with intelligence.[1]
Thus the lower causes are in one sense closer to their effects than
the higher, as being more readily affected by them; in another sense
more remote, as being less accessible to them by way of reversion.
In so far as the principles which compose it are considered as causes,
the entire world-order, extending from the One down to Matter,
appears as a convergent series, each successive cause being less able
to remain distinct from its effect; in so far as they are considered as
effects, it appears as a divergent series, each successive effect being
less able to identify itself with its cause. This doctrine, like so

[1] This concrete instance, viz. the relations obtaining between σῶμα, ψυχή and
νοῦς, seems to be the source of the general 'law'. The rest is a theoretical construction by analogy in the usual Neoplatonic manner. Cf. Porph. ἀφ. xxx.

much else in Pr., is but the hardening into an explicit law of what
is implicit in Plotinus. For the second half of it cf. Iamb. *de myst.*
59. 4 ff., and Pr. *in Tim.* I. 306. 9, where it is introduced in a report
of Amelius' views.

6. ὅσῳ δ᾽ ἂν ὑφειμένον . . . τοσούτῳ μᾶλλόν ἐστι . . . συμφυέστερον.
One is tempted to transpose μᾶλλον into the relative clause ; but
ὑφειμένον has itself a comparative force, and for μᾶλλον συμφυέστερον
cf. prop. 25, l. 35 n.

PROP. 131 applies to the henads the principle of prop. 18. This
argument is used by Pr. against some Platonists who denied knowledge to the gods but made them the causes of knowledge in others
(*in Parm.* 945. 8) ; and in general it enables him to ascribe to the
gods κατ᾽ αἰτίαν all the characters of the intelligible world. Syrianus
says similarly of the Forms that they are the first objects of their own
activity, *in Metaph.* 118. 8.

17. διότι δὴ κτλ. As the presence of δή suggests, διότι here
apparently = διό, ' wherefore '.

21. αὐτάρκες μόνον. μόνον is more likely to have been corrupted
to μέν (through the influence of the succeeding δέ) than *vice versa*.

26. ὧν δίδωσι. The genitive is the *lectio difficilior*, and cf.
supra, l. 16.

PROP. 132. The τάξεις of this proposition are not, like those of
prop. 130, vertical συστοιχίαι proceeding from a henad, but portions
of διακοσμήσεις, transverse strata or cross-sections of the universe.
The θεῖα γένη are the classes of henads enumerated in props. 162–5.
Cf. *Th. Pl.* VI. ii, where six orders of gods are arranged in two
triads, the last term of the higher triad being continuous with the
first term of the lower.

1. τῶν ὄντων : *comparatio compendiaria* for τῆς τῶν ὄντων ὑπάρξεως
(editors wrongly construe with ἡνῶσθαι).

5. συνάγει τὰ ἄκρα : cf. Plot. IV. iv. 23 [II. 71. 14] συνάπτον πως
τὰ ἄκρα ἀλλήλοις, of the sense organ ; Porph. ἀφ. 30. 11, &c.

PROP. 133 defines the relation of the henads to the One. This
relation is exactly parallel to that which subsists between intelligences and the Intelligence or between souls and the Soul (prop. 21).
The henads are of the same ' stuff ' as the One, and are the unfolding
of different aspects of its goodness : εἰ γὰρ ἐθέλοιμεν ἐξετάσαι, τί τὸ
ποιοῦν θεὸν νοητὸν ἢ νοερὸν ἢ ὑπερούσιον ἢ ἐγκόσμιον, οὐκ ἂν ἕτερον
οὐδὲν εὕροιμεν ἢ τἀγαθόν (*in Tim.* I. 360. 26). But though thus closely

linked to the One, they are not parts or attributes of it : the One has no parts, and but one attribute, goodness. Such an attempt to explain away polytheism at the expense of the unity of the supreme principle is definitely rejected by Pr., *in Parm.* 1066. 22 ff. For his Christian imitators it was naturally the only course, and they took it (see note on props. 151–9) ; but the scholastic doctrine that a plurality of attributes is somehow consistent with God's absolute unity seems to me more obscure and more self-contradictory than the pagan theory from which it derives.

16. οὗ τὴν ἑνιαίαν αἰτίαν τὸ πρῶτον προεστήσατο. The original reading of M cannot be fully deciphered, but it certainly had either οὗ or οὐ. The former is implied by W's version and is probably sound : misread as οὐ, it would account for the alteration to τὴν δέ in the other two families. On προεστήσατο see prop. 127, l. 31 n.

PROP. 134. The notion of a secondary and subordinate providence is a natural corollary to the wide extension of the term θεός (props. 128–9 n.), and was generally current in the Hellenistic world.[1] Pr. associates it especially with the Intelligence, perhaps because it serves to explain how the causal activity of intelligence can be said (as prop. 57 requires) to extend further down the scale of being than that of soul—by exercising providence it 'communicates itself to all things *qua* god', although it is not a henad. Cf. also *in Parm.* 967. 18, where authority for the doctrine is found in the *Laws* : *ibid.* 1047. 16 τῷ ἑαυτοῦ μὴ νῷ θεός ἐστιν ὁ νοῦς, καὶ τῷ ἑαυτοῦ μὴ θεῷ νοῦς ἐστιν ὁ ἐν αὐτῷ θεός: *dec. dub.* 142. 28 ff.

24. ὁ νοῦς . . . εἰς ταὐτὸν ἔρχεται τοῖς νοητοῖς: cf. prop. 167.

PROPS. 135, 136. By an exception to the general principle of prop. 62, that the lower order is always more numerous than the higher, the ὄντα (i.e. intelligible Forms prior to νοῦς) are identical in number with the henads, and there is a one-one correspondence throughout the two series. This looks like a survival from the original Neopythagorean conception of the henads (see above, p. 258), according to which they *were* the Forms or perhaps rather the 'unities' or πέρας-elements within the Forms. Pr. makes them transcend the Forms, but they are still related to these as their seminal sources (cf. *in Parm.* 811. 2 ff.).

[1] See [Plut.] *de fato*, c. 9, Apul. *de dogmate Plat.* I. 12, Nemes. *Nat. Hom.* c. 44, p. 167 f., and other passages quoted by Gercke in *Rhein. Mus.* N. F. 41 (1886), 285 f. Gercke is wrong in saying that developed Neoplatonism ' completely rejected this absurd idea '. Plotinus distinguishes πρόνοια ἡ ἄνωθεν from ἡ ἀπὸ τῆς ἄνω (III. iii. 4).

3. **τὰ μετέχοντα γένη τῶν ὄντων.** Each henad is participated directly by one '(real-)existent' or Form, indirectly by one *genus* of existents ', i.e. by whatever shares in or derives from the Form in question. The scope of the term γένη τῶν ὄντων here and in the next prop. clearly cannot be restricted to the logical categories. On the other hand these γένη are quite distinct from the γένη of props. 144, 145, which are the successive strata of reality or transverse series.

26. **ἡ κατ' ἀξίαν διανομή:** see prop. 122, l. 12 n.

PROP. 137 : see note on prop. 56, of which this is really an application. The intention is (1) to reconcile polytheism with Neoplatonic monism ; (2) to emphasize the continuity between the Forms and the henads, in virtue of which alone the latter are knowable.

PROP. 138. In prop. 129 the second hypostasis was treated as a unity, and we were told that the first participant in deity is νοῦς, in the wider sense of that term. In the present proposition account is taken of the triadic subdivision of the second hypostasis (see prop. 101 n.), and τὸ ὄν in the narrower sense thus appears as the first participant. That there is no further hypostasis between Being and Deity is proved in two ways : (*a*) from the fact that the Forms are, in the language of the *Philebus*, the first μικτόν, the first explicit manifestation of that duality of Limit and the Infinite which is implicit in the first hypostasis ; (*b*) from the fact that Being is, after Unity, the widest category.

9. **εἰ γὰρ . . . 10. εἴπερ.** The reading of the first family, εἰ γε . . . εἰ γάρ, yields a tolerable sense if we point after δέδεικται instead of after ἀκρότατον τὸ ὄν. But (1) the reference of τούτων in l. 11 is then obscured ; (2) B's εἰ γὰρ καί in l. 10 seems to betray itself as an accidental intrusion from the preceding line—which was then in turn altered, since the repeated εἰ γάρ made no sense.

14. **τὸ ὑπερούσιον μόνον.** The reading of the MSS., τὸ ὑπερούσιον ὄν, involves a formal contradiction which Pr. avoids ; and μόνον serves the argument better than the alternative remedies of deleting ὄν or reading ἕν. The twofold repetition of the syllable ον would make corruption easy.

19. **τὸ μὴ ὂν ὡς κρεῖττον τοῦ ὄντος :** in distinction from τὸ μὴ ὂν ὡς χεῖρον τοῦ ὄντος, which is Matter or στέρησις or passive potentiality. Cf. *in Parm.* 999. 19 ff.

PROP. 139. The loose-traditional use. of the terms θεός and θεῖον (props. 128-9 n.) is here justified (*a*) from the theory of secondary

COMMENTARY 273

providences (cf. props. 134, 141), (*b*) from the Iamblichean πάντα ἐν πᾶσιν principle (cf. prop. 103 n.) : the structure of each transverse stratum mirrors that of reality as a whole, and its first members may therefore be called 'gods'.

24. σώματα θεῖα εἶναί φαμεν. Plato had spoken of the stars as θεῖα γεννητά (*Rep.* 546 B), and from Aristotle onwards they are regularly referred to as τὰ θεῖα σώματα. Pr. denounces with unwonted passion the blind impiety of those who deny them to be divine, *in Crat.* cxxv. He considers them to be composed, not of the Aristotelian πέμπτον σῶμα (a theory which orthodox Platonists regarded as 'barbaric'), but of the four elements in a state of exceptional purity, *in Tim.* II. 42. 9 ff.: in the *Th. Pl.* he ascribes to them an ἄυλος φύσις (I. xix. 51). He also believes in θεῖα σώματα in the sense of material objects possessing magical properties (prop. 145).

25. ἀνεῖται: like ἀνήρτηται, ἀνάγεται, but with the additional idea of dedication. Cf. *Th. Pl.* III. xix. 153 τὸ φαινόμενον ὕδωρ . . . ταῖς ζωογόνοις ἀνεῖται δυνάμεσι, and Diehl's index to *in Tim.*, *s.v.*

PROP. 140. The 'divine presence' spoken of in this and the following propositions covers, I think, a variety of phenomena,[1] ranging from the ecstasy described by Plotinus to the manifestation of occult virtues in stones and herbs (cf. the passages quoted on props. 39 and 145). Pr.'s conception of its *modus operandi* reflects a general Hellenistic tradition which is common to pagan, Jewish, and (through Neoplatonism) Christian writers. The divine grace is as universal and as constant as the sunlight which is its traditional symbol ; but its consummation in any particular case is conditioned by the fitness of the recipient, who can receive only in the measure of his capacity. In this way it is sought to reconcile the theory of divine omnipresence with the existence of degrees of value (cf. prop. 98 n.). Cf. *Sophia Sal.* xii. 16 τοὺς ἀξίους αὐτῆς αὐτὴ (ἡ σοφία) περιέρχεται ζητοῦσα : Philo *de opif. mundi* 6, § 23 οὐ πρὸς τὸ μέγεθος εὐεργετεῖ (ὁ θεός) τῶν ἑαυτοῦ χαρίτων—ἀπερίγραφοι γὰρ αὐταί γε καὶ ἀτελεύτητοι· πρὸς δὲ τὰς τῶν εὐεργετουμένων δυνάμεις· οὐ γὰρ ὡς πέφυκεν ὁ θεὸς εὖ ποιεῖν, οὕτως καὶ τὸ γινόμενον εὖ πάσχειν : *Corp. Herm.* X. 4 ἐκλάμπει (ἡ τοῦ ἀγαθοῦ θέα) ἐπὶ τοσοῦτον, ἐφ' ὅσον δύναται ὁ δυνάμενος δέξασθαι τὴν ἐπεισροὴν τῆς νοητῆς λαμπηδόνος : Plutarch *de.gen. Socr.* 20, 589 B : Plot. VI. v. 11 *fin.*, VI. ix. 8 (II. 520. 2) : Porph. ἀφ. 26. 9 :

---

[1] Including actual apparitions of the gods. Both Pr. (*in Remp.* I. 39. 8) and Plot. (VI. v. 12 *fin.*) use the principle of ἐπιτηδειότης to explain why such apparitions are often seen by only one of a number of persons present—the others are, as modern spiritists would say, not sufficiently 'psychic'.

Iamb. *de myst.* 28. 18 : Sallust. 28. 10: Syrian. *in Metaph.* 109. 20 ff.: Basil *Tract. de Spiritu Sancto* IX. 22 (*P. G.* xxxii. 109 A) ὅσον αὐτὰ πέφυκεν (τὰ ὄντα μετέχει τοῦ θείου), οὐχ ὅσον ἐκεῖνο δύναται : ps.-Dion. *Div. Nom.* 3. 1: Erigena 905 B Migne. This is a favourite doctrine of the Cambridge Platonists, e.g. Benjamin Whichcote, *Sermons,* vol. iii, p. 102, ' It is the incapacity of the subject, where God is not . . . for God doth not withdraw Himself from us, unless we first leave Him : the distance is occasioned through our unnatural use of ourselves.'

9. οὔτε τότε παραγενόμεναι οὔτε πρότερον ἀπούσαι : cf. Plot. VI. v. 12 (II. 397. 29) οὐδ᾽ ἦλθεν, ἵνα παρῇ, ἀλλὰ σὺ ἀπῆλθες ὅτε οὐ πάρεστιν. εἰ δ᾽ ἀπῆλθες, οὐκ ἀπ᾽ αὐτοῦ—αὐτὸ γὰρ πάρεστιν—οὐδέ ποι ἀπῆλθες, ἀλλὰ παρὼν ἐπὶ τὰ ἐναντία ἐστράφης : Porph. πρὸς Γαῦρον 50. 21 Kalbfleisch : Pr. *dec. dub.* 94. 29 ff.

PROP. **141.** On the general notion of grades of providence see prop. 134 n. It is not very clear whether the συντεταγμένη πρόνοια is a *co-ordinate* providence, i.e. one exercised by the higher members of a transverse series towards the lower of the same series, e.g. by the general Soul towards particular souls ; or an *immanent* providence like that which the soul exercises towards the body. The use of the word συστοιχία in l. 23 is in favour of the latter view, which might be supported from *in Alc.* 372. 2 ff. τὸ γὰρ . . . προνοεῖν τῶν ἀτελεστέρων ὑπάρχει καὶ ψυχαῖς ὡς ψυχαῖς, ἐπεὶ καὶ ἡ κάθοδος αὐταῖς διὰ τὴν πρόνοιαν τῶν ἐν γενέσει πραγμάτων (cf. Plato, *Phaedr.* 246 B) ; but the other way of taking it enables us to give διακόσμησις (l. 23) its usual meaning of *transverse* series, and fits well with prop. 139, l. 26 f. ἵνα ἐν πάσῃ τάξει τὰ τοῖς θεοῖς ἀναλογοῦντα συνεκτικὰ καὶ σωστικὰ τῶν δευτέρων ὑπάρχῃ. In either case this proposition represents one more attempt to reconcile with divine transcendence the doctrine of an active providence. Cf. Erigena's theory of the twofold character of divine goodness : ' divina bonitas super omnia considerata dicitur non esse et omnino nihil est ; in omnibus vero et est et dicitur esse, quoniam totius universitatis essentia est ' (681 D Migne).

19. πᾶσα πρόνοια θείων. This reading seems to be required if the following τὰ μὲν . . . τὰ δέ are to be intelligible ; moreover, it is not easy to see how the *henads* can exercise a συντεταγμένη πρόνοια.

22. ὑπερήπλωται : see prop. 93, l. 6 n.

26. δύνανται. For the plural verb with neuter plural subject cf. props. 144, l. 23 ; 176, l. 3 ; 184, l. 28 (in the last passage Q omits the verb, in the others it offers the singular). Diehl notes only two examples of this construction in the *in Tim.,* but it is frequent

(if our MSS. can be trusted) in the *in Crat.* and in Hermeias' commentary on the *Phaedrus.*

PROP. 142 : see note on prop. 140.   The topic is elaborated in the *Parmenides* commentary, 842. 15 ff.

2. τούτοις.   This and the following ταῦτα refer to τὸ μετέχον, the change of number being dictated by convenience.   τοῖς οὖσιν, which seems to have stood originally in M, looks like a gloss or a conjecture : it is not recognized by W.

PROP. 143. Pr., like his master Syrianus (*in Metaph.* 8. 26, 185. 19 ff.), follows Plotinus in stressing the privative character of Evil, though he jibs at the Plotinian identification of Evil with Matter.[1] For the comparison of sin to a cloud which cuts us off from the sunlight cf. Iamb. *de myst.* 43. 5 αὐτοὶ ἑαυτοὺς ἀποστρέψαντες, ὥσπερ ἐν μεσημβρίᾳ φωτὸς κατακαλυψάμενοι, σκότος ἑαυτοῖς ἐπηγάγομεν καὶ ἀπεστερήσαμεν ἑαυτοὺς τῆς τῶν θεῶν ἀγαθῆς δόσεως, and Sallust. 26. 26 ff. It is interesting that Seneca uses the same comparison for other forms of evil (' hoc adversus virtutem possunt calamitates et damna et iniuriae, quod adversus solem potest nebula ', *Ep.* 92. 18).   For the flight of evil spirits before the divine light, cf. Celsus *ap.* Origen. *adv. Cels.* I. 60 ἐὰν δὲ θειοτέρα τις ἐπιφάνεια γένηται, καθαιροῦνται αἱ τῶν δαιμόνων ἐνέργειαι μὴ ἀντιβλέψαι δυνάμεναι τῷ τῆς θειότητος φωτί, and Iamb. *de myst.* 130. 8 ff.*.

14. ἐλλείψεως.   The unfortunate misreading ἐλλάμψεως has given rise to further corruptions (see crit. nn.) ; Cr. conjectured ἐκλείψεως, but failed to restore the rest of the passage.   The true text is preserved in BCD.

PROP. 144 : see note on props. 135-6. The thought is more fully developed in a striking passage of the *Timaeus* commentary, I. 209. 13 ff.   Pr. there affirms that in a sense everything, even Matter, is *directly* dependent upon the gods (by the principle of prop. 56), and suggests that the distinctness of the individual exists only for himself and not for the gods.

30. ἔρημον γενόμενον παντελῶς.   Edd. and translators take παντελῶς with ὑπεξίσταται, but cf. prop. 149, l. 25 παντελῶς ἔρημον.   For the doctrine compare [Arist.] *de mundo* 6, § 2 οὐδεμία δὲ φύσις αὐτὴ καθ' ἑαυτήν ἐστιν αὐτάρκης, ἐρημωθεῖσα τῆς ἐκ τούτου (sc. τοῦ θεοῦ) σωτηρίας.

PROP. 145 makes it clear that one purpose of the preceding

[1] For a detailed account of Pr.'s view see Schröder, *Plotins Abhandlung* Πόθεν τὰ κακά; 195 ff. and Whittaker[2], 234. . Apart from the *de mal. subsist.* the most important passages are *in Tim.* I. 373 ff., *in Parm.* 829 ff., and *Th. Pl.* I. xviii. 45 ff.

propositions is to provide a philosophical basis for the practice of theurgy.[1] The 'purgative' and other virtues ascribed to vegetables and minerals are not medical but magical, as appears from *in Tim.* I. III. 9 ff., *in Alc.* 377. 39 ff., and especially the newly discovered fragment περὶ τῆς καθ᾽ Ἕλληνας ἱερατικῆς τέχνης (*C. M. A. G.* VI. 148 ff.), where we are told that a single herb or stone may suffice to put us in contact with some mode of the divine activity—ἀπόχρη γὰρ πρὸς μὲν αὐτοφάνειαν τὸ κνέωρον, πρὸς δὲ φυλακὴν δάφνη, ῥάμνος, σκύλλα, κουράλιον, ἀδάμας καὶ ἴασπις, πρὸς δὲ πρόγνωσιν ἢ τοῦ ἀσπάλακος καρδία, πρὸς δὲ καθάρσεις τὸ θεῖον καὶ τὸ θαλάττιον ὕδωρ. This doctrine is Iamblichean (cf. *de myst.* 233. 10 ff.), and is borrowed, as Hopfner has shown, from Egyptian magic:[2] lists of symbolic stones, plants, animals, &c., are of frequent occurrence in the magical papyri, and several names[3] are common to Pr. and the papyri.—Pr. also uses the principle of this proposition to account for the existence of oracular sites and holy places (*in Tim.* III. 140. 19 ff.), and to justify astral determinism (*ibid.* 262. 6 ff.).

20. **μεστὰ δὲ πάντα θεῶν.** Cf. Arist. *de an.* 411 a 7 Θαλῆς ᾠήθη πάντα πλήρη θεῶν εἶναι: Plato, *Legg.* X. 899 B θεῶν εἶναι πλήρη πάντα. This venerable maxim is (as we might expect) a favourite with the later Stoics (e.g. Epict. *Diss.* III. xiii. 15, M.Aur. iii. 3). But the Platonizing author of the *de mundo* is careful to explain that it must be understood as referring to the power and not to the essence of the gods (6, § 3); and Pr., of course, understands it in this way (*in Tim.* III. 4. 23 ff.). Interpreting it in the light of the doctrine of σειραί, Pr. holds that each of the gods is present both θείως and δαιμονίως in each of the four elements, ἵνα πάντα ᾖ πανταχοῦ παντοίως (*ibid.* 171. 8). This quasi-pantheistic language is echoed by ps.-Dion. (e.g. *Eccl. Hier.* 1. 4), who transmitted it in turn to Erigena.[4]

PROP. 146. An application of props. 31 and 33, where see notes.

[1] Theurgy is nowhere explicitly referred to in the *El. Th.*; but compare prop. 39 n. and Introd., pp. xvii, xxii f., also Bidez, *Vie de Julien*, 77 f.

[2] One is reminded also of the popular books on the occult 'sympathies and antipathies' of animals, vegetables, and minerals which were current in the Hellenistic world from the second century B.C. onwards (cf. M. Wellmann, *Die Φυσικά des Bolos Demokritos* [Abh. Preuss. Akad. 1928]) But in these the 'sympathy' was usually an affinity between two physical organisms or objects, and their authors' interest was less often magico-religious than therapeutic or quasi-scientific.

[3] Of the stones mentioned in the fragment, σεληνίτης (*op. cit.* 149. 25), ἀδάμας and ἴασπις all occur in papyri (cf. Abt, *Apologie des Apuleius*, 190), as does the plant ἡλιοτρόπιον (*ibid.* 148. 10: cf. *Pap. Gr. Mag.* I. 1. 64). Jasper and coral are among the magic 'stones' dealt with in the 'Orphic' *Lithica* (267 ff., 510 ff.).

[4] Cf. Dörries, *Erigena u. der Neuplatonismus*, 40. D. fails to recognize that the 'pantheistic' phraseology often used by Erigena, no less than his assertions elsewhere of divine transcendence, has its ultimate source in Neoplatonism.

Similarly ps.-Dion., *Div. Nom.* 4. 14, τὸ ἀτελεύτητον ἑαυτοῦ καὶ ἄναρχον
ὁ θεῖος ἔρως ἐνδείκνυται διαφερόντως, ὥσπερ τις ἀΐδιος κύκλος . . . προιὼν
ἀεὶ καὶ μένων καὶ ἀποκαθιστάμενος.

Prop. **147** applies to the successive orders of gods the principle
laid down in prop. 112 to explain the continuity of the successive
strata of reality. Cf. *Th. Pl.* II. (vii.) 98, where Pr. extracts from
the passage about the sun in *Rep.* VI. the doctrine that the
monad or first term of the mundane order of gods, viz. the sun, is
supra-mundane; similarly the monad of the supra-mundane order
is intellectual, and that of the intellectual intelligible, while the
monad of the intelligible order is the One which is beyond intelligence.

Prop. **148** emphasizes the internal unity of the different orders of
gods, as the previous proposition did their continuity. The three
modes or aspects of unity which are here distinguished correspond
to the three types of whole and the three modes of subsistence
described in props. 67 and 65 respectively. It is on this ground that
Pr. justifies the triadic grouping of gods which fills so many pages of
the *Th. Pl.* and is mimicked in the hierarchy of ps.-Dion.

8. ἡ δὲ μεσότης . . . συνδεῖ . . . διαπορθμεύουσα : a reminiscence of
Plato, *Symp.* 202 E.

Prop. **149.** See notes on props. 61-2, prop. 86, and prop. 94.

Prop. **150.** The divine order is an order of universality, and the
lower henads 'proceed from' the higher as specific from generic
Forms; their functions are included in the functions of the higher
henads but do not exhaust them. This schematism is, of course,
quite foreign to the religious notions of the Greeks or any other
people; it marks the doctrine of henads as primarily an artificial
device for bridging, or concealing, the gulf which separates the One
from the world of Forms. On the general conception of the effect
as 'pre-embraced' in the cause see notes on props. 7 and 65.

16. καὶ γάρ seems to introduce an alternative demonstration (cf.
the use of ἐπεὶ καί in prop. 69, l. 33, prop. 80, l. 5).

οὕτως, if sound, qualifies ἄπειρον and is intended to exclude the
numerical infinity which is denied of the henads in the preceding
proposition.

21. ἦν γὰρ ἂν ἐκεῖνα περίληπτά κτλ. Q has preserved or restored
what is clearly the true reading; it has also been introduced conjecturally in some of the later copies of W. In the next line the
reading of BCD is a clumsy attempt to make sense of ἀπερίληπτα.

PROPS. 151-9 contain Pr.'s doctrine of the divine attributes, a doctrine which is among the most arid and formalistic parts of his system, but has nevertheless some historical importance. These attributes are not (as Professor Taylor seems to suggest) themselves henads : it is made clear in the *Th. Pl.* that each of them appears at successive levels in successive groups of henads (κατὰ πάσας τὰς θείας διακοσμήσεις, prop. 151, l. 27), so that there is, for example, a πατρικὸν αἴτιον among the 'intelligible' gods, another among the 'intellective', and so forth ; and even within a particular group each attribute may be represented by several 'gods' (e.g. in the intellective group τὸ πατρικόν consists of the triad Cronos—Rhea—Zeus, *Th. Pl.* V. ii–iii). The doctrine does, however, reflect the conception of the gods as 'functions of a first cause', which was increasingly current among educated pagans under the later empire,[1] although it was rejected by strict Plotinians as inconsistent with the pure unity of the One. Pr., attempting a compromise between the looser and the stricter view, conceives the causative potency which exists in the seminal unity of the One as progressively explicated in the successive grades of deity ; and he further conceives this explication as governed by the same triadic law which appears in the development of the later hypostases. τὸ πατρικόν and τὸ δημιουργικόν are represented as the sources of μονή (ὕπαρξις), respectively in its more generic and its more specific form ; τὸ γεννητικόν and τὸ ζωογόνον as respectively the sources of generic and specific πρόοδος (δύναμις) ; τὸ τελεσιουργόν and τὸ ἀναγωγόν as the sources of generic and specific ἐπιστροφή. Of these three pairs, the first belongs to the συστοιχία of πέρας and the second to that of ἀπειρία (*in Tim.* I. 441. 3 ff.) ; the third is presumably referable to τὸ μικτόν. There remain τὸ φρουρητικόν and its specific form τὸ καθαρτικόν, which seem to fall outside this schematism, but may perhaps be thought of as maintaining in being the triads created by the other six 'causes'.[2] The scheme will then be as follows :—

περατοειδῆ (unitary or static causes)	ἀπειροειδῆ (processive or dynamic causes)	μικτά (conversive causes)	(conservative causes ?)
generic form τὸ πατρικόν	τὸ γεννητικόν	τὸ τελεσιουργόν	τὸ φρουρητικόν
specific form τὸ δημιουργικόν	τὸ ζωογόνον	τὸ ἀναγωγόν	τὸ καθαρτικόν

[1] Cf. Nock, *Sallustius*, p. xlii ; and *supra*, p. 259 f.
[2] From prop. 158 it is clear that τὸ καθαρτικόν is the lowest of the eight.—The fourfold division of functions is older than Pr. His four pairs correspond to the

The names of these attributes are derived partly from Plato but mainly from the theosophical tradition of the *Chaldaean Oracles* and similar works. Several of them reappear as attributes of God in ps.-Dion., e.g. *Cael. Hier.* 7. 3 : he regards them as existing seminally within the divine unity, and protests against the opinion of those who made them θεοὺς τῶν ὄντων καὶ δημιουργούς (*Div. Nom.* 11. 6). The same view is taken by Nicolaus (Ἀνάπτ., p. 178, quoting the authority of ps.-Dion.) ; and by Psellus, who speaks of ἥ τε φρουρητικὴ ἥ τε ζωογόνος ἥ τε ἀναγωγική (δύναμις τοῦ θεοῦ), *de omnif. doct.* 15. In the West also it seems likely that the scholastic teaching on the divine attributes owes something to Proclus.

PROP. 151. πατήρ as an epithet of God is of constant recurrence in Hellenistic religious literature.[1] Plato called his demiurge ποιη-τὴν καὶ πατέρα τοῦδε τοῦ παντός (*Tim.* 28 C) ; but Pr. distinguishes the paternal function as higher than the creative (though lower than the ultimate causality of the One). In this he is following the *Chaldaean Oracles* (p. 25, Kroll), which distinguishes the πατήρ or πατρικὸς νοῦς from the lower τεχνίτης. According to *Th. Pl.* V. xvi. 276 f. the two differ not only (as here) in degree of generality but also in their *modus operandi* : τὸ πατρικόν, as exemplified in the παράδειγμα, produces αὐτῷ τῷ εἶναι, whereas the demiurge, who is predominantly a maker, produces τῷ ἐνεργεῖν. On the grades of τὸ πατρικόν compare *in Crat.* xcviii.

PROP. 152. τὸ γεννητικόν is the most generalized expression for the principle of emanation which governs the πρόοδος (prop. 25). It is noteworthy that by Proclus it is definitely regarded as a *good* function : see prop. 206 n.

22. ἀεννάους. I retain the spelling of the MSS., which is also found in the MSS. of *in Crat.* and some MSS. of *in Tim.*, and often elsewhere, e.g. in Porphyry's ἀφορμαί and the *Theologumena Arithmeticae.*

PROP. 153. τὸ τέλειον, which is one of the three marks of the Good in Plato's *Philebus* (20 D), is treated by Pr. as the causal principle of ἐπιστροφή, doubtless under the influence of the mystical associations of τελετή and kindred words. Certain τελεταρχαί having a τελεστικὴ ἰδιότης appear to have been mentioned in the *Chaldaean*

four triads of gods in Sallust. vi, οἱ ποιοῦντες, οἱ ψυχοῦντες, οἱ ἁρμόζοντες, and οἱ φρουροῦντες.
[1] A selection of examples will be found in J. Kroll, *Lehren des Hermes*[1], 31 f.

Oracles (Damasc. II. 125. 8, &c.).   Cf. also *Th. Pl.* I. xxiii. 58 ; and Plot. V. ix. 4 δεῖ τὰ πρῶτα ἐνεργείᾳ τίθεσθαι καὶ ἀπροσδεᾶ καὶ τέλεια· τὰ δὲ ὕστερα ἀπ᾽ ἐκείνων, τελειούμενα δὲ παρ᾽ αὐτῶν τῶν γεγεννηκότων δίκην πατέρων τελειούντων, ἃ κατ᾽ ἀρχὰς ἀτελῆ ἐγέννησαν.

PROP. 154. For φρουρεῖν (syn. συνέχειν, prop. 25, l. 2) cf. Damasc. II. 125. 15 ff., who quotes from the *Chaldaean Oracles* the lines

> φρουρεῖν αὖ πρηστῆρσιν ἑοῖς ἀκρότητας ἔδωκεν
> ἐγκεράσας ἀλκῆς ἴδιον μένος ἐν συνοχεῦσιν.

τὸ φρουρητικόν is identified by Pr. (*Th. Pl.* 205) with the Adrasteia of *Phaedr.* 248 C ; or with Uranus (*ibid.* 214-15).

10. ἀντεχόμενον. This reading is supported by *Th. Pl.* II. (ix). 105 (τὰ μεταξὺ) τῶν μὲν ὑπερεχόντων ὡς ἐφετῶν λιπαρῶς ἀντέχεται (cf. also V. xxxviii. 330).

PROP. 155. τὸ ζωογόνον is the especial attribute of Rhea-Cybele (Cornutus *Theol.* 6, p. 6. 7 Lang ; Sallust. 8. 3 ; Pr. *Th. Pl.* V. xi) ; it is also an epithet of Apollo-Helios (*Anth. Pal.* ix. 525 ; *Pap. Gr. Mag.* VII, l. 530).   Pr. makes it a subordinate form of τὸ γεννητικόν, connecting it with the charge of Plato's demiurge to the younger gods, τρέπεσθε κατὰ φύσιν ὑμεῖς εἰς τὴν τῶν ζῴων δημιουργίαν (*Tim.* 41 C, cf. *in Tim.* III. 227. 21).   Iamb. draws a similar distinction between the δυνάμεις γόνιμοι of the daemons and the δυνάμεις ζωοποιοί of the heroes (*de myst.* II. 1).   A 'zoogonic triad' seems to have been mentioned in the *Chaldaean Oracles* (Pr. *in Tim.* II. 107. 6 ; Psellus, *Hypotyposis* §§ 9, 11, 16, Kroll).

PROP. 156. According to *Th. Pl.* τὸ καθαρτικόν is especially associated with Κρόνος (explained as = καθαρὸς νοῦς, Plato *Crat.* 396 B) and with the mysterious triad of ἄχραντοι θεοί which Pr. elicited from the *Chaldaean Oracles*.   It is the fountain-head of the 'purificatory' virtues which are so prominent in the later Neoplatonist ethic.[1]   Pr., as his biographer tells us (*vit. Proc.* 18), devoted especial attention both to these and to the 'Chaldaean', Orphic and other ritual purifications, including sea bathing, which he practised 'unshrinkingly' at least once a month to an advanced age.

3. πόθεν . . . ἕξει τήν. These words were accidentally omitted in the archetype of the first family.   In BCD the sense has been

---

[1] Cf. Plot. I. ii. 3 ff.; Iamb. *ap.* Stob. I. xlix. 65 (59 H.); and O. Schissel v. Fleschenberg, *Marinos von Neapolis und die Neuplatonischen Tugendgrade*, *passim*.

mended by the insertion of κατ' before αἰτίαν; but it would seem
that in some MS. of this family the missing words were reinserted in
the margin, since in O and the *editio princeps*, in which the tradition
of M ²⁻³ is modified by further corrections from the first family,
they have got into the wrong place in the text.

PROP. 157 : see note on prop. 151.

PROP. 158. τὸ ἀναγωγόν is a character of Helios (ψυχῶν ἀναγωγεύς
Pr. *Hymn.* 1. 34, cf. Julian *Or.* iv. 152 A); of the Muses (*Hymn.* 2.
1); and of the Ἔρωτες (*ibid.* 4. 5). Iamb. too speaks of θεοὶ ἀναγωγοί
(*de myst.* VIII. 8), but he seems to make τὸ ἀναγωγόν a particular
grade of τὸ ἀποκαθαρτικόν (*ibid.* II. 5).

23. ὅλων = πάντων, as often in Pr. and Syrianus.

PROP. 159. The cosmogonic function of πέρας and ἀπειρία has
been dealt with in the note on props. 89–92. It is somewhat sur-
prising that the henads, which are ἑνικώταται and ἁπλούσταται (prop.
127), should be infected by this radical duality : πῶς σύνθετοι οἱ θεοί;
asks Nicolaus à propos of the present passage, and I confess I do
not know the answer.—The τάξεις or γένη of this proposition seem
to be not those defined in props. 162–5, but the classes of gods
grouped according to attribute : the πατρικοὶ θεοί are περατοειδεῖς, the
γεννητικοί are ἀπειροειδεῖς, and so forth.

PROPS. 160, 161. In the next group of propositions Pr. proceeds
to complete his account of the henads by classifying them according
to the principles in which they are immanent. But it is necessary
for him first to define what he means by 'true Being' or 'the
Intelligible', in which alone the highest class of henads is present,
and what he means by 'primal' or 'unparticipated' Intelligence, in
which henads of the second order express themselves. For Plotinus
Being and Intelligence had been co-ordinate and only logically distinguishable ; for Pr. all Intelligence is Being, but not all Being is
Intelligence (props. 101–2 n.). The Being which is not Intelligence
is in prop. 161 distinguished as τὸ ὄντως ὄν :¹ it is called 'intelligible'
not in the Plotinian sense as the content of the Intelligence, but as
the transcendent (ἀμέθεκτος) source of that content. On the relation
between intelligence and its objects see further prop. 167 n.

20. ὑπ' αὐτοῦ μετεχόμενον : apparently in the sense of *giving rise to*

¹ Elsewhere, however, this expression is used to include the participated Being
of ζωή and νοῦς, e.g. in prop. 88.

an immanent οὐσία. It is called ἀμέθεκτον just below, since it is not directly immanent. Cf. prop. 23 n.

PROPS. 162–5. The scheme of 'participation' implied in these propositions is as follows :

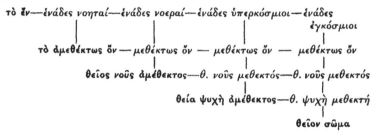

A still more elaborate scheme is given in the *Th. Pl.*, III. (vi). 131, where an additional class of gods, the ἑνάδες νοηταὶ καὶ νοεραί, is interpolated between the νοηταί and the νοεραί to correspond with the existence of ζωή as a distinct principle intermediate between τὸ ὄν and νοῦς. These 'intellective-intelligible' gods appear also in the commentaries on the *Timaeus, Parmenides* and *Cratylus*, and seem to have been mentioned in the lost commentary on the *Phaedrus* (*in Parm.* 949. 38): their absence from the *El. Th.* is perhaps a reason for ascribing to it a relatively early date. Another refinement which is missing from *El. Th.* is the subdivision of the supra-mundane class into ἀρχικοί or ἀφομοιωματικοὶ θεοί and ἀπόλυτοι θεοί (*Th. Pl.* VI *passim*, also *in Tim.*, *in Parm.* and *in Crat.*), giving in all six[1] classes of gods, which are arranged in two triads (*Th. Pl.* VI. ii.).

It is not easy to reconcile either classification with Pr.'s general account of the henads. We have been told that for each henad there is a particular real-existent and for each real-existent a particular henad (prop. 135): how, then, can a *group* of henads be participated by τὸ ἀμεθέκτως ὄν or by the unparticipated Intelligence or Soul, which should (by prop. 21) be single principles? Is not this, as Nicolaus puts it (p. 181), a case of πλῆθος πρὸ τοῦ ἑνός? Again, it seems perverse to call the highest class of gods νοητοί after we have been told that nothing divine is νοητόν (prop. 123, l. 32 f.) ; and to speak of some gods as 'above' and of others as 'within' the world-order, when we know from prop. 98 that all gods are in fact every-where and nowhere. Pr.'s defence on these latter counts is that

---

[1] On the significance of the hexad in such classifications see Bidez, *C.M.A.G.* VI. 100.

such descriptions are only applicable to the gods κατ' αἰτίαν, from the analogy of their participants ; but the truth seems to be that he is trying to dovetail into his system categories which were older than the transcendence theology and inconsistent with it, but were too deeply rooted in tradition and current usage to be easily ignored. Plato himself (*Tim.* 40 D) had spoken of the stars as θεοὶ ὁρατοὶ καὶ γεννητοί, and in Hellenistic times the belief in such gods was wide-spread.[1]   Hence two antitheses were early established in popular thought : the first between the astral divinities as 'sensible' gods and a higher class of 'intelligible' gods :[2] the other between the astral gods as οὐράνιοι or ἐγκόσμιοι and a higher god or gods who are ὑπερουράνιοι or ὑπερκόσμιοι.[3]   Three of Pr.'s classes were thus given in the tradition ; but they could be accommodated to the 'scientific' theology of post-Iamblichean Neoplatonism only by altering the meaning of the terms.   Pr.'s intelligible gods are not νοητά but the transcendent source of what is divine in νοητά ; his intra-mundane gods are not αἰσθητά but the transcendent source of what is divine in αἰσθητά ;[4] while the *Phaedrus* myth suggested that the supra-mundane order could be interpreted as the ultimate source of the soul's life (cf. Iamb. *de myst.* 271. 10).   In this way three out of the four strata of reality, intelligible Being, Soul and Body, were placed under divine patronage ; it remained—after Iamblichus had dis-tinguished the κόσμος νοερός from the κόσμος νοητός—to provide a source for the Intelligence by the introduction of νοεροὶ θεοί.   This seems to have been done in the fourth century, probably by Iam-blichus himself.[5]   Authority was found for it in the Platonic etymology of Κρόνος as καθαρὸς νοῦς (*Crat.* 396 B).

---

[1] Even the Jew Philo uses the fashionable language and speaks of θεοὶ ἐμφανεῖς τε καὶ αἰσθητοί (*de opif. mundi*, 7, § 27 [I. 8. 16 Cohn]).
[2] E.g. Max. Tyr. xi. 12 (ὁρατοί—ἀφανεῖς); Asclep. 53. 16 (sensibiles—intelligi-biles) ; Herm. *ap.* Stob. I. 293. 18 [750 H] (αἰσθητοί—νοηματικοί); Porph. *de abst.* II. 37 (ὁρατοί – ἀσώματοι), etc.
[3] E.g. Apul. *de dogm. Plat.* I. 11 (caelicolae—ultramundanus); Albin. c. xxviii (ἐπουράνιος—ὑπερουράνιος); Asclep. 65. 3. This local principle of classification suggests the school of Poseidonius (Cumont in *Arch. f. Religionswissenchaft*, IX [1906], 329) ; but cf. also the gods of the *Phaedrus* whose home is the ὑπερουράνιος τόπος. Plutarch (*def. orac.* 42, 433 D) says that the best philoso-phers refuse to identify the sun with Apollo, but regard it as ἔκγονον ἐκείνου καὶ τόκον, ὄντος ἀεὶ γιγνόμενον ἀεί.
[4] So, too, Iamblichus tries to explain away the sensible character of the intra-mundane gods (which afforded a dangerous handle to Christian controversialists), *de myst.* I. 19.
[5] In Sallustius vi *init.* we find a scheme identical in substance with that of *El. Th.*   After classifying gods as ἐγκόσμιοι or ὑπερκόσμιοι, S. proceeds to subdivide the latter class : τῶν δὲ ὑπερκοσμίων οἱ μὲν οὐσίας ποιοῦσι θεῶν (= Pr.'s νοητοί), οἱ δὲ νοῦν (= Pr.'s νοεροί), οἱ δὲ ψυχάς (= Pr.'s ὑπερκόσμιοι), καὶ διὰ τοῦτο τρεῖς ἔχουσι τάξεις, καὶ πάσας ἐν τοῖς περὶ τούτων λόγοις ἔστιν εὑρεῖν.   The reference in

17. τῆς ἀμεθέκτου πάσης ψυχῆς : εἰ μία ἡ ἀμέθεκτος ψυχή, σοφώτατε Πρόκλε, πῶς ὡς περὶ πολλῶν φῂς τὸ πάσης (Nicolaus *ad loc.*). I suspect that πάσης has been imported by a copyist from l. 22, where πᾶσα is legitimately used in reference to the ἀμέθεκτος ψυχή *plus* the μετεχόμεναι ψυχαί (cf. the diagrammatic table above).

19. ἡ ἀμέθεκτος ψυχὴ πρώτως ὑπὲρ τὸν κόσμον ἐστί. The doctrine that there is a Soul, or souls, transcending the world-order and distinguished from the World-Soul by the complete absence of any corporeal tie appears from *in Tim.* II. 105. 15 ff. and 143. 21 ff. to have been the invention of Iamblichus. But cf. also Plot. IV. iii. 4, where it is suggested that the World-Soul and the individual souls may be alike derived from an ultimate psychic unity, which is ἐφ' ἑαυτοῦ μὴ πίπτον εἰς τὸ σῶμα.

29. οὔτε γὰρ νοῦς ἄνευ ψυχῆς πάρεστί τινι τῶν ἐγκοσμίων σωμάτων : cf. Plato, *Phil.* 30 C σοφία . . . καὶ νοῦς ἄνευ ψυχῆς οὐκ ἄν ποτε γενοίσθην.

7. εἰ δύναμιν ἔχει προνοητικήν. The cautious form of expression may imply a doubt whether planetary influences are exercised by the planets themselves or only by their souls (cf. prop. 201). The reality of such influences was not doubted by Pr.: *in Tim.* III 58. 7 οἱ γὰρ καλούμενοι πλάνητες κοσμοκράτορές εἰσι καὶ ὁλικὴν εἰλήχασι δύναμιν: *Th. Pl.* VI. iv. 352. Plotinus had argued (II. iii. 7) that planetary conjunctions are merely or chiefly semantic and not causative ; but Pr. cites with seeming approval the opinion of οἱ ταῦτα δεινοί that eclipses, &c. are μεγάλων τινῶν ποιητικαὶ καὶ σημαντικαί (*in Tim.* III. 149. 16), although like Plotinus and Iamblichus he denies that the stars can be responsible for *evil* (*ibid.* 313. 13 ff.: cf. Plot. II. iii. 10, *de myst.* I. 18, Sallust. 18. 4 ff.). On planetary σειραί see prop. 204 n., and Bidez, *C. M. A. G.* VI. 143 ff.

M. *Of intelligences* (props. 166–83).

1. Classification of intelligences according to the principles which participate them (166).
2. General characters of νοῦς and the νοερὰ εἴδη (167–80).
3. Classification of participated intelligences as θεῖοι and νοεροί, with transition to souls (181–3).

PROP. 166. Corresponding to the three lowest classes of henads there are three grades of 'divine' intelligence : (*a*) the 'unpartici-

the last clause is probably to Iamblichus' lost work περὶ θεῶν. Cf. also Julian, *Or.* v. 166 A, where gods are classified as (*a*) νοητοί, (*b*) νοεροὶ καὶ δημιουργικοί, (*c*) ἐμφανεῖς.

pated' Intelligence ; (*b*) the supra-mundane intelligences, which
serve as a mean term between (*a*) and (*c*) ; (*c*) the intra-mundane
(planetary) intelligences. Cf. the table given above, p. 282. Besides
these there are intra-mundane intelligences which are not divine
(prop. 181), but are participated by daemonic and intermittently by
human souls (props. 183, 184). Iamblichus ascribes to the 'Egyptians'
(Hermetists) a slightly different classification ; καθαρόν τε νοῦν ὑπὲρ
τὸν κόσμον προτιθέασι, καὶ ἕνα ἀμέριστον ἐν ὅλῳ τῷ κόσμῳ, καὶ διῃρημένον
ἐπὶ πάσας τὰς σφαίρας ἕτερον (*de myst.* VIII. 4). An extra-mundane
and an intra-mundane Intelligence are already distinguished by
Albinus (*Didasc.* c. x), no doubt on the basis of the *Timaeus*. The
Chaldaean Oracles recognized a higher (transcendent) and a lower
(demiurgic) Intelligence. See further J. Kroll, *Lehren des Hermes*[1],
60 ff.

19. ὁ κόσμος ἔμψυχος ἅμα καὶ ἔννους ἐστί. Plato had called the
world-order ζῷον ἔμψυχον ἔννουν τε, *Tim.* 30 B.

20. τῶν ὑπερκοσμίων νόων. The triad is ὑπερκόσμιοι νόες, ἐγκόσμιοι
νόες, ἐγκόσμιοι ψυχαί : for participation τῶν ὑπερκοσμίων θεῶν (BCD,
renaissance copies, and edd.) a further intermediary would be
required.

PROP. 167. Pr.'s theory of the relation between the divine Intelligence and its objects is much more complicated than that of Plotinus.
It is most fully stated in the fifth book of the *Th. Pl.*, chs. i and v,
and in the commentary on the *Timaeus*, I. 321. 24 ff. and III. 100. 1 ff.
We may summarize it as follows :

(1) In some passages the two highest grades or aspects of Being,
τὸ ὄντως ὄν and ζωή, are described as πρώτως νοητόν : οὐχ ὡς πλήρωμα
τοῦ νοῦ προσαγορευόμενον νοητόν, ἀλλ' ὡς προαίτιον αὐτοῦ καὶ ἐφετὸν
αὐτῷ καὶ ἐραστόν, ἀσυντάκτως πρὸς αὐτὸν μονοειδῶς ὑφεστηκός (*Th. Pl.*
V. i. 248, cf. *in Tim.* III. 100. 7). This is the θεῖον νοητόν of prop.
161, which ' is not co-ordinate with the Intelligence but perfects it
without loss of transcendence.' It contains a cognitive subject only
κατ' αἰτίαν, and it is clear that it is itself called νοητόν only κατ' αἰτίαν,
as the source from which the highest Intelligence derives its content.
Hence it is ignored in the present proposition, and in one passage
(*in Parm.* 900. 26) it is expressly stated that the highest Intelligence
' has no intelligible object prior to it.'

(2) Below this is a νοῦς νοητός, in which, as in the Plotinian νοῦς,
subject and object are ἓν κατ' ἀριθμόν, i.e. only logically distinguish-
able : it is the lowest member of the 'intelligible' triad, and is

identified with the παντελὲς ζῷον of the *Timaeus* (*in Tim.* III. 101. 3). This seems to be the πρώτως νοῦς of prop. 160 and the ἀμέθεκτος νοῦς of props. 101, 166, 170.

(3) Below this, again, come a series of lower νόες which are not identical with their objects but know them κατὰ μέθεξιν, as reflected in themselves : καὶ γὰρ εἰς ἑαυτὸν εἰσιὼν εἰς ἐκεῖνον (τὸν πρὸ αὐτοῦ) χωρεῖ (πᾶς νοῦς), καὶ τῷ ἐν ἑαυτῷ νοητῷ τὸ πρὸ αὐτοῦ νοεῖ. καὶ οὕτως οὐκ ἔξω τοῦ νοῦ τὸ νοητόν· τὸ μὲν γὰρ ἐν ἑαυτῷ πᾶς νοῦς ἀδιάφορον ἔχει πρὸς ἑαυτόν, τὸ δὲ πρὸ αὐτοῦ πάλιν ἐν ἑαυτῷ νοεῖ (*Th. Pl.* V. v. 257). The highest of these is the δημιουργός of the *Timaeus* (*Th. Pl.* l.c., *in Tim.* I. 323).[1]

It appears that this elaborate hypothesis is the invention of Syrianus (*in Tim.* I. 310. 4, 322. 18, cf. Syrian. *in Metaph.* 110. 5) ; and that it was primarily intended to solve an exegetical difficulty which had always troubled commentators on the *Timaeus* (and still does so). As Pr. points out (*in Tim.* I. 323. 22), Plato sometimes speaks as if the δημιουργός were himself the model on which the sensible world was fashioned, sometimes as if the model were extraneous to him. The former interpretation had found many supporters, at least from the first century A.D. onwards (cf. prop. 20 n.) ; but that *Tim.* 39 E involves a separation between νοῦς and its objects was recognized by Amelius, and before him by Numenius (*in Tim.* III. 103. 18 ff.)—both of whom, however, tried to extract from the passage a *triad* of divine principles, an exegesis which Pr. rightly rejects. Plotinus has left us two discussions of this *locus vexatus*, one in the first of the collection of early notes put together by Porphyry as *Enn.* III. ix, the other in II. ix. 6 : the former is a rather hesitant attempt to interpret it on the Amelian lines, yet in a sense consistent with his own maxim οὐκ ἔξω τοῦ νοῦ τὰ νοητά ;[2] in the latter he definitely rejects the Amelian view, which he ascribes to the ·Gnostics *. Porphyry, according to Pr. (*in Tim.* I. 306. 31), made the δημιουργός a *soul* and his model νοῦς, thus giving the passage its natural interpretation without abandoning the Plotinian equation of νοῦς and νοητόν. Iamblichus' view of the matter was obscure even to Proclus, but the Amelian thesis was definitely revived by Theodore of Asine (*in Tim.* I. 309. 14). The theory of Syrianus and Proclus is thus the outcome of centuries of controversy :

---

[1] Elsewhere, however, the δημιουργός is described as ἀμέθεκτος νοῦς (*in Tim.* III. 101. 24, *Th. Pl.* V. xvi 275). I have found it impossible to bring Pr.'s various statements about the grades of νοῦς into complete congruity in detail.

[2] Cf. the qualifications of this maxim which are admitted in V. iv. 2 and VI. vi. 8.

it claims to reconcile Plotinus with Amelius, and the conflicting statements of Plato with each other, by showing that the παράδειγμα is in one sense outside and above the δημιουργός, in another sense immanent in him. Support was found for the solution in the *Chaldaean Oracles*, which appear to have contradicted themselves freely on this point: we find quoted from them on the one hand

σῆς ψυχῆς τεῖναι κενεὸν νόον ἐς τὸ νοητόν,
ὄφρα μάθῃς τὸ νοητόν, ἐπεὶ νόου ἔξω ὑπάρχει
(Damasc. I. 154. 24),

and on the other

οὐ γὰρ ἄνευ νόος ἐστὶ νοητοῦ, καὶ τὸ νοητὸν
οὐ νοῦ χωρὶς ὑπάρχει
(*ibid.* II. 16. 20, Pr. *in Tim.* III. 102. 10).

29. ἐκεῖνο. This reading is confirmed by ἀπ᾽ ἐκείνου below, and gives the natural contrast between αὐτό, 'the thing itself', and the τύπος.—The argument here is directed against the view of Longinus, who held (*in Tim.* I. 322. 24) that the παράδειγμα of the *Timaeus* was *lower* than the δημιουργός (whom he presumably identified, like Atticus and some modern interpreters, with the Form of the Good).

32. ἀφ᾽ οὗ [οὐ] πέπονθεν. If a negative were in place here, euphony and consistency alike would surely have dictated μή, not οὐ. But the sense requires an affirmative: that which *ex hypothesi* admits an impress of an object cannot be said not to be affected by it.

5. παράγον—7. γνώσεται. In this doubtful passage (of which both edd. make nonsense) M¹ offers an intelligible text, which I have followed except for omitting καί in l. 5 with Q. καὶ . . . μή cannot be translated 'not even' (Pr. would have written μηδέ); and Q's μὴ γινώσκον, suggested also by Cr., yields an unsatisfactory sense.

13. [τῷ νοοῦντι]. I take these words to be a gloss on αὐτῷ.

PROP. 168. Every intelligence is its own object; for it knows τὸ πρὸ αὐτοῦ only as reflected in itself. Hence the act of intellection always involves self-consciousness. Pr. in this proposition closely follows *Enn.* II. ix. 1 (I. 185. 10 ff.), where Plot. appears to be arguing against some previous writer who had distinguished two grades of intelligence, one which knows and a second which knows that the first knows, or else two successive moments in the intellective act, reflexive consciousness coming in 'as an afterthought' (ἐπινοίᾳ). Is the writer in question Numenius? He held that the first Intelligence ἐν προσχρήσει τοῦ δευτέρου νοεῖ (*in Tim.* III. 103. 29); and another distinction which is known to be Numenian, that

between νοῦς κινούμενος and νοῦς ἐν ἡσυχίᾳ, is discussed by Plot. in the same chapter.

PROP. 169. The 'existence' or substance of an intelligence is its intelligible content (νοητόν); its 'potency' is its power of intellection (νοῦς); its 'activity' is the act of intellection (νόησις). All three have that character of being a *totum simul* which for the Neoplatonists is the mark of eternity [1]: cf. Plot. V. i. 4 (II. 165. 28 ff.) and Porph. ἀφ. 44. 15. αἰών is already associated by Plato with the νοητά (*Tim.* 38 A) and by Aristotle with the divine νοῦς (*Metaph.* Λ 7, 1072 b 26 ff.)— indeed Porphyry's remark, παρυπέστη νῷ ὁ αἰών, is probably true as a statement of the historical origin of the concept of eternity.

PROP. 170. The substance of the argument, which in the editions is much obscured by textual corruptions, is as follows:—(1) All intelligences know all that they know in a simultaneous intuition (ἅμα), since their activity is eternal. But (2) no two intelligences have identical intuitions (ὁμοίως νοοῦσι): otherwise their being would be identical. The difference can only lie (a) in the sequence in which their knowledge presents itself (but this possibility is excluded by (1)); or (b) in the extent of their knowledge (but this would mean that some intelligences remained permanently ignorant of some things, since their knowledge, being eternal, cannot be increased like that of souls); or (c) in the point of view to which they relate their knowledge. (a) and (b) being disproved, (c) holds the field. Cf. Plot. V. viii. 4 (II. 235. 18) καὶ γὰρ ἔχει πᾶς πάντα ἐν αὑτῷ . . . ἐξέχει δ᾽ ἐν ἑκάστῳ ἄλλο, ἐμφαίνει δὲ καὶ πάντα: and Porph. ἀφ. 44. 11 ff. Pr. seems to conceive the '.dominant aspects' which characterize the thought of particular intelligences as analogous to specific differences within a genus: cf. prop. 177, and *in Tim.* II. 202. 7 τοῦ γὰρ ζῴου μετέχει μὲν καὶ ἄνθρωπος, καὶ ἔστιν ὅλον καὶ ἐν τούτῳ τὸ εἶδος, ἀλλ᾽ οὐ μόνον, ἀλλὰ καθ᾽ ἓν τὸ ὅλον, οἷον τὸ ἀνθρώπειον εἶδος, ὥστε μετὰ τοῦ ὅλου καὶ ἑνός τινος, ὅπερ ἐστὶν αὐτοῦ μόριον, πάρεστι τῷ μετέχοντι.

7. πάντα ἅμα νοήσει πᾶς. εἰ γὰρ κτλ. I can extract no sense from πᾶσι γὰρ κτλ. (MW), which previous editors print; and the readings of the other two families seem to be no more than clumsy attempts to emend πᾶσι.

17. εἰ μὴ ὁμοίως, ἢ ⟨μὴ⟩ πάντα νοεῖν ἕκαστον, ἀλλ᾽ ἕν. Here again

---

[1] Pr.'s argument on this point is formally circular: in this proposition νοῦς is said to be eternal because a *totum simul*, but in prop. 170 its character as a *totum simul* is inferred from its eternity.

I have had to fall back on conjecture. ἢ μὴ ὁμοίως ἢ πάντα .ν. ἐκ., ἀλλ' ἓν (M¹W) is plainly nonsense ; and the omission of the second ἤ in the other families and the printed editions restores only the appearance of sense— for τὸ μὴ ὁμοίως is not an outstanding possibility but an established fact.— In the next line ὅμως is confirmed by *in Tim.* III. 252. 3 τῶν πλείω μὲν ἑνός, οὐ πάντα δὲ ὅμως ἅμα νοουσῶν.
20. οὐδὲ γὰρ μεταβήσεται καὶ νοήσει ἃ μὴ πρότερον. The context makes it clear that this is what Pr. wrote. In the MSS. of the first family it has been supplanted by a gloss, which was later imported into M and so found its way into the printed editions.
27. αὐτῷ : sc. ἑκάστῳ νῷ.

PROP. 171. Between the pure unity of the One and the minimal unity of Matter Pr. recognizes six grades : (1) the henads, which are the transcendent sources of plurality ; (2) the intelligences, each of which is an actual plurality (as being a πλήρωμα εἰδῶν, prop. 177), but indivisible in space or time ; (3) souls, which are spatially indivisible but have their activity divided by time (prop. 191) ; (4) inseparable potencies and immanent Forms, which are infected by the spatial divisibility of body (prop. 190) ; (5) continuous corporeal magnitudes, which are divisible at any point (prop. 80) ; (6) discrete corporeal manifolds, which are actually divided in space. Plotinus (IV. ii. 1) and Porphyry (ἀφ. v) had made substantially the same distinctions, with the omission of the henads.

PROP. 172. See note on prop. 76, of which this is formally an application. Its Platonic source is the *Timaeus*, where the demiurge (νοῦς) is said to have created only ἀίδια.
18. αἰώνιος πάντῃ ὤν : sc. κατ' οὐσίαν καὶ κατ' ἐνέργειαν. The vulgate reading, αἰωνίως πάντα ὤν, involves an assertion which is both unproved and irrelevant to the argument.

PROP. 173. The Neoplatonists followed Aristotle in making the Intelligence its own object ; but they were nevertheless reluctant to cut it off from all knowledge of the spatio-temporal universe. Plotinus asserts that intelligence can contemplate (ὁρᾶν) ἢ τὰ πρὸ αὐτοῦ ἢ τὰ αὑτοῦ ἢ τὰ παρ' αὑτοῦ (VI. ix. 3 [II. 511. 29]), but without explaining how such contemplation of the lower is possible to it. Pr. finds the solution in the convenient principle πάντα ἐν πᾶσιν, οἰκείως δὲ ἐν ἑκάστῳ (prop. 103) : what the Intelligence knows is not the sensible world itself but the intelligible causes wherein the sensible is pre-embraced. Cf. *in Parm.* 964. 21 εἰ δὲ δὴ γιγνώσκων ὁ θεὸς ἑαυτὸν

αἴτιον ὄντα τῶν μετ' αὐτὸν γιγνώσκει καὶ ὧν αἴτιός ἐστιν, ἐντεῦθεν στησόμεθα καὶ πρὸς Ἀριστοτέλην, καὶ δείξομεν ὅπως ὁ κατ' αὐτὸν νοῦς, ἑαυτὸν εἰδὼς ὄντα πᾶσιν ὀρεκτόν, οἶδε καὶ τὰ πάντα ὅσα ὀρέγεται αὐτοῦ.

28. ἤδη γάρ. This seems on the whole the simplest correction of ἤ (or ἦ, or ᾗ) γάρ. The alternative is to retain ἤ and suppose that ἢ ὑπ' οὐδενός has fallen out after μετείχετο. ἦ γάρ, which Cr. prints, s nót in accordance with Pr.'s usage.

PROP. 174. Against the Christian doctrine of a deliberate creation in time the Neoplatonists maintained an emanative creation which is timeless and unwilled : the only creative power is contemplation or intuitive thought (θεωρία, νόησις), which at a certain level of being translates itself automatically into spatio-temporal terms. The classical exposition of this thesis is in the magnificent essay *Enn.* III. viii, where Plotinus says of φύσις very much what Pr. here says of νοῦς: τὸ οὖν εἶναι αὐτῇ ὅ ἐστι, τοῦτό ἐστι τὸ ποιεῖν αὐτῇ· ἔστι δὲ θεωρία καὶ θεώρημα, λόγος γάρ. τῷ οὖν εἶναι θεωρία καὶ θεώρημα καὶ λόγος, τούτῳ καὶ ποιεῖ, ᾗ ταῦτά ἐστιν (I. 334. 15). Elsewhere Plot. traces the creation of the sensible world back to νοῦς (e.g. V. ix. 3 [II. 250. 27] νοῦν ποιητὴν ὄντως καὶ 'δημιουργόν), or more usually to ψυχή (e.g. II. ix. 4). This apparent vagueness in the delimitation of function is characteristic of the Plotinian form of Neoplatonism as distinct from the Procline: in the philosophy of Plotinus there are, as Inge observes, no hard boundary lines drawn across the map of the universe, and it is often impossible to say at what point a particular moment of the πρόοδος takes its origin. Later the lines become more rigid as well as more numerous: accordingly we hear of a controversy between Porphyry, who made the creative principle a transcendent soul, and Iamblichus, who made it the intelligible world as a whole, each disputant claiming for his own view the authority of Plotinus (Pr. *in Tim.* I. 306. 31 ff.). For Pr. the creative principle κατ' ἐξοχήν is νοῦς: cf. prop. 34, l. 3 πρόεισι πάντα ἀπὸ νοῦ. But I cannot agree with Simon in seeing here 'the most important and the most real of all the differences which separate Proclus from Plotinus'[1]: what is really important is the conception, common to both writers, of creation as a by-product (παρακολούθημα, Plot. III. viii. 4) of contemplation. God creates because he thinks, but he does not think in order to create (*in Parm.* 791. 14).

Nicolaus argues against this theorem that if intellection be creation, then since each intelligence has intellection of itself and its priors

COMMENTARY 291

(prop. 167), each intelligence must create itself and its priors, which
is absurd. The answer to this is, of course, that contemplation of
the higher is creation *of the lower.*

14. [πᾶν] τὸ ὂν τὸ ἐν αὐτῷ. I take πᾶν, which is omitted by M¹W,
to be a doublet of τὸ ὄν.

PROP. 175. We have already seen (prop. 63 n.) that since the
human consciousness can enjoy intuitive thought only intermittently
Pr. finds himself obliged to posit certain higher souls as the permanent vehicles of νόησις. Of the nature of these higher souls more
will be said below (prop. 184 n.). Like the 'superconscious' of
Plotinus, they are a theoretical construction designed to strengthen
the continuity of the system at its weakest point, the point where
eternity passes over into time; but they differ from the Plotinian
superconscious in being non-human entities, not parts or aspects of
the human soul. As ἀεὶ 'κατὰ χρόνον νοοῦντα they are distinct from
our souls on the one hand and from the timeless intelligences on
the other: mediating between temporal and eternal activity, they
are analogous (as Pr. points out) to the ἀεὶ γινόμενα which mediate
between temporal and eternal being.

23. καὶ ὑφ' ὧν ἄρα κτλ. The words ἡ ἐνέργεια φασίν in [M]W are
clearly a gloss. There is more to be said for the genuineness of ἀεὶ
νοοῦντα just below: these words are found also in Q, they improve
the rhythm of the sentence, and the succeeding ἀεί would explain
their dropping out in the archetype of the first family.

PROP. 176. A perfect system of knowledge would be a perfect
type of organic unity: each part would involve, and be involved in
the existence of every other part,[1] yet without any blurring of the
articulations which keep each part distinct and unique. In the
content of a well-ordered human mind we may see an approximation
to such a unity-in-distinction; and if we think of this content as
grasped together in a single intuition instead of being surveyed
piecemeal we may get some notion of what 'intellection' is, and of
the mode of being of the Forms. This line of thought is attributed
by Syrianus (*in Metaph.* 87. 16) to 'the Pythagoreans' (compare
perhaps the opinion ascribed by Iamblichus to Numenius, Stob.
Ecl. I. xlix. 32 [866 H]). It is developed in several passages of the

[1] That individual 'truths' are scientifically worthless unless they carry a reference to the system as a whole is expressly recognized by Plotinus: IV. ix. 5
[II. 157. 23] ἔρημον δὲ τῶν ἄλλων θεωρημάτων οὐ δεῖ νομίζειν (τὸ μέρος). εἰ δὲ μή,
ἔσται οὐκέτι τεχνικὸν οὐδὲ ἐπιστημονικόν, ἀλλ' ὥσπερ ἂν καὶ εἰ παῖς λέγοι.

Enneads: for the intelligible world as unity-in-distinction cf. VI. iv. 14 *init.* and V. viii. 4; for the analogy of the sciences, IV. ix. 5, where, however, it is used to illustrate not (as here) the internal unity of pure mind, but the relation between Soul and the souls (so also Porph. ἀφ. xxxvii). The most elaborate discussion of the concept of unity-in-distinction is to be found in the *Parmenides* commentary, 751. 15 ff. From Pr. it was taken over by the Christian Neoplatonists, who made use of it to explain the doctrine of the Trinity (e.g. ps.-Dion., *Div. Nom.* 2. 5; Psellus *ap.* Bidez, *C. M. A. G.* VI. 165. 16; Nic. Cusan. *de docta ignorantia* 38. 24 Hoffmann-Klibansky).

3. τὰ νοερὰ εἴδη : i.e. the content of the νόες as distinct from the νοητὰ εἴδη which are above νοῦς and constitute τὸ ὄντως ὄν in the narrow sense: the latter have presumably a still more perfect unity. (Psellus, *de omnif. doct.* 25 understands by 'intellectual forms' here οἷον ψυχαί, νόες, ἄγγελοι, ἀρχάγγελοι, δυνάμεις, καὶ ὅσα τοιαῦτα, while he takes the εἴδη of the next proposition to be Platonic Forms like ἀγαθότης, ὁσιότης, &c. But *in Parm.* 757. 1 ff. seems to show that Pr. has Platonic Forms in mind in both propositions.)

19. τεκμηριοῦται. Elsewhere the mid. has the sense of τεκμαίρομαι, and the renaissance conj. τεκμηριοῖ (also suggested by Cr.) may be right, the corruption being due to dittography of the following καί.

30. τὸ γὰρ ... 31. ἀδιαστάτως. Failure to realize that these words are parenthetical is responsible both for the repetition of καὶ ἥνωται in BCDQ and for the διακεκριμένως of [M]W, which are two different but equally clumsy attempts to make sense of ἀμερίστως καὶ ἀδιαστάτως καὶ διακέκριται read without punctuation.

PROP. 177. There is a sense in which every intelligence contains the whole of the intelligible world (prop. 170). But the Forms, which are that world in its objective aspect, are organized as a hierarchy of genera and species, the generic Forms transcending the specific but embracing them seminally (cf. prop. 70 n.); and there must be a parallel grouping of intelligences. Each higher intelligence will contain one genus οἰκείως, the other genera and the species only implicitly; each of the more numerous lower intelligences will contain one species οἰκείως, the other species and the genera implicitly (cf. prop. 180). The creative power of each intelligence being correlated with the Forms which it possesses οἰκείως, it follows that the higher intelligences have greater power.

1. πλήρωμα. This seems to imply a complete 'set': cf. *in Tim.* III. 8. 18 τὸ αὐτόζωον πλήρωμά ἐστι τοῦ πλήθους τῶν νοητῶν ζώων, and Nock in Rawlinson, *Essays on the Trinity and the Incarnation*,

101 n. 3.   The word belongs especially to the vocabulary of Gnosticism, and appears to have been first introduced into Neoplatonism by Iamblichus (*de myst.* 28. 18).   It is a favourite term with Proclus.

PROP. 178 asserts of Forms what prop. 172 asserts of intelligences, and is proved in exactly the same way.   The question τίνων ἐστὶ καὶ τίνων οὐκ ἔστι τὰ εἴδη is more fully discussed by Pr. in the *Parmenides* commentary, 815 ff.   His general view is that there are Forms only of species, not of individuals : even human souls, which are imperishable individuals, are derived not severally from separate Forms, but collectively from the Forms of the various divine souls under which they are grouped (cf. prop. 204).   By an exception to the general principle, these divine souls have each a Form of its own, as have also the heavenly bodies.   There are no Forms of things which exist only as parts, e.g. eyes or fingers ; of accidental attributes like colour ; of artifacts (despite *Rep.* X) ; of practical τέχναι like weaving ; or of things evil.   This account of the matter goes back in part to Middle Platonist tradition (Albin. *Didasc.* c. ix), and does not differ substantially from that given by Plotinus, save in its greater precision.   Plotinus does indeed appear to assign a higher value to human individuality by linking each soul directly to an intelligence (IV. iii. 5) ; but Pr. is not to be understood as denying that such individuality is real and in its higher manifestations permanent, although the empirical individuality of the συναμφότερον is the temporary product of physical causes.

1. ᾗ φθαρτά.   The qualification is added because things which are individually perishable may be imperishable as a species, and so far traceable to a timeless cause (*in Parm.* 820. 26 ff.).

PROP. 179.   See note on prop. 86.   The number of intelligences is less than that of souls because, while every intelligence is permanently participated by a soul peculiar to it, there are also souls μεταβάλλουσαι ἀπὸ νοῦ εἰς ἄνοιαν (prop. 184) which have no permanent intelligence.

PROP. 180.   This supplements props. 170 and 177.   The primal Intelligence is, like all 'unparticipated' terms, a whole-before-the-parts ; each of the remaining intelligences is a whole-in-the-part (cf. prop. 67).   The same thing is said by Porphyry, ἀφ. xxii.

11. ⟨οὐχ⟩ ὡς ἐκ μερῶν ὑποστάς.   The insertion of a negative appears essential.   Otherwise we have, as Nicolaus points out, a flat contra-

diction both of prop. 171 and of the next sentence.—The following words, ἕκαστος . . . ἀπ' αὐτῶν, come from prop. 176 and seem to be a reader's marginal note: they have no satisfactory grammatical or logical connexion with the context.

PROPS. 181–3. This division of participated intelligences into the 'divine' and the 'purely intellectual' (which has already been made in prop. 111) does not coincide with the other division (prop. 166) into supra-mundane and intra-mundane: for since there are intra-mundane henads (prop. 165), some intra-mundane intelligences must be divine. If we combine the two we get three grades of partici-pated intelligence, (a) θεῖος ὑπερκόσμιος, (b) θεῖος ἐγκόσμιος, (c) νοερὸς ἐγκόσμιος. The present classification is an artificial grouping de-pendent on the classification of souls (see notes on props. 184–5).

16. οὐδὲ νοῦ μετέχουσαι (θείου). κατὰ λήθην τοῦ γραφέως παρελείφθη τὸ θείου (Nicolaus ad loc.). Otherwise the clause of course contra-dicts the enunciation.

N. *Of souls* (props. 184–211).

1. Classification of souls (184, 185).
2. General characters of souls as such: their being, life, know-ledge and participation by vehicles (186–97).
3. Periodicity of souls (198–200).
4. Characters and mutual relations of the classes of souls (201–4).
5. Descent of the particular souls, and doctrine of vehicles (205–11).

PROP. 184. The belief that the stars had souls which were divine passed from Plato (*Legg.* 899 B), through Stoicism, into the general body of Hellenistic thought:[1] cf. e.g. 'Hermes' *ap*. Stob. I. xlix. 5 [806 H]; Plot. VI. ix. 8 *init*.; Iamb. *ap*. Stob. I. xlix. 37 [888 H]; Hierocles *ap*. Phot. cod. 251. 461 b. The earlier writers are generally content to classify souls as divine and human, or as divine, human, and irrational. But as the development of the transcendence-theology progressively widened the gulf between man and god, there was as usual an increasing inclination to lay stress on the existence of mediating principles. For a Platonist, remembering his master's definition of τὸ δαιμόνιον as τὸ μεταξὺ θεοῦ τε καὶ θνητοῦ

---

[1] In popular thought it would hardly be distinguished from Aristotle's doctrine of astral intelligences or from the common belief in astral deities: the distinction is an artificial one required by the Neoplatonic world-scheme.

(*Symp.* 202 D), souls of this intermediate class are naturally δαίμονες.[1]
Demonology was made an especial object of study by Poseidonius
and his school; but it was already taken seriously in the Old
Academy, as we can see from the *Epinomis* and from the statement
of Plutarch (*def. orac.* 12, 416 C = Xen. fragm. 23) that Xenocrates
παράδειγμα τῷ λόγῳ ἐποιήσατο τὸ τῶν τριγώνων, θείῳ μὲν ἀπεικάσας τὸ
ἰσόπλευρον, θνητῷ δὲ τὸ σκαληνόν, τὸ δ' ἰσοσκελὲς δαιμονίῳ· τὸ μὲν γὰρ
ἴσον πάντη, τὸ δ' ἄνισον πάντη, τὸ δὲ πῆ μὲν ἴσον, πῆ δ' ἄνισον—where,
as in the present proposition, τὸ δαιμόνιον is the 'mean term' of a
triad.   Plotinus makes passing reference to the doctrine of daemons,
in the form given to it by Poseidonius, e.g. III. v. 6, IV. iii. 18 *fin.*;
but he seems to attach no metaphysical or practical importance to it.
Porphyry has much more to say about it (*de abst.* II. 37 ff.,[2] and the
fragments of the *de regressu animae* in Bidez, *Vie de Porphyre* 27* ff.).
One of the questions to which he desired an answer in his *Letter to
Anebo* was ' How are we to distinguish from one another gods, daemons, heroes and souls ?' (Iamb. *de myst.* 61. 11, 67. 1)—for with the
development of theurgy demonology was becoming a subject of the
liveliest practical interest.   Much of the demonological lore of
the Middle Ages goes back to the speculations of the post-Plotinian
Neoplatonism, to be found in such passages as Pr. *in Tim.* III.
155 ff., *in Alc.* 377 ff., and Olympiodorus *in Alc.* 15 ff. Creuzer.[3]

In the *El. Th.* there is no explicit mention of daemons, but it is
clear from *in Tim.* I. 142. 1 and other passages that they are to be
identified with the ψυχαὶ οὔτε θεῖαι οὔτε μεταβολῆς δεκτικαί.   They
are subdivided into ἄγγελοι, δαίμονες proper, and ἥρωες (*ibid.* III. 165.
11)—a classification which is as old as Celsus.[4]—The θεῖαι ψυχαί
include (*a*) the unparticipated Soul, which is extra-mundane (cf.
prop. 164, l. 19 n.) and corresponds to the third Plotinian hypostasis ;
(*b*) the immanent world-soul (*in Tim.* II. 290. 3) ; (*c*) the immanent
souls of the seven planets and of the fixed stars (*in Tim.* III.
255. 10) ; (*d*) those of the ' gods below the moon' (*ibid.*), i.e. the
descendants of Γῆ and Οὐρανός enumerated by Plato, *Tim.* 40 E.—

---

[1] Cf. Plut. *def. orac.* 10, 415 A ; 13, 416 E f. ; *Is. et Os.* 25.
[2] Cumont (*Religions Orientales*[4], 278 ff.) and Bousset (*Archiv f. Religionswissenschaft*, xviii [1915], 134 ff.) find Iranian influence in this passage, which
affirms the existence of evil demons under the presidency of an arch-devil
(προεστώς), and teaches that they creep into our bodies along with certain foods.
[3] Cf. Bidez, *C.M.A.G.* VI. 97 ff. ; and on Greek demonology in general Heinze,
Xenokrates, cap. ii, and Tambornino, *de antiquorum daemonismo.*
[4] *apud* Orig. *adv. Cels.* VII. 68.   On the pagan belief in ἄγγελοι see Dibelius,
Die Geisterwelt im Glauben des Paulus, 209 ff., and Bousset in *Archiv f. Religionswissenschaft*, xviii (1915), 170 ff., both of whom incline to regard it as independent
of Judaeo-Christian influence.

Human souls belong to the lowest of Pr.'s three classes, those which μεταβάλλουσιν ἀπὸ νοῦ εἰς ἄνοιαν (*in Tim.* II. 143. 29 ff., Syrian. *in Metaph.* 41. 30 ff.): the description is suggested by Plato, *Tim.* 44 AB.[1] Pr. follows Iamblichus (*apud* Stob. I. 372 ff. [886 ff. H]) in drawing more rigid distinctions of function between the three types of soul than Plotinus chose to make; and he is much more ready than Plotinus to insist on the lowly state of man: cf. notes on props. 194–5 and 211.—The principles of animal and vegetable life (ἄλογοι ψυχαί) are not in the *El. Th.* considered as souls at all : they are but εἴδωλα τῶν ψυχῶν (prop. 64 *fin.*). Pr. claims Plato's authority for this restricted use of the term soul: πολλαχοῦ δῆλός ἐστι καὶ ὁ Πλάτων ψυχὴν τὴν λογικὴν εἶναι τιθέμενος, τὰς δὲ ἄλλας εἴδωλα ψυχῆς, *Th. Pl.* III. (vi). 128. He denies that a human soul can become the soul of an animal, though it may be attached for a time to an animal body (*in Tim.* III. 294. 21 ff.).

PROP. 185. This is taken from Plato, *Phaedr.* 248 A. After describing the life of the ' gods ' (Pr.'s θεῖαι ψυχαί), Plato goes on αἱ δὲ ἄλλαι ψυχαί, ἡ μὲν ἄριστα θεῷ ἑπομένη καὶ εἰκασμένη ὑπερῆρεν εἰς τὸν ἔξω τόπον τὴν τοῦ ἡνιόχου κεφαλήν . . . ἡ δὲ τότε μὲν ἦρεν, τότε δ᾿ ἔδυ. The term ὀπαδός[2] comes from *Phaedr.* 252 C, whence it found its way into Philo (*Quis Rer. Div.* 15 § 76) and the Neoplatonists from Porphyry to ps.-Dionysius. We find a similar grading of souls in Iamblichus (*de myst.* 36. 9) and Syrianus (*in Metaph.* 41. 30 ff.) ; the latter ascribes it to οἱ θεολόγοι.

PROPS. 186, 187 hardly do more than summarize and apply to the soul the general results already reached in props. 15–17 and 47–9, where see notes.—For self-knowledge ἀπὸ τῶν αἰτίων cf. prop. 11, l. 15 n.—Besides the soul proper Pr. also recognizes an εἴδωλον ψυχῆς imparted by the soul to the body, inseparable from the latter and perishing with it[3] (cf. props. 64 *fin.*, 81–2, and *in Tim.* II. 285. 27) ; this corresponds to the ζῷον of Plotinus, and is identified by Pr. with the Aristotelian entelechy.

24. ἀνώλεθρός ἐστι καὶ ἄφθαρτος. The first term refers to annihilation by severance from the substrate, the second to dissolution into elements (cf. Arist. *Top.* 153 b 31).

---

[1] Cf. also Philo *de opif. mundi* 24 § 73 [I. 25. 5 Cohn] ἄνθρωπος, ὃς ἐπιδέχεται τἀναντία, φρόνησιν καὶ ἀφροσύνην

[2] Spelt ὀπαδός, on the analogy of ἕπομαι, in the MSS. both of *El. Th.* and of *in Tim.*

[3] For a qualification of this statement see prop. 209 n.

PROPS. **188–9.** The original meaning of ψυχή, as of the Latin *anima*, is 'life-breath': 'our ψυχή, being air, holds us together', as Anaximenes put it. Hence the close association in Greek thought of the notions of 'soul' and 'life': the word for 'alive' is ἔμψυχος, lit. 'ensouled'. The crowning 'proof' of immortality in the *Phaedo* turns on the impossibility of conceiving a dead soul, and ultimately on the assumption that soul is what Pr. calls αὐτόζως, possessed of life not accidentally but in its own right, so that it cannot be annihilated upon its separation from the body. This assumption is embodied in the traditional definition of soul as ζωὴ παρ' ἑαυτῆς ἔχουσα τὸ ζῆν (Porph. ἀφ. xvii, Iamb. *ap.* Stob. I. xlix. 32 [868 H]: cf. Plot. II. 136. 20). Pr. is not content to assume it : he attempts to prove it by showing that soul, as having self-knowledge, is self-constituted, and that its *esse* is *vivere* (prop. 189, cf. *in Tim.* III. 335. 14 ff.). But he has also to distinguish the soul as αὐτόζως from the Form of Life (*Phaedo* 106 D), which figures in his system as the middle term of the intelligible triad (cf. props. 101, 102 n.). This he does by making the soul at once ζωή and ζῶν (prop. 188), i.e. by giving it a life at once self-derived and derived from the transcendent Form of Life (*in Tim.* II. 128. 28).

24. οἷς ἂν παρῇ ζωῆς μεταδίδωσιν κτλ. : cf. *Phaedo* 105 D ψυχὴ ὅτι ἂν αὐτὴ κατάσχῃ, ἀεὶ ἥκει ἐπ' ἐκεῖνο φέρουσα ζωήν.—For the absence of will and calculation cf. Plot. IV. iii. 13. It is assumed here without proof, presumably on the strength of the general principle established in props. 26–7.

PROP. **190** is based on the well-known description of the making of the soul in the *Timaeus* : τῆς ἀμερίστου καὶ ἀεὶ κατὰ ταὐτὰ ἐχούσης οὐσίας καὶ τῆς αὖ περὶ τὰ σώματα γιγνομένης μεριστῆς τρίτον ἐξ ἀμφοῖν ἐν μέσῳ συνεκεράσατο οὐσίας εἶδος (35 A). This passage is the main source of the conception of the soul as the frontier between the two worlds, which gained wide currency from the time of Poseidonius onwards [1] and dominates the Neoplatonic psychology. The precise meaning of the 'indivisible' and 'divided' principles was, however, a matter of dispute, as we learn from Plutarch's περὶ τῆς ἐν Τιμαίῳ ψυχογονίας and Pr. *in Tim.* II. 152 ff. An Eratosthenes who is probably *not* the celebrated scientist made the soul a mixture of the incorporeal

---

[1] Cf. e g. Philo *de opif. mundi* 46 § 135 [I. 47. 8 Cohn], and *Corp. Herm.* I. 15. The *Chaldaean Oracles* called the soul ἀμφιπρόσωπος (*in Tim.* II. 130. 23). The doctrine has a long subsequent history. In Aquinas we read that the soul is 'in confinio corporum et incorporearum substantiarum, quasi in horizonte existens aeternitatis et temporis' (*Summa c. Gent.* II. 81).

and the corporeal; Numenius and many others, of the monad and the indeterminate dyad (this goes back to Xenocrates); Severus (after Poseidonius?), of the geometrical point and geometrical extension; Plutarch and Atticus, of the divine and the irrational; Plotinus, of intelligence and perception (cf. *Enn.* IV. viii. 7 *init.* : this view goes back to Crantor).[1] The strangest opinion is that ascribed to Theodore of Asine, that the soul is intermediate between a generic and a specific intelligence; this is said on the authority of Theodore, quoting Porphyry, quoting Antoninus 'the pupil of Ammonius', to have come 'from Persia'. Pr. himself understands the 'indivisible' class as representing the intelligible world in its transcendent being and the 'divisible' as its immanent manifestations or εἴδωλα in the material world. There are three grades of the latter: (*a*) αἴσθησις, which is the manifestation of νοῦς on the lower level; (*b*) φύσις (including the irrational life-principles), the manifestation of ζωή; (*c*) the ἔνυλα εἴδη, the manifestation of οὐσία (*in Tim.* II. 139. 14 ff.). This does not differ substantially from the Plotinian view as stated in *Enn.* IV. ii. 1 [2] and Porph. ἀφ. v. and xlii.

8. **κἂν ἐν ζωαῖς ὑφεστήκῃ.** ὑφεστάναι ἐν is commonly used by Pr. of existence *in a substrate*, and it is tempting to read ἐν ζώοις here. But the same difficulty occurs in the next clause, whether we read as BCD or as M¹W; so I have thought it better to understand both clauses as referring to the orders of existence in which divisible εἴδωλα arise (cf. last note).

PROPS. 191, 192. It has already been shown (props. 106, 107) that there must be a principle which participates both time and eternity, and is therefore at once a Being and a coming-to-be: this principle is now identified as μεθεκτὴ [3] ψυχή, which is thus again found to be intermediate between the two worlds. Cf. Plot. IV. iv. 15 (II. 61. 21) οὐδ' αἱ ψυχαὶ ἐν χρόνῳ, ἀλλὰ τὰ πάθη αὐτῶν ... καὶ τὰ

---

[1] These and other interpretations of the passage are fully discussed by A. E. Taylor *ad loc.* Much confusion has been caused by the assumption that the 'indivisible' and the 'divided' are identical with the 'same' and the 'other' respectively. I believe with Proclus and G. M. A. Grube (*Class. Philol.* 27 [1932], 80) that this identification is erroneous.

[2] An early essay, as is also IV. viii. In his later work Plotinus, with characteristic disregard of Platonic orthodoxy, often reckons the soul among the purely indivisible principles and claims for it full membership of the intelligible world : cf. Heinemann, *Plotin,* 172; Nebel, *Plotins Kategorien,* 17.

[3] The unparticipated Soul (as distinct from the world-soul), having no connexion with any body (prop. 196) and being assimilated to intelligence by the principle of prop. 112, is presumably pure Being, and eternal in activity as well as existence.

ποιήματα. The form of prop. 192 is influenced by Plato, *Tim.* 37 A λογισμοῦ δὲ μετέχουσα καὶ ἁρμονίας ψυχὴ τῶν νοητῶν ἀεί τε ὄντων ὑπὸ τοῦ ἀρίστου ἀρίστη γενομένη τῶν γεννηθέντων, where Pr. wrongly construes τῶν νοητῶν ἀεί τε ὄντων with ψυχή as a partitive genitive (*in Tim.* II. 294. 18). Further Platonic authority was found in the *Laws*, 904 A ἀνώλεθρον δὲ ὂν γενόμενον, ἀλλ' οὐκ αἰώνιον (cf. *in Tim.* I. 235. 17).

PROP. 193. Cf. Plot. IV. iii. 5 (II. 15. 9) αἱ ψυχαὶ ἐφεξῆς καθ' ἕκαστον νοῦν ἐξηρτημέναι.—Nicolaus asks here how soul can be at once self-constituted (prop. 189) and constituted by an intelligence. But the notion of the 'self-constituted' does not exclude derivation from a higher principle (see prop. 40 n.). A more serious difficulty is that we have been expressly told (props. 111, 175 *cor.*) that not all souls participate intelligence directly : how, then, can they be proximately derived from and proximately perfected by it ? We must apparently understand the 'proximate origination' of the present proposition as covering derivation through another member of the soul-order (prop. 204), προσεχῶς meaning merely that the intellectual order lies immediately above the psychic, in contrast with the remoter causes, ζωή, τὸ ὄν, and the henads. But the verbal inconsistency is significant : having adopted the Iamblichean doctrine of the grades of soul, Pr. nevertheless seeks to retain certain elements of the Plotinian tradition, which represented the human soul as in direct relation with the Intelligence ; and in combining the two he shows himself a little careless.

PROPS. 194, 195. Here again we have a piece of Plotinian [1] tradition which harmonizes imperfectly with Pr.'s general view of the status of the human soul. Though ultimately derived from Aristotle,[2] the doctrine that each soul possesses all the Forms (or, more strictly, the corresponding λόγοι) rests for Plotinus on the assumption that there is a super-conscious part of the human soul which 'abides above' and enjoys perpetual intuition : cf. e.g. *Enn.* III. iv. 3 (I. 263. 9) ἔστι γὰρ καὶ πολλὰ ἡ ψυχὴ καὶ πάντα, καὶ τὰ ἄνω καὶ τὰ κάτω αὖ μέχρι πάσης ζωῆς, καὶ ἐσμὲν ἕκαστος κόσμος νοητός, τοῖς μὲν κάτω συνάπτοντες τῷδε, τοῖς δὲ ἄνω τῷ νοητῷ, καὶ μένομεν τῷ μὲν ἄλλῳ παντὶ νοητῷ ἄνω, τῷ δὲ ἐσχάτῳ αὐτοῦ πεπεδήμεθα τῷ κάτω. This assumption is rejected by Pr. Consequently the universal knowledge of the

---

[1] Numenius seems to have assimilated the human soul to the Intelligence even more closely than Plotinus : cf. Stob. I. 365. 7 ff. [866 H].
[2] *de an.* iii. 8. 431ᵇ21.

Forms remains for him a potentiality which is never fully actualized in a human soul save in the interval between two incarnations : cf. prop. 190, l. 20 ἀγνοεῖ τὰ ὄντα ψυχή τις μένουσα ψυχή. And not only this, but even in its ideal actualization human science is still imperfect, knowing the Forms not as they are in themselves (νοητῶς), nor even as they are in the Intelligence (νοερῶς), but in concepts (λόγοι) which imperfectly reflect them (διανοητικῶς) : [1] καὶ οὔτε τὸν νοητὸν κόσμον ἐν ἡμῖν δεῖ τιθέναι, καθάπερ λέγουσί τινες (Numenius and Plotinus) . . . οὔτε μένειν τι τῆς ψυχῆς ἄνω ῥητέον . . . οὔτε ὁμοούσιον τὴν ψυχὴν ὑποθετέον τοῖς θεοῖς (in Parm. 948. 14, cf. 930. 26 ff. ; in Tim. II. 241. 29 ff.). Hence the need for theurgy. See also prop. 211 n. and Introd. p. xx.

33. οὐσιώδεις λόγους. The soul's essence is to be λογική, and the general λόγος which embraces the λόγοι both of sensible and of intelligible things is ἐνέργεια τοῦ οὐσιώδους τῆς ψυχῆς (in Tim. II. 299. 18).

Prop. 196. In discussing the relationship of the human soul to the world-soul Plotinus raises an ἀπορία (Enn. IV. iii. 4) : how is it that the human soul enjoys periods of freedom from incarnation, whereas the world-soul does not ? Must we not conclude that the former is the less deeply involved in Matter ? His tentative solution is that (a) both the human soul and the world-soul are in their highest reaches perpetually discarnate, merging into one with the intelligible Soul ; (b) in so far as it is incarnate the world-soul, unlike the human, organizes Matter without effort and without contamination. But he mentions another view which solved the ἀπορία by denying the assumption on which it rests : καίτοι τινές φασι τόδε μὲν (τὸ σῶμα) καταλείψειν (τὴν ἡμετέραν ψυχήν),[2] οὐ πάντη δὲ ἔξω σώματος ἔσεσθαι. This latter is the solution which Pr. adopts : no soul except the unparticipated Soul is ever wholly disembodied ; it is at all times in relation with an imperishable ' first body ' or ' first vehicle '. The history and significance of this theory is discussed in Appendix II. For the expression πρῶτον σῶμα (altered by Cr. to πρώτως σ.) cf. πρῶτον ὄχημα in the passage from Galen quoted on p. 316.

25. ἑκάστης is more likely to be a gloss on πάσης (explaining that it is used in the distributive sense) than vice versa.

Prop. 197. Pr. here ascribes to the soul a unity-in-distinction

[1] Contrast Plot. VI. v. 7 (II. 389. 24) νοοῦμεν ἐκεῖνα (sc. τὰ εἴδη) οὐκ εἴδωλα αὐτῶν οὐδὲ τύπους ἔχοντες.
[2] That Bréhier is wrong here in supplying τὴν τοῦ παντὸς ψυχήν is clear from the next sentence.

closely resembling that already discovered in the intelligence (prop.
176). It is contrasted with the latter as the more distinct with the
more unified, but it is not obvious in what precisely the difference
consists. Though lower than the indivisible principles (ἀμέριστα),
soul is nevertheless said to be without parts (ἀμερής);[1] and its distinguishable elements or aspects—substance (being), life and knowledge—are the same triad which we have already met in the intelligible
world (prop. 101), and have the same mutual implicitness which they
had there (prop. 103). This of course exemplifies the Iamblichean
principle πάντα ἐν πᾶσιν, οἰκείως δὲ ἐν ἑκάστῳ: but Pr. has hardly
made it clear what it is that is οἰκεῖον in the unity of soul.

16. ἡ ἄζως. If we read ζωῆς with MW and edd., there is no
proof that life as well as knowledge is involved in the soul's
substance.

18. ταῖς ἐνύλοις . . . 19. ζωαῖς: the principles of life in animals,
which lack self-consciousness and are εἴδωλα ψυχῆς, not αὐθυπόστατα.

PROP. 198. The physical universe is finite save in the sense that
finite bodies are potentially divisible *ad infinitum* (cf. prop. 94 n.).
And movement in a finite space can continue through an infinite
time only by returning periodically to its starting-point. Hence the
only movement which is both continuous and perpetual is a circular
movement, like that of the heavenly bodies. This theorem is
borrowed, like most of the Neoplatonic physics, from Aristotle
(*Phys.* Θ 8, 9), though in the propositions that follow it is applied in
a way quite foreign to him.

26. κατ' ἀριθμὸν πορεύεται. Time is an image of eternity κατ'
ἀριθμὸν ἰοῦσα, Plato, *Tim.* 37 D.

PROPS. 199, 200. The doctrine of the perpetuity and perfection
of circular motion was intended by Aristotle to apply only to the
movement of bodies in space, and especially of course to the movement of the stars. But it was naturally extended to the movement
of the planetary souls, and then (soul being the principle of motion
κατ' ἐξοχήν) to the movement of embodied souls in general. Confirmation of this was found in the οὐρανοῦ περιπολήσεις of the
Phaedrus (246 B ff., cf. Pr. *Th. Pl.* VI. iv. 351) and the account of

---

[1] This is the usual Neoplatonic view. Plato's unfortunate language about the
'parts' of the soul was explained as applicable to the soul not in its essence but
only in its relation to the bodily organs, or alternatively as referring to non-
quantitative parts, i.e. δυνάμεις (Porph. *ap.* Stob. I. 353 f. [842 ff. H]); Iamb. *ibid.*
367 ff. [872 ff. H]).

the 'circles in the soul' given in the *Timaeus* (36 B ff.). The cyclic period of a human soul is ' its proper life' (prop. 199, l. 1, cf. prop. 200, l. 33); this does not mean one human life, but one cycle of experience, i.e. the entire interval between the beginning of a 'descent' and the restoration of the soul to its original purity (ἀποκατάστασις, cf. Iamb. *Protrept.* 16. 5 Pistelli). Such an interval includes, according to Pr., a number of human lives,[1] and also the acquisition of the second 'vehicle' or 'garment' (intermediate between the immortal vehicle and the human body) and its sloughing off by a process of purification (*in Tim.* III. 237. 3, cf. *infra* prop. 209).

The period of the world-soul[2] is ' the whole of time '—by which Pr. means not, as one would naturally suppose, infinite time (for all cycles must of course be finite), but a complete cycle of *cosmic* experience, which ends in a universal ἀποκατάστασις and is followed by an infinite number of exactly similar cycles : cf. *in Tim.* III. 29. 18 (ὁ χρόνος) κυκλούμενος ... μετὰ τὴν πᾶσαν ἀνέλιξιν τῆς ἑαυτοῦ δυνάμεως ἀποκαθιστάμενος οὕτω καὶ τὰς τῶν ἄλλων ἀποκαθίστησι περιόδους : *ibid.* 278. 17 πάντα γὰρ ἀνελιττόμενα τὰ σχήματα τοῦ παντὸς ... ἀεὶ δὲ τὰ αὐτὰ σχήματα πάλιν καὶ πάλιν. Pr. chooses to describe such a period as ὁ σύμπας χρόνος because of *Tim.* 36 E (ἡ ψυχή) θείαν ἀρχὴν ἤρξατο ἀπαύστου καὶ ἔμφρονος βίου πρὸς τὸν σύμπαντα χρόνον. Its time is really the least common multiple of the times of all other periodic movements ; Pr. finds it to be expressed in the 'nuptial number' of the *Republic* (*in Tim.* III. 93. 22 ff.).—This doctrine of world-cycles each culminating in an ἀποκατάστασις is traceable in Middle Platonism, which may be conjectured to have derived it from Poseidonius ; it seems to be the result of reading Stoic[3] ideas into the *Politicus* myth (as was done by Severus *apud* Pr. *in Tim.* I. 289. 6 and by the author of the Hermetic *Asclepius*) and into *Tim.* 39 D

---

[1] Cf. *Phaedr.* 248 E f., where the minimum interval is said to be three thousand years, including three incarnations. The 'return to the appropriate star' of which Plato speaks in the *Timaeus* (42 B) can take place after one incarnation ; but Pr. explains that this is not a complete ἀποκατάστασις (*in Tim.* III. 291. 17 ff.).

[2] That by ἡ πρώτη ὑπὸ χρόνου μετρουμένη ψυχή Pr. intends the world-soul, and not the 'unparticipated' or supra-mundane Soul, is clear from *in Tim.* II. 289.

[3] Doubtless ultimately Babylonian, at least as regards the astral side of the doctrine (cf. Bidez, *Bérose et la grande année*, in Mélanges Paul Frédéricq, 9 ff.). Reitzenstein's interesting contention (*Studien zum Antiken Synkretismus*, 66), that the *Politicus* myth itself (in which the notion of astral conjunctions plays no part) directly reflects oriental religious tradition, seems to me not proven. It is, indeed, a singular and possibly significant fact (*ibid.* 56) that Berosus (*apud* Sen. *N. Q.* iii. 29. 1), Proclus and the astrologer Antiochus agree with the *Mahabharata* in associating the cosmic ἀποκατάστασις with a conjunction in Cancer, though Greek authorities were not unanimous on this point (see Kroll's note in his edition of Pr. *in Remp.*, II. 386). The *Mahabharata* is, however, generally thought to be posterior, at least in its present form, to Alexander's invasion of India, and may therefore incorporate Greek ideas.

([Plut.] *de fato* 3).[1] It is apparently accepted by Plotinus (V. vii. 1–3 and IV. iii. 12), though it does not play an important part in his system.

5. περιοδικῶς ἀνακυκλεῖται : cf. *Tim.* 37 A αὐτὴ (ἡ ψυχή) ἀνακυκλουμένη πρὸς αὑτήν.

PROPS. 201, 202 distinguish the three types of soul κατὰ τὴν ἐνέργειαν, and assign their order of rank. But the distinction κατ' οὐσίαν which has been made in props. 184–5 is already based on their difference of function, and the present theorems add little to what has been said already. On the notion of subordinate providences see prop. 134 n.

6. συμφυῶς : cf. props. 63, l. 3, 182, l. 8 ; and *in Tim.* III. 269. 31 τὰς θειοτάτας τῶν ψυχῶν . . . πλέον ἡνῶσθαι ταῖς ὑπὲρ αὐτὰς ἀμερίστοις οὐσίαις, ὧν ἐξήρτηνται συμφυῶς. φυσικῶς (MW) seems always to mean in Pr. either 'physically' (opp. ψυχικῶς, νοητῶς) or 'by the method of physics' (opp. μαθηματικῶς, θεολογικῶς).

8. ἐν τῷ ψυχικῷ πλάτει. The term πλάτος, the literal equivalent of the 'planes' of modern theosophy, is a favourite one with Pr. I have failed to discover any example of this use of the word earlier than Syrianus (*in Metaph.* 6. 30, &c.).

PROP. 203. Cf. props. 61–2 n. By a similar argument Psellus proves that men are more numerous than angels, *de omnif. doctrina* 19. Pr. finds the principle implied in *Timaeus* 42 D, where Plato says that *a number of* souls were 'sown' by the demiurge in each of the planets (*in Tim.* III. 261. 12 ff.).

PROP. 204. This is founded on the passage of the *Timaeus* referred to in the last note. Plato seems to have intended the souls sown in the planets to be the future inhabitants of their respective stars ; but Pr. understands them to be human souls which are placed under the 'hegemony' of particular planetary souls, 'in order that they may have them as saviours from the errors incidental to temporal process, and may call upon them as their especial patrons' (*in Tim.* III. 280. 20). He is thus enabled to father on Plato much of the current doctrine of planetary astrology and planetary cultus (cf. prop. 165, l. 7 n.). Each soul derives from its planet (or other divine patron[2]) its peculiar aptitudes ; but on its own free will depends the

---

[1] But Pr. rightly distinguishes the world-period from the Great Year of *Timaeus* 39 D, which is merely the ἀποκατάστασις of the planetary system (see Taylor *ad loc.*).

[2] 'Divine souls' include other than planetary souls (prop. 184 n.), although it is

choice of a life suitable to its aptitudes and the good or bad use which it makes of the life it has chosen (*in Tim.* III. 279. 11 ff.). Souls which 'recognize their god' by choosing the appropriate life are the true children of the gods, and to such inspiration comes (*ibid.* 159. 20 ff.); they may even identify themselves with their gods and become their earthly representatives, as the human hero Asclepius was of the god Asclepius (*ibid.* 166. 14 ff.). This union with the planetary god is mediated by the homonymous planetary daemons (*in Alc.* 382. 15 ff.).

Prop. **205.** The 'vehicles' (ὀχήματα) of this and the following propositions are the imperishable 'first bodies' of prop. 196. For the origin of the term ὄχημα see Appendix II, p. 315 ; it was evidently so familiar to Pr.'s readers that he thinks it unnecessary to explain its meaning. The present theorem may have been suggested by Arist. *de gen. anim.* 736 b 31 ὡς δὲ διαφέρουσι τιμιότητι αἱ ψυχαὶ καὶ ἀτιμίᾳ ἀλλήλων, οὕτω καὶ ἡ τοιαύτη (*sc.* τοῦ πνεύματος) διαφέρει φύσις. Pr.'s meaning is, however, quite different from Aristotle's. He extends to the vehicle (and so indirectly to the irrational soul and the earthly body) the planetary influence which has already been shown to govern the character of the souls themselves: from the soil in which the soul was originally sown the vehicle takes its quality (*in Tim.* III. 305. 4 ff., *in Parm.* 822. 16 ff.). Hence presumably the origin of the 'temperaments': persons under the patronage of Saturn have a saturnine composition, the clients of Jupiter are jovial, and so forth (cf. Servius on *Aen.* VI. 714; 'Hermes' *apud* Stob. I. v. 14 [174 f. H.]).

9. τῆς ὅλης: not the 'universal Soul' of Plotinus, but (as the context shows) the planetary or other divine soul to which the particular soul in question is attached. For ὅλαι ψυχαί in the plural cf. *Th. Pl.* 126.

Prop. **206.** The question whether the human soul can attain a final release from the 'circle of birth', as in the Orphic-Pythagorean and the Indian doctrine, was one on which the Neoplatonists were not unanimous. There is, I think, no definite affirmation of such a release in the *Enneads*, and it would not be easy to reconcile with the Plotinian theory of the soul as the frontier-principle between time and eternity. Porphyry, however, seems to have asserted in the *de regressu animae* (fragm. 11 Bidez = Aug. *Civ. Dei* X. 30,

of these that Pr. chiefly thinks when he speaks of θεῖαι ψυχαί. Cf. *in Tim.* III. 264. 30 ff.

XII. 27, &c.) that the soul, at any rate the soul of the philosopher, *will* eventually be released for ever. Later we find the contrary opinion, that souls cannot 'leave the body once for all and remain through all time in idleness', maintained by Sallustius [1] (who is very probably following Iamblichus here): he supports it (*a*) by the argument from function, that souls have their natural citizenship in the body; and (*b*) by the consideration that since the number of souls is finite and new souls cannot be added to a universe already perfect, the earth would on the Porphyrian theory eventually be depopulated. Pr. takes the same view as Sallustius, but relies on the more general argument that an eternal life cannot start from, or finish at, a point in time. He holds with Syrianus that while self-will causes some human souls to descend more often than is necessary, cosmic law requires that each shall descend at least once in every world-period (*in Tim.* III. 278. 10 ff.).[2] Consistently with this, he rejects the Pythagorean and Gnostic view that such descent is in itself sinful, a notion which had found a place even in the teaching of Plotinus. It is true that in one passage (*de mal. subsist.* 210. 30 ff.) he uses, like Plotinus (V. i. 1), the Pythagorean term τόλμα in this connexion; but elsewhere he definitely treats the descent as a necessary part of the soul's education (*dec. dub.* 114. 36 ff., cf. Plot. IV. viii. 5) or as a necessary cosmic service, ἐπ' εὐεργεσίᾳ μὲν τῶν ἀτελεστέρων ψυχῶν, προνοίᾳ δὲ τῶν σωτηρίας δεομένων (*in Alc.* 328. 29, cf. *in Tim.* III. 324. 4 ff., Plot. IV. iii. 17).

20. οὐδὲ γὰρ κτλ. Something seems to have fallen out here, for it is hardly credible that Pr. should have omitted to mention the Porphyrian view that the perpetual sojourn with the gods *follows* the series of incarnations. The Christian doctrine that the endless sojourn above is preceded only by a *finite* experience of this world is, of course, excluded from consideration by the assumption that the soul's life is endless *a parte ante* as well as *a parte post.*—For οὐδέ . . . οὐδέ as an equivalent of οὔτε . . . οὔτε in late Greek, see Nock, *Sallustius*, p. cviii.

23. τοῖς σώμασι: i.e. the earthly body and the other χιτῶνες ἐνυλότεροι, not the immaterial πρῶτον σῶμα, which the soul retains even ἐν τοῖς θεοῖς. The meaning may have been made clear in the missing clause.

[1] C. xx. The suggestion of 'idleness' looks like a hit at popular Christian theology.
[2] In the *Cratylus* commentary, c. cxvii, he makes an exception for certain 'heroic' souls like Heracles, which 'spend many periods' in the intelligible world—hence no doubt their rarity in this one.

PROP. **207**. This is founded on *Timaeus* 41 D f., where the demiurge is said to have mounted the souls upon the stars 'as on vehicles'; Pr. understands Plato to mean that the 'first body' is created by νοῦς, the unmoved cause (as it must be, if it is to be imperishable), *in Tim.* III. 238. 2.

PROP. **208**. For the immateriality of the 'first body' cf. *Th. Pl.* III. (v); for its impassibility, *in Tim.* II. 60. 2 ff. The former character follows from the latter by the principle of prop. 80; the latter is essential to its perpetuity, as is also its freedom from the risk of disruption. The earlier tradition, which identified the 'first body' with the πνεῦμα, can hardly have ascribed these properties to it[1]; the possibility arose only with the distinction of the imperishable 'luminous' vehicle from the perishable 'pneumatic' vehicle (see Appendix II, p. 320). Pr.'s doctrine is reflected in Psellus's statement that the angels have immaterial and impassive bodies, in contrast with those of demons (Pr.'s 'pneumatic' vehicles), which are ἔνυλά πη καὶ ἐμπαθῆ (*de operatione daemonum* 8, 837 B f. Migne).[2]

PROP. **209**. The connexion of the vehicle with the lower functions of the soul is traditional and goes back ultimately to Aristotle's doctrine of πνεῦμα: see Appendix II, p. 315 f. Accordingly, for the earlier Neoplatonists, the question of the immortality of the vehicle was bound up with that of the immortality of the irrational soul. Middle Platonists like Atticus and Albinus had held, according to Pr. *in Tim.* III. 234. 9 ff., that both[3] were mortal; Porphyry, that both survived bodily death but were eventually resolved into the firmament[4]; Iamblichus, that both were immortal.[5] The first two opinions were based on the explicit statement of Plato, *Tim.* 69 C; the second provided, as the first did not, for the physical punishments in Hades of which Plato had spoken and for the possibility of

[1] 'Hermes', however, *apud* Stob. I. 410. 23 [988 H], speaks of 'incorporeal envelopes' of the soul.
[2] Psellus is also influenced, as Bidez points out, by Porphyry's distinction (*apud* Pr. *in Tim.* II. 11) between 'fiery' and 'earthy' δαίμονες, who become for him respectively angels and demons.
[3] It is possible that Pr. is reading into these writers the belief in a pneumatic vehicle. In his extant *Handbook* Albinus speaks only, like Plato, of the fleshly body as the ὄχημα of the incarnate soul (c 23) and of the stars as the ὀχήματα of discarnate souls (c. 16).
[4] See Appendix II, p. 318 f. This is also the usual view of Plotinus. Cf. the perishable ψυχή of the curious myth in Plut. *de facie*, 28, 943 A ff., which Reinhardt *Kosmos u. Sympathie* 318 ff. refers to Poseidonius.
[5] The immortality of the irrational soul was already affirmed, if we can trust Olympiodorus *in Phaed.* 124. 15 Norvin, by Speusippus and Xenocrates.

a discarnate soul making an irrational choice of its next life; while Iamblichus' view met the Aristotelian objection that a soul must be the ἐντελέχεια of *some* body, and was supposed to be confirmed by *Tim.* 41 D f. (cf. prop. 207 n.). Pr. combines the second and third doctrines by positing both an immortal vehicle and a perishable one which survives bodily death, and by attaching the irrational soul to the latter while holding that certain ἀκρότητες τῆς ἀλόγου ζωῆς or roots of unreason are imperishable—a view perhaps suggested by Plot. VI. vii. 3 ff.

The perishable vehicle is ἐκ παντοδαπῶν χιτώνων συγκείμενον (*in Tim.* III. 298. 1): it consists of successive layers of the four elements, which are successively attached to the immortal vehicle in the course of the soul's descent and discarded in the reverse order during the ascent (*ibid.* 297. 21 ff.). The Platonic 'source' of this lies in a misunderstanding of *Tim.* 42 C συνεπισπώμενος τὸν πολὺν ὄχλον καὶ ὕστερον προσφύντα ἐκ πυρὸς καὶ ὕδατος καὶ ἀέρος καὶ γῆς: but the idea seems to have been elaborated under the influence of the Poseidonian eschatology, and perhaps indirectly of the mystery-religions.[1]

The word χιτών seems to have been originally an Orphic-Pythagorean term for the *fleshly* body. In this sense it is used by Empedocles, fragm. 126 Diels, σαρκῶν ἀλλόγνωτι περιστέλλουσα χιτῶνι, with which may be compared Plato *Gorg.* 523 C ff., where the fleshly body is described as an ἀμφίεσμα which the soul takes off at death. The clean linen tunic of the Orphic votary perhaps symbolized the purity of his 'garment of flesh'.[2] It may have been this ancient usage which suggested to the Valentinian Gnostics the idea that the 'coat of skins' (χιτὼν δερμάτινος) in *Genesis* iii. 21 meant the fleshly body.[3] In Philo we meet a slightly different application of the metaphor: he speaks of δόξα, φαντασία and the other 'parts of the irrational soul' as the χιτῶνες which envelop[4] τὸ λογικόν (*Leg. Alleg.*

---

[1] The descent through the successive elements recalls a much discussed phrase in Apuleius' account of the Isiac mysteries, 'per omnia vectus elementa remeavi' (*Metam.* xi. 23). An alternative, and commoner, doctrine is that the increasing burden of impurity is acquired during the descent *through the seven planetary spheres* (Porph. *apud* Stob. II. 171. 2 [388 H]; Iamb. *de myst.* VIII. 6; Macrob. *in Somn. Scip.* I. 11–12, etc.). This is plausibly traced by Bousset, *Archiv f. Religionswissenschaft*, xviii (1915), 134 ff., to Gnostic-Hermetic circles (cf. esp. *Corp. Herm.* I. 25).

[2] I owe this suggestion, as well as the Philo reference, to the kindness of Professor Taylor.

[3] Irenaeus, *cont. haer.* i. 5, § 5 (*P. G.* VII. 501) [= Tertull. *adv. Valentinianos*, xxiv (*P. L.* II. 578)]. See also the passages from Clement cited by Bernays, *Theophrastos' Schrift über Frömmigkeit*. n. 9.

[4] χιτών regularly means physical envelope or membrane in Aristotle and the medical writers.

III. 15 f.). Plotinus uses Plato's word ἠμφιέσθαι of the incarnate soul (I. vi. 7 *init.*); but not, I think, χιτών.—The first to speak of the *pneumatic* body as a χιτών is, so far as I know, Porphyry.[1] For him the body of flesh and blood has become 'the last garment' (*de abst.* II. 46). It is curious that he twice applies to the latter the not very obvious epithet δερμάτινος (*ibid.* I. 31, II. 46): Bernays may be right in thinking that he is influenced here by the Valentinian interpretation of the passage in *Genesis*, especially as he quotes *Genesis* elsewhere[2] in a citation from Numenius, a writer who shows knowledge of Valentinianism.

22. καθαρὰ καὶ γυμνὴ κτλ. The extensive omission at this point in M and the printed texts has led to the corruption of ἀπεικονίζεται (l. 26), συμφυῆ (l. 29), and ἐφιέμενα (l. 33), copyists failing to realize that ὀχήματα (l. 24) is the subject of all the succeeding verbs down to συνεπαίρεται (l. 32).

26. ταῖς ἑαυτῶν περιφοραῖς. The proper movement of the vehicle is circular, like that of νοῦς and the heavenly bodies: *in Tim.* II. 72. 14 τὸ ἡμέτερον ὄχημα ... κινεῖται κυκλικῶς, ὅταν διαφερόντως ὁμοιωθῇ πρὸς τὸν νοῦν ἡ ψυχή· μιμεῖται γὰρ τὴν νοερὰν ἐνέργειαν ἥ τε τῆς ψυχῆς νόησις καὶ ἡ κυκλοφορία τῶν σωμάτων, ὥσπερ τὰς ἀνόδους καὶ καθόδους τῶν ψυχῶν ἡ κατ' εὐθεῖαν κίνησις. Cf. Plot. II. ii. 2 (I. 132. 10) and Plato, *Tim.* 35 C, 40 A, 43 A.

33. παντοίως συμμεταβάλλει. Yet the συμφυὲς ὄχημα is ἀμετάβλητον κατ' οὐσίαν (prop. 207). The apparent contradiction is explained in the next proposition.

31. παθαινομέναις : cf. note on prop. 80.

PROP. 210. The immaterial vehicle of the human soul is spherical (*in Tim.* II. 72. 14),[3] like the human skull,[4] the stars and the universe itself *. Hence, perhaps, the curious opinion ascribed (wrongly, as it seems) to Origen,[5] that we shall be resurrected with round bodies. Daemons, too, have spherical vehicles, but the lower

---

[1] The fiery χιτών of *Corp. Herm.* X. 18, which is *first assumed* by νοῦς (the higher soul) when it leaves the mortal body, belongs to a different circle of ideas: it is akin to the Pauline 'incorruptible body' and the Isiac 'garment of light'. For the Neoplatonist, as for the Orphic, the χιτών is always something acquired in the soul's descent and thereafter sloughed off.

[2] *de ant. nymph.* 10.

[3] According to Olympiodorus *in Alc.* p. 16 it is egg-shaped, having been distorted out of perfect sphericity by its association with the material body.

[4] Plato, *Tim.* 44 D. According to some opinions the ὄχημα had its seat in the skull (Damascius *apud* Suid. s.v. αὐγοειδές).

[5] See Addenda et corrigenda,

sort have material bodies as well (*in Crat.* 35. 22, *Th. Pl.* III. (v). 125 f.). The immaterial vehicles are naturally invisible in the state of purity, but by the addition of the successive 'garments' they become visible in various shapes: cf. Porph. *de ant. nymph.* 11 παχυνθέντος δ' ἐν αὐταῖς (ταῖς ψυχαῖς) τοῦ πνεύματος ὑγροῦ πλεονασμῷ ὁρατὰς γίνεσθαι. καὶ ἐκ τῶν τοιούτων αἱ συναντῶσαί τισι κατὰ φαντασίαν χρώζουσαι τὸ πνεῦμα εἰδώλων ἐμφάσεις: also *de abst.* II. 47 and Origen *adv. Celsum* II. 60 (892 A Migne). These passages suggest that ὁρᾶται and φαντάζεται in the present proposition refer to apparitions of the souls of the dead (or of daemons, cf. *in Tim.* I. 395. 29, &c.). On the changing shapes of daemonic vehicles see App. II, p. 319.

PROP. 211. The final proposition is directed consciously—as is shown by the language [1] and by the parallel passage in the *Timaeus* commentary—against the well-known theory of Plotinus that a part of the human soul remains 'above', so that we are at all times potentially in direct communion with the intelligible world and potentially divine (IV. viii. 8, V. i. 10). Plotinus admits that this theory is foreign to the school tradition (παρὰ δόξαν τῶν ἄλλων, IV. viii. 8 *init.*): it was devised, as Pr. says (*in Parm.* 948. 18), in order to maintain the continuity of the soul with the νοητά. Theodore of Asine accepted it (Pr. *in Tim.* III. 333. 28), as did Damascius after-wards (II. 254. 6). But it seems to have been rejected by Iamblichus (Pr. *in Tim.* III. 334. 3),[2] who is followed in this by most of the later Neoplatonists. Pr.'s objections to the theory are (*a*) that it breaks the unity of the soul, the supposed higher part being either indistinguishable from νοῦς [3] or at any rate wholly different in kind from the lower; (*b*) that it is inconsistent with the facts of human sin and misery (so Iamblichus *apud* Pr. *in Tim.* l.c.). He also points out (*in Tim.* l.c.) that it conflicts with the statement of the *Timaeus* (43 C f.), that *both* the 'circles in the soul' are thrown out of gear by the experience of sense life, and that of the *Phaedrus* (248 A), that the

---

[1] ἄνω εἶναι and ἐν τῷ νοητῷ εἶναι are the regular Plotinian terms for what Pr. has hitherto described as θεοῖς ἕπεσθαι or ἐν τοῖς θεοῖς εἶναι. And ἄτοπον . . . . μὴ κρατεῖν τῶν ἄλλων δυνάμεων looks like a retort to Plot. II. 152. 9 ff. τὸ δὲ ἐν τῷ αἰσθητῷ εἰ κρατοῖ κτλ.

[2] The passage from Damascius (II. 259. 12), which Cr. cites as evidence that Iamb. adopted the Plotinian view, refers only to the divine souls. From Hermeias *in Phaedr.* 160. 1 ff. Couvreur we may infer that Syrianus agreed with Iamb. and Pr., since this commentary is based on a course of lectures by Syrianus.

[3] According to Plot. νοῦς is at once a part of us and that to which we aspire: μέρος γὰρ καὶ οὗτος ἡμῶν καὶ πρὸς τοῦτον ἄνιμεν, I. i. 13 *fin.* Here, as elsewhere, the scholastic spirit of later Neoplatonism demanded a more precise delimitation of frontiers.

charioteer, who symbolizes what is highest in us, sinks to earth with his horses. On the significance of the humbler status assigned to the human soul by later Neoplatonism as compared with Plotinus, see Introd., p. xx.

Appendix I

The Unknown God in Neoplatonism *

It has been maintained by Eduard Norden in a learned and brilliant book [1] that neither the expression ἄγνωστος θεός nor the idea which it represents is genuinely Greek. If this is so, we have in the Neoplatonic doctrine of the unknowableness of God a clear example—for Plotinus possibly the only clear example—of that oriental influence on Neoplatonism to which Vacherot and Zeller attached a wide if vague importance, and whose nature Bréhier and others have recently attempted to determine with more precision. Consequently it seems worth while briefly to re-examine the evidence on this point.

That the actual phrase ἄγνωστος θεός occurs in no writer of purely Hellenic culture is (I believe) true, but as regards Plotinus irrelevant ; for the phrase, so far as I know, occurs nowhere in the *Enneads*.[2] It is frequent in Gnostic writings, and Norden produces good reasons for regarding it as specifically Gnostic. Did Plotinus, while avoiding the *word*, borrow the *thought* from the Gnosis, either directly or through the mediation of Numenius [3] or Philo [4] ? Such a filiation is undoubtedly possible : as *Enn.* II. ix. shows, Plot. knew a good deal about the Gnosis though he intensely disliked it ; and he was accused in his own day of plagiarizing from Numenius (Porph. *vit. Plot.* 17). But before assuming that the Gnosis is the principal or the only source of this Neoplatonic doctrine it may be well to recall

---

[1] *Agnostos Theos*, 1913: see esp. pp. 84, 109, and cf. Reitzenstein, *H.M.-R*[3]. 298.

[2] He comes nearest to it in V. iii. 13 (II. 196. 12) πολὺ γὰρ αὐτὸ (τὸ ἕν) ποιοῦμεν, γνωστὸν (ὄν), 14 (197. 15) οὐδὲ γνῶσιν οὐδὲ νόησιν ἔχομεν αὐτοῦ. γνῶσις is never used by Plot. in the Gnostic sense : it is always either a synonym of ἐπιστήμη or a quite general term for knowledge.

[3] Cf. Numen. *apud* Euseb. *Prep. Ev.* XI. 22 τὸν πρῶτον νοῦν, ὅστις καλεῖται αὐτὸ ὄν, παντάπασιν ἀγνοούμενον παρ' αὐτοῖς (sc. τοῖς ἀνθρώποις). There is some reason to think that N. was acquainted with the Gnosis (Norden 109). But he was also acquainted with Plato.

[4] Cf. *de mon.* 6 (V. 11 C.W.), *de mutat. nom.* 2 (III. 158). I agree, however, with Schröder, Whittaker and Inge that there is no clear evidence that Plot. had read Philo.

(*a*) that Plot. had, or thought he had, authority for it in two passages of Plato ; (*b*) that the *meaning* of the doctrine in Neoplatonism is quite different from its meaning in Gnosticism.

(*a*) The Platonic passages in question are *Parm.* 142 A οὐδ' ὀνομά-ζεται ἄρα οὐδὲ λέγεται οὐδὲ δοξάζεται οὐδὲ γιγνώσκεται, οὐδέ τι τῶν ὄντων αὐτοῦ αἰσθάνεται, and *Epist.* vii. 341 C–D ῥητὸν γὰρ οὐδαμῶς ἐστιν ὡς ἄλλα μαθήματα, ἀλλ' ἐκ πολλῆς συνουσίας γιγνομένης περὶ τὸ πρᾶγμα αὐτὸ καὶ τοῦ συζῆν ἐξαίφνης, οἷον ἀπὸ πυρὸς πηδήσαντος ἐξαφθὲν φῶς, ἐν τῇ ψυχῇ γενόμενον αὐτὸ ἑαυτὸ ἤδη τρέφει . . . εἰ δέ μοι ἐφαίνετο γραπτέα θ' ἱκανῶς εἶναι πρὸς τοὺς πολλοὺς καὶ ῥητά, τί τούτου κάλλιον ἐπέπρακτ' ἂν ἡμῖν ἐν τῷ βίῳ; The former of these (which is not noticed by Norden) was understood as referring to the supreme God not only by Plotinus[1] but, as I have tried to show elsewhere,[2] by the Neo-pythagorean school as early as the first century A.D., and probably also in the Old Academy : if I am right in this, the interpretation must be independent of Gnostic influence. The other passage, from *Epist.* vii, is quoted by Plot. and interpreted by him as meaning that the One is unknowable save in a *unio mystica* which does not yield any communicable knowledge (VI. ix. 4 : cf. VI. vii. 36). For the Neoplatonists this text seems to be the primary[3] source of the epithet ἄρρητος which in Pr. is regularly associated with ἄγνωστος.[4]

(*b*) It is important to make clear—as Norden does not always do —the different senses in which ἄγνωστος and cognate terms are used of God or the gods. A god may be (i) unknown because foreign or nameless, as in the altar inscription cited by Norden from Hierony-mus' commentary on *Titus* i. 12 'Diis Asiae et Africae, diis ignotis et peregrinis'[5]; or (ii) unknown to mankind in general owing to the necessary limitations of human knowledge ; or (iii) unknown to all who have not enjoyed a special revelation or initiation ; or (iv) un-

---

[1] V. i. 8 (II. 172. 3 ff.). Cf. Syrian. *in Metaph.* 55. 26 τἀγαθὸν ἄγνωστόν ἐστι καὶ ὑπὲρ πᾶσαν ἐπιστήμην, ὡς ἐν Παρμενίδῃ σαφῶς ὁ Πλάτων βοᾷ : Pr. *Th. Pl.* V. xxviii. 308.

[2] *Class. Qu.* 22 (1928), 135 ff.

[3] The word belongs also to the terminology of the Mysteries.

[4] *El. Th.* prop. 123, l. 25, *in Crat.* 32. 23, *Th. Pl.* II. xi. 110 etc. : cf. Synes. *Hymn.* iv. 226. ps.-Dion. *Epist.* 3 etc. Albinus, on the other hand, combining the Good of *Epist.* vii with the demiurge of the *Timaeus*, describes it as ἄρρητος καὶ τῷ νῷ μόνῳ ληπτός (*Didasc.* c. x : cf. Max. Tyr. 140. 1 ff. Hobein).

[5] Here, it seems to me, belong the references in the Babylonian hymns to gods, goddesses and many other things as 'known and unknown'. Norden concludes from these references that the Babylonians worshipped 'unknown gods' : but are we justified in inferring more than that the Babylonians recognized the possible existence of gods outside their own cultus, and included them in their prayers as a precautionary measure? As regards the Graeco-Roman world, it is significant that we have no evidence at all (apart from the passage in *Acts*) that cultus was ever offered to *an* unknown god (in the singular). Cf. further Nock, *Sallustius*, p. xc, n. 211.

known and unknowable in his essence, but partially knowable by inference from his works or analogy with other causes; or (v) unknown and unknowable in his positive character, but definable by negations; or (vi) unknown and unknowable, but accessible in a *unio mystica* which is not properly speaking knowledge, being supralogical. Of these six doctrines, the first has no real connexion with the others, and may here be dismissed. The second is the ordinary position of the Greek sceptic, which is already expressed in the famous fragment of Protagoras' work *Concerning the Gods*. There is nothing either oriental or explicitly mystical about it. The remaining four may be regarded as different ways of escaping from the sceptical position while maintaining and even heightening the belief in divine transcendence which is implicit in scepticism as the positive correlate of its insistence on human limitation.[1] Of these, the escape by special revelation is characteristically eastern; it gave Gnosticism its name, and is exemplified in such passages as *Evang. Matth.* xi. 27. The complete absence of this doctrine from the *Enneads* marks Plotinism as being a philosophy and not a religion.

The other three 'ways', the way of analogy, the way of negation and the way of ecstasy, are all of them expounded in the *Enneads*; but all three already formed part of the Platonist tradition before Plotinus, as appears from Albinus *Didasc.* c. x, where they are clearly stated and distinguished. Albinus, like Plot. and Pr., connects the way of analogy with the simile of the sun in *Rep.* VI, the way of ecstasy with Diotima's teaching in the *Symposium* and the 'suddenly kindled fire' of *Epist.* vii. For the way of negation he cites no Platonic authority; but his illustration, ὅπως καὶ σημεῖον ἐνοήσαμεν κατὰ ἀφαίρεσιν ἀπὸ τοῦ αἰσθητοῦ, ἐπιφάνειαν νοήσαντες, εἶτα γραμμήν, καὶ τελευταῖον τὸ σημεῖον, points to a Neopythagorean source. I have little doubt that the Neopythagoreans found it where Pr. finds it,[2] in the first 'hypothesis' of the Platonic *Parmenides*; in any case it is the logical consummation of Plato's regressive dialectic, and I see no reason for ascribing to it an oriental origin. With the ways of analogy and ecstasy the case is less clear, since they are not peculiar to the Platonic tradition. Philo's teaching about ecstasy, though influenced by Plato,[3] is in its fundamental character non-Platonic,

[1] On scepticism as the forerunner of Neoplatonism see M. J. Monrad in *Philos. Monatshefte*, 24 (1888), 156 ff.
[2] *Th. Pl.* II. v. 93 ἐν δὲ τῷ Παρμενίδῃ διὰ τῶν ἀποφάσεων τὴν τοῦ ἑνὸς πρὸς πάντα τὰ μετ' αὐτὸ διαφορὰν ἐνεδείξατο.
[3] The verbal parallelisms between *Quis Rer. Div.* § 249 ff. and Plato, *Phaedr.* 240 A–250 C and 265 B make this certain. Cf. Leisegang, *Der Heilige Geist*, I. i. 163 ff.; R. M. Jones in *Class. Philol.* 21 (1926), 102.

being based on the popular notion of the withdrawal or suppression of the ecstatic's own spirit and the invasion of some δαίμων from without.[1] And the idea that God may be known 'by his power' or 'through his works' is a commonplace of later Hellenistic speculation.[2] It is futile to seek a single source for concepts so vague and so widely diffused as these, or even to label them definitely as 'Greek' or 'oriental'. But in the school tradition inherited by Plotinus from Middle Platonism and from such men as Numenius they appear in close association with Platonic texts and in a form which may be called specifically Platonic. And it is only within this tradition that they have any real philosophical basis. The way of analogy is valid only if the sensible world is εἰκὼν τοῦ νοητοῦ θεὸς αἰσθητός: the way of ecstasy is significant only if man is in his innermost nature already potentially identical with God.[3] To derive the unknowable One of Neoplatonism from the ἄγνωστος θεός of Gnosticism, or the Plotinian ecstasy from the Philonic, is, it seems to me, to be deceived by words and commit the common fallacy of arguing from coincidence of language to identity of thought. The Plotinian doctrine and the others are solutions of the same problems; but they are not the same solutions.

APPENDIX II

The Astral[4] Body in Neoplatonism.

The modern mystery-religions, and especially that singular amalgam of discredited speculations known as theosophy, have made us familiar with the theory that mind and body are linked together by a *tertium quid*, an inner envelope of the soul, which is less material than the fleshly body and survives its dissolution, yet has not the pure immateriality of mind. This doctrine is popularly regarded as oriental. But it has, in fact, a very long history in European thought reaching back from the Cambridge Platonists in the seventeenth century to Porphyry and Iamblichus in the fourth, and traceable

---

[1] Bréhier scarcely exaggerates when he says ' On chercherait vainement, dans toutes les œuvres de Philon, un seul passage où il accepte l'ecstase au sens que les mystiques donnent à ce mot' (*Les Idées Philosophiques et Religieuses de Philon*, 204).

[2] For examples see Norden, *op. cit.* Poseidonius may perhaps have given the thought philosophical currency, but was hardly its originator.

[3] Cf. *Class. Qu.* 22. 141 f.

[4] The *term* ἀστροειδές seems not to occur in this connexion earlier than Proclus: previous writers speak of a ' luminous ', ' ethereal ' or ' pneumatic ' body. But the theory that it is of like stuff with the stars has its source in Aristotle, and its connexion with the soul's sojourn in the firmament goes back ultimately to Plato.

thence to an origin in the classical period of Greek philosophy. How far and at what points in this long course it was modified by oriental influences it is difficult to say; for the Christian period the question is complicated by the Pauline doctrine of the 'spiritual body', which had a different origin from the Greek ὄχημα-πνεῦμα theory but is often fused with it by Christian Platonists. Such oriental influence as went to the shaping of the pagan Greek concept was, so far as I can judge, secondary and rather late[1]; its *origin* can be explained, as I hope to show below, without assuming any importation of ideas from outside the circle of Hellenic speculation. There is, indeed, a superficial analogy between the Greek doctrine and the σῶμα τέλειον (also referred to as πνεῦμα) of the so-called 'Mithras-liturgy', a concept which Reitzenstein[2] traces to an Iranian source; cf. also the ἀθάνατον σῶμα of *Corp. Herm.* XIII. 3 and the Gnostic 'garment of light'.[3] But whereas the Greek theory aims at providing a bridge between soul and body, and accordingly ascribes an astral body to all souls (whether as a permanent possession or as something acquired in the course of the descent to generation), the magician, the Hermetist and the Gnostic are trying to make a bridge between God and man; for them the immortal body is acquired *by initiation*, and by putting it on, man becomes a god. The nearest analogue to this in any Neoplatonist is the *prophetic* πνεῦμα which according to Porphyry (*apud* Euseb. *Prep. Ev.* V. 8. 12) comes from the divine power, enters into man and speaks through his mouth, using his soul as its 'basis'; but this prophetic breath belongs to Porphyry's earlier belief, and seems to be unconnected with the use of πνεῦμα in his later writings and in the other Neo-platonists.—More to the point is Clement's statement (*Strom.* II. 20. 112–13) that the Basilidian Gnostics believed in a προσηρτημένον πνεῦμα or προσφνὴς ψυχή which was the organ of passion; with this Bousset[4] compares the ἀντίμιμον πνεῦμα of the *Pistis Sophia*, bestowed during the soul's descent by the five planetary Rulers, and identified with the Platonic 'cup of forgetfulness'. Unfortunately

---

[1] The form which it eventually assumed in Neoplatonism is obviously influenced (*via* Poseidonius?) by the astral mysticism which came into the Hellenistic world from Babylonia both directly and by way of Egypt; but this affected the application rather than the substance of the thought.

[2] *H.M.-R*[3]. 178 f. He also identifies the ἴδιος δαίμων of the magicians and the οἰκεῖος δαίμων of Porph. *vit. Plot.* 10 with the 'heavenly body' of Iranian religion.

[3] Bousset, *Hauptprobleme der Gnosis* 303. The Neoplatonists use the term χιτών, but they apply it always to the *perishable* πνεῦμα: see above, prop. 209 n.*

[4] *Hauptprobleme* 365 ff. Does a trace of the same doctrine appear in Plotinus' report of the Gnostic teachings, *Enn.* II. ix. 5 (I. 189. 15)? If so, Plotinus did not recognize it as akin to the Greek theory.

we know very little of these speculations, which appear not to have been central in Gnosticism. How far they either influenced or were influenced by the development of the Greek ὄχημα-πνεῦμα theory is not easily determined; that they originated the latter I find it impossible, after a survey of the very abundant Greek evidence, seriously to credit.

Origin of the theory.[1]

(a) The Neoplatonists of course claim to find authority in Plato for this as for their other doctrines. The passages to which they chiefly appeal[2] are *Phaedo* 113 D ἀναβάντες ἃ δὴ αὐτοῖς ὀχήματά ἐστιν: *Phaedr.* 247 B τὰ μὲν θεῶν ὀχήματα ἰσορρόπως εὐήνια ὄντα ῥᾳδίως πορεύεται, τὰ δὲ ἄλλα μόγις : *Tim.* 41 E ἔνειμεν θ᾽ ἑκάστην (ψυχήν) πρὸς ἕκαστον (ἄστρον), καὶ ἐμβιβάσας ὡς ἐς ὄχημα τὴν τοῦ παντὸς φύσιν ἔδειξεν: and *ibid.* 44 E, 69 C. But the first of these passages evidently refers to certain boats which convey the souls of the dead on Acheron, and the second is part of the imagery of the charioteer and the two horses; in *Tim.* 41 E the stars are compared to chariots, and in the other two *Timaeus* passages the ordinary mortal body is called the soul's chariot. These casual and unrelated metaphors could not by themselves suggest to the most perverse mind a theory of astral bodies. There is, however, one passage in Plato which does appear to point in this direction, viz. *Legg.* 898 E f., where he discusses the manner in which we may suppose the stars to be guided by their souls, and suggests as one possibility the interposition of a fiery or aerial body as a *tertium quid.*[3]

(b) With somewhat more justice Pr. claims the authority of Aristotle : ὄχημα . . . πνευματικόν, οἷον καὶ Ἀριστοτέλης ὑπέλαβε (*in Tim.* III. 238. 20) ; cf. Themistius' commentary on the *de anima*, p. 32 (Berlin edition) παρὰ Πλάτωνι μὲν τὸ αὐγοειδὲς ὄχημα ταύτης ἔχεται τῆς ὑπονοίας, Ἀριστοτέλει δὲ τὸ ἀνάλογον τῷ πέμπτῳ σώματι. This refers to Aristotle's doctrine of the πνεῦμα which is the seat of

---

[1] For many of the references in the following paragraphs I am indebted to a paper by R. C. Kissling, ' The ὄχημα-πνεῦμα of the Neoplatonists and the *de Insomniis* of Synesius of Cyrene ', *Amer. Journ. of Philology* 43 (1922), 318 ff. Kissling rightly insists on the dual origin of the doctrine in the Platonic ὄχημα and the Aristotelian πνεῦμα ; but he does not explain how the two came to be connected. About the later theory I have learned much from Hopfner's *Gr.-Aeg. Offenbarungszauber* and from the admirable chapter in Bidez's *Vie de Porphyre*, 88 ff.

[2] Iamb. *apud* Stob. I. 374. 1 [892 H] ; Pr. *in Tim.* III. 235. 23, 238. 2, 268. 3 ; *in Remp.* II. 257. 18.

[3] ἢ πόθεν ἔξωθεν σῶμα αὐτῇ πορισαμένη πυρὸς ἤ τινος ἀέρος, ὡς λόγος ἐστί τινων, ὠθεῖ βίᾳ σώματι σῶμα. Hence, probably, the later dogma that δαίμονες have bodies of fire or air (*infra*, p. 319, n. 1).

the nutritive and sensitive soul and the physiological condition of φαντασία, and is 'analogous to that element of which the stars are made', i.e. to the πέμπτον σῶμα (*de gen. anim.* 736 b 27 ff.). The Aristotelian πνεῦμα is still far from being an 'astral body'; it is an element in the body as we know it, is common to all animals, and is transmitted in the act of procreation. But certain features of the later ὄχημα-πνεῦμα are clearly derived from this source : its function as 'carrier' of the irrational soul, its special connexion with φαντασία,[1] its quasi-immateriality, and its 'innate' character (it is συμφυές as Aristotle's πνεῦμα is συμφυτόν, though not in the same sense).

(*c*) Who it was that first linked together the star-vehicles of the *Timaeus* and the starry πνεῦμα of Aristotle, we do not know ; but we can make a guess at the circumstances and the motive of the combination. The earliest extant passage where the terms ὄχημα and πνεῦμα are actually conjoined is perhaps Galen *de placitis Hippo-cratis et Platonis*, p. 643 f. Müller (quoted by Reinhardt, *Kosmos u. Sympathie* 190). After expounding the Poseidonian[2] theory of φωτοειδὲς πνεῦμα as mediating vision Galen adds : εἰ δὲ καὶ περὶ ψυχῆς οὐσίας ἀποφήνασθαι χρή, δυοῖν θάτερον ἀναγκαῖον εἰπεῖν, ἢ τοῦτο εἶναι τὸ οἷον αὐγοειδές τε καὶ αἰθερῶδες σῶμα [λεκτέον αὐτὴν] εἰς ὅ, κἂν μὴ βούλωνται, κατὰ ἀκολουθίαν ἀφικνοῦνται Στωϊκοί τε καὶ Ἀριστοτέλης, ἢ αὐτὴν μὲν ἀσώματον ὑπάρχειν οὐσίαν, ὄχημα δὲ τὸ πρῶτον αὐτῆς εἶναι τουτὶ τὸ σῶμα, δι᾽ οὗ μέσου τὴν πρὸς τἆλλα σώματα κοινωνίαν λαμβάνει. This passage is suggestive in two ways. In the first place the doctrine appears here not as an arbitrary piece of occultism, like the ἀντίμιμον πνεῦμα of the *Pistis Sophia*, but as having a physiological basis, and the epithet αὐγοειδές is brought into connexion with the Poseidonian teaching about the affinity between the sun's rays (αὐγαί) and the organ of vision. Secondly, the doctrine appears as a modification of the cruder view according to which the soul is itself πνεῦμα.[3] It in fact offered a compromise, on the one hand,

---

[1] Cf. Porph. ἀφ. 13. 12 ἐναπομόργνυται τύπος τῆς φαντασίας εἰς τὸ πνεῦμα, with Mommert's note ; Synes. *de insomniis* 135 D ; Iamb. *de myst.* III. 14.

[2] A Poseidonian development of the traditional Stoic theory of πνεῦμα as mediating perception in general, for which cf. *Stoic. Vet. Fragm.* II 716, 773 f., 856, 861, 863, 866 Arnim.

[3] Cf. *Stoic. Vet. Fragm.* II. 774, 885 : the ultimate basis is the primitive thought that the soul is the life-breath. Such views were not confined to the materialist schools. Heraclides Ponticus, Platonist though he was, is said to have described the soul as an οὐράνιον σῶμα of luminous substance (Diels, *Dox. Gr.* 213, 214, 388) ; and similar opinions are attributed by Alexander Polyhistor (*apud* Diog. Laert. 8. 28) to the Pythagoreans, and by Iamblichus (*apud* Stob I. 366. 25 [870 H]) to ' some of the Aristotelians '. Primitive ideas die hard. and after their apparent death they tend to survive in attenuated forms. That the ' pneumatic ' vehicle is in one aspect an attenuated survival of the ' pneumatic ' soul is further suggested by the equation in Synesius (*de insomn.* 137 D), and perhaps in Porphyry

between Plato's conception of the soul as separable from its earthly body and Aristotle's insistence that it can exist only as the ἐντελέχεια of some organism; on the other, between the immaterialist psychology of both Plato and Aristotle and the Stoic πνεῦμα-psychology. It enabled the eclectically minded to hold that the soul was immortal yet an ἐντελέχεια, and incorporeal yet inseparable from the πνεῦμα. One can readily understand that the hypothesis was found attractive by serious thinkers in the period of the early Empire, an age whose philosophical ideal was to reconcile Stoicism with the *Timaeus* and both with Aristotle.

(*d*) Some further testimonies to the existence of the theory prior to the rise of Neoplatonism may be noticed here. The author of [Plut.] *de vita et poesi Homeri* affirms on the authority of ' Plato and Aristotle ' that the soul at death takes with it τὸ πνευματικόν, which acts as its ὄχημα (c. 128). This writer's date is unknown ; Diels, *Dox. Gr.* 99, places him in the second century A.D. Simplicius *in Phys.* 964. 19 ff. (Diels) cites and answers the objections raised by Alexander of Aphrodisias against the doctrine of the ὄχημα : this implies that the theory was well known by the beginning of the third century A.D. (about the date of Galen's death). Again, the Hermetist *apud* Stob. I. 410. 18 ff. [988 H] speaks of certain ' mists ' (ἀέρες) which are the incorporeal envelope (περιβόλαιον) of the soul ; and *Corp. Herm.* X. 13, 17 of the πνεῦμα as the soul's περιβολή (or ὑπηρέτης), in which it ὀχεῖται. Both these Hermetists are influenced by Poseidonian views, and are certainly pre-Plotinian. In the third century two Christian writers, Origen (*adv. Celsum* II. 60, 892 A Migne) and Hippolytus (*Philosoph.* 568. 14 Diels), mention the αὐγοειδὲς σῶμα : the former uses it, like the Neoplatonists,[1] to explain the possibility of apparitions of the dead. Finally, Iamblichus *apud* Stob. I. 378 [904 H] ascribes to ' the school of Eratosthenes and Ptolemy the Platonist and others ' the opinion that the soul is permanently embodied and passes into the earthly body from others ' of finer stuff ' (λεπτότερα). The reference to Ptolemy the Platonist tends to confirm what has been suggested in the last paragraph ; for if he is rightly identified with Ptolemaeus Chennos of Alexandria, he belonged to the same age and the same eclectic school as Galen, and wrote both on Aristotle and (probably) on the *Timaeus*.[2] On the

before him, of the terms ψυχικὸν πνεῦμα and πνευματικὴ ψυχή (cf. Mau, *Religions-philosophie Kaiser Julians* 111 ff.).

[1] Cf. *supra*, prop. 210 n.

[2] Cf. A. Chatzis, *Der Philosoph u. Grammatiker Ptolemaios Chennos* (*Studien z. Geschichte u. Kultur d. Altertums*, VII. 2).

other hand if the Eratosthenes referred to is the celebrated scientist of Cyrene (as Hirzel assumes), the theory or more likely some vague anticipation of it goes back to the third century B.C.; but this identification is doubted, not without reason, by Wachsmuth and Knaack *

The Astral Body in Plotinus and Porphyry.

Plotinus accepted the hypothesis of the λεπτότερον σῶμα; but he does not explicitly connect it with the ὀχήματα of the *Timaeus*,[1] and he did not, like the authorities last cited, regard it as συμφυτόν—to do so would have been a dangerous concession to the ἐντελέχεια view of the soul's function. It is acquired, according to him, in the οὐρανός in the course of the soul's descent;[2] and it is presumably discarded there when the soul reascends to the intelligible world.[3] A passing reference elsewhere[4] to the πνεῦμα suggests that he probably identified it with the astral body; but it is evident that he attached little philosophical importance to either concept.—Porphyry, like Plotinus, believed that the astral body was acquired in the οὐρανός (ἀφ. 13. 8, πρὸς Γαῦρον XI. 3); but he thought the subject worthy of a much more elaborate treatment than his master had accorded it. He connects the πνεῦμα closely with the irrational soul,[5] which in Augustine's citations from the *de regressu animae* is called 'anima spiritalis'. Originally of an 'ethereal' substance, in the course of its descent the πνεῦμα is progressively darkened and thickened as it absorbs moisture from the air,[6] until it finally becomes fully material and even visible (ἀφ. 14. 4 ff., *de ant. nymph.* 11). After death it is hampered in its efforts to rise by this moist and heavy element, which may carry it down to a place of punishment, and the irrational soul with it (ἀφ. *l.c.*); but theurgy, or (more surely) philosophy, will help it to reascend (*de regressu animae,*

---

[1] He does, however, in one passage use ὀχεῖσθαι of the soul's relation to it (III. vi. 5 *fin*. [I. 283. 20 ff.]).

[2] IV. iii. 15 *init*. (cf. also 9). This passage recalls the Poseidonian 'Himmelfahrt', and the essay in which it occurs is one which contains several definite echoes of Poseidonian speculation. He mentions in the same essay the theory of the συμφυτὸν σῶμα, but does not adopt it: cf. *supra* prop. 196 n.

[3] IV. iii. 24.

[4] II. ii. 2 (I. 132. 10): the πνεῦμα attached to the soul has perhaps (ἴσως) the same sort of movement as the stars.

[5] Cf. p. 316, n. 3. It is not certain that Porph. ever spoke of the πνεῦμα as an ὄχημα: Pr. *in Tim.* III. 234. 20 may be accommodating to his own terminology his report of Porph.'s views. Augustine, however, whose chief or only source for the doctrine seems to be Porphyry, knows the term 'vehiculum' (*Epist.* 13, § 2 Migne).

[6] A similar doctrine seems to have appeared in the *Chaldaean Oracles* (47 Kroll = Pr. *in Tim.* III. 234. 26 ff.).

fragm. 2 Bidez). It will eventually be dissolved again in the οὐρανός together with the irrational soul (Porph. *apud* Pr. *in Tim.* III. 234. 18). δαίμονες have a misty (ἀερῶδες) πνεῦμα,[1] which alters its form in response to their momentary imaginings,[2] and thus causes them to appear to us in ever changing shapes (πρὸς Γαῦρον VI. 1), sometimes acting the parts of gods or higher spirits or the souls of the dead (*de myst.* III. 31).—All this (with the possible exception of the speculation about the changing shapes of daemons) is, as Bidez says,[3] obviously unoriginal; much of it may go back to Poseidonius' account of the descent of the soul (conceived as being itself a πνεῦμα) from the οὐρανός.[4]

Later elaboration of the theory,

(*a*) The substitution of theurgy for the personal mysticism of Plotinus enhanced the importance of the astral body; for theurgy operated in the borderland between mind and matter, claiming to produce spiritual effects by material means, and it could be explained that such effects were mediated by the psychic envelope. In the *de mysteriis* (III. 14) the αἰθερῶδες καὶ αὐγοειδὲς ὄχημα is the recipient of divine φαντασίαι and the organ of mediumship, as the 'anima spiritalis' already is in Porph. *de regressu an.*, fragm. 2. Such φαντασίαι can be perceived by means of the luminous envelope (τοῖς αὐγοειδέσι περιβλήμασιν) even when the eyes of the body are covered (Pr. *in Remp.* I. 39. 9; Hermeias *in Phaedr.* 69. 7 ff. Couvreur). Similar ideas appear in Synesius *de insomniis* 142 A ff., and Nemesius *Nat. Hom.* 201 Matth. The ὄχημα must first, however, be 'purged' by theurgy (Synesius l.c. and Hierocles *in Carm. Aur.* 479 ff. Mullach, cf. Pr. *in Tim.* III. 300. 16: Porph. l.c. says the same of the 'anima spiritalis').

(*b*) We have seen that there were two distinct traditions about the astral body: the one represented it as permanently attached to the soul ('Eratosthenes and Ptolemy the Platonist', followed by

---

[1] Cf. Plot. III. v. 6 (I. 275. 21) πολλοῖς δοκεῖ ἡ οὐσία τοῦ δαίμονος καθ' ὅσον δαίμων μετά τινος σώματος ἢ ἀέρος ἢ πυρὸς εἶναι. This is also the usual view of Christian writers from Tatian (*or. ad Graecos* 15) onwards: cf. Hopfner, *Gr.-Aeg. Offenb.* I. § 201 f. Others assigned daemons to all the elements, with corresponding elemental bodies (*de myst.* V. 12 : cf. Bidez, *C.M.A.G* VI. 97 ff.). Hence the 'elementals' of medieval belief, and the use of στοιχειό for 'demon' in modern Greek (H. Diels, *Elementum*, 56).
[2] Modern theosophy has, oddly enough, the same theory about its 'astral entities'; cf. the passage from Annie Besant, *The Ancient Wisdom*, quoted by Bidez, *C.M.A.G.* VI. 98, n. 3.
[3] *Vie de Porphyre*, 94.
[4] We must also reckon seriously with the possibility of secondary Iranian or Gnostic influence at this point (cf. notes on props. 184 and 209).

Iamblichus *apud* Pr. *in Tim.* III. 234. 32 ff., and Hierocles *in Carm.
Aur.* 478 Mullach) ; the other, as acquired in the course of the soul's
descent and discarded in the reascent (Plotinus, Porphyry, and the
Chaldaean Oracles).[1] The divergence was involved with the vexed
question of the immortality of the irrational soul, whose vehicle is
the astral body (*in Tim.* III. 238. 5 ff. : see above, prop. 209 n.).
Proclus, following Syrianus, characteristically combines the two views
by assuming the existence of *two ὀχήματα* (*in Tim.* III. 236. 31 ff.,
298. 12 ff. ; *El. Th.* props. 196, 207-9).[2] The higher (συμφυὲς or
αὐγοειδὲς or ἀστροειδὲς) ὄχημα is immaterial,[3] impassible and imperishable ; it corresponds in its perpetuity to the enduring root of unreason
in the human soul which survives every purgation. This is the
'vehicle' into which Plato's demiurge puts the soul (*Tim.* 41 E).
The lower (πνευματικὸν) ὄχημα is a temporary accretion, composite
of the four elements (cf. *Tim.* 42 B)[4] ; it is the vehicle of the irrational soul proper and, like it, survives bodily death but is eventually
purged away. Pr. thinks that the dwellers on the high places of the
earth in the myth of the *Phaedo* are souls with the lower ὄχημα
awaiting their full ἀποκατάστασις (*in Tim.* III. 309. 26). By this
theory he escapes the dilemma (*ibid.* 299. 16) of either affirming
with Plotinus the existence of human souls completely disembodied
(contrary to Plato *Phaedo* 113 D and *Phaedr.* 247 B),[5] or ascribing
full immortality to the irrational soul with Iamblichus (contrary to
Plato *Tim.* 69 C and *Rep.* 611 B ff.). In the *Th. Pl.*, III. (v). 125 f.,
he accommodates this distinction of the two ὀχήματα to the threefold
classification of souls : divine souls, he tells us, have only the
luminous ὄχημα ; daemons have also the pneumatic or elemental

---

[1] The former view (which was adopted also by Origen, *de princip.* II. ii) connects
itself naturally with Aristotelian psychology, the latter with the 'Himmelfahrt'
and astral mysticism.— Sometimes various grades of body are supposed to be successively acquired in the descent : Macrob. *in Somn. Scip.* I. 12. 13, Aeneas of
Gaza, *Theophr.* p. 59, cf. perhaps Iamb. *apud* Stob. I. 385. 5 [926 H]. So Pr.
analyses his lower ὄχημα into a series of χιτῶνες (*El. Th.* prop. 2 9, etc.)

[2] Psellus *Expos. orac. Chald.* 1137 C has, as Kroll points out, no real justification for ascribing this refinement to the *Chaldaean Oracles.*

[3] So also the ὄχημα of Hierocles (who attributes his doctrine to the Pythagoreans but may really have derived it from the Athenian Neoplatonist Plutarchus)
is ἄϋλον, *in Carm. Aur.* 478.

[4] Compare also the second *soul*, composite of the four elements, in which
Plotinus' Gnostic adversaries believed (*Enn.* II. ix. 5 [I. 189. 15]). In positing
his two ὀχήματα Pr. may have been influenced by this two-soul theory, which
appears in the *de myst.* (VIII. 6) as a Ἑρμαϊκὸν νόημα (cf. Reitzenstein, *Poimandres*
306, n. 1).

[5] Other objections to this view (*in Tim.* III. 267. 28 ff.) were (*a*) that it
deprived the human soul of its natural function (cf. Sall. xx, quoted on prop. 206),
(*b*) that it made it superior to the star-souls which are perpetually embodied (cf.
Plot. IV. iii. 4, quoted on prop. 196).

ὄχημα: human souls have both the ὀχήματα and the fleshly body as well.

I cannot attempt to trace in detail the further history of the astral body. It remained a regular tenet of Neoplatonism so long as Neoplatonism survived in any form : we meet it not only in the last representatives of the Athenian school, Damascius, Simplicius, and Priscianus, but in Alexandrian Platonists such as Hermeias (*in Phaedr.* 69. 7), Olympiodorus (who holds, like some modern theosophists, that it is egg-shaped (!), *in Alc.*, p. 16 Cr.), and Philoponus (who reproduces the Procline distinction between the two ὀχήματα, *de anima*, p. 12 ff. Hayduck). With the Byzantine renaissance it emerges again in the works of Psellus and Nicephorus Gregoras, along with much else of Neoplatonic occultism.[1] In the Latin West it appears as the ' luminosi corporis amictus ' of Macrobius (*in Somn. Scip.* I. 12. 13), and the ' leves currus ' of Boethius (*Consol. Philos.* III. 9), and remains a familiar idea throughout the Middle Ages. How deeply it impressed the imagination of Dante may be seen from *Purgatorio* xxv. 88 ff. Even in the later seventeenth century it found a learned champion in Ralph Cudworth, who devoted to its explanation and defence a lengthy section of his *Intellectual System.*

[1] See Svoboda, *Démonologie de M. Psellos*, 17 ff. ; and Bidez's introduction to the *de operatione daemonum, C.M.A.G.* VI. 97 ff.

NOTE.—*In the Index Verborum large and small figures refer respectively to pages and lines of text, small roman numerals to pages of Introduction.*
An obelus indicates that the word occurs more than twice in the same Proposition: in such cases only the first occurrence is given.

INDEX VERBORUM

324 INDEX VERBORUM

18 166.17 ἀναφαίρετος 94.18 ἄσβε-
στος 78.22 αὐτόζως 166.12 ἐπείσα-
κτος 176.16 πρώτη 92.3† 164.16
plur. 166.8 182.24 ζ. ἄλογοι 182.20
ἔνυλοι 172.18 cf. s.v. νοερός
ζωογονία 136.17
ζωογονικός 136.14
ζωογόνος : τὸ ζ. def. 136.12†
ζῷον 26.20 66.19.20 128.9,13
ζωοποιεῖν 80.2 164.27 pass. 182.29
ζωοποιός 128.11 176.15
ζωτικός 42.1 164.24 172.1.3 ζωτικῶς
40.27 92.16,26

H

ἡγεῖσθαι praeesse 8.29 28.17 al. τὸ
ἡγούμενον 86.21
ἡγεμονεῖν 90.5 104.13 112.12 176.22
ἡγεμονικός 98.9 178.13
ἡνωμένως vide s.v. ἑνοῦν

Θ

θάνατος 94.11
θεῖος 100.24 106.24† 114.12† 118.12,
29 122.7,29† 126.10† 128.22,32,34
132.27 140.8,14† 176.37 compar.
98.7 138.29 superl. 114.15 τὸ θεῖον
106.10 108.1,25,32 110.22 112.25,33
124.34 142.1 160.12 162.9 178.7,14
180.18 τὸ πρώτως θ. 122.31 τὰ θεῖα
114.23 118.7 124.19 126.12 132.16
134.13,22 cf. s.vv. ἀριθμός γένος
γνῶσις δύναμις ἑνάς νοητός νοῦς σῶμα
τάξις φῶς ψυχή θείως 176.9,12
θέμις 108.18 110.28
θεοειδής 114.15
θεός def. 100.9† dist. νοῦς 118.20†
θ. ὁ πρώτιστος (πρῶτος) 102.9 118.10†
θεοί 98.19,26 100.16-144.8 passim
144.19 158.19 160.17 162.1† 176 passim 178.11,32 180.2,17† sunt
plures θ. 100.12† attributa deorum
182.26-188.29 θ. πρώτιστοι 142.5
θ. νοητοί, νοεροί, ὑπερκόσμιοι, ἐγκόσμιοι
140.28-144.8 cf. s.vv. ἀγαθότης ἑνάς
πλῆθος
θεότης 122.5 136.17 142.30 160.10
176.21 θ. γεννητική 134.14 θ. καθαρτική, φρουρητική al. 128.8†
θεωρεῖν 64.3 pass. 62.20
θεώρημα 154.28

I

ἰδέα 86.12
ἰδιάζειν 154.11
ἴδιος 134.15 186.30 al.
ἰδιότης 24.12 74.3 86.9† 88.26 al.
conj. δύναμις 150.29
ἰδίωμα 86.26 118.13,28

ἰδρύειν 176.13 med. 116.26 148.6
pass. 44.4 98.3 106.27
ἴσος : τὸ πρώτως ἴσον 26.19
ἱστάναι 136.7 intrans. 16.20 52.31
στῆναι εἴς τι 4.14 ἵστασθαι ἔν τινι
48.24 50.13 118.26 κατά τι 160.2
ἐστήξεται 26.27

K

καθαίρειν 182.31
καθαρός 182.22
καθαρότης 86.32 136.8,23† 154.9
κάθαρσις 128.8 182.27
καθαρτικός 128.8,11 τὸ κ. dist. τὸ
φρουρητικόν 136.23† dist. τὸ ἀναγωγόν 138.20†
καθέκαστα, τά 70.19
καθήκειν descendere 124.2 128.18
κάθοδος 180.26 182.21
κάλλος 60.16
καλός : τὸ πρώτως κ. 26.19
καταδεέστερος (opp. κρείττων) 10.29
14.13 28 8,13.27 al.
καταδέχεσθαι 70.27
καταλάμπειν (c. acc.) 140.28 142.3,13
pass. 126.10
καταληπτικός 108.30
κατατάσσειν 88.16
κατεξανίστασθαι 126.17
κατιέναι (in generationem) 180.15,28
182.16,19 184.10†
κέντρον 130.13
κινεῖν 16.9† 18.21† 22.4† 30.15 72.13,
18 144.5 148.21 168.22 174.4 176.4
182.25 πρῶτον κινοῦν 16.18 τὸ ἑαυτὸ κινοῦν 18.21 τὸ πρώτως κινούμενον
16.21,24 174.21 τὸ ἀεὶ κινούμενον
172.23†
κίνησις 16.16 30.15,16 36.14 42.5
52.10 72.7† 92.9,10 114.29 172.26,
28 174.4†,13,21
κινητικός 18.22 176.14 κ. ἑαυτοῦ 18.32
92.2
κινητός 22.4
κληροῦσθαι 98.9
κοινωνεῖν 4.4 6.9,11 38.13 96.6 κ.
πρός τι 20.18
κοινωνία 24.13 32.19 36.6† 74.29 96.17
112.6 130.11
κομίζεσθαι 128.5
κοσμεῖν 12.13,14 80.2 126.25 132.33
κόσμος 88.4 142.19,28 144.1,17,19
κρατεῖν 106.17,19 140.3 148.25 184.18
κρατητικός 106.14,17
κρείττων 8.11,27 10.14 al. τὸ κρ. def.
14.15 κρειττόνως 20.10 62.21 110.12
κρίσις 164.27
κρύφιος 84.9 106.11,28 134.11 140.29
κύκλιος 86.17 κύκλῳ 12.9,18 16.16
36.16 κατὰ κύκλον 40.10
κύριος 42.28 44.31 κυρίως 70.28 72.2

330 INDEX VERBORUM

ὑποκεῖσθαι 78.17   ὑποκείμενον 42.32†
48.8,9 68.5 162.26†   ὑπ. πάντων
68.27 ψυχώσεως 68.28 plur. 60.27
66.17 68.1,17 166.6
ὑπομένειν 2.17 4.4
ὑπόστασις 30.30 32.8 34.11 44.31
52.16 76.15 78.6 84.24 86.18,23
92.10 96.18 saepe   ὑπ. αὐτοτελής
60.21† 100.25   μετεχομένη 26.23
νοερά 22.2 166.30 176.10
ὑποστάτης 52.7 56.16 150.16 168.31
ὑποστατικός 20.8 28.24† 54.12,24 58.5
60.23 al.
ὑποστρωννύναι 106.16 118.6 176.11
ὕφεσις 34.8 40.1 56.35 60.12 86.20
110.33 112.3 114.5 116.33   καθ'
ὕφεσιν 60.23 86.10 178.30   κατ'
ἐσχάτην ὕφ. 64.11
ὑφιέναι: ὑφειμένος (opp. κρείττων) 20.6
28.15 68.11,15 112.23 al.
ὑφιστάναι trans. 8.12 26.22 30.14
32.1,11 34.1,5,6 saepe   infin. ὑφιστάνειν 30.2 134.17   intrans. et med.
4.24 12.33 20.8,17 26.29 34.16 saepe
ὑφεστός (v.l. -ώς) 6.8 18.27 52.15
70.18
ὑψηλότερα, τά 116.8

Φ

φαντάζεσθαι 184.7
φέρεσθαι 144.6 150.4
φθάνειν (intrans.) 118.29 122.16
φθαρτά, τά 156.33 158.1
φθείρεσθαι 46.21,23 156,28 162.27
182.13
φοιτᾶν πάντα διὰ πάντων sim. 154.7,22
172.13
φρουρά 136.4,28†
φρουρεῖν 118.14 pass. 136.5,8
φρουρητικός 128.9   τὸ φ. ἐν τοῖς θεοῖς
def. 136.1 dist. τὸ καθαρτικόν 136.23†
φυλάττειν 14.7 30.29 110.31 112.11
154.9
φύσις (hypostasis) 24.23† 96.27 genus
rerum 20.21† 50.5   indoles alicuius
22.7 98.6 100.2 110.23   ἡ τοῦ παραγομένου φ. syn. τὸ παραγόμενον sim.
8.1 12.20 14.6 20.8 al.   φ. αἰώνιος
52.29   ἀκίνητος 22.14   μεριστή 96.26
μεριστή 76.10   νοερά 22.2 σωματική
58.30 98.21,29 122.22.33   αἱ πολλαί
φ. 24.24,32   τῇ φύσει opp. χρόνῳ
4.27   κατὰ φύσιν 4.32 8.24 10.17
28.30 al.   παρὰ φύσιν 108.17
φυτόν 128.9,12
φῶς, θεῖον 126.10,14 162.4

X

χαλᾶν 108.2
χαρακτηρίζειν 148.27   pass. 92.21 106.
32 138.28
χειρόνως 62.22
χιτῶνες vehiculi 182.17
χορηγεῖν 10.20 20.3 68.7,12 108.11
164.28 pass. 20.4,20
χορηγία 116.23
χορηγός 136.17 138.6
χρονικός 48.28 54.1 172.27 174.32
180.23
χρόνος 50.25–54.3 passim 80.19 94.3†
96.1,6 124.31 148.9 150.4 152.26†
166.27† 168.15† 172.23† 174.4,8
χρόνων χρ. 52.6   ὁ ἀεὶ χρ. 52.15   ὁ
σύμπας χρ. 174.12†   χρ. ἄπειρος 78.14
180.21,27   περιοδικός 174.18   χρόνῳ
opp. τῇ φύσει 4.28   χρόνῳ (ὑπὸ χρόνου) μετρούμενα 48.16† 50.1† 94.22†,
34 148.2 168.2 174.3,10†
χωρεῖν capere 88.17   vadere 134.8
χωρίζειν 10.21 18.17 162.19,28
χωρισμός 18.3
χωριστός 18.7† 76.14† 86.27† 108.3,
17 140.22 144.17 162.13 166.3,12
χωριστῶς 76.12,23,28 88.2

Ψ

ψυχή 22.1† 24.25† 56.8† 58.31 60.15
68.26,29 98.20† 122.26 128.8 142.29†
148.21 154.29† 160.5–184.20 passim
tria genera ψυχῶν 160.21 162.1   ψ.
ἀμέθεκτος 142.18†   conj. ὑπερκόσμιος
144.14   ψ. θεία 114.13† 160.5–162.12
passim 176.1–180.14 passim   λογική
128.14   μεθεκτή 166.26 168.9,11
170.18†   μερική 96.25,27 176.19–
184.20 passim   νοερά 98.20,29 ποτὲ
νοοῦσα 154.1   ὅλη 96.26,28 180.9
πρώτη (πρωτίστη) 24.26,32   26.18
πρώτη ὑπὸ χρόνου μετρουμένη 174.12†
ὑπερκόσμιος, ἐγκόσμιος 144.10† 174.1,7
ψυχῆς ἔλλαμψις 62.11   τὸ τῆς ψ. ἀκρότατον 184.17 cf. s. v. ὀπαδός
ψυχικός (ἀριθμός sim.) 98.19 100.7
176.8,31   τὸ ψ. 178.7   ψυχικῶς
122.30 162.1 176.8
ψυχοῦν 170.21†
ψύχωσις 68.28 plur. 60.15

Ω

ὡσαύτως: ἀεὶ ὡσ. ἔχειν 124.10 144.5
156.31 τὸ οὐχ ὡσ. 126.2

[*Numerals above the line refer to footnotes.*]

ADDENDA ET CORRIGENDA

p. xii. On the *Chaldaean Oracles* H. Lewy's book, *Chaldaean Oracles and Theurgy* (Cairo, 1956), is indispensable though not everywhere convincing; on their relationship to Neoplatonism see W. Theiler, *Die chaldaeischen Orakel und die Hymnen des Synesios* (Halle, 1942), and my paper in *J.R.S.* 37 (1947), reprinted in *The Greeks and the Irrational*, 283 ff.

pp. xiii–xxvi. For the evidence regarding lost works of Proclus, and a comprehensive account of his system, see now the long and careful article by R. Beutler in Pauly-Wissowa, s.v. 'Proklos'. L. J. Rosán, *The Philosophy of Proclus* (New York, 1949), expounds Proclus' teaching faithfully for Greekless readers, but without providing much historical background.

pp. xxiii–iv. On the unsolved problem of the missing links between Iamblichus and Proclus see most recently J. Daniélou, 'Eunome l'Arien et l'exégèse néo-platonicienne du *Cratyle*', *R.E.G.* 69 (1956), 412 ff., who assigns a major role to Nestorius, and, *contra*, É. Évrard, 'Le Maître de Plutarque d'Athènes et les origines du néoplatonisme athénien', *L'Ant. Class.* 29 (1960), 108 ff., 391 ff.

pp. xxvi–xxxiii. Cf. now R. Klibansky, *The Continuity of the Platonic Tradition during the Middle Ages* (Warburg Institute, 1939); and H. D. Saffrey, O.P., 'Le Chrétien Jean Philopone et la survivance de l'école d'Alexandrie au sixième siècle', *R.E.G.* 67 (1954), 396 ff.

p. xxix. A fragment of the *Elements of Theology* has now turned up in an Arabic version by Abu Uthmān (*fl. c.* A.D. 914). It appears among a collection of ten short treatises preserved in an eleventh-century MS. at Damascus, where they are attributed to Alexander of Aphrodisias, and published by A. Badawi, *Aristū 'inda l-'Arab*, Cairo 1947. That the treatise in question is in fact a translation of *El. Th.* props. 15–17, plus some supplementary matter, was simultaneously pointed out by B. Lewin, *Orientalia Suecana* 4 (1955) 101 ff., and by S. Pinès, *Oriens* 8 (1955), 195 ff. Collation of Lewin's French translation of the treatise with my text of Proclus reveals various blunders on Abu Uthmān's part, but no fresh readings of any interest and no decisive evidence for determining the relationship

of Abu Uthmān's exemplar to the existing families of Greek MSS. (an omission shared with BCDM at p. 18.24 is inconclusive, since it could have originated independently owing to homoeoteleuton). The supplementary matter in the treatise is presumably due to a Greek or Syriac intermediary; it is most unlikely that any of it goes back to the original text of the *Elements*.

A larger fragment of the *Elements* in Arabic has recently been identified by Pinès in an Istanbul MS., but is as yet unpublished. This contains 20 propositions (including the three previously known) and is likewise attributed to Alexander of Aphrodisias. See Pinès's forthcoming paper in the *Journal asiatique*.

On Petritsi's Georgian version of the *Elements* see addendum to p. xlii.

p. xxx. On the *Liber de causis* and Aquinas' commentary on it (in which he quotes extensively from *El. Th.*) see Saffrey's edition of the commentary (Fribourg-Louvain, 1954), pp. xv–xxxvii. Degen's hypothesis about the origin of Albertus Magnus' additions to the *Liber de causis* appears to be mistaken.

pp. xxxiii–xli. For a detailed description and history of some of these MSS.—those which contain *Th. Pl.*, viz. nos. 1, 2, 24, 25, 26, 28, 30, 33, 34, 37, 38—see now H. D. Saffrey, 'Sur la tradition manuscrite de la *Théologie platonicienne* de Proclus', in *Autour d'Aristote, recueil d'études offert à Monseigneur A. Mansion* (Louvain, 1955), pp. 395–415. Among other interesting points, Saffrey shows that no. 26 (*Riccardianus graec.* 70) has marginalia in the hand of Ficino, and that no. 33 (*Monacensis graec.* 547) was annotated throughout by Bessarion, who seems to have collated it with no. 2 (*Marcianus graec.* 403). To my list of secondary MSS. should be added *Phillipicus* 1505 (Berolinensis graec. 101), chart., saec. xvi; according to Saffrey it is a copy of no. 33.

p. xlii. Since I wrote my introduction Petritsi's Georgian version of the *Elements* has been published by Dr. S. Qaukhchishvili (Kauchtschischwili) in *Ioannis Petritzii Opera*, tomus I (Tbilissi, 1940), and his commentary in tomus II. I owe it to the generous co-operation of Dr. D. M. Lang, Reader in Caucasian Studies at the School of Oriental and African Studies, that I am now able to provide some further information about it. The book proved to be unobtainable in this country, but during a visit to the U.S.S.R. Dr. Lang was enabled by the friendly help of the Georgian Academy of Sciences to procure a çopy, and he has been good enough to translate for me

from the Georgian over fifty selected passages. Unfortunately, Petritsi's version does not reflect its Greek exemplar at all closely. It is a free translation, and in addition it exhibits many errors which are unlikely to go back to the Greek. Some of these are evidently due to a failure to follow Proclus' reasoning, while others, such as the total omission of prop. 149, may well have been introduced by peccant Georgian copyists. (Qaukhchishvili's careful edition is based on ten Georgian manuscripts, but he states that the best codex, written in the thirteenth century, was not available to him.) For these reasons it has only limited value for the reconstitution of the Greek text. It can, however, be shown with certainty that Petritsi's exemplar belonged to the MPQW group, with which he shares numerous characteristic errors, whereas I have nowhere found him erring in the sole company of BCD. As between M(W) and (P)Q the Georgian seems to be more or less neutral: errors otherwise peculiar to M or MW reappear in Geo at pp. 64.29, 94.6, 138.17; on the other hand it reproduces a characteristic error of Q at p. 102.11.

Very occasionally, in the passages I have examined, Geo seems to point to a good reading which has vanished from the direct tradition. The clearest instance is at p. 148.7–8, where Geo has '*each one* will know all things simultaneously. But *if* it should be known to it in parts. . . .' This confirms my correction πᾶς. εἰ (πᾶσι MW, πάντα BCD, τό Q). The following variants also seem worth recording:

p. 14.6: καὶ τὴν φύσιν τῶν ὄντων om. Geo, perhaps rightly (cf., however, *Th. Pl.* 73.10 ἄπαντα τὰ ὄντα καὶ πάσας τὰς τῶν ὄντων φύσεις).

p. 22.1: 'spiritual existence' Geo, perhaps pointing to my conjecture ψυχική (ψυχή PQArg.: ψυχῆς BCDOW: deficit M).

p. 80.20: 'is eternal being' Geo (= ἀεὶ ὄν ἐστι Q: ὄν om. cett.). But in the next line Geo does not recognize Q's πᾶσιν.

p. 92.8–9: 'the movement inherent in it' Geo, showing that BCD's παρ' ἑαυτῇ stood in the archetype.

p. 114: after prop. 128 Geo inserts an additional proposition beginning 'Every divine and diabolic (? = δαιμονία) soul exercises thought in a variable way, and no intelligence does so in an immutable fashion.' This cannot be authentic: it contradicts props. 170 and 184, and the terms δαίμων, δαιμόνιος, are not used in the *El. Th.* I have no clue to its origin.

p. 124.19: 'Each providence of the divine sort' Geo, apparently confirming my correction θείων (θεῶν MSS).

p. 144.32: Geo rightly omits the negative (as M primitus).

p. 180.24: 'it cannot ever have a beginning' Geo, supporting Q's ἀρχήν ποτε.

p. 182.17: 'ascends in company with its soul' Geo, pointing to my correction συνανάγεται (συνάγεται MW: συνάπτεται Q).

On the life and writings of Petritsi, who had been a pupil of Psellus at Byzantium, see M. Tarchnishvili, *Geschichte der kirchlichen georgischen Literatur* (= Studi e Testi, vol. 185, Vatican City, 1955) 211-25. His interest in Neoplatonism is further attested by his translation of Nemesius, *de natura hominis*, into Georgian.

p. xlii. William of Morbecca's translation has now been published, without apparatus criticus, by C. Vansteenkiste in *Tijdschrift voor Philosophie* 13 (1951), 263-302 and 491-531. A critical edition by Dr. Helmut Boese is in preparation.

p. 216. For a comparison between Proclus' 'monadology' and that of Leibniz cf. J. Trouillard, 'La Monadologie de Proclus', *Rev. philos. de Louvain* 57 (1959) 309 ff.

p. 221. That the triadic formulation of the three 'moments', immanence, procession, and reversion, is not the personal invention of Proclus is confirmed by W. Theiler, *Porphyrios und Augustin* 33, who shows that they appear as a triad in Marius Victorinus (A.D. *c.* 360), *hymn. iii* (P.L. 8, 1144 A 6), and more than once in Augustine; he supposes the source to be a lost work of Porphyry.

pp. 222 f. The technical usages of the word ἐπιτηδειότης deserve a fuller note, if only because Liddell and Scott's Lexicon gives no hint of their existence. Three such usages are to be distinguished.

1. *Inherent capacity for acting or being acted upon in a specific way.* This seems to go back to Philo the Megaric, *c.* 300 B.C. (*apud* Alex. *in Anal. Pr.* 184.6 ff. Wallies and Simp. *in Cat.* 195.33 ff. Kalbfleisch), from whom it was taken over by the Stoics (Simp. *in Cat.* 242.4 ff. = *SVF* III. 217). It persists into late antiquity as a supplement to the Aristotelian theory of potentiality (cf. *El. Th.* 74.19, 164.25, and *in Alc.* 420.33 (= 122.7 Cr.) τὴν κατ' ἐπιτηδειότητα δύναμιν) or as an alternative to it (cf. especially Philoponus *in de an.* 107.26-109.6). This usage, which in itself is quite non-mystical, is discussed by Professor Sambursky (to whom I owe some of these references) in his *Physical World of Late Antiquity*, chap. iv.

2. *Inherent affinity of one substance for another*: Poseidonius *apud* Strabo 764 C; Plut. *Symp.* 5.3, 676 B; Plut. *comm. not.* 13,

1065 B. This is a specialized application of sense (1) within the framework of the doctrine of occult sympathies. It served in the last resort to 'explain' otherwise unaccountable instances of συμπά-θεια. Thus 'Democritus' (i.e. Bolos of Mendes) speaks of ὁκόσα (τῶν ἀψύχων) ἀναιτιολογήτως ἐπιτετήδευται τοῖς ἐμψύχοισι (p. 4.7 Gemoll). And it was invoked to account for action at a distance: Iamb. de myst. 5.7 quotes the view that τις ἐπιτηδειότης τοῦ ποιοῦντος πρὸς τὸ πάσχον συγκινεῖ τὰ ὅμοια καὶ ἐπιτήδεια, ὡσαύτως κατὰ μίαν συμ-πάθειαν διήκουσα καὶ ἐν τοῖς πορρωτάτω ὡς ἔγγιστα οὖσι.

3. *Inherent or induced capacity for the reception of a divine in-fluence.* This further specialization of the term appears first, so far as I know, in *Corp. Herm.* 16.15 and Porph. *ad Marc.* 19 παρα-σκευαστέον δὲ αὐτὸν (sc. τὸν νοῦν) καὶ κοσμητέον εἰς καταδοχὴν τοῦ θεοῦ ἐπιτήδειον. Here it perhaps expresses no more than the old idea that only persons in a 'state of grace' can perceive the divine presence (cf. Eur. *Bacch.* 502 and my note *ad loc.*). But from Iam-blichus onwards it is linked with the occult virtues ascribed in Egyptian magic to certain stones, herbs, and animals as carriers of συνθήματα θεῖα: cf. *de myst.* 5.23 and Pr. *in Tim.* I. 139. 23 ff. This theory formed the basis of the theurgic art of calling down gods to animate statues or human mediums (*de myst.* 5.23, p. 233. 10 ff., cf. my *Greeks and the Irrational,* 292 ff.).

There is thus a progressive development from an innocent philo-sophical sense to a purely magical one.

p. 224. For the notion of αὐθυπόστατα cf. also Porph. *hist. phil.* fr. 18 Nauck, where νοῦς is καθ' ἑαυτὸν ὑφεστῶτα, and the remarks of Theiler, *Porphyrios und Augustin* 15. But Pr. *in Tim.* I. 277.8 does not prove that the *term* αὐθυπόστατος goes back to Crantor: the quotation is not verbatim.

As to the correlation of ἐν ἄλλῳ (χείρονι) with ὑπ' ἄλλου (κρείτ-τονος), I ought to have pointed out that the starting-point of this association is Plato, *Tim.* 52 C.

p. 237. As Rosán observes (*Philosophy of Proclus* 91 n. 84), the analogy between the three kinds of whole and the triad ἀμέθεκτον-μετεχόμενα-μετέχοντα breaks down as soon as we press it. He offers (p. 142) a different and much more complicated explanation.

p. 241. Cf. also Aristotle, *Phys.* 259 b 32–260 a 19.

pp. 252 f. On the origins of the triad τὸ ὄν-ζωή-νοῦς and its place in the system of Plotinus (which is more considerable than my note

would suggest) see now the important paper of P. Hadot in *Les Sources de Plotin* (Entretiens Hardt, tome V) 107–41, and the discussion on it. On the later elaborations, which are influenced by the *Chaldaean Oracles*, see W. Theiler, *Die Chald. Orakel* 4 ff.

p. 254. The notion of 'naming by predominance' is as old as Antiochus (*apud* Cic. *Tusc.* V. 22), and may even be said to go back to Anaxagoras (cf. Ar. *Phys.* 187 b 1–7); but Numenius seems to have been the first to apply it systematically to relations within the intelligible world. That its application to the triad τὸ ὄν–ζωή–νοῦς is older than Proclus is shown by its occurrence in Marius Victorinus, *adv. Arium* iv. 5 (P.L. 8, 1116 D 4), where it is said of this triad 'haec tria accipienda ut singula, sed ita ut qua suo plurimo sunt, hoc nominentur et esse dicantur' (quoted by Hadot, *Les Sources de Plotin* 127).

pp. 257–60. The henads have been usefully discussed by Beutler (P.-W. s.v. 'Proklos', cols. 217–23) and by L. H. Grondijs, 'L'Âme, le nous et les hénades dans la théologie de Proclus', *Proc. R. Netherlands Academy*, N.S. 23.2 (1960). But the question of their origin and of their exact status in the late-Neoplatonic world-scheme has not been fully cleared up. On at least one point my account is wrong: the opinion attributed at *in Parm.* 1066.16 to τινὲς τῶν ἡμῖν αἰδοίων, that the first hypothesis of the *Parmenides* applies to the gods or henads, cannot be that of Syrianus; for Syrianus found the gods in the *second* hypothesis (*ibid.* 1061. 20–1063. 1), as does Proclus himself. It seems that the αἰδοῖοι, and therefore the doctrine of henads, must be earlier than Syrianus.

p. 275. For the historical background of the 'divine light' cf. W. Beierwaltes, *Lux Intelligibilis* (diss. München, 1957); for the use of the metaphor in late antiquity, Nock, *Sallustius* p. xcviii n. 6, xcix n. 10; for its significance in theurgy, C. M. Edsman, *Ignis Divinus* (Lund, 1949) 205–19, and Lewy, *Chaldaean Oracles and Theurgy* 192 ff., 418 ff.

p. 286. On Numenius' view of the relation between the divine Intelligence and its objects, and Plotinus' criticism of it, see my paper in *Les Sources de Plotin*, pp. 13–16 and 19–21.

p. 296. For the human soul as μεταβάλλουσα ἀπὸ νοῦ εἰς ἄνοιαν cf. Hierocles *in carm. aur.* 471 b Mullach μέση γὰρ οὖσα ἡ τοῦ ἀνθρώπου οὐσία τῶν τε ἀεὶ νοούντων τὸν θεὸν καὶ τῶν μηδέποτε νοεῖν πεφυκότων ἄνεισί τε πρὸς ἐκεῖνα καὶ κάτεισι πρὸς ταῦτα νοῦ κτήσει καὶ

ADDENDA ET CORRIGENDA

ἀποβολῇ: Theiler, *Porphyrios und Augustin* 22, argues that the doctrine goes back to Porphyry.

p. 308. The view that the 'vehicle' of the human soul is spherical appears in Aristides Quintilianus, *de musica* 63.31 Jahn, who perhaps draws on Porph.; and seems to have been known to Plotinus, though he does not commit himself to it: cf. *Enn.* IV. iv. 5. 18 Henry–Schwyzer (where the σφαιροειδῆ σχήματα would seem to be the vehicles of individual souls rather than the bodies of stars) and II. ii. 2. 21 ἴσως δὲ καὶ παρ' ἡμῖν τὸ πνεῦμα τὸ περὶ τὴν ψυχὴν τοῦτο ποιεῖ (where, despite Harder, τοῦτο ποιεῖ surely = συνέπεται λεπτὸν καὶ εὐκίνητον (19) like the stars, as the καὶ shows: the pneumatic envelope is εὐκίνητον because spherical?).

The belief that we shall be resurrected with spherical bodies (σῶμα αἰθέριόν τε καὶ σφαιροειδές) was condemned as heretical by the Council of Constantinople in 553. It is ascribed to the Origenists by Cyril of Scythopolis, *vita Cyriaci* 230. 7 ff. Schwartz. But it has been shown by H. Chadwick, *Harv. Theol. Rev.* 41 (1948) 94 ff., and by A.-J. Festugière, *Rev. sci. philos. et théol.* 43 (1959) 81 ff., that the extant works of Origen do not support the charge; the 'heavenly bodies' of *de orat.* 31, p. 397.3 ff. Koetschau, which are said to be spherical, are simply stars.

pp. 310–13. On the 'Unknown God' in Neoplatonism and elsewhere see now A.-J. Festugière, *La Révélation d'Hermès Trismégiste* IV (Paris, 1954) 1–140. The outcome of his full and detailed inquiry is to confirm the view that the doctrine is genuinely Greek and has its main root in an interpretation of Plato.

p. 314. G. Verbeke, *L'Évolution de la doctrine du pneuma du stoïcisme à S. Augustin* (Paris–Louvain, 1945), brings together a wealth of interesting material on the various uses of the word πνεῦμα, philosophical, medical, Jewish, Gnostic and Christian; but his view that the theory of the 'pneumatic envelope' originated in Egypt (p. 313 ff.) is hardly supported by sufficient evidence.

pp. 317 f. To the passages which testify to the existence of a belief in 'astral bodies' prior to the rise of Neoplatonism should be added Macrobius *in Somn. Scip.* 1.11.12 and 1.12.13, which almost certainly goes back to Numenius (cf. *Les Sources de Plotin* 8–10): here the soul acquires a *sidereum* (ἀστροειδές) or *luminosum* (αὐγοειδές) *corpus* in the course of its descent through the planetary spheres. And we should add also Hierocles *in carm. aur.* 478 b Mullach

τὸ αὐγοειδὲς ἡμῶν σῶμα, ὃ καὶ "ψυχῆς λεπτὸν ὄχημα" οἱ χρησμοὶ καλοῦσι, where the words in inverted commas are evidently a quotation from the *Chaldaean Oracles* (Lewy, *Chald. Oracles and Theurgy* 178 n. 7).

As to Eratosthenes, F. Solmsen, 'Eratosthenes as Platonist and Poet,' *T.A.P.A.* 73 (1942) 201 ff., makes a good case for thinking that the person intended by Iamblichus is indeed the scientist of Cyrene (who was, as he shows, interested in the interpretation of the *Timaeus*), but denies that the passage refers to 'astral bodies'. On the latter point he is surely mistaken: no one familiar with the language of Neoplatonism is likely to doubt that *for Iamblichus* the λεπτότερα σώματα which he contrasts with earthly bodies (στερέα or ὀστρεώδη σώματα) are the etherial or pneumatic envelopes: cf. the Chaldaean oracle quoted above; Plot. II. ii. 2. 19 quoted in addendum to p. 308; Augustine, *de gen. ad litt.* 7. 15 *subtilioris naturam corporis*; Pr. *in Remp.* I. 119. 10 ff., II. 187. 10 ff. But Eratosthenes may have said no more than that the soul is permanently embodied; the rest may well be the interpretation put on his words by Ptolemaeus Chennos, or even by Iamblichus himself.

ADDITIONAL NOTE.

Since my first edition a further portion of Proclus' *Parmenides* commentary has been discovered in William of Morbecca's Latin translation and published by R. Klibansky and C. Labowsky in *Plato Latinus* III (1953); the Greek original of the three *opuscula* hitherto known only in Latin has been largely recovered by H. Boese (1960); the *Alcibiades* commentary has been re-edited by L. G. Westerink (1954), and the *Hymns* by E. Vogt (1957). The contribution which these publications make to our knowledge of Proclus' thought is usefully summarized by W. Beierwaltes, *Philos. Rundschau* 10 (1962), 49 ff.